GenderSpeak

Personal Effectiveness in Gender Communication

THIRD EDITION

Diana K. Ivy
Texas A&M University–Corpus Christi

Phil Backlund
Central Washington University

Boston   Burr Ridge, IL   Dubuque, IA   Madison, WI   New York
San Francisco   St. Louis   Bangkok   Bogotá   Caracas   Kuala Lumpur
Lisbon   London   Madrid   Mexico City   Milan   Montreal   New Delhi
Santiago   Seoul   Singapore   Sydney   Taipei   Toronto

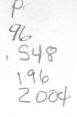

The **McGraw·Hill** Companies

Mc
Graw
Hill **Higher Education**

Publisher: *Phillip A. Butcher*
Sponsoring editor: *Nanette Giles*
Editorial Coordinator: *Josh Hawkins*
Senior marketing manager: *Leslie Oberhuber*
Producer, Media technology: *Jessica Bodie*
Project manager: *Ruth Smith*
Lead production supervisor: *Randy L. Hurst*
Designer: *George J. Kokkonas*
Lead supplement producer: *Marc Mattson*
Photo researcher: *Natalia Peschiera*
Associate art editor: *Carin C. Yancey*
Cover and interior designer: *Kay Fulton*
Typeface: *10/12 Palatino*
Compositor: *Carlisle Communications, Ltd.*
Printer: *Quebecor World Fairfield Inc.*

Library of Congress Cataloging-in-Publication Data

Ivy, Diana K.
    [Exploring genderspeak]
    Genderspeak : personal effectiveness in gender communication / Diana K. Ivy, Phil
Backlund.--3rd ed.
        p. cm.
    Includes index.
    ISBN 0-07-248393-8 (alk. paper)
    1. Communication--Sex differences. I. Backlund, Phil. II. Title
P96.S48I96 2004
305.42'01'4--dc22

                                                                    2003059687

www.mhhe.com

To Important Women
Hazel, Carol, and Karen
DKI

To Judy, Shane, Ryan, Matt,
Kari, Emily, and Madison
PB

About the Authors

DIANA K. IVY received her undergraduate degree in speech communication and theatre from Texas Wesleyan University in her hometown of Fort Worth, Texas. After serving Wesleyan for four years as Assistant Director of Admissions, Ivy pursued graduate education in the Department of Communication at the University of Oklahoma. Concentrating on instructional and interpersonal communication there, she received her M.A. in 1984 and her Ph.D. in 1987. Ivy's first faculty position was in the Department of Speech Communication at Southwest Texas State University, where she received the Professor of the Year Award from the Nontraditional Student Organization and the departmental Outstanding Teacher Award. She then served four years as Basic Course Director in the Department of Communication at North Carolina State University. Currently, Ivy is a Professor of Communication at Texas A&M University-Corpus Christi, where she has served as Director of the Women's Center for Education and Service and as a Faculty Senator. In 2002, Ivy was named Outstanding Gender Scholar of the Year by the Southern States Communication Association.

PHILIP M. BACKLUND received his undergraduate degree in business administration and a master's degree in speech communication from Humboldt State University (California). His first academic position took him to the University of Alaska in Fairbanks as an assistant professor. After spending two years in that interesting environment, he and his family moved to Denver, Colorado, where he pursued his Ph.D. in speech communication at the University of Denver. During his graduate program, he taught full- and part-time for Arapahoe Community College. After receiving his Ph.D., he and his growing family moved to Utica, New York, where he taught at Utica College. After two years in New York, he and his family returned to the west to Central Washington University, where he is currently a professor of communication studies. The students of Central Washington University have twice honored Phil with the Associated Students' Distinguished Professor of the Year Award and once as Most Inspirational Professor. Phil enjoys family activities, basketball, and windsurfing.

Contents

Part One
COMMUNICATION, GENDER AND EFFECTIVENESS

Part Three
LET'S TALK: INITIATING AND DEVELOPING RELATIONSHIPS

Chapter 4. Choosing and Using Gendered Language 153

Part Four
THE CONTEXTS FOR OUR RELATIONSHIPS: PERSONAL EFFECTIVENESS IN ACTION

Preface

"The battle of the sexes." "The war between men and women." Ever tire of hearing those kinds of dichotomizing references? We tire of militaristic images when it comes to the sexes and how they relate to one another; that's one of the motivations for writing *GenderSpeak: Personal Effectiveness in Gender Communication* in the first place, and for continuing to update and revise it. Language that pits women against men, that over-emphasizes gender differences and ignores similarities just doesn't help advance our culture or edify our lives. We grant that some sex and gender differences can be interesting, so we talk about some of them in this text. But the goal is to bridge gaps in understanding between the sexes, to encourage a dialogue about ways that we are similar *and* different.

As in past editions of this text, we remain firmly committed to the receiver orientation to communication and the personal effectiveness approach, as outlined in Chapter 1. We continue to believe in the power of adopting a receiver orientation because of its ability to help students take others' perspectives, to better understand themselves, and to improve communication in their personal and professional relationships. We often see students struggle with this orientation to communication, because many of them are used to thinking about improving communication skills from a sender perspective. They have been taught that a communicator's goal is to be as clear and understandable as possible with others. But less often have they been taught that they are responsible for the effect or impact of their communication on others. Understanding that perspective and learning to adapt one's communication to others form the basis of the receiver orientation that we embrace in the text and in our teaching. Once students understand this perspective, ponder it, and then attempt to use it in their interactions with others, most come to see its value and the potential for receiver-oriented communication to transform (or at least enhance) their relationships.

In the first sections of the text, we encourage students to consider the myriad of influences—from physiology to culture to media—that affect their communication with women and men. Most important, as students explore this information, they are challenged to learn about themselves in ways that may expand their individual conceptions of what it is to be a woman or a man. As students explore attitudes and stereotypes, gender identity development and self-esteem, and mediated influences, they may come to a greater understanding of themselves, and may see that differences between the sexes are not so great as some might suggest.

One section of the text continues to distinguish us from most competitors—the inclusion of chapters on interpersonal communication and the role of gender in the initiation and development of relationships. For many students, learning more about gender and relationships is their main reason for taking a gender communication course. So we continue to believe in the importance of discussing trends and challenges posed when we explore relational waters.

Another element we have retained in the third edition relates to our grounded or application-oriented approach. Over the years we have found that students find value in the concrete, the applicable, the reality-based. If your students are like ours, they are cognizant of the fact that they need a theoretical, research-driven background on a given topic. But what they really seek is a translation of that information into a recognizable, useful form. Another way of saying this is that, in the area of gender communication especially, students continually seek empowerment. They seek ways they can use what they learn to more effectively establish and improve their relationships with others. Some textbooks merely report research results without offering possible interpretations of the findings or applications of the information. The result of this practice is that the reader or the instructor must act as an interpreter, making sense of research findings that are often contradictory and providing avenues for practical application to daily life. One of the things we continue to do in *GenderSpeak* is to depict realistic events in the lives of students, offer explanations for those events via cutting-edge research, and then provide a range of communicative options students may employ for enhanced personal effectiveness in their interactions and relationships.

We also continue our efforts to speak to college students using language and examples they find provocative. Students have demonstrated to us that they are much more likely to embrace this content and allow it to challenge their relational lives because the language is accessible, current, and engaging. The text has been written primarily for college undergraduates enrolled in courses focusing on the effects of gender on the communication process. Such courses may be represented in university curricula as upper-division courses, while at community colleges, for example, they may be more introductory in nature. *GenderSpeak* is appropriate for both these levels. While some prior exposure to basic concepts and theories of interpersonal communication will serve the reader well, this exposure is not requisite to an understanding of the content of this text.

Organization of the Third Edition

Readers will notice a more streamlined, tightly organized version of our text this time. We worked very hard to not fall into a trend that many authors experience when doing multiple revisions of a text—a tendency for books to expand as they are revised, such that teachers end up with massive amounts of information to weed through or decisions to make about what *not* to cover. An "expanding text-book waistline" creates an organizational problem for instructors and over-whelms students, so we put this edition on a treadmill and slimmed it down to a more workable size. We retained the general four-part structure, but have re-structured related areas of content that appeared in early chapters and stream-lined our approach to make the book more accessible for student readers and more teachable for instructors.

Colleagues using the book across the country remarked that they found the Epilogue useful in the second edition, but wondered why it was "buried" at the end of the book. We took their advice this time around and moved this contex-tual and historical information to the front of the book as a Prologue instead. It now serves as a nice grounding or contextual exercise to help students realize how far we have come in terms of equality for the sexes. (It also prompts us to ponder how much further we have to go.) The third edition hosts a 10-chapter-plus-Prologue organization, which is more easily covered over the course of a semester or quarter.

Part One, "Communication, Gender and Effectiveness" contains an overview of the communication process, including our emphasis on the receiver of communication, a discussion of key terminology, and a description of the var-ious components within the personal effectiveness approach. Part Two, "Influ-ences on Our Choices," encourages readers to explore the many influences that shape their identities, attitudes, expectations, and communication as women and men. This section is based on an assumption that students must first understand what is influencing them—in terms of choices they make about themselves and about communication—before they can work to improve their communication skills and their relationships. Specific topics of discussion include the "nature versus nurture" argument; gender identity development as affected by family, school, and peers; and the influence of mediated communication on sex and gen-der. We have combined Chapters 2 and 3 from the second edition, in an effort to eliminate overlapping content and streamline the book.

"Let's Talk: Initiating and Developing Relationships" is the title of Part Three, which continues to be one of the most unique aspects of the text. This section begins with an in-depth discussion of language—language used *about* the sexes that influences our perceptions of ourselves and of others, as well as language used *between* the sexes in relationships. We then continue our fo-cus, as in the second edition, on the role of gender communication in the ini-tiation, development, maintenance, and sometimes termination of personal relationships.

Once the building blocks of gender communication and relationship devel-opment are conveyed, students proceed into the final section of the text. In Part Four, "The Contexts for Our Relationships: Personal Effectiveness in Action," five chapters explore ways in which gender communication affects and is af-fected by the following contexts or life-situations: friendships (same-sex and cross-sex), intimate or romantic relationships, the workplace, and educational settings. A chapter within this section also investigates the "down side" of human relationships—power abuses in the forms of sexual harassment, sexual assault, and partner violence.

What's New in the Chapters?

- Chapter 1 contains an expanded discussion of current and historical types of feminisms, such as third-wave feminism, and an introduction to transgenderism, as contrasted with transsexualism and transvestitism.
- In Chapter 2 we explore gender identity development, with particular attention paid to androgyny and gender transcendence, and expand on Chapter 1's discussion of transgenderism. We also offer an expanded treatment of the influences on gender identity development, such as family, school, peers, clothes, and toys.
- The media chapter includes a new discussion of male and female images in hip-hop and rap music and music video, as well as an expanded discussion of men's depictions in advertising and the potential effects of male objectification and commodification. Updated research appears on women's and men's television roles, as well as the effect of such depictions on relationships.
- The newly revised interpersonal chapter explores the role of flirtatious communication in the initiation of relationships. We also provide updates on cyber-relationships, with specific topics of emphasis such as identity management through technology, ways that on-line users establish virtual relationships, and the pros and cons of translating virtual relationships into face-to-face ones.
- The romantic relationships chapter, Chapter 7, includes an expanded discussion of the importance of communication and metacommunication in on-going, committed relationships. An extensive discussion of gender and conflict is provided in this edition, including an exploration of the demand-withdraw pattern as it pertains to women and men.
- Chapter 9 on workplace communication contains an updated discussion of the continued controversy over affirmative action and its effects on women's and men's hiring and career advancement. We also provide research on ways professionals attempt to balance or juggle career, home, and family.
- The education chapter provides recent findings of AAUW surveys, in terms of how girls are improving their achievement and self-esteem in schools. Updates on educational sexual harassment and legal developments, especially as pertains to peer harassment, are also included.

Pedagogical Features

Each chapter contains nine pedagogical features to serve as aids for instructors and students alike. We have retained six features that worked well in the second edition. These include *Case Studies* to introduce each chapter, with the exception of Chapter 8. In this chapter on power abuses, case studies are embedded for each of the three main topics. In some instances, case studies represent actual events that occurred or emerged from discussions in our gender communication class-rooms. The case study device is used not only to gain attention from readers as they delve into a new topic, but also to orient or alert the reader to the nature of the discussion that lies in the next pages. *Hot Topics* sections follow case studies, as a means of helping students realize the scope of the chapter. These bulleted phrases serve as topical chapter outlines, which students can use in preparation for exams or to simply check their understanding of chapter content.

A popular feature new to the second edition, which we have retained for the third, is the *Celebrity Quote*. We have updated these fascinating (and sometimes appalling) quotes related to concepts discussed on our pages. These "pearls of wisdom" come from film and television personalities, athletes, political figures, musicians, and historical figures. We also retained the chapter-end *Summaries*, as well as the series of *Discussion Starters* which instructors may use as a means of generating class discussion over chapter content, as actual assignments, or as thought provokers for students to consider on their own time. Finally, complete *References* to research cited within the text appear at the end of each chapter. Students may find these references useful as they prepare assignments and/or conduct their own research projects. Instructors may use the references to gather additional material for their own research or to supplement instruction.

In an effort to make this third edition of *GenderSpeak* more user-friendly for students, we have created three new pedagogical features. The first is a variation on the *Recap Box* from the second edition; the revised devices, boxed features entitled *Remember . . .* , go beyond a simple listing of key terms to provide brief definitions for students' review. These boxes appear intermittently within each chapter as a reminder to students of important concepts they will want to retain.

We have also created a new feature entitled *'Net Notes*, in which we introduce Websites related to chapter content. For example, in our discussion of gender and media in Chapter 3, we provide Website addresses and information on a computer-generated news anchor, as well as sites devoted to female hip-hop artists. The final new pedagogical feature is the *Hot Button Issue* box, in which we pose ideas to challenge students' thinking related to sex and gender. One such *Hot Button Issue* box appears in the chapter on romantic relationships, where we explore the difference between sexual safety and sexual correctness, specifically one university's attempt to make sexual relations between its students more safe and consensual. These boxes often raise controversial issues—not in a way that advocates a particular stance but that makes students think for themselves.

With this edition of *GenderSpeak*, we also introduce an on-line instructor's manual and test bank that will assist faculty members in their teaching of gender communication courses. The Website address is <http://genderspeakinst. pageout.net>. Included in the material for instructors are sample syllabi (for both a semester and a quarter system); chapter outlines, which can be used as lecture notes; exercises to help students better understand and retain textbook information; a section termed "Paths of Most Resistance," in which we discuss chapter topics that may engender defensiveness or resistance in students (from our years of experience in teaching the course); and a test bank of multiple-choice questions that can be used to construct exams. The test bank portion of the Website is password-protected for test security purposes. We invite you to visit the Website for the third edition of *GenderSpeak*, and encourage your feedback on the effectiveness of the site and suggestions for improvement.

Acknowledgments

This project has certainly been a team effort; thus there are many people to acknowledge and thank. The authors wish to thank the many folks we've been privileged to work with at McGraw-Hill, including our sponsoring editor, Nanette Giles, editorial assistant Sarah Watts, editorial coordinator Josh Hawkins, project manager Ruth Smith, photography researcher Natalia Peschiera, and designer George Kokkonas. We also wish to thank our original editor on this project, Hilary Jackson, because without her enthusiasm, support, advice, and vision, this book would never have seen the light of day, nor the prospect of going into second and third editions.

We are grateful to our colleagues in the field of communication whose advice and encouragement throughout the review process for this text were invaluable. Reviewers who helped shape the third edition include: Bernardo Attias, California State University, Northridge; Anne E. Boyle, University of Maryland; Marcia D. Dixson, Indiana-Purdue University, Fort Wayne; Brian R. McGee, Texas Tech University; Carol Morgan, Wright State University; Linda M. Pledger, University of Arkansas at Little Rock; Pamela D. Schultz, Alfred University; and Judith Termini, Gallaudet University.

First and second edition reviewers to thank include: Elizabeth Altman, University of Southern California; Janis Andersen, San Diego State University; Cynthia Begnal, Pennsylvania State University (whose enthusiasm continually encouraged us); Cynthia Berryman-Fink, University of Cincinnati; Diana Carlin, University of Kansas; Dan Cavanaugh, Southwest Texas State University; Judith Dallinger, Western Illinois University (whose detailed reviewing over the course of the project contributed greatly to the outcome); Pamela Dunkin, Southern Oregon State University; Karen Foss, Humboldt State University; Karla Kay Jensen, Texas Tech University; Anthony Mulac, University of California, Santa Barbara; Jamey A. Piland, Trinity College, Washington, DC; Robert Smith, University of Tennessee, Martin; Helen Sterk, Marquette University; and Julia Wood, University of North Carolina, Chapel Hill.

Thanks also go to our colleagues in the Departments of Communication at Texas A&M University-Corpus Christi and Central Washington University, for their unwavering support and for being kind to us when we told them yet another book-revision story. We are particularly indebted to Nada Frazier Cano, graduate student of Texas A&M University-Corpus Christi, for her brilliant work on the second edition Epilogue (now third edition Prologue). And a very special thanks goes to our dear friend and support system extraordinaire, Steve Beebe, Southwest Texas State University, for his advice, empathy, good humor, and encouragement of fellow authors.

No project for the benefit of college students has probably ever succeeded without the help of college students. We have many to thank at both A&M-Corpus Christi and Central Washington for being sources of inspiration for the creation and revision of this textbook. Students of gender communication deserve our thanks for providing the motivation to write this text and the "fuel" for a good deal of its content.

Finally, we thank our families and friends for their listening ears, thought-provoking questions, lively arguments, and persistent belief in this book and its authors.

Diana K. Ivy

Phil Backlund

GenderSpeak

Personal Effectiveness in Gender Communication

The Impact of Social Movements on Gender Communication:

You Must Know Where You've Been to Know Where You're Going

Throughout your college career, you've written papers, given presentations, and taken exams. Think back to the most recent exam you took. Imagine that, because of effective teaching and students' hard work, everyone in your class received a score of 100 percent. Yet when you review a posting of the grades in the class, something is amiss. The men's scores reflect 100 percent, but each woman in the class receives a grade of 72 percent. The teacher records As for the male students and Cs for the female students. How can this be? We use this scenario to exemplify the point that women make approximately 72 cents for each man's dollar of pay, as an annual wage (U. S. Department of Labor, Women's Bureau, 2002). As a culture, we've come a long way with regard to sex and gender equity, as a result of a lot of effort throughout our history, but we also have a long way to go.

The chapters you will read in this text focus on contemporary gender communication, but before you plunge in, it's important to recognize some of the historical and cultural events that have shaped where we are today. In this prologue, we survey history, examine women's and men's movements, and take a look at some of the individuals who have contributed to social, economic, and

*This prologue benefited from the significant contributions of a guest author, Nada Frazier Cano.

political changes that have affected and will continue to affect gender communication. But it is beyond the scope of this prologue to focus on each and every social movement that has had an impact. If we fail to mention individuals or movements you deem significant, we hope you will use the omission as a beginning point for class discussion.

LEARNING "HERSTORY"

Regardless of whether you personally embrace feminism, much of what you do and enjoy today is a result of actions of and advocacy by feminists. Some of you no doubt have grown up taking equality for granted; fortunately, it may be all you have ever known. But it is because of dedicated feminists that many of you are sitting in this classroom today.

It's impossible to detail every significant feminist in American history. The truth is that we simply don't know or don't have information about each significant advocate of women's rights and civil rights. Those we do know about are not representative of all who fought to get us where we are today. It's important to remember, especially with respect to women and members of minority groups, that most were considered the property of privileged men. They were not always afforded educational opportunities and often were denied a voice. Those we discuss here somehow made their way into the annals of history, but they are by no means the only ones who made valuable contributions. While history books today are much more inclusive than they've ever been, many would argue they are still "his story," as opposed to "her story." Let's begin by focusing on developments in the realm of education.

Men, Education, and Women—in That Order

When you enter class today, look around you. Notice the number of university students who would once have been barred from the education you are receiving today. Who's responsible for the fact that education is expanding and becoming accessible to everyone? How did it happen? Have you ever wondered what it was that motivated women and minority persons to openly challenge their social status and work so passionately for basic human rights?

In Colonial times American women, under the guidance of men, focused on their "helpmeet" role, which centered on economically essential household production (Theriot, 1996, p. 17). In 1778 a Quaker grammar school opened to educate rural mothers responsible for teaching their children (Bernikow, 1997). Emma Hart Willard is often considered the first important female educator in America (Weatherford, 1994). In 1818 Willard appealed to the New York state legislature to allocate taxes for the education of young women, an outlandish concept at the time. Her request was denied. Most legislators were shocked that Willard proposed to teach anatomy; they believed that her curriculum was contrary to God's will for women. She later founded the Troy Female Seminary in New York state, which incorporated an unprecedented mathematics and science curriculum that sought to provide women with an education comparable to men's (Lunardini, 1994; Weatherford, 1994).

The first public high school for girls opened in 1824 in Worcester, Massachusetts. In Connecticut, a Quaker, Prudence Crandall, was arrested and convicted of defying Connecticut's "black law" (Weatherford, 1994, p. 93) when she dared to educate "negro girls" in her boarding school (Bernikow, 1997, p. 127). All shops and meeting houses in the town were closed to her and her pupils. Doctors would not treat them, the well on her property was filled with manure, and rotten eggs and stones were hurled at her home. In 1834 Crandall's school was set ablaze and burned to the ground.

In 1837 Mary Lyon founded Mount Holyoke Female Seminary in South Hadley, Massachusetts, which was the first institution to educate women who were not from the upper class. In 1837 Oberlin College began to admit women students, as did Antioch College in 1853 and Vassar College in 1865 (Bernikow, 1997). However, these progressive steps were still far from ensuring women's equality in education.

Dr. Edward Clarke, a professor at the prestigious Harvard Medical School, was vehemently opposed to the formal education of women, claiming that higher education harmed not only women but their offspring as well. Doctors who followed Clarke's teachings included S. Weir Mitchell, a then-famous neurologist, who treated Charlotte Perkins Gilman, a commercial artist and writer, and instructed her to "Live as domestic a life as possible. Have but two hours of intellectual life a day. And never touch pen, brush, or pencil as long as you live" (Bernikow, 1997, pp. 153, 154). Gilman defiantly recovered from Mitchell's "cure" and wrote about it in her short story *The Yellow Wallpaper* (1890), which fictionalized her mental breakdown and contained a radically feminist thesis for the time.

In 1908 teachers in New York City, who were struggling for equal pay for equal work, were forced to resign when they married. School authorities were even known to search the schools for pregnant teachers. Henrietta Rodman, a high school English teacher, argued that teachers should be fired for misconduct, but that "marriage is not misconduct." She was suspended when she wrote a letter to the *New York Tribune* protesting the Board of Education's "mother-baiting," and in 1916 she went on to form the Teachers' League, later to become the American Federation of Teachers (Bernikow, 1997, p. 148).

The First Wave of Feminism

England's Mary Wollstonecraft is regarded as one of the first feminists. Her book *A Vindication of the Rights of Woman*, which called for women's equality with men, is still widely studied today. Abigail Smith Adams, wife of the second U.S. president, John Adams, and the mother of sixth president, John Quincy Adams, is considered an early feminist as well. She is credited with writing letters in 1776 to her husband while he was at the Continental Congress, prodding him to "remember the ladies" (Lunardini, 1994, p. 16). However, the Constitution originally barred women, African Americans, American Indians, and many poor people from participation. For years after the Constitution was adopted women were legally subjugated to their husbands. According to the laws in most states, a married woman "literally did not own the clothes on her back"; her husband legally possessed her and everything she earned (Weatherford, 1994, p. 222).

Married women could not sign contracts or obtain credit. The first middle-class women employed by the federal government in the Patent Office received paychecks made out to their husbands (Weatherford, 1994).

> *Women are systematically degraded by receiving the trivial attentions which men think it manly to pay to the sex, when, in fact, men are insultingly supporting their own superiority.*
>
> *—Mary Wollstonecraft,*
> *British feminist*

Suffragists: The Early Equality-Seekers

Imagine that as you leave class today you go to vote in the student government elections, only to find that men are allowed to vote but the women on campus are being turned away, arrested, and imprisoned for trying to vote. This was what America was like less than 100 years ago. The origins of feminism can be found in antislavery (abolitionist) and temperance campaigns (Humm, 1992). One of the initial launching grounds for women's organized efforts was the first national antislavery convention in New York in 1837. Celebrated female abolitionists at the time included Lucy Stone, Angelina Grimke, Sarah Grimke, Lucretia Mott, Elizabeth Cady Stanton, and Susan B. Anthony. Mott was a delegate at the World Antislavery Convention in London, where American women were excluded from participation and forced to sit in the balcony behind a curtain (Greenspan, 1994). After this event Mott's and Stanton's activism for women's equality, particularly their efforts to win women's right to vote, intensified.

On July 19, 1848, the first Women's Rights Convention was held in Seneca Falls, New York, with some 300 women and men attending. (Feminists worldwide celebrated the 150th anniversary of this historic convention in 1998 with another convention on women's rights at Seneca Falls.) Mott and Stanton, along with other early feminists—Jane Hunt, Mary McClintock, and Martha Wright—advocated changes in social policy including equality between husbands and

'Net Notes

Here's a site that overviews the life and times of Elizabeth Cady Stanton and Susan B. Anthony, two prominent figures in the first wave of the women's rights movement: **www.pbs.org/stantonanthony**

wives and women's suffrage. Stanton wrote the "Declaration of Sentiments," modeled after the Declaration of Independence, which stated, "We hold these truths to be self evident, that all men *and women* are created equal" (Ruth, 1990, p. 460). It further listed 18 legal grievances and called for major reforms in suffrage, marriage, and inheritance laws (Greenspan, 1994).

As is the case today with feminists, varying opinions on issues emerged that led to the establishment of two distinct suffrage organizations: the National Woman Suffrage Association (NWSA), founded by Susan B. Anthony and Elizabeth Cady Stanton; and the American Woman Suffrage Association (AWSA), founded by Lucy Stone (Carver, 1999). In 1847, Stone graduated first in her class at Oberlin College, but she was forced to sit in the audience while a male student read her valedictory speech. She is also known for retaining her birth name rather than taking her husband's name when she married. Women who followed her lead became known as "Lucy Stoners" (Bernikow, 1997, p. 287). Members of NWSA argued that as long as women were denied their rights, all other issues had to be secondary. The AWSA disagreed with a "radical" nationwide suffrage movement and instead focused on enacting changes in individual state constitutions (Lunardini, 1994).

Feminists' discontent intensified in 1870 when the Fifteenth Amendment to the Constitution ensured former male slaves the right to vote but did not extend that right to women (Lunardini, 1994). As a result, the national election of 1872 was fraught with controversy, even by today's standards. Although she didn't have the legal right to vote, activist Victoria Woodhull, called "Mrs. Satan" by her many opponents, ran for president of the United States (Bernikow, 1997, p. 7). Woodhull's bid for the presidency ended when she was arrested by a moral crusader, Anthony Comstock, for disseminating "obscene" material through the mail, although she was eventually acquitted under First Amendment protections (Lunardini, 1994, p. 92). The material Comstock found obscene was Woodhull's writings that advocated free love, shorter skirts for women, and legalized prostitution. History has tagged Woodhull a "sex radical" suffragist, but her insistence that private issues emerge into public and political debate broadened the reach of the suffrage movement (Frisken, 2000).

Also during the 1872 election, Susan B. Anthony and hundreds of women attempted to vote, knowing that it was against the law (Lunardini, 1994). Anthony was arrested for daring to cast a vote, tried in a U.S. District Court, convicted, and ordered to pay a $100 fine (Weatherford, 1994). Anthony was not allowed to speak at her trial; the law deemed her incompetent to testify because she was a woman. There were other "subversive" attempts to vote: Dr. Mary Walker dressed in men's clothes and tried to vote in Oswego, New York; and Sojourner Truth tried to vote in Battle Creek, Michigan—both to no avail (Bernikow, 1997).

Women continued to fight for the right to vote, but success would not come easily. Suffragists organized massive rallies and demonstrations, staged boycotts and hunger strikes, destroyed property, chained themselves to public buildings, and carried out other acts of civil disobedience (Neft & Levine, 1997). Thousands continued to march; the White House was picketed six days a week; and over a period of two militant years, 500 women were arrested (Bernikow, 1997).

Other notable early feminists were Harriett Tubman and (as already mentioned) Sojourner Truth. Tubman, an escaped slave, is best known for running the Underground Railroad, but she was also a feminist, a nurse, and a spy for the North during the Civil War (Ventura, 1998). Tubman is credited with leading a raid, in 1863, that freed 750 slaves, and she became the first American woman to lead troops into battle in the Civil War (Greenspan, 1994). At the Women's Rights Convention of 1851, Sojourner Truth made one of her marks on history. Truth was the only woman of color in attendance, and amid the jeers of hostile men she delivered her famous "Ain't I a Woman" speech (Greenspan, 1994, p. 237). Truth, a preacher, suffragist, and abolitionist, was born a slave, was sold away from her parents, and was traded numerous times. When she was an adult, her children were sold away from her (Ventura, 1998). Truth dedicated her life to activism against slavery and for segregation and women's rights.

After decades of activism, in 1920 the Nineteenth Amendment, granting women the right to vote, was finally ratified into law. Many of you probably were unaware of the fact that white women and women of color did not have the right to vote in this country until 50 years after black men (former slaves) were granted their right to vote. Once women obtained the right to vote the public's interest in women's rights waned and, collectively, feminism lay dormant for years, until World War II changed everything.

> *It pisses me off when women, for whatever reason, don't use the word "feminist" when they are all benefiting from the great feminists who struggled and suffered and worked to give us everything women now enjoy—including the right to vote, to bring a lawsuit, the right to custody in a divorce—everything. I feel it is my responsibility to use that word because of all the sacrifices women have made.*
>
> *—Cybill Shepherd, actor*

Enter "Rosie the Riveter"

World War II sent men off to war and motivated women to enter the workforce to fill jobs in industry. More than 6 million women went to work outside the home for the first time, with the majority employed in factory or clerical jobs in war-related industries (Neft & Levine, 1997). "Rosie the Riveter" became a national symbol for women's contributions to the war effort (Colman,

1995). Some employers still refused to hire women, causing the War Department, in 1943, to distribute the booklet *You're Going to Employ Women*. The publication advised employers as follows: "In some respects women workers are superior to men. Properly hired, properly trained, properly handled, new women employees are splendidly efficient workers. The desire of a new worker to help win the war—to shorten it even by a minute—gives her an enthusiasm that more than offsets industrial experience" (Colman, 1995, p. 73). Women became employed as welders, electricians, mechanics, police officers, lawyers, statisticians, journalists, and boilermakers. They operated streetcars, taxis, cranes, buses, tractors, and planes.

Job opportunities for women dried up in 1945 when the war ended. Women were terminated in order to ensure jobs for men returning home from the war. Propaganda from government and industry tried to sell women on the idea that it was their patriotic duty to return home and take care of their husbands and children. Those women who attempted to keep their wartime jobs were laid off or forced into lower-paying jobs. Women who wanted or needed employment were encouraged to find traditional women's jobs as teachers, nurses, or clerical workers. The obvious message to women was that it was their role or duty to focus on husband, children, and home. And for many, home they went and home they stayed (Colman, 1995).

The Civil Rights Movement

Life in Montgomery, Alabama, in 1955 was much different from what it is today. Racism was rampant; racist and segregationist rules and practices were the norm. African Americans riding city buses had to enter the front of a bus to pay a fare, and then get off and enter the bus again from the rear door. They were also required to give up their seats if white people were standing (Lunardini, 1994). Rosa Parks, a mild-mannered African American seamstress in her mid-forties, was seated in the first row of the section for blacks when the white section filled up, leaving a white man without a seat (Ventura, 1998). Parks was arrested for failing to follow the bus driver's instructions to surrender her bus seat to the white man (Lunardini, 1994; Ventura, 1998). She was found guilty of the offense but refused to pay her fine and appealed the decision. Both Parks and her husband lost their jobs and received threats to their lives (Ventura, 1998). Within three days of Park's arrest, African Americans in Alabama began a massive bus boycott that continued for a year until Alabama's state and city bus segregation policies were found unconstitutional (Lunardini, 1994).

From this point on, Martin Luther King, Jr., and other civil rights leaders began to vehemently demand overdue civil rights reforms. Women and men fought for racial progress by joining organizations such as the Students' Nonviolent Coordinating Committee (SNCC) and Students for a Democratic Society (SDS). Soon Martin Luther King, Jr., Malcolm X, John F. Kennedy, and Robert Kennedy would all be assassinated. Some young men would head off to fight the Vietnam War while others would protest it by proclaiming we should "make love, not war." For many, the 1960s were about change and challenging "the establishment." For some, it was a time of sexual revolution—a revolution with a profound impact on relationships and communication between women and men.

The Sexual Revolution

Later chapters in this text explore gender communication in intimate relationships, but again, relevant historical events have had a profound effect on our modern relationships. For example, women have practiced birth control in one form or another throughout history, though not always legally. Margaret Sanger was among the first to make the connection between reproductive rights and women's economic and social equality. She felt that birth control was the key to women's equality (Ventura, 1998). In 1914 Sanger began publishing a journal entitled *Woman Rebel*. Even though it contained no specific information about contraceptives, it violated laws of the time and led to Sanger's arrest and indictment by an all-male grand jury. In 1916 she opened a clinic in Brooklyn where, in only 10 days before the police shut it down and arrested Sanger, 500 women were given diaphragms smuggled in from Europe (Weatherford, 1994). While upholding the laws of the day, courts did allow physicians to prescribe contraceptives for women and condoms for men to prevent venereal disease (Lunardini, 1994). By 1938 federal courts altered obscenity laws. Sanger and her associates opened a network of 300 birth control clinics nationwide, and in 1942 they established the Birth Control League, which would later become the Planned Parenthood Association (Lunardini, 1994).

In 1960 the Food and Drug Administration approved the manufacture and sale of "the pill" as a new form of contraception, which quickly became the keystone of the so-called sexual revolution (Lunardini, 1994, p. 297). Many people believe that this one innovation, in the form of a simple pill, helped make the ideas of women's liberation more practical and acceptable to a wider range of American women. In 1965 the Supreme Court ruled that states could not ban the distribution of contraceptives to married people; in 1972 the right to purchase contraceptives was extended without regard to marital status (Weatherford, 1994). For many, the sexual revolution marked the first time that women could freely explore their sexuality without being concerned about becoming pregnant.

The sexual revolution accompanied the escalation of a "singles" culture, including the hippie movement's advocating of "free sex" and the "swinging" lifestyle of the 1970s, which led to a higher rate of cohabitation and switching of sexual partners (Lunardini, 1994, pp. 297–298). Since the 1960s, the number of American heterosexual, nonmarried couples living together has increased by approximately 600 percent (Neft & Levine, 1997). Approximately half a million couples cohabited in 1960; by 1994 that figure had grown to 3.6 million. The gay rights movement emerged as well during this period, opening discussions on sexuality and the oppression of homosexuals in society. In 1973 the American Psychiatric Association officially declassified homosexuality as a psychiatric disorder (Bernikow, 1997). Yes, the times, they were a changing, as Bob Dylan sang.

The Second Wave of Feminism

In 1953 French writer and philosopher Simone de Beauvoir published *The Second Sex*, which "argued that women—like all human beings—were in essence free but that they had almost always been trapped by particularly inflexible and limiting conditions. Only by means of courageous action and self-assertive creativity could a woman become a completely free person and escape the role of the inferior 'other' that men had constructed for her gender" (McKay, Hill, & Buckler, 1995, p. 1055).

The Second-Class Status of Women

Author of several books on women's history, Louise Bernikow (1997) describes the status of U.S. women before 1965:

> Married women could not establish credit in their own names, which meant no credit cards or mortgages or other financial transactions were possible without a husband's agreement. Newspapers carried sex-segregated help-wanted ads. Employers routinely assigned certain jobs to women, others to men, with the women's jobs paying far less. There were few women in law or medical school and few visibly prominent in those professions. Under most state laws, women were routinely not allowed to be administrators of estates. Working women who became pregnant could be fired. An employer who insisted that in order to keep her job, a female employee have sex with him or submit to fondling was not breaking the law. (pp. 43–44)

In 1961 President John F. Kennedy appointed Eleanor Roosevelt to chair the Commission on the Status of Women (Weatherford, 1994). The report from this commission documented discriminatory practices in government, education, and employment and included recommendations for reform. Many states followed suit and identified discrimination at the state level. Hundreds of daily situations exemplified the second-class status of women in our society.

Here's an example. We have it on good authority that some (and we emphasize the word *some*) students (over the age of 21, of course) have been known to occasionally frequent a bar or dance club. Today most would not consider that as unusual. However, in the nineteenth and much of the twentieth century, women who frequented bars were generally assumed to be prostitutes. Businesses wanting a respectable reputation either banned women or provided a separate ladies' lounge. During World War II millions of women entered bars for the first time to join men in smoking and drinking. In 1948 an unsuccessful lawsuit was filed attempting to overturn legislation that prohibited women from working as bartenders unless their husband or father owned the bar. Some states even maintained legislation into the 1970s that prohibited women from sitting at a bar, rather than at a table (Weatherford, 1994).

At the recommendation of the president's Commission on the Status of Women, Congress passed the Equal Pay Act of 1963, which was the first national legislation for women's employment since the progressive era. However, it has proved rather difficult to enforce (Lunardini, 1994). The Civil Rights Act of 1964 prohibited private employers from discriminating on the basis of race, color, religion, national origin, or sex.

Net Notes

If you are interested in viewing documents produced during the women's liberation movement, check out a Website entitled *Sweet 16 to Saggy 36: The Saga of American Womanhood* at: **http://scriptorium.lib.duke.edu/wlm**

The Problem That Has No Name

In 1963 American author Betty Friedan, a graduate of Smith College who shortly after graduation had married and begun raising her family, helped awaken the feminist movement with the publication of her book *The Feminine Mystique*. Friedan wrote of the "problem that has no name," which she described as a vague feeling of discontent and aimlessness (p. 15). Friedan's book helped break the silence on issues such as unequal salaries, limited opportunities, and women's powerlessness in family and society (Lunardini, 1994). Friedan argued that editors of women's magazines, advertising experts, Freudian psychologists, social scientists, and educators "contributed to a romanticization of domesticity she termed 'the feminine mystique' " (Kerber & De Hart, 1991, p. 505). She further asserted that women should help themselves out of their malaise and take positive steps to reassert their identities (Lunardini, 1994). Quickly Friedan became a celebrity with a mission.

For those of you who often fly on airplanes, think about the diversity you now see among flight attendants. Did you know that up until the late 1960s, flight attendants (called stewardesses at the time) were forced to resign when they reached their early thirties, gained too much weight, or married? When hired, they were expected to be the "American image of the wholesome 'girl-next-door,' which meant white and attractive in a feminine, youthful sense" (Tobias, 1997, p. 88). Betty Friedan testified against the airlines' inherent sex discrimination policies and further disclosed the bottom line: airlines saved substantial amounts of money by firing women before they had time to accumulate pay increases, vacation time, and pension rights (Friedan, 1963).

Getting Their Acts Together

In 1966 Friedan and 27 other women attending the Third National Conference of the Commission on the Status of Women in Washington, D.C., founded the National Organization for Women, commonly referred to as NOW (NOW, 1998). NOW committed itself to "take action to bring women into full participation in the mainstream of American society" (Friedan, 1963, p. 384). The organization clearly communicated that women were ready for action *now*. NOW's current membership rolls exceed 500,000, with more than 550 chapters in the 50 states and the District of Columbia (NOW, 2001). NOW's priorities include winning economic equality and securing it with a constitutional amendment guaranteeing equal rights for women; championing abortion rights, reproductive freedom, and other women's health issues; and opposing racism, fighting bigotry against lesbians and gays, and ending violence against women.

Other organizations, such as the Women's Equity Action League (WEAL), were formed to further women's issues. In 1987 the Feminist Majority was founded to promote "equality for women and men, non-violence, social justice and economic development and to enhance feminist participation in public policy" with a mission to "empower feminists to win equality for women at the decision-making tables of the state, nation, and the world" (Feminist Majority, 1998, p. 1).

Ms. Gloria Steinem

"Gloria Steinem's name is synonymous with feminism" (Ventura, 1998, p. 160). Steinem is certainly one of the most renowned feminists. She was a leading activist in the early days of NOW, and in 1971 she joined Bella Abzug and Shirley Chisholm to found the National Women's Political Caucus (Weatherford, 1994). This group encourages women to become involved as officeholders, volunteers, political appointees, convention delegates, judges, and committee members (Lunardini, 1994). Steinem then created *Ms.* magazine, the first mainstream feminist magazine in American history (Ventura, 1998). In 1971 the preview issue of *Ms.* hit the stands, and the initial 300,000 copies were sold out within 10 days (Thom, 1997). The *Ms.* Foundation for Women, organized in 1972, supports the efforts of women and girls to govern their own lives and influence the world around them (*Ms.* Foundation for Women, 1998).

Feminist activists made numerous other groundbreaking accomplishments in a short period of time. In 1969 San Diego State University established the first baccalaureate degree program in women's studies (Lunardini, 1994). In 1970 the first congressional hearings on sex discrimination in education were held. In 1972 Title IX of the Education Omnibus Act passed, penalizing educational institutions for sex discrimination in schools. In 1973 the Supreme Court's decision in *Roe* v. *Wade* legalized abortion. In 1975 the Equal Credit Opportunity Act made credit more available to women. That same year the Rhodes Scholarship Foundation, which funded undergraduate study at Oxford University, no longer excluded women from consideration as Rhodes scholars (Bernikow, 1997). In 1981 Sandra Day O'Connor was appointed the first female justice on the U.S. Supreme Court. In 1983 Sally Ride became the first female astronaut. In 1984 Geraldine Ferraro became the first female vice presidential candidate, as Walter Mondale's running mate in his bid for the presidency. Granted, there were lots of changes, but women still did not have the same, full equal rights as men.

The Equal Rights Amendment (ERA)

Much as gaining the right to vote had brought first wave feminists together to focus on a common goal, ratification of the Equal Rights Amendment (ERA) united many second wave feminists. You may not realize that the ERA was first introduced to Congress in 1923 (Andersen, 1997). For almost 50 years it lay dormant. The 1972 version of the ERA states, "Equality of rights under the law shall not be denied or abridged by the United States or by any State on account of sex"

(Kerber & De Hart, 1991, p. 547). By an overwhelming majority, both houses of Congress passed the ERA in 1972. Shortly thereafter, 28 of the 38 states needed had ratified the ERA (Lunardini, 1994). Phyllis Schlafly, a staunchly conservative voice of the time, rallied others in opposition to the ERA, predicting the destruction of the family, among other things. A campaign known as STOP-ERA spread fear that women would be drafted and might have to serve in combat if the ERA passed (Andersen, 1997; Lunardini, 1994). In 1982 the ERA failed, just 3 states shy of the 38 needed for ratification. In 1983 the amendment was reintroduced to Congress, but its passage is still pending (Kerber & De Hart, 1991). If the ERA had passed, perhaps it wouldn't have taken until the year 1999 for a woman to be named NASA's first female shuttle commander (Dunn, 1999) and the year 2001 for women to pilot combat missions, as they did in the United States' war on terrorism.

> *The fight for the Equal Rights Amendment] is about a socialist, anti-family political movement that encourages women to leave their husbands, kill their children, practice witchcraft, destroy capitalism, and become lesbians.*
>
> *—Pat Robertson, televangelist and former presidential candidate*

No Such Thing as "THE" Feminists

Despite rumors to the contrary, feminism is still alive and well in the United States, and internationally; however, it continues to confront misunderstanding and opposition as a movement and a philosophy. One way to reduce or contain the power of something is to disassemble it. In our history we've seen whole treaties devoted to dismantling nuclear weaponry, for example. One way to reduce the perceived power of a movement, such as civil rights or feminism, is to suggest that members of the movement should be one cohesive group, all in agreement, all using the same rhetoric, and all dedicated to the same causes. When it is inevitably discovered that disagreement or diversity exists within the ranks, then the movement can be criticized and the causes ignored, because "they can't even agree among themselves."

There are many "feminisms," meaning different interpretations or approaches to achieving the goal of sexual equality. Some view this as a splintering or disintegration of feminism rather than a representation of a movement or ideology that has diversity at its core, both historically and in contemporary times. It's inaccurate to refer, as media pundits are prone to do, to "*the* feminists," because the phrase assumes that all feminists should appear en masse or speak up with completely united voices about an issue (Gillespie, 1998). When feminists differ in their particular brand of feminism or in their political or social views, these differences don't signal the demise of a movement. Feminism has always been diverse; the belief in the value of diverse approaches and voices is a strength of feminism, not a weakness. It's interesting, for example, that people don't fret over the demise of such organizations as political parties when their members disagree on key issues.

To attempt to place each and every feminist in a tidy, clearly discernible philosophical box is limiting at best and inaccurate at worst. Yet there are certain ideologies within different subsets of feminism. Currently, three strands of feminism predominate: liberal, socialist, and radical (Andersen, 1997). *Liberal feminism* has a long history and can be defined as "the theory of individual freedom for women" (Humm, 1992, p. 407). The focus of liberal feminism is on social and legal reform through policies designed to create equal opportunities for women. *Socialist feminism* contends that patriarchy and capitalism interact to create women's oppression, to further define women as the property of men, and to exploit them for the purposes of profit (Andersen, 1997). And finally, *radical feminism* "argues that women's oppression comes from being categorized as an inferior class on the basis of gender. What makes this feminism radical is that it focuses on the roots of male domination and claims that all forms of oppression are extensions of male supremacy" (Humm, 1992, p. 408). This movement embraces a separatist philosophy of radical lesbian feminism, which promotes a woman-centered world that excludes men.

Popular writings and media sound bites communicate a multitude of feminist messages, including ecofeminism, which combines interests in women's and environmental issues (Eve Online, 1998; Van Gelder, 2002); womanism (a label that now applies specifically to the feminism of African American women; Humm, 1992); Christian feminism; academic feminism; power feminism (Wolf, 1993); equity feminism (Hoff Sommers, 1994); pod feminism; postideological feminism (Faludi, 1995); multicultural feminism (Lehrman, 1992); dissident feminism (Paglia, as in Madigan, 1995); and mass-movement feminism (Hogeland, 2001). Certain strands of feminism have faded into history while others have emerged and become prominent. It is not uncommon, however, for feminist

---

'Net Notes

The Feminist Majority and the National Organization for Women are viable, activist, and highly visible national and international organizations. Many chapters of NOW exist on university campuses. For more information on these organizations, contact:

www.feminist.org

www.now.org

philosophies or viewpoints to blend or overlap at times and for various strands to share members, because, as we've stated, no one guiding perspective can be identified as *the* feminist perspective.

With the diversity of feminism and the blurring of feminist camp lines, some women felt (and still feel) alienated by the movement. Women who work inside the home and enjoy more traditional family styles often feel that they have little in common with feminists. Some feminists perpetuate mistrust by not validating those women who truly want to be traditional housewives and mothers (Lunardini, 1994). While many feminists still vehemently push to further their causes and gain choice, they are sometimes perceived as having violated the feminist golden rule by devaluing the choices of women who follow more traditional paths.

> *I'm proud to be a life-long one [feminist]. It's as natural as breathing, feeling, and thinking. Never go back, never apologize, and never forget we're half the human race.*
>
> *—Bella Abzug, political activist*

The Third Wave of Feminism

Some critics contend that feminism is dead or "stolen" (Hoff Sommers, 1994) or that we have moved into a "post-feminist" existence because feminism is no longer necessary (Denfeld, 1995; Roiphe, 1993). However, Pulitzer Prize-winning journalist Susan Faludi, author of *Backlash: The Undeclared War against American Women* (1991) and *Stiffed: The Betrayal of the American Man* (2000), contends that each time women move toward equality, a backlash occurs to restrain them, as was the case for the first and second waves of feminism. A backlash, according to Faludi, is not an organized conspiracy but a subtle yet persuasive campaign against feminist objectives which emerges in attempts to rescind many of the gains previously made by the women's movement. It is a deceptive force that permeates American culture via national and local politics and the mass media, and it prompts women to question whether equality is what they really want. A backlash will identify feminism as the devil incarnate and feminists as miserable, lonely, childless, and emotionally unstable.

In her book *Faces of Feminism: An Activist's Reflections on the Women's Movement*, Sheila Tobias (1997) describes a feminist movement for the twenty-first century that emerged in the 1990s from women in their twenties and thirties who continue to be proud to call themselves "the third wave" (p. 252). These young feminists emphasize collective action to effect change and embrace the diversity represented by various feminisms. They focus on inclusion; a multicultural emphasis; and strive to address problems stemming from sexism, racism, social class inequality, and homophobia (Baumgardner & Richards, 2000; Renzetti &

'Net Notes

For more information on third wave feminism, contact:
www.io.com/~wwwave

Curran, 1995). As Leslie Heywood and Jennifer Drake explain in their book *Third Wave Agenda* (1997), third wave feminism draws from the struggles of past waves but is not a mere extension of a past movement.

Just as other strains of feminism have had their critics, third wave feminism has been scrutinized. Some scholars charge that an overemphasis on age and generational differences associated with the movement works against effective political reform and makes "crucial conversations impossible" (Hogeland, 2001, p. 117). Others are in the process of exploring and critiquing the movement's emphasis on the self, rather than on accomplishing positive change through collectivism (Shugart, 2001; Shugart, Waggoner, & Hallstein, 2001). Still others question the movement's reliance on celebrity and media images and its close association with popular culture, in that some of its icons are television characters such as Ally McBeal, fashion models such as Kate Moss, and musicians and actors such as Alanis Morissette and Courtney Love (Bellafante, 1998; Dow, 1996; Shugart, et al., 2001). As a reporter for *Time* magazine, Ginia Bellafante (1998) suggests, "If feminism of the '60s and '70s was steeped in research and obsessed with social change, feminism today is wed to the culture of celebrity and self-obsession" (p. 57). If you are interested in learning more about third wave feminism, we recommend two books that provide insight into the movement: Barbara Findlen's *Listen Up! Voices from the Next Generation of Feminists* (1995) and Rebecca Walker's *To Be Real: Telling the Truth and Changing the Face of Feminism* (1995).

As we said earlier in this prologue, no matter whether you call yourself a feminist or embrace feminist ideals, you are now likely to be more aware of the opportunities and freedoms you enjoy that are a direct result of feminists' hard work, determination, and dedication to equality. None of us arrived where we are today without the help and work of others. Finally, let's explore the development of men's movements to see how their contributions continue to affect relationships and communication between women and men.

WHAT ABOUT "HIS STORY?"

As women's movements have progressed, men's lives have also changed significantly, often as a result of that progress. In Chapter 2, we discuss the fact that many men enjoy privilege based on their biological sex. Privilege, however, varies from man to man, depending on ethnicity, race, social class, age, physical ability, and sexual orientation (Renzetti & Curran, 1995). Men's movements, like women's movements, are not made up of one central group united around a common cause; they reflect a rich diversity of issues and followers. Some movements aren't really considered movements at all, especially if you believe that movements result when people come together to fight injustice. We'll call them movements in this prologue, but some groups view themselves more as efforts to improve the human condition through societal, political, and personal change. As we did for women's movements, we also look at men's movements from a historical standpoint, since they have affected and will continue to affect gender communication.

Early Male Supporters of Women's Rights

Historically in the United States, men have benefited from a patriarchally constructed (or male-dominated) society. However, there have always been exceptional men who fought societal trends and supported women and women's causes. Frederick Douglass, James Mott, and Henry Blackwell openly advocated women's suffrage when it certainly wasn't stylish to do so (Bernikow, 1997). After making a passionate speech at the Seneca Falls Convention, antislavery leader Frederick Douglass was maligned in Syracuse newspapers, which first called him a "wimp," then referred to him as an "Aunt Nancy" (Kimmel, 1997, p. 58). James Mott, a Quaker businessperson, cochaired the women's rights meeting at Seneca Falls with his suffragist wife, Lucretia Mott. Henry Blackwell, a persistent advocate of women's rights, helped his wife, Lucy Stone, and daughter, Alice Stone Blackwell, publish *The Woman's Journal* (Bernikow, 1997). In 1910 Max Eastman, an instructor in philosophy at Columbia University, cofounded the Men's League for Woman Suffrage (Kimmel, 1997). While these men weren't chaining themselves to fences for women's suffrage, the public support they offered was exceptional for the time.

Effects of the Sexual Revolution on Men

Over time male sex and gender roles have evolved, if not as dramatically or visibly as women's. Noted author James Doyle (1995) identifies three developments that challenged traditional views of the male gender role: technological advances, distrust of established institutions, and the women's movement. As the industrial revolution changed our society from an agrarian to a technological, service-oriented basis, men's role as providers (or "hunters," as they once were in hunter-gatherer cultures) diminished.

In the 1960s and 1970s social conflicts such as the Vietnam War, antiwar protests on college campuses, the beating of demonstrators at the Democratic National Convention in Chicago in 1968, and the killing of four students at Kent State University turned many against the government (Doyle, 1995). The 1960s saw a convergence of the civil rights movement, the women's movement, the antiwar movement, and the new left movement (Astrachan, 1986). When respect for the traditionally masculine role of soldier declined with America's increasing disillusionment with the military and the government, men experienced a significant shift in role. Along with the women's movement, this shift made it a confusing time to decide just what being a man meant. However, some people believe that the process of reconsidering sex roles and opening up new avenues of communication between men and women was a necessary and healthy development. Professor and Vietnam veteran Terry Anderson (1995) contends, "Feminists confronted sexism, provoked men to reconsider their views, and along the way brought about men's liberation. Men have the freedom to choose whether to be the provider, the decision-maker, to stay at home with the children, or to remain single" (p. 419).

Men Raised Consciousness Too

We most often think of consciousness-raising as an activity of the women's liberation movement. However, the men's movement (actually more a trend than a movement per se) in the 1970s involved consciousness-raising groups, most often focusing on individual growth. These groups "triggered changes in the lives of a few participants, but none excited people to the collective action that affected the whole society, as many women's gatherings did" (Astrachan, 1986, pp. 290–291). Up to the mid-1980s, most men actively participating in men's groups held a single guiding ideology: the elimination of the belief that one sex is superior to the other, or the eradication of sexism (Doyle, 1995). Men considered profeminist agreed generally with the feminist critique of patriarchy and organized themselves collectively to change men's behavior and attitudes (Mechling & Mechling, 1994). In 1975 the First National Conference on Men and Masculinity was held in Knoxville, Tennessee. Associations such as the National Organization for Men against Sexism (originally called the National Organization for Changing Men) were founded during this time (Astrachan, 1986).

Profeminist men (many of whom simply call themselves feminists) are still active today (Messner, 1998). The male coauthor of your textbook is one of them. Groups of profeminists may well be active on your campus. University profeminist men often organize Take Back the Night marches, which are programs that honor survivors of rape and sexual assault; present programs on sexual assault to fraternities, dorms, and athletic teams; and teach and take courses on masculinity (Kimmel, 1997). They also initiate and join campus groups such as Men Acting for Change (MAC), Men Opposed to Sexist Tradition (MOST), Men against Sexual Harassment (MASH), Men against Sexual Assault (MASA), and Men against Rape and Sexism (MARS) (Kimmel, 1997). Hobart College in Geneva, New York, started a men's studies academic program in 1997, but it has been criticized for offering "fluff" and "touchy-feely" courses that are more like therapy than legitimate content courses. That is the same criticism that has been leveled at women's studies programs for decades.

A Movement of Fathers

Another movement of men in the 1960s and 1970s involved fathers' rights in divorce and child custody cases. In Colonial times fathers retained domestic control and defined and supervised their children's development; wives were expected to defer to their husbands (Furstenberg, 1988, as in Skolnick & Skolnick, 1997). Until the middle of the nineteenth century, if "marital disruption" occurred the father was typically awarded custody because fathers "were assumed to maintain control over marital property (of which the children were a part)" (Furstenberg, 1988, p. 224). During this period women often died in childbirth, leaving their widowed husbands responsible for their children. The children were most often turned over to another woman in the family to raise. With the industrial revolution, public and private spheres became more separate—men worked in the outside world and women worked in the home attending to the needs of the children (Doyle, 1995).

By the end of the century women predominantly were awarded custody of their children because women were believed to possess superior parenting skills (Furstenberg, 1988). The courts subsequently adopted a "tender years presumption," meaning that during a child's younger years she or he needed a mother more than a father (Renzetti & Curran, 1995, p. 217). This dramatically shifted custody decisions in favor of mothers and against fathers, a practice that still continues in today's courts. This trend has led many men around the country to challenge the courts and move for equal custody and parenting rights. Attorney and activist Andrew Kimbrell (1995) asserts that as men promote a national fatherhood policy, it is just as important to change our culture's view of men and fatherhood as it is to change laws and public policy. Support groups and activist organizations have been formed, such as Fathers United for Equal Rights, U.S. Divorce Reform, the Coalition Organized for Parental Equality (COPE), Divorced American Men Unite (DAMU), and the National Congress for Men (NCM).

We are living at an important and fruitful moment now, for it is clear to men that the images of adult manhood given by the popular culture are worn out; a man can no longer depend on them. By the time a man is thirty-five he knows that the images of the right man, the tough man, the true man which he received in high school do not work in life.

—Robert Bly, author

There Are Some "Wild Men" Out There

Another contemporary social movement is most often referred to simply as the men's movement, but its more elaborate name is the mythopoetic movement. The most noteworthy spokesperson for the mythopoetic movement is the author and poet Robert Bly. Bly's best-selling book *Iron John* (1990) utilizes mythology and Grimm's fairy tales to help men find the "community inside the psyche" (p. 227). This means that men are encouraged to seek out different parts or roles within themselves.

Bly and other advocates of mythopoetics promote men's self-discovery and masculinity through nature and tribal rituals. At retreats called "wildman gatherings," men beat drums, tearfully hug one another, dance in ritualistic circles, smear one another's bodies with mud, and huddle around a campfire howling (Kimbrell, 1995, p. 133; Natharius, 1992). One goal of such gatherings is to encourage men to explore the complicated relationships most have with their fathers, engaging the psychological and emotional wounds left over from childhood. In turn, the hope is that these men will become better fathers to their own children.

The Million Man March

On October 16, 1995, an estimated 400,000 men attended the Million Man March on the federal mall in Washington, D.C. (*USA Today*, 1996). Organized by the controversial head of the Nation of Islam, Louis Farrakhan, the march was intended to rally the black community and strengthen black families by emphasizing the role of fathers. Farrakhan (1998) described the event as "A Holy Day of Atonement and Reconciliation"; he called for "one million disciplined, committed, and dedicated Black men, from all walks of life in America, to march in Washington, D.C." (p. 1). Emphasizing the need for fathers to bolster black family life, Farrakhan asserted that "as men, we must recognize and unconditionally atone for the absence, in too many cases, of the Black male as the head of the household, positive role model and building block of our community. We believe that we must atone for, and establish positive solutions to, the abuse and misuse of our women and girls" (p. 1). Since that time, similar marches among African American women and, more recently, a rally for black youth in Harlem, have worked to strengthen African Americans' self-esteem and pride and to build community (Bekker, 1997).

Keeping Those Promises

Most of you have probably heard of Promise Keepers, a movement based on fundamental Christian traditions and beliefs. While the movement has lost a great deal of steam since the 1990s, it is still active and viable. Bill McCartney, a successful head football coach at the University of Colorado, and his friend Dave Wardell conceived of the organization in 1990 as they were driving to a dinner held by the Fellowship of Christian Athletes (McCartney & Diles, 1995). The two discussed the idea of filling a stadium with Christian men coming together for the purpose of Christian discipleship. Their idea came to fruition, and the first Promise Keepers conference was attended by 4,200 men in July 1991. Since that time, more than 3.5 million men have attended nearly 100 Promise Keepers' conferences in stadiums and arenas (Kellner, 2000).

In its mission statement, Promise Keepers is described as a "Christ-centered ministry dedicated to uniting men through vital relationships to become Godly influences in their world" (Promise Keepers, 1998, p. 1). The promises these men make are intended to guide them toward Christ, to transform them as people, and to challenge them to assume active leadership roles within their own families (Dobson et al., 1994; Silverstein, Auerbach, Grieco, & Dunkel, 1999). Small discussion groups are intended to draw men into a closer relationship with Christ, and stadium events motivate men to pursue spiritual growth (Promise Keepers, 1998).

The Promise Keepers movement is not without controversy. Promise Keepers' stance on homosexuality is that the Bible "clearly teaches that homosexuality violates God's creative design for a husband and wife and that it is a sin" (Promise Keepers, 1998, p. 1). Although the organization declares that it is not politically motivated in any way, others disagree. Conason, Ross, and Cokorinos (1996), writing in *The Nation,* assert that "Promise Keepers appears to be one of the most sophisticated creations of the religious right" (p. 19), which includes such highly conservative factions as the Christian Coalition, a group with a definite political agenda.

Some suggest that the high point for the Promise Keepers movement may have come in 1997, when approximately 1 million men attended the Stand in the Gap rally in Washington, D.C. Since that time, attendance at rallies has declined, leading to a shift to more arena settings than stadiums and more emphasis on men's groups within local churches (Dooley, 2001). The organization has suffered financial woes, closed several regional offices, and downsized its staff. However, the Promise Keepers are still alive and well, with rallies planned well into the twenty-first century, along with book and tape projects and the development of a family-friendly Internet service provider (Kellner, 2000; Morley, 2000).

Many women applaud the efforts of Promise Keepers to strengthen men's roles in the family unit. However, other women are concerned that the movement may be attempting to turn back the clock. The National Organization for Women organized a Promise Keepers Mobilization Project in order to monitor the activities of the group (NOW, 1997). Many feminists (not just members of NOW) are concerned because of the possibility that exhortations to men to reclaim some "rightful" place as family and societal leaders will imperil gains toward equality achieved thus far. If a man asserts a "divine right" to be head of the household and make decisions for his wife and children, no matter the preference of other family members, for many people this conjures up images of power and domination, not leadership.

It will be interesting to track the progress of the several men's movements, including the Promise Keepers, into this new century. Will the mythopoetic wild men still be around? Will we see growth in men's studies programs on college campuses? Will fathers win more custody suits and change the trend in the courts? Will there be more marches on capitals in the name of one sex or the other? We suspect that women's and men's movements will continue, but it might be interesting to see if a "human" movement emerges in the new millennium.

GENDER COMMUNICATION: LOOKING FORWARD

Why have we included so much information on women's and men's movements in this prologue? Relevant historical events that shape gender communication are either skimmed over or not taught at most levels of secondary school. In some school districts, parents strongly affirm traditional sex roles and believe that controversial topics such as women's movements, homosexuality, and the Vietnam War are to be avoided (Loewen, 1995). Even in colleges and universities today, often only students enrolled in specialized courses in women's history are exposed to this important material.

It's important to understand how our current state of gender communication came to be, to realize that there is a historical context for why women and men relate to one another as they do. When you hear feminists discuss disparity in wages between the sexes or men argue for fathers' rights, knowing some of the historical details that preceded the status quo facilitates more effective gender communication. When you embrace racial diversity, it's important to comprehend what people of color have historically encountered. When you participate in intimate relationships and grapple with reproductive issues, you gain perspective on the history of birth control and controversies surrounding reproductive rights. When you hear that less than 40 percent of eligible voters in the United States actually vote these days, perhaps you will wonder if suffragists are rolling over in their graves.

When you study the theories and effective tools of gender communication we explore in this text, we hope that looking at our past will help you plan your future. And as for that class where men received a 100 percent grade and women a lower score, those of you who received the unfair marks can just be thankful you didn't take this class in the 1970s—your score would have been 58 percent, and you would have failed.

References

Andersen, M. (1997). *Thinking about women: Sociological perspectives on sex and gender* (4th ed.). Boston: Allyn & Bacon.

Anderson, T. (1995). *The movement and the sixties: Protest in America from Greensboro to Wounded Knee.* New York: Oxford University Press.

Astrachan, A. (1986). *How men feel: Their response to women's demands for equality and power.* Garden City, NY: Anchor Press/Doubleday.

Baumgardner, J., & Richards, A. (2000). *Manifesta: Young women, feminism, and the future.* New York: Farrar, Straus and Giroux.

Bekker, S. (1997, October 26). Sending a message of solidarity: Civil rights issues voiced at Million Woman March. *Corpus Christi Caller Times*, pp. A1, A14.

Bellafante, G. (1998, June 29). Feminism: It's all about me! *Time*, 54–62.

Bernikow, L. (1997). *The American women's almanac: An inspiring and irreverent women's history.* New York: Berkley Books.

Bly, R. (1990). *Iron John: A book about men.* Reading, MA: Addison-Wesley.

Carver, M. (1999, October). *Lucy Stone: Apostle for a "New Woman."* Paper presented at the 22nd Conference of the Organization for the Study of Communication, Language, and Gender, Wichita, KS.

Colman, P. (1995). *Rosie the riveter.* New York: Crown.

Conason, J., Ross, A., & Cokorinos, L. (1996, October 7). The Promise Keepers are coming: The third wave of the religious right. *The Nation,* 11–19.

Denfeld, R. (1995). *The new Victorians: A young woman's challenge to the old feminist order.* New York: Warner.

Dobson, J., Bright, B., Cole, E., Evans, T., McCartney, B., Palau, L., Phillips, R., & Smalley, G. (1994). *Seven promises of a Promise Keeper.* Colorado Springs: Focus on the Family.

Dooley, T. (2001, September 29). Renewing the promise: Men's group downsizes venues, expands spiritual horizons. *The Houston Chronicle.* (Online.)

Dow, B. J. (1996). *Prime-time feminism: Television, media culture, and the Women's Movement since 1970.* Philadelphia: University of Pennsylvania Press.

Doyle, J. (1995). *The male experience* (3rd ed.). Madison, WI: Brown & Benchmark.

Dunn, M. (1999, July 18). Woman will be in charge when Columbia launches this week. *Corpus Christi Caller Times,* pp. A1, A5.

Eve Online. (1998, November 14). What is ecofeminism anyway? *Ecofeminist Visions Emerging.* (Online.) Available: http://www.enviroweb.org/eve/what.html

Faludi, S. (1991). *Backlash: The undeclared war against American women.* New York: Crown.

Faludi, S. (1995, March). "I'm not a feminist but I play one on TV." *Ms.,* 30–39.

Faludi, S. (2000). *Stiffed: The betrayal of the American man.* New York: William Morrow.

Farrakhan, L. (1998, November 16). Second opinion. *Minister Louis Farrakhan on the Million Man March.* (Online.) Available: http://users.aol.com/camikem/eyeview/millionman.html

Feminist Majority. (1998, November 18). The Feminist Majority. *Feminist Majority Foundation Home Page.* (Online.) Available: http://www.feminist.org/welcome/fm_1987–88.html

Findlen, B. (1995). *Listen up! Voices from the next feminist generation.* Seattle: Seal Press.

Friedan, B. (1963). *The feminine mystique.* New York: Laurel.

Frisken, A. (2000). Sex in politics: Victoria Woodhull as an American public woman, 1870–1876. *Journal of Women's History, 12,* 89–111.

Furstenberg, F. F., Jr. (1988). Good dad—bad dads: Two faces of fatherhood. In A. Cherlin (Ed.), *The changing American family.* New York: Urban Institute Press.

Gillespie, M. A. (1998, May–June). The backlash boogie. *Ms.,* 1.

Greenspan, K. (1994). *The timetables of women's history: A chronology of the most important people and events in women's history.* New York: Simon & Schuster.

Heywood, L., & Drake, J. (1997). *Third wave agenda: Being feminist, doing feminism.* Minneapolis: University of Minnesota Press.

Hoff Sommers, C. (1994). *Who stole feminism? How women have betrayed women.* New York: Simon & Schuster.

Hogeland, L. M. (2001). Against generational thinking, or, some things that "third wave" feminism isn't. *Women's Studies in Communication, 24,* 107–121.

Humm, M. (Ed.). (1992). *Modern feminisms: Political, literary, cultural.* New York: Columbia University Press.

Kellner, M. A. (2000). Keeping their promises. *Christianity Today, 44,* 21.

Kerber, L., & De Hart, J. (1991). *Women's America: Refocusing the past* (3rd ed.). New York: Oxford University Press.

Kimbrell, A. (1995). *The masculine mystique: The politics of masculinity.* New York: Ballantine Books.

Kimmel, M. (1997, November–December). Real men join the movement. *Ms.,* 52–59.

Lehrman, K. (1992, March 16). The feminist mystique—*Backlash: The undeclared war against American women* by Susan Faludi/*Revolution from within: A book of self-esteem* by Gloria Steinem. *The New Republic,* 30–34.

Loewen, J. (1995). *Lies my teacher told me: Everything your American history textbook got wrong.* New York: Touchstone.

Lunardini, C. (1994). *What every American should know about women's history.* Holbrook, MA: Bob Adams.

Madigan, T. J. (1995, Spring). Camille Paglia on free thought, feminism, and iconoclasm. *Free Inquiry,* 5–8.

McCartney, B., & Diles, D. (1995). *From ashes to glory.* Nashville: Thomas Nelson.

McKay, J., Hill, B., & Buckler, J. (1995). *A history of western society, volume II: From absolutism to the present* (5th ed.). Boston: Houghton Mifflin.

Mechling, E., & Mechling, J. (1994). The Jung and the restless: The mythopoetic men's movement. *Southern Communication Journal, 59,* 97–111.

Messner, M. A. (1998). The limits of the "male sex role": An analysis of the men's liberation and men's rights movements' discourse. *Gender & Society, 12,* 255–276.

Morley, P. (2000). The next Christian men's movement. *Christianity Today, 44,* 84–86.

Ms. Foundation for Women. (1998). What does the *Ms.* Foundation for Women do? (Online.) Available: http://www.ms.foundation./org/ms/msdo97.html

Natharius, D. (1992, October). *From the hazards of being male to fire in the belly: Are men finally getting it and, if so, what are they getting?* Paper presented at the meeting of the Speech Communication Association, Chicago, IL.

National Organization for Women (NOW). (1997, October). NOW promises "no surrender" to right-wing Promise Keepers. *NOW National Times,* p. 1.

National Organization for Women (NOW). (1998, November 18). The history of the National Organization for Women. *National Organization for Women (NOW) Home Page.* (Online.) Available: http://www.now.org/history/history.html

National Organization for Women (NOW). (2001). Frequently asked questions. *National Organization for Women (NOW) Home Page.* (Online.) Available: http://www.now.org

Neft, N., & Levine, A. (1997). *Where women stand: An international report on the status of women in 140 countries, 1997–1998.* New York: Random House.

Promise Keepers. (1998, October 14). Mission statement. *Official Promise Keepers Site.* (Online.) Available: http://www.promisekeepers.org.html

Renzetti, C., & Curran, D. (1995). *Women, men and society* (3rd ed.). Boston: Allyn & Bacon.

Roiphe, K. (1993). *The morning after: Sex, fear, and feminism on campus.* Boston: Little Brown.

Ruth, S. (1990). *Issues in feminism: An introduction to women's studies.* Mountain View, CA: Mayfield.

Shugart, H. A. (2001). Isn't it ironic?: The intersection of third-wave feminism and generation X. *Women's Studies in Communication, 24,* 131–168.

Shugart, H. A., Waggoner, C. E., & Hallstein, D. L. O. (2001). Mediating third-wave feminism: Appropriation as postmodern media practice. *Critical Studies in Media Communication, 18,* 194–210.

Silverstein, L. B., Auerbach, C. F., Grieco, L., & Dunkel, F. (1999). Do Promise Keepers dream of feminist sheep? *Sex Roles, 40,* 665–688.

Skolnick, A., & Skolnick, J. (1997). *Family in transition* (9th ed.). New York: Longman.

Theriot, N. (1996). *Mothers and daughters in nineteenth-century America: The biosocial construction of femininity.* Lexington: University of Kentucky Press.

Thom, M. (1997). *Inside Ms.: 25 years of the magazine and the feminist movement.* New York: Henry Holt.

Tobias, S. (1997). *Faces of feminism: An activist's reflections on the women's movement.* Boulder, CO: Westview.

USA Today. (1996, February 16). Washington's great gatherings. *USA Today.* (Online.) Available: http://www.usatoday.com/news/index/nman006

U. S. Department of Labor, Women's Bureau. (2002). Earnings differences between women and men. In P. J. Dubeck & D. Dunn (Eds.), *Workplace/women's place: An anthology* (2nd ed.) (pp. 57–63). Los Angeles: Roxbury.

Van Gelder, L. (2002, Spring). It's not nice to mess with mother nature: Ecofeminism 101. *Ms.*, 57–59.

Ventura, V. (1998). *Sheroes: Bold, brash, and absolutely unabashed superwomen.* Berkeley, CA: Conari.

Walker, R. (1995). *To be real: Telling the truth and changing the face of feminism.* New York: Anchor.

Weatherford, D. (1994). *American women's history: An A to Z of people, organizations, issues, and events.* New York: Prentice-Hall.

Wolf, N. (1993). *Fire with fire: The new female power and how to use it.* New York: Fawcett Columbine.

PART ONE

COMMUNICATION, GENDER AND EFFECTIVENESS

CHAPTER ONE

GENDER JARGON AND EFFECTIVE COMMUNICATION:

Learning to Talk the Talk

Hot Topics

- What gender communication is and why you are studying it
- Meanings of such terms as sex, gender, gender identity, androgyny, sexual orientation, heterosexism, homophobia, and transgender
- What feminism, patriarchy, and sexism mean today
- How uncertainty affects gender communication and motivates us in relationships
- How to communicate from a receiver orientation
- What it means to be personally effective in communication with women and men
- How values are associated with gender communication that leads to successful and satisfying relationships

WHAT IS GENDER COMMUNICATION?

You can hardly log onto the Internet, open a magazine or newspaper, or turn on the television these days without coming across a discussion of "problems that plague the sexes." Lots of people are talking about societal issues dividing women and men, whether these issues involve situations of professional communication between coworkers of both sexes, confusion over interpersonal signals, competing messages of homemaking versus a career, or verbal exchanges that result in violence. One thing is certain: Communication between women and men is a popular topic of conversation, study, and research—more now than ever, it seems. But is this popular topic all there is to the term *gender communication?* What is encompassed by the term? Just what *is* this topic you're going to read about and study?

First you need to understand that we're putting the words *gender* and *communication* together to form a modern label for an ancient phenomenon. Gender communication is a unique, fascinating subset of a larger phenomenon known as communication. From our perspective, not all communication is gender communication.

Here's a simple way to understand this perspective on gender communication: **Gender communication is communication *about* and *between* men and women.** The front part of the statement—the "about" aspect—involves how the sexes are discussed, referred to, or depicted, both verbally and nonverbally. The back part of the definition—the "between" aspect—is the interpersonal dimension of gender communication, and it's a bit harder to understand.

We believe that communication becomes *gendered* when sex or gender overtly begins to influence your choices—choices of what you say and how you relate to others. For example, two students could be talking about a project for class. The students could be both male, both female, or of opposite sexes. The sex composition of the communicators doesn't matter in a judgment of whether gender communication is going on or not. Thus far, the conversation about the class project doesn't necessarily involve gender communication. But what happens if the conversation topic shifts to a discussion of political issues especially relevant to women, or whom the interactants are dating, or opinions regarding parenting responsibilities? For these topics, the awareness of one's own sex, the other person's sex, or both may come into play; thus gender communication is occurring. Notice that we said "may come into play," because the topic doesn't always dictate whether or not gender communication is occurring.

Take another example: You may be talking with someone about the weather or some local current event. The topic isn't related to sex or gender, but as the conversation progresses you find that you are becoming attracted to the other person. You become acutely aware of your own and the other person's sex. *Now* we would say that gender communication is happening. Examples can also be found in situations that don't involve attraction. Suppose you merely become aware, during a conversation, that you are presenting a "female view" of something and are seeking a "male view," or vice versa. That sounds like playing into stereotypes, but in some situations you may become aware that your own slant on something is overtly affected by your sex or gender. Can you see the difference between these two examples and the first example of classmates discussing a project? When sex or gender becomes an overt factor in your communication, when you become conscious of your own or another person's sex or gender, then gender communication is operating.

However, some scholars believe that gender is an all-encompassing designation, a personal characteristic so pervasive that communication cannot escape its effects. In this view, all communication is gendered (Spender, 1985; Thorne, Kramarae, & Henley, 1983; Wilson Schaef, 1981). These viewpoints—our more restricted approach to gender communication and the more pervasive perspective—aren't necessarily contradictory. You can study gender communication and operate from both perspectives. In other words, the information in this text can be applicable whether one views gender communication as a specific form of communication or whether one believes that all communication is gendered. Essentially, there is no "right" conceptualization of the relationship between gender and communication; it's too complicated a topic for a "right" or "wrong" approach.

WHY STUDY GENDER COMMUNICATION?

Gender communication is *provocative, popularized, pervasive, problematic,* and *unpredictable*—which makes it fascinating to study.

Provocative: Gender communication is *provocative* because we're all interested in how we're perceived, how we communicate with other human beings, and how others respond to us. We're all especially interested in communication with members of the other sex, for several reasons—the most obvious being that we cannot experience the other sex firsthand. Also, we're interested in the possible rewards that may result from effective gender communication.

Popularized: Have you read any of the popular books that claim the sexes are from different planets or different cultures? We've said that gender communication is a hot topic in our culture, as is evidenced by the many books, television shows, Websites, films, and songs devoted to it. But we need to separate popularized material from scientific or research-based information about gender and communication. They both have their place, and we draw from each in this textbook. Since you're more likely to be aware of the popularized treatments of gender, we offer a balance by reviewing research findings that provide meaningful insights into sex, gender, and communication.

Pervasive: Gender communication is *pervasive,* meaning that interaction with women and men occurs every day, every hour. The sheer number of contacts we have with members of the other sex heightens interest in the effects of sex and gender on the communication process. When those contacts affect us in profound ways, such as in social or work relationships, the importance of these relationships and the pervasiveness of our interactions with significant people further necessitate improved understanding of gender communication.

Problematic: Saying that gender communication is *problematic* doesn't mean that all gender communication centers around problems, but that it is complicated. Communication itself is complex; it's not a simple process that can be accomplished just because we're human beings who learned language at some early age or because we've been talking all our lives. When you add sex and gender (like other forms of human diversity) into the communication process, you expand the complexity because now there is more than one way of looking at or talking about something.

Unpredictable: Gender communication is *unpredictable* in that societal norms, rules, and roles have changed dramatically and seem to change more every day. For example, often our students talk about their difficulties with seemingly simple rituals, such as dating etiquette. Female students reveal their own inconsistency, in that they want a guy to treat them to a night out, but they also like offering to pay for themselves. Male students complain, "If I open the car door for my date, she'll think that I don't respect her as a competent, 'liberated' woman who can take care of herself. But if I don't open the car door, she'll think that I was raised by wolves and have no manners at all." In these situations and countless others, lessons people learned while growing up come into conflict with changes in society, leaving confusion as to what is appropriate behavior.

If you have reason to believe that communication between men and women is so confusing that maybe it isn't worth trying to improve, or that you'll just stumble along until the right person automatically understands what you say, think, and feel, we have a better suggestion: Hang in there with this course you're taking and this book you've been assigned to read. We not only summarize research-based and popularized information in this text, but also provide practical suggestions about how to apply the knowledge to your life experiences. Your textbook authors and your instructor want you not only to *know* the current information on gender communication, but also to be able to *use* the information to enhance your communication skills and enrich your relationships. The first thing to know is the lingo.

GENDER JARGON

Many gender-related terms are assigned different meanings, primarily by the media. Your own experience also may give you meanings that differ from textbook terminology. So to reduce the potential for confusion, we offer you here some common gender communication terms and their most commonly used meanings. Becoming more skilled in your communication with men and women begins with the use of current, sensitive, accurate language.

Is It Sex or Is It Gender?

You've probably already heard the terms *sex* and *gender* used interchangeably, and some people think the terms are indeed interchangeable. For the sake of clarity, however, we use them in this text with exclusive meanings. For our purposes, the term *sex* means the biological and physiological characteristics that make us female or male. At some points in this text we use the term *sex* to refer to sexual activity between men and women, but it will be clear to you whether the term is meant as a categorization of persons or an activity.

The term used most often in this text (even in the title) is *gender.* Most narrowly, gender refers to psychological and emotional characteristics of individuals. You may understand these characteristics to be masculine, feminine, or androgynous (a combination of both feminine and masculine traits). But gender encompasses more than this. Defined broadly, the term *gender* includes personality traits, but it also involves psychological makeup; attitudes, beliefs, and values; sexual orientation; and gender identity (defined below).

Gender is culturally constructed: that is, one's femaleness or maleness is more extensive than the fact of being born anatomically female or male. What is *attached* or *related* to that anatomy is taught to you through our culture, virtually from the time you are born. In their book on gender and society, Thorne, Kramarae, and Henley (1983) explain, "gender is not a unitary, or 'natural' fact, but takes shape in concrete, historically changing social relationships" (p. 16). Culture, with its evolving customs, rules, and expectations for behavior, has the power to affect your perception of gender. For example, if you were raised in the Middle East, your views regarding the status and role of women in society will be quite different from what they would be if you were raised in the United States. Perhaps you grew up with strict rules for appropriate male-

> *I can't stand people that can't stand one of the sexes. We've only got two. Why would you dislike one of them?*
>
> *—Drew Barrymore, actor*

female behavior, such as, "Men ask women out on dates; women do not call men for dates." When you encounter members of other cultures (or your own culture, for that matter) who do not adhere to clearly drawn gender lines or who operate on the basis of rules different from your own, then the notable difference may reinforce your original conception of gender or cause it to change.

The American dualistic view of gender is not the only way culture is conceived in all societies. Devor (1992) describes Aboriginal cultures which have multiple gender categories and accept the idea that gender may be changed without altering one's biological sex. Some native peoples in North and South America have legitimate social categories for persons who wish to define their own gender, regardless of their biological sex.

In studying communication about and between women and men, it is helpful to use the term *sex* as a biological determination and *gender* as something that is culturally constructed. Sex is binary: there are only two choices. However, there are many choices when it comes to gender. Thus, you'll see references in this text to the "opposite or other sex," meaning a comparison between female and male. If you understand the notion of gender as a broad-based, multifaceted concept, then you understand why there is no such thing as an "opposite gender."

Viewing gender as culturally constructed allows one to change or reconstruct gender. This is a powerful idea. For example, the way you see the gender of "male, masculine" or "female, feminine" is not the way you *have* to see it. You can learn to see it differently and more broadly if you discover new information. This is discussed more thoroughly in Chapter 2; but for now, consider these examples: What if a guy discovers that "being a man" doesn't mean that he has to be strong and emotionally nonexpressive? He might decide that he's tired of always being the strong one, that he'd rather express his emotions and get some help instead. A woman might realize that her ability to climb the ladder of professional success is stronger than her nurturing instinct, so she chooses a career over motherhood as her primary life's work. Might these discoveries alter one's vision of gender? Possibly, but these people don't merely replace one stereotypical trait with another; they expand their options and find new ways of seeing themselves in relation to others. That's one of the goals of this text—to give you different ways of seeing things, including gender.

Here's one more example to clarify the notion of gender-as-constructed. While genetic research brings choosing the sex of one's child closer to a reality every day, most of us still will have no control over the sex of our children. However, we have much to do with the development or construction of the child's gender. What's the first question most people ask when they hear the news that a baby has been born? Generally, the first reaction is, "Is it a boy or a girl?" "Pink or blue?" Imagine if you asked a new mother, "Is it a boy or a girl?" and the answer was, "Yes." (That's not the usual response, so you might conclude that the new mother must still be suffering the effects of childbirth!) But once we find out the biological sex of the child, different sets of expectations, attitudes, and treatments—what can be termed stereotypical gender "baggage"—are called up in our brain and enacted. Thus, friends present the proud parents with a baseball mitt for a male baby and a doll for a female baby. People talk to girl babies and boy babies quite differently. If gender were not societally induced or constructed, we would not feel the need to align the sex of a child with a particular object or color, or to alter our style of communication.

One of the more provocative illustrations of these ideas can be found in "X: A Fabulous Child's Story" by Lois Gould (1972). Gould offers a fictional account of a child named X whose parents participated in an experimental study by not revealing to anyone the biological sex of the child. The story progresses from infancy through childhood, as X plays with other children, goes to school and deals with sex-specific bathrooms, and is pronounced mentally healthy by a psychiatrist. What is most fascinating in this story is people's reactions to X. Adults and children alike in the story had extreme difficulty in coping with not knowing the child's sex. It was as if they didn't know how to behave without sex-based information to guide them. Students who read this story also reveal discomfort in not knowing the sex of the child.

Biological sex suggests several things about how women and men communicate and are communicated with, but biology isn't destiny, and that's the powerful potential of studying gender communication. A person's sex isn't easily changed, but a person's concept of gender is far more open to change and development.

Remember. . .

GENDER COMMUNICATION: Communication about and between women and men.

SEX: A biological designation of being female or male.

GENDER: A cultural construction which includes biological sex (male or female), psychological characteristics (femininity, masculinity, androgyny), attitudes about the sexes, and sexual orientation.

Gender Identity, Androgyny, and Sexual Orientation

In this text, we use the term *gender identity* as a subset of gender to refer to the way you view yourself, how you see yourself relative to stereotypically feminine or masculine traits. Your self-esteem may be connected, in part, to your gender identity, meaning that sometimes people's self-esteem is affected when they measure themselves against some ideal or stereotype of what a woman or man is supposed to be.

Many people are more comfortable viewing themselves as androgynous, meaning that they possess and blend traits typically associated with one sex or the other. *Androgyny* is a term made popular by gender scholar Sandra Bem (1974); the term is derived from the Greek *andros,* meaning man; and *gyne,* meaning woman. Androgynous women aren't necessarily masculine or sexless; likewise, androgynous men aren't necessarily effeminate, gay, or asexual. This form of gender identity simply involves a blending of sex-associated traits, rather than an adherence to only those traits associated with femininity or masculinity (Lippa, 2002).

Another component of gender is your general perception of appropriate roles for women and men in the society of which you are a member. The term *gender identity* thus encompasses not only your vision of self but your vision of the roles or functions for human beings within a given culture. While your gender identity is affected by your sex and your gender, it is within your power to change this identity. But what about a remaining element within the broad-based view of gender—an element which, in the view of many, you have no control over?

To use the term *sexual preference* to designate a person as heterosexual, homosexual, or bisexual is to use outdated terminology. The word *preference* implies that a person *chooses* his or her sexuality, that a person can make a conscious decision about sexuality. The prevailing view is that one's *sexual orientation,* that is, to whom one is sexually attracted or with whom one has sexual relations, is a characteristic of a person, not a person's choice (Majors, 1994). Many members of the gay and lesbian community in this country and abroad contend that they were born gay, not shaped into homosexuality by life's experiences or societal factors. Whatever your view of this issue of choice or no choice, being inclusive, sensitive, and contemporary in language usage requires referring to a person's sexuality as an orientation, not a preference.

Discriminatory attitudes and behavior which communicate the belief that heterosexuality is superior to homosexuality or bisexuality are termed *heterosexist* (Griffin, 1998). Often this form of discrimination manifests itself by omission, rather than by commission—it's not what you say; it's the assumption you communicate by what you leave out or don't say. The following question will illustrate what we mean here: Have you ever heard an instructor use a real or hypothetical example involving homosexuals to illustrate or clarify a principle or concept in a class? Even today, in a world that is more enlightened about different forms of sexuality, when an instructor casually provides an example depicting, say, the dating behaviors of a homosexual couple, the reactions of students across the room may be such that the instructor can't continue. Students often seem so taken aback by a reference such as "John and Bob out on a first date" that the lesson, the point of the example, becomes lost. Has this happened at your institution? When one of the authors of this textbook tries to use homosexual examples in courses on gender and interpersonal communication, the giggles across the room, the strange looks that pass between students, and the chatter that invariably ensues obstruct the point. Thus an instructor's choice to use—primarily, if not exclusively—examples of heterosexual interaction to clarify information about human communication, as well as students' protestations at merely raising an example involving homosexual individuals, may represent heterosexism of omission (Heinz, 2002). Instances of more obvious, concrete discrimination against anything not heterosexual represents heterosexism of commission.

Some confusion surrounds the term *homophobia*. We have found three usages of this term: (1) Homophobia can refer to a general fear of persons who are homosexual in sexual orientation. (2) The term may also describe the fear of being labeled a homosexual. (3) Within homosexual communities, homophobia may be used to mean behavior or attitudes that indicate self-hatred or severe loss of self-esteem. In these cases, the homosexual individual, out of anger or hatred for her or his orientation, acts or thinks in ways that direct this anger onto the self.

A final term warrants attention in this section—persons describing themselves as *transgender*. You may be unfamiliar with this term because it is rather new, but more and more is being written and discussed about this form of identity. First, don't make the mistake of confusing this term with others, like transvestitism (cross-dressing), hermaphroditism (being born with both male and female genitalia), or transsexualism (being biologically of one sex but identifying psychologically with the other, often resulting in the altering of one's biological sex through medical methods). Gender scholars Ekins and King (1997) offer this distinction: Transvestite and transsexual "identities were/are hidden identities. The male transsexual and the male transvestite in public seek to pass as women—not to be read as a transsexual or transvestite. In contrast, the trans-

Hot Button Issue

"GENDER BLURRING"

Ah, the good old days when men were men and women were women and you knew the difference. But were those days really that good? While we may sometimes yearn for a simpler time, a time when navigating the gender and relationship waters was less complicated, was it really preferable to what we have now? Images of a man, a woman, maleness, and femaleness are more blurred today than they were in the past. Might that be seen as a good thing? Is it a welcome freedom for individuals to create their own genders, released from the confines of societal definitions for how they're supposed to behave, feel, and express themselves?

Remember. . .

GENDER IDENTITY: A view of the self relative to feminine or masculine traits, as well as one's vision of the roles or functions for people within a given culture.

ANDROGYNY: A blending of masculine and feminine personality traits.

SEXUAL ORIENTATION: To whom one is sexually attracted or with whom one has sexual relations.

HETEROSEXISM: Discriminatory attitudes and behavior communicating the belief that heterosexuality is superior to homosexuality or bisexuality.

HOMOPHOBIA: A general fear of homosexual persons; a fear of being labeled a homosexual; a homosexual's behavior or attitudes that indicate self-hatred or severe loss of self-esteem.

TRANSGENDER: A unique gender identity not confined by traditional notions of masculinity or femininity.

---

gender identity breaks down the gender dichotomy by mixing and matching its characteristics in any combination. It is also a more open identity in that transgenderists are perceived as neither male nor female" (p. 341).

As author of *Transgender Warriors* Leslie Feinberg (1997) explains, transgender identity involves "the right of each individual to express their gender in any way they choose, whether feminine, androgynous, masculine, or any point on the spectrum between. And that includes the right to gender ambiguity and gender contradiction." Transgender persons strive to challenge the patriarchal, traditional idea of gender—in essence, taking the concept of gender-as-constructed to its fullest extent. For example, Lennard Davis (2000) writes about a conversation with his son, who explained that he was transgender. He didn't mean that he was homosexual or desirous of a sex-change operation, but simply that he didn't want to comply with the boundaries of binary sex (only two choices) or the societal confines of gender. He wanted to be free to dress as he pleased, express himself as he wanted, and associate with whom he pleased, not necessarily in line with what was expected from a biological male.

As we said, we are all learning about what is meant by the term *transgender.* But for now, try to understand it as referring to an identity that seeks to cross genders, to transcend the confines and expectations of sex and gender, in order to construct a personal and unique form of gender.

Feminism (The "F-Word"), Patriarchy, and Sexism

When you first saw the term *feminism* in the heading for this section, what thoughts or images came to mind? Did you react by saying, "Oh no, not this stuff again!"? Did you think of the women's liberation movement of the 1960s and 1970s? Did the unfortunate term *femi-Nazi,* made popular by Rush Limbaugh in the early 1990s, come to mind? In our prologue to this book, we considered feminism from a historical perspective, starting with the first wave (suffrage) and then going on to the second wave (beginning with the women's liberation movement) and a fairly new development—a third wave of feminism. For our purposes in this chapter, it's very illuminating to find out what people, especially college students, know and think about feminism these days.

We first heard the term *feminist* referred to as the new "F-word" by a colleague; you too may have seen or heard this reference in recent years (DeFrancisco, 1992). When students in gender communication classes are asked, "Do you believe that women and men should receive equal opportunities and treatment in all facets of life?" they reply with a confident, hearty affirmative. When they are asked, "Are you a feminist?" the response is much more convoluted, with the most prevalent reaction being, "Well, no, I wouldn't call myself a feminist." Research suggests that although people may believe in equality, which is the basic tenet of feminism, many do not consider themselves feminists and do not want to be called this F-word (Basden Arnold, 2000; Bellafante, 1998; McIntosh, 2000; Twenge, 1997; Williams & Wittig, 1997; Wolf, as in Barta, 1997).

Why does feminism conjure up visions, among men *and* women, of angry, radical, bra-burning, man-hating, humorless, masculine women storming out of the headquarters of the National Organization for Women (NOW) to try to gain superiority over men? These negative connotations in large part come from selective images the media have transmitted (and continue to transmit) to the mass audience (hooks, 2000). For example, did you know that there are no documented accounts of actual bra-burning among "women's libbers" in the late 1960s? Only one incident was remotely connected to this concept—a protest against the Miss America pageant of 1968 during which protesters threw their bras into a trash can. Yet the image of feminists as bra-burners made headlines (Wallis, 1989).

One of the strongest feminist voices of our time is bell hooks, whose book *Feminism Is for Everybody* (2000) goes a long way toward clearing up confusion about what feminism is and is not. She describes another attempt in the past to discredit or marginalize the movement: "Embedded in the portrayal of feminists as man-hating was the assumption that all feminists were lesbians. Appealing to homophobia, mass media intensified anti-feminist sentiment among men"

Hot Button Issue

"DON'T CALL ME A FEMINIST!"

We realize that most of you reading this material likely form a negative mental image when you hear a reference to "feminism." Yet in our experience with college students, once they understand the basic tenets of the feminist movement, they find themselves in agreement. Is there a better term, one that is less divisive or negative? One that would rally people around the issues rather than turn them off?

(p. 68). We still see evidence of this today, when students reveal that they associate feminism with lesbianism, assuming that all feminists are homosexual and therefore man-haters. Let's clear up the confusion: First, not all feminists are female; second, not all female feminists are lesbians; and finally, we don't know of any lesbian feminists who hate men.

In the most basic sense, a feminist is a person—male or female—who believes in equality, especially sex and gender equality. In calling for people to "come closer to feminism," hooks (2000) cites her favorite definition of the term: "Feminism is a movement to end sexism, sexist exploitation, and oppression" (p. viii). She goes on to say that "the movement is not about being anti-male. It makes it clear that the problem is sexism" (p. viii). She describes sexism as being perpetrated by both men and women who are socialized from birth to accept sexist ideas and actions. Well-known feminist author Susan Faludi (1991) suggests, "Feminism's agenda is basic: It asks that women not be forced to 'choose' between public justice and private happiness. It asks that women be free to define themselves—instead of having their identity defined for them, time and again, by their culture and their men" (p. xxiii). Authors of *Manifesta: Young Women, Feminism, and the Future,* Baumgardner and Richards (2000) describe feminism as being "exactly what the dictionary says it is: the movement for social, political, and economic equality of men and women. Feminism means that women have the right to enough information to make informed choices about their lives" (p. 56).

In a more specific sense, feminism involves a reaction to institutionalized and internalized sexism, to power imposed by a male-dominated system or *patriarchy* (derived from a Greek word meaning "of the fathers"; hooks, 2000; hooks, Vaid, Steinem, & Wolf, 1993). Gender scholar Dale Spender (1985) describes patriarchy as a self-perpetuating society "based on the belief that the male is the superior sex" (p. 1). Often patriarchal practices or attitudes are referred to as *sexist,* typically pertaining to discriminatory treatment of women. But the term *sexism* simply means the denigration of one sex and the exaltation of the other, or, stated another way, valuing one sex over the other. Thus, sexism does not refer exclusively to devaluing women, just as racism does not refer exclusively to the denigration of one specific race in preference for another. Given this definition of sexism, there can be no such thing as "reverse sexism," even though some people have used this term to refer to discriminatory treatment of men.

> *The word, and the concept of feminism was a gift because it gave me a sense of identity and a way of defining how I wished to live my life. It was critical to finding a way out.*
>
> —*Betty Buckley,*
> *actor and singer*

[Feminism's] gift is the idea that a girl can be whoever she wants, that she too can grow up to be president. Its gift is the faith that both my children—my daughter and my son—can be free to be their best selves. But with the gift comes the responsibility to fulfill its promise, to stand up as a woman, if not for your own sake, then for the sake of those who come next.

—Susan Estrich, attorney, professor, and author

Perhaps you believe that our society is not male-dominated or that patriarchy or sexism is okay because "that's just the way it is." Maybe you feel that no opportunities have been denied to either sex or that neither sex has endured particular suffering during your lifetime. But stop and think for a moment, not only on a personal level but globally. Which sex is still underrepresented among decision makers, such as political leaders and judges, and among highly paid corporate executives? Which sex still holds more of the lowest-paying jobs and earns 72 cents to the other's dollar of wages? (U. S. Department of Labor, Women's Bureau, 2002) Conversely, which parent is most often denied child custody in divorce proceedings, simply because of that parent's sex? Perhaps you haven't yet seen any overt instances of sex discrimination in your personal life. But what about missed opportunities—those jobs, benefits, rewards, or relationships that did not come your way merely because someone held a limited view of which sex is best suited for a certain circumstance?

Today, individuals have many options for gender communication and behavior. This relatively recent development stems from changing roles, a wider and more tolerant view

Remember . . .

FEMINISM: A movement or philosophy based on a belief in sex and gender equality.
PATRIARCHY: A societal system of male domination.
SEXISM: The denigration of one sex and the exaltation of the other; valuing one sex over the other.

of what is considered appropriate behavior, and increased opportunities for both men and women. Many of the changes in societal expectations, opportunities, and relational patterns resulted (and continue to result) from the work of feminists and their supporters. If you don't already have a viewpoint toward feminism or established conceptualizations of the terms we've discussed in this section, this course you're taking and text you're reading may lead you to some interesting thinking along these lines. Now that you have mastered some of the basic gender-related lingo, let's move on to how those terms are put to use in the communication process.

COMMUNICATION: A COMPLEX HUMAN PROCESS

Communication is a word that you hear frequently, especially since technology has become so sophisticated that we can easily and quickly interact around the world. As the channels for communicating have expanded, so have the meanings of the term *communication*. In fact, two communication theorists in the 1970s isolated 126 definitions of communication (Dance & Larson, 1976). For our purposes, here's a fairly basic perspective of communication.

Human communication isn't static; it's an ongoing, dynamic process of sending and receiving messages for the purpose of sharing meaning. To accomplish this purpose, people use both *verbal* and *nonverbal* communication (including body movement, physical appearance, facial expression, touch, and tone of voice). Communication flows back and forth simultaneously, both verbally and nonverbally, between *sender* and *receiver* (DeVito, 2000; Wood, 2001).

In the comic strip shown here, depicting a conversation between Nancy and Sluggo, Nancy can be labeled the *sender* and Sluggo the *receiver*. Nancy initiates a conversation by asking Sluggo a question. Sluggo receives the message and responds verbally and nonverbally. Note Nancy's confused nonverbal reaction in the second frame. The conversation continues as messages are exchanged between sender and receiver. The point of the cartoon is that even though messages have been transmitted between sender and receiver, effective communication may not be the end result. Two additional components related

NANCY reprinted by permission of United Feature Syndicate, Inc.

Remember. . .

COMMUNICATION: The ongoing and dynamic process of sending and receiving messages for the purpose of sharing meaning.

VERBAL COMMUNICATION: The sending and receiving of messages, in the form of words, so as to create shared meaning.

NONVERBAL COMMUNICATION: The sending and receiving of messages without words, as in the use of body movements, eye contact, and facial expressions, so as to create shared meaning.

SENDER: The initiator or source of a message.

RECEIVER: The listener or recipient of a message.

to this basic perspective of communication warrant brief explanation: *uncertainty reduction* and the *receiver orientation to communication*.

Reducing Uncertainty about Others

In the introductory paragraphs of this chapter, unpredictability was listed as one of the reasons for studying gender communication. Let's explore this a bit further. Humans like to be able to form expectations and to predict how others will behave. These expectations and predictions are comforting; thus, they are powerful motivators in human interaction. On the basis of their past and ever-expanding experiences, people strive to anticipate a situation, predict how certain behaviors will lead to certain reactions from others, act accordingly, and reap rewards from the situation. Charles Berger and his colleagues have contributed a significant amount of research about this process of *uncertainty reduction*. According to these researchers, when people cannot form adequate expectations and are unable to predict what will happen in situations, they experience uncertainty (Berger & Bradac, 1982; Berger & Calabrese, 1975). One reaction to this discomfort is to communicate to gain information and reduce uncertainty.

Can you imagine how the notion of uncertainty reduction applies to communication between women and men? Can you see it operating in your own communication? As we said earlier, communication between the sexes has changed dramatically and is still changing. The factors contributing to the changes are contributing to uncertainty, too. The world has become a smaller place—with almost instant access to other people and other cultures, we now have more of a global community. The likelihood is increasing that you will become friends in college with someone whose culture is vastly different from your own and that you will travel abroad or use technology to communicate with people worldwide. As advanced technology, greater mobility, and easier access have resulted in greater diversity within our own culture, the complexity of communication has compounded. These factors significantly increase our uncertainty about how to communicate effectively.

Consider this example of a male-female encounter: Amber sees Mario across the room at a party and is attracted to him. From watching him at a distance, she thinks that he may have come to the party alone, but she feels uncertain. She doesn't know Mario and doesn't know if he's dating someone steadily, or even if he's married, for that matter. Amber's uncertainty is high, but not high enough to keep her from finding out some information about Mario. She learns from Jason, the host, that Mario is single, but Jason doesn't know if Mario came with a date or not. So Amber's uncertainty is somewhat reduced, leading her to try a more direct method. She strikes up a conversation with Mario, showing that she finds him interesting, and learns that he came to the party alone. While her uncertainty about Mario hasn't completely disappeared, it has been significantly reduced via communication.

Reducing uncertainty and increasing predictability about communication with others are perplexing tasks. Sex roles in our society have shifted dramatically. For example, men and women alike are taking longer to marry today than in past generations. More women are entering the workforce and more men are actively involving themselves in childrearing, so that even the very basic roles such as breadwinner, homemaker, childcare-giver and the like have changed. As these roles evolve and the rules governing people's behavior fall by the societal wayside, you may experience high uncertainty, low predictability, and resulting confusion, possibly even disillusionment. This often generates a "take your best guess" mentality. If your best guess fails, you are once again reminded of the unpredictable nature of gender communication.

Becoming Receiver-Oriented in Your Communication

While the roles of sender and receiver in the communication process are both important, we believe that the receiver's interpretation of the sender's message makes the difference between shared meaning and misunderstanding. Thus, the approach we advocate is termed the *receiver orientation to communication*. What the sender *intends* to convey is important, but it is less important than what the receiver *thinks is being conveyed,* or how the receiver interprets the message. You may clearly understand your intentions in what you say, but a listener may take your message differently from what you originally intended. The result of not being receiver-oriented can sound like this: "What do you MEAN, I'm late in calling you? I said I'd call you AROUND five o'clock. Six-thirty IS around five o'clock!" In an instance like this, obviously the sender intended something different from the receiver's interpretation. Being receiver-oriented—stopping, *before* you give a message, to think about how it will be understood by a listener— can greatly enhance your skill as a communicator.

When one is misunderstood, a typical response is to think that the receiver is at fault for not understanding the message. This reaction becomes particularly relevant to gender communication when you consider how often women report that they do not understand men, because men do not react like women. And men get frustrated when women do not communicate or interpret communication like men. Here's our proposition to you:

> If people would spend more time figuring out how a listener will best hear, accept, understand, and retain a message and less time figuring out how they want to say something to please themselves, then their communication with others would vastly improve.

This sounds like a "golden rule of communication," doesn't it? Do you currently communicate from this perspective, even though you didn't know what to call it? Think of it this way: If you talk, but no one is there to listen or receive what you say, has communication occurred? Some people will say yes; at the very least the sender has communicated with the self. But others will argue that without a listener, communication does not occur, and that the receiver is therefore the most necessary link in the communication process. Again, this is part of the receiver orientation to communication.

If communication breaks down (as it seems to do regularly), who is at fault? Rarely is the sender completely to blame for a breakdown. Sometimes the best forethought, insight, experience, and skill applied to a situation still lead to misunderstanding on the part of a receiver. But in a receiver-oriented view of communication, the sender is responsible for communicating in a manner that will be most easily understood by the receiver; the receiver's responsibility is to attempt to understand the intent of the sender. Communication researchers Beebe, Beebe, and Ivy (2004) frame the receiver orientation as a skill of adaptation—a critical skill for an effective communicator to develop. They explain, "When you adapt a message, you make choices about how best to formulate a message and respond to others to achieve your communication goals. Adapting involves appropriately editing and shaping your responses so that your messages are accurately understood by others and so that you achieve your goal without coercing or using untruthful information or other unethical methods" (pp. 24–25).

Here's an example to help clarify receiver-based communication. Bonnie sees Clyde outside class and wants to start up a conversation with him. She says, "Hey, Clyde, that was pretty funny in class today when the professor called on you just as you were about to nod off to sleep!" Clyde, feeling self-conscious and embarrassed, replies angrily, "Oh, so everybody got a big laugh out of that, huh?" You can see that this conversation is not going the way Bonnie intended; she just meant to lightly tease Clyde to get a conversation going. Clyde took Bonnie's statement as criticism, as though she were making fun of him. Obviously, in this situation, the message intended and sent did not equal the message received. Who would you say is most responsible for the miscommunication in this situation?

In terms of a receiver orientation to communication, we could say that the sender, in this case Bonnie, should have used more caution. If she'd thought about the effect her humorous line could have on Clyde, she might have considered a different approach, one that wouldn't appear to Clyde as though she were poking fun at his expense. Perhaps she could have merely made a general funny comment about class, rather than one that involved Clyde personally.

Now, if you are saying to yourself, "That Clyde must be one touchy character; he really overreacted and missed the boat," you are adopting a sender orientation to communication. Again, you are emphasizing what was *said* rather than how it was *taken.* Let's consider a more serious example, one involving gender communication that has more dire consequences than Bonnie and Clyde's misunderstanding.

Before a board meeting at a local corporation, a few executives are milling about, drinking coffee and talking about the upcoming meeting. Maria says good morning to a coworker, Jerry, as he comes up to her on her way to the boardroom. He says, as he puts his arm around her waist, "You know, you are a breath of fresh air in this joint, because I sure like a little perfume and soft skin next to me in the morning. Makes the workday go a lot easier, don't you think? Why don't you sit by me at this meeting?" Maria is so taken aback that she cannot respond, except to extract herself from Jerry's grasp, collect her wits, and get ready for the board meeting. Maria views Jerry's comments as a form of sexual harassment—unprofessional and inappropriate communication in the workplace. That may or may not be how Jerry intended it. Perhaps he communicates to female coworkers in a sexualized manner on purpose, to belittle them or assert his own male prowess. Or perhaps he believes that he was simply complimenting Maria, trying to make her feel more comfortable before the meeting started or merely offering some harmless teasing to break the tension of the morning.

While we recognize that this example of sexual harassment is rather dramatic, and that you may have reacted strongly to it, we offer it here for a reason. Instances of sexual harassment constitute prime illustrations of what we mean by taking a receiver orientation to communication. Whether or not a sender of a message intends to be harassing is not the main issue; what matters more is how the target or receiver of the message interprets it. The topic of sexual harassment is dealt with more fully in subsequent chapters. Just realize for now that in most situations, instead of defending your intentions when you communicate poorly or inappropriately, you can learn lessons for the next time. Considering in advance how a receiver will interpret your message will go a long way toward improving your skills as a communicator. This stance is especially critical for gender communication, which is highly complex. It's advisable in every situation, as illustrated in these examples, to focus on the receiver of your message *before, during,* and *after* you communicate.

You will find the receiver orientation to communication reiterated throughout this text, so comprehending this perspective is a key to understanding the remaining chapters. But we want you to recognize that the receiver orientation is only one perspective within the communication discipline; there are several other ways to view communication, including the traditional sender-based perspective. However, we are firmly committed to the belief that a receiver orientation is the most fruitful approach, especially when the communication process is complicated by the effects of gender. This orientation, together with a focus on uncertainty reduction, form the basis of our approach to enhancing your gender communication skills—the *personal effectiveness approach.*

Remember. . .

UNCERTAINTY REDUCTION: A motivation to seek and use information to lessen uncertainty or unpredictability in human encounters.

RECEIVER ORIENTATION TO COMMUNICATION: An approach to communication that places more emphasis on a receiver's interpretation of a message than a sender's intentions in communicating.

THE PERSONAL EFFECTIVENESS APPROACH TO GENDER COMMUNICATION

Have you ever had difficulty communicating with someone of the other sex? Of course; everyone has. Have you ever wished that you were better at gender communication? What does "better" mean? We continually conduct surveys at our universities to understand students' concerns about gender communication. Here are a few of our male students' questions and concerns:

"In a conversation with a woman, when a problem's solved, why does the woman still want to continue the conversation?"
"My wife says that men don't listen. I think that women listen too much."
"In a serious situation, would women rather that guys get emotional and make everyone else upset, or not show emotion and risk making someone else upset later?"

From female respondents to our surveys, we receive questions like these:

"When guys say, 'I'll call you,' what do they really mean?"
"Why is it that men find it so difficult to say what they mean if emotional aspects are involved? Is it that they are afraid of what other men will say? Or is it because they feel they will be viewed as less of a man?"
"Guys usually want sex from women. So after a woman goes to bed with a man, why does he talk as though he no longer respects her?"

There is no lack of advice from the popular press and no lack of personal opinions on problems related to gender communication. Through our classroom experience and research, we have developed our own point of view—the *personal effectiveness approach*. Becoming "better" at gender communication depends on becoming a more personally effective communicator.

We will all have many different relationships in our lives. Each relationship consists of three things: the self, the other person, and the situation. Which of these three things do you have the most direct control over? Clearly, yourself. You can exert some control over the situation, and now and then you can influence another person. But with some self-awareness, learning, and skill, you can be proactive and improve your ability to control your own communication behavior.

You already control your own communication behavior to some degree. However, you may not control it as well as you would like. Did you ever find yourself saying or doing something (especially with someone of the other sex!) and thinking, "Where did *that* come from?" Occasionally, we all feel that we aren't in control of things around us, that we merely react to people and circumstances. But at other times, we do plan something and it does work. So you already do have some control and you already know some things about communication and gender. You've experienced some level of success, but you've also had some failures. Becoming more personally effective involves developing greater control over your own communication behavior and a greater ability to influence the development and success of relationships.

We believe that adhering to the principles of the personal effectiveness approach can help you improve your success in relating to others. Personal effectiveness begins with knowledge and a perception of yourself and your own tendencies, extends to your knowledge of the "rules" of society, and includes your knowledge of the communication process. It also involves judgments that other people make about you. Let's examine these components one at a time.

Personal Effectiveness: Your Own Perception

At various times, you may have looked at how some people communicate and thought, "They are good at this; I wish I were that good." Then you probably looked at others and thought, "They need some help." No one can be effective *all* of the time, but each of us can be effective *more* of the time. The following four elements work together to help you be more effective more of the time.

1. Repertoire

You have been communicating for a number of years and have developed patterns of communication that feel natural to you. Within these patterns are communication behaviors that you frequently use. Some work most of the time, some don't, and sometimes you may not know which to use. But few of us want to be the kind of person who always communicates or responds a certain way— like a "default mode"—no matter whom we're dealing with or what situation we're in. For most of us, that's taking a comfortable pattern or behavior too far, and it can quickly land us in a communicative and relational rut. One of the goals of personal effectiveness is to expand the range of behaviors or repertoire at your disposal. You want an enlarged communicative "bag of tricks" from which to choose when you confront various communication situations so that you're not locked into a predictable pattern. The expanded repertoire is especially helpful in those uncomfortable situations that involve members of the other sex. The rest of this text offers many ways to expand your repertoire, with special emphasis on how this expansion process can enhance your gender communication and your relationships.

2. Selection

Once you have expanded your repertoire, you need to know which behavior to choose. In subsequent chapters, we talk about selecting the most appropriate behavior for various circumstances. For now, just realize that the selection depends on an analysis of your goals, the other person's goals, and the situation. Decisions are also based on what you might value. At the end of this chapter, we outline some values that can be applied to selecting your communication behaviors for female-male relationships in particular.

3. Skill

To be personally effective, you also need the skill to perform a behavior so that another person accepts it and responds positively. We spend a good deal of time in this text discussing skills as an element of personal effectiveness, and applying this element to various situations you may encounter. We also encourage you to observe others, ask questions of your instructor and classmates to find out how they deal with certain situations, and then develop and practice your communication skills to enhance your view of yourself and your relationships.

4. Evaluation

This element involves your ability to judge your own success. You need to be able to assess your efforts to see if they have been effective in the way you wanted, and to use this information to adapt your behavior the next time. If you don't evaluate, you won't know what to change; you might continue to make the same mistake over and over.

These four elements are central to your perception of your personal effectiveness. You will be more successful in gender communication if you:

1. Develop a wider range of communication behaviors from which to choose.
2. Know how to analyze a situation and select the most appropriate behaviors from your repertoire.
3. Perform those behaviors with skill.
4. Carefully evaluate the result.

As we said at the beginning of this section, personal effectiveness only begins with a perception of self. It also includes the views that others may have of you as an individual. The next section describes personal effectiveness as a social judgment.

Personal Effectiveness: Others' Perceptions

People interact with each other and make judgments about effectiveness all the time. If you think about it for a minute, you've probably been involved in conversations with people and then walked away thinking, "So much for *that*" or "What a head case." To take another example, suppose you ask someone, "What time is it?" and he or she responds "Tuesday." You're likely to call into question that person's effectiveness. On the other hand, if the conversation goes smoothly you are likely to judge her or him as "pretty good at this." The point here is that only part of a judgment of effectiveness comes from the viewpoint of the communicator; the remainder rests with the person who receives the communication.

This means that one fundamental aspect of becoming more personally effective is to increase the number of times you are positively regarded or evaluated by people who communicate with you. Let's say that you have observed someone else interacting in an effective way with a member of the other sex and you wish to imitate this behavior. For example, suppose one of your friends is especially skilled at first conversations—the exchange that occurs when people first meet. You'd like to get better at this kind of communication, so you add your friend's behavior to your own "bag of tricks" (*repertoire*) and try it out in a subsequent encounter (*selection*). In a way, you are practicing new communication *skills* on others. This is something that happens all the time; many of us notice how others behave, then adopt their behavior, adjust it to fit our own style, and try it out on others. The last step is to *evaluate* the results of this experiment. When you do this, it is wise to go further than just your own reactions or judgments of effectiveness; you will want to seek honest feedback from others—including, at times, the person or persons directly involved in the encounter. You may want other friends to observe you and give you feedback as to the appropriateness and effectiveness of your communication, or you may just tell someone later about the encounter and ask what that person thinks. You may even want to ask, at the moment or at some later point, what the receiver of your communication thinks or thought about your behavior. It doesn't hurt to get a simple "perception check" on how one is coming across. That may sound crazy to you—too forced, or too much trouble for something that ought to be simple. But this is exactly how most of us go about developing any skill. If you want a to develop better golf swing, make a better pasta dish, or write a better research paper, it's likely that you'll go through this process, with the final step being both self-evaluation and evaluation by others to help you improve for the future. The process of developing personally effective communication skills works much the same way.

Remember. . .

PERSONAL EFFECTIVENESS: An approach to communication that begins with knowledge of self, extends to an understanding of societal rules and expectations, and includes the development of greater control over one's communication behavior.

REPERTOIRE: A range of communicative behaviors from which to choose in social situations.

SELECTION: The ability to choose appropriate communication for any given situation.

SKILL: The ability to enact selected communication behaviors to achieve desired results.

EVALUATION: Reflecting on one's communication and seeking feedback from others, so as to improve in future situations.

Our point in presenting the personal effectiveness approach to gender communication is that you may experience some change while taking this course and reading this text. We don't suggest that you learn to "figure people out" merely to get more of what you want. We *do* suggest that you develop yourself, that you change your behaviors for the better. If you want to be more personally effective, you may need to communicate differently from the way you do now. Ideally, you will feel more empowered by what you learn from this text and the course you're taking. The goal is to become more effective, to increase your repertoire of communication behaviors, and to know when and how to use those behaviors. You will want to further develop your ability to analyze what is going on and to communicate in a way that is beneficial for you and those you encounter. As a result, you'll find your communication with both men and women more satisfying.

VALUES TO GUIDE YOUR CHOICES

How do you make wise choices in gender communication? Not making wise choices has probably gotten a lot of us into trouble. An assessment of your personal values, with regard to human beings and relationships, can be useful. To close this chapter, we did just that: We developed a list of values relevant to gender communication, and we offer them as a useful guide for you as you enhance your communication ability and personal effectiveness.

Value 1: Equality of Power

Some relationships function successfully with an uneven distribution of power (e.g., parent-child, mentor-protégé, employer-employee), although abuses of power exist within these relationships as well as within other types. However, when an imbalance of power isn't necessarily societally induced or an appropriate expectation for a relationship—as in marriage, dating and romantic relationships, work relationships, or friendships—an ideal or goal to work toward is an even distribution of power or control. Empowerment—power *to* rather than power *over*—involves a shared approach to power or control that capitalizes on the strengths of each partner in a relationship (Bate & Bowker, 1997; Thorne, Kramarae, & Henley, 1983).

Value 2: Talking about It Makes It Better

We believe profoundly in the power of communication to help solve the problems we face. You've probably heard or read news reports about people who have difficulty verbally expressing anger and frustration and who wind up using physical violence as a means of solving problems. Granted, not all problems can be solved through communication; in some instances, time is needed and talk may only make things worse. But in most situations, talking it over is absolutely critical to effectiveness in relationships. The willingness and ability to sit down and talk about the topic at hand, the relationship, each other's feelings, and possible solutions to problems are critical to personal effectiveness.

Value 3: Confirmation and Acceptance

Research suggests that a basic dimension within every communication situation is a feeling of acceptance or rejection (Beebe, Beebe, & Redmond, 2002; Cissna, Garvin, & Kennedy, 1990; Sieburg, 1969). When we talk with someone, we can go away saying, "That person accepted me and what I had to say," or we can experience rejection or indifference. The communication of confirmation is a very important part of establishing satisfying relationships, since a relationship doesn't progress if someone feels rejected.

Value 4: Freedom of Choice

When we talk about becoming more personally effective and developing more successful relationships, we include the possibility that you will influence or persuade someone else. With that possibility comes more responsibility. A value we hold central to this process is the freedom of the other person to choose his or her own line of action. People often manipulate the emotions of their partners to get what they want, restricting the partner's freedom to choose. While the information in this text may help you become more persuasive in your relationships, you should use these skills in a manner that respects the right of each person to choose her or his own response to persuasive attempts.

Value 5: Being Open-Minded and Willing to Change

Have you ever talked with people who are completely closed-minded? It's frustrating and frequently we have a reaction like, "Oh, what's the use? They'll never change their minds anyway, so there's no point in even talking." That's not a desirable reaction in effective communication. In connection with value 4, a basic dimension of personal effectiveness is the belief on the part of other people that we are open to influence and change. In a relationship, the more each person believes that the other person can be influenced, the more both are likely to communicate. So it's important to be open to persuasion. We don't suggest that you believe everything people tell you or do everything people ask of you; but if there is sufficient cause, it's okay to change your mind. Open-mindedness and the ability to change are positive values for all relationships.

Value 6: Treating Another Person as an Individual

Stereotyping is hard to avoid. Can you imagine starting from scratch with every person you meet, never using past experiences as a clue to what to expect? Consider for a minute how you expect college professors to do certain things when they walk into a classroom, and how you expect salespersons to behave in certain ways when you enter a store. In some ways, stereotypes help reduce our uncertainty and increase our ability to predict what will happen. But sometimes stereotypes seriously limit the range of possibilities. For example, what if you applied an inaccurate stereotype to a person from another culture, only to discover that you misjudged the person and possibly lost out on a unique friendship?

Let's be even more specific: In your relationships, should you stereotype women and men on the basis of their sex? We suggest not—not just because there are so many differences between people, but because no one likes to be treated like a stereotype. A man doesn't like to be told that he is just another unfeeling, inexpressive male. No woman likes to be told that "all women are too emotional." No one likes to be told, "You are just like everyone else." In the first place, we are all different and our differences need to be recognized and celebrated. Second, actions based on stereotypes do nothing to advance a relationship. Third, stereotypes can negatively affect someone's self-esteem. When possible, treat people as individuals, not categories.

CONCLUSION

In this opening chapter, we offered a definition of gender communication and described it as provocative, popularized, pervasive, problematic, and unpredictable. We also explained key terms so that you would more fully understand the gender jargon used in the remainder of this textbook. We explored the communication process from a receiver orientation and introduced the personal effectiveness approach to gender communication. As we stated, one goal of this text is to help you develop greater personal effectiveness so that you understand more of what is happening when women and men communicate. This process begins with a fuller awareness and understanding of your own communication behavior, so that you can better predict the potential impact of your communication on other people. If you can do that, you will be better at selecting the best option from your repertoire of communication behaviors and enacting that option with skill. Finally, we want to develop your ability to evaluate your communication with others and to explain why things work out the way they do, because these steps are critical to personal effectiveness as a communicator.

Discussion Starters

1. Think about how roles have changed for men and women in our society. What roles did your parents model for you when you were growing up? What attitudes have you developed about appropriate roles for women and men in our society? As you continue to mature, will you assume different roles from your same-sex parent?

2. What comes to mind when you hear the term *Women's Liberation Movement*? What comes to mind when you hear the term *feminism*? Do you consider yourself a feminist? Why or why not?

3. Think of something you consider really sexist. It could be a policy or practice, or something that you saw, read, or heard. What was your reaction to this sexist stimulus at the time? What is your reaction now? If your reactions are different, why are they different?

4. Recall a situation in which your interpretation of a message (as the receiver) did not match a person's intentions (as the sender). It could be something simple, such as a miscommunication over the time or place where you were supposed to meet someone; or it could be something more serious, such as misunderstanding an instructor's explanation of an assignment. Analyze that situation: Was it a same-sex or mixed-sex

conversation? What do you think the sender of the message intended to communicate? How did you, as the receiver, interpret the message? What was said or done during the conversation that was the primary cause of misunderstanding? How was the situation resolved? In terms of a receiver orientation to communication, what could the sender in the conversation have done to make the situation better? How could you, as the receiver, have reduced the potential for misunderstanding?

5. How are your values reflected in your communication? Consider the six values presented in this chapter. Which of these values are already consistent with yours? Which ones represent new ideas for you? Are there values that you would add to our list?

References

Barta, C. (1997, March 27). More women are learning to use "f" word—feminism. *Corpus Christi Caller Times*, pp. B1, B9.

Basden Arnold, L. (2000). "What is a feminist?" Students' descriptions. *Women & Language, 23,* 8–18.

Bate, B., & Bowker, J. (1997). *Communication and the sexes* (2nd ed.). Prospect Heights, IL: Waveland.

Baumgardner, J., & Richards, A. (2000). *Manifesta: Young women, feminism, and the future.* New York: Farrar, Straus, & Giroux.

Beebe, S. A., Beebe, S. J., & Ivy, D. K. (2004). *Communication: Principles for a lifetime* (2nd ed.). Boston: Allyn & Bacon.

Beebe, S. A., Beebe, S. J., & Redmond, M. V. (2002). *Interpersonal communication: Relating to others.* (3rd ed.). Boston: Allyn & Bacon.

Bellafante, G. (1998, June 29). Feminism: It's all about me! *Time,* 54–62.

Bem, S. L. (1974). The measurement of psychological androgyny. *Journal of Consulting and Clinical Psychology, 42,* 155–162.

Berger, C. R., & Bradac, J. J. (1982). *Language and social knowledge: Uncertainty in interpersonal relationships.* London: Edward Arnold.

Berger, C. R., & Calabrese, R. J. (1975). Some explorations in initial interaction and beyond: Toward a developmental theory of interpersonal communication. *Human Communication Research, 1,* 99–112.

Cissna, K. N., Garvin, B. J., & Kennedy, C. W. (1990). Reliability in coding social interaction: A study of confirmation. *Communication Reports, 3,* 58–69.

Dance, F. E. X., & Larson, C. E. (1976). *The functions of human communication.* New York: Holt, Rinehart, & Winston.

Davis, L. J. (2000, March 24). Gaining a daughter: A father's transgendered tale. *Chronicle of Higher Education,* pp. B4–B6.

DeFrancisco, V. (1992, March). *Position statement: How can feminist scholars create a feminist future in the academic environment?* Paper presented at the Tenth Annual Conference on Research in Gender and Communication, Roanoke, VA.

DeVito, J. A. (2000). *The interpersonal communication book* (9th ed.). New York: Addison Wesley.

Devor, H. (1992). Becoming members of society: Learning the social meanings of gender. In M. Schaum & C. Flanagan (Eds.), *Gender images: Readings for composition* (pp. 23–33). Boston: Houghton Mifflin.

Ekins, R., & King, D. (1997). Blending genders: Contributions to the emerging field of transgender studies. *The International Journal of Transgenderism, 1.* [Excerpt derived from Paul, E. L. (2002). *Taking sides: Clashing views on controversial issues in sex and gender* (2nd ed.) (pp. 340–347). New York: McGraw-Hill/Dushkin.]

Faludi, S. (1991). *Backlash: The undeclared war against American women.* New York: Crown.

Feinberg, L. (1997). *Transgender warriors: Making history from Joan of Arc to Dennis Rodman.* Boston: Beacon.

Gould, L. (1972, December). X: A fabulous child's story. *Ms.,* 105–106.

Griffin, G. (1998). Understanding heterosexism—the subtle continuum of homophobia. *Women & Language, 21,* 33–39.

Heinz, B. (2002). Enga(y)ging the discipline: Sexual minorities and communication studies. *Communication Education, 51,* 95–104.

hooks, b. (2000). *Feminism is for everybody: Passionate politics.* Cambridge, MA: South End Press.

hooks, b., Vaid, U., Steinem, G., & Wolf, N. (1993, September–October). Let's get real about feminism: The backlash, the myths, the movement. *Ms.,* 34–43.

Lippa, R. A. (2002). *Gender, nature, and nurture.* Mahwah, NJ: Erlbaum.

Lipson, J. (2001). Pay equity: Fact or fiction? *American Association of University Women's Outlook, 95,* 14–18.

Majors, R. E. (1994). Discovering gay culture in America. In L. A. Samovar & R. E. Porter (Eds.), *Intercultural communication: A reader* (4th ed.) (pp. 148–154). Belmont, CA: Wadsworth.

McIntosh, T. (2000, Winter). Fear of the f-word. *Bust,* 38–39.

Sieburg, E. (1969). *Dysfunctional communication and interpersonal responsiveness in small groups.* Unpublished doctoral dissertation, University of Denver, Denver, CO.

Spender, D. (1985). *Man made language* (2nd ed.). London: Routledge & Kegan Paul.

Thorne, B., Kramarae, C., & Henley, N. (1983). Language, gender, and society: Opening a second decade of research. In B. Thorne, C. Kramarae, & N. Henley (Eds.), *Language, gender, and society* (pp. 7–24). Rowley, MA: Newbury.

Twenge, J. M. (1997). Attitudes toward women, 1970–1995. *Psychology of Women Quarterly, 21,* 35–51.

U. S. Department of Labor, Women's Bureau. (2002). Earnings differences between women and men. In P. J. Dubeck & D. Dunn (Eds.), *Workplace/women's place: An anthology* (2nd ed.) (pp. 57–63). Los Angeles: Roxbury.

Wallis, C. (1989, December 4). Onward, women! *Time,* 80–89.

Williams, R., & Wittig, M. A. (1997). "I'm not a feminist, but . . . ": Factors contributing to the discrepancy between pro-feminist orientation and feminist social identity. *Sex Roles, 37,* 885–904.

Wilson Schaef, A. (1981). *Women's reality: An emerging female system in the white male society.* Minneapolis: Winston.

Wood, J. T. (2001). *Communication mosaics: A new introduction to the field of communication* (2nd ed.). Belmont, CA: Wadsworth.

PART TWO

INFLUENCES ON OUR CHOICES

CHAPTER TWO

BECOMING A WOMAN, BECOMING A MAN, AND BECOMING A PERSON:

Biological and Social Influences on Gender Identity Development

CASE STUDY: ANYTHING SOUND FAMILIAR?

"I guess it's going to happen sooner or later—probably in my lifetime—that a woman will become president of the United States. But it's just hard to think about or imagine; how will she deal with all the aggressive congressmen trying to get her to see things their way? How will she respond to partisan criticism?"

"Will she react more emotionally to things than male presidents, especially if she's PMSing? For example, would a female president find it more difficult than a male president to order a bombing that might wipe out civilians as well as the target?"

"I think we need to start off with a female vice president, just so we can get used to the idea before a woman gets elected to the top office."

"I don't think women belong in combat, because they're simply not as strong as men. I'm not sexist or anything, but I just don't want to see women on the front lines getting blown up. What if we had a situation where women soldiers were killed or taken prisoner or something?"

"That *DID* happen—it happened in the Persian Gulf war and in Afghanistan. I think a couple of female Marines were killed in those conflicts. Why is it harder for you to think of a woman being a POW or a casualty than a man?"

"I don't think men and women should compete against each other in sports, simply because male athletes are generally stronger, bigger, faster, etc. It just wouldn't be fair competition. In the long run, it could be deflating or demotivating for the women. And they could really get hurt."

"But I know some women who could kick just about any guy's butt in just about any sport. What about them? Should they be kept out of the top sports and the big money, just because they're women?"

"If it's so hard to imagine coed sports like football or boxing, why not start out with less confrontational sports, like golf, tennis, swimming, or even bowling? Start integrating those, with girls and guys playing against each other in tennis matches, golf tournaments, and swim meets. Sports will never be integrated if we don't start off when we're young—in the schools."

The examples above are exchanges that have occurred over recent years in the classes of the authors of this textbook. We need not mention the sex of the speakers, because the opinions expressed are held by the women and the men who take our courses. Do you detect any leaps on the part of the students—that is, do you find them starting with a biological property and then either relying on or rejecting a social interpretation of that property to develop an opinion? For example, we still hear quite often comments about a female president making decisions when she's menstruating. The stereotypical leap from this monthly biological process to impaired brain functioning has not gone away.

Some people believe that because biological differences between women and men are natural and uniquely human, they are something to be appreciated, not played down or resented. These biological properties "make the world go 'round," so why be concerned about them? Others believe that biological sex differences are fairly insignificant; the real issue is the social interpretation of those differences. For example, communication scholar Peter Andersen (1998) supports the notion that biology is not destiny, suggesting that "a thorough review of the evidence on sex differences reveals that they are a function of culture, biology, and their interaction" (p. 98). Sometimes the interpretation is that the sexes are more biologically alike than different. But at other times, society uses biological differences as a disguise or excuse for discrimination.

Of the many internal and external factors that influence communication with members of the opposite sex, biological and social factors have a profound, if sometimes subconscious, psychological effect on your gender identity and communication. When you read the information about biological and social influences that follows, think about the following things: (1) the extent to which your biological sex (being male or female) is a part of your identity; (2) how you have been shaped by social interpretations of that biology; (3) your psychological response to these first two things, in terms of how you have formed your gender identity; and (4) how you communicate that identity to others.

Hot Topics

- How social interpretations of biological sex differences can lead to communication based on stereotypes
- Changing definitions of masculinity and femininity
- Social interpretations of anatomical sex differences such as sexual organs, reproductive functions, and judgments of physical strength

- Social interpretations of hormonal differences related to nurturance, aggression, and cycles
- Research on sex differences in brain functioning and cognitive ability
- Theories of gender identity development
- Gender transcendence, androgyny, and the expanded communication repertoire
- The impact of families, clothes, toys, peers, and schools on gender identity development

WHAT'S FEMININE? WHAT'S MASCULINE?

Since gender is a social construct based on social interaction, definitions of femininity and masculinity can and do change according to the needs of the society that creates the definition (Deaux & Lafrance, 1998). When American society was organized more closely around agriculture, the differences between masculine and feminine were less distinct (Cancian, 1989). Women and men assumed responsibility for the family and for economic survival. Since the husband's work was in the same physical location as that of the wife (or very close to it), the two were much more interdependent. This interdependence created, to a degree, a sense of shared and relatively equal responsibility for the family. However, when factories emerged and men began to work in a location outside the home, the concept of separate gender identities expanded greatly. Men's working environment and separateness led to an impersonal, public, and utilitarian attitude. Women remained at home and became more directly associated with the personal, the private, the nurturing, and the emotional. References to women as weak, decorative, inferior, negative, and trivial emerged at that time (Monedas, 1992).

As society slowly changed, so did definitions of femininity and masculinity. Qualities that had been important to women in agricultural life, such as ambition, strength, and decisiveness, slowly faded from the feminine gender identity. Qualities important to men in agricultural society such as emotionality, nurturance, and interdependence (essential to family life) likewise diminished from the masculine gender identity. As women were confined to the private domain, femininity was redefined as nurturing, relational, and caring for others. As men became more removed from the home, masculinity was redefined to include independence, aggressiveness, self-control, and achievement (Cancian, 1989).

Stereotyping: He-Men and She-Women?

Social psychologist Douglas Kenrick and his colleagues suggest: "Stereotyping is a cognitively inexpensive way of understanding others: By presuming that people are like other members of their groups, we avoid the effortful process of learning about them as individuals" (Kenrick, Neuberg, & Cialdini, 2002, p. 399). Stereotypical definitions of masculinity and femininity have been explored widely in research. According to gender researchers Borisoff and Merrill (1998), the stereotypical woman is soft-spoken (when she speaks at all), emotional, subjective, self-effacing, uncertain, humble, compliant, and submissive. Femininity results in warm and continued relationships with men, a sense of maternity, interest in caring for children, and the capacity to work productively and continuously in female occupations (Devor, 1992). These descriptions imply that women be heterosexual, which in turn requires women to focus on their attractiveness to men.

The stereotypical man is an ineffective listener, emotionally inexpressive, categorical and certain in his language use, and dominating in discussions (Borisoff & Merrill, 1998). In his classic research, psychologist Joseph Pleck (1981) suggests that masculinity in our society is conveyed by one or more of the following:

1. Displaying success or high status in one's social group
2. Exhibiting a manly air of toughness, confidence, and self-reliance
3. Demonstrating aggression, violence, and daring
4. Avoiding anything associated with femininity

These descriptions require men to organize themselves and society in a hierarchical manner. Competition is driven by a goal of individual achievement, and it requires participants to show a degree of emotional insensitivity to others' pain or losses. This stereotype leaves little room for relationships.

The societal conditions that gave rise to the current stereotypical definitions of masculinity and femininity occurred more than a hundred years ago, and these conditions have changed a great deal in the past three decades. Yet the definitions themselves have been slower to change. Riesman (1990) notes that the "institutionalized roles of husband and wife continue to provide a blueprint for marriage, situating men's work primarily in the public sphere and women's in the private sphere" (p. 51). Femininity remains linked to the home, family, emotional expressiveness, and caring for others. Masculinity continues to focus on the public area of work and is associated with power and dominance, emotional reserve, and productivity (Wood, 1994).

Have you ever been talked to or treated a certain way, merely because of your sex? Can you recall a situation when someone sized you up because you were a woman or a man, and then talked to you on the basis of a stereotype of your sex? Here are some common examples. People assume that because men tend to have more muscle mass than women, all men can lift all kinds of heavy things. Men are often called on to help people move, help rearrange bulky furniture, or lift heavy boxes and other objects. Many men have strained their backs or, worse, developed hernias and detached retinas from all the lifting they are "supposed" to be able to do. Why assume that a guy always has such strength or, for that matter, *wants* to do physical labor? If you are a woman, have you ever taken your car to a service center for repairs and been treated by the mechanic as though you don't speak English? (Yes, men are sometimes treated this way too, but usually there seems to be an expectation that men can understand cars better than women.) People who don't know you may assume a lot about you, simply because of your sex. And we all know of more serious examples of sexual stereotyping and discriminatory treatment than these.

In Chapter 1 we discussed uncertainty reduction as a motivation for communicating. When people are uncertain and don't know you as an individual, they communicate with you on the basis of extremely limited information—your sex and other physical attributes that can be perceived with the senses. In the absence of more extensive information, people tend to rely on socially learned stereotypes which provide some basis for how to proceed. Communication scholars Canary and Emmers-Sommer (1997) provide this insight: "Stereotypes can offer a means to explain sex and gender differences on at least two levels: (1) as a way to predict men's and women's behavioral differences; and (2) as a way that people establish baselines for expectations about other people's behavior" (p. 3). Stereotypes based on biological sex become intertwined with social influences embedded within one's culture. If someone always stops at a stereotype without exploring what makes you a unique person, you probably won't like that treatment. Stereotypes can be useful, but they are typically exaggerated, inaccurate, and unfavorable, and they are very difficult to dislodge.

The Changing Face of Masculinity

In an article with the interesting title "Thicker Thighs by Thanksgiving," Ann Dobosz (1997) examines American men's magazines such as *Men's Health*, *Details, Maxim*, and *Men's Fitness*, which focus on self-improvement and include diet tips, columns on relationships, advice about sex, health updates, and information on how be more masculine. Men's magazines are catching up to what women's magazines have been doing for years. The danger, as Dobosz points out, is that the focus on "shaving creams, sexual performance, and well-toned abs may create a men's culture as warped and obsessive as women's mass culture" (p. 91). Is that what we want?

Michael Segell (1996) commented on the changing definitions of masculinity in an article for *Esquire*, entitled "The Second Coming of the Alpha Male." He argues for the utility of certain traditional aspects of masculinity such as fearlessness and the ability to mask emotions, take risks, and be aggressive. According to Segell, aggression and dominance (male characteristics), not sensitivity and submissiveness (female characteristics), contribute to superior self-esteem in both men and women. However, author Cooper Thompson (1992) maintains that taken to an extreme, masculinity promotes violence. For example, he found that high school boys use the word *fag* as their most humiliating put-down. If a boy is called a fag, he is perceived as weak or timid and therefore not masculine enough to suit his peers. There is enormous pressure for him to fight back, and not being tough at these moments only proves the allegation. Thompson believes that boys must learn different patterns because the cost of being masculine is high, in that toughness increases stress and the risk of physical injury and early death.

Harvard psychologist and author of the book *Real Boys: Rescuing Our Sons from the Myths of Boyhood* William Pollack (1998) stresses the nurture side of the debate about boys' development by focusing on socialization and the way a culture genders its males. He finds more merit in that discussion than in the nature side, or the argument that boys are they way they are because of testosterone rather than social conditioning. Pollack believes that boys need instruction in and support for emotional release, including such emotions as joy, sadness, and fear, not just anger. He critiques what he calls the "boy code" and the "mask of masculinity," described as a "kind of swaggering attitude that boys embrace to hide their fears, suppress dependency and vulnerability, and present a stoic front" (Pollack, as in Kimmel, 1999, p. 89). Many experts agree that boys need to express a range of emotions and learn nonviolent means of resolving conflicts. They must learn to show vulnerability (or not to be afraid of it), ask for help, be gentle and nurturing, and be more open to those attitudes and behaviors that have traditionally been labeled as feminine. We realize that changing long-standing cultural definitions of masculinity has not been and will not be easy. Awareness of options and support for those options are necessary to make change possible.

The Changing Face of Femininity

Cultural definitions of femininity have historically included negative characteristics, reviewed earlier in this chapter. Has this changed? One study examined meanings for *feminine* and *femininity* throughout the twentieth century (Greene, 1997). The author concluded that although times have changed and definitions have moved from negativity to a celebration of the feminine, the cultural belief in distinct genders makes it likely that future meanings of femininity will be influenced by their biological roots. In similar research, Lueptow, Garovich, and Lueptow (1995) compared gender stereotypes held by more than 3,600 college students over a 17-year period—from 1974 to 1991. Contrary to predictions and despite dramatic changes in sex roles and attitudes during this time, perceptions of gender-typed personality traits increased slightly. However, other studies offer evidence that perceptions, particularly about femininity, are changing somewhat and in a positive direction (Jackson, Fleury, & Lewandowski, 1996; Pennell & Ogilvie, 1995). Views of what it means to be feminine continue to change, from self-definitions to ideas about body image, athleticism, clothing, and nonconformity, so that today a wider range of behaviors, attitudes, and choices may be viewed as "feminine."

Most people simply cannot live up to the ideal or the stereotypical images of masculinity and femininity, as commonly defined. The frustration and disillusionment that may set in when the ideal is not reached can have lasting effects on an individual's self-esteem (Bate & Bowker, 1997). The more one consciously learns about options in defining and living out one's femininity and masculinity, the easier it is to select a definition that fits one's own personality, needs, and goals.

Remember . . .

STEREOTYPE: A presumption that someone is like members of a group, rather than an individual.

MASCULINITY: Stereotypical personality and psychological traits associated with being male, such as independence, competitiveness, and aggressiveness.

FEMININITY: Stereotypical personality and psychological traits associated with being female, such as affiliativeness, cooperativeness, and nurturance.

BIOLOGICAL SEX AND SOCIAL INTERPRETATIONS

Biological differences between men and women continue to be hot topics these days. Discussions of brain functioning, hormonal effects, and anatomical abnormalities are regular fodder for magazines, newspapers, Websites, and television talk shows. The headline on the cover of a recent issue of *U.S. News and World Report* reads, "Boys: The Weaker Sex?" followed by "Why girls do better in the real world." Inside, reporter Anna Mulrine (2001) explores the current status of the age-old nature-nurture argument, examining gaps between the sexes and their biological and social causes.

While this chapter will inform you about some biological sex differences, those differences are neither our central focus nor critical to our approach to gender communication. We won't suggest that one sex is physically superior to the other. Indeed, we don't want to make too much out of biological differences, because we've seen that they sometimes become a cop-out. It's easy to confine a discussion of gender to biological differences and leave it at that, without exploring more deeply the ramifications or consequences of those differences. This view implies that somehow biology gives us permission to behave in a certain way—even if that way is discriminatory or inappropriate. For many of us who study gender communication, this is not a workable stance. So while we want to explore the biology, we are most interested in how communication is affected by the social translations of that biology.

"Innies" and "Outies": Anatomical Differences and Social Interpretations

Some of the biological findings described in this section may be quite familiar to you, while some may surprise you. We challenge you to think about the social interpretations of the biology in ways that you might not have thought of before now. Think also about how those interpretations are reflected in communication between women and men.

Sexual Organs

Since your first class in human biology, you have known that the combination of XX chromosomes creates a female fetus and the XY combination creates a male, in the majority of instances. (There are some exceptions, but we'll leave these for others to

> *The male is by nature superior, and the female inferior; the one rules, and the other is ruled. The lower sort are by nature slaves, and it is better for them as for all inferior that they should be under the rule of a master.*
>
> —*Aristotle, Greek philosopher*

explain.) Early on, human embryos develop both male and female sex organs, but the presence of the extra X or Y chromosome causes the secretion of hormones and the differentiation of sex organs. The fetus starts to form internal female or external male genitalia at around three or four months into development (Crawford & Unger, 2000; Devor, 1989).

Think for a moment about the consequences of that simple differentiation of genitalia. Consider the interesting parallel between the sexes' genitalia and their roles in society. For centuries the male penis has been viewed as a symbol of virility—an external, outward sign of men's strength and their ability to assert themselves in the world. The externality of men's sexual organs has been interpreted socially to identify men as the actors, doers, leaders, and decision makers in many aspects of life, such as relationships, work, and politics. In contrast, the internal genitalia of women are associated with the more passive, submissive profile that women have traditionally assumed—a profile endorsed by men, and often, society in general. The social interpretations of women's sexual organs identify women as reactors, receivers, followers, and beneficiaries of men's decisions.

Maybe you have never considered these parallels before; maybe your reaction to these ideas is: "The world has changed; these depictions of women and men are past history, so why draw the parallel to sexuality?" If that's what you're thinking, then congratulate yourself. We agree that, for many people, these profiles no longer apply and thus the biological parallel doesn't apply either. But at times you may be painfully reminded that within many institutions in society—business, education, politicals—more than mere echoes of this "historical" view of women and men still exist.

Reproductive Functions

While the sexual organs represent the more obvious anatomical sex differences, perhaps the most profound difference rests in the sexes' reproductive functions. Researchers Bermant and Davidson (1974) define biological sex as "separateness: a division of reproductive labor into specialized cells, organs, and organisms. The sexes of a species are the classes of reproductively incomplete individuals" (p. 9). We know that it takes both eggs and sperm to rectify this "incompleteness," so this is not the differentiating reproductive function to which we refer. What makes the sexes so different in this regard is the woman's capacity to carry a developing fetus for nine months, give birth, and nurse an infant. These tasks have long been protected, even to the extent that turn-of-the-century medical information warned women against too much thinking or exercise so as not to divert blood away from their reproductive systems (Borisoff & Merrill, 1998; McLoughlin, Shryer, Goode, & McAuliffe, 1988). The reproductive capabilities of men and women have more profound social translations than any other biological property or function.

To explain that last statement, allow us to re-create for you a segment of a rather lively discussion that occurred at a gathering of friends. We were talking about biological sex differences when one of the men commented that sex differences exist in their current form because of centuries of *hunter-gatherer cultures.*

These were societies in which the men combed the land, hunted the food, and protected their families from danger, while the women had the birthing and child-rearing duties and developed tools to gather and carry the food. This separation of labor formed the basis of a social structure that worked very well; thus it continued into modern times, in the opinion of our friend. But this explanation of sex differences is more important than a mere anthropological lesson; the point is that because of simple biology, whole societal structures were set in place. Did you ever think that so much might rest on the capacity to reproduce? This is a prime example of what we mean when we say that biological factors contribute to a wide range of social norms and expectations.

> *On the one hand, we'll never experience childbirth. On the other hand, we can open all our own jars.*
>
> *–Bruce Willis, actor*

Did you ever stop to consider how arbitrary the decision might have been—the decision that women would give birth to babies? Whether you believe the decision was made by a divine entity or occurred as an accident of evolution is not the focus of our discussion here. However you believe it occurred, what if the decision had been made in the reverse? Have you ever thought about what kind of world we'd be living in if conception, pregnancy, birthing, and nursing were biological capabilities of men? Would men still be seen as actors, doers, and decision makers and women as reactors, receivers, and decision followers? Would the power structure that accompanies going out into the world and making a living versus staying at home with children be reversed as well? How would communication between men and women be affected?

Medical knowledge and technology have progressed to the point that women, in particular, can benefit from alternatives to their own biology—alternatives that continue to change our social structure. Although they are still able to carry and give birth to babies, women now have several methods of preventing conception. In fact, some observers contend that the development and accessibility of the birth control pill contributed more than other events or discoveries to altering male-female dynamics in recent U.S. history (Hain, 1997). In addition, if women do become pregnant, they do not necessarily have to be the biologically designated primary childcare-givers once the baby is born. Many women choose to return to work (or must work because of economic constraints) or pursue other endeavors. These choices affect how the sexes view each other, as well as how they communicate.

These days in two-parent families, some fathers are choosing to take time off from their jobs after a baby's birth or even quit their jobs to care for their children. But according to data from the U.S. Census Bureau, fathers provide primary childcare for preschoolers in only about 20 percent of marriages (Cummins, 2000). Men who make this choice face some interesting consequences. For instance, a colleague of ours resigned his tenured faculty position at a university to be the primary caregiver for his children while his wife continued her highly successful career as an attorney (Cavanaugh, 1997). Granted, you have to be in a financially secure position to even consider such a choice; many families simply cannot afford to sacrifice one income. But for those who can, articles citing the experiences of stay-at-home dads and Mr. Moms, as well as publications with helpful advice for fathers, are more prevalent now than a decade ago (Bernstein, 1996; Cooper, 2000; Libby, 2000; Marin, 2000; Walsh, 2002; White, 1998). From a social perspective, the reactions to stay-at-home dads are most interesting. These men report varied responses from women and a good deal of expected razzing from men. One dad reported that it was very tough at first because people kidded him about being Mr. Mom, relatives placed bets on when he'd go back to work, and mothers at the playground rebuffed him (Steinberg, 1995).

What is the social backlash for women who don't follow the more traditional path of motherhood? Have you heard criticism leveled at women who choose not to have children or who return to their careers while their children are still quite young? Often these women are ridiculed for "rocking the biological boat" and for being "selfish." If a man chose not to father any children or not to become the primary caregiver for a newborn because it would disrupt his career goals, do you think that he would receive as much criticism as women who make the same choices? In sum, even though it isn't as unusual as it once was to see women returning to work after giving birth and men choosing to be primary childcare-givers, statistics indicate that this profile of the family is still much more an aberration than the norm (Steinberg, 1995).

The Measure of Strength

When the subject of biological sex differences is introduced, students are quick to comment about issues surrounding physical strength and endurance. Heightened by events in America's campaign against terrorism and other military conflicts, such topics as biological attributes of male and female soldiers, differing standards of fitness, and women in front-line combat generate provocative discussions (Diamond, 1997; Hamilton, 1997; Schafer, 1998). A common theme in these discussions is whether women, whose bodies are higher in fat and lower in muscle in comparison to men's, have the strength and endurance necessary for combat or other sustained military action. Some people contend that if women are able to endure childbirth, they ought to be able to handle combat. What do some experts say about muscle versus fat composition, strength, and sex differences?

According to research, across adult age groups, men's body fat tends to average around 10 percent less than women's (Bailey & Bishop, 2001; Dolnick, 1991). Scientists attribute this difference primarily to the fact that the female body needs to protect a fetus. Besides men's higher concentration of muscle, four other factors give men more natural strength than women: (1) a greater oxygen-carrying capacity; (2) a lower resting heart rate; (3) higher blood pressure; and (4) more efficient methods of recovering from physical exertion (Stockard & Johnson, 1980). Because of these characteristics, men have long been thought of as the stronger sex, and women as the weaker sex. But let's take a closer look at determinations of strength.

Hot Button Issue

"WOMEN IN THE MILITARY"

For some people, the presence of women in the American armed forces is still a hot button issue. Even though women have served in the military for decades, debate continues over what roles they should play, whether they should have equal access to all military situations (including ground combat and male-dominated ships at sea), and differing standards for physical ability. Is this a hot button issue for you, one for which you hold strong opinions?

Strength is defined in *Webster's* dictionary as force, invulnerability, or the capacity for exertion and endurance. If you examine strength in terms of invulnerability or endurance, then the argument that strength is sex-typed breaks down a bit. Research documents the following differences between males and females:

1. Male fetuses experience many more developmental difficulties and birth defects, average an hour longer to deliver, and have a higher death rate than female fetuses.
2. For the 15 leading causes of death in the United States, men have higher death rates than women.
3. Women outlive men by 7 to 8 years.
4. Men do not tend to see themselves as ill or susceptible to disease or injury, but they are actually more susceptible than women.
5. Men generally drive more recklessly than women, causing three out of every four traffic fatalities.
6. In some sports requiring extreme levels of endurance (such as ultramarathons and dogsled racing), women are catching up to and surpassing men (Cahow, 1997; Dolnick, 1991; Jacklin, 1989; McLoughlin et al., 1988).

Could it be that the notion of male strength has more to do with social interpretations than biological fact? The answer to that question is no if you equate strength with higher muscle mass, but yes if you equate strength with invulnerability and endurance. Most often a determination of strength depends on the individual, not the sex.

> *I want a little boy to say, forty years from now, "I want to run like Marion Jones," not Carl Lewis or Michael Johnson.*
>
> —*Marion Jones, Olympic gold medalist*

We've all seen some women who were stronger (in terms of muscle strength) than some men and vice versa. But it's fascinating to realize how many social expectations and stereotypes are based on biology.

Social Interpretations of "Raging" Hormones

When people think about or comment on biological differences between the sexes, most often those differences are attributed to hormones (Jacklin, 1989). However, as hormonal studies become more frequent and use more sophisticated methods, they produce inconsistent results. We still do not know exactly what effects hormones have on human behavior. Some of the complexity results from not knowing where genetics leaves off and environment begins.

You may already be aware that all humans have the three main groups of hormones—androgens, estrogens, and progestrogens—but at varying levels. Here, for simplicity's sake, we have chosen to explore those hormones most associated with masculinity (androgens, and specifically testosterone) and femininity (estrogen). We've pared some complex information down to three key elements: hormonal effects on nurturance, aggression, and cycles. These functions are the most distinctive for the sexes and have the most significant social interpretations.

Nurturance

Stereotypically, nurturance is associated with women's role as mothers, but it is defined as the "giving of aid and comfort to others" (Maccoby & Jacklin, 1974, pp. 214–215). Research by Anke Ehrhardt found a relationship between female hormones and the inclination to nurture. Ehrhardt and colleagues (1980; 1984) examined young girls who had been prenatally "masculinized" by receiving large doses of androgens (male hormones) from drugs prescribed for their mothers. These subjects rarely fantasized or daydreamed about marriage and pregnancy, nor did they show much interest in caring for small children. They more often gave career a higher priority than marriage in discussions of future plans, generally liked to play and associate with boys more than girls, and were more likely to exhibit high levels of physical energy. These studies and other evidence led researchers to link hormones and nurturance.

But many researchers argue that the ability to nurture goes beyond biology. Sex role researchers Stockard and Johnson (1980) caution that "hormonal influence helps prompt the appearance of and interest in nurturing behavior, but social situations and interactions also exert an influence, making it possible for males as well as females to nurture" (p. 137). Such experiences as participation in childbirth, early contact between parents and infants, and even whether one has younger siblings may affect one's ability to nurture. Psychologists Crawford and Unger (2000) suggest that a "nurturing personality" can be developed simply when adults are put into nurturing roles (p. 349). Given this information, why does society so readily associate femininity with the ability to nurture and comfort, as though men were incapable of doing so? Granted, the association between motherhood and nurturance is deeply ingrained in our culture; thus, it is a reasonable connection. But does it have to be the only connection?

If a man finds that he has a nurturing tendency at least as strong as that of his wife or partner, should his masculinity be threatened? Think about why, until recently, mothers were almost always awarded custody of children in divorce proceedings, regardless of which parent was actually the better nurturer. Conversely, if a woman isn't particularly fond of children and isn't at all interested in motherhood, does this mean that she has a hormonal deficit or that she is somehow less feminine than women who want to nurture children? It's easy to see how hormonal functioning can lead to labels and stereotypes for the sexes—labels that affect our opportunities and influence our choices in communication.

Aggression

Aggressive behavior may be learned, but research indicates that hormones influence aggressive behavior (Lippa, 2002; Snowbeck, 2001). Aggressiveness has been long viewed as a male characteristic related to androgens (primarily testosterone), and passivity as related to a lack of androgens in the female system (Maccoby & Jacklin, 1980). Stockard and Johnson (1980) reviewed investigations of boys and girls who received high dosages of androgens (male hormones) before birth. In these studies, both male and female subjects had higher energy levels than a control group and preferred boys' games, toys, sports, and activities. Female subjects exhibited "tomboy" characteristics and behaviors and were more likely to start family fights than control group female subjects. However, professor of medical science Anne Fausto-Sterling (1992) discovered that many studies attempting to link male aggression and testosterone levels produced contradictory results; thus the relationship between hormones and aggression was questionable. So researchers continue their attempts to understand this relationship better.

Why do we still tend to associate masculinity with aggressive behavior and femininity with passive behavior? Could it again be the case that judgments about aggression and the sexes have more to do with social influences than biological fact? Think about the messages that many little boys receive—messages from their mothers and fathers, siblings, peers, and the media. In addition to those messages about strength that we discussed in an earlier section, boys are warned not to "act like a sissy" and are chastised for anything resembling feminine behavior. One of the worst insults people can level at a boy or a man is to call him a girl or a woman. (Remember the Hans and Frans "girly man" skits on *Saturday Night Live?*) You see fathers, uncles, and older brothers teaching young boys to stick up for themselves, to develop aggressive attitudes by playing contact sports, to rough-and-tumble with the best of them, and not to "throw like a girl." Granted, things are changing and not all families raise their male children in this manner, but for some reason the stereotype of the male as aggressor is still around.

Many men are not particularly proud of the legacy of aggression. In fact, they're working hard to turn this legacy around because the expectation that they will be constantly strong and aggressive constitutes a burden they'd rather not carry. They seek alternatives to expected behavior and resent the implication that being a "real man" means being aggressive, competitive, emotionally aloof or detached, and in control all the time. Interesting recent research suggests that men's testosterone levels vary according to their personal relationships. One study found that married men, particularly married men who are fathers of new-borns, have lower testosterone levels than unmarried men. Another study found that divorced men had higher testosterone levels than their married counter-parts. Scientists conducting the studies will not speculate as to what causes the decrease (Barry, 2002).

Now consider the flip side of aggression. What happens when girls carry tomboyish behaviors into adulthood? How do most people react when women behave aggressively? Unfortunately, many people react negatively, as though a woman who expresses this stereotypically masculine trait is experiencing a hor-monal imbalance or simply behaving inappropriately. Occasionally, off-base, derogatory insinuations about sexual orientation are made. Some men are threat-ened or put off by aggressive women, because they don't welcome another con-text for competition. Also, some women are put off by unexpected aggressive behavior in other women. For example, if a female manager were to argue aggressively with her coworkers or boss, interrupt the verbal contributions of colleagues, or aggressively strive to achieve a promotion, think about whether she would be viewed through the same lens as a man behaving similarly.

What about aggression and sports? Acting out aggression on the football field, in the hockey arena, or in the boxing ring is encouraged, expected, and rewarded in men. But, as more women's sports gain prominence and respectability, how do people view athletic aggression by females? Is this one of very few arenas in which female aggression is rewarded? Does it look the same and is it received as well as aggression in male athletes?

This front is changing as we speak. Female athletes competing in tradition-ally male sports are gaining popularity and acceptability in society every day (Phillips, 1997). Examples include U.S. women's teams that have won Olympic gold medals in ice hockey, basketball, softball, and soccer; the success of a pro-fessional women's basketball league (the WNBA); the introduction of female ref-erees into the NBA; the admission of two female professional golfers into the PGA; and the increasing popularity of women's professional boxing, due to the efforts of athletes like Leyla Ali and Christy Martin (Fried, 1997; Hoffer, 1997; Howard, 1997; Lasswell, 1996; Salter, 1997; Starr & Rosenberg, 1997).

Most people encourage female verbal and physical aggression in the sport-ing context, as long as that aggression isn't aimed at male competitors. Maybe you think this statement is harsh, but can you think of any sports that allow direct, physical competition between women and men? Apart from the occasional anomaly—such as the famous "battle of the sexes" tennis match between Billy Jean King and Bobby Riggs in 1973, occasional female race car drivers in the Indy 500, a female place kicker who had a short stint in college football, and a fe-male pitcher with a mean fastball who burned up minor league baseball in the summer of 1998—few women are given the opportunity to compete against men in either professional or collegiate sports. No contact sports on these levels, such as football, basketball, soccer, rugby, wrestling, or hockey, place the sexes in di-rect competition with each other. Neither do many noncontact sports, with the exception of mixed doubles matches in tennis, some endurance races (often called ultramarathons), and dogsledding. Perhaps a continued rise in popularity of women's sports, to the degree that they become more commonplace instead of exceptions to the rule, will affect people's stereotypical notions about aggression.

Cycles

When we think of biological cycles, we typically associate them with women's biology in general and with premenstrual syndrome (PMS) in particular. Three decades ago, the medical profession largely attributed women's menstrual discomfort (e.g., irritability, headaches, cramps, bloating, and mood swings) to hypochondria. In Ramey's (1976) groundbreaking research on PMS, 60 percent of subjects reported experiencing menstrual discomfort. When enough research documented women's reports of menstrual problems over time, the medical community researched the malady, reversed its position, and declared PMS a disease (Richmond-Abbott, 1992). Some scholars believe that labeling PMS a disease has given the condition credibility, but it has also reinforced an old stereotype. Dramatic accounts of outlandish, overemotional, even violent behavior, as well as exaggerated images of women unable to meet their responsibilities have been attributed to PMS. There's even a T-shirt with the message, "I Have PMS and ESP. That Makes Me A Bitch Who Knows It All." In their book on women's psychology, Crawford and Unger (2000) state: "The view that their reproductive cycle makes women vulnerable to psychological problems helps to limit women, to define them as dangerous and deviant, and to exclude them from a role in society equal to that of men" (p. 535). At the same time that diagnosing the condition legitimized women's complaints as reality, not folklore, it gave society more impetus to question women's abilities.

One example emerges from the United States' military conflicts in recent years—questions about women's ability to participate with men in life-threatening combat, a topic mentioned earlier in reference to physical strength. Some of the arguments about the effects of women's cycles on mental functioning relegate women to background or support positions in times of conflict. Accusations are made that because women's bodies cycle and their hormones "rage," they cannot be trusted to pilot F-16s, withhold information if captured, or make decisions as to when weapons should be fired. Please realize that it is not our intent here to take a stance about women and combat. The point is that social interpretations of women's cyclical biology negate or call into question women's ability in many contexts.

The warning most commonly cited about this issue is, "Would you want the hand of a woman with PMS on the button to detonate a nuclear bomb?" (Kleiman, 1992, p. 2E). This question implies that women are such victims of their own biology that they could not possibly be relied on in critical situations. What is most interesting here is that the same argument could be made about men's levels of testosterone and aggressive behavior. Do men's hormonal functioning and their bent toward aggression better equip them to "put the hand on the button"? If this statement seems comical to you, it's probably because such an argument is hardly ever made. While society is quick to link hormonal functioning with debilitation in women, the same cannot be said for men.

But what about the notion of a male biological cycle? The male cycle is more than a mere notion, according to research. In the mid-1970s researchers began to

Hot Button Issue

"A MALE PERIOD"

This is one of those topics that makes men feel squeamish while women want to laugh. When we broach this subject with students in our gender communication classes, invariably one or more of the women will swear that her boyfriend or husband has some sort of hormonal cycle, something akin to the female menstrual cycle. While there's no physical manifestation of the cycle, these men seem to go through regular, predictable periods of irritability, sensitivity, and depression. The female students suggest that if their men were to be tested at those times, a lowered level of testosterone and other male hormones would probably be detected. If you are female, do you agree with our female students? If you are male, do you see evidence of a cycle in yourself, or do you think this idea is completely nuts?

investigate male hormonal functioning as evidence of a male cycle. Ramey (1976) found that men displayed regular variations in emotions over each 24-hour period within a 6-week time frame. Ramey also detected a 30-day cycle for men's hormonal functioning. During these cycles, men's physical strength, emotionality, and intellectual functioning were affected. Doreen Kimura (1987), in internationally noted research, identified a tentative link between seasons of the year and men's cognitive functioning. According to Kimura, in the spring, when testosterone levels are lower, men's mathematical and analytic skills are enhanced. These abilities decrease in the fall when testosterone levels are higher. The popular press picked up on this research, having fun comparing women's monthly periods to what it called men's seasonal "commas" (Kleiman, 1992, p. 1E). Other researchers have investigated the possibility of a male menopause, noting a link between depleted testosterone levels and depression (Fischman, 2001).

What if, a few years from now, evidence overwhelmingly documents the existence of a male cycle? What would be the social reaction to such news? Do you think that jobs, opportunities, responsibilities, and social roles would change to reflect this biological "instability" in men? Could this alter communication between women and men in some way? We don't know the answers to these questions, but if this scenario becomes a reality, it is likely that the social interpretations of the biology will be far more interesting than the biology itself.

Mind Over Matter: Are Men's and Women's Brains Really Different?

Current information regarding sex differences and brain functioning has caused more than mild controversy. As one researcher suggests, "This is a politically charged area of research because the stakes are high for the more and less cognitively able" (Paul, 2002, p. 93). Brain functions are extremely complex, tied to hormonal functioning, affected by environmental and social factors, and related to cognitive abilities (Halpern, 2000). This is not meant to be an introductory lesson in physiology, so we will review only the primary research findings, emphasizing their social interpretations.

Brain Functioning

Some researchers report sex differences in brain size, glucose metabolism counts, and cerebral blood flow (Gur et al., 1982; Gur et al., 1995; Halpern, 2000). But others conclude that studies in this area actually show minimal differences (indicating that the sexes' brains are actually more similar than different) and are used primarily to engender divisiveness (Bleier, 1984; Gibbons, 1991; Tavris, 1992). Prolific gender scholar Celeste Condit contends that a good deal of research on sex differences and the brain is biased in its assumptions and faulty in its methods, constituting a form of "bad science" (1996, p. 87).

Research has shown that the human brain has two hemispheres, housing various capabilities. The left hemisphere is primarily responsible for the production of language; the right hemisphere manages spatial ability. Studies have attempted to find a relationship between hemisphere dominance and sex, hypothesizing that hormones cause women's and men's brains to develop differently. It has long been thought—and many people still contend—that men perform better on tests of spatial skills while women excel on tests of verbal ability, as a result of hormonal and brain functioning (Kimura, 2000). Since most social interpretations of the information on brain functioning relate to cognitive ability, let's explore this area before considering those interpretations.

I have a brain and a uterus, and I use both.

—Patricia Schroeder, former congresswoman

Cognitive Ability

Almost anything one reads about sex differences in cognitive ability includes a review of a report by the psychologists Benbow and Stanley (1980) of years of research on math abilities in gifted girls and boys. A consistent pattern emerged over two decades of conducting this research: boys outscored girls on the math portions of the SAT. This finding led to the conclusion that male dominance in math was related to hemispheric specialization in the brain, that is, that the right hemisphere was more fully developed in men than in women. Recent research supports the notion that differing cognitive ability is related to the use of various areas of the brain (Gorski, as in Thornton, 1992; Gur, as in Bowden, 1995).

However, social scientists on the nurture side of the nature-nurture argument have other explanations for sex differences in cognitive functioning, insisting that social and environmental factors affect the picture. These researchers have found that since boys are expected to excel in math, they are encouraged and coached by parents and teachers. Taking more advanced math courses in school and participating in athletics improves boys' math and spatial abilities as well, whereas attitudes and anxiety about the difficulty of math inhibit girls' achievement (Baenninger & Newcombe, 1995; Eccles, 1989; Linn & Petersen, 1986). Some research also points a finger at the media, such as magazines and television talk shows, for hyping studies that find brain differences in the sexes while ignoring those that reveal similarities (Bing, 1999).

Concerning verbal ability, the general opinion for decades was that females outperformed males in such areas as language acquisition, vocabulary, spelling, writing, and verbal expressiveness. But again, research has produced findings to the contrary. Researchers now believe that if there once was a gap in verbal abilities and math and spatial abilities between the sexes due to brain differences and hormonal functioning, this gap has all but disappeared (Crawford & Unger, 2000; Hall, 1987; Holden, 1991; Hyde & Linn, 1988). If the human brain hasn't changed, what explains the finding that the sexes perform more similarly in specific areas now than in times past?

One explanation relates to changing times and changing parents. Perhaps more parents have backed away from the old stereotypes and now believe that female and male children can do anything, given encouragement, support, and education (Shapiro, 1990). Another explanation regards educational systems. If teachers demonstrate sex bias in their instruction, such as coaching boys in math while sending messages to girls that say "you probably won't be good at this," these biases have ways of becoming reality. Teachers who refrain from sex-biased behaviors are helping students to maximize their potential, regardless of expectations for their sex (Ehrenreich, 1992). Educational institutions that offer and encourage mathematical and spatial curricula for all children help to enhance these abilities (Baenninger & Newcombe, 1995). In sum, societal shifts are affecting students' vision of what they can accomplish, and the gender gap in cognitive ability is narrowing.

This is a hopeful trend, in that it will affect the way we think about the sexes' abilities. Maybe the stereotype that "women talk too much"—a myth that most people don't connect with biologically superior verbal ability—will die a well-deserved death. Maybe the image of the "strong, silent type" of man will deservedly fade away, too. Maybe male-dominated fields related to math and spatial skills, such as engineering, science, and technology, will open up even further to women. Maybe men will feel more comfortable in fields traditionally filled by women, such as teaching and other helping professions that rely heavily on verbal abilities. These are a lot of maybes, but the thought that things are changing, stereotypes are fading, and past expectations are loosening should give you a feeling of relief and a sense of freedom. Does this information make you feel that way? If it doesn't, if the changes feel threatening, what might be some causes for your concern? It's interesting to ponder how we can be influenced by biological sex differences, but also how we can choose to interpret biology and communicate with others as a result.

> ## *Remember . . .*
>
> **BIOLOGICAL SEX:** Being born male or female.
>
> **REPRODUCTIVE FUNCTIONS:** The sexes' differing abilities to conceive, carry, give birth to, and nurture offspring.
>
> **HUNTER-GATHERER CULTURES:** Ancient societies in which men's and women's roles were distinguished according to who provided food, protected the family from danger, and gave birth to and reared children.
>
> **PHYSICAL STRENGTH:** A societally derived judgment based on physical characteristics such as muscle mass, invulnerability, and endurance.
>
> **NURTURANCE:** The stereotypically female trait of giving aid and comfort to others.
>
> **AGGRESSION:** The stereotypically male trait of asserting or inflicting force.

SOCIAL INFLUENCES ON PSYCHOLOGICAL GENDER

In the first major section of this chapter we talked about biological sex differences; note that here we have switched the focus to psychological variables or *gender identity*. Recall from Chapter 1 that the term *sex* is generally used to refer to maleness and femaleness based on biology, whereas *gender* is a much broader psychological and cultural construct. Gender is culturally based and socially constructed from psychological characteristics; it also contains such things as attitudes and beliefs, sexual orientation, and perceptions of appropriate roles for women and men in society. *Gender identity* is a subset of gender that refers to the way you view yourself, how you see yourself relative to stereotypically feminine or masculine traits.

Learning to Be Girls and Boys

The development of gender understanding in young children is fascinating because they believe gender to be changeable (Devor, 1992). (Ah, the wisdom of children.) They see gender not as being based on anatomy, but as a role that can be changed, much like changing a hairstyle. As children start to understand themselves as individuals separate from others, they begin to understand that others see them and respond to them as particular people of a particular sex.

Theories of Gender Identity Development

Theories have been generated to explain the phenomenon of gender identity development, or how one becomes "gendered." We will summarize some of the more prominent theories and then explore the connection between gender identity and gender communication.

Social Learning Theory

Social psychologists Walter Mischel (1966) and Albert Bandura (1971; 1986) are noted for their research on social learning theory as an explanation for human development. This theory suggests that children learn gender-related behavior from their social contacts, primarily their parents and peers. Through a process known as identification, children model the thoughts, emotions, and actions of others. This role modeling has a powerful effect on how children see themselves and on how they form gender identities.

A related practice involves a sort of trial-and-error method in which children learn what behaviors are expected of each sex. Some behaviors in little girls and boys are rewarded by parents, teachers, peers, and other agents of socialization; the same behaviors enacted by the opposite sex are punished. As children continue to receive positive and negative responses to their behaviors, they generalize to other situations and come to develop identities as girls or boys (Lippa, 2002; Peach, 1998).

One problem with this theory is the suggestion that children develop according to gender stereotypes; some theorists consider this idea a limited or confining view of human development. For example, what if a little girl rejects stereotypical girlish behavior because she likes the status or acceptance she sees little boys receiving? When she wants to imitate their behavior in order to gain their status, it may not work for her the same way it does for them. She might be labeled a tomboy, perhaps gaining some acceptance, but also receiving occasional ridicule. If she patterns her behavior after same-sex models, it is possible that she will not receive the respect, power, and status she wants. If a little boy is surrounded predominantly by models of the opposite sex, like his mother and most of his preschool and elementary school teachers, what happens if he closely follows their behavior? He may be chastised, ostracized, and labeled effeminate or a "sissy." These examples illustrate what some people consider a weakness in the theory—its emphasis on gender stereotypes as guides for behavior and identity development.

However, we know that our sense of identity is affected by how we imitate or learn from our parents. Think about the person you patterned your behavior after; was it your mom or your dad, or was it both? Did you pattern yourself more after a same-sex parent or an opposite-sex parent? Maybe an important model for you when you were growing up was a sibling, a grandparent, or some other significant person. Maybe you didn't grow up with two parents. As our culture continues to diversify, the number of single-parent families is growing. If you've experienced this family profile, what effect do you think the focus on one parent had on your notions about gender?

An example illustrates this idea of modeling your behavior after that of your parents. This story has been around awhile, but it's a good one. A woman describes how she always followed in her mother's footsteps, especially in the kitchen. It seems that she recalled her mother always cutting one end off a ham before putting it in a pan to bake. That was the way her mother did it, so that was the proper way to bake a ham. She prepared hams this way in her own home and taught her daughter to do so as well. One holiday when the three women (we'll call them the grandmother, the mother, and the granddaughter) were gathered in the kitchen preparing the holiday meal, the grandmother saw the granddaughter religiously cut off one end of the ham before putting it in a pan to bake. The granddaughter thought nothing of it; that's just the way you cooked a ham. The grandmother burst out laughing, finally realizing what the granddaughter was doing. The granddaughter responded that her mother had taught her that this was how you baked a ham. Wasn't it "grandma's way"? When the grandmother explained that the only reason she lopped off one end of the ham was that back then she didn't own a pan big enough for a large ham, these women laughed at themselves for their years of misguided tradition.

Cognitive Development Theory

One prominent gender identity theory results primarily from the work of Lawrence Kohlberg. According to Kohlberg (1966), as children's minds mature, they gain an understanding of gender roles and self-identity without external reinforcement (in contrast to the suggestions of social learning theory). Kohlberg's theory essentially is that children socialize themselves into feminine or masculine identities via progress through four stages of mental ability. In stage 1, very young children are beginning to recognize sex distinctions, but they cannot attach a sex identity to a person. They are likely to say such things as "Daddy is a girl." In stage 2, children learn their own sexual identity, as well as how to identify other people's sex correctly (Ruble, Balaban, & Cooper, 1981). They now understand that their own maleness or femaleness is unchangeable. In stage 3, children learn that there are "ground rules" for sex roles, or guidelines for sex-typed appropriate behavior, that stem from one's culture. Children become motivated to behave in accordance with those rules, persuading others to conform, too. For example, girls want to wear ruffly, "girly" clothing, and boys are appalled at the thought of playing with dolls. At this point, children begin to value and imitate those behaviors associated with their own sex, more so than behaviors associated with the other sex.

This progress continues into stage 4, when children separate their identities from those of their primary caregivers (typically their mothers). For boys, the importance of their fathers' identity and behavior is compounded. But because girls cannot separate themselves from the mother's female identity, they remain at stage three, unlike their male counterparts who progress through all four stages. In essence, a girl's development is stunted because her sex identity is the same as her mother's. Can you anticipate any problems with this theory? A major criticism of the theory has to do with its use of a male model of development that is then generalized to all humans. The model suggests that girls' development is somehow less complete or advanced than boys'.

Gender Schema Theory

Gender schema theory, primarily advanced by psychologist Sandra Bem (1983), states that once a child learns an appropriate cultural definition of gender, this definition becomes the key structure around which all other information is organized. A schema is a cognitive structure that helps us interpret the world. In cultures that adhere closely to traditional gender differentiation, gender schemas are likely to be complex and elaborate. Before a schema can be formulated and gender-related information can be viewed through it, the child must be old enough to identify gender accurately. When a girl learns that cultural prescriptions for femininity include politeness and kindness, she incorporates these traits into her emerging schema and begins to behave in a polite and kind way. Gender schemas provide prescriptions for how to behave and can strongly influence a child's sense of self-esteem.

As children develop a gender schema, they increasingly use it as an organizing perspective. A schema related to a child's own sex appears to develop first, and it becomes more complex and detailed than schemas for the other sex. Using his or her own schema, a child takes in new information, plans activities, and chooses roles. The development of and subsequent adherence to gender schemas may help us understand why it is so difficult to dislodge gender-stereotypical thinking.

Bem's (1993) work on gender socialization expands gender schema theory by describing the effects of culture on the acquisition of gender. According to Bem, every culture contains assumptions about behavior that are part of its social institutions. She maintains that three fundamental, culturally shared beliefs exist regarding males and females:

1. Females and males are totally different and opposite beings.
2. Males are superior to females.
3. Biology produces natural and inevitable gender roles.

Despite evidence against gender polarization and biological predestination, these beliefs remain prevalent. Bem notes that most children accept these beliefs without recognizing that alternatives are possible. As these children grow older, they cannot envision a society organized differently.

Gilligan's Gender Identity Development Theory

Carol Gilligan (1982) challenged human development theorists in her groundbreaking book *In a Different Voice: Psychological Theory and Women's Development.* Gilligan's theory expands previous views of human development to account for both female and male paths to gender identity. In a nutshell (which does not do justice to this theory), the core of identity development rests within the mother-child relationship. The female child connects and finds gender identity with the mother, but the male child must find identity by separating himself from this female caregiver. Thus—unlike male development, which stresses separation and independence—female identity revolves around interconnectedness and relationships. As communication researchers Wood and Lenze (1991) explain, "This results in a critical distinction in the fundamental basis of identity learned by the genders. For men, the development of personal identity precedes intimacy with others, while for females, intimacy with others, especially within the formative relationship with the mother, is fused with development of personal identity: the two are interwoven processes" (p. 5).

Gilligan's theory offers insight into how men and women function. But Gilligan's critics claim that the theory focuses too heavily on female development, and that it implies an advantage for females who can identify with a same-sex caregiver, while merely drawing occasional comparisons with how the process works for males. How, then, does one make sense of all these theories? Does a "best" theory of gender identity exist?

While the theories we've reviewed contribute significantly to our understanding, they tend to dichotomize, focusing on maleness and femaleness. This focus diminishes the broader concept of gender, relegating it to an "either-or" discussion of sex. Another problem is that each theory tends to focus primarily on childhood development or how children discover gender and corresponding social expectations. What we believe to be more interesting for our discussion of gender communication is a model that begins with how we experience gender as children, but shifts to how we progress or transcend that experience later in life. A theory of transcendence offers real insight into how adults negotiate and renegotiate their gender identities, over time, given experiences and education.

Gender Transcendence and Androgyny

Several researchers have developed, expanded, and refined a theory of gender identity development called *gender transcendence*. Our discussion begins with the notable contributions of psychologist Joseph Pleck, in a comparison between traditional sex-role identity development theory and gender transcendence.

In traditional views of development, the term *sex role* is defined as "the psychological traits and the social responsibilities that individuals have and feel are appropriate for them because they are male or female" (Pleck, 1977, p. 182). The emphasis here is on the two designations—masculine and feminine. Masculinity involves instrumental or task-oriented competence and includes such traits as assertiveness, self-expansion, self-protection, and a general orientation of self *against* the world. Femininity is viewed as expressive or relationship-oriented competence, with corresponding traits that include nurturance and concern for others, emphasis on relationships and the expression of feelings, and a general orientation of self *within* the world (Eccles, 1987; Parsons & Bales, 1955).

Critics of traditional views of development believe that the prevailing theories perpetuate the dichotomy between males and females and limit individuals' options regarding identity. Gender transcendence theory responds to this criticism. Within transcendence theory, Pleck (1975) envisions a three-stage sequence of gender identity development. The first two stages resemble Kohlberg's (1966) cognitive development model. However, stage 3 represents the point where transcendence theory departs from the more traditional theories. Stage 3 occurs when individuals experience difficulty because the rules of behavior no longer seem to make sense or because they begin to suspect that they possess both expressive (feminine) and instrumental (masculine) abilities.

At this point, individuals may "transcend" their understanding of the norms and expectations of gender to develop "psychological androgyny in accordance with their inner needs and temperaments" (Pleck, 1975, p. 172). (As we discussed in Chapter 1, "transgender" persons may have accomplished gender transcendence, in that they have moved past traditional role definitions and no

---

'Net Notes

It's inappropriate to equate transgenderism with transvestitism or trans-sexualism, although there is some overlap between these forms of identity. For an interesting Website on transgenderism, try **www.susans.org,** the official Website for Susan's Place, which offers a wide variety of transgender resources, including chat rooms, links to other sites, and reading suggestions.

---

longer rely on those definitions when determining their own behavior or assessing the behavior of others.) When transcendence occurs, the "individual heads toward a resolution. . ., which in terms of gender-role development involves the integration of one's masculine and feminine selves into self-defined gender-role identity" (Eccles, 1987, p. 232). Communication researcher Harold Barrett (1998) describes the shift in emphasis from biological sex to psychological gender this way: "The emphasis now is less on determination of role by sex—male versus female—and more on awareness of gender plurality in an individual's nature" (p. 83). The notion of "gender plurality" is another way to conceive of gender transcendence.

Like other theories of gender identity development, transcendence theory begins with a discussion of child development. However, it emphasizes adolescence as a period when traditional definitions of what is male and female are likely to be challenged for the first time. The theory then tracks into adult development, as changing values, social pressures, and life events (e.g., marriage, new jobs, parenting, retirement) cause adults to reevaluate their gender identities. Transcendence, then, may occur in adolescence and adulthood; however, not everyone experiences it. Some people continue throughout adulthood to adhere to traditional roles and definitions of what is female and male, and they manage this quite successfully.

Androgyny, which we discussed briefly in Chapter 1, is related to this notion of gender transcendence. Androgyny is more understandable if you envision a continuum with masculinity placed toward one end, femininity toward the other end, and androgyny in the middle. You don't lose masculine traits or behaviors if you are androgynous, or somehow become masculine if you move away from the feminine pole. Androgyny is an intermix of the feminine and the masculine. Some androgynous individuals may have more masculine traits than feminine, and vice versa.

> *If I'm androgynous,*
> *I'd say I lean toward*
> *macho-androgynous.*
>
> *—John Travolta, actor*

Perhaps a diagram will clarify the idea of androgyny further (see Figure 2.1). At the top are two bell curves labeled "masculinity" and

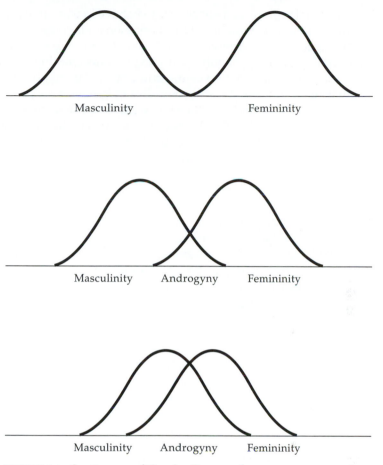

FIGURE 2-1. Continuum of Gender Transcendence.

"femininity." If you adopt a traditional view of sex roles, you fall under one of these two curves depending on your sex. In the middle, you see that the bell curves have merged somewhat, so that their overlap represents androgyny. As individuals continue to challenge traditional sex-typed roles and experience gender transcendence, they widen their identities to include male and female traits and behaviors. Over time, the androgynous identity continues to widen, as depicted in the expanded androgynous area at the bottom.

While their identity expands, gender-transcended individuals' repertoire of communication behavior also has the capacity to expand. This should sound familiar, since it is fundamental to the personal effectiveness approach to gender communication. In Chapter 1, we explained how effective individuals develop a wider range of communication behaviors from which to choose, know how to analyze a situation and select the best behaviors from their repertoire, enact those behaviors, and evaluate the results. Because the process of gender transcendence causes an individual to incorporate feminine and masculine traits into a unique blend, that individual is more likely to choose to behave in ways that aren't confined by traditional, stereotypical notions of how men and women are *supposed* to behave. For example, an androgynous male may be more likely than a masculine type of male to talk about and openly express his emotions because he does not buy into the notion that revealing emotions is "unmanly." Androgynous individuals tend to expand their repertoires of behavior; in general, they are adaptive to situations and comfortable with communicative options— options that become extremely helpful in the complicated realm of gender communication (Bem, 1987; Eccles; 1987; Greenblatt, Hasenauer, & Friemuth, 1980; Kelly, O'Brien, & Hosford, 1981). Results from a study in which subjects indicated strong identification with both masculine and feminine traits (i.e., androgyny) led the researchers to suggest that "androgyny may be a new gender ideal" (House, Dallinger, & Kilgallen, 1998, p. 18).

Another advantage of an androgynous orientation involves how you see and respond to others—an important component of the receiver orientation to communication. To be your most receiver oriented, you need to be able to accept people for what makes them unique. Because androgynous individuals have expanded views of sex roles and corresponding behavior, they tend to be more generally accepting and less judgmental of others whose behavior deviates from social expectations for the sexes.

What is your reaction to the theory of gender transcendence and the concept of androgyny? Some of you may be thinking that the theory reduces the importance of masculinity or femininity, that it waters down unique, important properties of being female or male. If you have these thoughts, you're not alone. The idea is to view androgyny as you would a glass that is half full, rather than half empty. Rather than taking away from the distinctiveness of the sexes, androgyny is a way of recognizing and celebrating qualities of the masculine and the feminine—a way of making these qualities *human,* rather than options for one sex but not the other.

We've made the case for gender transcendence and androgyny, but of course there are some cautions regarding this information. First, while we believe that androgyny and repertoire expansion fit together logically, we don't mean to suggest that the *only* way to expand the communication repertoire is to adopt an androgynous gender identity. A person who aligns himself or herself with a traditionally feminine or masculine gender identity may still expand the communication repertoire. In many situations, this individual may behave appropriately and be viewed as an effective communicator. It's important to keep in mind that, while we consider an androgynous person more likely to develop a greater repertoire than a traditionally sex-typed person, this is just a trend, not a hard and fast rule.

The second caution is, in a sense, a reverse of the first. We don't mean to insinuate that *all* androgynous people are *automatically* effective communicators in *all* situations, just because they embody masculine and feminine traits and behaviors. As you are becoming aware, there are neither easy answers nor "quick fixes" in gender communication. We believe that gender transcendence broadens your approach and enhances your repertoire and that it is a desirable position from which to communicate with others, but it offers no guarantees.

Remember . . .

GENDER IDENTITY DEVELOPMENT: The way one develops one's gender, with regard for feminine traits, masculine traits, or a blend of both.

SOCIAL LEARNING THEORY: Children learn gender-related behavior from their social contacts, primarily their parents and peers.

COGNITIVE DEVELOPMENT THEORY: Children socialize themselves into feminine or masculine identities as they progress through various stages of mental ability.

GENDER SCHEMA THEORY: Once children learn appropriate cultural definitions of gender, these definitions become key structures around which all other information is organized.

GILLIGAN'S GENDER IDENTITY THEORY: The core of gender identity development rests within the mother-child relationship; it involves the development of connectedness in girls and autonomy in boys.

GENDER TRANSCENDENCE: A rejection of traditional gender identities (masculine or feminine); an integration of feminine and masculine selves into a self-defined gender identity.

ANDROGYNY: An intermix or blending of feminine and masculine traits.

THE EFFECTS OF SOCIALIZATION ON GENDER IDENTITY DEVELOPMENT

The process of developing gender identity involves acquiring information about cultural norms and roles for men and women (a social function), then adjusting one's view of self, one's role in society, and one's behavior in response to those norms (a psychological function). Some prefer to call this *socialization*, defined as the process through which individuals learn their culture, develop their potential, and become functioning members of society (Lindsey & Christy, 1997). The primary vehicle for socialization is communication. Socialization recurs throughout the life cycle and includes gender identity development as only one facet. For example, a person can experience socialization upon moving to another state or country, changing jobs, or encountering new relationships. For our purposes in this discussion, focusing on gender identity within the larger framework of socialization helps us understand how we come to develop our sense of self, our own vision of appropriate roles and behavior for women and men, and our patterns in gender communication.

The Family as a Primary Socializing Agent

Our society is never finished socializing us, and the family is by far the most significant agent of socialization. Family communication scholar Virginia Satir (1972; 1988) views the family as a factory where "peoplemaking" occurs. This is a useful perspective because families do create people, not just children. The family context (including the communication within it) continues to shape and mold an adult throughout her or his life. The family has the ability to influence the gender identities of the people it makes by reinforcing the status quo or by offering a broader view of how to be a boy or girl, man or woman.

Gender differences in the treatment of female and male children begin *before* birth. While parents indicate that their first priority is to have a healthy baby, a preference for one sex over the other is prevalent. Across the globe, most couples prefer male over female children, especially for a first or only child—a finding that has not changed much since the 1930s (Basow, 1992; Beal, 1994; Moen, 1991; Pooler, 1991). For example, the Chinese tradition of preferring sons over daughters continues, as reflected in the Chinese proverb, "Raising a daughter is like weeding another man's garden" (Carmondy, 1989). In some countries, such as China, India, and other Asian nations, this preference results in the underreporting of female births, female infanticide, neglect of female infants, abortion of female fetuses, and many abuses as underground overseas adoption services flourish (Lloyd, 1994; Park & Cho, 1995). Adding to concerns about sex preferences are technological developments which offer a high rate of success in choosing the sex of a child. One technique, Microsort, is a procedure that helps couples conceive a baby of their preferred sex 65 to 90 percent of the time (Joyce, 1999).

After the birth of a child, the family maintains the major responsibility for socializing the child during the critical years of life, even when other socializing influences exist. In the family, the child gains a sense of self, learns language, and begins to understand norms of interaction with parents, siblings, and significant others. Research over multiple decades has explored sex-typing of babies. In studies of infants of similar weight, length, and health, both parents described sons as big, tough, strong, firm, and alert, while daughters were described as cheerful, gentle, delicate, soft, and awkward (Rubin, Provensano, & Luria, 1974; Stern & Karraker, 1989).

Sex-typed socialization continues as children grow and mature. Research indicates that fathers are significantly more likely than mothers to differentiate between their sons and daughters and to encourage more traditional sex-specific behavior in their sons (Fagot & Leinbach, 1995; Hardesty, Wenk, & Morgan, 1995). Parents tend to engage in more physical, rough play with sons (Lindsey & Mize, 2001; Ross & Taylor, 1989); to maintain closer physical proximity to daughters (Bronstein, 1988); and to believe that girls need more help than boys (Snow, Jacklin, & Maccoby, 1983). Girls are encouraged to participate in activities that keep them close to their homes and families, while boys are given more opportunities for play and other activities away from home and independent of adult supervision, a finding that holds in both Western and non-Western cultures (Erwin, 1992). Research on patterns of interaction shows differential treatment of children based on the sex of the child, in that parents do not speak the same way to daughters as they do to sons (Bellinger & Gleason, 1982; Buerkel-Rothfuss, Covert, Keith, & Nelson, 1986; Eisenberg, 1996). Finally, one study found that assertiveness in daughters was viewed less positively than assertiveness in sons, while appropriate interpersonal communication skills were viewed more favorably in daughters than in sons (Leaper, Anderson, & Sanders, 1998).

I'VE SHIFTED MY PARENTAL ROLE FROM GIVING MY KIDS A PERFECT CHILDHOOD TO LIMITING THE STUFF THEY'RE GOING TO TELL A THERAPIST...

Mothers—historically and currently—have played the key role in the socialization of children in most two-parent families, but researchers have explored the importance and nature of fathers' involvement (Bacorn, 1992; Gerstel & Gallagher, 2001). Studies suggest that both boys and girls develop less traditionally sex-stereotyped attitudes about male and female roles when their fathers are highly involved in childcare (Sagi & Sharon, 1984). Extensive interaction between father and child is also associated with the development of androgyny in children (Lavine & Lombardo, 1984). Feminist scholar bell hooks (2000) credits feminism for its role in highlighting the importance of the father's role. She suggests, "One of the most positive interventions feminist movement made on behalf of children was to create greater cultural awareness of the need for men to participate equally in parenting not just to create gender equity, but to build better relationships with children" (p. 75). Besides the positive effects of fathers, one study found that fathers' involvement in the lives and development of their children (both biological and adopted) had a significant positive effect on the fathers' social connections, family ties, and work satisfaction (Eggebeen & Knoester, 2001).

Is it possible to raise children who do not conform to gender identity stereotypes? Sandra Bem's experience shows that it's possible, but not easy. In her book *An Unconventional Family*, Bem (1998) describes her and her husband Daryl's efforts to raise "gender-liberated children," a process which involved "inoculating them early enough and effectively enough against the culture" (pp. 308, 309). Family communication scholars Beebe and Masterson (1986) describe the difference between *person-centered* and *position-centered families*. Position-centered families focus on the position or role each person holds in the family, whereas person-centered families place a high value on the individuality of each member. The person-centered approach tends to discourage sex-typed development while enhancing a child's ability to behave flexibly in a role.

Secondary Agents of Socialization

We are definitely affected or socialized by the gender roles that were enacted in our families. Because of parents' influence on children's understanding of gender, many modern parents are trying a nongendered approach. They are giving children gender-neutral toys, games, and books in efforts to avoid the more traditional items that often perpetuate stereotypes (like Barbie, GI Joe, and traditional fairy tales) (Messner, 2000; Morgan, 1993). In this section, we address the socializing effects of clothing, toys, peer relationships, and teachers as role models. The media also have a significant impact on chidren's gender identity development—a topic that we'll save for later chapters. For now, think about the things you played with as a child and the relationships in the neighborhood or at school that had the most effect on your view of what it means to be a man or a woman in our culture.

Clothes and Toys

The first things acquired for an infant are clothes and toys. When the sex of a baby is not known, friends and family members try to buy sex-neutral gifts, like yellow receiving blankets or green bibs. Color-coded and sex-typed clothing of infants and young children is still quite prevalent (Fagot, Rodgers, & Leinbach, 2000; Pomerleau, Bloduc, Malcuit, & Cosette, 1990). One study found that more than 90 percent of infants observed in a shopping mall could be readily categorized by sex according to the characteristics of their clothing (Shakin, Shakin, & Sternglanz, 1985). Sex-specific clothing provides the initial labels to ensure that children are responded to "appropriately." Is this necessary?

Along with clothing, toys and play are powerful forces of socialization (Berkowitz, Gerali, & Skillin, 1999; Caldera & Sciaraffa, 1998; Messner, 2000). For girls, probably the most popular and influential toy of recent times is the Barbie doll. Barbie and her variations, introduced across the years (e.g., "Multicultural Barbie," "Baywatch Barbie," and "Barbie for President 2000"), continue to be a subject of much research and discussion, in terms of the doll's impact on young girls, how they see themselves, and how they develop notions of femininity and attractiveness (DuCille, 1994; Jacobs & Shaw, 2000; Kluger, 2000; Rand, 1998). The Mattel company recently received letters of outrage over its perceived sexist toy manufacturing and marketing, when it introduced its line of Barbie computers for girls (with hardware in pink, no less) and Hot Wheels computers for boys (in the expected blue). The Hot Wheels computer package came complete with logic, math, anatomy, and computer art software, while Barbie software packages focused on fashion design, story-making, and ocean discovery (Shore, 2001).

Toys for girls encourage domesticity, interpersonal closeness, and social orientation, whereas boys receive not only more categories of toys but toys that are more complex and more expensive and that foster self-reliance and problem solving (Hughes, 1994; Leaper, 1994). Children's advertisements in catalogs and on television reinforce gender typing in toys. Next time you go to a toy store, note how the aisles are organized and how pictures on the boxes suggest the way girls and boys should use the toys. Boys receive more sports equipment, tools, and vehicles. Girls receive dolls, fictional characters, and children's furniture. According to one team of researchers, "Parents and other adults encourage sex-type play by selecting different toys for female and male children, even before the child can express her or his own preference" (Pomerleau, Bloduc, Malcuit, & Cossette, 1990, p. 365). Parental expectations and gender stereotypes are revealed by the kinds of toys parents provide for their children (Campenni, 1999).

Some scholars believe that children construct a great deal of their sense of gender through play, primarily in groups and thus under the influence of social relationships (Messner, 2000). Regarding the games children play, boys' games are usually more complex, competitive, and rule-governed than girls' games and allow for a larger number of participants (Ignico & Mead, 1990). Girls' games, such as hopscotch or jump rope, are more structured and are played in small groups with a modicum of competitiveness. While boys' play is generally directed toward power, self-reliance, using talk to hold center stage, vying for status, and asserting themselves, girls' play reveals affiliation, interdependence, interaction, cooperativeness, communication as relationship building, and responsiveness to others (King, Miles, & Kniska, 1991; Maltz & Borker, 1982). In the United States, children hear more negative messages about boys who engage in girl-style play than girls who engage in boy-style play, meaning that it's still better to be a "tomboy" than a "sissy." Overall, girls have more freedom of action beyond the sex-defined boundaries.

Peers and School

As children get older, they are gradually introduced into the world outside the family. Parents' gender expectations at home become extended into the child's social world. Parents initiate the first relationships for their children and for the first few years of life, children prefer to play with children of a similar age, sex unspecified. Often this is related to proximity, meaning that we tend to play with other kids from our neighborhood or building, since they're close by and handy. The sex of the child doesn't matter much until we start school, when our preference for playmates changes quickly. Activities and games in schools tend to be strongly related to gender roles and are powerful agents of socialization (Lindsey & Christy, 1997).

Schools have a major responsibility for ensuring that children are educated in the ways of society, but many accomplish it in a manner that perpetuates gender stereotypes (Lindsey & Christy, 1997). Schools tend to be set up for what are generally seen as masculine values: competitive, independent work involving initiative. While schools may offer cooperative learning activities with shared participation, they still stress individual achievement. How often were you graded as a group in school? Schools' and teachers' differential treatment of the sexes is explored in more depth in Chapter 10.

Instructional researchers Sadker and Sadker (1994) asked children at all grade levels, "What would it be like to become a member of the opposite sex?" Both boys and girls preferred their own sex, but girls found the prospect of becoming boys intriguing and were willing to try it out for a while. Boys, on the other hand, found the prospect of becoming girls intensely disgusting and humiliating. One boy even said, "If I were turned into a girl today I would kill myself." Do schools perpetuate the privileging of one sex over the other? How much

---

Remember . . .

SOCIALIZATION: The process through which individuals learn their culture, develop their potential, and become functioning members of society.

PERSON-CENTERED FAMILIES: Families that place a high value on the individuality of each member.

POSITION-CENTERED FAMILIES: Families that focus on the position or role each person holds in the family.

---

socialization and gender identity development should be appropriately accomplished through schooling? What should happen if family socialization and school socialization come into conflict, as in a situation where gender-neutral toys and games are the norm at home, but sex-specific or sex-segregated play rules the day at school?

Socialization theories stress the importance of peer interactions. Sex segregation and the influence of peer groups increase throughout the school years through play, games, and schooling. Sex boundaries are closely watched and enforced by peers (Maccoby, 1994). It's common to hear boys say, "Only sissies play with girls!" Throughout schooling, the worlds of boys and girls become that much more divided and each sex learns less about the other (Inhoff, Halverson, & Pissigati, 1983). A major consequence is that "boys and girls will meet in adolescence virtually as strangers, having learned different styles of interaction" (Fagot, 1994, p. 62). The lack of cross-sex interaction impoverishes both sexes and results in restricted gender identities.

CONCLUSION

Learning to be a woman or man is both interesting and problematic. This section of the text is about influences on your choices. Biological influences discussed in this chapter affect your view of self. Social influences, as well as your own attitudes about appropriate roles for others to assume in society, shape your view of self. Out of these biological and social influences, you form a psychological response—your gender identity—which is expressed in your communication with others. Developing personal effectiveness in gender communication starts with introspection—with a long, hard look at yourself in terms of your sex and your gender identity. As you learn more about the effects of gender on the communication process, your identity may begin to change. Or you may become more comfortable with your current view of self, so that it solidifies. We challenge you to answer the following questions for yourself, either after reading this chapter or this text, or after taking a course in gender communication: What is your current gender identity? What aspects of your biology most affect this identity? What social influences most shaped your identity? Are you in the process of changing your gender identity? How does your communication (particularly with members of the opposite sex) clue people as to your gender identity? How can you become more personally effective in communicating who you are to others?

Discussion Starters

1. On a sheet of paper, list 10 of the most common adjectives describing women; then list 10 for men. Discuss in class whether these adjectives reflect stereotypes or "real" traits. Have people's stereotypes for the sexes changed? In what ways? What does it mean now, in the twenty-first century, to be feminine? masculine?

2. Think about the reproductive capacities of women. What if someday science and technology were to progress to the point where men could carry a fetus and give birth? It sounds crazy now, but what if they could someday? Would they still be "men"? After all, what is the real definition of a man? A woman?

3. What if more research continued to document the existence of a male cycle and the medical community labeled it TS, for "testosterone syndrome"? Do you think that the existence of a male hormonal cycle is possible? Specifically, how would a male cycle affect perceptions of women and men in society? How would it affect gender communication?

4. Consider the various theories of gender identity development that were discussed in this chapter. What are the main strengths of social learning theory, cognitive development theory, gender schema theory, Gilligan's theory, and gender transcendence theory? Their main weaknesses?

5. Of the various agents of socialization discussed in this chapter—family, clothes, toys, peers, and school—what do you think has had the greatest impact on your gender identity? If, for example, the greatest influence on you was your family, do you adhere to stereotypical masculine or feminine traits learned in your family, or has your identity transcended gender?

References

Andersen, P. A. (1998). Researching sex differences within sex similarities: The evolutionary consequences of reproductive differences. In D. J. Canary & K. Dindia (Eds.), *Sex differences and similarities in communication* (pp. 83–100). Mahwah, NJ: Erlbaum.

Bacorn, C. N. (1992, December 7). Dear dads: Save your sons. *Newsweek,* 13.

Baenninger, M. A., & Newcombe, N. (1995). Environmental input to the development of sex-related differences in spatial and mathematical ability. *Learning and individual differences,* 7. [Excerpt derived from Paul, E. L. (2002). *Taking sides: Clashing views on controversial issues in sex and gender* (2nd ed.) (pp. 97–107). New York: McGraw-Hill/Dushkin.]

Bailey, C., & Bishop, L. (2001). *The complete fit-or-fat book.* New York: Galahad.

Bandura, A. (1971). Social-learning theory of identificatory processes. In D. A. Goslin (Ed.), *Handbook of socialization theory and research.* Chicago: Rand McNally.

Bandura, A. (1986). *Social foundations of thought and action: A social cognitive theory.* Englewood Cliffs, NJ: Prentice-Hall.

Barrett, H. (1998). *Maintaining the self in communication.* Incline Village, NV: Alpha & Omega.

Barry, E. (2002, July 14). Testosterone rises and falls with a man's familial relationships. *Boston Globe,* as reported in *Corpus Christi Caller Times,* p. A23.

Basow, S. (1992). *Gender: Stereotypes and roles* (3rd ed.). Pacific Grove, CA: Brooks/Cole.

Bate, B., & Bowker, J. (1997). *Communication and the sexes* (2nd ed.). Prospect Heights, IL: Waveland.

Beal, C. R. (1994). *Boys and girls: The development of gender roles.* New York: McGraw-Hill.

Beebe, S. A., & Masterson, J. T. (1986). *Family talk: Interpersonal communication in the family.* New York: Random House.

Bellinger, D. C., & Gleason, J. B. (1982). Sex differences in parental directives to young children. *Sex Roles, 8,* 1123–1139.

Bem, S. L. (1983). Gender schema theory and its implications for child development: Raising gender-aschematic children in a gender-schematic society. *Signs, 8,* 598–616.

Bem, S. L. (1987). Masculinity and femininity exist only in the mind of the perceiver. In J. M. Reinisch, L. A. Rosenblum, & S. A. Sanders, (Eds.), *Masculinity/femininity: Basic perspectives* (pp. 304–311). New York: Oxford University Press.

Bem, S. L. (1993). *The lenses of gender: Transforming the debate on sexual inequality.* New Haven, CT: Yale University Press.

Bem, S. L. (1998). *An unconventional family.* New Haven, CT: Yale University Press. [Excerpt derived from Paul, E. L. (2002). *Taking sides: Clashing views on controversial issues in sex and gender* (2nd ed.) (pp. 308–315). New York: McGraw-Hill/Dushkin.]

Benbow, C. P., & Stanley, J. C. (1980). Sex differences in mathematical ability: Fact or artifact? *Science, 210,* 1262–1264.

Berkowitz, S. J., Gerali, S., & Skillin, K. (1999, October). *Mind games: An exploratory study of games, gender, and socialization.* Paper presented at the meeting of the Organization for the Study of Communication, Language, and Gender, Wichita, KS.

Bermant, G., & Davidson, J. M. (1974). *Biological bases of sexual behavior.* New York: Harper & Row.

Bernstein, E. (1996, January 21). At-home dads: Increasingly, men are giving up careers to take care of children. *Corpus Christi Caller Times,* pp. G1, G3.

Bing, J. (1999). Brain sex: How the media report and distort brain research. *Women & Language, 22,* 4–12.

Bleier, R. (1984). *Science and gender: A critique of biology and its theories on women.* New York: Pergamon.

Borisoff, D., & Merrill, L. (1998). *The power to communicate: Gender differences as barriers* (3rd ed.). Prospect Heights, IL: Waveland.

Bowden, M. (1995, January 27). Science offers proof: Men and women do not think alike. *Corpus Christi Caller Times,* p. A4.

Bronstein, P. (1988). Father-child interaction: Implications for gender role socialization. In P. Bronstein & C. P. Cowan (Eds.), *Fatherhood today: Men's changing role in the family* (pp. 107–126). New York: John Wiley.

Buerkel-Rothfuss, N. L., Covert, A. M., Keith, J., & Nelson, C. (1986). *Early adolescent and parental communication patterns.* Paper presented at the meeting of the Speech Communication Association, Chicago, IL.

Cahow, K. L. (1997, Fall). Survival tactics. *Spohn Quarterly,* 12–16.

Caldera, Y. M., & Sciaraffa, M. A. (1998). Parent-toddler play with feminine toys: Are all dolls the same? *Sex Roles, 39,* 657–668.

Campenni, C. E. (1999). Gender stereotyping of children's toys: A comparison of parents and nonparents. *Sex Roles, 40,* 121–138.

Canary, D. J., & Emmers-Sommer, T. M. (1997). *Sex and gender differences in personal relationships.* New York: Guilford.

Cancian, F. (1989). Love and the rise of capitalism. In B. Risman & P. Schwartz (Eds.), *Gender in intimate relationships* (pp. 12–25). Belmont, CA: Wadsworth.

Carmondy, D. L. (1989). *Women and world religions.* Englewood Cliffs, NJ: Prentice-Hall.

Cavanaugh, D. (1997). Personal communication, November.

Condit, C. (1996). How bad science stays that way: Brain sex, demarcation, and the status of truth in the rhetoric of science. *Rhetoric Society Quarterly, 26,* 83–109.

Cooper, M. (2000). Being the "go-to guy": Fatherhood, masculinity, and the organization of work in Silicon Valley. *Qualitative Sociology, 23,* 379–405.

Crawford, M., & Unger, R. (2000). *Women and gender: A feminist psychology* (3rd ed.). New York: McGraw-Hill.

Cummins, H. J. (2000, June 18). Carving their niche as at-home fathers puts pressure on men. *Minneapolis-St. Paul Star Tribune,* as reported in *Corpus Christi Caller Times,* pp. H1, H3.

Deaux, K., & Lafrance, M. (1998). Gender. In D. T. Gilbert, S. T. Fiske, & G. Lindzey (Eds.), *The handbook of social psychology,* Vol. 1 (4th ed.) (pp. 788–828). New York: McGraw-Hill.

Devor, H. (1989). *Gender blending: Confronting the limits of duality.* Bloomington: Indiana University Press.

Devor, H. (1992). Becoming members of society: Learning the social meanings of gender. In M. Schaum & C. Flanagan (Eds.), *Gender images: Readings for composition* (pp. 23–33). Boston: Houghton Mifflin.

Diamond, J. (1997, February 2). Military closing fitness gender gap. *Corpus Christi Caller Times,* p. A17.

Dobosz, A. M. (1997, November-December). Thicker thighs by Thanksgiving. *Media,* 89–91.

Dolnick, E. (1991, July-August). Super women. *Health,* 42–48.

DuCille, A. (1994). Dyes and dolls: Multicultural Barbie and the merchandising of difference. *Differences: A Journal of Cultural Studies, 6,* 46–68.

Eccles, J. S. (1987). Adolescence: Gateway to gender-role transcendence. In D. B. Carter (Ed.), *Current conceptions of sex roles and sex typing* (pp. 225–241). New York: Praeger.

Eccles, J. S. (1989). Bringing young women to math and science. In M. Crawford & M. Gentry (Eds.), *Gender and thought: Psychological perspectives* (pp. 36–58). New York: Springer.

Eggebeen, D. J., & Knoester, C. (2001). Does fatherhood matter for men? *Journal of Marriage and Family, 63,* 381–393.

Ehrenreich, B. (1992, January 20). Making sense of la difference. *Time,* 51.

Ehrhardt, A. A. (1984). Gender differences: A biosocial perspective. In T. B. Sonderegger (Ed.), *Psychology and gender* (pp. 37–57). Lincoln: University of Nebraska Press.

Ehrhardt, A. A., & Meyer-Behlburg, H. (1980). Prenatal sex hormones and the developing brain: Effects on psycho-sexual differentiation and cognitive functions. *Annual Progress in Child Psychology and Child Development,* 177–191.

Eisenberg, A. R. (1996). The conflict talk of mothers and children: Patterns related to culture, SES, and gender of child. *Merrill Palmer Quarterly, 42,* 438–458.

Erwin, P. (1992). *Friendship and peer relations in children.* Chichester, UK: John Wiley.

Fagot, B. (1994). Peer relations and the development of competence in boys and girls. In C. Leaper (Ed.), *Childhood gender segregation: Causes and consequences* (pp. 53–66). San Francisco: Josey-Bass.

Fagot, B., & Leinbach, M. D. (1995). Gender knowledge in egalitarian and traditional families. *Sex Roles, 32,* 523–526.

Fagot, B. L., Rodgers, C. S., & Leinbach, M. D. (2000). Theories of gender socialization. In T. Eckes & H. Trautner (Eds.), *The developmental social psychology of gender* (pp. 65–89). Mahwah, NJ: Erlbaum.

Fausto-Sterling, A. (1992). *Myths of gender: Biological theories about women and men* (2nd ed.). New York: Basic Books.

Fischman, J. (2001, July 30). Do men experience menopause? *U.S. News & World Report, 47.*

Fried, C. (1997, Fall). One on one. *Sports Illustrated's Women Sport,* 70–73.

Gerstel, N., & Gallagher, S. K. (2001). Men's caregiving: Gender and the contingent character of care. *Gender & Society, 15,* 197–217.

Gibbons, A. (1991). The brain as "sexual organ." *Science, 253,* 957–959.

Gilligan, C. (1982). *In a different voice: Psychological theory and women's development.* Cambridge, MA: Harvard University Press.

Greenblatt, L., Hasenauer, J. E., & Friemuth, V. S. (1980). Psychological sex type and androgyny in the study of communication variables: Self-disclosure and communication apprehension. *Human Communication Research, 6,* 117–129.

Greene, S. (1997). Psychology and the re-evaluation of the feminine. *Irish Journal of Psychology, 18,* 367–385.

Gur, R. C., Gur, R. E., Obrist, W. D., Hungerbuhler, J. P., Younkin, D., Rosen, A. D., Skolnick, B. E., & Reivich, M. (1982). Sex and handedness differences in cerebral blood flow during rest and cognitive activity. *Science, 217,* 659–661.

Gur, R. C., Mozley, L. H., Mozley, P. D., Resnick, S. M., Karp, J. S., Alavi, A., Arnold, S. E., & Gur, R. E. (1995). Sex differences in regional cerebral glucose metabolism during a resting state. *Science, 267,* 528–531.

Hain, P. (1997). Personal communication, October.

Hall, E. (1987, November). All in the family. *Psychology Today,* 54–60.

Halpern, D. (2000). *Sex differences in cognitive abilities* (3rd ed.). Mahwah, NJ: Erlbaum.

Hamilton, H. E. (1997, November). *Women's bodies, women's voices: Images of technology in the combat exclusion debate.* Paper presented at the meeting of the National Communication Association, Chicago, IL.

Hardesty, C., Wenk, D., & Morgan, C. S. (1995). Paternal involvement and the development of gender expectations in sons and daughters. *Youth and Society, 267,* 283–297.

Hoffer, R. (1997, Fall). Pow! *Sports Illustrated's Women Sport,* 74–81.

Holden, C. (1991). Is the "gender gap" narrowing? *Science, 253,* 959–960.

hooks, b. (2000). *Feminism is for everybody: Passionate politics.* Cambridge, MA: South End Press.

House, A., Dallinger, J. M., & Kilgallen, D. L. (1998). Androgyny and rhetorical sensitivity: The connection of gender and communicator style. *Communication Reports, 11,* 11–20.

Howard, J. (1997, Fall). So good, so fast: How did the U.S. women shoot past the rest of the world in soccer? *Sports Illlustrated's Women Sport,* 68–69.

Hughes, F. P. (1994). *Children, play, and development.* Boston: Allyn & Bacon.

Hyde, J. S., & Linn, M. C. (1988). Gender differences in verbal ability: A meta-analysis. *Psychological Bulletin, 104,* 53–69.

Ignico, A. A., & Mead, B. J. (1990). Children's perceptions of the gender-appropriateness of physical activities. *Perceptual and Motor Skills, 71,* 1275–1281.

Inhoff, G. E., Halverson, C. F., Jr., & Pissigati, K. A. L. (1983). The influence of sex-role stereotypes on children's self- and peer-attributions. *Sex Roles, 9,* 1205–1222.

Jacklin, C. N. (1989). Female and male: Issues of gender. *The American Psychologist, 44,* 127–134.

Jackson, L. A., Fleury, R. E., & Lewandowski, D. A. (1996). Feminism: Definitions, support, and correlates of support among female and male college students. *Sex Roles, 34,* 687–693.

Jacobs, A. J., & Shaw, J. (2000). Legend of the doll. *Entertainment Weekly,* 16.

Joyce, C. (1999, May 14–16). Special delivery: Science is perfecting a way to select the sex of your next child. *USA Weekend,* 6–7.

Kelly, J. A., O'Brien, G. G., & Hosford, R. (1981). Sex roles and social skills in considerations for interpersonal adjustment. *Psychology of Women Quarterly, 5,* 758–766.

Kenrick, D. T., Neuberg, S. L., & Cialdini, R. B. (2002). *Social psychology: Unraveling the mystery* (2nd ed.). Boston: Allyn & Bacon.

Kimmel, M. (1999, October/November). What are little boys made of? *Ms.,* 88–91.

Kimura, D. (1987). Are men's and women's brains really different? *Canadian Psychology, 28,* 133–147.

Kimura, D. (2000). *Sex and cognition.* Boston: MIT Press. [Excerpt derived from Paul, E. L. (2002). *Taking sides: Clashing views on controversial issues in sex and gender* (2nd ed.) (pp. 94–96). New York: McGraw-Hill/Dushkin.]

King, W. C., Jr., Miles, E. W., & Kniska, J. (1991). Boys will be boys (and girls will be girls): The attribution of gender role stereotypes in a gaming situation. *Sex Roles, 25,* 607–623.

Kleiman, C. (1992, January 23). Males and their raging hormones. *Raleigh News and Observer,* pp. 1E, 2E.

Kluger, B. (2000, May 7). Kids can learn about Washington at Politicians R Us. *New York Times* News Service, as reported in *Corpus Christi Caller Times,* pp. A24, A25.

Kohlberg, L. (1966). A cognitive-developmental analysis of children's sex-role concepts and attitudes. In E. E. Maccoby (Ed.), *The development of sex differences* (pp. 82–173). Stanford, CA: Stanford University Press.

Lasswell, M. (1996, February 7–13). Women's hockey comes into its own, as Team USA makes its move to win one of the sport's first Olympic medals. *TV Guide,* 18–22.

Lavine, L. O., & Lombardo, J. P. (1984). Self-disclosure: Intimate and nonintimate disclosures to parents and best friends as a function of Bem sex-role category. *Sex Roles, 11,* 735–744.

Leaper, C. (1994). Exploring the consequences of gender segregation on social relationships. In C. Leaper (Ed.), *Childhood gender segregation: Causes and consequences* (pp. 76–86). San Francisco: Josey-Bass.

Leaper, C., Anderson, K., & Sanders, P. (1998). Moderators of gender effects on parents' talk to their children: A meta-analysis. *Developmental Psychology, 34,* 3–27.

Libby, L. (2000, December 31). Hubby homemakers: It's a guy thing: At-home dads play by their own rules. *Corpus Christi Caller Times,* pp. H1, H3.

Lindsey, E. W., & Mize, J. (2001). Contextual differences in parent-child play: Implications for children's gender role development. *Sex Roles, 44,* 155–176.

Lindsey, L. L., & Christy, S. (1997). *Gender roles: A sociological perspective* (3rd ed.). Upper Saddle River, NJ: Prentice-Hall.

Linn, M. C., & Petersen, A. C. (1986). A meta-analysis of gender differences in spatial ability: Implications for mathematics and science achievement. In J. S. Hyde & M. C. Linn (Eds.), *The psychology of gender: Advances through meta-analysis* (pp. 67–101). Baltimore: Johns Hopkins University Press.

Lippa, R. A. (2002). *Gender, nature, and nurture.* Mahwah, NJ: Erlbaum.

Lloyd, C. (1994). Investing in the next generation: The implications of high fertility at the level of the family. In R. Casses (Ed.), *Population and development: Old debates, new conclusions.* Washington, DC: Overseas Development Council.

Lueptow, L. B., Garovich, L., & Lueptow, M. B. (1995). The persistence of gender stereotypes in the face of changing sex roles: Evidence contrary to the sociocultural model. *Ethology & Sociobiology, 16,* 509–530.

Maccoby, E. E. (1994). Commentary: Gender segregation in childhood. In C. Leaper (Ed.), *Childhood gender segregation: Causes and consequences* (pp. 87–97). San Francisco: Josey-Bass.

Maccoby, E. E., & Jacklin, C. (1974). *The psychology of sex differences*. Stanford, CA: Stanford University Press.

Maccoby, E. E., & Jacklin, C. (1980). Sex differences in aggression: A rejoinder and reprise. *Child Development, 5*, 964–980.

Maltz, D. N., & Borker, R. (1982). A cultural approach to male-female miscommunication. In J. J. Gumpertz (Ed.), *Language and social identity* (pp. 196–216). Cambridge, England: Cambridge University Press.

Marin, R. (2000, January 2). More stay-at-home fathers now come out of the kitchen. *New York Times* News Service, as reported in *Corpus Christi Caller Times*, p. A18.

McLoughlin, M., Shryer, T. L., Goode, E. E., & McAuliffe, K. (1988, August 8). Men vs. women. *U.S. News & World Report*, 50–56.

Messner, M. A. (2000). Barbie girls versus sea monsters: Children constructing gender. *Gender & Society, 14*, 765–784.

Mischel, W. (1966). A social learning view of sex differences in behavior. In E. E. Maccoby (Ed.), *The development of sex differences* (pp. 56–81). Stanford, CA: Stanford University Press.

Moen, E. (1991). Sex selective eugenic abortion: Prospects in China and India. *Issues in Reproductive and Genetic Engineering, 4*, 231–249.

Monedas, M. (1992). Men communicating with women: Self-esteem and power. In L. A. M. Perry, L. H. Turner, & H. M. Sterk (Eds.), *Constructing and reconstructing gender: The links among communication, language, and gender* (pp. 197–208). Albany: State University of New York Press.

Morgan, R. (1993, November/December). Raising sons: We know our dreams for our daughters; what about our sons? *Ms.*, 36–41.

Mulrine, A. (2001, July 30). Are boys the weaker sex? *U.S. News & World Report*, 41–47.

Park, C. B., & Cho, N. (1995). Consequences of son preference in a low-fertility society: Imbalance of the sex ratio at birth in Korea. *Population and Development Review, 21*, 59–84.

Parsons, T., & Bales, R. (1955). *Family, socialization, and interaction process*. New York: Free Press.

Paul, E. L. (Ed.). (2002). *Taking sides: Clashing views on controversial issues in sex and gender* (2nd ed.). New York: McGraw-Hill/Dushkin.

Peach, L. J. (1998). Women in culture: Introduction. In L. J. Peach (Ed.), *Women in culture: A women's studies anthology* (pp. 1–12). Malden, MA: Blackwell.

Pennell, G. E., & Ogilvie, D. M. (1995). You and me as she and he: The meaning of gender-related concepts in other- and self-perception. *Sex Roles, 33*, 29–57.

Phillips, J. (1997, July-August). A new season for women's sports. *Ms.*, 86–88.

Pleck, J. H. (1975). Masculinity-femininity: Current and alternative paradigms. *Sex Roles, 1*, 161–178.

Pleck, J. H. (1977). The psychology of sex roles: Traditional and new views. In L. A. Cater, A. F. Scott, & W. Martyna (Eds.), *Women and men: Changing roles, relationships, and perceptions* (pp. 181–199). New York: Praeger.

Pleck, J. H. (1981). *The myth of masculinity*. Cambridge, MA: MIT Press.

Pollack, W. (1998). *Real boys: Rescuing our sons from the myths of boyhood*. New York: Owl Books.

Pomerleau, A., Bloduc, D., Malcuit, G., & Cossette, L. (1990). Pink or blue: Gender stereotypes in the first two years of life. *Sex Roles, 22*, 359–376.

Pooler, W. S. (1991). Sex of child preferences among college students. *Sex Roles, 25*, 569–576.

Ramey, E. (1976). Men's cycles (They have them too you know). In A. Kaplan & J. Bean (Eds.), *Beyond sex-role stereotypes*. Boston: Little Brown.

Rand, E. (1998). Older heads on younger bodies. In H. Jenkins (Ed.), *The children's culture reader* (pp. 382–393). New York: New York University Press.

Richmond-Abbott, M. (1992). *Masculine and feminine: Gender roles over the life cycle* (2nd ed.). New York: McGraw-Hill.

Riesman, C. (1990). *Divorce talk: Women and men make sense of personal relationships.* New Brunswick, NJ: Princeton University Press.

Ross, H., & Taylor, H. (1989). Do boys prefer daddy or his physical style of play? *Sex Roles, 20,* 23–31.

Rubin, J. Z., Provensano, F., & Luria, Z. (1974). The eye of the beholder: Parents' views on sex of newborns. *American Journal of Orthopsychiatry, 44,* 312–319.

Ruble, D. N., Balaban, T., & Cooper, J. (1981). Gender constancy and the effects of sex-typed televised toy commercials. *Child Development, 52,* 667–673.

Sadker, M., & Sadker, D. (1994). *Failing at fairness: How America's schools cheat girls.* New York: Scribner's.

Sagi, A., & Sharon, N. (1984). The role of the father in the family: Toward a gender-neutral family policy. *Children & Youth Services Review, 6,* 83–99.

Salter, S. (1997, November 3). Women refs will blaze a difficult trail. *Corpus Christi Caller Times,* p. A15.

Satir, V. (1972). *Peoplemaking.* Palo Alto, CA: Science and Behavior Books.

Satir, V. (1988). *The new peoplemaking.* Mountain View, CA: Science and Behavior Books.

Schafer, S. M. (1998, March 1). Recruits, sergeants differ on coed training. *Corpus Christi Caller Times,* pp. A17, A18.

Segell, M. (1996, October). The second coming of the alpha male. *Esquire,* 12–17.

Shakin, M., Shakin D., & Sternglanz, S. H. (1985). Infant clothing: Sex labeling for strangers. *Sex Roles, 12,* 955–964.

Shapiro, L. (1990, May 28). Guns and dolls. *Newsweek,* 56–65.

Shore, R. B. (2001). Matellin' them off. *Bitch, 13,* 17.

Snow, M. E., Jacklin, C. N., & Maccoby, E. E. (1983). Sex-of-child differences in father-child interactions at one year of age. *Child Development, 54,* 227–232.

Snowbeck, C. (2001, September 9). The many moods of testosterone. *Pittsburgh Post-Gazette,* as reported in *Corpus Christi Caller Times,* p. C7.

Starr, M., & Rosenberg, D. (1997, March 24). She's breaking the ice. *Newsweek,* 67.

Steinberg, L. (1995, June 18). Mr. Moms find same rewards, pressures as women. *Corpus Christi Caller Times,* pp. G1, G3.

Stern, M., & Karraker, K. H. (1989). Sex stereotyping in infants: A review of gender labeling studies. *Sex Roles, 20,* 501–522.

Stockard, J., & Johnson, M. (1980). *Sex roles.* Englewood Cliffs, NJ: Prentice-Hall.

Tavris, C. (1992). *The mismeasure of woman.* New York: Simon & Schuster.

Thompson, C. (1992). A new vision of masculinity. In M. Schaum & C. Flanagan (Eds.), *Gender images: Readings for composition* (pp. 77–83). Boston: Houghton Mifflin.

Thornton, J. (1992, March). His brain is different. *Self,* 114–116, 164, 166.

Walsh, B. (2002, June 16). Becoming emotional providers: More men are realizing the importance of being involved in their children's lives. *Corpus Christi Caller Times,* pp. H1, H4.

White, D. (1998, July 12). Stay-at-home dad shares sacrifices, rewards of new role. *Corpus Christi Caller Times,* pp. H1, H3.

Wood, J. T. (1994). Engendered identities: Shaping voice and mind through gender. In D. R. Vocate (Ed.), *Intrapersonal communication: Different voices, different minds* (pp. 145–168). Hillsdale, NJ: Erlbaum.

Wood, J. T., & Lenze, L. F. (1991). Gender and the development of self: Inclusive pedagogy in interpersonal communication. *Women's Studies in Communication, 14,* 1–23.

CHAPTER THREE

PICTURES, PORNO, AND POP:
Gender and Mass Media

CASE STUDY: A DAY IN THE LIFE

It's 6:30 A.M., the clock radio alarm goes off, and a couple of people on a morning talk-radio show are chatting away. Rey shuts off the alarm, rolls out of bed, and begins his morning routine. Over his usual bowl of cereal, he scans the local newspaper and *The Wall Street Journal,* reading stock indexes with interest and making a mental note to check the stock exchange on the Internet later in the day. While shaving, he turns on the Weather Channel for a quick check of the local forecast, then switches to a 24-hour cable news source for the latest headlines. Then Rey reviews his schedule for the day on his palm pilot. Before he leaves the house, he checks his combo VCR/DVD player and satellite dish setup to make sure it will correctly record the network nightly news (which he tapes every weekday because he doesn't leave work in time to see the broadcast), as well as a few of his favorite television programs. If something comes up at work, he might not get home to catch these shows, so it's better to tape them than miss them.

On the drive to work, Rey tunes in his car radio and checks back with the talk-radio program. An air personality says, "Well, scandals are nothing new in politics. . . ." Rey decides he's heard enough and is more in the mood to listen to a CD. About halfway between his home and the office, Rey puts the CD on pause and uses his cell phone to call ahead to the office and check in with his secretary so he can anticipate what will be happening when he gets there. She says it's pretty quiet, but that a few faxes did come in overnight; they're on his desk for him to read when he gets there. He cues up the CD again and notices he's reached that point in the drive where he passes a bank's digital billboard calculating increases in the national debt.

Rey arrives at the office; his secretary is on the phone, so he swings by the central mailboxes and picks up his mail, including more messages and a couple of magazines he subscribes to. When he gets to his desk, the light on his phone is blinking, indicating that he has voice mail messages. He takes off his coat, lays the mail on top of the faxes on his desk, and thumbs through the first couple of ads in one of his magazines. Then he picks up the phone and dials in his code to start listening to voice mail messages while, at the same time, punching the start-up key on his computer. The computer screen fires up and a mail icon with the statement, "You've got mail," appears. Once he's gone through the 10 or so voice mail messages and noted on his digital pocket recorder who to call back, he begins to read the interoffice e-mail. Later he'll log onto the Internet to read his other e-mail—postings to an electronic bulletin board he subscribes to as well as messages from colleagues across the country, the occasional family member, and a buddy who's now working in Australia. He hopes that just before lunch he'll remember to use his Web browser to check the latest stock trends. He'd love to knock off early today to catch the newest action film, but no doubt something would come up and his secretary would page him. There's nothing so irritating as somebody's beeper going off in a movie theatre. Too much going on, too many things and people to deal with, too little time.

HEY—wasn't technology supposed to SAVE us time? Do you think Rey, who is bombarded by media and surrounded by technological innovations, feels that they keep him informed and save him time or that they impinge on his time? Is Rey running the media or are the media running him? By the way, you proba-bly think that Rey is some hotshot financial guy or corporate honcho—he's actually a high school principal, and this is an average day.

How much media and technology do you consume each day? What influ-ence do media and technology have on you? What messages about the sexes are communicated via the media you consume? That's the topic of this chapter.

Hot Topics

- Theories of media effects on consumers
- The impact of stereotypical depictions of women and men in advertisements on attitudes about the sexes
- Gendered messages in prime-time television programming
- Communication about the sexes from daytime soap operas and talk shows
- Gender bending in film and how men's and women's film roles affect viewers
- The pervasive influence of pornography and the effects of its consumption on women's and men's attitudes and relationships
- Portrayals of the sexes in song lyrics and music video

THE POWER OF MEDIATED COMMUNICATION: EFFECTS ON OUR LIVES

Perhaps no other force influences our daily lives more than media. Parents are hugely important, teachers have significant impact, friends affect us in profound ways but, over time, media may have the strongest effect of all. Consider how often you compare real life—work, family, relationships—to how these things are depicted in various media. It's common to hear someone refer to something on television, such as, "I don't trust that guy I went out with last night; he reminds me of that guy in the Dell computer commercials," "My wife and I have arguments kind of like that couple on (name a sitcom—*any* sitcom)" or "I felt as if I'd stepped into a sad country-and-western tune." Media are highly influential in how they communicate messages about women and men.

A Bombardment of Media

How much media did Rey, in our opening case study, experience in an average morning? Your modern existence is jammed full of mass communication every sunrise to sunset, but just how are you affected by it? You are bombarded with forms of mass communication every day and the effects of this bombardment are dramatic, as research documents (Calloway-Thomas, Cooper, & Blake, 1999; Lindlof, 1991; Press, 1991a).

As a college-educated person, you are probably an above-average critical consumer of mass communication—that is, you consciously select mediated messages to take in or to filter out. However, a great deal of mediated information is absorbed unconsciously, even by the most critical consumers. Few of us have time in our busy lives to focus attention on all the mediated messages we receive in a typical day and make conscious decisions about their effects. This critical thinking process becomes a skill we use less often as we take in more and more mediated information. Just how this absorption affects us has been the subject of a good deal of attention among media researchers.

Approaches to Studying the Effects of Media Consumption

In the 1970s, media scholar Gaye Tuchman (1979) described an explosion of media research, as mass media grew exponentially during the years between World War II and the beginning of the 1980s. Several research approaches and theories have emerged that attempt to explain how media affect consumers.

Hypodermic Needle or Direct-Effects Theory

This early theory viewed the mass audience as consuming mediated messages passively and directly. The image was a hypodermic needle that injected mass communication directly into the veins of noncritical consumers (Campbell, Martin, & Fabos, 2003). This theory offered an inadequate, overly simplistic explanation of media effects because it ignored how other factors might influence the process.

Minimal-Effects Model

With increasing sophistication in social scientific techniques came dissatisfaction with direct-effects theory. Media theorists began to argue that consumers were only minimally affected by mediated messages, and that they selectively exposed themselves to media messages and selectively retained those messages that reinforced or were consistent with their own behaviors, attitudes, and values. This theory suggested that consumers were less at the power of persuasive media than had previously been thought (Campbell et al., 2003).

Uses and Gratifications Theory

Media expert John Vivian (2003) describes the uses and gratifications approach as a theory that no longer viewed mass audiences as passive sponges but active users of media. The theory describes how consumers are motivated to use various media and what gains, rewards, or gratifications they receive from such consumption. Media researchers have applied uses and gratifications theory to better understand such things as the uses people make of television news or commercial advertising (Rayburn, Palmgreen, & Acker, 1984), the pleasure people derive from soap operas (Hayward, 1997), and the effects of listening to children's music (Christenson, 1994).

Agenda-Setting Research

The seeds of agenda-setting research date back to the 1920s and the early work of Walter Lippmann, who suggested that media "create pictures in our heads" (as in Campbell et al., 2003, p. 523). A contemporary of Lippmann's, Robert Park, proposed that the media do not merely report, reflect, or dramatize what is important in society but actually guide what we think is important (Vivian, 2003). The media generate awareness of issues; thus, media may not dictate attitudes or stances on issues, but they have the power to affect what we think about. In essence, viewers may allow a media outlet to set an agenda for what should be most important to them (Heaton & Wilson, 1995).

Cultivation Theory

Cultivation theory suggests that media consumption " 'cultivates' in us a distorted perception of the world we live in, making it seem more like television portrays it, than it is in real life" (Bittner, 1989, p. 386). The media blur reality and fantasy, what life is really like and how it is represented on television and in movies, magazine ads, romance novels, etc. Media scholar George Gerbner and various colleagues are among the most prominent researchers who have developed cultivation theory to better understand how the social reality of violence and crime is related to the media's depiction of it (Gerbner, 2003; Gerbner, Gross, Eleey, Jackson-Beeck, Jeffries-Fox, & Signorielli, 1977; Gerbner, Gross, Morgan, & Signorielli, 1980; Signorielli & Morgan, 1990). Gerbner, who began his investigations of televised violence in the late 1960s, contends that a typical American child will see 32,000 on-screen murders before she or he turns 18 (as in Vivian, 2003). Cultivation theory suggests, for example, that some children who see violent mediated images will expect that they can repeat those acts of violence in their lives, without consequences or harm to others. One need only check recent newspaper headlines to see evidence of this theory in action, as children have harmed and, in some instances, killed other children by replicating wrestling moves or other violent acts, believing that the victim will spring back up or be unharmed by their actions (Levin & Carlsson-Paige, 2003; Potter, 2003).

Cultural Studies Approaches

Just as minimal-effects research approaches developed in reaction to earlier techniques, cultural studies approaches to understanding media effects developed out of a reaction to what was perceived as too much data-gathering,

---

Remember. . .

HYPODERMIC NEEDLE/DIRECT-EFFECTS THEORY: An early theory of media effects which proposed that the mass audience passively and directly consumed mediated messages.

MINIMAL-EFFECTS THEORY: The suggestion that consumers are only minimally affected by mediated messages; consumers selectively expose themselves to media messages and selectively retain those that reinforce or are consistent with their own behaviors, attitudes, and values.

USES AND GRATIFICATIONS THEORY: A theory that describes how consumers are motivated to use various media and what gains, rewards, or gratifications they receive from such consumption.

AGENDA-SETTING THEORY: The proposition that viewers allow media outlets to set an agenda for what should be most important to them.

CULTIVATION THEORY: A theory that the media cultivate distortions in consumers and blur the line between reality and fantasy.

CULTURAL STUDIES APPROACHES: Interpretive and intuitive approaches to studying media effects; researchers explore how media and culture reflect patterns in daily life.

---

number-crunching, and trend-charting in social scientific research. Cultural studies approaches are more interpretive and intuitive; researchers "try to understand how media and culture are tied to the actual patterns of communication in daily life" (Campbell et al., 2003, pp. 525–526). Everyday cultural symbols, as found in print and visual media, are analyzed for their power to make meaning, to create and communicate reality, and to help people understand their daily existence. Researchers are particularly interested in issues of race, gender, class, and sexuality, and the inequities involved. As an example of this approach to media effects research, gender scholars Garner, Sterk, and Adams (1998) examined the advice about sexual etiquette given in teenage women's magazines over a twenty-year span. They concluded that even though society had changed a great deal in terms of sexuality and roles for women, little had changed in these magazines' messages about sexual etiquette. Young women were encouraged to be subordinate to men and to avoid being sexually aggressive. Cultural studies research taps the often subtle effects that media can have in shaping a culture.

ADVERTISING: SELLING A PRODUCT OR SELLING SEXISM?

Advertising is a huge and pervasive industry. You may have thought of advertisements merely as interruptions in your favorite television programs or radio broadcasts or as filler in magazines, but advertisers are getting craftier and more desperate to get their products and services into your view. Ads come through unprompted on your fax machine, play in your ear when you're on hold on the telephone, precede movies you see in theatres, introduce the videos and DVDs you rent or purchase, and appear as product placements in TV programs and films, as when a character is depicted typing on a particular brand of computer or drinking a name-brand beer (Twitchell, 2000). Ads are digitized to appear behind the batter's box or in the middle of a football field, and the images and products change as you watch the televised sporting event. If you're attending a major sporting event, you'll see ads on the blimp flying overhead. Ads clutter Websites, line the walls of buses and subways, and provide often unwanted "color" on your road trip, in the form of billboards. In the decade between 1991 and 2001, the amount of ad space in a one-hour prime-time television program had risen by three minutes; this means that almost a *third* (approximately 16 minutes, 8 seconds) of the time you were watching your favorite TV program, you were actually watching ads (Campbell et al., 2003). Estimates indicate that you are exposed to more than 3,000 ads *each day*—each wanting to persuade you and separate you from your money (Simon, 2000/2001).

Advertising has a powerful effect that goes well beyond the purpose of selling products to consumers; it affects our culture and our views (Cortese, 1999). A great deal of research has been conducted on the ways women and men are depicted in print and electronic advertisements, as well as the messages these ads communicate to media consumers. A good deal of these depictions evoke stereotypes. Media researchers Wells, Burnett, and Moriarty (1998) explain that *stereotyping* "involves presenting a group of people in an unvarying pattern that lacks individuality and often reflects popular misconceptions" (p. 49). Let's look at some of the various stereotypical portrayals of the sexes in ads, including a few exceptions, and then consider the overall effects on consumers.

Babes in Bras: Female Depiction in Advertising

Programmatic research spanning two decades by marketing professors Alice Courtney and Thomas Whipple (1974, 1980, 1983, 1985) forms the basis for the claim that advertising has a major impact on individuals' views of gender. From the compiled results of numerous studies, Courtney and Whipple produced a comprehensive list of female *gender stereotypes* in advertising. Subsequent national and international research has expanded the list, which we provide below (Artz, Munger, & Purdy, 1999; Browne, 1998; Hall, Iijima, & Crum, 1994; Lin, 1997; Liu, Inoue, Bresnahan, & Nishida, 1998; Mwangi, 1996; Simonton, 1995):

1. Fewer depictions of women, in general, than men
2. Women in isolation, particularly from other women
3. Women in sleepwear, underwear, and lingerie more than in professional clothing
4. Young girls portrayed as passive and in need of help
5. Women as representatives for kitchen and bathroom products
6. Women appearing more than men in ads for personal hygiene products
7. An abundance of women serving men and boys
8. Medical ads depicting male physicians interacting with hysterical female hypochondriacs

9. Women more often depicted in family- and home-oriented roles than in business roles
10. Young housewives shown performing household duties, whereas older men act as product representatives who give advice to housewives
11. Women portrayed as decorative, nonfunctioning entities
12. Women depicted as being obsessed with physical attractiveness
13. Fewer depictions of older women than older men
14. Fewer depictions of minority women than minority men
15. Fewer women than men advertising expensive luxury products
16. Few women depicted actively engaged in sports
17. Ads overtly critical of feminist rights and issues
18. Women's body parts, especially genitalia, featured in ads rather than the whole body
19. Frequent decapitated images of women; women often pictured only from the mouth or neck downward (as though they don't have brains)
20. Women in depictions of bondage, such as being embedded in inanimate objects or bound with tape, fabric, or rope.

One study examined television ads that ran during the 1999 Super Bowl and found that sexist, stereotypical images of women abounded, leading the author to conclude that "advertising has apparently decided that the benefit of crudely impressing men trumps the disadvantages of dishonoring women" (Garfield, 1999, p. 1).

Perhaps some of you are familiar with the work of Jean Kilbourne, particularly her educational films. Kilbourne's first film, *Killing Us Softly*, was released in 1979, and she continues to produce research and films which support her assertion that advertising presents women almost exclusively in one of two roles: housewife or sex object (Kilbourne, 1999). Her examples include women pathologically obsessed with cleanliness and ridding

> *We grew up founding our dreams on the infinite promise of American advertising. I still believe that one can learn to play the piano by mail and that mud will give you a perfect complexion.*
>
> —Zelda Fitzgerald, author

their husbands' shirts of "ring around the collar," and thin, tall, long-legged mannequin-like women with perfect skin and no signs of aging.

In particular, women of color fare poorly in ads, both in the quantity of depictions and the quality of the roles (Bramlett-Solomon, 2001). According to author Gail Baker Woods (1995), "Less than 20 percent of all ads with blacks feature black women. When they are seen, black women are often portrayed as 'jive'-talking, sassy 'sisters' or overweight, wise-cracking, church-going women" (p. 28). Hispanic, Asian American, and Native American women are represented in ads less than African American women, who are represented less than white women. When women of color appear in ads, often they are expected to conform to standards of white beauty (Cortese, 1999; Wilson & Gutierrez, 2003).

An Exercise in Ad Analysis

Look at the billboard advertisement reproduced in Figure 3.1. Some of you might think there's nothing inherently wrong or sexist about this advertisement. The ad is simply catching the eye of motorists in Dallas, Texas, and effectively selling a product. However, others may look at this ad and think, "Not another scantily clad woman selling beer!" Using the following set of questions, analyze this ad. Supply your own answers to the questions first; then we'll provide our perspective.

1. Who is the target audience for this product?
2. What's being sold here, beer? Sexuality? Leisure? Status?
3. Is there anything unusual in the fact that only a woman appears in this ad, given that men are the predominant beer drinkers in the country?
4. What is your interpretation of the clothing the woman is wearing (or lack thereof)?
5. Do you find anything sexist in her body position, meaning her prone position on the billboard?
6. What is your interpretation of the positioning of the beer bottle underneath the woman's body?
7. What is the meaning of the caption, "Tap into the cold, Dallas"?

FIGURE 3-1.

Compare your answers with those of your classmates to see how subjective a judgment of sexism can be.

Here's our interpretation of this advertisement: Since more men than women drink beer, it's safe to assume that this ad is geared more toward a male target audience than a female audience. It's a sexist ad for many reasons, the main one being that it represents yet another attempt on the part of advertisers to use a woman's sexuality for profit. What's really being sold here is the woman and her sexuality, not beer (Hall, Iijima, & Crum, 1994). If that weren't the case, then why not show just the beer bottle and the caption? The message to men is, "If you drink this brand of beer, you'll attract a woman who looks like this, who'll dress like this and lie down for you like this." What messages do women get from a huge billboard like this?

Our interpretation is reinforced by the vulnerable position of the woman (in only a bathing suit) lying on her back with one arm up, which conveys a sexual, submissive message. The fact that she is on top of a cold beer bottle suggests sexual imagery, since it's easy to construe the neck of the beer bottle, intentionally placed underneath and between her legs, as a phallic symbol. These kinds of images are prevalent in alcohol ads (Kilbourne, 1999). Concerning the caption, one wonders if it is the beer that is to be tapped or the woman. Research shows convincingly that men's attitudes about sexual aggression and their perceptions of women's sexual interest in men are affected by sexual images of women in the media (Jansma, Linz, Mulac, & Imrich, 1997; MacKay & Covell, 1997; Milburn, Mather, & Conrad, 2000; Mullin, 1995).

At this point you may disagree with us or wonder if we don't get out much. We realize that no one is likely to pull off a Dallas freeway to critique this billboard. Perhaps the argument could be made that, in isolation, this one ad isn't sexist. But what about the trend for advertisers to display women, typically in revealing attire, draped across the hoods of cars or posed in various suggestive positions with objects such as oversized beer bottles or shiny motorcycles between their legs? What's being communicated when these kinds of ads appear with such regularity?

Some manufacturers have changed their approach to advertising products for female consumers—the operant word in this statement being *some*. Laura Zinn (1991), a writer for *Business Week*, describes ads for women's products that show promise, such as those for Maidenform lingerie and Nike's women's athletic wear. Since increasing numbers of women are making sports and exercise a significant part of their lives, Nike and Reebok ads in particular have wisely reflected the trend toward less sexist advertising. These companies have made serious, laudable, successful attempts to communicate to female consumers that they understand them and find them important—but they are the exception, not the rule. When men and women appear together in ads, women still are too often portrayed less than fully clothed and as sexy, flirtatious, and vulnerable. We don't see sexism lurking at every turn, but we do worry about the prevalence of sexual images of women being used to sell all kinds of products—especially products geared to men.

Advertising's Effects on Women

Sexist and stereotypical ad portrayals have severe negative effects on women (Martin & Gentry, 2003; Romaine, 1999). Kilbourne (1998) states: "A woman is conditioned to view her face as a mask and her body as an object, as *things* separate from and more important than her real self, constantly in need of alteration, improvement, and disguise. She is made to feel dissatisfied with and ashamed of herself, whether she tries to achieve 'the look' or not. Objectified constantly by others, she learns to objectify herself" (p. 129). Research on American college students shows that "up to two thirds of young women and one third of young men experience significant dissatisfaction with their body size, shape, condition, or appearance in relation to most advertising campaigns" (Raeback-Wagener, Eickenhoff-Schemeck, & Kelly-Vance, 1998, p. 29). Studies continue to reveal our culture's obsession with thinness, as reflected in advertising (Lavine, Sweeney, & Wagner, 1999; Lee, 1995; Myers & Biocca, 1992; Posavac, 1998). The results are consistent and overwhelming:

1. Women receive many times more advertising messages about thinness and body shape than men.
2. The volume of these ads in prominent magazines and on television is staggering.
3. The trend toward severe thinness is inescapable in ads, creating an ever-widening gap between the weight of an average American woman and the ideal.
4. Thin female models are perceived to be more attractive than average-weight or overweight models in ads.
5. The majority of African American models, including supermodels Tyra Banks and Naomi Campbell, are slim, although the standard of thinness isn't as extreme among black women as among other racial and ethnic groups.
6. The pressure to be thin is not as great for men as for women, as evidenced by the higher number of average-weight and overweight male models in ads in comparison with females.
7. Young women's images of their bodies become distorted when they are presented with images of an ideal body shape. (Many simply believe that they cannot be thin enough, and they suffer poor health and loss of self-esteem trying to achieve the media's unreal perfect body.)
8. The term *heroin chic* was coined late in the 1990s to describe the gaunt, unhealthy look of many top fashion models. Kate Moss is the poster child for this look; she is also one of the top models in the world, admired by countless numbers of young women.

We've all heard the phrase "sex sells," but women's sex *really* sells, as ads prove time and time again. Many of us have grown weary of women's bodies and sexuality being used in every possible way to draw a viewer's or reader's attention and sell a product—*any* product.

Mixed Signals Create Confusion

People are confused by images in the media; at times, this confusion has consequences for their relationships and communication. Many men wonder if women want to be treated as equals and professionals, as traditional helpmates and caregivers, or as sex kittens, because the media readily provide continuous, seemingly acceptable images of each.

One source of confusion is the cover pictures on women's magazines and the contradictory headlines describing the magazine's contents. Extremely thin female models, their breasts squeezed into outfits that create cleavage, appear on the covers—opposite headings such as "How to Get Your Boss to Take You Seriously." In ads found in various print sources, the images of women create a paradox that is compounded by reading the copy accompanying the ad (Jackson, 1991; Sullivan & O'Connor, 1988). For example, an ad meant to depict a typical day in the life of a professional career woman shows her dressed in a business suit with briefcase in hand, but the copy says she'd really like to be anywhere but at work; she's on the job, but actually thinking of her man. In a controversial move, two traditional women's magazines—*Redbook* and *Ladies' Home Journal*—recently began to include sex-oriented columns and features, in an effort to boost lagging sales. Opposite cover photos of wholesome women and, quite often, their children, you'll now find headings like "What Your Sex Dreams Say about You" and "Grown-Up Sexxx: He Needs It, You'll Love It" (Kuczynski, 2000, p. A25).

Probably the best, and most insidious, example of mixed signals in advertising has been perpetrated by the makers of Virginia Slims cigarettes, whose ads first emerged during the heyday of the women's liberation movement. The early television and print ads were done in sepia tones, to look like old-fashioned movie reels or still photographs. In the TV ads, a male voice-over described how some women in history got into trouble for being rebellious and smoking. These ads then cut to modern-day images of women, accompanied by the motto (originally sung) "You've come a long way, baby, to get where you got to today!" The point was to illustrate how women's status had improved in American society because women were finally allowed to smoke. Current versions of these ads can legally appear only in magazines and on billboards because of laws restricting cigarette advertising. Ads depict youthful, attractive women doing fun, active things (as active as you can be with a cigarette in your hand), while using the language of liberation. The paradox comes when you compare the visual images with the wording across the ads, such as "Now's your chance to tell the world just how far you've come" and repeated sentences, just under the name Virginia Slims and next to the cigarette pack, such as "It's a *woman* thing" and "Find Your Voice." (That voice will sound like gravel the longer one smokes.) This ad campaign has long been criticized by health care officials and feminists alike, who are outraged by the fact that a tobacco company continues to ignore women's health issues and packages the product as though it epitomizes liberation, women's rights, and feminism, when in fact smoking their product actually enslaves women (Cortese, 1999; Kilbourne, 1998; Steinem, 1990). Is the company trying to convince young women that smoking equals liberation and that it's a "woman's thing" to smoke? What do teenage and adolescent girls think when they see these ads?

Studs in Suits: Male Depiction in Advertising

Just as there are female stereotypes in advertising, male gender stereotypes also appear. More research has been conducted on depictions of women, but several studies provide interesting revelations about men in advertisements.

Corporate Success, Great Dad, and Angry Guy

Studies in the 1980s showed that men were typically portrayed in ads as dominant, successful professionals in business settings or engaged in having fun in settings away from home (Courtney & Whipple, 1983). They were still portrayed this way in the 1990s, but a new trend depicted men involved in domestic tasks such as taking care of children, preparing family meals, and doing household chores (Craig, 1992; Richmond-Abbott, 1992). In addition, men were more often presented as sex objects and in decorative, nonfunctional roles that had no relation to the product being sold (Lin, 1997).

While some people think that ads depicting men as sex objects are realistic and humorous, others see them as male-bashing. A Hyundai ad of a few years ago was particularly memorable, if for no other reasons than its blatant role reversal and sexual innuendo—and the fact that it was hugely successful. In the ad, two women critique men who get out of fancy sports cars, saying that one "must be compensating for a shortcoming." When a man arrives in a sensible Hyundai, one woman says to the other, admiringly, "I wonder what he's got under *his* hood." Researcher Philip Patterson (1996) views this ad as an example of what he calls *power babe commercials* in which "women enjoy the upper hand over men" (p. 93). He is critical of two prominent stereotypes of men in advertising, which he calls *Rambo* and *Himbo depictions:* "The image of men in advertising is either that of a 'Rambo,' solo conqueror of all he sees, or a 'Himbo,' a male bimbo" (p. 94). These stereotypical, overdrawn images of men persist today.

Another trend emerged in advertising during the late 1990s and into the new century—the "angry guy." Media scholar Jackson Katz (2003) describes a trend toward depictions of violent white males in advertising for a wide range of products. Katz detects recurring themes in magazine advertising: "The angry, aggressive, White, working-class male as antiauthority rebel; violence as genetically programmed male behavior; the use of military and sports symbolism to enhance the masculine identification and appeal of products; the association of muscularity with ideal masculinity; and the equation of heroic masculinity with violent masculinity" (p. 352). He cites examples such as white rap artist Eminem, who epitomizes the angry white male with attitude, shown most often scowling, overly serious, or in violent poses. Other common depictions include men in uniforms with their weapons or gear—both military and sporting. Coinciding with the rising popularity of professional wrestling, hypermasculinized male wrestlers can be seen on television touting the glories of the latest vacuum cleaner.

A few years ago, we got a letter from a professor whose class used our textbook and found an omission in the media chapter. The students saw no list of male stereotypes that corresponded to Courtney and Whipple's list of depictions of women. So the class created one, and we think it's well worth reprinting. According to Lynn Wells's students at Saddleback College in Mission Viejo, California (to whom we're grateful), depictions of men in ads include the following:

1. Stud or cowboy, like the Marlboro man
2. Jock, who can perform in all sports
3. Handyman, who can fix anything
4. Young and hip, as in ads for sports drinks
5. Handsome ladies' man, as in beer commercials
6. Kind and grandfatherly, as in insurance ads
7. Professional, knowledgeable
8. Couch potato man
9. Blue-collar worker, sometimes seen as a sex symbol
10. Androgynous, as in Calvin Klein ads
11. Romantic, coffee-drinking man
12. Fonzie type, Joe Cool
13. Helpless, as in the "Got Milk" commercials
14. Just a kid, who needs a woman to save him.

What advertising types can you add to this list?

Advertising's Effects on Men

Most people prefer not to relate to men as though they were stereotypes. But it's hard not to wonder if men actually want to avoid being stereotyped, given that so many macho images of men still pervade many media, from magazine ads depicting rugged men in their pickup trucks to infomercials pushing the latest exercise equipment.

If you're a male, what's your reaction to an ad in which a scantily clad man is depicted as a sex object? (Some people would argue Calvin Klein's, Versace's and other magazine ads fit this description.) What about the now infamous Diet Coke ad of the early 1990s, in which a hunky, sweaty construction worker removes his shirt and downs a Diet Coke to the delight of the women working next door, who watch the clock for their "Diet Coke break"? As one female columnist wrote, "For a lot of us, this ad is sweeter than a thermos full of sugar substitute for a whole lot of reasons. Most obvious: It is so grand to take off the placemats and turn those tables" (Loohauis, 1994, p. 5C). If you're a male, do you notice male-objectifying ads more than or in a different way from, for example, Victoria's Secret lingerie ads, which began appearing on television in the late 1990s? Do these ads make you feel bad about yourself in comparison with some stud women swoon over? Or do you find them refreshing and realistic because men are shown as sexy and women show their "appreciation"?

Many scholars believe that men are the next targets for an all-out assault on self-esteem, mainly because the market for assaulting women's self-esteem—forcing them to buy products and services ranging from simple beauty remedies to full-scale plastic surgery—is saturated, profits maxed out (Lin, 1997). We continue to see a significant increase in ads showing barely clothed men with perfect bodies, skin, hair, and teeth, touting the products and services that can get men that way. These ads encourage men to think of themselves as sex objects (Dobosz, 1997). Michelle Cottle (2003), editor of *Washington Monthly* magazine, admits taking a guilty pleasure in reading *Men's Health* magazine. In her article "Turning Boys into Girls," Cottle describes a trend she sees in men's advertising:

> My affection for *Men's Health* is driven by pure gender politics—by the realization that this magazine, and a handful of others like it, are leveling the playing field in a way that *Ms.* can only dream of. With page after page of bulging biceps and Gillette jaws, robust hairlines and silken skin, *Men's Health* is peddling a standard of male beauty as unforgiving and unrealistic as the female version sold by those dewy-eyed pre-teen waifs draped across the covers of *Glamour* and *Elle*. *Men's Health* is on its way to making the male species as insane, insecure, and irrational about physical appearance as any *Cosmo* girl. (p. 68)

You may find you've become so desensitized to sexually objectifying ads—of both men and women—that you hardly notice them any more. Since sexually objectifying female ads don't seem to be going away, do you think it's a form of equality to objectify men sexually in ads? Will ads like these develop or increase in men an irrational concern with appearance, image, and sex appeal?

Lessons From the Small Screen: Television and Gender

Ninety-nine percent of American households have at least one television set; most have more than one set (Vivian, 2003). At the turn of the new century, approximately 70 percent of American television-viewing households were cable subscribers, 90 percent had a least one VCR, and about one-third had DVD players (Campbell et al., 2003). The average number of hours per week spent watching television exceeds the average 40-hour work week (Goldberg, 1998). Video recording has greatly expanded the impact of television by allowing consumers to tape and watch cable and network programming when convenient—a practice known as *time shifting*. New *black box technologies*, including such brands as Replay and TiVo, broaden the time frame in which a viewer can tape a show. They allow viewers to record onto the box itself, which acts much like a computer hard drive and is capable of much greater storage than tapes or CDs but is less bulky (Campbell et al., 2003). We've all no doubt seen futuristic ads in which someone handles all of life's needs (such as banking, purchasing groceries and clothing, and communicating with others) through the use of a telephone, television, and computer interface. Soon those won't be futuristic ads;

they'll reflect reality. Since it's unlikely that exposure to programming will decrease anytime soon, it seems reasonable that depictions of the sexes on television will continue to have an impact on the viewing audience.

Television: Mirroring Reality or Creating It?

Television is a rapidly changing industry; it's likely that some of the television shows we refer to in this chapter will be off the air by the time you read this material. But one thing will remain—a chicken-or-egg argument about whether the media merely reflect what is happening in society or actually create issues and trends that then become relevant in society. Perhaps it's a bit of both.

Hot Button Issue

"Reflecting or Leading?"

What's your basic view of the role or function of the media? What should they contribute to society? Should advertisements, television programming, films, and music simply reflect what exists in our society or endeavor to affect culture in a positive way? Is it possible to do both?

Media outlets tend to engender strong opinions in their consumers. For example, you may or may not be aware of the controversy that has surrounded the Abercrombie and Fitch catalog in recent years, related to its portrayal of life on college campuses. Male and female students (as well as some androgynous, non-sex-identifiable individuals) are depicted in various states of undress and in situations implying a great deal of sexual ambiguity. For instance, two women and one man are depicted on campus, outdoors, in their underwear, in what appears to be a romantic interlude or ménage à trois. Another page touts the "well-equipped campus necessity"—a refrigerator fully stocked with only beer, wine, and liquor. Flipping through the pages of this catalog, you would think that all college students do is frolic about half-naked and drunk and have sex with various partners of both sexes. You tell us—does that reflect your life as a college student?

Other controversies surround violence that has erupted and has later been linked to some form of mediated stimulus. In one incident a young man was killed when he stretched out on the center stripes of a busy street and was run over by a car; he was mimicking a scene from the movie *The Program,* in which football players did this as a means of building character and team camaraderie. One television program (now made into a feature-length film), *Jackass,* is built on such a premise—that people will copy stupid, even dangerous, feats they see acted out on television or are dared to perform. And we've all heard acts of violence later described as being media-inspired, such as shootings at public schools inspired by violent imagery in rock and rap music. Are the media simply mirroring harsh, cruel reality, or do they lead people to do foolish and terrible things? What do you believe is the responsibility of the media? Do they exist simply to document cultural reality, or do they play a role in creating it?

To support the idea that the media reflect reality, one could argue that the economic pressures and changing lifestyles of young professionals in the early twenty-first century are reflected in various prime-time programs, such as the long-running sitcom *Friends*. On the other hand, many researchers support the view that the media drive or create culture, believing that television actually expands viewers' range of behaviors. Probably the best example of this view was the hit series *Seinfeld*, which media scholars believe at once expanded language and created a whole new way of relating to friends, jobs, parents, lovers, and life in general (Stark, 2000a). Yet another school of thought contends that television programming, for the most part, neither reflects nor creates reality; rather, its exaggerated portrayals and overly dramatized situations are nowhere near the realities of most people's lives. (Maybe *Alias* is a good example of this perspective.) In this view, television programs and other forms of media serve purely as escapism and entertainment for consumers, as uses and gratifications theory suggests (Rubin, 1986).

While it's beyond our focus in this book to delve deeply into the effects of television viewing on children and adolescents, research continues to show that television has a lot of power to shape girls' and boys' visions of themselves and their notions about how men and women behave (Barner, 1999; Douglas, 1995b; Powell & Abels, 2002; Ward & Rivadeneyra, 1999). Whether as an adult you tend to relate more to traditional portrayals or to groundbreaking characterizations of the sexes, one implication is that our communication with relational partners, as well as our attitudes about gender and behavior in relationships, is influenced, in varying degrees, by sitcoms and television dramas.

> *I find television very educational. Every time someone switches it on I go into another room and read a good book.*
>
> —Groucho Marx, actor and comedian

The Changing Roles of Men in Prime Time

To better understand depictions of the sexes in prime-time television programming, media scholar Marvin Moore (1992) conducted an extensive survey of depictions of families in American prime-time television programming from 1947 to 1990. Moore analyzed 115 prime-time programs and found that 94 percent of the families in the programs were white and two-thirds involved a traditional married couple, with or without children. Little has changed in prime-time programming at the start of the twenty-first century. Sitcoms and dramas are still primarily about white, young to middle-aged, middle-class America, with male roles outnumbering female roles (Butsch, 2003; Elasmar, Hasegawa, & Brain, 1999; Harwood & Anderson, 2002). A quick look at prime-time TV listings proves the point. What are the predominant male roles in prime-time television, and what message does the perpetuation of such roles send to the viewing audience?

The Kinder, Gentler Male Character

From the 1990s and to the first few seasons of television in the twenty-first century, a feminized or reconstructed male has emerged in prime-time programming (Craig, 1992). These male characters aren't buffoons or wimps but likable, masculine men who struggle to understand themselves, communicate with the women in their lives, and be better parents. Several highly successful shows capitalizing on this trend include *Mad About You*, *Everybody Loves Raymond*, and *ER*. The multifaceted male roles have proved popular with male and female viewers alike, but the trend mostly reflects an effort to reach women in the viewing audience, since women constitute the majority of prime-time television viewers, as well as the primary shoppers for households. (Never underestimate the power of the dollar to control even such things as television characters.)

The Non-PC Male Character

Another trend in depictions of males in prime-time television is what media scholar Robert Hanke (1998) calls the *mock-macho sitcom*. These sitcoms "address white, middle class, middle-aged men's anxieties about a feminized ideal for manhood they may not want to live up to, as well as changes in work and family that continue to dissolve separate gender spheres" (p. 76). Shows like the huge hit in the 1990s, *Home Improvement*, mock machismo while preserving masculinity, in that they simultaneously present "male comic television actors who ridicule their own lack of self-knowledge" and men who are "objects of laughter" (p. 76). The main male character is usually a devoted husband and father who is an equal partner with his wife, but who often goofs up and admits he doesn't understand women (Stark, 2000a). This characterization has also been called the *playful patriarch* (Traube, 1992).

Breakthrough TV Roles for Men

Other male characters reflect blended roles, in the sense that more shows today than in the past depict multidimensional, complicated men. The epitome of this trend can be found in Detective Andy Sipowicz of *NYPD Blue* (Douglas, 2000). While Sipowicz has expressed sexist and racist attitudes over the years, has frequented prostitutes during his prerecovery days as an alcoholic, is quick to anger, and often uses brutal methods of interrogation, his character also has sympathetic dimensions. You'd probably call him a macho guy, but his emotional side, his subtle ways of responding to bittersweet moments, endear the character (and the actor) to the viewing audience. Sipowicz may be one of the most integrated, richly portrayed male characters in television.

Breakthrough roles related to sexual orientation were more prevalent at the turn of the new century than in decades past, and gay men's roles have emerged with greater range and impact. The highly successful *Will and Grace*, a show about a close relationship between a straight woman and a gay man, and *Queer As Folk* on cable TV both have gay male leading and supporting characters and continue to achieve greater viewer acceptance (Hart, 2003). Eric McCormack, who plays the character of Will, described *Will and Grace* at the Emmy Awards of 2002 as follows: "It's not girlfriend/boyfriend; it's not girlfriend/girlfriend;

"We rarely watch television. Most of our free time is devoted to sex."

it's that delicious something in between." These shows aren't without their critics, many of whom include gays and lesbians who resent *Queer As Folk* because of its stereotypical or caricatured portrayals of gay men (Gilbert, 2001). Yet the popularity of these shows indicates either a greater acceptance of homosexuals in our society or a simple recognition that homosexuality exists in our culture—a show with homosexual characters and plotlines may be more accepted because people are simply more used to the idea.

The Slower-to-Change Roles of Women in Prime Time

From *Buffy the Vampire Slayer*, *Sabrina the Teenage Witch*, and *Alias*, one might get the strong impression that June Cleaver and Lucy Ricardo are long gone. But are these extreme images rather than the typical depiction of the female character on prime-time television?

Underrepresented and Traditional: Women's Roles over Time

In the 1970s, Tuchman and colleagues described women's presence on prime-time television as a "symbolic annihilation" (Tuchman, Daniels, & Benet, 1978). Several studies examining trends in the portrayal of women in prime-time television programming offer evidence that the annihilation is far from over (Lindsey, 2003). Media researchers Greenberg and Collette (1997) examined new-season programming over a span of about 30 years, operating on the assumption that if patterns of male dominance in prime-time programming were to change, evidence of the change would emerge in new programs. Across the 27 seasons they reviewed, women were consistently underrepresented, women appeared in far more traditional roles (wife, mother) than nontraditional roles, and new female characters were predominantly young or middle-aged.

Another study analyzed 10 of the most popular prime-time sitcoms in the United States from the 1950s to the 1990s, focusing on such variables as the depiction of equal sex roles, dominance of certain characters, stability of family relationships, and family satisfaction (Olson & Douglas, 1997). The results documented a good deal of fluctuation in gender-role portrayals across the 40-year span, with a general decline in both the quantity and quality of female roles. Women's roles toward the end of the span reflected less positive characterizations than in earlier times.

We referred to Marvin Moore's work in the previous section on men's portrayals. Moore's (1992) analysis of families in 1980s prime-time television was critical of portrayals of women. He asserted that, whereas television programs depicted men in nontraditional roles, indicating that men have the freedom to choose different paths for themselves without societal sanctions, women's changing roles in society were largely ignored. The reality was that huge numbers of women entered the workforce during the 1980s, to support themselves and subsidize the family income, but representations of working women were few and far between. Moore found that mothers and wives in family series were rarely identified as having occupations; they were predominantly home-centered and were supported by their male counterparts in the shows. His primary example was Claire Huxtable, the leading female character in one of the most successful

---

'Net Notes

You may have heard of Ananova, a computer representation of a woman, who anchors the news on her Website, **www.ananova.com.** Her two-minute news broadcasts attract Web users for more than just news; the site also offers electronic searches and online shopping. Ananova is supposed to be a "liberated" computer-generated woman. At a virtual news conference in 2000, Ananova said, "Just because I am good-looking, some people think I am a bimbo. But I want to be judged on what I do and not on my looks." Check out the site, and *you* be the judge.

sitcoms of the decade, *The Cosby Show*. She was a successful lawyer, but she rarely referred to her job and was rarely depicted in a legal setting.

In one of the most comprehensive studies of prime-time television programming, media scholars Signorielli and Bacue (1999) conducted a content analysis of samples of dramatic programs broadcast between the fall of 1967 and the spring of 1998. They focused on gender trends in two primary areas: recognition (quantity and frequency of appearances) and respect (types and breadth of roles). Regarding recognition, they found that although women's presence in prime-time programming increased over time, women were still greatly underrepresented relative to their numbers in the U.S. population. Regarding respect, they found that women appeared most often in sitcoms and least often in action, adventure, and crime programs, which tend to receive more respect or to be taken more seriously than sitcoms by the viewing public. Women were still depicted as younger than their male counterparts; however, more women were presented as employed outside the home and in more prestigious occupations than in the past. Finally, women depicted in traditionally male jobs (e.g., law enforcement) or gender-neutral jobs (e.g., sales) increased significantly between 1970 and 1998.

Women Juggling Home and Work

A good deal of research has examined how contemporary working women are depicted in prime-time television, with specific regard to tension between a female character's personal life and her work (Douglas, 1995b; Dow, 1996; Vande Berg & Streckfuss, 1992). Although working women are central characters or significant family members many more times in today's prime-time television programs than in decades past, they are still outnumbered by depictions of men, and the programs are more likely to emphasize women's love lives over their working lives (Signorielli & Kahlenberg, 1999; Steenland, 1995).

Media and gender researcher Phyllis Japp (1991) was among the first to explore this trend. She found that the typical emphases for TV's working women are their relationships with men (and, for some, their relationships with their children) and the tension created when they juggle work and these relationships. While this tension constitutes a reality for many contemporary women, the personal and relational elements in female television characters' lives receive more emphasis or airtime than the professional, career-oriented elements. This sends a message that no matter how professional or successful a woman becomes, what matters most, what really makes a woman acceptable or unacceptable in American consciousness is her relationship with a man (Shalit, 1998). Probably no other program epitomizes this tendency more than *Ally McBeal*, which ended its highly successful run in 2002 (Elber, 2002).

Breakthrough TV Roles for Women

Spin-offs of the *Star Trek* series broke new ground in depictions of women (Kim, 1995; Luong, 1992). In the more recent shows, unlike the original series, most of the women's roles were high-ranking officers, doctors, security specialists, engineers, and scientists. In fact, in January 1995 the cover of *Entertainment Weekly* magazine pictured actress Kate Mulgrew, in uniform as Captain Kathryn Janeway of the Starship Enterprise in the *Star Trek: Voyager* series, with a caption that read, "Boldly Going Where Only Men Have Gone Before." Action-adventure roles have increased for women, in such shows as *Xena: Warrior Princess*, *Buffy the Vampire Slayer*, and *Alias*; however, action-adventure television remains a male-dominated form of entertainment (Signorielli & Bacue, 1999).

Certainly the characters Roseanne Connor and Murphy Brown can be seen as groundbreakers for women's roles. The lead character in *Roseanne* was a contra-diction—a challenge to the social norm of femininity, a struggling, outspoken, blue-collar worker, and a sarcastic yet devoted wife, mother, and sister (Douglas, 1995a; Faludi, 1991; Rowe, 1990). The central character in *Murphy Brown* has been studied for many reasons, primarily because she was one of the first strong, inde-pendent, career-minded, persistently single female characters (since *The Mary Tyler Moore Show*) who developed over time and seemed to defy stereotypes (Dow, 1996). At the same time, she was a recovering alcoholic and had some unattrac-tive, negative dimensions, such as her abrasiveness with people. As Diane English, cocreator of the sitcom, told a reporter, "I had never seen a strong, competent woman on television who also had the courage of her convictions, who wasn't try-ing to please everyone, who allowed herself to be rude and who didn't edit her-self. These are traits you would normally find in a man. I really, basically, wrote Murphy as a man in a skirt" (Clark, 1993, p. 5C).

An important, if controversial, breakthrough role was the character played by Ellen DeGeneres in the prime-time sitcom *Ellen*. Much has been written about this role and this show, as well as the courage of the actress-comedian, who came out to the television audience both personally and through her on-screen per-sona (Cagle, 1998; Hubert, 2003). No matter what your sexual orientation or your views on gay rights, it's hard to disagree that *Ellen* had a significant impact on the television landscape.

While there are other breakthrough women's roles on television, probably none generated more interest and "heat" at the turn of the century than the four female characters on HBO's hit series *Sex and the City* (Mansfield, 2000; Tucker, 2002). Some of our male students who have seen the cable show ask us, "Do women really talk that way about men and sex?" The answer is that some women (probably more than you think) really do talk that bluntly about sex and men, and some women don't. Although little scientific research exists yet on the effects of these particular media portrayals, it's easy to speculate (from avid watching of the show) about messages sent to viewers. Our obser-vation is that the show seems to send mixed signals. On the one hand, view-ers get strong messages of women's liberation, specifically that it's fine (even wonderful) to be single, have and raise a baby on your own, break up with men who aren't right for you instead of feeling pressure to marry, and divorce if you're unhappy. On the other hand, it's clear from just a few episodes that these four women are focused more on their romances than their careers or other aspects of their lives. Even though their friendship with each other is the pri-mary focus of the program, the almost constant subject of conversations and plotlines is men—how to get them, what to do with them, whether or not to keep them, and when it's time to move on to the next one. Again, as in many other prime-time TV shows, the message is that men are the most important thing women can talk about; men are what make women's lives interesting and complete. We understand that sentiment, but is it a balanced, accurate representation of women? What women's roles do you think are missing from current prime-time programming?

The Influence of Social Issues Programming

The term *social issues programming* refers to the kind of prime-time informational show that tackles a social or political issue, such as gun control legislation, reproductive rights, or gay marriage. This type of television is nothing new in daytime fare; however, daytime discussions typically occur within an already established format, such as a talk show or a local interview program with invited guests or panelists. In the 1990s networks and cable companies were challenged to explore social issues not only through a movie-of-the-week format, but also through extended prime-time evening talk shows, "town hall debates," and informative panel discussions and forums.

The Agenda-Setting Potential of Social Issues Programming

Social issues programming is both similar to and different from newsmagazine shows such as *Dateline NBC, 20/20, 48 Hours,* and the grandparent of them all, *60 Minutes.* These types of programming are similar in that they are nonfictional and usually involve reporters as hosts and typical or average people as guests or subjects of investigation. Another aspect common to both formats is the agenda-setting function they serve for the mass audience. If a network devotes one of its prime-time slots to a town hall debate on political scandal or a forum on juvenile crime, it sends a clear signal to the viewing public that "this topic is *really* important." The main difference between the two types of programming is the range of topics—newsmagazines usually cover several topics in one episode, whereas social issues programs typically focus in depth on one general issue. Of special interest for our purposes are programs that have the potential to instruct the viewing public and to set an agenda as to which gender issues are most important.

One Network's Provocative Social Issues Program

One way to understand social issues programming is to consider a highly provocative program that was broadcast on ABC in the mid-1990s. News anchor Peter Jennings hosted a forum called *Men, Sex, and Rape* that featured two panels of experts placed in a small auditorium—six female experts on one side of the stage, six male experts on the other side. The show's producers even divided the audience seating by sex to further dramatize how women and men tend to hold polarized opinions on the issue of sexual assault and rape. The male lineup included such experts as author Warren Farrell; John Leo, a columnist for *Time* and other magazines; and Florida attorney F. Lee Bailey. (Note that this program took place before O. J. Simpson's trial, through which F. Lee Bailey became a household word. It also took place before John Gray's book *Men Are From Mars, Women Are From Venus* became a best-seller; otherwise, Gray would have no doubt been included on the men's panel.) The female panel included such experts as Pulitzer-prize-winning author Susan Faludi; Naomi Wolf, author of

The Beauty Myth and other books that have made her a central voice of third-wave feminism (see the Prologue); Catharine MacKinnon, a feminist attorney at the University of Michigan School of Law; and Mary Koss, whose important research on sexual assault and rape we review in Chapter 8.

Here's the gist of the 90-minute program. After Jennings's brief introduction, the program cut to a short video clip of a scantily clad woman entertaining a room full of men at what looked like a bachelor party. Jennings then asked the panelists for their reactions to the tape, followed by their comments about both stranger and acquaintance rape. The discussion included such aspects as how men and women view rape and respond to rape education efforts differently, methods of education and prevention, treatment for survivors, rehabilitation for rapists, and legal matters. Exchanges between panelists occasionally turned to banter, such as when one of the female panelists responded to Warren Farrell's defensive comments about men with something along the lines of, "You just don't get it, do you?" At several key points in the program, Jennings turned to audience members for prearranged comments on the subject or for personal stories of sexual assault and rape.

Are Viewers Getting the Social Message?

We don't mean to sound cynical or jaded, but it's highly likely that social issues programming continues to air on various networks and cable channels less because of social conscience—a desire to advance our culture—than because of economics. In essence, such shows are produced because they're cheap. The same is true of newsmagazine shows: they don't cost much to produce and don't involve big salaries for actors or expensive locations. For example, in the spring of 2002, ABC's *Nightline* presented a five-part series of programs on gay issues. The title of the series was "A Matter of Choice?" and the programs explored whether sexual orientation is genetic or a function of social conditioning.

Little has been written on the effects of this type of programming; however, two studies have been conducted to determine viewers' reactions to dramatizations of social issues. Mass media researcher Andrea Press (1991b) studied women's reactions to an episode of the television drama *Cagney and Lacey* in the 1980s. The episode dealt with abortion, reproductive rights, and justice. Specifically, Press found that women's language and views about abortion were affected by the language used and the views expressed in the episode. This study indicated that television programming could serve an educational function, if only to cause viewers to talk about an issue in a different way.

Communication researchers Wilson, Linz, Donnerstein, and Stipp (1992) examined the effects of viewing a television movie about acquaintance rape on attitudes about rape. Overall, the results of the study indicated that the film served an educational function for viewers. More specifically, male and female viewers of varying ages (ranging from 18 to around 50) altered their perception of the problem of date rape after seeing the television movie. Afterward, viewers were less likely to blame female survivors of date rape, more likely to perceive women as being coerced into sexual activity, and more concerned about the seriousness of date rape as a societal problem.

What effects does this form of programming have on the American viewing public? First, social issues programs utilize an accessible medium—the home television set—to introduce topics in a way that is likely to catch people's attention. Second, these programs have the potential to educate the public on issues of increasing importance and to provide new ways to think about those issues. Viewers may understand an issue more profoundly when a television program explores it. Finally, a social issues program is likely to spark healthy dialogue about an issue after the broadcast.

However, these programs may also present only one side of an issue, reflecting certain biases of the reporters, the networks or cable companies, or the commercial sponsors. Whether social issues programmers feel a responsibility to provide evenhanded treatments of issues; whether these programs actually affect people's attitudes and, more important, their behavior; and exactly to what extent the programs influence women, men, and the communication between them represent provocative research challenges.

Daytime Television: Not Just for Women Anymore

Daytime television viewers are a mix of people—full-time homemakers, teenagers, people who work part-time, college students (some of whom arrange their class schedules around their favorite soaps), shift workers home during the day, and others who record their favorite programs to watch at their leisure. In this section, we discuss two formats of daytime programming—soap operas and talk shows—with special regard for what these programs communicate about women and men.

As the Culture Turns

Daytime dramas have been popular with radio and television audiences for many decades, and research on their effects dates back to the 1940s (Campbell et al., 2003). An estimated 40 million viewers tune in daily to their soaps (Whitmire, 1996). If ardent followers miss a program, publications like *Soap Opera Digest* and a multitude of Websites will supply the details. Before we go further in this discussion, let's address a popular misconception—that soap operas are watched exclusively by women. Daytime television programming has been, and still is to a great extent, targeted to the perceived needs and circumstances of women. However, as VCRs have become widely available and affordable, the audience for soap operas has broadened. Nielsen's statistics estimate that 30 percent of the audience for soap operas is male (Hayward, 2003). Some of our male students reveal, albeit somewhat reluctantly, that they regularly watch certain soaps.

A great deal has been written about soap operas, primarily on the functions they serve in society, the predominant roles male and female family members play in the plots, communication between characters, and viewers' perceptions of the parallels between soaps and real life (Freud Loewenstein, 1993; Irwin & Cassata, 1993; Mumford, 1995; Scodari, 1998; White, 1995). Media researchers Livingstone and Liebes (1995) consider soap operas an extension of childhood fairy tales: "Dilemmas of identity, emotional anxieties, and other personal conflicts do not all reach resolution at the end of childhood. Thus, once grown ups have left behind the period when they may legitimately listen to fairy tales, other forms of popular culture are needed" (p. 157).

By applying psychoanalytic theory to the plotlines of contemporary soap operas, Livingstone and Liebes found that mother characters were positive influences in sons' lives, but were nonexistent for or psychologically distant from their daughters. In addition, marriage is often portrayed as an important goal for female characters (much less so for male characters), but the marriages most often turn out to be temporary and unsatisfying. Soap opera producers realize that what they offer viewers is a happily-ever-after fantasy, but they provide female characters who do not achieve that fantasy or who achieve it but don't get to keep it very long. The researchers found that in the soaps, as in prime-time programming, men play dominant roles and are portrayed as the center of women's existence. Even for career-oriented female characters, romances and families take precedence over jobs; they derive their identities from their relationships with male characters, and those relationships are seldom successful (Rogers, 2003). Soaps serve a therapeutic function for viewers, who can identify with the life experiences of the characters. But for the most part, soaps reinforce stereotypical gender roles that can be limiting to both men and women (Livingstone & Liebes, 1995).

Author Laura Stempel Mumford (2000) contends that a "paternity plot" drives most soap operas; the obsession with learning who is the father of whom communicates to mass audiences that fatherhood, not motherhood, is the key factor in a social realm. Rather than marriage and child-raising, questions of paternity are prevalent, as Mumford explains: "On the soaps, as in real life, paternity is more than a biological fact. It means inheritance of name and property, defines kinship patterns, and seems to carry the weight of loyalty, family traits, and even day-to-day behavior. The assimilation of all family members into the family of the father is so complete that, for example, a woman who marries into a family often takes on whatever traits are typical of the new family" (p. 253). Again, media and social critics are concerned about the power of such a pervasive form of programming to communicate gender roles and societal values.

From Phil to Oprah to Jerry

What do talk shows communicate to modern women and men? Are these shows examples of how men and women are supposed to talk to each other? (We *really* hope not.) Do these talk shows set an agenda for their viewers?

Since there are between 20 and 30 nationally syndicated daytime (and a few prime-time and late-night) talk shows on the air, the impact of these shows cannot be denied (Heaton & Wilson, 1995; Moorti, 2003). The original modern talk show, *The Phil Donahue Show*, and its revolutionary successor *The Oprah Winfrey Show*, provided a platform for discussions of women's issues (Shattuc, 1997; Stark, 2000b). Naomi Wolf, discussing the early effects of talk shows, noted, "That daily act of listening, whatever its shortcomings, made for a revolution in what women were willing to ask for; the shows daily conditioned otherwise unheard women into the belief that they were entitled to a voice" (as in Heaton & Wilson, p. 45). Even though there are still more female than male viewers because more women are at home during the day, the audience for talk shows expanded during the 1990s to include greater numbers of men. Some observers suggest that this may be related to the inclusion (and encouragement) of more conflict and controversy on such programs as *The Jerry Springer Show.*

Feminist media critic Roseann Mandziuk (1991) contends that talk shows seriously delimit gender boundaries. The intimate nature of talk programs corresponds with the cultural stereotype that women are supposed to be sensitive, nurturing, and responsive. This intimacy is exemplified by relationships among hosts, guests, and audiences, the camera close-ups of tearful guests who are commended for their brave emotional displays as they recount personal narratives on national television, the accessibility of some shows to people who telephone, and the occasional personal disclosure or reaction of the host. The format also reinforces women's existence, thus "genderizing" this programming. The spontaneity of discussion limited by interruptive commercial breaks mirrors the realities of women's multitask existence. And the fact that there's never enough time to give full treatment to any issue sends a message, primarily to women, that "conversation is never finished" and that "there is always more to be learned, always another talk show to seek out for information on another day" (Mandziuk, 1991, p. 13).

Mandziuk also suggests that talk shows, particularly those broadcast during the day, may actually instruct women what they should worry about; in other words, the programs serve an agenda-setting function. What are the possible ramifications of believing that "being a man trapped inside a woman's body" is one of the most critical issues facing contemporary women? While some topics may be deemed outlandish or trivial, such as a problem with a husband who likes to dress in women's lingerie or a girl who flirts with her sister's boyfriend, other topics may make some women wonder if they're supposed to be worried about these issues. A greater problem ensues when the larger general public "ghettoizes" important issues, such as reproductive rights, sexual harassment, and childcare, by labeling them women's issues rather than societal or human issues.

Heaton and Wilson (1995) suggest, "The very same stereotypes that have plagued both women and men for centuries are in full force. Instead of encouraging changes in sex roles, the shows actually solidify them" (p. 45). The men on these programs are certainly not God's gifts to womankind, and the women fare no better: "If there is a man for every offense, there is certainly a woman for every trauma. Most women on talk TV are perpetual victims presented as having so little power that not only do they have to contend with real dangers such as sexual or physical abuse, but they are also overcome by bad hair, big thighs, and beautiful but predatory 'other' women" (Heaton & Wilson, 1995, pp. 45–46).

Have you ever considered the instructive potential or the agenda-setting function of daytime talk shows? Perhaps you recall talking about particular shows in your college classes or in conversations with friends, dates, or your spouse. Have your perceptions about women and men—their gender roles and issues—been influenced by one of these talk shows?

Remember . . .

STEREOTYPE: A recurring depiction in the media that puts people into narrowly defined categories.

GENDER STEREOTYPES: Recurring depictions of men and women that place them in narrowly defined roles.

HEROIN CHIC: The term coined for the gaunt, unhealthy look of top fashion models in the 1990s and beyond.

POWER BABE COMMERCIALS: Ads that depict women objectifying men or enjoying having the upper hand over men.

RAMBO DEPICTION: A male stereotype in advertising, in which a man is depicted as a conquering hero.

HIMBO DEPICTION: A male stereotype in advertising, in which a man is depicted as a bumbling idiot or fool—a male bimbo.

TIME-SHIFTING: Using media technology to tape and watch cable and network programming when convenient.

BLACK-BOX TECHNOLOGY: Technology that expands the time frame in which a viewer can tape a show; viewers record onto the box itself, which has much greater storage capacity than traditional technologies.

MOCK-MACHO SITCOM: A television situation comedy with a central theme of mocking or making fun of a middle-aged man's anxieties.

PLAYFUL PATRIARCH: A male leading character in a sitcom who is typically a devoted husband and father, but who often goofs up and admits that he doesn't understand women.

SOCIAL ISSUES PROGRAMMING: A prime-time informational show that tackles a social or political issue.

LESSONS FROM THE BIG SCREEN: FILM AND GENDER

Here's an interesting exercise. Imagine that you have to put together a time capsule, a snapshot of American life representing your time on earth, something that future generations might stumble upon and use to better understand their heritage. No doubt you'd turn to media to help you fill the capsule; no doubt you'd include some movies. The question is: Which movies would you include and why? Another question: If only three movies would fit in the capsule, which three would you include? Would you include films from different genres, such as a western, a romance, and a horror movie? Would you include a classic like *Casablanca*, a futuristic film like *Star Wars*, or a movie that depicts your version of typical American life? It's interesting to share responses to this exercise (and it makes for good dinner conversation). But what's most intriguing is people's answers to this question: Why did you pick that movie? Responses tend to reveal people's value systems; people pick certain films so that things they care most about in life can be communicated to future generations. What would your choices say to future generations about your view of the sexes?

Gender in the Movies

Film has the power to communicate gender roles. It may not give blatant messages about the roles women and men play in society or about how we communicate in relationships, but the more subtle messages that we see and hear repeatedly are likely to sink in on some level and affect us. On the most basic level, if a subject is dramatized on the big screen, it's there for a reason; it has to be important, right? The potential effect on children is even greater, as evidenced by the significant impact of Disney films on kids (Matti & Lisosky, 1999). Research has found time and again how various forms of media, including film, affect children's views of themselves, how male and female characters are supposed to behave, who are the good guys and the bad guys, and so on (Hoerrner, 1996; Van Evra, 1990).

One phenomenon in film that stirs up a good deal of talk and controversy, not surprisingly, has to do with gender. Before we begin discussing that topic, here are a few questions for you to think about: Have you seen any movies that affected how you interact with members of the opposite sex, at work or in your social or family life? Was there a memorable movie that changed your views about women's and men's roles or that changed one of your relationships? Might it have been *Sleepless in Seattle*, *Titanic*, or *You've Got Mail*? (Or were those simply "date flicks"?) Can movies affect you in this way?

One for the Capsule

For the authors of this textbook, one such memorable, outlook-altering movie was *Tootsie*, a film that to this day conjures up confused but pleasant thoughts about gender roles. If you haven't seen this movie, rent it, but until then, here's a synopsis of the plot. Dustin Hoffman plays Michael, an actor who desperately wants work but whose opportunities are limited because he has a reputation for being difficult. When his agent tells Michael that no one will hire him, Michael sets out to prove him wrong by auditioning for a role in a popular soap opera. The twist is that the role is for a woman, so Michael auditions in drag as an actress named Dorothy Michaels. After landing the part, Michael encounters a number of sticky situations because of his hidden identity. The stickiest situation arises when Michael realizes that he's falling for Julie, another actress on the soap, played in the movie by Jessica Lange. As Michael (via Dorothy) becomes good friends with Julie, he is confronted with how to admit the deception and still have a chance with her.

One amazing aspect of this movie is how Dustin Hoffman's portrayal of Dorothy, through the character of Michael, becomes real to viewers, so real that when Michael reveals his true identity in one of the final scenes, audiences are sad because they are going to miss Dorothy. Another fascinating aspect of this movie was that it fulfilled a fantasy for many people—walking in the opposite sex's shoes, seeing how members of that sex are treated, and getting to know an attractive member of the opposite sex without the hang-ups and pressures that often accompany romantic relationships. It was also intriguing to think about the opportunity of putting one's newfound insight into the opposite sex to work in a relationship. As Michael explained to Julie in the last scene of the movie, "I was a better man with you, as a woman, than I ever was as a man. I've just got to learn to do it without the dress."

The film *Tootsie* frames the rest of our discussion nicely, because it exemplifies *gender bending*, a term referring to media depictions in which characters' actions belie or contradict what is expected of members of their sex. But our use of this term is not limited to people who have masqueraded in films as members of the opposite sex. The example of *Tootsie* serves to start our thinking, but gender bending doesn't necessarily imply actors in drag.

Buddies on a Dead-End Road

Thelma & Louise was a groundbreaking gender-bending film on many counts; one critic described it as "a butt-kicking feminist manifesto" (Schickel, 1991, p. 52). It was an open-road buddy film, but with female instead of male buddies (Glenn, 1992; Kroll, 1991). One of the most laudable effects of this film was that it sparked a great deal of discussion. In fact, it still sparks discussion. Although the film opened in May 1991, people still talk about it and media critics and scholars still write about it.

Few if any people who saw this film came out of theatres saying, "What a cute, funny little movie." Some people were outraged at what they considered an inappropriate level of violence in the film, although only one person gets shot. While the film contains violent images, critics maintained it had nowhere near the violence depicted in other films of the day. As one reporter explained, "The real source of the outrage was the fact that the violence was directed at men. [Susan] Sarandon (aka Louise) said that the controversy showed 'what a straight, white male world movies occupy. This kind of scrutiny didn't happen with that Schwarzenegger thing [*Total Recall*, 1990] where he shoots a woman in the head and says 'Consider that a divorce!' ' " (Bowers, 1997, p. 74)

Female audiences for this movie had complex emotions and varied reactions (Cooper, 2000). Some cheered what they perceived to be payback, especially in a scene with a piggish trucker and his rig. At the same time, many felt odd to be applauding revenge, as one film journalist explained: "For some, it allowed an understanding as to why some women remain in abusive relationships and some women snap. For others, it was terrifying to realize that they themselves were applauding violent retribution, at least for the moment, in the dark anonymity of the theater" (Hoffman, 1997, p. 69).

Besides the dominant images and "radical" behaviors of the female leads, the portrayal of male characters in *Thelma & Louise* was atypical for the movies. This portrayal led to claims of male-bashing, based on contentions that the male characters were unrealistic and exaggerated, particularly because they were repeatedly vanquished by the two women. One critic for the New York *Daily News* asserted that the movie justified violence, crime, and drunken driving and was "degrading to men, with pathetic stereotypes of testosterone-crazed behavior" (Johnson, as in Schickel, 1991, p. 52). Film researcher Robert Glenn (1992) suggests, "Feminists have perpetuated a behavioral definition of sexism that has been fictionalized and lampooned for more than a decade in films and television.

Thelma & Louise effectively reconstructs these identifiable caricatures in order to paint an extremely unflattering portrait of men as insensitive and ignorant savages who treat women as functional objects to be used and manipulated" (p. 12). From this viewpoint, the caricatures or overdrawn images of men in the film were created to further highlight the victimization of the two female characters.

What messages about women and men did audiences get from this movie? Some people came away thinking that women were winning some kind of war against male oppression, that they were retaliating against unacceptable male behavior in like fashion. This is a gender-bending message taken to an extreme. However, some film critics and feminist scholars, although they believe that *Thelma & Louise* made a significant statement about relationships between men and women in the 1990s, contend that it was not a triumphant women's rights movie. They point out that the film depicts the desperation of women in modern times—women who counter the powerlessness they feel with some very isolated, extreme actions, but who, in the long run, are still out of power in a patriarchal system (Klawans, 1991; Leo, 1991; Shapiro, 1991). This theme is epitomized by the ending (which we won't give away).

Gender Bending, Post-*Thelma & Louise*

A few movies have followed the trail blazed by *Thelma & Louise*. These include *A League of Their Own*, *Waiting to Exhale*, *The First Wives Club*, *Boys on the Side*, and *Blue Crush*, an all-girl surfing movie that opened in the summer of 2002. While none of these has a scene as violent as what occurs in the first half-hour of *Thelma & Louise*, all of them have female leads in tight-knit groups of friends who face difficult choices, experience disappointing relationships, and rebuild their lives. One movie of the late 1990s that fits the description gender-bending is *GI Jane*, in which a naval officer becomes the first woman admitted into the navy's Seal training program, one of the most challenging programs in the armed forces. The character rails against double standards—one set of standards for men and an easier set for women. She realizes she's a token player in a political game, but she is determined to set a precedent that women can succeed in such a program and make a valuable contribution in combat (Butler, 1997). Another gender-bending role, in some opinions, is Lara Croft in *Tomb Raider* (Solomon, 2001). This film, which grew out of a video game, depicts a no-nonsense female action hero battling her way through precarious situations—a role typically reserved for a Stallone, a Willis, or a Schwarzenegger.

Can you think of some gender-bending movies that depict men in non-stereotypical, non-drag roles? *Kramer vs. Kramer* and *Mr. Mom*, in the early 1980s could be examples of gender-bending films. In both films, the main male characters are fathers raising their children without a mother (In *Kramer*, the mother has left. In *Mr. Mom*, she had taken a lucrative full-time job). One of our favorite gender-bending movies is *Mrs. Doubtfire*—first, because we love Robin Williams; and second, because the movie was just great fun. This movie is a gender bender more because of its portrayal of fatherhood than because Williams dresses as a woman for much of it. Unlike Hoffman's character in *Tootsie*, Williams's character didn't take on a woman's persona for the purpose of gaining some empathy for womankind.

History documents the power of the media to make sweeping changes in a culture. Will other gender-bending films exploring these issues further appear in the twenty-first century and make a significant impact? This is unpredictable; but in any case, gender-bending movies challenge us to think further and deeper and in ways that may be new to us. They challenge us to take an inventory of our attitudes and expectations about women and men. They ask us to reconsider how we communicate with one another and how we derive pleasure out of our relationships.

THE COMMUNICATIVE POWER OF PORNOGRAPHY

We usually don't begin our coverage of a topic with a disclaimer or an apology, but this subject is different—*really* different. Pornography is a topic that continues to generate a great deal of research and writing, and there is no way we can do justice to that body of information in this short section. Many books and articles offer insightful analyses of the pervasiveness of pornography in modern life, its effects on how women and men are viewed in our culture, and its impact on everyday relationships. All we offer here is a snapshot—a highly condensed introduction to the topic—just to get you thinking about pornography, perhaps in a way you haven't thought before.

Multiple Definitions of Pornography: The Beginnings of Controversy

A specific, universally agreed-upon legal definition of pornography doesn't exist. In legal contexts, *obscenity* is the term used, but not all pornographic material meets the legal standard of obscenity (deGrazia, 1992; Tedford, 2001). Sometimes the term *erotica* is confused with pornography, although erotica pertains to material that portrays sex as an equal activity involving mutual sensual pleasure, not activity involving power or subordination (Crawford & Unger, 2000; Steinem, 1983). Strictly speaking, erotic material isn't pornographic, but material that some people deem pornographic may also contain erotica. (We told you this was a complicated topic.) Scholars have offered descriptions of what the term *pornography* might encompass, even tracing the term to its linguistic roots:

> Numerous attempts have been made to define pornography and to distinguish it from what some consider its more acceptable form—"erotica." The word pornography comes from the Greek "writings of prostitutes" (*porno* = prostitute and *graphein* = to write). In recent definitions, material has been classified as pornography when the producer's intent is to elicit erotic responses from the consumer, when it sexually arouses the consumer, or when women characters are degraded or demeaned. Pornography has been distinguished from erotica depending upon whether the material portrays unequal or equal power in sexual relations. (Malamuth & Billings, 1984, pp. 117–118)

Some people would take two elements from this definition—the phrases "intent to elicit erotic responses" and "sexually arouses the consumer"—and call them something other than pornography. In their minds, material that accomplishes these two purposes falls into the realm of erotica or sexual expression; it moves out of that realm and into pornography when it degrades or demeans people. But that can be a very fine line at times, can't it? If two people watch the same sexual scene in a film, for instance, one may find it sexually arousing while the other thinks the sexual activity is degrading—to the actors, to one sex or the other, or as a whole.

> *The difference between pornography and erotica is lighting.*
>
> —*Gloria Leonard, publisher, High Society magazine*

Catherine MacKinnon and Andrea Dworkin are prominent feminist activists on a variety of fronts, especially through their writings about the serious negative effects of pornographic images on women's lives and American culture in general. MacKinnon and Dworkin made one of the most tangible contributions to the antipornography effort to date by trying to get a civil rights bill, in the form of an antipornography ordinance, passed in Minnesota in the 1980s. The definition of pornography in this bill was written from the standpoint of women's victimization—understandably, given the very small numbers of men who are victimized in pornography. MacKinnon and Dworkin's definition is as follows:

> "Pornography" means the graphic sexually explicit subordination of women through pictures and/or words, including by electronic or other data retrieval systems, that also includes one of more of the following: (1) Women are presented dehumanized as sexual objects, things, or commodities. (2) Women are presented as sexual objects who enjoy humiliation or pain; or as sexual objects experiencing sexual pleasure in rape, incest, or other sexual assault; or as sexual objects tied up, cut up, mutilated, bruised, or physically hurt. (3) Women are presented in postures or positions of sexual submission, servility, or display. (4) Women's body parts—including but not limited to vaginas, breasts, or buttocks—are exhibited such that women are reduced to those parts. (5) Women are presented being penetrated by objects or animals. (6) Women are presented in scenarios of degradation, humiliation, injury, or torture, shown as filthy or inferior, bleeding, bruised, or hurt in a context that makes these conditions sexual. The use of men, children, or transsexuals in the place of women is also pornography for purposes of this law. (as in Gillespie et al., 1994, p. 44)

Representing another viewpoint is Nadine Strossen, author of the book *Defending Pornography: Free Speech, Sex, and the Fight for Women's Rights* (2000), and one of the most outspoken critics of antipornography efforts. In Strossen's view, "Pornography is a vague term. In short, it is sexual expression that is meant to, or does, provoke sexual arousal or desire" (p. 18). She goes on to critique other definitions: "In recent times, the word 'pornography' has assumed such negative connotations that it tends to be used as an epithet to describe—and con-demn—whatever sexually oriented expression the person using it dislikes. As one wit put it, 'What turns me on is erotica, but what turns you on is pornogra-phy!' " (p. 18). In her book, Strossen differentiates between pornography that is destructive and degrading and that which is merely sexually arousing. She still considers the latter pornography, but acceptable pornography.

Types of Readily Accessible Pornography

One other distinction in terminology is important before going further. *Hard-core pornography* depicts or describes intercourse and other sexual practices (e.g., oral sex, anal sex). In *soft-core pornography*, such acts are implied but not fully or ex-plicitly acted out on a screen or displayed on a page. According to Malamuth and Billings (1984), "both soft- and hard-core pornography present women as animalistic and in need of control. Women also are portrayed as easily accessi-ble objects intended for possession" (p. 122).

In the next few paragraphs, we present divergent viewpoints on pornogra-phy. But before doing so, we have some questions for you to consider: Before you dismiss or downplay this discussion because you don't believe yourself to be a consumer of pornography, think again. If you adopt a broad definition of pornography as material that provokes sexual desire, then what can be consid-ered pornographic takes on a much wider frame. For example, do you consider HBO's *Sex and the City* pornography? How about *Playboy* and *Penthouse* maga-zines? Are they somehow in a different, more acceptable category than *Hustler* magazine? If the depictions in *Playboy* are sexually arousing, do they qualify as pornographic? How about the swimsuit issue of *Sports Illustrated*? (Uh-oh, we've just tread on some sacred ground.) Believe it or not, there is considerable opin-ion that the swimsuit issue actually is soft-core porn, just packaged in a sports magazine to make it appear more socially acceptable (Davis, 1997). If you deem something pornographic because it contains images that exploit, objectify, and denigrate, then advertising images that we see every day in *Time*, *Vogue*, and *Es-quire* could be considered pornographic (Caputi, 2003). What about the stripping and dancing in so-called "gentleman's" clubs? Is this erotic, but not porno-graphic, even though it may be sexually arousing to the viewers?

We continue to go through this exact process in our own minds as we struggle to decide what should and should not be considered pornographic. Something might be pornographic, but does that necessarily make it harmful, degrading, and dangerous for society? Does pornography serve some useful purpose? We have our own personal answers to all these questions, but what's most important for our dis-cussion is this: Concerned adults must deal with these questions and others about pornography carefully and thoughtfully. Sexually explicit, arousing material is all around us and available for our consumption any hour of the day, especially as *cyberporn* on the Internet (Barak, Fisher, Belfry, & Lashambe, 1999; Goodson, McCormick, & Evans, 2000, 2001). What you consume, what you believe consent-ing adults have the right to consume, and what adults should protect children from consuming are very important decisions each individual should make.

Multiple Camps for a Complex Issue

As we've said, there are different ways of looking at the issue of pornography. One thing to remember is that the two main camps we discuss below aren't really opposing sides of the issue. You can be in more than one camp regarding pornography. The two main groups—antipornography and anticensorship—both talk about the topic of pornography, but they talk about it in very different ways. The antipornography people do not consider themselves pro-censorship; the anticensorship people do not consider themselves pro-pornography.

Voices from the Anti-Pornography Camp

Dworkin (1986), in an address before the Attorney General's Commission on Pornography, stated the following (be forewarned about the language and graphic descriptions):

> In this country where I live, every year millions and millions of pictures are being made of women with our legs spread. We are called beaver, we are called pussy, our genitals are tied up, they are pasted, makeup is put on them to make them pop out of a page at a male viewer. Millions and millions of pictures are made of us in postures of submission and sexual access so that our vaginas are exposed for penetration, our anuses are exposed for penetration, our throats are used as if they are genitals for penetration. In this country where I live as a citizen real rapes are on film and are being sold in the marketplace. And the major motif of pornography as a form of entertainment is that women are raped and violated and humiliated until we discover that we like it and at that point we ask for more. (p. 277)

Dworkin's descriptions may sound harsh, but many of us are shielded from such degrading images of women. Those images exist; they are readily consumed by people every day. In fact, pornography is a multibillion-dollar industry—some estimates place it at $10 billion a year (Peach, 1998; Steinem, 1997). Because of the pervasiveness and easy accessibility of the Internet, coupled with the slow responses of governments regarding the regulation of what appears in cyberspace, the porn industry is experiencing enormous success and profits. Researchers Fisher and Barak (2001) suggest: "Spectacular growth in availability of sexually explicit material on the Internet has created an unprecedented opportunity for individuals to have anonymous, cost-free, and unfettered access to an essentially unlimited range of sexually explicit texts, still and moving images, and audio materials" (p. 312).

Don't get the idea that Dworkin is in favor of censorship; she and MacKinnon believe that the pornography issue really has nothing to do with censorship—it has to do with respect (Dworkin, 2000). As Dworkin explains, "The mindset has to change. It's not a question of looking at a magazine and censoring the content. It's a matter of looking at the social reality, the subordination of women necessary to create the magazine, and the way that the magazine is then used in the world against women" (as in Gillespie et al., 1994, pp. 37, 38). Law professor Mari Matsuda commented about the censorship issue, in relation to pornography: "We need to get away from male-centered notions of free speech. We should say that pornography, sexual harassment, racist speech, gay-bashing, anti-Semitic speech—speech that assaults and excludes—is not the same as the forms of speech deserving protection. Why is it that pornography, which undermines women's equality, is singled out for absolute protection?" (as in *Pornography*, 1994, p. 42). Gloria Steinem (1997) takes a similar view; in an article responding to the film *The People vs. Larry Flynt*, she asked, "Why can feminists speak against everything from wars and presidents to tobacco companies, yet if we use our free speech against pornography, we are accused, in Orwellian fashion, of being against free speech?" (p. 76)

> *I would like to see all people who read pornography or have anything to do with it put in a mental hospital for observation so we could find out what we have done to them.*
>
> —*Linda Lovelace, actor in "adult" films*

Voices from the Anti-Censorship Camp

Strossen (2000) describes herself as a feminist who is "dedicated to securing equal rights for women and to combating women's continuing second-class citizenship in our society," but she "strongly opposes any effort to censor sexual expression" (p. 14). She and other activists believe that if you suppress women's sexuality, you actually oppress them. Strossen describes the position of many members of the anticensorship camp: "We are as committed as any other feminists to eradicating violence and discrimination against women. But we believe that suppressing sexual words and images will not advance these crucial causes. To the contrary, we are convinced that censoring sexual expression actually would do more harm than good to women's rights and safety" (p. 14). Performance artist Holly Hughes contends that being a consumer of pornography doesn't mean that "I'm going to go out and do everything I see. To be anticensorship doesn't mean that you are not offended. But the antidote to speech that you find disturbing is more speech" (as in *Pornography*, 1994, p. 43).

Author Sallie Tisdale (1992), in an article entitled "Talk Dirty to Me: A Woman's Taste for Pornography," provides an interesting personal glimpse into the anti-censorship view. She describes her journeys into adult video stores, the fear and discomfort she feels while selecting porn tapes, and the bashful way she later views these videos at home. She believes the tapes have educational value, that she learns a great deal about her own sexuality from them, and she's certainly not in favor of any efforts to censor her viewing pleasure. But she makes a distinction between viewing consensual sex in a video and viewing violence against women or degrading images of them. While we would not put Malamuth and Billings (1984) in the anti-censorship camp, they describe others' views that coincide with Tisdale's: "Some of those who see pornography as sexual communication interpret its function in light of consumers' needs. Accordingly, pornography affects only the realm of fantasy or provides desirable information often lacking in many people's sex education" (p. 118).

Where to Put Up Your Tent

If you're having trouble deciding which camp to align yourself with, you're not alone. Elements of both positions have merit, we realize. There are well-known, outspoken feminists who adopt what could be perceived as a middle position. One of these is Marilyn French, author of eight books including *The War Against Women* (1992). In a discussion in *Ms.* magazine, French admitted that she considered Dworkin and MacKinnon's ordinance against pornography a form of censorship. She suggested: "There may be some of us who would defend the First Amendment rather than see these [pornographic] magazines end—I'm one of them. But the problem is never, never going to be solved unless we start thinking about what this stuff means to men. You cannot make a movie or write a book that defends the practices of the Holocaust or that exalts black slavery. But you can make a movie, you can write a book that shows any kind of torture, enslavement, or murder of women. How come?" (as in Gillespie et al., 1994, p. 36)

The Crux of the Matter: Pornography Is Personal

We have two purposes in presenting this material on pornography to you: first, to help you better understand the complexities of the issue through a discussion of diverse viewpoints; and second, to challenge you to think about the impact of pornography in your own life. Now before you start to think, "Hey, don't accuse me of looking at that kind of stuff," we realize, as we've said before, that many of you reading this text think of pornography only in a hard-core sense and that you choose not to consume it. What concerns us more, as textbook writers and teachers of gender communication courses, is the subtle soft-core porn that permeates our existence, because even soft-core porn includes stereotyping of women as subordinate sex objects and men's playthings (Jensen, 1991).

The barrage of sexual images we consume daily—in song lyrics and music videos (as we explore in the final section of this chapter), television and film images, advertisements in magazines and newspapers, images in comic books, cartoon strips, and cyberspace—simply must have some effect. As research shows and our students consistently confirm for us, the amount and type of mediated sexual images we consume shape our views of the sexes and our behavior (Jansma, Linz, Mulac, & Imrich, 1997; Senn, 1993). In one study of undergraduates' reactions to pornographic videos, male students reported greater sexual arousal and enjoyment than female students; also, more male students than female students believed the videos to be acceptable and not degrading (Gardos & Mosher, 1999). In research that reviewed 46 studies (85 percent of which were done in the U.S.) conducted between 1962 and 1995 on the effects of pornography consumption, media scholars Oddone-Paolucci, Genuis, and Violato (2000) found evidence of a link between consumption of pornography and a propensity toward violence in relationships. Research has definitively documented a link between consuming degrading, powerless, hypersexualized images in pornography and engaging in abusive behavior toward others (Bergen, 2000; Malamuth, Addison, & Koss, 2000). Mediated messages really do affect how we believe we are supposed to behave toward one another, what we expect from each other in relationships (both platonic and romantic), how we communicate our desires and needs (especially in sexual situations), and how much respect we develop for ourselves and others.

Here's a concrete example; you might think it an extreme case, but it involves a male student, just like someone sitting in one of your classes. A few years ago, one of the TV newsmagazine shows did a story on a support group for users of pornography—a group of about 30 male students at Duke University that began as a small group of guys in a campus dorm having regular informal discussions about sex and the effects of pornography on their lives. The camera taped one of the weekly discussions, and the men's revelations were startlingly honest. Viewers at the time were shocked that pornography could so permeate these young men's lives, so debilitate their relationships with women and their feelings of self-esteem. One student's admission was particularly painful and memorable: he described a sexual encounter with a woman he was very interested in. They'd been out a couple of times but had not yet had sex. He was highly attracted to the woman and wanted to be intimate with her, but when the opportunity to have sex with her arrived, to his embarrassment he was unable to become aroused and get an erection. He then explained how he enabled himself to function in the situation by imagining the woman beneath him as a pornographic image of a woman from a magazine. Only when he shut his eyes, tuned out the real person he was with, and vividly imagined the graphic magazine picture did he become aroused. He was worried that this suggested his sexual future—that he was doomed to a life of being aroused not by real people but by mediated images—and also mortified by his impersonal, distant behavior with the woman. He could not continue the relationship after this experience and had had no other sexual encounters at the time the group met.

What's your reaction to this story? Do you know people who seem to be more comfortable with pornography than with real lovers or their own sexuality? Should sexual fantasy and reality blend, rather than exist as separate entities that inhibit one's ability to function? We worry on a macro or societal level about how pornographic images—hard- and soft-core—harm women and men, how they keep women "in their place," as sexualized commodities to be purchased and used for gratification, and how they add to the pressure men feel to be sexual performers. But we worry more on a micro level; we worry about people like these students at Duke who might now be considered sex addicts. We wonder how some men can say that they respect their wives when they regularly frequent strip clubs or adult film houses, become aroused by the dancers or images, and then come home wanting to have sex with their wives. What's the role of pornography in these men's lives? And we cannot help but believe (as the research documents) that the enormous problem of violence, such as date rape and sexual assault, in romantic situations is connected to the all-pervasive pornography, ready and waiting for your consumption.

> ## Remember . . .
>
> **GENDER BENDING:** A media depiction in which a character's actions belie or contradict what is expected for members of her or his sex.
>
> **OBSCENITY:** The legal term used in reference to pornographic material.
>
> **EROTICA:** Material that portrays sex as an equal activity involving mutual sensual pleasure, not power or subordination.
>
> **PORNOGRAPHY:** Material produced with an intent to elicit erotic responses from a consumer, to sexually arouse a consumer, to degrade or demean women characters in a sexual manner, or to portray unequal power in sexual activity.
>
> **HARD-CORE PORNOGRAPHY:** Material that depicts or describes intercourse and other sexual practices (e.g., oral sex, anal sex).
>
> **SOFT-CORE PORNOGRAPHY:** Material in which sexual acts are implied but not fully or explicitly acted out or portrayed.

WE COULD MAKE BEAUTIFUL MUSIC TOGETHER. . .

Music is a powerful force in our culture; its influence pervades our existence. In this final section of the chapter, we examine how song lyrics and music videos communicate images of men and women.

From Pop to Rock to Rap to Country: The Women and Men of Song Lyrics

Sometimes when you listen to a song you want to concentrate on the lyrics; you attend to the words from a more critical standpoint. But at other times you simply like the rhythm, beat, and musical performance, so you tune out the lyrics. Have you ever read the lyrics to a particular song and said to yourself, "Oh *that's* what they're saying"? This is much easier to do nowadays, because full transcripts of words often accompany CDs. Sometimes, however, you find yourself humming or singing along with a song on the radio or on a favorite CD when you suddenly realize what the words really are. You become acutely aware that what you're singing with or listening to isn't something you'd like to repeat in *any* company, especially mixed company.

There are just about as many ways to process music as there are people who listen to it. But consider the possibility that music, specifically song lyrics depicting the sexes, may have more impact on you than you realize. In reporting his research about the content and impact of song lyrics, music scholar Peter Christenson (1993) contends, "Even though the 'message' of popular music resides as much in its 'sound' as in its words, and even though lyrics are often—perhaps usually— ignored during the listening process, the words matter" (p. 2). The repetition of songs in a typical radio day and on CDs is likely to reinforce the lyrics in listeners' psyches. What do these lyrics communicate about women and men?

Gender Trends in Lyrics

Research over the past few decades has found some interesting trends in gender and song lyrics. In the 1970s, scholars Freudiger and Almquist (1978) examined images and gender-role depictions of men and women in song lyrics in three genres of popular music. They reviewed the top 50 hits on *Billboard's* charts for country, soul, and easy listening and found, first, that women more than men were the focus of lyrics across all three genres. Second, women were rarely criticized and were most often positively portrayed in these lyrics, but they were described primarily as stereotypes: submissive, supportive, and dependent. In contrast, when men were mentioned in lyrics—especially in songs written from a female perspective—they were portrayed in a more negative and critical light, especially in country music. Men's depictions also reflected stereotypical traits: aggression, consistency, action, and confidence.

In the 1980s, studies identified stereotypical portrayals of women in American popular music, portrayals that are still prevalent today. Communication scholars Butruille and Taylor (1987) detected "three recurring images of women: The Ideal Woman/Madonna/Saint, the evil or fickle Witch/Sinner/Whore, and the victim (often dead)" (p. 180). Some of these images date back to early religious customs and beliefs about the sinful versus virginal nature of woman. As communication researcher Janet Wyman (1993) suggests, "The virgin/whore dichotomy is destructive to women not only because it polarizes, and thus limits their sexual identity, but because neither category is particularly flattering. The virgin/whore dichotomy stifles the social power of women since both the virgin and the whore are in powerless positions" (pp. 6–7). Interestingly enough, one explanation for the popularity of the late Tejano singer Selena was her ability to combine saint and sinner, meaning that she presented a sexual, sensual image through dress and demeanor along with a "good girl" quality and a strong connection to family (Willis & Gonzalez, 1997).

One trend in the 1990s and later has been female artists' lyrics describing difficult choices, abusive situations, and destructive relationships (Sellnow, 1999). While some scholars contend that women's music is just as focused on romantic relationships as it has always been, others believe that the newer women's bold representations of brutality and degradation they've experienced in relationships communicate an unprecedented honesty. For example, Alicia Keys' "Fallin'" describes a woman who keeps falling in love with a man who isn't good for her, Liz Phair's "Johnny Feelgood" is about a woman's obsession with an abusive man, Ani DiFranco's "Lost Woman Song" asserts a woman's right to an abortion, and Tori Amos' "Silent All These Years" and Fiona Apple's "Sullen Girl" describe recovery after rape (Browne, 1998; Farley, 1997; Papazian, 1996; Perry, 2003). In a study of violence in relationships conveyed in song lyrics, media scholar Jennifer Maxwell (2001) found that subjects who reported having experienced multiple forms of abuse in their lives interpreted lyrics to a particular song (Natalie Merchant's "I May Know the Word") literally. They believed that the song was a literal representation of sexual assault, rape, and battering. By contrast, subjects who had not experienced abuse interpreted the song in a more abstract way, as a depiction of conflict

Women are really empowering themselves in politics and in every facet of life now. Music tends to represent what's going on with youth, and the youth of America felt really frustrated a few years ago, and you had these angry alterna-bands. Now you have a lot of females who are stepping up to represent women in America or women in the world, becoming role models for young girls.

—*Sheryl Crow, singer and songwriter*

over decision making in a relationship. The experiences we have in life definitely affect how we respond to and interpret song lyrics.

Sex and Degradation in Songs

Christenson (1993) explored similarities and differences in the way men and women are depicted in song lyrics. He suggests that both sexes are often portrayed as emotional and dependent, because of "the natural tendency of popular music songs, no matter who is singing them, to take on a sad, bittersweet tone" (p. 15). But he does see persistent gender stereotypes, particularly in negative depictions of women in popular music. His comparison of sexual imagery in songs by the Rolling Stones, Donna Summer, and Marvin Gaye with imagery in the songs of such groups of the 1980s and 1990s as 2 Live Crew, Motley Crüe, and Guns 'n' Roses revealed a trend toward more explicit and graphic representations of sexual activity and more dramatically degrading images of and actions toward women.

Scholars of pop culture in the 1980s asserted that of all forms of popular music, rock provided the most derogatory, sexist images of women (Harding & Nett, 1984). However, in the view of many, rap and hip-hop have overtaken rock as the most misogynistic forms (hooks, 1992, 1994; Leland, 1992; Wood, 1998). Although some rap and hip-hop artists focus on racial and political issues and attempt to show positive images of relationships in their music, other artists are notorious for their depictions of men as all-powerful aggressors and women as virtual sex slaves (Krohn & Suazo, 1995). Lyrics penned and performed by the controversial Eminem have contributed to the view that rap and hip-hop are inherently anti-woman. A study of listeners' reactions to music revealed that subjects believed sexually explicit rap music to be more patently offensive than sexually explicit non-rap music (Dixon & Linz, 1997). The researchers suggest that because rap artists tend not to use "softening strategies" (such as poor pronunciation of offensive words, excessively loud music to muffle explicit language, and double entendres to soften offensive ideas), the rap songs used in the study may have seemed more blatantly offensive when compared with non-rap songs (p. 234). Some of the lyrics depicting men as brutal terrorizers and users of women communicate skewed, nonrepresentative images that do nothing to improve relationships between the sexes.

Free-lance music critic Jeff Niesel (1997) offers a helpful distinction to avoid labeling all rap and hip-hop as woman-hating. He distinguishes alternative rap from gangsta rap:

> When I first started listening to rap music in the early 1990s, I found that the gender paradigms presented there had more in common with David Lee Roth and the masculine posturing of male athletes. . . their macho attitudes were often alienating and presented views of women with which I could not identify. Shortly afterward, I realized that there was an alternative to gangsta rap. These artists, by blurring the boundaries between male and female and between black and white, they suggested that for political activism to be truly successful, coalitions must be built across the lines that divide people according to race, gender, and class. For "alternative" rappers, rap music had the most potential of any music to inspire social change, and, unlike gangsta rappers who separated racism and poverty from sexism, alternative rappers explicitly included women, demonstrating that for their work to be considered effectively political, race activists need to include rather than exclude feminists. (pp. 240–241)

Some scholars believe that the most productive site for activism, particularly for accomplishing societal change in terms of gender equality, is the youth music culture (Heywood & Drake, 1997).

It's interesting to consider what effects song lyrics have on your perceptions or expectations of members of your sex and the opposite sex. If you can easily remember the lyrics to a popular song (as opposed to formulas for your math exam), it's clear that they're permeating your consciousness on some level. So while we might not regulate our relationships according to what we hear in song lyrics, those lyrics do affect all of us in some way. Do you think your own attitudes and gender communication can be shaped or affected by the messages contained in song lyrics? What about the effects of graphically violent and sexually explicit messages on noncritical consumers, such as adolescents and children? Can children actually learn brutality through music? We can agree that music is not the sole or primary socializing agent of children, but it's safe to say that along with the violent, degrading images children see in other forms of media, some popular music contributes to the problem. Popular music can also be a constructive force—an energizing impetus for positive change.

Sex Kittens and He-Men in Music Videos

What happens when visual images in music videos reinforce the messages of song lyrics? As one researcher put it, "Music videos are more than a fad, more than fodder for spare hours and dollars of young consumers. They are pioneers in video expression, and the results of their reshaping of the form extend far be-yond the TV set" (Aufderheide, 1986, p. 57). Since MTV went on the air in 1981 and quickly infiltrated American households, the music video industry has sky-rocketed (Vivian, 2003). So have profits in the music industry—an industry that wasn't floundering but wasn't booming either before the innovation of music video. Nowadays the music video industry has sparked so much attention and has become such a vehicle for boosting sales that artists feel compelled to create and market videos to accompany their songs.

Gender and Race in Music Video

As media scholar Joe Gow (1996) explains, although music video has been praised for its innovativeness, it has also been criticized for its stereotypical depictions of relationships between women and men and between people of different racial groups. In fact, not too long after music video was introduced into this country (having first emerged in Europe in the 1970s), researchers be-gan to investigate the extent of gender and ethnic stereotyping in music videos (Peterson, 1987; Seidman, 1992; Sherman & Dominick, 1986).

In music videos of the 1980s, women were predominantly depicted as deco-rations and sex objects; female artists such as Tina Turner and Madonna most of-ten portrayed themselves in seductive clothing and situations in their videos (Vincent, 1989). Media specialists Brown and Campbell (1986) assessed race and sex differences in music videos on MTV and *Video Soul*, a program broadcast by the cable channel Black Entertainment Television. They found "indications of per-sistent stereotypes of women as less active, less goal-directed, and less worthy of attention" (p. 101). Black and white women were significantly less often portrayed in professional settings in comparison with men of these races, a finding corrob-orated by subsequent research (Seidman, 1992; White, 2000). Brown and Camp-bell concluded, "White men, primarily by virtue of their greater numbers, are the center of attention and power and are more often aggressive and hostile than help-ful and cooperative. Women and blacks are rarely important enough to be a part of the foreground" (p. 104). Media researchers Sherman and Dominick (1986) had similar results; they concluded, "Music television is a predominantly white and male world. Men outnumber women by two to one" (p. 84).

Research in the 1990s found little evidence of increased equity in music videos. An analysis of 40 music videos regularly broadcast on MTV produced the following results:

1. Men appeared in videos twice as often as women.
2. Men were significantly more aggressive and dominant in their behavior than women.
3. Women were highly sexual as well as subservient in their behavior.
4. Women were often targets of explicit and aggressive sexual advances (Sommers-Flanagan, Sommers-Flanagan, & Davis, 1993).

A study of the 100 most popular MTV videos of the early 1990s produced more bad news for women (Gow, 1996). In these videos, five times as many men as women held lead roles. Women most often appeared performing their music for the camera or dancing while lip-synching a song, suggesting that, in contrast to men's musical talent, women's appearance, sexiness, and physical talents were more important or emphasized. Men were most often shown performing in earnest in recording studios or on sound stages, but they also held several other lead roles, in comparison with the narrow range of roles for women. Perhaps you have seen the documentary film *Dreamworlds: Desire/Sex/Power in Rock Video*, by Sut Jhally (1990), which explores music video's hypersexualized images of women. In many videos, especially rock videos, women appear as mere sex objects designed to please men—as "legs in high heels," according to Jhally.

On a more positive note, an interesting study of country music video showed a progression in the way female country music stars are depicted (Andsager & Roe, 1999). Male country artists outnumber female country artists by three to one, and female artists still do not have the same status as their male counterparts. However, the enormous success of such women as Shania Twain, Mary Chapin Carpenter, and LeAnn Rimes led the country music industry to declare 1997 the "Year of the Woman." Also, music videos by female artists portrayed women more progressively and less stereotypically. As they gain popularity and economic success, female artists are able to assume more control over the content of their videos; thus, more positive, current, and well-integrated portrayals emerge. In contrast, the study found that music videos by male country artists continued to include many of the same female stereotypes as in past decades.

Images of women in hip-hop videos have shown some progress as well. Media scholar Imani Perry (2003) discusses early hip-hop videos, which contained many sexually objectifying and degrading images of women. Perry describes these images as "women dressed in swimsuits"; "scantily clad" women dancing in male artists' videos; "half-nude women"; women as "commodities," much like the property surrounding them (e.g., luxury cars, Rolex watches, diamond medallions); women as "vacuous, doing nothing but swaying around seductively, their eyes averted from the camera, thereby allowing the viewer to have a voyeuristic relationship to them"; and clear references to the "culture of strip clubs and pornography," in that "women dance around poles" and "porn actresses and exotic dancers are often featured in the videos" (pp. 137–138).

However, Perry detects a change in the video imagery, which she attributes to feminist music artists who have broken new ground. Feminists have had a presence in hip-hop music since the 1980s—examples include Salt 'n Pepa and Queen Latifah—but many more female artists have emerged to carry the torch of respectability and equality. Among the numerous feminist artists and groups releasing antisexist hip-hop songs are Mary J. Blige, Lauryn Hill, Destiny's Child, Missy Elliot, Erykah Badu, Alicia Keys, and India.Arie. Perry cites India.Arie's early hit song and video, entitled "Video," in which Arie critiques the type of women typically appearing in music videos. Perry contends that there is a difference between presenting oneself as a sexual object, there for the pleasure of others, and presenting oneself as a sexual subject, a sexual human being worthy of respect. She also acknowledges "tension between texts" meaning that for every feminist hip-hop artist there is someone like Lil Kim, whom Perry

---

'Net Notes

Here's a hip-hop music Website that focuses on the cultural contributions of female artists:

www.b-gyrl.com. The site is primarily about music, but it also offers links to articles on authors, activists, and entrepreneurs who are trying to effect social change.

---

describes as a "master of shock appeal" (pp. 140, 141). One conclusion we might reach is that the genre of hip-hop music is in transition—at least as far as female artists are concerned—with all the inconsistencies of an entity experiencing growing pains.

Is Seeing Believing or Is Hearing Believing?

Do music videos have an impact beyond that of song lyrics? Media scholar Roger Desmond (1987) points out that "Music videos, with their capacity for both verbal and visual coding, and their tendency to dramatize the themes of lyrics, do add a potential for learning and arousal beyond the realm of music lyrics" (p. 282). While disagreement exists as to the exact added effects of visual images produced by music videos, there is considerable agreement that the combined visual and auditory channels have profound effects on memory and recall. And for some observers, this is a real concern when the lyrics and accompanying video images are sexist, racist, violent, and degrading. Calling it a "concern" is an understatement for many feminists, who believe that music videos and degrading song lyrics the music industry regularly distributes and profits from are among the most serious contributors to women's lower status and violence against women in our culture. If you think this is an exaggeration, consider the results of some recent research: one study found that exposure to sexual imagery in music videos was linked to an acceptance of interpersonal violence; people who enjoyed and absorbed sexual images in videos were more likely to believe that certain forms of violence in relationships, such as sexual intimidation and assault, were acceptable (Kalof, 1999).

Media scholar Susan Douglas (1995b), whose work we discussed in the section on prime-time television, describes her concerns about music video and its effects on future generations:

> What will be dramatically different for my little girl is that she will be less sheltered from images of violence against women than I was. Now the actual or threatened violation of women permeates the airwaves and is especially rampant on a channel like MTV. The MTV that initially brought us Culture Club, "Beat It," and Cyndi Lauper switched, under the influence of market research, to one of the most relentless showcases of misogyny in America. If MTV is still around in ten years, and if its images don't change much, my daughter will see

woman after woman tied up, strapped down, or on her knees in front of some strutting male hominid, begging to service him forever. These women are either garter-belt-clad nymphomaniacs or whip-wielding, castrating bitches: they all have long, red fingernails, huge breasts, buns of steel, and no brains; they adore sunken-chested, sickly looking boys with very big guitars. Worse, they either want to be or deserve to be violated. Anyone who doesn't think such representations matter hasn't read any headlines recently recounting the hostility with which all too many adolescent boys treat girls, or their eagerness to act on such hostilities, especially when they're in groups with names like Spur Posse. (pp. 302–303)

Music video is a pervasive form of media, particularly in the lives of young people. However, it is not as pervasive or intrusive into your day as music that you hear on the radio as you're driving to class or to work, or that you turn on instantly when you walk through the door of your dorm room or home. Turning on the television or tuning in to music videos implies more conscious choice and action than merely listening to background music. But think for a moment about the whole effect—the very powerful effect of combining visual images with musical sound, a beat, and lyrics. Whether or not you actually watch every second of the average three-minute music video or really attend to the lyrics of a song, you still receive the message. Somewhere your brain is processing the information, sometimes on a conscious level but usually on a subconscious level.

Do you think that taking in so many stereotypical, sexist messages has some effect on you? We encourage you to think about how the music you listen to and the videos you watch (if you watch them) affect your view of self, your attitudes about sex roles in society, the expectations you form (especially regarding members of the opposite sex), and your gender communication within relationships.

CONCLUSION

You may not feel that you have reached the status of a media expert, but we suspect that you know more about the forms of media that surround you every day than you did before you read this chapter. When you think about the many media outlets and methods that have the potential to influence you, you may feel almost overwhelmed. But your knowledge can empower you to better understand the effects of media messages about gender. We hope that you not only have more knowledge about mass communication, but that you are able to more critically assess the role media play in your life. That critical assessment enables you to make thoughtful choices about just how much you will allow the media to affect you.

Think about whether you have some standards for romantic relationships and where those standards came from. Do your expectations reflect romance as portrayed in movies or between characters on television? When you think about communication between marital partners, do you think about your parents, your married friends, or married characters on soap operas or prime-time television shows? If you were to describe a relationship or use it as an example, would you mention a couple from real life or a couple shown brawling on some talk show? Now that you're more aware of the wide range of mediated images that could be considered pornographic, do you think any of those readily accessible images have affected your expectations about relationships?

When you're feeling down, are there certain songs and musical artists that either help you feel your pain more fully or help raise your spirits? Have you ever watched TV characters go through some trauma, such as the death of a loved one, an angry exchange between friends, or the breakup of an important relationship, and then later used the characters' dialogue about the experience in your own life? We encourage you to take more opportunities to consciously decipher media influence, particularly in reference to gender communication. The more you understand what's influencing you, the more ready you'll be to dive into new relationships or to strengthen your existing ones.

Discussion Starters

1. When your favorite magazine arrives at your door or when you decide to buy the newest issue at a store, don't plunge into it right away. Try this exercise first: Thumb through the magazine, paying special attention to the advertisements. How many ads depict members of your sex? How many depict members of the opposite sex? Analyze an ad the way we analyzed the billboard showing a woman on the beer bottle. Do you see the ad in a different light after having analyzed it in this manner? What does the ad communicate about gender?

2. What's your favorite prime-time television show? Think of several reasons why this show is your favorite. Do your reasons have to do mostly with the characters, the setting or scenery, the plotlines, or something else? Now think about a prime-time television show that you watched and hated. What was so irritating about that show? Are there any gender issues affecting your decision about your favorite and least favorite TV shows?

3. After having read the section in this chapter about talk shows, try to watch one or record one on videotape. What issue is being discussed on the talk show? Is the host of the talk show a man or a woman? Do you think the sex of the host makes a difference? Would an opposite-sex host have put a different spin on the topic of the particular show you watched? If so, why? Can you see the agenda-setting function of media at work in this talk show?

4. Have your views on pornography changed at all as a result of the information in this chapter? Think about the different definitions of pornography and then think about media you consume—magazine ads, television shows, films, music videos. How much of these media could be classified pornographic? What role, if any, has pornography played in your developing understanding of gender?

5. Assess your music collection. Who do you listen to—predominantly artists of the same sex as you or of the opposite sex? If there's a pattern, why do you think the pattern exists? Then pick one CD or cassette tape and play the cut on it that you are the least familiar with. Listen carefully and try to take in every word of the lyrics. Did you hear anything for the first time? Did you realize that this song was actually on this tape?

6. Think about the most sexist music video you've ever seen. What makes this video memorable? Was it sexist toward men, women, or both? How was sexism conveyed in the video? Who was the artist? What do you think the connection is between the artist and the sexism inherent in the video?

References

Andsager, J. L., & Roe, K. (1999). Country music video in country's Year of the Woman. *Journal of Communication, 49,* 69–82.

Artz, N., Munger, J., & Purdy, W. (1999). Gender issues in advertising language. *Women & Language, 22,* 20–26.

Aufderheide, P. (1986). Music videos: The look of sound. *Journal of Communication, 36,* 57–77.

Baker Woods, G. (1995). *Advertising and marketing to the new majority.* Belmont, CA: Wadsworth.

Barak, A., Fisher, W. A., Belfry, S., & Lashambe, D. R. (1999). Sex, guys, and cyberspace: Effects of Internet pornography and individual differences on men's attitudes toward women. *Journal of Psychology & Human Sexuality, 11,* 63–91.

Barner, M. R. (1999). Gender stereotyping and intended audience age: An analysis of children's educational/informational TV programming. *Communication Research Reports, 16,* 193–202.

Bergen, R. K. (2000). Exploring the connection between pornography and sexual violence. *Violence & Victims, 15,* 227–234.

Bittner, J. R. (1989). *Mass communication: An introduction* (5th ed.). Englewood Cliffs, NJ: Prentice Hall.

Bowers, M. (1997, May 23). *Thelma & Louise* debuts. *Entertainment Weekly,* 74.

Bramlett-Solomon, S. (2001, October). *Rarely there but redefining beauty? Black women in fashion magazine ads.* Paper presented at the meeting of the Organization for the Study of Communication, Language, and Gender, San Diego, CA.

Brown, J. D., & Campbell, K. (1986). Race and gender in music videos: The same beat but a different drummer. *Journal of Communication, 36,* 94–106.

Browne, B. A. (1998). Gender stereotypes in advertising on children's television in the 1990s: A cross-national analysis. *Journal of Advertising, 27,* 83–96.

Browne, D. (1998, August 14). Modern maturity. *Entertainment Weekly,* 78–79.

Butsch, R. (2003). Ralph, Fred, Archie, and Homer: Why television keeps re-creating the white male working-class buffoon. In G. Dines & J. M. Humez (Eds.), *Gender, race, and class in media* (2nd ed.) (pp. 575–585). Thousand Oaks, CA: Sage.

Butler, R. W. (1997, August 24). Films hold misogyny to light. *Corpus Christi Caller Times,* p. F5.

Butruille, S. G., & Taylor, A. (1987). Women in American popular song. In L. P. Stewart & S. Ting-Toomey (Eds.), *Communication, gender, and sex roles in diverse interaction contexts* (pp. 179–188). Norwood, NJ: Ablex.

Cagle, J. (1998, May 8). As gay as it gets? *Entertainment Weekly,* 26–32.

Calloway-Thomas, C., Cooper, P. J., & Blake, C. (1999). *Intercultural communication: Roots and routes.* Boston: Allyn & Bacon.

Campbell, R., Martin, C. R., & Fabos, B. (2003). *Media and culture: An introduction to mass communication* (updated 3rd ed.). Boston: Bedford/St. Martin's.

Caputi, J. (2003). Everyday pornography. In G. Dines & J. M. Humez (Eds.), *Gender, race, and class in media* (2nd ed.) (pp. 434–450). Thousand Oaks, CA: Sage.

Christenson, P. G. (1993, February). *The content of popular music.* Paper presented at the meeting of the Western States Communication Association, Albuquerque, NM.

Christenson, P. G. (1994). Childhood patterns of music uses and preferences. *Communication Reports, 7,* 136–144.

Clark, K. R. (1993, January 6). Role models. *Dallas Morning News,* pp. 5C, 14C.

Cooper, B. (2000). "Chick flicks" as feminist texts: The appropriation of the male gaze in *Thelma & Louise. Women's Studies in Communication, 23,* 277–306.

Cortese, A. J. (1999). *Provocateur: Images of women and minorities in advertising.* Lanham, MD: Rowman & Littlefield.

Cottle, M. (2003). Turning boys into girls. In A. Alexander & J. Hanson (Eds.), *Taking sides: Clashing views on controversial issues in mass media and society* (7th ed.) (pp. 68–74). Guilford, CT: McGraw-Hill/Dushkin.

Courtney, A. E., & Whipple, T. W. (1974). Women in TV commercials. *Journal of Communication, 24,* 110–118.

Courtney, A. E., & Whipple, T. W. (1983). *Sex stereotyping in advertising.* Lexington, MA: Lexington Press.

Craig, R. S. (1992, October). *Selling masculinities, selling femininities: Multiple genders and the economics of television.* Paper presented at the meeting of the Speech Communication Association, Chicago, IL.

Crawford, M., & Unger, R. (2000). *Women and gender: A feminist psychology* (3rd ed.). New York: McGraw-Hill.

Davis, L. R. (1997). *The swimsuit issue and sport: Hegemonic masculinity in Sports Illustrated.* Albany: State University of New York Press.

deGrazia, E. (1992). *Girls lean back everywhere: The law of obscenity and the assault on genius.* New York: Random House.

Desmond, R. J. (1987). Adolescents and music lyrics: Implications of a cognitive perspective. *Communication Quarterly, 35,* 276–284.

Dixon, T. L., & Linz, D. G. (1997). Obscenity law and sexually explicit rap music: Understanding the effects of sex, attitudes, and beliefs. *Journal of Applied Communication Research, 25,* 217–241.

Dobosz, A. M. (1997, November-December). Thicker thighs by Thanksgiving. *Ms.,* 89–91.

Douglas, S. J. (1995a). Sitcom women: We've come a long way. Maybe. *Ms.,* 76–80.

Douglas, S. J. (1995b). *Where the girls are: Growing up female with the mass media.* New York: Random House.

Douglas, S. J. (2000). Signs of intelligent life on TV. In S. Maasik & J. Solomon (Eds.), *Signs of life in the U.S.A.: Readings on popular culture for writers* (pp. 260–264). Boston: Bedford/St. Martin's.

Dow, B. J. (1996). *Prime-time feminism: Television, media culture, and the Women's Movement since 1970.* Philadelphia: University of Pennsylvania Press.

Dworkin, A. (1986). Pornography is a civil rights issue. In A. Dworkin (Ed.) (1993), *Letters from a war zone.* Brooklyn, NY: Lawrence Hill.

Dworkin, A. (2000). Against the male flood: Censorship, pornography, and equality. In D. Cornell (Ed.), *Feminism & pornography* (pp. 19–38). New York: Oxford University Press.

Elasmar, M., Hasegawa, K., & Brain, M. (1999). The portrayal of women in U.S. primetime television. *Journal of Broadcasting & Electronic Media, 44,* 20–34.

Elber, L. (2002, May 19). TV's romance with "Ally" comes to a welcomed end. Associated Press, as reported in *Corpus Christi Caller Times,* p. D5.

Faludi, S. (1991). *Backlash: The undeclared war against American women.* New York: Crown.

Farley, C. J. (1997, July 21). Galapalooza! Lilith Fair—a traveling festival featuring female folk-pop stars—is rocking the music world. *Time,* 60–64.

Fisher, W. A., & Barak, A. (2001). Internet pornography: A social psychological perspective on Internet sexuality. *Journal of Sex Research, 38,* 312–323.

French, M. (1992). *The war against women.* New York: Summit.

Freud Loewenstein, A. (1993, November-December). Sister from another planet probes the soaps. *Ms.,* 76–79.

Freudiger, P., & Almquist, E. M. (1978). Male and female roles in the lyrics of three genres of contemporary music. *Sex Roles, 4*, 51–65.

Gardos, P. S., & Mosher, D. L. (1999). Gender differences in reactions to viewing pornographic vignettes: Essential or interpretive? *Journal of Psychology & Human Sexuality, 11*, 65–83.

Garfield, B. (1999, February 1). Chauvinist pigskin: Ad Review—Superbowl advertisers set the world back 30 years with naked appeals to guys. *Advertising Age, 1*.

Garner, A., Sterk, H. M., & Adams, S. (1998). Narrative analysis of sexual etiquette in teenage magazines. *Journal of Communication, 48*, 59–78.

Gerbner, G. (2003). Television violence at a time of turmoil and terror. In G. Dines & J. M. Humez (Eds.), *Gender, race, and class in media* (2nd ed.) (pp. 339–348). Thousand Oaks, CA: Sage.

Gerbner, G., Gross, L., Eleey, M. F., Jackson-Beeck, M., Jeffries-Fox, S., & Signorielli, N. (1977). TV violence profile no. 8: The highlights. *Journal of Communication, 27*, 171–180.

Gerbner, G., Gross, L., Morgan, M., & Signorielli, N. (1980). The "mainstreaming" of America: Violence profile no. 11. *Journal of Communication, 30*, 10–29.

Gilbert, M. (2001, July 1). Avoiding the soapbox: "Queer as Folk" presents an unapologetic celebration of life in all its varied forms. *The Boston Globe,* as reported in *Corpus Christi Caller Times,* p. J4.

Gillespie, M. A., Dworkin, A., Shange, N., Ramos, N., & French, M. (1994, January-February). Where do we stand on pornography? *Ms.,* 33–41.

Glenn, R. J., III. (1992, November). *Echoes of feminism on the big screen: A fantasy theme analysis of "Thelma & Louise."* Paper presented at the meeting of the Speech Communication Association, Chicago, IL.

Goldberg, R. (1998, November). If not now, when? *Premiere,* 86–88.

Goodson, P., McCormick, D., & Evans, A. (2000). Sex on the Internet: College students' emotional arousal when viewing sexually explicit materials on-line. *Journal of Sex Education and Therapy, 25*, 252–260.

Goodson, P., McCormick, D., & Evans, A. (2001). Searching for sexually explicit materials on the Internet: An exploratory study of college students' behavior and attitudes. *Archives of Sexual Behavior, 30*, 101–118.

Gow, J. (1996). Reconsidering gender roles on MTV: Depictions in the most popular music videos of the early 1990s. *Communication Reports, 9*, 151–161.

Greenberg, B. S., & Collette, L. (1997). The changing faces on TV: A demographic analysis of network television's new seasons, 1966–1992. *Journal of Broadcasting & Electronic Media, 41*, 1–13.

Hall, C., Iijima, C., & Crum, M. J. (1994). Women and "body-isms" in television beer commercials. *Sex Roles, 31*, 329–337.

Hanke, R. (1998). The "mock-macho" situation comedy: Hegemonic masculinity and its reiteration. *Western Journal of Communication, 62*, 74–93.

Harding, D., & Nett, E. (1984). Women and rock music. *Atlantis, 10*, 60–77.

Hart, K-P. R. (2003). Representing gay men on American television. In G. Dines & J. M. Humez (Eds.), *Gender, race, and class in media* (2nd ed.) (pp. 507–607). Thousand Oaks, CA: Sage.

Harwood, J., & Anderson, K. (2002). The presence and portrayal of social groups on prime-time television. *Communication Reports, 15*, 81–97.

Hayward, J. (1997). *Consuming pleasures: Active audiences and serial fictions from Dickens to soap opera.* Lexington: University of Kentucky Press.

Hayward, J. (2003). Consuming pleasures: Active audiences and soap opera. In G. Dines & J. M. Humez (Eds.), *Gender, race, and class in media* (2nd ed.) (pp. 507–521). Thousand Oaks, CA: Sage.

Heaton, J. A., & Wilson, N. L. (1995, September/October). Tuning in to trouble. *Ms.,* 44–51.

Heywood, L., & Drake, J. (1997). Introduction. In L. Heywood & J. Drake (Eds.), *Third wave agenda: Being feminist, doing feminism* (pp. 1–20). Minneapolis: University of Minnesota Press.

Hoerrner, K. L. (1996). Gender roles in Disney films: Analysing behaviors from Snow White to Simba. *Women's Studies in Communication, 19,* 213–228.

Hoffman, A. (1997, October). *Thelma & Louise:* What do you do when the American dream fails you? *Premiere, 69.*

hooks, b. (1992). *Black looks: Race and representation.* Boston: Sound End Press.

hooks, b. (1994). *Outlaw culture: Resisting representations.* New York: Routledge.

Hubert, S. J. (2003). What's wrong with this picture? The politics of Ellen's coming out party. In G. Dines & J. M. Humez (Eds.), *Gender, race, and class in media* (2nd ed.) (pp. 608–612). Thousand Oaks, CA: Sage.

Irwin, B. J., & Cassata, M. (1993, November). *Cultural indicators: Families on daytime television.* Paper presented at the meeting of the Speech Communication Association, Miami, FL.

Jackson, K. (1991, September 14). Have you come a long way, baby? *Dallas Morning News,* pp. 1C, 3C.

Jansma, L. L., Linz, D. G., Mulac, A., & Imrich, D. J. (1997). Men's interactions with women after viewing sexually explicit films: Does degradation make a difference? *Communication Monographs, 64,* 1–24.

Japp, P. M. (1991). Gender and work in the 1980s: Television's working women as displaced persons. *Women's Studies in Communication, 14,* 49–74.

Jensen, S. (1991, January-February). Pornography does make women sex objects. *Utne Reader, 13.*

Jhally, S. (1990). *Dreamworlds: Desire/sex/power in rock video.* Amherst: University of Massachusetts Communication Service Trust Fund. (Videotape)

Kalof, L. (1999). The effects of gender and music video imagery on sexual attitudes. *Journal of Social Psychology, 139,* 378–385.

Katz, J. (2003). Advertising and the construction of violent white masculinity. In G. Dines & J. M. Humez (Eds.), *Gender, race, and class in media* (2nd ed.) (pp. 349–358). Thousand Oaks, CA: Sage.

Kilbourne, J. (1998). Beauty and the beast of advertising. In L. J. Peach (Ed.), *Women in culture: A women's studies anthology* (pp. 127–131). Malden, MA: Blackwell.

Kilbourne, J. (1999). *Can't buy my love: How advertising changes the way we think and feel.* New York: Touchstone.

Kim, A. (1995, January 20). Star trip: A new "Trek," a new network, a new captain—and (red alert!) she's a woman. *Entertainment Weekly,* 14–20.

Klawans, S. (1991, June 24). Films: *Thelma & Louise. The Nation,* 862–863.

Krohn, F., & Suazo, F. (1995). Contemporary urban music: Controversial messages in hip-hop and rap lyrics. *ETC: A Review of General Semantics, Summer,* 139–155.

Kroll, J. (1991, June 24). Back on the road again. *Newsweek, 67.*

Kuczynski, A. (2000, March 5). Selling it all: "Red hot sex" and a stellar tuna casserole. *New York Times* News Service, as reported in *Corpus Christi Caller Times,* p. A25.

Lavine, H., Sweeney, D., & Wagner, S. H. (1999). Depicting women as sex objects in television advertising: Effects on body dissatisfaction. *Personality and Social Psychology Bulletin, 25,* 1049–1058.

Lee, M. (1995, November). No more waifs. *The Progressive, 13.*

Leland, J. (1992, June 29). Rap and race. *Newsweek,* 47–52.

Levin, D. E., & Carlsson-Paige, N. (2003). The Mighty Morphin Power Rangers: Teachers voice concern. In G. Dines & J. M. Humez (Eds.), *Gender, race, and class in media* (2nd ed.) (pp. 359–366). Thousand Oaks, CA: Sage.

Leo, J. (1991, June 10). Toxic feminism on the big screen. *U.S. News and World Report, 20.*

Lin, C. A. (1997). Beefcake versus cheesecake in the 1990s: Sexist portrayals of both genders in television commercials. *Howard Journal of Communications, 8,* 237–249.

Lindlof, T. R. (1991). Qualitative study of media audiences. *Journal of Broadcasting and Electronic Media, 35,* 23–42.

Lindsey, K. (2003). In their prime: Women in nighttime drama. In G. Dines & J. M. Humez (Eds.), *Gender, race, and class in media* (2nd ed.) (pp. 625–632). Thousand Oaks, CA: Sage.

Liu, W. Y., Inoue, Y., Bresnahan, M. J., & Nishida, T. (1998, November). *Eat, drink, man, woman: Sex and occupational role stereotypes in prime time commercials in Japan and Taiwan.* Paper presented at the meeting of the National Communication Association, New York, NY.

Livingstone, S., & Liebes, T. (1995). Where have all the mothers gone? Soap opera's replaying of the Oedipal story. *Critical Studies in Mass Communication, 12,* 155–175.

Loohauis, J. (1994, March 16). Now, here's a pause that really refreshes. *Dallas Morning News,* pp. 5C, 13C.

Luong, M. A. (1992, October). *Star Trek: The Next Generation: Boldly forging empowered female characters.* Paper presented at the meeting of the Speech Communication Association, Chicago, IL.

MacKay, N. J., & Covell, K. (1997). The impact of women in advertisements on attitudes toward women. *Sex Roles, 36,* 573–583.

Malamuth, N. M., Addison, T., & Koss, M. (2000). Pornography and sexual aggression: Are there reliable effects and can we understand them? *Annual Review of Sex Research, 11,* 26–91.

Malamuth, N. M., & Billings, V. (1984). Why pornography? Models of functions and effects. *Journal of Communication, 34,* 117–129.

Mandziuk, R. (1991, February). *Cementing her sphere: Daytime talk and the television world of women.* Paper presented at the meeting of the Western States Communication Association, Phoenix, AZ.

Mansfield, S. (2000, May 26–28). Sarah's sexy success. *USA Today Weekend,* 6–7.

Martin, M. C., & Gentry, J. W. (2003). Stuck in the model trap. In A. Alexander & J. Hanson (Eds.), *Taking sides: Clashing views on controversial issues in mass media and society* (7th ed.) (pp. 58–67). Guilford, CT: McGraw-Hill/Dushkin.

Matti, C. L., & Lisosky, J. M. (1999). In search of sandbox dreams: Examining the decision-making of Disney's female and male animated heroes. *Women & Language, 22,* 66.

Maxwell, J. P. (2001). The perception of relationship violence in the lyrics of a song. *Journal of Interpersonal Violence, 16,* 640–661.

Milburn, M. A., Mather, R., & Conrad, S. D. (2000). The effects of viewing R-rated movie scenes that objectify women on perceptions of date rape. *Sex Roles, 43,* 645–664.

Moore, M. L. (1992). The family as portrayed on prime-time television, 1947–1990: Structure and characteristics. *Sex Roles, 26,* 41–61.

Moorti, S. (2003). Cathartic confessions or emancipatory texts? Rape narratives on *The Oprah Winfrey Show.* In G. Dines & J. M. Humez (Eds.), *Gender, race, and class in media* (2nd ed.) (pp. 522–533). Thousand Oaks, CA: Sage.

Mullin, C. R. (1995). Desensitization and resensitization to violence against women: Effects of exposure to sexually violent films on judgments of domestic violence victims. *Journal of Personality & Social Psychology, 69,* 449–459.

Mumford, L. S. (1995). *Love and ideology in the afternoon: Soap opera, women, and television genre.* Bloomington: University of Indiana Press.

Mwangi, M. W. (1996). Gender roles portrayed in Kenyan television commercials. *Sex Roles, 34,* 205–214.

Myers, P. N., Jr., & Biocca, R. A. (1992). The elastic body image: The effect of television advertising and programming on body image distortions in young women. *Journal of Communication, 42,* 108–133.

Niesel, J. (1997). Hip-hop matters: Rewriting the sexual politics of rap music. In L. Heywood & J. Drake (Eds.), *Third wave agenda: Being feminist, doing feminism* (pp. 239–253). Minneapolis: University of Minnesota Press.

Oddone-Paolucci, E., Genuis, M., & Violato, C. (2000). A meta-analysis of the published research on the effects of pornography. *The Changing Family and Child Development.* (Book of selected papers from the International Congress on the Changing Family and Child Development, Calgary, AB.) Aldershot, England: Ashgate.

Olson, B., & Douglas, W. (1997). The family on television: An evaluation of gender roles in situation comedy. *Sex Roles, 36,* 409–427.

Papazian, E. (1996, November-December). Woman on the verge. *Ms.,* 38–45.

Patterson, P. (1996). Rambos and Himbos: Stereotypical images of men in advertising. In P. Lester (Ed.), *Images that injure* (pp. 93–96). Westport, CT: Praeger.

Peach, L. J. (1998). Women and popular culture I: Advertising, print media, and pornography. In L. J. Peach (Ed.), *Women in culture: A women's studies anthology* (pp. 119–127). Malden, MA: Blackwell.

Perry, I. (2003). Who(se) am I? The identity and image of women in hip-hop. In G. Dines & J. M. Humez (Eds.), *Gender, race, and class in media* (2nd ed.) (pp. 136–148). Thousand Oaks, CA: Sage.

Peterson, E. E. (1987). Media consumption and girls who want to have fun. *Critical Studies in Mass Communication, 4,* 37–50.

Pornography: Does women's equality depend on what we do about it? (1994, January-February). *Ms.,* 42–45.

Posavac, H. D. (1998). Exposure to media images of female attractiveness and concern with body weight among young women. *Sex Roles, 37,* 1–10.

Potter, W. J. (2003). On media violence. In A. Alexander & J. Hanson (Eds.), *Taking sides: Clashing views on controversial issues in mass media and society* (7th ed.) (pp. 34–46). Guilford, CT: McGraw-Hill/Dushkin.

Powell, K. A., & Abels, L. (2002). Sex-role stereotypes in TV programs aimed at the preschool audience: An analysis of *Teletubbies* and *Barney & Friends. Women & Language, 25,* 14–22.

Press, A. L. (1991a). *Women watching television: Gender, class, and generation in the American television experience.* Philadelphia: University of Pennsylvania Press.

Press, A. L. (1991b). Working-class women in a middle-class world: The impact of television on modes of reasoning about abortion. *Critical Studies in Mass Communication, 8,* 421–441.

Raeback-Wagener, J., Eickenhoff-Schemeck, J., & Kelly-Vance, L. (1998). The effect of media analysis on attitudes and behaviors regarding body image among college students. *Journal of American College Health, 47,* 29–40.

Rayburn, J. D., Palmgreen, P., & Acker, T. (1984). Media gratifications and choosing a morning news program. *Journalism Quarterly, 61,* 149–156.

Richmond-Abbott, M. (1992). *Masculine and feminine: Gender roles over the life cycle* (2nd ed.). New York: McGraw-Hill.

Rogers, D. D. (2003). Daze of our lives: The soap opera as feminine text. In G. Dines & J. M. Humez (Eds.), *Gender, race, and class in media* (2nd ed.) (pp. 476–481). Thousand Oaks, CA: Sage.

Romaine, S. (1999). *Communicating gender.* Mahwah, NJ: Erlbaum.

Rowe, K. (1990). Roseanne: Unruly woman as domestic goddess. *Screen, 31,* 408–419.

Rubin, A. M. (1986). Uses and gratifications. In J. Bryant & D. Zillmann (Eds)., *Perspectives on media effects*. Hillsdale, NJ: Erlbaum.

Schickel, R. (1991, June 24). Gender bender. *Time*, 52–56.

Scodari, C. (1998). "No politics here": Age and gender in soap opera "cyberfandom." *Women's Studies in Communication, 21*, 168–187.

Seidman, S. A. (1992). An investigation of sex-role stereotyping in music videos. *Journal of Broadcasting and Electronic Media, 36*, 209–216.

Sellnow, D. D. (1999). Music as persuasion: Refuting hegemonic masculinity in "He Thinks He'll Keep Her." *Women's Studies in Communication, 22*, 66–84.

Senn, C. Y. (1993). Women's multiple perspectives and experiences with pornography. *Psychology of Women Quarterly, 17*, 318–341.

Shalit, R. (1998, April 6). Canny and Lacy: Ally, Dharma, Ronnie, and the betrayal of post-feminism. *The New Republic*, 27–32.

Shapiro, L. (1991, June 17). Women who kill too much. *Newsweek*, 52–56.

Shattuc, J. (1997). *The talking cure: TV talk shows and women*. New York: Routledge.

Sherman, B. L., & Dominick, J. R. (1986). Violence and sex in music videos: TV and rock and roll. *Journal of Communication, 36*, 79–93.

Signorielli, N., & Bacue, A. (1999). Recognition and respect: A content analysis of prime-time television characters across three decades. *Sex Roles, 40*, 527–544.

Signorielli, N., & Kahlenberg, S. (1999, November). *Television's world of work in the nineties*. Paper presented at the meeting of the National Communication Association, Chicago, IL.

Signorielli, N., & Morgan, M. (1990). *Cultivation analysis: New directions in media effects research*. Newbury Park, CA: Sage.

Simon, C. (2000/2001, December/January). Hooked on advertising. *Ms.*, 54–59.

Simonton, A. J. (1995). Women for sale. In C. M. Lont (Ed.), *Women and media: Content, careers, criticism* (pp. 143–164). Belmont, CA: Wadsworth.

Solomon, M. (2001, October). Let us now praise famous women. *Premiere*, 14.

Sommers-Flanagan, R., Sommers-Flanagan, J., & Davis, B. (1993). What's happening on music television? A gender role content analysis. *Sex Roles, 28*, 745–753.

Stark, S. (2000a). A tale of two sitcoms. In S. Maasik & J. Solomon (Eds.), *Signs of life in the U.S.A.: Readings on popular culture for writers* (pp. 236–241). Boston: Bedford/St. Martin's.

Stark, S. (2000b). *The Oprah Winfrey Show* and the talk-show furor. In S. Maasik & J. Solomon (Eds.), *Signs of life in the U.S.A.: Readings on popular culture for writers* (pp. 241–248). Boston: Bedford/St. Martin's.

Steenland, S. (1995). Content analysis of the image of women on television. In C. M. Lont (Ed.), *Women and media: Content, careers, criticism* (pp. 179–189). Belmont, CA: Wadsworth.

Steinem, G. (1983). Erotica vs. pornography. In G. Steinem (Ed.), *Outrageous acts and everyday rebellions* (pp. 219–230). New York: Holt, Rinehart and Winston.

Steinem, G. (1990, July-August). Sex, lies, and advertising. As reprinted in the spring 2002 issue of *Ms.*, 60–64.

Steinem, G. (1997, March-April). What's wrong with this picture? *Ms.*, 76.

Stempel Mumford, L. (2000). Plotting paternity: Looking for dad on the daytime soaps. In S. Maasik & J. Solomon (Eds.), *Signs of life in the U.S.A.: Readings on popular culture for writers* (pp. 249–259). Boston: Bedford/St. Martin's.

Strossen, N. (2000). *Defending pornography: Free speech, sex, and the fight for women's rights*. New York: New York University Press.

Sullivan, G. L., & O'Connor, P. J. (1988). Women's role portrayals in magazine advertising: 1958–1983. *Sex Roles, 18,* 181–189.

Tedford, T. L. (2001). *Freedom of speech in the United States* (4th ed.). New York: Strata.

Tisdale, S. (1992, February). Talk dirty to me: A woman's taste for pornography. *Harper's,* 37–46.

Traube, E. (1992). *Dreaming identities: Class, gender, and generation in 1980s Hollywood movies.* Boulder, CO: Westview.

Tuchman, G. (1979). Women's depiction by the mass media. *Signs, 4,* 528–542.

Tuchman, G., Daniels, A. K., & Benet, J. (Eds.) (1978). *Hearth and home: Images of women in the mass media.* New York: Oxford University Press.

Tucker, K. (2002, January 4). Opposite of "sex." *Entertainment Weekly,* 56–57.

Twitchell, J. B. (2000). Plop, plop, fizz, fizz. In S. Maasik & J. Solomon (Eds.), *Signs of life in the U.S.A.: Readings on popular culture for writers* (pp. 202–209). Boston: Bedford/St. Martin's.

Vande Berg, L. R., & Streckfuss, D. (1992). Prime-time television's portrayal of women and the world of work: A demographic profile. *Journal of Broadcasting and Electronic Media, 36,* 195–208.

Van Evra, J. (1990). *Television and child development.* Hillsdale, NJ: Erlbaum.

Vincent, R. C. (1989). Clio's consciousness raised? Portrayal of women in rock videos, re-examined. *Journalism Quarterly, 66,* 155–160.

Vivian, J. (2003). *The media of mass communication* (6th ed.). Boston: Allyn & Bacon.

Ward, L. M., & Rivadeneyra, R. (1999). Contributions of entertainment television to adolescents' sexual attitudes and expectations: The role of viewing amount versus viewer involvement. *Journal of Sex Research, 36,* 237–249.

Wells, W., Burnett, J., & Moriarty, S. (1998). *Advertising principals and practice.* Upper Saddle River, NJ: Prentice Hall.

Whipple, T. W., & Courtney, A. E. (1980). How to portray women in TV commercials. *Journal of Advertising Research, 20,* 53–59.

Whipple, T. W., & Courtney, A. E. (1985). Female role portrayals in advertising and communication effectiveness: A review. *Journal of Advertising, 14,* 4–8.

White, L. A. (2000, November). *A reinvestigation of sex-role stereotyping in MTV music videos.* Paper presented at the meeting of the National Communication Association, Seattle, WA.

White, S. E. (1995). A content analytic technique for measuring the sexiness of women's business attire in media presentations. *Communication Research Reports, 122,* 178–185.

Whitmire, T. (1996, September 8). Soap opera study finds plenty of sex, not much talk of birth control. *Corpus Christi Caller Times,* p. A7.

Willis, J., & Gonzalez, A. (1997). Reconceptualizing gender through intercultural dialogue: The case of the Tex-Mex Madonna. *Women & Language, 20,* 9–12.

Wilson, B. J., Linz, D., Donnerstein, E., & Stipp, H. (1992). The impact of social issue television programming on attitudes toward rape. *Human Communication Research, 19,* 179–208.

Wilson, C. G., & Gutierrez, F. (2003). Advertising and people of color. In G. Dines & J. M. Humez (Eds.), *Gender, race, and class in media* (2nd ed.) (pp. 283–292). Thousand Oaks, CA: Sage.

Wood, J. T. (1998). *But I thought you meant . . . : Misunderstandings in human communication.* Mountain View, CA: Mayfield.

Wyman, L. M. (1993, November). *The virgin/whore dichotomy of sexual powerlessness: Vampire bitches, brides, and victims in Bram Stoker's Dracula.* Paper presented at the meeting of the Speech Communication Association, Miami, FL.

Zinn, L. (1991, November 4). This Bud's for you. No, not you—her. *Business Week,* 86–87.

PART THREE

Let's Talk:
Initiating and
Developing
Relationships

CHAPTER FOUR

CHOOSING AND USING GENDERED LANGUAGE

CASE STUDY: WATCH YOUR LANGUAGE

Most societies use distinctions of biological sex as a significant way to understand the world around them. People, objects, and ideas are commonly characterized as inherently male or female (Devor, 1992). Some languages, such as Spanish and French, have sex-linked designations. For example, in Spanish, a table is feminine (*la mesa*) and a floor is masculine (*el piso*). In these languages, sex is a legitimate way to classify objects and people. Sex, then, becomes a nearly universally accepted organizing construct. Since the English language does not categorize objects this way, instead using *"a," "an,"* and *"the,"* which imply no sex, many English-speakers ask why. Why, for example, is a table feminine and a floor masculine in other languages? Is there some property inherent in the inanimate object that links it to a designation of sex? Likewise, one might question the conventional English usage of female terms for ships or boats. The only explanation we've heard is that a ship is a vessel; women are vessels in that they can carry fetuses—but that explanation is pretty weak. In fact, the British shipping industry in an attempt to modernize, decided that as of March 2002 it would no longer refer to a ship as *"she,"* but would rather say *"it,"* according to Lloyd's List, a British newspaper that has covered the shipping industry since 1734.

Have you ever thought about language—how yours originated and how it has changed and evolved over time? (We assume that the language you used in junior high is not the same language you're using today, as a college student.) Have you ever wondered why some languages seem so foreign and unintelligible? And why are many people so protective of language and resistant to attempts to update it, as though the words they used were a central part of their identity? Why is it important to change one's language in the first place?

This chapter offers an in-depth examination of language because *the language we choose to use reveals to others who we are.* We put language under a microscope in this chapter, because as much as some people discount its importance, the language you choose to use is your primary tool of communication, your primary method of communicating who you are to others, of becoming known by them. That puts language at the center of what most of us find incredibly important.

Hot Topics

- The power of choosing and using language
- Language, sexist language, and the interrelationship between language and thought
- Reasons for using nonsexist language
- Forms of sexist language, such as man-linked terms and generic pronouns
- Sexual language and what it communicates about men and women
- Linguistic practices that reflect bias, such as married names and titles for women and men
- The relational and content axiom of communication (the functions of conversation)
- Vocal properties and linguistic constructions that communicate tentativeness
- Ways that men and women manage conversation

CHOOSING YOUR LANGUAGE

Choosing and *using* in the title of this chapter refer to our view of using language by choice. Many people use language out of habit—they talk the way they've always talked, simply because they've always talked that way. These people rarely think about the influence of language on their view of self, their relationships, and their communication. After reading this chapter, maybe you won't be one of these people.

This chapter scrutinizes language in order to examine its powerful influences on communication. We explore language in a way that parallels the definition of gender communication: communication *about* and *between* women and men. We first focus on language that is used to communicate *about* the sexes—language others use to communicate about you, as well as language you might use to communicate about others. The latter part of the chapter explores language used to communicate *between* the sexes, in terms of how sex and gender affect your choice of language as you communicate with others.

People, in general, are resistant to changing their language. Sometimes it seems that we hold onto language just like we hold onto old, worn-out luggage. We don't really know why this is, but we find that students often resist language reform. Although research shows that women tend to be more accepting of nonsexist language reform than men, many women are resistant, perhaps not realizing that language reform and social reform go hand in hand (Parks & Roberton, 1998a).

Students sometimes suggest that, rather than wasting time talking about language, people should concentrate on issues that have more serious consequences—such as equal pay for equal work and reproductive and family rights. We agree that equal opportunity, wage gaps, and other political and economic

'Net Notes

We all could use a little vocabulary expansion—whether for speaking or writing. We found a few useful Websites that focus on language:

www.celerity.co.uk/words This site will increase your word power, so that you don't end up being an "ultracrepidarian" (one who speaks or acts outside one's experience, knowledge, or ability).

www.peevish.co.uk/slang/news Described as a "monster online dictionary," this site contains the latest slang words and their definitions; categories include rap slang and crime and prison slang (Morreale, 2002, p. 9).

www.worddog.com Need help with a speech or term paper? This site offers editing software that suggests alternatives for ambiguous words, redundancies, and overworked expressions. It also provides links to dictionaries, encyclopedias, and quotations on the Web. (It opens with a barking dog.)

www.logophilia.com/Word/Spy This site is a guide to the "pseudo-postmodern jargon that is the backdrop of today's new economy" (Kang, 2001, p. 121). Newly coined words are provided, as well as older terms that have experienced a resurgence in modern times.

www.dictionary.com If you seek a definition for a word, type the word in at this site and it will provide several definitions from multiple reputable dictionaries, so that you can compare meanings. The site will also translate words, phrases, or an entire Web page from one major European language (including English) into another (Morreale, 2000).

www.pnl.gov/ag/usage/bias This site offers guidelines on how to use bias-free oral and written communication, avoiding discriminatory or negative language.

issues affecting the sexes are extremely important. But politics and economics aren't the focus of this text; gender communication *is*. Think about it this way: if language is at the base of our culture, and if that language is flawed or biased, then that flawed, biased language is what we use to communicate about so-called bigger issues. Why not address problems in the very language of the issues?

Another response we hear occasionally in classroom discussions or when we make professional speeches about language and gender is that aspects of sexist language, such as using *he* as a pronoun to stand for all people, are such picky, minor things to spend one's energy on. What's the big deal? In fact, a recent study at a midwestern university found that nearly half of the students surveyed were supportive of nonsexist language usage, but 32 percent were ambivalent and 21 percent were actually opposed to nonsexist language usage (Parks & Roberton, 1998b). We ask you to keep an open mind, because the many examples of outdated, sexist, exclusive language we give in this chapter should illustrate the magnitude of the problem. The *cumulative* effect on our culture of all these "picky" points about language is enormous.

LANGUAGE: A POWERFUL HUMAN TOOL

What Is Language? What Is Sexist Language?

A *language* is a system of symbols (words or vocabulary) governed by rules (grammar) and patterns (syntax) common to a community of people. Authors Graddol and Swann (1989) suggest that language is both personal and social, that it is a "vehicle of our internal thoughts" as well as a "public resource" (pp. 4–5). Our thoughts take form when they are translated into language, but sometimes language is inadequate to express our thoughts or, particularly, our emotions. Have you ever seen or felt something that you just could not put into words? When you want to extend yourself to someone else, to communicate who you are and what you think and feel, language becomes incredibly important.

Noted Australian gender scholar Dale Spender (1985) describes language as "our means of ordering, classifying and manipulating the world. It is through language that we become members of a human community, that the world becomes comprehensible and meaningful, that we bring into existence the world in which we live" (p. 3). Language has power because it allows us to make sense out of reality, but that power can also be constraining. If you don't have a word for something, can you think about it? Have you ever considered that maybe your thinking might be limited by your language? There might be a whole host of "realities" that you have never thought of because there are no words within your language to describe them.

> *Who ever thought up the word "mammogram"? Every time I hear it, I think I'm supposed to put my breast in an envelope and send it to someone.*
>
> —*Jan King, comedian*

Two researchers who investigated this notion were Edward Sapir and his student Benjamin Lee Whorf. They developed what has come to be called the *Sapir-Whorf Hypothesis*, which suggests an interrelationship between language and thought. Whorf (1956) hypothesized that "the forms of a person's thoughts are controlled by inexorable laws of pattern of which he [she] is unconscious" (p. 252). In this view, human thought is so rooted in language that language may actually control what you can think about. Language and gender scholar Julia Penelope (1990) put it this way: "What we say *is* who we are" (p. 202).

Thus language is a powerful tool in two ways: it affects how you think, shaping your reality; and it allows you to verbally communicate what you think and feel, to convey who you are to others. In the discussion of terminology in

Chapter 1, we defined *sexism* as attitudes, behavior, or both that denigrate one sex to the exaltation of the other. It follows, then, that *sexist language* is verbal communication that conveys those differential attitudes or behaviors. As Bobbye Sorrels (1983) puts it in *The Nonsexist Communicator*, "A basic sense of fairness requires the equal treatment of men and women in the communication symbols that so define the lives of the people who use them. Sexist communication limits and devalues all humans" (pp. 2–3).

Much of what research has exposed as sexist language reflects women's traditional lower status or the patriarchal nature of our society. In fact, some scholars contend that English and other male-dominated languages cause women to be a "muted group." Communication scholar Cheris Kramarae (1981), who first generated muted-group theory, explains it as follows:

> Women (and members of other subordinate groups) are not as free or as able as men are to say what they wish, when and where they wish, because the words and the norms for their use have been formulated by the dominant group, men. So women cannot as easily or as directly articulate their experiences as men can. Women's perceptions differ from those of men because women's subordination means they experience life differently. However, the words and norms for speaking are not generated from or fitted to women's experiences. Women are thus "muted." Their talk is often not considered of much value by men. . . . Words constantly ignored may eventually come to be unspoken and perhaps even unthought. (p. 1)

Our intent in this chapter is to explore the English language, wonderful and flawed as it is—not to blame anyone, not to suggest that men use language purposefully to oppress women and maintain their status, and not to make readers feel defensive about how they use language. We all inherited a male-dominated language, but it is not a mystical entity that cannot be studied or changed (Romaine, 1999). In fact, English has changed a great deal, according to three of the most influential scholars of language in the United States. Miller, Swift, and Maggio (1997) discuss many advances within recent American culture, citing such sources as the *American Heritage Book of English Usage* and the *American Heritage Dictionary*, which document successful efforts at ridding the language of sexism.

Language may control some people, but it need not control you. Think of language as something that has tremendous influence on us, but remember that we can *choose* how to use it and how to influence *it*. In this chapter, we examine various aspects of language that research has deemed sexist, as well as efforts individuals have made to eliminate the sexism. Some of these reforms you've already learned, so you may think there was never another way of expressing the ideas in question. After reading this chapter, you may decide to inventory your language and make some changes, because some aspects are outdated. Or you may realize that some ways you've used language in the past could be taken as sexist, although you didn't realize it until now. That happens to the best of us.

WHY USE NONSEXIST LANGUAGE?

Inventorying your language and making some changes takes work, but not a lot of work, given the benefits you'll experience. But first, you have to sign on to do the work. Below we give you a few reasons for incorporating nonsexist language into your communication repertoire.

Reason 1: Nonsexist Language Demonstrates Sensitivity

Sensitivity seems like an obvious reason for using nonsexist language, but it may be more obvious in spirit than in practice. While you may have a basic philosophy that variations among people are worthy of respect, you may communicate in a manner that contradicts your philosophy—either out of ignorance (because you just didn't know any better) or out of nonchalance (thinking that sexist communication is "no big deal"). Maybe you simply feel that subtle forms of sexist language that have developed into habits will take too much time and effort to change. Maybe you believe that if people get the wrong impression of you from your language, either they'll take the time to learn the truth or they won't—and if they won't, they aren't worth your energy in the first place. But remember that spoken and written communication are ways of extending oneself into the world, of getting to know others and being known by them. If you want to present yourself as a caring, sensitive individual who believes in a basic system of fairness for everyone, doesn't it seem logical for your language to reflect that desire?

Reason 2: Nonsexist Language Reflects Nonsexist Attitudes

Even though we aren't sure about the exact relationship between language and thought, it's clear that a relationship exists. So if you communicate in a sexist manner—whether or not you are aware that a particular usage is sexist, and regardless of your intentions—it is possible that you have some sexist attitudes. That conclusion may seem rather strong, but if thoughts are indeed influenced by language and if language affects the quality of thought, then sexist language may be linked to sexist thoughts. Stop and think for a moment: Can you safely say that your communication, both oral and written, is free from sexist language? A tougher question is this: If your communication contains some sexist usages, could someone claim that you have sexist attitudes?

Reason 3: Nonsexist Language Is Basic to the Receiver Orientation to Communication

Hardly any other topic we discuss in this text pertains more to the principles of receiver orientation to communication (explained in Chapter 1) than sexist language. Simply put, if a listener perceives your language to be sexist, then in terms of a receiver orientation to communication, that is a legitimate judgment—one you need to think about. For example, if you say, "If a person is in trouble, he should feel confident calling on a policeman for help," a listener may interpret your use of male language as sexist because it might insinuate (1) that only men are persons, and (2) that only men are police officers. You may not mean anything sexist or demeaning in your message, but if your message is interpreted by a listener as sexist, you can't erase it, can you? The communication is *out there*, and undoing it or convincing a listener that you meant otherwise takes 10 times as long as if you'd applied a little thought before speaking.

Reason 4: Nonsexist Language Is Contemporary

One set of goals within higher education is that on graduation, students will be able to think, write, and converse in a manner befitting a highly educated person. Using outdated, sexist language undermines that goal. The reality we all share is that the roles women and men can fulfill have changed a great deal. Because these changes have occurred and are likely to keep occurring, language should evolve to reflect current society. Since the 1970s, academic and scholarly publishing standards have been explicit about nonsexist usage: sexist language doesn't get into print. We encourage you to inventory your spoken and written language in efforts to exorcise sexism, if you haven't done so already, so that you will be viewed as educated and contemporary.

Reason 5: Nonsexist Language Strengthens Expression

Another benefit of nonsexist language is a better writing style. Linguist Rosalie Maggio (1988; 1992), author of two books containing alternatives for biased English words and phrases, suggests: "One of the most rewarding—and, for many people, the most unexpected—side effects of breaking away from traditional, sexist patterns of language is a dramatic improvement in writing style" (1988, p. 164). Some students balk at our suggestion that they rid their talk of even the most subtle forms of sexism. They believe that nonsexist language is cumbersome, that it "junks up" one's speaking and writing with a bunch of extra words, just to include everybody. However, once they learn and begin to practice simple methods of avoiding sexist, exclusive means of expression, they readily admit that it does make their communication more clear and dynamic.

Remember...

LANGUAGE: A system of symbols (words or vocabulary) governed by rules (grammar) and patterns (syntax) common to a community of people.

SAPIR-WHORF HYPOTHESIS: A supposition about the interrelationship between language and thought.

SEXIST LANGUAGE: Verbal communication that conveys differential attitudes or behaviors with regard to the sexes; language that demonstrates that one sex is valued over the other.

SEXIST LANGUAGE: FORMS, PRACTICES, AND ALTERNATIVES

This section is divided into two main areas: *forms* of sexist language and sexist *practices* that involve language. The first area has to do with language that is sexist in and of itself. In the second area, it's not the words themselves that are sexist but the traditions inherent in how we use language. When we explain each sexist form or practice, we also offer a nonsexist alternative. As you work through this information, take inventory of your own communication habits by asking, "Does my communication contain any of these sexist language forms or practices?" If you find that it does, you will want to note the nonsexist alternatives.

Forms of Sexist Language

Manmade Everything

Words or phrases that include *man*, as though these terms should be generic and stand for all persons, are referred to as man-linked terminology— a form of sexist language that has diminished but still has not disappeared (Miller, Swift, & Maggio, 1997; Steinem, 1995). The term *man* or its derivative *mankind* in reference to all persons creates ambiguity and confusion when one doesn't know whether the term refers to a set of male persons or to all persons in general (Graddol & Swann, 1989). (Even more confusing is the term *he-man!*)

Originally, *man* was derived from a truly generic form, similar to the term *human*. Contrary to popular belief, the term *woman* did not derive from the term *man*, nor did *female* derive from *male* (Hardman, 1999). The terms for female-men (*wifmann*) and male-men (*wermann*) developed when the culture decided that it needed differentiating terms for the sexes (McConnell-Ginet, 1980). Maggio's (1988) dictionary of gender-free terminology provides Greek, Latin, and Old English terms for human, woman, and man. In Greek, the terms are *anthropos*, *gyne*, and *aner*; in Latin, *homo*, *femina*, and *vir*; and in Old English, *man*, *female*, and *wer* (pp. 176–177). The problem is that *man* should be a designation only for *male* persons, not *all* persons. Research shows that masculine mental images arise when the term *man* is used. Again, not only does this term exclude women, it reinforces the problematic idea that male is the standard.

Even though the word *human* contains *man*, it is derived from the Latin *homo*, meaning all persons. The term *human* does not evoke masculine-only imagery as the term *man* does (Graddol & Swann, 1989; Maggio, 1988). Man-linked terms include expressions such as *man the phones* or *manned space flight* as well as numerous words that have *man* attached to or embedded within them (e.g., repairman), which convert the term into a role, position, or action that an individual can assume or make (Palczewski, 1998). Unfortunately, people see the masculine part of the term and instantaneously form the perception that the word describes something masculine only. If you are thinking, "People make too big a deal of this 'mailman, fireman, policeman' thing," look at Figure 4-1 to see how many commonly used man-linked terms there are. Maggio (1988) cautions, however, that not

FIGURE 4-1. Man-Linked Terminology and Alternatives

Term	Alternative	Term	Alternative
adman	advertising executive; ad executive	man in the moon	face in the moon
airman	aviator; pilot	mankind	mankind; humanity
anchorman	anchor; newscaster	manmade	artificial; handmade; synthetic
bail/bondsman	bail or bond agent	manned space flight	space flight
bogeyman	bogey; bogey monster	man of few words	silent type
base man	base player	man of the house	homeowner
bellman/bellboy	attendant; luggage handler; bellperson	man of the world	sophisticate
businessman	businessperson; business executive or leader	man-of-war	warship
cameraman	camera operator	man on the street	average person; common person
cattleman	rancher; cattle owner	man overboard	overboard; person overboard
caveman	prehistoric person; neanderthal	manpower	staff power; work force
chairman	chair; chairperson	manservant	servant; butler; valet; maid
churchman	churchgoer	man the phones	answer the phones
committeeman	committee member	man-to-man	one-to-one; person-to-person
congressman	senator; representative; legislator; congressperson	man your battle stations/positions	assume your battle stations; go to your positions
con man	con artist	marksman/rifleman	sharpshooter
councilman	council member	may the best man win	may the best person win
doorman	doorkeeper; porter	men working	people working; workers
draftsman	drafter	modern man	modern people; modern civilization
everyman	common person; typical or ordinary person	no-man's land	limbo; dead zone; void
fisherman	fisher	one-upmanship	going one better; one-up tendency; dominance
foreman	supervisor; foreperson	patrolman	patroller; patrol officer; trooper
frenchman (other nations)	french native (native of other nations)	penmanship	handwriting
freshman	first-year student	policeman	police officer; cop
frontiersman	pioneer; settler	Renaissance man	Renaissance person; all-around expert
garbageman/trashman	garbage or trash collector; sanitation worker	repairman	repairer; servicer; technician
G-man	government or federal agent	salesman	salesclerk; clerk; salesperson
groomsman	wedding or groom's attendant	self-made man	independent person; self-made person; entrepreneur
gunman	killer; assassin; shooter	serviceman (military)	soldier; member of the armed forces
handyman	odd jobber; repairer	snowman	snow figure or person
hit man	hired killer; hired gun	spaceman	astronaut; space explorer
layman	layperson; laity; lay worker	spokesman	spokesperson; speaker
mailman/postman	mail carrier; postal worker	sportsman	sports enthusiast; athlete; good sport
man	human; humans; person; persons; people	statesman	politician; citizen; patriot
man about town	worldly person; socialite; jet-setter	stunt man	stunt person; stunt performer; daredevil
man a post	fill a post; staff a post	under/upperclassman	undergraduate; first-year student; sophomore, etc.
man-eating	flesh eating; carnivore	unman	unnerve; frighten; disarm
man for all seasons	all-around expert; Renaissance person	unmanned	unstaffed; uninhabited
manhandle	mistreat; rough up	unsportsmanlike	unsporting; unfair
manhole	sewer; utility hole	watchman	guard; security guard; sentry
manhood	pride; strength	workman's compensation	worker's compensation
man-hours	staff hours	workmanship	work; handiwork; artisanry
manhunt	chase; fugitive search		

> *I'm just a person trapped inside a woman's body.*
>
> *—Elaine Boosler, comedian*

all words containing *-man* or *-men* are sexist. Some examples she provides are *amen, emancipate, manager, maneuver, manipulate, ottoman,* and *menstruation.*

Alternatives to *man* (e.g., *people, persons, individuals*), the simplest being *human* (and its derivatives *human being, humanity,* and *humankind*), are becoming more commonplace in everyday language (Miller, Swift, & Maggio, 1997). Figure 4-1 shows some of these alternatives. Note that only a few call for the addition of *person* to the term; for some, adding *person* to a word signals a feminine rather than a generic form (Aldrich, 1985). Some of the alternatives to masculine terms may seem awkward or even ridiculous, but over time you will probably come to wonder how anyone could argue with such simple changes.

Antimale Bias in Language

Language scholar Eugene August (1992) describes three forms of antimale language in English: gender-exclusive language, gender-restrictive language, and language that evokes negative stereotypes of males. First, August explores the equating of *mother* and *parent,* suggesting that the terms are often used interchangeably, whereas the term *noncustodial parent* is almost always synonymous with *father.* He suggests that males are also excluded terms describing victims, such as the expressions *wife abuse* and *innocent women and children.* This language implies that males cannot be victims of violence, rape, and abuse. The second category, gender-restrictive language, refers to language that limits men to a social role. August's examples include language that strongly suggests to boys the role they are to play and chastises them if they stray from that role or do not perform as expected (e.g., *sissy, mama's boy, take it like a man,* and *impotent*). In the final category, August claims, "negative stereotyping is embedded in the language, sometimes it resides in people's assumptions about males" (p. 137). As evidence of this tendency, August cites terms linked to crime and evil, such as *murderer, mugger, suspect,* and *rapist*—terms he contends evoke male stereotypes that are "insulting, dehumanizing, and potentially dangerous" (p. 132). In reference to the term *rape,* August discusses the fact that the majority of rapes are committed by males on female victims; however, the bias comes in with the assumption of a female victim, ignoring rapes perpetrated against men in our culture.

The Perpetual Pronoun Problem

Think about what you were taught regarding pronouns. If you were taught that the masculine pronoun *he* (with its derivatives *his, him,* and *himself*) was perfectly acceptable as a generic term for all persons, both female and male, then you got an outdated lesson. Research from the 1970s to the present provides convincing evidence that the generic *he* isn't generic at all; it's masculine and conjures up masculine images (Gastil, 1990; Hamilton, 1988; Moulton, Robinson, & Elias, 1978; Romaine, 1999; Stinger & Hopper, 1998).

One of the most illuminating early studies on this topic was conducted by gender psychologist Wendy Martyna (1978) who investigated college students' use of pronouns by asking them to complete sentence fragments, both orally and in writing. The students were required to provide pronouns to refer to sex-indefinite nouns, as in the statement, "Before a judge can give a final ruling, _____." Fragments depicting typically male occupations or roles included such terms as *doctor, lawyer, engineer,* and *judge;* feminine referents included *nurse, librarian, teacher,* and *babysitter;* neutral fragments used such nouns as *person, individual,* and *student.* The participants also were asked to reveal what image or idea came to mind as they chose a certain pronoun to complete a sentence.

In a nutshell, college students in Martyna's research continually read sex into the subjects of sentence fragments and responded with sex-specific pronouns. The nurses, librarians, teachers, and babysitters were predominantly *she,* while the doctors, lawyers, engineers, and judges were *he.* The neutral subjects most often received the pronoun *they.* If the pronoun *he* had truly been a term indicating all persons, then *he* would have been the pronoun of choice no matter what role the sentence depicted. In conjunction with their choices of pronouns, students reported sex-stereotyped images that came to mind when they read the fragments.

Martyna's results underscore the fact that people (at least in American culture) can hardly function without knowing the sex of a person. If they aren't told the sex, they generally assign one based on stereotypes and, granted, on the numbers of persons in our society who hold the majority of certain positions and roles. So, if you argue that when you say *he* you are including everyone and that neither sex is implied, listeners may tell you that you are referring to men only and excluding women completely. Further, your language implies that male is the standard; if this were not the case, then why didn't you use *she?* In terms of a receiver orientation to communication, your listeners have a point.

If you think that Martyna's study is so dated that the results couldn't apply to today's college students, think again. At two universities—one on the east coast and the other on the west coast—we repeated and extended Martyna's study, hoping to find that contemporary college students were attuned to the problem of sexist pronouns (Ivy, Bullis-Moore, Norvell, Backlund, & Javidi, 1995). On the contrary, the results were virtually the same. For terms such as *lawyer, judge,* and *engineer,* students responded predominantly with masculine pronouns and imagery, while *nurses, librarians,* and *babysitters* were female.

We also asked subjects about their exposure to nonsexist language instruction in high school and college. Results showed that in both high school and college students received mixed messages regarding pronoun usage. For every lesson on the use of inclusive, nonsexist pronouns, students recalled a counter-lesson telling them that the pronoun *he* was an acceptable substitute for all persons. It's obvious that people aren't getting a clear message about nonsexist language. This lack of clarity in education may lead people to resort to stereotypes in their language.

Besides the fact that generic masculine pronouns aren't really generic, other negative consequences of using this form of exclusive language have emerged from research. Studies show that exclusive pronoun usage (1) places undue emphasis on men over women; (2) maintains sex-biased perceptions; (3) shapes people's attitudes about careers that are appropriate for one sex but not the other; (4) causes some women to believe that certain jobs and roles aren't attainable; and (5) contributes to the belief that men deserve higher status in society than women do (Briere & Lanktree, 1983; Brooks, 1983; Ivy, 1986; Stericker, 1981; Stinger & Hopper, 1998).

The Pronoun Solution

Is there a pronoun that can stand for everyone? Some scholars have attempted to introduce new words, or *neologisms*, into the language primarily for the purpose of inclusivity. Such *neologisms* as *gen, tey, co, herm*, and *heris* are interesting, but they haven't had much success in being adopted into common usage. Interestingly enough, in 2003 the president of the student government at Smith College, an all-women's institution in Massachusetts, proposed a constitutional change to the document governing students at that college. In an effort to be sensitive to transgender persons, the proposal involved changing all references to *she* and *her* in the constitution to *the student*. Dozens of other American colleges and universities are grappling with language in their documents and communication, in order to more sensitively communicate to persons who consider themselves transgender. (For a reminder of what a transgender identity entails, see Chapters 1 and 2.)

If you want to refer to one person—any person of either sex—the clearest, most grammatical, nonsexist way to do that is to use either *she or he, he/she*, or *s/he* (Kennedy, 1992). A recent study found that texts using paired pronoun forms (e.g., *he or she*) were rated more favorably than texts which alternated male and female pronouns by paragraph or chapter; however, the alternate-pronouns approach was more effective in reducing sexist attitudes (Madson & Hessling, 1999). Other ways to avoid excluding any portion of the population in your communication are to omit a pronoun altogether, either rewording a message or substituting an article (*a, an*, or *the*) for the pronoun; to use *you* or variations of the indefinite pronoun *one*; or to use the plural pronoun *they* (Maggio, 1988; Miller, Swift, & Maggio, 1997).

The Lady Doctor and the Male Nurse

A subtle form of sexist language, called *marking*, involves placing a sex-identifying adjective in front of a noun to designate the reference as somehow different or deviant from the norm (LaRocque, 1997; Romaine, 1999;

West, 1998). Examples of this practice include *woman* or *lady doctor, male secretary, female boss, female soldier,* and *lady lawyer.* Such sex marking is limiting, discriminatory, and unnecessary. (Remember how Ben Stiller's character was ridiculed in the movie Meet the Parents for being a *male nurse*?) Why does one need to point out the sex of a doctor, lawyer, or boss? The implication is that one incarnation of a role or position is the norm, whereas a person of the opposite sex in that role or position is an aberration or "not normal." Such language can have an isolating, chilling effect on the person who is "not the norm." The use of marking terms appears to be changing as more people enter professions previously dominated by members of the opposite sex.

References to sports teams commonly reflect this sexist practice of marking. Male teams or groups use the generic or mascot name (e.g., Professional Golf Association, Longhorns), and female teams or groups are marked by sex (e.g., Ladies' Professional Golf Association, Lady Longhorns; Miller, Swift, & Maggio, 1997). If there were no sexism in language, these associations would either not be identified by sex at all or would have parallel names, such as the Men's National Basketball Association (MNBA) and the Women's National Basketball Association (WNBA). (Would that lead to the formation of the "Gentlemen's Professional Golf Association"?!) We understand that, in many instances, this practice merely reflects the fact that male teams existed long before female teams and thus were assigned the generic or mascot name. But perhaps long-held traditions should be revisited (especially if those traditions are exclusive). Some university athletic programs are working to counter this form of sexism, insisting that references to teams be parallel and include no sex-based markers.

How's Trix?

Adding a suffix such as *-ette, -ess, -enne,* or *-trix* to form a feminine version of a supposed male term is another subtle form of sexist language that appears to be making its rightful exit from common usage (Miller, Swift, & Maggio, 1997). The suffix "perpetuates the notion that the male is the norm and the female is a subset, a deviation, a secondary classification. In other words, men are 'the real thing' and women are sort of like them" (Maggio, 1988, p. 178). Does it really matter if the person waiting on a table at a restaurant is female or male? Does someone who is admired need to be called a *hero* or a *heroine*? We guarantee you that our female students would rather be called a *dude* than a *dudette*! Such terminology makes a person's sex too important, revealing a need to know the sex to determine how to behave or what to expect.

How can sexist suffixes be avoided? Figure 4-2 provides a list of appropriate alternatives to words with feminine endings. One can simply use the original term and omit the suffix. If there is a legitimate reason for specifying sex, a pronoun can be used, as in "The actor was performing her monologue beautifully, when someone's watch alarm went off in the theater."

FIGURE 4-2. Feminine Suffixes and Alternatives

actress	actor
adulteress	adulterer
ambassadress	ambassador
anchoress	anchor
authoress	author
aviatrix or aviatress	aviator
bachelorette	single person
comedienne	comedian
equestrienne	equestrian
governess	governor
heiress	heir
heroine	hero
hostess	host
justess	justice
laundress	laundry worker
majorette	major
murderess	murderer
poetess	poet
sculptress	sculptor
songstress	singer
starlet	star
stewardess	flight attendant
suffragette	suffragist
usherette	usher
waitress	waiter, waitron, waitstaff, or server

Speaking of a Higher Power. . .

Saying that the topic of sexism in religious language is "sticky" is a major understatement. It is not our intent here to uproot your religious beliefs (or even to assume you have religious beliefs that need uprooting), but merely to provide "food for thought."

In their book about language and the sexes, Miller and Swift (1991) explain that within the Judaeo-Christian tradition, religious scholars for centuries have insisted that the translation of such an abstract concept as a deity into language need not involve a designation of sex. According to these researchers, "the symbolization of a male God must not be taken to mean that God really is 'male.' In fact, it must be understood that God has no sex at all" (p. 64). To one dean of the Harvard Divinity School, masculine language about God is "a cultural and linguistic accident" (Stendahl, as in Miller & Swift, 1991, p. 67). As one rabbi put it, "I think of God as an undefinable being; to talk about God in gender terms, we're talking in terms we can understand and not in terms of what God is really like" (Ezring, as in Leardi, 1997, p. H1).

The problem, at least for religions relying on biblical teachings, is that early translations of scriptures from the ancient Hebrew language into Old English rendered masculine images of deity, reflecting the culture of male superiority at the time (Kramarae, 1981; Schmitt, 1992). Thus the literature is dominated by the pronoun *he* and by such terms as *father* and *kingdom*. Linguistic scholars contend that much of the original female imagery was lost in modern translation or was omitted from consideration by the canonizers of the Bible (Miller & Swift, 1991; Spender, 1985). The Old Testament says that humans were created in God's image—both male and female. It is interesting, then, that we have come to connect masculinity with most religious images and terms. Also interesting, as August (1992) contends, is the "masculinization of evil," the fact that male pronouns and images are most often associated with Satan, such as a reference to the *Father of Lies*. August says, "Few theologians talk about Satan and her legions" (p. 139).

Are you uncomfortable enough at this point in your reading to say to yourself, "Come on now; you're messing with religion. Enough is enough"? That's understandable, because religion is a deeply personal thing. It's something that a lot of us grew up with; thus its images and teachings are so ingrained that we don't often question them or stop to consider where some of the traditions originated. However, questioning the language of religion doesn't mean that one is questioning his or her faith.

A few religions have begun to lessen male dominance in their communication. Scholars Jones and Mills (2001) explain: "Judaism has been unprecedented in its efforts to include women in a traditionally patriarchal religion. Over the past thirty years the language of ancient rituals and ceremonies, sacred to the faith, have been altered and re-written to include women" (p. 58). In some Christian sects, the masculinity *and* femininity of God are beginning to receive equal emphasis, as in one version of the Apostles' Creed which begins, "I believe in God the Father and Mother almighty, maker of heaven and

Hot Button Issue

"STAY OUT OF SCRIPTURE?"

Our discussion of sexism in religious language may raise some hairs on the back of your neck, because religion, to many of us, is something deeply felt and rooted in tradition. Many people feel that changing the language in current translations of the Bible is akin to (or worse than) altering Shakespeare. If you are a person within the Christian tradition, which is grounded in biblical teachings, do you feel that your faith or your ability to worship would be shaken if more female language or gender-neutral terms appeared in the Bible? Would you trip over such language, or would you see it as a welcome change? Is it political correctness gone amok, or an opportunity for more people to relate to biblical teachings?

earth." In January 2002, publishers of a leading version of the Bible (in terms of sales) in the U.S., the New International Version (NIV), announced that they would begin producing editions that contained more inclusive language (Gorski, 2002). Not all references to *men* will be changed to *people*, nor will male references to God be removed. What will change is that gender-specific language will be altered when it's evident that the original text didn't intend any gender. For example, some references to *sons* will be changed to *children* and *brothers* into *brothers and sisters*. These kinds of reforms are interesting and are increasing in number, but they are unnerving to many people (Leardi, 1997).

Chicks, Cupcakes, and Pansies

There are many derogatory terms for human beings, unfortunately. But did you know that using terms for animals, food, and plants as labels for men and women can be interpreted as demeaning and sexist? Maggio (1988) points out, "Using animal names to refer to people is neither sensitive nor very socially attractive. Names of foods are also used for people, and while many of them purport to be positive, ultimately they are belittling, trivializing, and make objects of people" (pp. 182–183). One of our students felt very demeaned when a male classmate told her she looked like "a delicious piece of cheesecake." While he protested that he was only trying to offer a compliment, she did not feel complimented. The comment made her flustered, embarrassed, and angry. In this example, was the guy an unwitting victim of circumstance, a complete jerk, or just misunderstood? Maybe the woman was hypersensitive and didn't take him the "right" way. Should she have just laughed it off, or was she right in making an issue of it to try and teach him a lesson? What's the best interpretation of what occurred, from a receiver orientation to communication?

Figure 4-3 lists some terms for animals, food, and plants that are commonly used in reference to people. Note that the lists for women are longer than the lists for men, because these kinds of references are used more often for women. Keep in mind one important point: this category of language usage is especially connected to the context of the communication, as well as to the relationship between the persons involved. For example, romantic partners may develop pet names for each other, including some of the terms listed in Figure 4-3. Some women take no offense at being called "chicks," while others will be offended by the reference to a baby animal—helpless and innocent. Exercise caution here: Only in certain contexts and within certain relationships—those in which two people's feelings and regard for each other are mutually understood—should animal, food, and plant terms be construed as endearments for persons.

Reduced to a Body Part

Language about sexuality profoundly affects how women and men perceive the sexes, as well as how they communicate with each other. Most of us know that reducing a human being to his or her sexuality is a loathsome, degrading

FIGURE 4-3. Animal, Food, and Plant Terms for Persons

Animal Terms		Food Terms		Plant Terms	
Women	Men	Women	Men	Women	Men
fox, vixen	fox, wolf	honey	honey	rose, rosebud	pansy
pig, hog, sow	pig	sugar	sugar	clinging vine	
lamb	lamb	cookie	cookie	buttercup	
dog	dog	pumpkin	pumpkin	sweet pea	
bitch	stag (party)	honey bun	honey bun	petunia	
tiger	tiger	cupcake	cupcake	daisy	
pussy	pussy	baby cakes	beefcake	honeysuckle	
cat (cat fight)	cat, tomcat	cheesecake	big cheese	violet	
sex kitten	ass, jackass	candy	candy ass		
kitty	gorilla, big ape	cutie pie	cutie pie		
dumb ox	big ox	muffin	(stud) muffin		
chicken	chicken	jelly roll	meat		
chick	cock	tomato	meathead		
chickadee	turkey	sugar lips	sweetmeat		
bird	old goat	peach	hot dog		
silly goose	snake	cherry	wiener, weenie		
bunny	worm	lamb chop	tube steak		
mouse	rat	pudding	cream puff		
beaver	weasel	dish	jelly		
filly	stud	brown sugar	bone		
old mare	buck	marshmallow	top banana		
black widow	bear or teddy bear	tart			
cow	bull	lollipop			
heifer	squirrel	tidbit			
broad (pregnant cow)		morsel			
bearded clam		taco			
tuna					
hen ("he's henpecked")					
shrew (a mouse-like mammal)					
claws ("her claws are out")					

practice that can be personally devastating to the recipient of such language. While most people refrain from this practice individually, that may not be true when people are out with a group of friends. The group sees someone interesting, attractive, or not so attractive—and that's when the language can turn ugly, perhaps under the guise of "it's all in good fun." But think about what is actually happening in these instances. A person, most likely without his or her knowledge, is being sexually objectified or turned into a body part, for adulation or derision, by the group's language. One attempt to justify this behavior is the claim, "We were just admiring the person." Most of us would rather be deprived of this kind of admiration.

We defer a good deal here to the important work of linguist Robert Baker in the 1980s, who was interested in conceptions of women in American culture. Although men also are described in sexualized terms, significantly more sexual terms identify women than men. For example, one study uncovered 220 terms for sexually promiscuous women and only 22 terms for sexually promiscuous men (Stanley, 1977). Baker (1981) contends that the following categories of terms are recognized as "more or less interchangeable with 'woman' " (p. 167):

1. Neutral terms, such as *lady, gal,* and *girl*
2. Animal terms
3. Words that describe playthings or toys, such as *babe, baby, doll,* and *cuddly*
4. Clothing terms, such as *skirt* or *hem*
5. A whole range of sexual terms.

In reference to Baker's category 5, think of how many terms exist in our language that are based on anatomy, but that may be used to describe the whole person. Some of the less graphic terms that describe women's anatomy or sexual behavior and are interchangeable with the word *woman* include *snatch, twat, pussy, beaver, cherry, a piece, box, easy, some* (as in "getting some"), *slut, whore,* and a *screw* or *lay.* Here's some male sexual lingo: *prick, cock, male member, dick, tool,* and a *screw* or *lay.* Obviously, there are more terms than these, but we leave those to your imagination rather than putting them in print.

> *My mother never saw the irony in calling me a son-of-a-bitch.*
>
> —Jack Nicholson, actor

Anthropologist Michael Moffat (1989) studied the use of language by residents of university dormitories and found that one-third of young men in the study, in conversations with other men, consistently referred to women as "chicks, broads, and sluts," reflecting what Moffat termed a "locker-room style" of communication about women (p. 183). We don't believe that only men use sexually demeaning terminology in reference to women. We've heard women call or refer to other women by a few of the terms listed above, but typically just

Hot Button Issue

"DIRTY WORDS"

We realize that many of you do not use the language we discuss (so bluntly) in this section of the chapter. But in specific situations, such as when you were really down over being dumped from an important relationship or when you were frustrated or furious, perhaps you've found yourself using language you wouldn't ordinarily use. You probably also know people who do use this kind of language, even if you don't use it yourself. How have you reacted when you've heard friends or acquaintances equate people with their sexual organs or body parts? Should language be an emotional release for people? Stated another way, is there is a place and time for foul or degrading language? Does it depend on who's around to hear you?

the ones that imply sexual promiscuity (e.g., *slut, easy*). Do you agree that conceiving of a person in sexual terms is demeaning and sexist?

Two recent studies examined college students' use and perceptions of sexual language (Murnen, 2000). In the first study, male and female students were asked to self-report the kinds of sexual language they used to describe others. Results showed that men in the study were much more likely than women to use (1) sexually degrading terms in reference to opposite sex genitalia, and (2) highly aggressive terms to refer to sexual intercourse. In a follow-up study, subjects listened to either two men or two women conversing about having sex with someone they'd met the night before. Both male and female speakers who used degrading sexual language were evaluated negatively by the listeners; however, in highly degrading conversations, the object of the degradation was judged as less intelligent and less moral than those persons who were spoken of in more respectful terms. The researcher concluded that use of sexual language is affected by gender and that one's attitudes toward members of the opposite sex, as well as about sexual activity, are revealed by one's choice of language.

Another form of sexual language describes sexual activity, with an emphasis on verbs and their effect on the roles women and men assume sexually. Baker's synonyms for sexual intercourse, as generated by his students in the early 1980s, include *screwed, laid, had, did it, banged, slept with, humped,* and *made love to.* Feminist theorist Deborah Cameron's (1985) discussion of sexual language adds the verb *poked* to the list. Author Jonathon Green (1999) offers such metaphorical language for intercourse as *jumped someone's bones* or *bod, bumped uglies, gave a tumble,* and *knocked boots.* Our students have generously offered such contemporary references as *hooked up with, got some from, got some play, made (someone), took,* and even *mated.*

Remember. . .

MAN-LINKED TERMINOLOGY: The use of words or phrases that include *man* as a generic term to stand for all persons.

ANTIMALE BIAS: Language use that excludes men, restricts the roles for and perceptions of men, and evokes negative stereotypes of men.

GENERIC PRONOUN: Use of a masculine pronoun as a term to stand for all persons.

NEOLOGISM: A new word introduced into a language.

MARKING: Placing a sex-identifying adjective in front of a noun to designate the reference as somehow different or deviant from the norm.

FEMININE SUFFIX: Adding a suffix to a male term to form a female term.

According to Baker, the sexism in these descriptions comes from the placement of subjects that precede some of the verbs and the objects that follow them. Sentences like "Dick screwed Jane" and "Dick banged Jane" describe men as the doers of sexual activity, while women are almost always the recipients. When a female subject of a sentence appears, the verb form changes into a passive rather than an active construction, as in "Jane was screwed by Dick" and "Jane was banged by Dick"—the woman is still the recipient (pp. 175–176). Baker labels "inadequate" the argument that the linguistic tendency to describe males as active and females as passive reflects the fact that men's genitalia are external and women's genitalia are internal. If active sexual roles for women were the norm or were more accepted, Baker contends, the verb *to engulf* would be in common usage. Cameron (1985) proposes that the term *penetration* as a synonym for the sexual act suggests male origins; if a woman had set the term, it might have been *enclosure.*

Students in the early twenty-first century believe that the dichotomy of male-active, female-passive sexuality is changing, as is the corresponding language. They offer a few active constructions for women's sexual behavior (largely related to woman's being on top in heterosexual intercourse, e.g., *to ride*). However, they admit that even in our postmodern times, more negative judgments are communicated about women who behave actively or dominantly in intercourse than about men who behave submissively. Changes are taking place in the sexual arena, but the language hasn't kept pace.

Sexist Linguistic Practices

The Name Game

Many of us believe that our names are an integral part of our identity. Why, then, should a married woman be expected to give up her last name, part of her identity, to adopt her husband's? The practice of wives taking husbands' names isn't necessarily sexist; what is sexist is the expectation that a married woman is supposed to or must take a man's last name. (This is one problem that most gay couples can happily avoid.) For some heterosexual women, assuming a husband's last name is something they've looked forward to all their lives. For others, this custom identifies the woman as property; actually, that was the historic intent behind the practice. But have you ever realized that all last names are male, since a woman's birth name is, almost without exception, the last name of her father? If a baby isn't given the father's last name, it is given the last name of the mother, which, in almost all cases, is the last name of the mother's father, and so on. Some people have altered this process to give themselves an autonomous identity. For example, feminist author Julia Penelope used to be Julia Stanley, but she dropped her father's last name (Stanley) and began using her middle name, Penelope, as a last name (Spender, 1985).

> *I bet that women who keep their own names are less apt to keep their husbands.*
>
> —*Andy Rooney, commentator on CBS's 60 Minutes*

People in many countries struggle with the issue of married names (Arichi, 1999). Only recently in the U.S. have some women begun to choose to retain their maiden names when they marry, rather than adopt their husbands' last name—a choice that has caused many a prenuptial argument (Foss, Edson, & Linde, 2000). However, these women are in the minority; according to some statistics, 90 percent of American married women choose to adopt their husbands' last name (Brightman, 1994). The remaining 10 percent tend to be younger and well-educated. Of that group, 5 percent use a hyphenated name, 3 percent use their maiden name as a middle name (as in Senator Hillary Rodham Clinton and Bush Cabinet member Christine Todd Whitman), and the remaining 2 percent use only their maiden name.

One study shows that Americans have mixed perceptions of married women who use their maiden names. A professor of language surveyed more than 10,000 people in 12 states and discovered that married women who kept their maiden names were perceived as "more likely to be independent, less attractive, less likely to make a good wife or mother, more feminist, younger, better educated, more likely to work outside the home, more outspoken, more self-confident, less likely to enjoy cooking, and less likely to go to church" (Murray, as in " 'Feminist' stereotype persists," 1998, p. H1).

If you're female and you expect to marry someday, what do you think would happen if you asked your future husband to take *your* last name? If you're male, what would happen if your future wife asked you to take *her* last name rather than taking yours? Do you know of men who have taken their wives' last name? We can't think of any married couples who go by only the wife's last name—Jane Smith and Joe Jones becoming Jane and Joe Smith. We do know many couples who use both last names or who have combined their last names into a new family name. But the name game can become very tense if children come along. Again, the point is to be able to *choose* language that suits you and your relationships.

Euphemisms and Metaphors

The English language contains a great many expressions about the sexes that go seemingly unnoticed, but that form subtly sexist patterns. These expressions are usually in the form of *metaphors* or *euphemisms*—more comfortable substitutes for other terms. One of the most influential authors on the topic of euphemistic language is Robin Lakoff, whose research of the 1970s continues to have an impact today. Lakoff (1975) explored euphemisms for the word *woman*, such as *lady* and *girl*, and their connotations. Depending on the context, these three terms can either be synonyms or opposites (Kruh, 1992; Romaine, 1999). While many people think of *lady* as a term of respect that puts a woman on a pedestal, to others it suggests negative qualities such as being frail, scatterbrained, sugary sweet, demure, flatterable, and sexually frigid or repressed. If you're female, maybe you can recall instances in which an authority figure warned you to "Act like a lady!" Did you know what that meant, and did you then know how to act? However, more recently third wave feminists have co-opted the term, redefining it with irony, metaphor, and sassiness, as in descriptions of female musicians and artists (Fudge, 2001).

Connotations of the word *girl* have changed a great deal in recent years. Many adult women in the 1970s and 1980s reported feeling patronized and disrespected when they were referred to as *girls*. The term connoted childishness, innocence, and immaturity—and most women don't want to be thought of in those terms. However, starting in the 1990s and continuing today, more positive meanings for *girl* have emerged (especially for women in their teens and twenties). Some of this trend relates to the "alternative culture's Riot Grrrl movement, an effort by new female bands in the early '90s to reclaim the brash, bratty sense of self-control that psychologists claim girls lose just before puberty" (Bellafante, 1998, p. 60). The Spice Girls in England and the slogan "girl power" were among the early contributors to this shift in language. Many positive efforts and projects across the country continue to use *girl*-language as a means of enhancing young girls' self-esteem and their sense that they are not powerless in the world.

The confusion in this regard arises partly because there's no acceptable female equivalent term for *guy*. When males are called *guys*, females are called *girls*, rather than *gals* or *women* (or *dolls*, as in the musical *Guys and Dolls*). Think about what would happen if you were to say to a group of men, "Good morning, boys!" It could

> *It's okay to say "girls." Women want to be called girls. You can't say, "To all the old ladies I've loved before."*
>
> *—Enrique Iglesias, singer*

be seen as a friendly greeting connoting male camaraderie or a derogatory, condescending euphemism for men. Which terms are most appropriate really depends on the context in which you find yourself.

A Parallel Universe

Symmetry or *parallelism* in language is the use of gender-fair terms in referring to the sexes. Maggio (1988) cites three ways in which terms are asymmetrical and sexist. The first involves words that may appear parallel (or equal) but in actuality are not. An example that seems to be on its rightful way out is the dreaded statement "I now pronounce you man and wife" (LaRocque, 1997; Miller, Swift, & Maggio, 1997). If you don't see anything wrong with this statement, look closer. The man is still a man, but the woman is now a wife, with the connotation that she is relegated to that one role while he maintains a complete identity. How different would the connotation be if the traditional statement were "I now pronounce you woman and husband"?

A second type of asymmetry relates to terms originally constructed as parallel whose meanings have changed with common usage and time, so that the feminine form has a negative connotation (Romaine, 1999). Examples include *governor-governess, master-mistress, sir-madam,* and *bachelor-spinster* or *old maid*. A man who governs is a *governor*, but *governess* has come to mean a woman who takes care of someone else's children. You can certainly see the gap between meanings in the second and third examples—*mistress* and *madam* have taken on negative, sexual connotations while the masculine forms still imply power and authority. The last example is dramatic—as men grow older and stay single, they remain *bachelors* while women degenerate into *spinsters* and *old maids*. The tendency in our culture to compliment a man for his ability to stay single while ridiculing a woman for being unmarried is changing but is still quite real (Connelly, 1998).

The third type of asymmetry involves acceptable words, but their use is unacceptable because it alters the equality (Lakoff, 1975; Maggio, 1988). Two prime examples emerged from news stories about the American war on terror, which dominated the turn of the new century. In December 2001, CNN's news commentator Wolf Blitzer made the following comment: "Scores of Afghans, including many Afghan women, were turned away from food supply locations." In January 2002, a reporter for ABC included this statement in his coverage of the first American military casualties in the conflict: "Seven Marines were killed, including the first U.S. woman." During the Persian Gulf War, considerable discussion emerged about women's roles in the conflict. Much was made of the fact that female soldiers were experiencing the most direct combat of any female military personnel thus far, and the question continually asked was: Is America ready to see its female soldiers brought home in body bags? One news report during the Persian Gulf War read as follows: "A small number of American soldiers were taken captive by the Iraqi soldiers; one of the prisoners is believed to be a woman."

These are prime examples of violations of parallel usage because the language depicts men as the norm and the female Afghan citizens, female American Marine, and female P.O.W. as aberrations. The presence of men in these situations is a given or the rule; the presence of women deserves extra attention and special language because women are the exceptions to the rule. But this kind of attention is limiting and unnecessary; the language makes women outsiders. Adhering to nonsexist principles of parallelism would result in the following altered statement about the slain Marines: "Seven Marines were killed, including one woman and six men." Do you think women have been in the Marine Corps and other military organizations long enough now that we no longer need to call special attention to them?

Out of Order

Have you heard the traditional saying "ladies first"? While some people still operate by this standard in such matters as opening doors, "ladies first" isn't a predominant pattern in language. When you put language under the microscope, you find that male terms are almost always communicated first and female terms second, as in the following: his and hers; boys and girls; men and women; men, women, and children; male and female; husband and wife; Mr. and Mrs. Smith; the duke and duchess of Windsor; king and queen; the president and first lady; brothers and sisters. (Three exceptions are the traditional greeting, "ladies and gentlemen," references to the "bride and groom," and a mention of someone's parents, as in "How are your mom and dad doing?") Putting the masculine term first gives precedence to men and implies that women were derived from men or are secondary to them (Frank & Treichler, 1989; Hardman, 1999; Miller & Swift, 1988). The simple suggestion here is that you try to alternate which term you say or write first when you use these constructions in communication. If you're sharp, you've noticed that, in this text, for every "women and men" and "she or he," a "men and women" and "he or she" appears. It's a small correction in one's language and few may notice it, but it will make your communication more gender-sensitive.

Titles and Salutations

The accepted male title, *Mr.*, doesn't reflect a man's marital status. Mr. Joe Schmoe can be single, married, divorced, or widowed. The titles for women include *Miss, Mrs.*, and *Ms.*, which have been called *nubility titles*, a term derived from *nubile*, meaning sexually attractive or marriageable (Romaine, 1999, p. 123). What differentiates *Miss* and *Mrs.* is marital status, but this is only a fairly recent usage. Until the nineteenth century, the two terms merely distinguished female children and young women from older, more mature women (Spender, 1985). History isn't clear about why the function of the titles changed, but some scholars link it to the beginning of the industrial revolution, when women began working outside the home. Supposedly, working obscured a woman's tie to the home, so the titles provided clarity (Miller & Swift, 1991). Because of the patriarchal nature of language, people deemed it necessary to be able to identify whether or not a woman was married, though it was not necessary to know a man's relationship to a woman.

To counter this practice, women began to use the neologism *Ms.* a few decades ago, although the term has existed as a title of courtesy since the 1940s (Miller & Swift, 1991). People of both sexes resisted the use of *Ms.* when it first came on the scene, claiming that it was hard to pronounce. But is it any harder to pronounce than *Mrs.* or *Mr.*? Some women today choose not to use the title because they believe it links them with feminists, a connection they consider undesirable. Others use *Ms.* for exactly that reason—its link with feminism—and to establish their identity apart from men. Our male and female students alike report that *Ms.* is well accepted and commonly used, although some mistakenly believe that *Ms.* is a title referring exclusively to divorced women.

Regarding written salutations and greetings, for many years the standard salutation in a letter to someone you did not know (and did not know the sex of) was "Dear Sir" or "Gentlemen." If you only knew the last name of a person in an address or if the first name did not reveal the sex of the person, the default salutation was "Dear Mr. So-and-So." But that sexist practice is changing because of questions about why the masculine form should stand for all people. The terms *Sirs* and *Gentlemen* no more include women than the pronoun *he* or the term *mankind*.

What are your nonsexist options for salutations? Sometimes a simple phone call or e-mail to the organization you want to contact will enable you to specify a greeting. An easier way to fix this problem is to use terms that don't imply sex, such as: (Dear) Officers, Staff Member, Personnel, Members of the Department, Managers, Resident, Subscriber, Director, Executives, and the like. It may seem awkward the first time you use terminology like this. If it is more comfortable for you to use a sex-identified term, then use inclusive references such as *Ms./Mr.,*

Remember. . .

EUPHEMISM: A more comfortable term that substitutes for another term.

METAPHOR: Use of language to draw a comparison; the nonliteral application of language to an object or action.

SYMMETRICAL OR PARALLEL LANGUAGE: Use of language that represents the sexes in a balanced and fair manner.

ORDER OF TERMS: Language usage that alternates which sex appears or is said first.

TITLES: Designations such as *Mr.* or *Ms.* before a person's name.

SALUTATIONS: Letter or memo greetings that often contain sexist, exclusively male language.

Sir or Madam, and *Madams and Sirs*. We suspect that a man's reaction to *Dear Madam or Sir* won't be as negative as that of a woman who sees *Dear Sir* in her letter. Other alternatives include omitting a salutation altogether, opting for an opening line that says "Greetings!" or "Hello!" or structuring a letter more like a memo, beginning with "To the Director," "Regarding Your Memo of 9/7," or "TO: Friends of the Library" (Maggio, 1988, p. 184). We caution against using the trite, overused "To Whom It May Concern"; your letter may end up in the trash simply because "no one was concerned."

USING LANGUAGE: ONCE YOU CHOOSE IT, HOW DO YOU USE IT?

Now that you understand what we mean by choice in language, here comes the real challenge: the actual use of language in everyday interactions with others. We now move on to the *between* aspect of language—communication *between* the sexes, not *about* them. Experience and research tell us that men and women often have difficulty communicating with each other. Before we explore how women and men communicate, let's explore why they communicate.

An Axiom of Communication

Three communication scholars—Watzlawick, Beavin, and Jackson (1967)—developed a set of *axioms*, or basic rules, about how human communication operates. They proposed, as one axiom, that "Every communication has a content and a relationship aspect such that the latter classifies the former and is therefore a metacommunication" (p. 54). The *content* aspect of communication is what is actually said or the information imparted from one communicator to another. The *relational* aspect of the message is termed *metacommunication* (communication about communication) because it tells the receiver how the message should be interpreted and communicates something about the nature of the relationship between the interactants. For example, a simple "hello" spoken in a warm tone of voice conveys a sense of friendship and familiarity, whereas a hollow, perfunctory tone may indicate a more formal and impersonal relationship. Tone of voice, in this case, serves as metacommunication; that is, it indicates how the message should be interpreted and gives clues about the relationship. The content element is generally conveyed through verbal communication, whereas the relational element primarily takes the form of nonverbal communication. Watzlawick, Beavin, and Jackson suggested that rarely do interactants deliberately define the nature and state of their relationship; thus the relational elements of messages are usually conveyed in subtle, unspoken, and unconscious ways.

Even the simplest exchange has a relational and a content dimension. If a complete stranger walked toward you on the sidewalk, made eye contact, and said "Hi; how's it going?" you might reply with some minimal greeting like "Okay, thanks." But if someone you knew was walking down the hallway at school and extended the same greeting, although you might answer the same way, your response would probably sound and look different from your response in the exchange with the stranger. In both interactions, the content of the message is a basic greeting, but the relational aspects signal a difference in the relationship between you and the stranger versus you and the school acquaintance.

Women, Men, and the Relational versus Content Approach to Communication

On the basis of Watzlawick, Beavin, and Jackson's axiom, we suggest that a fundamental difference exists in what many women and men believe to be the function or purpose of communication. (Granted, this is a generalization, and there are exceptions.) Specifically, men tend to approach conversation more with the intent of imparting information (content aspect) than to convey cues about the relationship (relational aspect). In contrast, women tend to view conversation more as an indication of relationship than as a mechanism for imparting information. This does not mean that every time a man speaks, he is conveying information only; on the contrary, *every* message carries content and relational meanings. Nor does it mean that women communicate only relationally, without ever exchanging any real information. What it does mean is that men may use communication primarily for information exchange rather than for relationship development. Think about it. Male friendships more often develop in the form of *doing*, rather than *talking*. Women like to *do* as well as *talk*, but their relationships with other women are more often maintained via conversation than by doing things together. This represents a fundamental sex difference before women and men even meet, and it may set us up for conflict when we communicate.

Here are some real-life examples to illustrate this supposition—which we call the *relational versus content approach to communication*. On hearing an explanation of these approaches, a colleague said, "Is this like the other morning when my wife and I woke up before we had to actually get up, and she said, 'Let's just lie here and talk,' and I didn't have anything to talk *about*?" Similarly, a friend explained that a man she'd been seeing gave her the "silent treatment" one evening at her house. She asked him a couple of times if anything was wrong and he politely replied, "No," but he continued to be quiet. In frustration, she finally accused him of holding something back; she assumed he didn't care about her or they would be talking. His response was that he just didn't have anything to say, but that obviously he must care about her because "After all, I'm *here*." A student recalled a recent argument he'd had with his partner: "We'd been talking about something that happened a few nights before, and it led to an argument. When I felt that I'd explained my side of the story sufficiently and that we'd argued enough, I simply said, 'There's nothing more to say. End of discussion.' This made her furious, and I couldn't figure out why. She wanted to continue talking about the incident, my side of it, her side of it, what the argument meant about our relationship, and I just wanted the conversation *over*."

These examples illustrate men's and women's different views of the uses or functions of conversation. Many times women want to talk just to reinforce the fact that a relationship exists and that the relationship is important. What is actually being said is usually less important than the fact that a conversation is taking place. Conversely, men generally approach conversation from a functional standpoint. A conversation functions as a means of exchanging information or content, not as a reinforcement of the relationship.

No wonder men often think that women talk on and on about nothing. No wonder women often think that men's relationships (and sometimes, men themselves) are superficial. What's going on here? It's not that women are insecure chatterboxes who have nothing better to do than carry on long, pointless conversations because they need relational reinforcement. And it's not that men are relationally aloof clods who don't need reinforcement of a relationship or can't manage even a simple conversation to save their souls. What's going here is that, in general, women and men use communication for different purposes and get their "relational goodies" in different ways.

What Does the Research Say?

Research and theory support the supposition that men and women tend to approach conversation from different functional perspectives. However, some of the terminology and research approaches vary across disciplines.

Videotaped Conversation Research

To test the relational versus content supposition, we conducted two experiments to see if observers would assign different purposes or reasons for people's engagement in conversation. Both involved scripted videotaped conversations between two opposite-sex classmates. The first video depicted acquaintances chatting before class started. In this scene, a male student recognized a female classmate as someone from a previous class. They slowly remembered each other and the earlier class, discussed problems with the current class, and ended the conversation as the female student agreed to lend her class notes to the male student. At various points, a facilitator stopped the tape during breaks in the conversation and asked subjects to complete items on a questionnaire. When asked, "What do you think the purpose of this conversation is?" a majority of the female respondents suggested relational purposes (such as "to become friends rather than just acquaintances" and "to introduce something larger, perhaps a date or studying together for a test"). Most male respondents suggested content purposes, indicating that the conversation served the function of venting complaints and arranging for the loan of notes.

A different group of students responded to a second video. In this video the setting was the same—an encounter before class—but the script involved a female student telling a male classmate about a club she'd been to and about a party she was going to with some friends. The conversation ended just before class started, with the guy deciding to go to the party with the female student and her friends. As in the first study, female subjects saw primarily relational purposes in the conversation, offering such comments as, "They're establishing 'extra interest' at this point" and "It seems like they're trying to get to see each other outside of class, as maybe more than just friends." Male subjects attributed content purposes more than relational purposes; they made comments such as, "She's telling him about a party," and "They're catching up on what they've been doing." While these studies are from the perspective of an observer or eavesdropper rather than someone involved in the conversation, the findings do lend support to the relational versus content approach to communication.

Interpersonal Communication Motives

Communication researchers continue to explore the purposes of talk, specifically people's motives for engaging in conversation (Kondo, 1994; Myers, Martin, & Mottet, 2002; Rubin & Martin, 1998). Rubin, Perse, and Barbato (1988) propose that while interpersonal communication research has been thorough in its examination of *how* interaction occurs, it has been less thorough in attempting to understand *why* people choose to interact. Thus Rubin and colleagues studied more than 500 subjects ranging in age from 12 to 91, attempting to discover whether people communicated for such purposes as wanting to be included by others, extending and receiving affection, simply relaxing, needing companionship, or controlling situations and other people. They detected a significant sex difference. Female subjects reported being "more likely to talk to others for pleasure, to express affection, to seek inclusion, and to relax" (p. 621). Men reported communicating more to exert control over a situation rather than to express affection or seek inclusion. Results from this study support the contention that, in many cases, men's and women's motives or purposes for engaging in conversation differ.

Tannen's Contributions

In her book *That's Not What I Meant!*, sociolinguist Deborah Tannen (1986) describes sex differences in communication in terms of messages (actual content) versus metamessages (cues about how to interpret messages and about the relationship), using language similar to the axiom proposed by Watzlawick et al. (1967). She posits that "women are often more attuned than men to the metamessages of talk. When women surmise meaning in this way, it seems mysterious to men, who call it 'women's intuition' (if they think it's right) or 'reading things in' (if they think it's wrong). The difference in focus on messages and metamessages can give men and women different points of view on almost any comment" (Tannen, 1986, as in Coates, 1998, pp. 435–436, 437). In her second book, *You Just Don't Understand*, Tannen (1990) describes men's and women's talk in ways that parallel the relational versus content supposition. The female style, which she calls *rapport-talk*, is women's "way of establishing connections and negotiating relationships" (p. 77). The male style or *report-talk* "is primarily a means to preserve independence and negotiate and maintain status. This is done by exhibiting knowledge and skill and by holding center stage through verbal performance such as storytelling, joking, or imparting information" (p. 77).

What's Preferable—Relational or Content Communication?

Neither the relational nor the content approach is necessarily preferable. Remember that every message—no matter how brief or trivial—has both content and relational elements. The difference seems to lie in a person's view of the function or purpose of a given message. Watzlawick, Beavin, and Jackson believed that in healthy relationships, content and relational aspects were balanced. By contrast, a "sick" relationship could be characterized by communication focused too narrowly on the relational dimension, so that even the simplest messages became interpreted as statements about the relationship. Likewise, relationships in which communication degenerated into mere information exchange could also be termed "sick" (p. 53).

Throughout this text we encourage you to expand your options for communicative behavior into a more fully developed repertoire. An understanding of male and female approaches to talk is illuminating, but an important goal is to develop an integrated or balanced approach derived from the best attributes of both. Such an approach recognizes that certain times, situations, and people require different kinds of communication. Skill is involved in determining which communicative approach—relational or content—is better, given the dictates of the situation. In this manner, men could strengthen their male friendships through conversation rather than relying primarily on action or shared activities. Such conversation would provide good experience that could carry over into their relationships with women. Likewise, more women could realize that in many of their relationships with men, talk may not be the primary way to develop the relationship. Women might become more comfortable in approaching conversation with men more on the basis of content, rather than expecting the conversation to reveal how men feel about them or how men view the relationship. The ideal would be to respond to each other as effectively as possible, unencumbered by what is expected or stereotypical for each sex.

> ## *Remember. . .*
>
> **AXIOM OF COMMUNICATION:** Basic rules or law-like statements about how human communication operates.
>
> **RELATIONAL APPROACH:** The view that communication functions primarily to establish and develop relationships between interactants.
>
> **CONTENT APPROACH:** The view that communication functions primarily for information exchange between interactants.
>
> **METACOMMUNICATION:** Communication about communication.
>
> **INTERPERSONAL COMMUNICATION MOTIVES:** A line of research that focuses on why people communicate, that is, what function or purpose communication serves for people.
>
> **RAPPORT TALK:** Tannen's term for a female style of communicating, based on the motivation of establishing connections between people.
>
> **REPORT TALK:** Tannen's term for a male style of communicating, based on the motivation of preserving independence and gaining and maintaining status.

LANGUAGE USAGE BETWEEN WOMEN AND MEN

This final section of the chapter examines ways in which language is used in communication *between* women and men—*how* we communicate. Researchers have described the male style of communication as direct, succinct, personal, and instrumental, and the female style as indirect, elaborate, and affective, that is, reflecting emotions and attitudes (Mulac, Bradac, & Gibbons, 2001). Studies have produced contradictory results regarding some linguistic patterns of the sexes, but in general female patterns have been found weaker, more passive, and less commanding of respect in comparison with male styles. Some researchers consider linguistic sex differences profound enough to form *genderlects*, defined as "speech that contains features that mark it as stereotypically masculine or feminine" (Hoar, 1992, p. 127). As language expert Anthony Mulac (1998) puts it, "There are two abiding truths on which the general public and research scholars find themselves in uneasy agreement: (a) Men and women speak the same language, and (b) men and women speak that language differently" (p. 127).

Vocal Properties and Linguistic Constructions

Vocal properties are aspects of the production of sound related to the physiological voice-producing mechanism in humans. *Linguistic constructions* reflect speech patterns or habits; they are communicative choices people make.

How Low Can You Go?

The *pitch* of a human voice can be defined as the highness or lowness of a particular sound produced when air causes the vocal cords to vibrate. Physiological structures related to voice production are configured so that women tend to produce higher-pitched sounds and men tend to produce lower-pitched sounds. But scholars have uprooted some notions about physiological sex differences and voice production, especially with regard to singing, suggesting that differences may have more to do with social interpretations than with physiology alone (Brownmiller, 1984; Graddol & Swann, 1989). Research indicates that women and men are equally capable of producing high pitches, but that men have been socialized not to use the higher pitches for fear of sounding feminine (Henley, 1977; Kramer, 1977; Pfeiffer, 1985).

In comparison with the low melodic tones that most men are able to produce, the so-called high-pitched female whine has drawn long-standing societal criticism (McConnell-Ginet, 1983); this has led to, as Cameron (1985) puts it, "a widespread prejudice against women's voices" (p. 54). In a patriarchal society such as ours, men's lower-pitched voices are deemed more credible and persuasive than women's. Gender scholar Nancy Hoar (1992) suggests, "Women who aspire to influential positions are often advised to cultivate lower-pitched voices, voices that communicate authority" (p. 130). Examples are readily found in network and cable news shows, in which the few women who serve as substitute or weekend anchors, as well as those who report or offer commentary, tend to have (or develop) lower-pitched voices than women in the general population.

Men with higher-pitched voices are often ridiculed as effeminate. Their "feminine" voices detract from their credibility and dynamism, unless another physical or personality attribute somehow overpowers or contradicts that judgment. (Mike Tyson, former heavyweight boxing champion, is one example of this.)

Indications of Tentativeness

A great deal of research shows that women are far more *tentative* in their communication than men, and this tentativeness can undermine women's messages, making women appear uncertain, insecure, incompetent, powerless, and less likely to be taken seriously (Carli, 1990; Graddol & Swann, 1989; Lakoff, 1975; McConnell-Ginet, 1983). However, other studies suggest that factors such as culture, status and position in society, the goal or intent of the communicator (e.g., to create rapport between interactants or to facilitate conflict), and the nature of the group in which communication occurs (same-sex or mixed-sex) have much more impact than sex on stylistic variations (Aries, 1996; Mulac et al., 2001; Swann, 1998; Weatherall, 1998; Yaeger-Dror, 1998).

One vocal property that indicates tentativeness is *intonation*, described by sociolinguist Sally McConnell-Ginet (1983) as "the tune to which we set the text of our talk" (p. 70). Research is contradictory as to whether a rising intonation (typically associated with asking questions) is more indicative of a female or a male style. In the 1970s, Robin Lakoff contended that a rising intonation was unique to English-speaking women whose intent was to receive confirmation from others. An example can be found in the simple exchange, "What's for dinner tonight?" followed by the answer, "Spaghetti?" The intonation turns the answer into a question, as if to say "Is that okay with you?" However, research conducted by one expert in language and education, Carole Edelsky (1979), indicated that the interpretation of a rising intonation depended on the context in which it was used. Contradictory research findings led feminist scholar Julia Penelope (1990) to conclude: "Women are said to use. . . structures that are servile and submissive ('polite'), tentative, uncertain, emotionally exaggerated, and self-demeaning. These alleged traits represent a stereotype of how women talk, *not* the way we do talk" (pp. xxii–xxiii).

A linguistic construction related to tentativeness is the *tag question*, as in "This is a really beautiful day, don't you think?" The primary function of the tag question is to seek agreement or a response from a listener (Fishman, 1980; Zimmerman & West, 1975). Lakoff (1975) believed that tag questions serve as an "apology for making an assertion at all" (p. 54). She attributed the use of tag questions to a general lack of assertiveness or confidence about what one is saying, more indicative of the female style than the male style. Some research supports a connection between women's style and the use of tag questions (Carli, 1990; Zimmerman & West, 1975), but other research finds no evidence that tag questions occur more in female speech than in male speech, nor that tag questions necessarily function to indicate uncertainty or tentativeness (Holmes, 1990; Roger & Nesshoever, 1987). Tag questions may operate as genuine requests, as considerate attempts to include others in the conversation, or as efforts to "forestall opposition" (Dubois & Crouch, 1975, p. 292; Romaine, 1999). As Spender (1985) points out, it is inappropriate to view tag questions as always indicating hesitancy, as evidenced by her example, " 'You won't do that again, *will you?' " (p. 9).

Qualifiers, *hedges*, and *disclaimers* are other linguistic constructions generally interpreted as indicating tentativeness and stereotypically associated with women's speech. *Qualifiers* include *well, you know, kind of, sort of, really, perhaps, possibly, maybe,* and *of course. Hedging* devices include such terms as *I think (believe, feel), I guess, I mean,* and *I wonder* (Carli, 1990; Holmes, 1990; Spender, 1985). *Disclaimers* are typically longer forms of hedges that act as prefaces or defense mechanisms when one is unsure or doubtful of what one is about to say (Beach & Dunning, 1982; Hewitt & Stokes, 1975). Disclaimers generally weaken or soften the effect of a message. Examples of disclaimers include such statements as "I know this is a dumb question, but. . ." and "I may be wrong here, but I think that. . ."

Two linguists—Janet Holmes (1990), who studied speech patterns in New Zealand; and Deborah Cameron (1985), who studied tentativeness in Londoners' speech patterns—conclude that sex-typed interpretations of tentativeness must be made within the given context in which the communication occurs, as do researchers in the United States (Mulac et al., 2001; Mulac & Lundell, 1986; Ragan, 1989; Sayers & Sherblom, 1987). Holmes (1990) discovered, for example, that men and women were equally likely to use tentative linguistic devices, depending on the needs or mandates of the particular situation. Cameron (1985) found that male subjects exhibited tentative communication when placed in certain roles, such as facilitators of group interaction. Male and female subjects in O'Barr and Atkins's (1980) study of courtroom communication used the entire range of indicators of tentativeness with equal frequency, except for tag questions.

An overabundance of tentative forms of expression in one's communication can be interpreted as a sign of uncertainty and insecurity. But tentative language may also have positive, facilitative uses; these kinds of expressions need not be identified with one sex or the other. As gender scholar Alice Deakins (1992) suggests, "women's style" or "powerless style" may be "interpreted as cooperative, consensual, and leaderless" (p. 155). For example, a manager who has high status within an organization might use disclaimers or hedges in attempts to even out a status differential, foster a sense of camaraderie among staff members, and show herself or himself as open to employees' suggestions and ideas.

Managing to Converse

Have you ever considered how conversation is organized or "managed"? *Conversation management* involves several variables, but one interesting vein of research has to do with indicators of conversational dominance.

Conversation typically occurs in *turns,* meaning that one speaker takes a turn, then another, and so on, such that interaction is socially organized (Sacks, Schegloff, & Jefferson, 1978). Two noted sociologists, West and Zimmerman, have conducted significant research into how turn-taking is accomplished. When people take turns talking, they may experience *overlaps,* defined as "simultaneous speech initiated by a next speaker just as a current speaker arrives at a possible turn-transition place"; and *interruptions,* which are "deeper intrusions into the internal structure of the speaker's utterance" (West & Zimmerman, 1983, pp. 103–104). Interruptions and overlaps have been interpreted as indicating disrespect, restricting a speaker's rights, serving as devices to control a topic, and revealing an attitude of dominance and authority (Marche & Peterson, 1993; Weiss & Fisher, 1998). Overlaps are considered less egregious than interruptions because overlapping someone's speech may be seen as supportive—as trying to reinforce or dovetail off of someone else's idea. Interruptions more often indicate dominance and power plays because they cut off the speaker in midstream and suggest that the interrupter's comment is somehow more important or insightful.

In the most widely cited study of adult conversations, Zimmerman and West (1975) found few overlaps and interruptions within same-sex interactions. However, in cross-sex conversations more interruptions occurred than overlaps, and 96 percent of the interruptions were made by males. West and Zimmerman compared their findings for male and female interruptive behavior to that seen in parent-child interactions; they suggest that "the use of interruptions by males is a *display* of dominance or control to the female (and to any witnesses), just as the parent's interruption communicates an aspect of parental control to the child and to others present" (1975, as in Coates, 1998, p. 172).

Other early research revealed definite evidence of male conversational dominance in terms of initiating topics, working to keep the conversation focused on those topics, talking more often and for longer durations, offering minimal responses to women's comments, and using more declaratives than questions (Edelsky, 1981; Fishman, 1983). However, later studies have gone beyond sex effects to explore the complexity of dominance in such contexts as face-to-face interaction, same-sex and mixed-sex dyads and groups, marital dyads, and

Remember. . .

GENDERLECTS: Language containing specific, consistent features that mark it as stereotypically masculine or feminine.

VOCAL PROPERTIES: Aspects of the production of sound related to the physiological voice-producing mechanism in humans.

LINGUISTIC CONSTRUCTIONS: Speech patterns or habits; communicative choices people make.

PITCH: The highness or lowness of a particular sound made when air causes the vocal cords to vibrate.

TENTATIVENESS: Forms of language, typically used by women, which indicate hesitation or speculation and which can make them appear uncertain, insecure, incompetent, powerless, and less likely to be taken seriously.

INTONATION: Use of pitch that creates a pattern or that sends a specific message, such as a rising pitch to indicate a question.

TAG QUESTION: A linguistic construction related to tentativeness, which involves adding a brief question onto the end of a statement.

QUALIFIER, HEDGE, & DISCLAIMER: Linguistic constructions related to tentativeness, which preface or accompany a message so as to soften its impact or deflect attention away from the statement.

CONVERSATION MANAGEMENT: The way a conversation is organized or conducted in a series of turns.

OVERLAP: A linguistic construction typically associated with conversational dominance, in which one person begins speaking just as another person finishes speaking.

INTERRUPTION: A linguistic construction typically associated with conversational dominance, in which one speaker intrudes into the comments of another.

electronic conversations. Researchers now suggest that many nonverbal, contextual, and cultural factors, such as perceptions of power and status, seating arrangements, and sex-typed topics, affect judgments of dominant or powerless styles (Aries, 1998; Herring, Johnson, & DiBenedetto, 1998; Robey, Canary, & Burggraf, 1998; Smythe & Huddleston, 1992; Swann, 1998; Tannen, 1994).

News talk shows on television, such as *Larry King Live* (CNN), *Hardball* (MSNBC), and *The O'Reilly Factor* (Fox News) are prime opportunities to observe conversation management (or, many times, mismanagement). The displays of vocal dominance and competitiveness among male and female guests are fascinating in these forums. Male speakers and hosts often dominate female speakers. However, the more seasoned female guests have learned techniques for controlling the topics they respond to and raise with hosts, for holding their turns at talk longer, and for minimizing interruptions from other guests or the host. Take a break some time from all that studying you do every night and tune in to one of these programs. See if you can detect the elements we describe, as well as other linguistic and vocal devices that are used to manage conversation.

CONCLUSION

In this chapter on language, we've explored some influences existing in your world that profoundly affect your gender communication. You first need to understand how you are influenced before you can choose to lessen or negate an influence. This chapter has given you more than a few things to think about, because when you put something under a microscope, you see it in a new way. We have tossed a lot at you for one main reason: so that you won't use language by default or habit but will instead *choose* to use language that accurately reflects who you are and how you think. Now that you've read this material, do you understand what we meant by the *cumulative* effect we mentioned in the introductory paragraphs of this chapter?

This chapter has challenged you to consider more fully how communication is used to talk *about* the sexes, as well as why and how communication occurs *between* them. We first explored the nature of language and some reasons for using nonsexist language; then we reviewed several forms and practices related to sexist language, as well as nonsexist alternatives. Regarding communication *between* the sexes, we examined relational and content approaches to determine whether the sexes view communication as serving different functions or purposes. We then focused on vocal properties and linguistic constructions that continue to be studied for what they reveal about the sexes and how we communicate. As we said in the introduction to this chapter, the goal was to focus on language and its important role in gender communication, to offer ways that you can expand your linguistic options, and to challenge you to *choose* and *use* language in a more inclusive and unbiased way in order to enhance your personal effectiveness in gender communication and your relationships.

Discussion Starters

1. What were you taught in junior high or high school about sexist language? Do you remember any reactions you had at the time to what was taught? If you received no instruction on nonsexist language, why do you think this information wasn't included in your education? Have you been taught something similar or contradictory in college about sexist language? (Or have you perhaps been taught nothing at all?) How does previous teaching you received on this topic compare with the information in this chapter?

2. Why do you think a neologism like *Ms.* made its way into the language whereas nonsexist pronouns like *tey*, *gen*, and *herm* have not been accepted? What does it take, in your opinion, for a new term to be accepted in society? If you wanted to introduce new words into the language, what would they be and how would you go about it?

3. Sexism in religious language is one of the more difficult topics to explore and discuss. For some people, it is an affront to put the language used to convey their deeply personal religious beliefs under the microscope. What are your views on this subject? First, do you think that religious language is male-dominated? If so, do you think this language should be reexamined? Or do you think religious language should be an exception within the larger topic of sexist language?

4. Think of two people—a woman and a man—whose communication styles correspond most closely (or stereotypically) to the relational and content approaches presented in this chapter. What aspects of each person's communication make him or her stand out in your mind as an example?

5. In light of the information in this chapter on conversation management, assess your own style of communication. How often do you communicate in questions? How often do you communicate in statements? Do you use questions because you earnestly want answers, or to ensure that you'll get a response and the conversation will continue? Are you more likely to be interrupted or to interrupt someone else? How do you respond to other people's overlaps and interruptions? Do you use a lot of tag questions, hedges, and disclaimers in your communication? Think about classroom communication. Do you find yourself saying things like, "This might be a dumb question, but. . ." or "I could be wrong, but. . ."? If so, do you believe that these elements weaken your effect and make you appear tentative or powerless?

References

Aldrich, P. G. (1985, December). Skirting sexism. *Nation's Business*, 34–35.

Arichi, M. (1999). Is it radical? Women's right to keep their own surnames after marriage. *Women's Studies International Forum, 22*, 411–415.

Aries, E. (1996). *Men and women in interaction*. New York: Oxford University Press.

Aries, E. (1998). Gender differences in interaction: A reexamination. In D. J. Canary & K. Dindia (Eds.), *Sex differences and similarities in communication: Critical essays and empirical investigations of sex and gender in interaction* (pp. 65–81). Mahwah, NJ: Erlbaum.

August, E. R. (1992). Real men don't: Anti-male bias in English. In M. Schaum & C. Flanagan (Eds.), *Gender images: Readings for composition* (pp. 131–141). Boston: Houghton Mifflin.

Baker, R. (1981). "Pricks" and "chicks": A plea for "persons." In M. Vetterling-Braggin (Ed.), *Sexist language: A modern philosophical analysis* (pp. 161–182). New York: Rowman & Littlefield.

Beach, W. A., & Dunning, D. G. (1982). Pre-indexing and conversational organization. *Quarterly Journal of Speech, 67*, 170–185.

Bellafante, G. (1998, June 29). Feminism: It's all about me! *Time*, 54–62.

Briere, J., & Lanktree, C. (1983). Sex-role related effects of sex bias in language. *Sex Roles, 9*, 625–632.

Brightman, J. (1994). Why Hillary chooses Rodham Clinton. *American Demographics, 16*, 9–11.

Brooks, L. (1983). Sexist language in occupational information: Does it make a difference? *Journal of Vocational Behavior, 23*, 227–232.

Brownmiller, S. (1984). *Femininity*. New York: Simon & Schuster.

Cameron, D. (1985). *Feminism and linguistic theory*. New York: St. Martin's.

Carli, L. L. (1990). Gender, language, and influence. *Journal of Personality and Social Psychology, 59*, 941–951.

Connelly, S. (1998, August 2). Single women still viewed as incomplete. *Corpus Christi Caller Times*, p. H1.

Deakins, A. H. (1992). The *tu/vous* dilemma: Gender, power, and solidarity. In L. A. M. Perry, L. H. Turner, & H. M. Sterk (Eds.), *Constructing and reconstructing gender: The links among communication, language, and gender* (pp. 151–161). Albany: State University of New York Press.

Devor, H. (1992). Becoming members of society: Learning the social meanings of gender. In M. Schaum & C. Flanagan (Eds.), *Gender images: Readings for composition* (pp. 23–33). Boston: Houghton Mifflin.

Dubois, B. L., & Crouch, I. (1975). The question of tag questions in women's speech: They don't really use more of them, do they? *Language in Society, 4,* 289–294.

Edelsky, C. (1979). Question intonation and sex roles. *Language in Society, 8,* 15–32.

Edelsky, C. (1981). Who's got the floor? *Language in Society, 10,* 383–421.

"Feminist" stereotype persists about wives who choose to keep maiden name. (1998, July 12). *Corpus Christi Caller Times,* pp. H1, H3.

Fishman, P. M. (1980). Conversational insecurity. In H. Giles, W. P. Robinson, & P. M. Smith (Eds.), *Language: Social psychological perspectives* (pp. 1 27–132). New York: Pergamon.

Fishman, P. M. (1983). Interaction: The work women do. In B. Thorne, C. Kramarae, & N. Henley (Eds.), *Language, gender, and society* (pp. 89–101). Rowley, MA: Newbury.

Foss, K., Edson, B., & Linde, J. (2000). What's in a name? Negotiating decisions about marital names. In D. O. Braithwaite & J. T. Wood (Eds.), *Case studies in interpersonal communication* (pp. 18–25). Belmont, CA: Wadsworth.

Frank, F. W., & Treichler, P. A. (1989). *Language, gender, and professional writing: Theoretical approaches and guidelines for non-sexist usage.* New York: Modern Language Association.

Fudge, R. (2001). Grrrl, you'll be a lady soon. *Bitch, 14,* 22–24.

Gastil, J. (1990). Generic pronouns and sexist language: The oxymoronic character of masculine generics. *Sex Roles, 23,* 629–641.

Gorski, E. (2002, February 3). Christian leaders debate new gender-neutral Bible translation. Knight Ridder Newspapers, as reported in *Corpus Christi Caller Times.*

Graddol, D., & Swann, J. (1989). *Gender voices.* Cambridge, MA: Basil Blackwell.

Green, J. (1999). *The big book of filth.* London: Cassell.

Hamilton, L. C. (1988). Using masculine generics: Does generic "he" increase male bias in the user's imagery? *Sex Roles, 19,* 785–799.

Hardman, M. J. (1999). Why we should say "women and men" until it doesn't matter any more. *Women & Language, 22,* 1–2.

Henley, N. M. (1977). *Body politics: Power, sex, and nonverbal communication.* Englewood Cliffs, NJ: Prentice-Hall.

Herring, S. C., Johnson, D. A., & DiBenedetto, T. (1998). Participation in electronic discourse in a "feminist" field. In J. Coates (Ed.), *Language and gender: A reader* (pp. 197–210). Malden, MA: Blackwell.

Hewitt, J. P., & Stokes, R. (1975). Disclaimers. *American Sociological Review, 40,* 1–11.

Hoar, N. (1992). Genderlect, powerlect, and politeness. In L. A. M. Perry, L. H. Turner, & H. M. Sterk (Eds.), *Constructing and reconstructing gender: The links among communication, language, and gender* (pp. 127–136). Albany: State University of New York Press.

Holmes, J. (1990). Hedges and boosters in women's and men's speech. *Language and Communication, 10,* 185–205.

Ivy, D. K. (1986, February). *Who's the boss?: He, he/she, or they?* Paper presented at the meeting of the Western Speech Communication Association, Tucson, AZ.

Ivy, D. K., Bullis-Moore, L., Norvell, K., Backlund, P., & Javidi, M. (1995). The lawyer, the babysitter, and the student: Inclusive language usage and instruction. *Women & Language, 18,* 13–21.

Jones, K. T., & Mills, R. (2001). The rhetoric of heteroglossia of Jewish feminism: A paradox confronted. *Women & Language, 24,* 58–64.

Kang, Y. P. (2001, April 27). What to surf: Net cetera. *Entertainment Weekly,* 121.

Kondo, D. S. (1994). A comparative analysis of interpersonal communication motives between high and low communication apprehensives. *Communication Research Reports, 11,* 53–58.

Kennedy, D. (1992). Review essay: She or he in textbooks. *Women & Language, 15,* 46–49.

Kramarae, C. (1981). *Women and men speaking.* Rowley, MA: Newbury.

Kramer, C. (1977). Perceptions of female and male speech. *Language and Speech, 20,* 151–161.

Kruh, N. (1992, April 29). What name should you wear? Girl, lady, or woman—the terms mean more than you think. *Dallas Morning News,* pp. 1C, 2C, 3C.

Lakoff, R. (1975). *Language and woman's place.* New York: Harper & Row.

LaRocque, P. (1997, April 7). Sexism slips into language. *Dallas Morning News,* p. 13A.

Leardi, J. (1997, September 28). Is God male or female? For some, issue of God and gender is subject to debate. *Corpus Christi Caller Times,* pp. H1, H3.

Madson, L., & Hessling, R. M. (1999). Does alternating between masculine and feminine pronouns eliminate perceived gender bias in a text? *Sex Roles, 41,* 559–576.

Maggio, R. (1988). *The nonsexist word finder: A dictionary of gender-free usage.* Boston: Beacon.

Maggio, R. (1992). *The bias-free word finder.* Boston: Beacon.

Marche, T. A., & Peterson, C. (1993). The development and sex-related use of interruption behavior. *Human Communication Research, 19,* 388–408.

Martyna, W. (1978). What does "he" mean? Use of the generic masculine. *Journal of Communication, 28,* 131–138.

McConnell-Ginet, S. (1980). Linguistics and the feminist challenge. In S. McConnell-Ginet, R. Borker, & N. Furman (Eds.), *Women and language in literature and society* (pp. 3–25). New York: Praeger.

McConnell-Ginet, S. (1983). Intonation in a man's world. In B. Thorne, C. Kramarae, & N. Henley (Eds.), *Language, gender, and society* (pp. 69–88). Rowley, MA: Newbury.

Miller, C., & Swift, K. (1988). *The handbook of nonsexist writing* (2nd ed.). New York: Harper & Row.

Miller, C., & Swift, K. (1991). *Words and women: New language in new times.* New York: HarperCollins.

Miller, C., Swift, K., & Maggio, R. (1997, September-October). Liberating language. *Ms.,* 50–54.

Moffat, M. (1989). *Coming of age in New Jersey.* New Brunswick, NJ: Rutgers University Press.

Morreale, S. (2000, August). Morreale's mailbag: Research resources for students. *Spectra,* National Communication Association newsletter.

Morreale, S. (2002, March). Morreale's mailbag: Internet resources for students. *Spectra,* National Communication Association newsletter.

Moulton, J., Robinson, G. M., & Elias, C. (1978). Sex bias in language use: "Neutral" pronouns that aren't. *American Psychologist, 33,* 1032–1036.

Mulac, A. (1998). The gender-linked language effect: Do language differences really make a difference? In D. J. Canary & K. Dindia (Eds.), *Sex differences and similarities in communication: Critical essays and empirical investigations of sex and gender in interaction* (pp. 127–155). Mahwah, NJ: Erlbaum.

Mulac, A., Bradac, J. J., & Gibbons, P. (2001). Empirical support for the gender-as-culture hypothesis: An intercultural analysis of male/female language differences. *Human Communication Research, 27,* 121–152.

Mulac, A., & Lundell, T. L. (1986). Linguistic contributors to the gender-linked language effect. *Journal of Language and Social Psychology, 5,* 81–101.

Murnen, S. K. (2000). Gender and the use of sexually degrading language. *Psychology of Women Quarterly, 24,* 319–327.

Myers, S. A., Martin, M. M., & Mottet, T. P. (2002). Students' motives for communicating with their instructors: Considering instructor socio-communicative style, student socio-communicative orientation, and student gender. *Communication Education, 51,* 121–133.

O'Barr, W. M., & Atkins, B. K. (1980). "Women's language" or "powerless language"? In S. McConnell-Ginet, R. Borker, & N. Furman (Eds.), *Women and language in literature and society* (pp. 93–110). New York: Praeger.

Palczewski, C. H. (1998). "Tak[e] the helm," man the ship . . . and I forgot my bikini! Unraveling why woman is not considered a verb. *Women & Language, 21*, 1–8.

Parks, J. B., & Roberton, M. A. (1998a). Influence of age, gender, and context on attitudes toward sexist/nonsexist language: Is sport a special case? *Sex Roles, 38*, 477–494.

Parks, J. B., & Roberton, M. A. (1998b). Contemporary arguments against nonsexist language: Blaubergs (1980) revisited. *Sex Roles, 39*, 445–461.

Penelope, J. (1990). *Speaking freely: Unlearning the lies of the fathers' tongues*. New York: Pergamon.

Pfeiffer, J. (1985). Girl talk, boy talk. *Science, 85*, 58–63.

Ragan, S. L. (1989). Communication between the sexes: A consideration of sex differences in adult communication. In J. F. Nussbaum (Ed.), *Life-span communication: Normative processes* (pp. 179–193). Hillsdale, NJ: Erlbaum.

Robey, E. B., Canary, D. J., & Burggraf, C. S. (1998). Conversational maintenance behaviors of husbands and wives: An observational analysis. In D. J. Canary & K. Dindia (Eds.), *Sex differences and similarities in communication* (pp. 373–392). Mahwah, NJ: Erlbaum.

Roger, D., & Nesshoever, W. (1987). Individual differences in dyadic conversational strategies: A further study. *British Journal of Social Psychology, 26*, 247–255.

Romaine, S. (1999). *Communicating gender*. Mahwah, NJ: Erlbaum.

Rubin, R. B., & Martin, M. M. (1998). Interpersonal communication motives. In J. C. McCroskey, J. A. Daly, M. M. Martin, & M. J. Beatty (Eds.), *Communication and personality: Trait perspectives* (pp. 287–308). Cresskill, NJ: Hampton.

Rubin, R. B., Perse, E. M., & Barbato, C. A. (1988). Conceptualization and measurement of interpersonal communication motives. *Human Communication Research, 14*, 602–628.

Sacks, H., Schegloff, E. A., & Jefferson, G. (1978). A simple systematic for the organization of turn taking for conversation. In J. Schenkein (Ed.), *Studies in the organization of conversational interaction* (pp. 7–55). New York: Academic.

Sayers, F., & Sherblom, J. (1987). Qualification in male language as influenced by age and gender of conversational partner. *Communication Research Reports, 4*, 88–92.

Schmitt, J. J. (1992). God's wife: Some gender reflections on the Bible and biblical interpretation. In L. A. M. Perry, L. H. Turner, & H. M. Sterk (Eds.), *Constructing and reconstructing gender: The links among communication, language, and gender* (pp. 269–281). Albany: State University of New York Press.

Smythe, M. J., & Huddleston, B. (1992). Competition and collaboration: Male and female communication patterns during dyadic interactions. In L. A. M. Perry, L. H. Turner, & H. M. Sterk (Eds.), *Constructing and reconstructing gender: The links among communication, language, and gender* (pp. 251–260). Albany: State University of New York Press.

Sorrels, B. D. (1983). *The nonsexist communicator*. Englewood Cliffs, NJ: Prentice-Hall.

Spender, D. (1985). *Man made language* (2nd ed.). London: Routledge & Kegan Paul.

Stanley, J. P. (1977). Paradigmatic woman: The prostitute. In D. L. Shores (Ed.), *Papers in language variation*. Birmingham: University of Alabama Press.

Steinem, G. (1995, September-October). Words and change. *Ms.*, 93–96.

Stericker, A. (1981). Does this "he or she" business really make a difference? The effect of masculine pronouns as generics on job attitudes. *Sex Roles, 7*, 637–641.

Stinger, J. L., & Hopper, R. (1998). Generic *he* in conversation? *Quarterly Journal of Speech, 84*, 209–221.

Swann, J. (1998). Talk control: An illustration from the classroom of problems in analysing male dominance of conversation. In J. Coates (Ed.), *Language and gender: A reader* (pp. 184–196). Malden, MA: Blackwell.

Tannen, D. (1986). *That's not what I meant!* London: Dent.

Tannen, D. (1990). *You just don't understand.* New York: William Morrow.

Tannen, D. (1994). *Gender and discourse.* New York: Oxford University Press.

Watzlawick, P., Beavin, J. H., & Jackson, D. D. (1967). *Pragmatics of human communication.* New York: W. W. Norton.

Weatherall, A. (1998). Re-visioning gender and language research. *Women & Language, 21,* 1–9.

Weiss, E. H., & Fisher, B. (1998). Should we teach women to interrupt? Cultural variables in management communication courses. *Women in Management Review, 13,* 37–44.

West, C. (1998). When the doctor is a "lady": Power, status and gender in physician-patient encounters. In J. Coates (Ed.), *Language and gender: A reader* (pp. 396–412). Malden, MA: Blackwell.

West, C., & Zimmerman, D. H. (1975). Women's place in everyday talk: Reflections on parent-child interaction. In J. Coates (1998) (Ed.), *Language and gender: A reader* (pp.165–175). Malden, MA: Blackwell.

West, C., & Zimmerman, D. H. (1983). Small insults: A study of interruptions in cross-sex conversations between unacquainted persons. In B. Thorne, C. Kramarae, & N. Henley (Eds.), *Language, gender, and society* (pp. 102–117). Rowley, MA: Newbury.

Whorf, B. L. (1956). Science and linguistics. In J. B. Carroll (Ed.), *Language, thought, and reality.* Cambridge, MA: Massachusetts Institute of Technology Press.

Yaeger-Dror, M. (1998). Factors influencing the contrast between men's and women's speech. *Women & Language, 21,* 40–46.

Zimmerman, D. H., & West, C. (1975). Sex roles, interruptions and silences in conversation. In B. Thorne & N. Henley (Eds.), *Language and sex: Difference and dominance* (pp. 105–129). Rowley, MA: Newbury.

CHAPTER FIVE

GENDER AND RELATIONSHIPS:
Developing Potential into Reality

CASE STUDY: CHOOSING AND BEING CHOSEN

Debbie wasn't the greatest athlete when she was a kid. The best athletes always got to choose sides for kickball during elementary school recess, and invariably Debbie was among the last to be chosen by one of the two captains. (You couldn't really call it "choosing" at that point—it was just a matter of who was left and which side had to take her.) Anticipating recess and her inevitable humiliation planted early seeds of an ulcer.

Not much changed in this regard as Debbie grew up. In college, when she tried to play intramural sports, she found that her spirit was willing but her flesh was weak. She was the proverbial "alternate" on the volunteer team. Debbie was successful in other areas, however. She was a fairly good student, making mostly A's and B's, because she found subjects she liked to study. She chose a major that suited her. It turned out that team sports weren't her "thing"; academics were.

What about a social life? After all, isn't that the reason most everyone goes to college in the first place? (Just kidding.) Debbie had lots of friends, mostly college women she met in the dorms and classmates who shared her major. But when another dateless Saturday night rolled around, Debbie decided that something HAD to change. She studied feminism in some of her courses; she'd read about women's liberation in history class. She could sit idly by, weekend after weekend, waiting for Mr. Right (or Mr. Right Now) to get lost on campus, find his way to her room to ask for directions, take one look at her and fall head over heels, and beg her to go out with him. Or she could take the reins and make her own future relationships happen. We're pleased to report that Debbie is now a successful business owner and happily married with two perfect children and a husband who adores her. (We felt a need to provide a Hollywood ending.)

What's the point of this story? We all face choices in life—choices we make and choices others make concerning us. These choices have a significant impact on who we are and who we become. A wise person once said, "There are no such things as right and wrong decisions; there are only decisions." But we all want to make the wisest decisions possible, because our decisions guide our lives and we know we'll have to live with the consequences.

For most of us, relationships bring us life's greatest satisfactions. Probably more than anything else in life, relationships bring us our highest highs and, sad to say, our lowest lows. This chapter examines the bases of choices regarding relationships and the forms of communication that facilitate those choices. Rather than hoping or believing that if you wait long enough or experiment enough, the perfect friend, dating partner, or mate will find his or her way to you, this chapter suggests a more proactive (rather than reactive) strategy. Relationship initiation and development are based on *choice—choosing* and *being chosen*. You clearly can't have close, personal relationships with everyone, so you must choose. On the flip side, it is very flattering to be chosen and can be very painful not to be.

Hot Topics

- The role of information in the process of choosing and being chosen
- Barriers or roadblocks to success in relationships
- The ups and downs of initiating relationships in cyberspace
- The role of attraction, physical appearance, proximity, and similarity in the initiation of relationships
- Strategies to reduce uncertainty about potential relationships
- Initial contact, first conversations, and flirting
- How sex differences in communication skills such as self-disclosure, empathy, listening, and nonverbal expressiveness and sensitivity influence the development of relationships
- Communicating to effect change in relationships

BETTER INFORMATION = BETTER CHOICES

When we talk with students about the process of choice in relationships or who chooses whom and why, it seems to come down to one thing: not physical appearance, not opposites attract, but *information*. Most of the time, people choose people they *know the most about*. What is the source of this information? *Communication*. The information you gather may be based on communication—verbal or nonverbal, conscious or unconscious, intentional or unintentional. The better and more complete your information, the better your choices. Initiating relationships depends more on information gathered through the communication process than on any other factor, even physical appearance (no matter what the media and the fashion industry would have you believe).

The basic process works like this: You observe, you communicate, you evaluate, you make choices, you act. How relationships develop and change and who takes responsibility for these tasks are questions many of our students have pondered, yet most are not fully aware of the information they use to make their choices. Understanding how the process works and, more important, understanding how women and men deal with relational issues are critical.

> *Relationship is a pervading and changing mystery . . . brutal or lovely, the mystery waits for people wherever they go, whatever extreme they run to.*
>
> —Eudora Welty, author

At various stages in a developing relationship, you will make decisions about the future of the relationship. These instances may be seen as *choice points*. Imagine that you have a superficial friendship with someone at work. However, you think the person is interesting and decide that a more personal friendship might be possible. By making that decision, you have exercised some control over the direction of the relationship. You've decided to accelerate the rate of change and move the relationship from one level to another. Each of us has faced decisions such as whether to turn an acquaintance into a friend, a friendship into something deeper, or a romantic relationship back to a friendship (good luck). Choice points such as these occur frequently, and the decisions that arise from them have an obvious impact on the quality of the relationship.

Before going further, let's clarify our use of the terms *relationship* and *relational partner*. There are all kinds of relationships, and the word *relationship* is widely used. When we use the word *relationship* in our gender communication classes, students typically think of dating or romantic relationships rather than other kinds. We discuss in this chapter some elements that pertain more to dating or romantic relationships. But there are many concepts and research findings that apply to relationships in general—all kinds of relationships. When we use the term *relational partner*, it does not necessarily suggest a romantic relationship; nor does it imply the permanence implied by the term *marital partner*. It is simply a means of identifying the two people in a relationship.

RELATIONSHIP ROADBLOCKS

Sometimes relationships work very well; at other times, they just don't go well at all. Before exploring aspects of gender communication that enhance relationship initiation and maintenance, let's examine some common barriers to healthy, satisfying relationships.

Roadblock 1: High Expectations

In Chapter 3, we discussed the impact of the media on our behavior. It's fairly clear that movies, television shows, and romance novels set us up for unrealistic expectations regarding relationships, especially romantic ones. The media frequently depict attractive, beautiful people engaged in fun, seemingly worry-free, and highly physical romantic relationships. The media rarely show these relationships six months or a year later, as they have developed over time, nor do they usually depict the work necessary to make relationships successful. The sexes may fantasize about the perfect mate, but we know that nobody's perfect. So sometimes when we set unrealistically high expectations for others and for our relationships, we really set ourselves up for a fall.

Roadblock 2: This Should Be Easy

You know now that communication isn't a natural thing that you can do successfully just because you've been communicating all your life. So why do we sometimes think it ought to be so easy to just relax and talk to someone? Why, in reality, is communication so difficult in relationships—especially in important relationships? Effective communication isn't easy, and the more you have riding on the success of your relationship, the more difficult communication seems to be.

Roadblock 3: Fear of Failure

This is the reverse of Roadblock 2: the fear of failing at relationships so stymies some people that they don't even try make friends, much less date. They talk the most to their dog. Failure is part of the relational process, however painful it might be. And, even though this is a cliché, we do learn from failure.

Roadblock 4: If I Just Relax, a Good Relationship Will Find Me

Even though we believe in a proactive approach to relationships, there are rare times when things just happen. You aren't thinking about dating anyone, you don't expect to meet someone wonderful, and—bingo—Ms. or Mr. Incredible comes into the picture. But there's no predicting this process, and you may be setting yourself up for some lonely times if you merely wait and expect friendship or romance to find you. A proactive, balanced approach of introspection, planning, patience, developing communication skills, and maybe a bit of faith is likely to generate better results than just waiting for something to happen.

Roadblock 5: The "Bozos"

Many people become tongue-tied when they talk to someone they are attracted to and interested in. Nothing seems to work, weird sentences come out of their mouths, they forget their own names, they break into a sweat, and things generally go from bad to worse. Men and women alike, articulate in every other situation, may suddenly get an attack of the "bozos" when they face an attractive person. The "bozos" happen to all of us at one time or another, and they can stop an interesting relationship from ever getting off the ground. But with a better understanding of gender communication and more practice in developing your relational skills, your "bozo" moments will be fewer.

Roadblock 6: It's Got to Happen Now!

As Carrie Fisher wrote in *Postcards from the Edge,* "Instant gratification takes too long." Some people express a desire to have a remote control for relationships, so they can zip and zap, getting what they want when they want it. Probably all of us could use a bigger dose of patience in our relationships. Solid, successful relationships of all kinds take time to nurture and develop. Wanting too much too soon (and sometimes getting it) can be a big problem. Not taking adequate time to nurture a relationship can sabotage a potentially wonderful relationship before it has had its chance.

> *It doesn't matter whether your partner is the same sex or the opposite sex, all of it is tough.*
>
> —*Lynda Bird Johnson, elder daughter of President Lyndon B. Johnson*

Roadblock 7: Giving Up Too Much Just to Have a Dating Relationship

Advisers in university residence halls describe a problem that they see regularly: some students (more often female than male) are too willing to compromise themselves sexually or in other ways in order to get a dating relationship started. Are women more likely than men to want dating or romantic relationships, or is this just a stereotype? Women often feel tension between the traditional message that they should have a man in their lives and the modern message of careerism and autonomy. Sometimes this desire for acceptance causes people to do things they really don't want to do. No one should have to bend to pressure or be motivated by the desire to impress another person or to achieve some form of social status.

Remember. . .

CHOICE POINTS: Moments in a relationship when you make decisions about its future.

RELATIONSHIP: Any type of partnering between two people, e.g., friendships, workplace connections, romantic or committed partnerings.

RELATIONAL PARTNER: A term to identify the two people in a relationship—any relationship, not just a romantic or committed one.

STAGE 1: IS THERE A RELATIONSHIP GOLD MINE OUT THERE? PROSPECTING AND BEING A PROSPECT

Initiating relationships is a process similar to prospecting for gold. Like a prospector, you are looking for something that will add value to your life (if not actually make you rich!). Like a prospector, you go out into the "field" and examine "samples" for possible value to you. If a sample (person) looks interesting, you can examine him or her more closely. But there is at least one big difference—while you are examining prospects, they could be examining you. You are a prospect as well as a prospector.

Prospecting—whether for gold or for a relationship—is an active process. This is very different than the attitude of waiting for something to happen suggested by the expression, "If it's meant to be, it will be." The proactive approach presented here puts you in charge of your relationships: you neither wait for something to happen nor blame something or someone if it doesn't happen. Did you ever see the bumper sticker, "So many men, so little time"? In your lifetime, you have the potential to initiate and develop hundreds of relationships. Whether you entered college immediately after leaving high school or started your college career later in life, college is a prime time for experiencing various kinds of relationships, and it presents numerous opportunities for initiating relationships.

Seeing and Being Seen

The first part of stage 1 in relationship development, normally, is seeing others and being seen. Information gathered through observations guides your first choices, but when men and women go prospecting, what do they look for? What features catch the eye and spark the imagination? Research suggests that we form impressions and make judgments about people in the first 10 seconds after meeting them (Burch, 2001). What impression do you make when someone first meets you?

We like to ask our male and female students what they look for in potential dating partners; their responses are amazingly similar. Both sexes seem to look for people who are physically appealing (but not so exceptionally gorgeous that they are unapproachable), who look nice (usually that means nonthreatening, well-groomed, etc.), who show an appropriate degree of self-confidence, who smile a lot and have a good sense of humor, who aren't too afraid or too macho to show interest, and who will impress their parents and friends. It's interesting that this list doesn't include being "Joe Stud" or looking like "Molly Model."

Not Being Seen: Prospecting in Cyberspace

Obviously, seeing a person is not the only way a relationship can begin. The Internet, for example, has vastly increased opportunities for relationship development; it has also had an impact on users' general understanding of romantic relationships (Adelman & Ahuvia, 1992; Breznican, 2000; Maurstad, 1996; Stone, 1999). Communication scholar Malcom Parks, who has done research on the formation of relationships through the Web, states: "One of the great things about the Net, for both good and bad, is that it allows you to find and communicate with people of a common interest unusually quickly and on a tremendous scale" (as in Maurstad, 1996, p. A17). For many people, a major advantage of cyber-relating is that it lessens the importance of physical appearance in relationship initiation. As one Internet user comments, "Eloquence makes me beautiful on line" (Markham, 1998, p. 203).

Interestingly, some research appears to indicate that sex differences diminish in computer-mediated communication. One study found that women were at less of a disadvantage in computer-mediated communication than in face-to-face communication and could be more participative and direct (McConnell, 1997). Other research determined that, besides reducing the importance of physical traits, computerized communication increases the significance of rapport and similarity and allows more freedom from gender-role constraints (Cooper & Sportolari, 1997). However, some gender-related trends emerge in cyber-communication (Yates, 1997). For example, online conversations between men and women tend to be male-dominated and the topics tend to be male-oriented (Sutton, 1996; Warnick, 1999). Men's online communication style tends to contain more assertions than questions, more self-promotion, more challenges, and more sarcasm; women's style tends to contain questions, apologies, and a personal (rather than factual) orientation.

One of the most interesting aspects of Internet communication is the possibility of altering one's identity and gender bending (Turkle, 1995). It is possible for people to take on totally different identities online, to present themselves as a member of the opposite sex, and to "walk on the wild side" in relative safety. Thus you may never know exactly with whom you are communicating; you and the other person may both be experimenting. (We've all heard or read horror stories of innocent people who were duped by predators on the Internet.) People who meet on the Internet must be careful if they arrange to meet in person. Many Internet relationships fail to survive the first face-to-face meeting. However, we have students who spend hours on the Internet, go out on computer dates, develop deep relationships, and in some cases, fall in love. Internet relationships can be just as meaningful and significant as in-person relationships (Markham, 1998; Walther & Tidwell, 1996).

Being Attracted to a Prospect

Just what is attraction? According to students, it can be "lust," "a sort of chemistry between you and another person," "wanting to have sexual intercourse with another person," and "liking someone—not just physically, but for personality traits." You can see from these responses that some people use the term *attraction* to apply to platonic friendships, in which one person is attracted to another on a nonphysical, nonsexual basis, whereas others associate attraction with sexual interest. *Attraction* has been defined as a motivational state that causes someone to think, feel, and behave in a positive manner toward another person (Berscheid, 1985). More specifically, *sexual attraction* could be considered

---

'Net Notes

Two Websites provide a battery of tests you can take to determine such things as your IQ, what breed of dog you're most like, your "aura," and, most pertinent to our discussion of relationships in this chapter, your "romantic sensibilities" (Limpert, 2002, p. 70). At **www.emode.com,** you can take a "Passion Predictor" quiz; you can also find out which Hollywood star your personality would be best suited for by taking the "Celebrity Matchmaker" test. The Spark site **(www.thespark.com)** offers 10 personality tests and is highly interactive. For example, the "Love Quiz" asks you questions, then provides profiles of other people (no names, just handles) who live in your area and scored similar results on the quiz.

"animal attraction"—being drawn to another person because you want to have sexual contact with her or him. You may or may not actually fulfill that desire, but the attraction is felt nonetheless. For our purposes in this chapter, let's use a broader interpretation: *interpersonal attraction* is the degree to which you want to form and possibly maintain an interpersonal relationship with another person (Beebe, Beebe, & Ivy, 2004). That relationship might be a same-sex or cross-sex friendship, a relationship with a coworker, a romantic relationship (nonsexual), or a sexual relationship.

Attractive Territory Ahead

Where does attraction start? Its source can be found in a concept of nonverbal communication known as *proximity.* As social psychologist Sharon Brehm explains, "To meet people is not necessarily to love them, but to love them we must first meet them" (2001, p. 61). Proximity relates to the space (territory) around you and the physical distance between you and someone else, the amount of time you spend physically near that person, how easily you can gain access to her or him, and how physical closeness affects the relationship. While it is possible to be attracted to someone you've never met and will probably never meet, realistically you are more likely to be attracted to someone if you perceive that there are opportunities to be around that person (Guerrero, Andersen, & Afifi, 2001; Kenrick, Neuberg, & Cialdini, 2002; Knapp & Hall, 2002). Some researchers have refined the idea of proximity or physical distance as *communication distance,* defined as the "number of members of their communication networks an initiator and his or her potential partner would have to go through to reach each other" (Berscheid & Reis, 1998, p. 204). This concept extends proximity by taking into account social context, patterns of expectations, and electronically mediated communication. In other words, you are more likely to be attracted to people you have the *opportunity* to interact with.

Proximity can increase or decrease your opportunity for attraction—that's simple enough. Now it's a matter of turning proximity to your advantage. Have you ever stationed yourself in the hallway to get a chance to talk with a certain special person? Or have you ever taken up a dangerous sport or a crazy hobby, just because a certain person participates in that activity? This is the "just happened to run into you at the gym" approach. If you have done any of these things, then you've been putting proximity to work for you. If you're currently in or have been in a long-distance relationship, then you know firsthand the challenges that not being near your relational partner can create (Blake, 1996; Van Horn et al., 1997).

Checking Out the Prospects

One prospecting strategy for gathering information about other people is to go out and observe them. You look at others; they look at you. Research suggests that in heterosexual encounters, women play the dominant role by scanning male prospects. They initiate most of the contact, primarily through the use of nonverbal signaling behaviors (Trost & Alberts, 1998). Typically, this is accomplished by making eye contact with a man they are interested in and either smiling or prolonging the eye contact to indicate approachability (Howell, 1996). While men do most of the physical approaching to initiate an encounter, they usually approach only after a woman has indicated nonverbally that an approach would be welcome.

Are the sexes different in terms of how much importance they place on physical appearance as a determinant of attraction? Social psychologist Alan Feingold (1990) reviewed approximately 50 studies supporting the finding that men value physical attractiveness most in a potential partner, whereas women value personality, intelligence, kindness, sensitivity, and a sense of humor more than looks. Subsequent research has borne out these findings (Feingold, 1992; Kenrick, Groth, Trost, & Sadalla, 1993; Kenrick, Sadalla, Groth, & Trost, 1990). Do these research findings match your own experience? How does someone's physical appearance affect you with regard to initiating relationships, or in relationships others initiate with you?

Another interesting point regarding attraction is that you may see someone you consider physically attractive but remain unattracted to him or her. We are not necessarily attracted to people who have a pleasing appearance. Haven't you ever seen someone who was beautiful but just didn't stir you in any way? Social psychological research in the 1970s produced a fascinating observation of human behavior that has stood the test of time and has come to be known as the *matching hypothesis* (Bar-Tal & Saxe, 1976). This research indicates that although you may appreciate the appearance of someone who is stunningly good-looking, you usually have relationships (and partnerships) with people you feel are similar in physical attractiveness to you. An average-looking heterosexual man may appreciate the physical appearance of a very good-looking woman, but he is more likely to be attracted to, date, and marry a woman he believes is at a level of attractiveness similar to his own.

Liking People Who Are Like You

Perhaps you have heard the cliché "Opposites attract." Probably more accurate is the notion that opposites attract, but the attraction typically doesn't last. Some people may be interested in others who are radically different from them—mainly because the differences are intriguing. But often these relationships don't last, because as the initial intrigue fades, the differences become obstacles, sometimes insurmountable.

Most of us prefer *similarity* over difference in relationships. Research indicates that under most circumstances, you will generally be more interested in someone whose upbringing, attitudes, beliefs, and values are more similar to yours than different (Kenrick et al., 2002; Shaikh & Kanakar, 1994; Sharma & Kaur, 1995; Waldron & Applegate, 1998). Social psychologists Berscheid and Reis (1998) put it aptly: "The most basic principle of attraction is familiarity. As opposed to the unfamiliar, familiar people usually are judged to be safe and unlikely to cause harm" (p. 205). One study of teenagers found that similarities in appearance, sex, age, and race highly influenced interpersonal attraction and choices for beginning conversations (Aboud & Mendelson, 1998). Research involving dating partners and college roommates found that similarity in the emotional dimensions of a relationship (comfort, ego support, conflict management, sincerity, and warmth) were more important than other dimensions of attraction and contributed to greater relationship satisfaction (Burleson, Kunkel, & Birch, 1994; Varnadore, Howe, & Brownlow, 1994).

How can you turn this information into a strategy—both for choosing and for being chosen? It's a good idea to place yourself in the company of people

---

Remember...

ATTRACTION: A motivational state that causes someone to think, feel, and behave in a positive manner toward another person.

SEXUAL ATTRACTION: Feeling drawn to another person because you want to have sexual contact with her or him.

INTERPERSONAL ATTRACTION: The degree to which you want to form and possibly maintain an interpersonal relationship with another person.

PROXIMITY: The space (territory) around you; the physical and psychological distance between you and others.

COMMUNICATION DISTANCE: The number of members of communication networks potential partners have to go through to reach each other.

MATCHING HYPOTHESIS: The tendency to form relationships, particularly romantic relationships, with persons you feel are similar in physical attractiveness to you.

SIMILARITY: The tendency to be interested in someone whose upbringing, attitudes, beliefs, and values are more similar to yours than different.

who seem similar to you and learn to what extent those similarities actually exist. For example, if you think that bar or club scenes are great opportunities for socializing with people who are fun, you are more likely to find someone with similar attitudes if you look in a bar or club than elsewhere. If your religious values are such that you believe attending church is important, then your chances of finding someone with similar values and beliefs are greater in a church setting than other places.

A Closer Inspection of the Prospect

What do people look for in a romantic partner? An article in *Ebony* magazine cited the following attributes as important: appearing approachable, increasing an intrigue factor (meaning that you project yourself as an interesting and captivating person), dressing to enhance but not entice, not getting lost in the crowd, having good conversational skills, exuding confidence, combining independence with a touch of vulnerability, staying in good physical shape, having a good sense of humor, and being positive about life in general (Turner, 1990). The list includes but is not obsessive about physical appearance; more personality traits are listed than physical characteristics. How do you get information about someone's personality?

Strategies for Gaining Information

As you perceive other people and begin to learn about them, understanding the role of information in this process may be helpful. Recall our discussion in Chapter 1 about *uncertainty reduction*. To briefly review, communication researchers have found that some situations, like meeting new people or forging new levels of relationships with people we already know, generate a degree of uncertainty for most of us. In an effort to reduce our uncertainty and make ourselves more comfortable, we respond by seeking information (Berger & Calabrese, 1975; Berger & Douglas, 1981; Douglas, 1990). Reducing uncertainty by gaining information enables *choice*—the choice you will make about whether or not to proceed with someone, as well as the choice someone else will make about you. (Although we describe uncertainty reduction mainly in the context of new relationships, ongoing relationships also generate uncertainty at certain points, and the strategies for reducing uncertainty apply in those instances as well.)

Three general strategies emerge for reducing uncertainty, all of which are based on information. The strategies are progressive, meaning that people usually start with the first and progress through the other two. Anywhere along the line, however, you can choose to break off the search for information if you deem it too risky or if you discover something that leads you to think the relationship will not be rewarding. First, people engage in *passive strategies*— observing others, most of the time without them knowing it. If you are thinking about making friends with someone, you may watch to see whom that person hangs out with and what they do. The more observations you make, the more you know.

The second category, *active strategies,* require more action than observation and typically involve a third party or another indirect means of gaining information. The most obvious strategy is to ask other people about someone—what the person is like, what he or she does, if the person is involved with someone at the time, and so on. Another active strategy, although it sounds a bit manipulative, is to stage situations to gain information about how another person responds. For example, someone at a party could walk around with an empty drink cup, just to see if she or he is noticed and if an offer for a refill is extended. Relationship experts Guerrero, Andersen, and Afifi (2001) recount an example provided by one of their female students. She wrote a note asking for a meeting, signed it "a secret female admirer," and placed it on her boyfriend's car. She wanted to know if her boyfriend would tell her of the letter and if he would meet the supposed admirer. As it turns out, the boyfriend never mentioned the letter to the girlfriend, but neither did he make the "rendezvous."

The most direct method of reducing uncertainty is an *interactive strategy,* which involves asking the "object of one's affection" direct questions or engaging her or him in conversation, either one-on-one or in a group. This strategy is considered the most risky, and for most of us it takes self-confidence and nerve, but it seems to be the most reliable, straightforward, and time-efficient method of getting information.

"We met in a recovery program, with separate, yet compatible, addictions."

Reprinted by permission of Donna L. Barstow.

Remember. . .

UNCERTAINTY REDUCTION: Human responses to low predictability and high uncertainty about other persons and circumstances.

PASSIVE STRATEGY: A strategy for reducing uncertainty by gaining information through observing people, but not directly communicating.

ACTIVE STRATEGY: A strategy for reducing uncertainty that involves a third party or another indirect means of gaining information.

INTERACTIVE STRATEGY: A strategy for reducing uncertainty that engages the interested party directly in communication, either one-on-one or in a group, to gain more information.

STAGE 2: ENGAGING THE PROSPECT—CONVERSATIONS

There is no clear-cut line between the first and second stages; they merely have some identifying characteristics. Stage 2 consists of the opening interactions of a relationship. Each person has made the initial choice in favor of the other person and has indicated a willingness to begin to interact and learn about the other. In this stage, people expend a good deal of energy trying to get the other person to think well of them. Here are a few strategies to help accomplish that goal.

Digging In and Discovering More

Most decisions about whether to act further on one's attraction are made in the first few minutes of a conversation, so a lot rides on that first encounter (Redmond & Vrchota, 1997). Your interest—and we use the word *interest* as an extension of attraction—now demands that you communicate verbally. What are the best ways to begin and develop an effective conversation?

Conversation Starters

Conversations have to start somewhere and there has to be an opening verbalization. Everyone laughs at the pickup lines of the 1960s and 1970s, such as "What's your sign?" "Haven't I seen you somewhere before?" and "What's a nice girl like you doing in a place like this?" In fact, the book *How To Pick Up Girls!* (1970) offered men a list of opening lines that were supposed to guarantee success with women. Here are a few of the more laughable ones: "You're Miss Ohio, aren't you? I saw your picture in the paper yesterday." "Do you have change for a 10?" "What kind of dog is that? He's great-looking." "Here, let me carry that for you. I wouldn't want you to strain that lovely body of yours." "Please pass the ketchup." "Didn't I meet you in Istanbul?" (Weber, 1970, pp. 72–78).

Opening lines can be funny to think and talk about, but they can reduce effective communication to a gimmick. Packaged opening lines are inconsistent with the principles underlying the receiver orientation to communication because they generally sidestep the process of adapting one's communication to the situation and to the receiver of the message. Why would someone use a line? Sometimes it is simply easier—people who might be nervous sometimes resort to trite beginnings just to get the ball rolling. For these reasons, we grant that lines or conversation-openers may be useful at times. Opening lines could be intended simply as conversation starters, not necessarily as an effort to pick up or hit on someone. Conversation-openers that reflect a thoughtful, sincere attempt at interaction can serve as an icebreaker for you and someone you're interested in. Maybe you know some things to say that have received relatively positive responses in past conversations. Perhaps you've observed something about the other person that you can comment on, such as a book the person is carrying that might lead into a conversation about college classes, or a T-shirt the person is wearing from a place you've visited or a favorite sports team.

Gender psychologists Kleinke, Meeker, and Staneski (1986) found that more than 90 percent of their subjects believed it was just as appropriate for a woman to open a conversation with a man as the reverse. In their study, college students generated examples of conversation-starters that they had heard or used, including things men might say to women and women might say to men. Then the researchers surveyed more than 250 college students to learn their preferences for these openers, which were divided into general and situation-specific categories.

The five general openers (in descending order) most preferred for women to use to initiate conversation were: (1) "Since we're both sitting alone, would you care to join me? (2) "Hi." (3) "I'm having trouble getting my car started. Will you give me a hand?" (4) "I don't have anybody to introduce me, but I'd really like to get to know you." (5) "Can you give me directions to (anywhere)?" The five least preferred openers (with the worst listed first) for women to use were: (1) "Didn't we meet in a previous life?" (2) "It's been a long time since I had a boyfriend." (3) "Hey baby, you've got a gorgeous chassis. Mind if I look under the hood?" (We're not kidding.) (4) "I'm easy. Are you?" (5) "What's your sign?" Did you notice that the five preferred openers are really just common ways to get someone talking, rather than suggestive, manipulative lines that make the other person feel uncomfortable or set up?

In this study, the five preferred openers that men might use with women were as follows: (1) "Hi." (2) "Hi. My name is _____." (3) "I feel a little embarrassed about this, but I'd like to meet you." (4) "That's a very pretty (sweater, dress, etc.) you have on." (5) "You have really nice (hair, eyes, etc.)." The five least preferred general openers for men to use (again, the worst is listed first) were: (1) "Is that really your hair?" (2) "You remind me of a woman I used to date." (3) "Your place or mine?" (Some things never change.) (4) "I'm easy. Are you?" (5) "Isn't it cold? Let's make some body heat." Both women and men in the study agreed that cute, flippant conversational openings were less effective than direct or nonthreatening, innocuous ones.

Asking Great Questions

If you wonder what makes a good conversationalist, the best answer we can provide is this: learn to ask great questions. Notice that we said "great" questions, not just questions. A great question is, first, tailored as much as possible to the recipient. Unlike a job interview, in which an interviewer may bombard an applicant with as many questions as time allows, a social encounter requires a kinder, gentler approach. Use whatever you can observe about the person and the situation to help you formulate questions that will draw the other person out. Basic informational questions (e.g., "Where are you from?" "What do you do for a living?") help break the ice, but "yes-no" questions or questions that can be answered with a single word don't extend a conversation. Also, avoid questions that might be perceived as too personal.

> *A study in the Washington Post says that women have better verbal skills than men. I just want to say to the authors of that study: Duh.*
>
> –Conan O'Brien, *television talk show host*

The second skill that helps develop conversational ability relates to listening. Many people go through the motions of asking questions, but they don't really listen to the answers. They may find themselves repeating questions they've already asked, embarrassing themselves and turning off the person they're trying to impress. It's important to listen intently when someone responds to your question, then pose a follow-up question that shows you're really listening and interested—not a statement that takes the focus away from the other person. Although some people become uncomfortable talking about themselves or their views, most of us enjoy the attention and feel that genuine interest is being shown.

Studies have found that more women than men ask questions to generate conversation in social situations (Coates, 1993; Lindsey & Zakahi, 1996, 1998). But we all need to develop and hone our conversational skills so that one person isn't responsible for getting a conversation off the ground and keeping it aloft. The skill of asking great questions doesn't happen like magic or overnight—time, maturity, and experience will help you improve your conversational ability.

The Art and Skill of Flirting

Is it typical of you to be unaware that someone likes you? How do you detect that someone is interested in you, either for a friendship or romantically? How do you show your interest in another person? Are you likely to reveal your interest through nonverbal means first, rather than coming right out and declaring undying love and affection? What exactly does it mean to flirt?

Hot Button Issue

"FLIRTING IS A TRICKY BUSINESS"

You've lived a number of years now, so we don't have to tell you that flirting is a tricky business. Some people suggest that among heterosexuals, it's a woman's job to flirt and a man's job to pick up on that flirtation and choose to do or not do something about it. But the situation is not really that simple, is it?

We call this a hot button issue to make a point: one person's flirtation is another person's sexual harassment. These days, you have to be very careful when you show romantic interest in another person. Since Americans' working lives take up increasingly significant amounts of time, many people find their social and romantic outlets through coworkers (Fine, 1996). But developing a romantic relationship with a colleague is a delicate endeavor, particularly if the colleague is your boss, you are his or her boss, or status differences exist for other reasons. Flirting at the office might seem perfectly harmless to you, but a more important point is whether or not the object of your flirtation also sees it as harmless.

Books on professional behavior will warn you to stay away from romantic entanglements at the office—period—no matter if both of you are on the same level within the organization. We understand this suggestion, but we realize that sometimes office liaisons just happen, and they can lead to wonderful relationships. We know of many colleagues who met their spouses at work or through professional circles. But the books' advice on flirting at the office is sound: be very, *very* careful with any kind of public demonstrations of interest. You never know who's looking and how that behavior may come back to haunt you.

Flirting is a popular term for a long-standing phenomenon: showing attraction to and interest in another person. We suggest caution here, however, because not all flirting is an indication of interest (Egland, Spitzberg, & Zormeier, 1996). Researchers have found that "people may flirt because they see it as innocent fun, they want to make a third party jealous, they want to develop their social skills, or they are trying to persuade someone to do something for them" (Guerrero et al., 2001, p. 185).

No matter what type of relationship is being initiated, most of us usually convey our interest in others nonverbally, rather than strolling up to someone and saying, "I find you interesting" (Abrahams, 1994; Grammer, 1990). One study conducted in singles bars identified fifty-two (!) nonverbal cues that heterosexual women use to signal their interest in men. At the top of this list of cues were smiling, surveying a room with the eyes, and increased physical proximity (Moore, 1985). People are also more likely to preen; they may adjust their clothing, fidget with their hair, and alter their posture in the presence of an attractive person (Daly, Hogg, Sacks, Smith, & Zimring, 1999; Grammer, Knuck, & Magnusson, 1998; Scheflen, 1965).

Communication scholars Trost and Alberts (1998) provide a fascinating discussion of heterosexual courtship, flirting, and sex differences, which they explain from a biological or evolutionary perspective. While the details of their argument would take us beyond the scope of our current discussion, these researchers do provide evidence from a body of work on the topic, and their conclusions are illuminating. The general conclusion from studies is that women are more dominant or more in control of the flirting process than men. Specifically, research is consistent in four findings: (1) women are more skilled at encoding and decoding flirtatious nonverbal behaviors; (2) women exhibit a wide variety of flirting behaviors that are used to signal their interest to men they desire to attract; (3) women have a widely developed repertoire of rejection strategies; and (4) women who exhibit flirtatious behaviors will typically be approached by men.

Before you start getting defensive, think about how flirtation actually seems to work in real life. As we suggested earlier, in the section on attraction, women typically initiate the process of "seeing and being seen" by nonverbally signaling their interest in a man. For decades, research on nonverbal communication has determined that women tend to give off more nonverbal cues than men and to decipher the cues of others with more accuracy than men (Knapp & Hall, 2002). Typically, if a woman is attracted to and interested in a man, she will show that interest nonverbally, leaving it to the man to pick up on her cues, decipher them as indications of interest, and make a decision to approach or not approach (Arliss, 2001). (This puts a lot of pressure on the man!) Granted, flirting doesn't always work this way. Some women tease and give off miscues (Kowalski, 1993); men sometimes misread cues (Abbey, 1982, 1987, 1991; Koeppel, Montagne, O'Hair, & Cody, 1999; Mongeau, 1992). Men may not reciprocate women's interest, and women are certainly capable of charging right up to men and declaring their interest verbally. But Trost and Albert's research findings are illuminating; ponder them and then see if they match your experience.

Once you've put yourself out there so as to see and be seen, you've been attracted and attractive, you've flirted, you've opened a conversation—perhaps with some scintillating, prepared lines or well-thought-out questions—you've listened to responses to your questions, and you've followed up those responses with other questions or comments. Now what? If those first conversations were successful enough to make you feel that there is real potential with someone, congratulations! Now you have more work to do.

STAGE 3: DEVELOPING THE CLAIM AND ESTABLISHING THE RELATIONSHIP

As a relationship develops, a judgment of *communicative competence* (meaning how effectively and appropriately one communicates) appears to outweigh other factors, such as appearance or similarity, in determinations of relationship satisfaction (Bell & Roloff, 1991; Flora & Segrin, 1999; Miczo, Segrin, & Allspach, 2001). Thus it is important to work to establish effective communication behaviors and patterns if you want a relationship to succeed—any kind of relationship. If we asked men and women, "What types of communication are most critical to the success of a relationship," would they generate similar lists? A few forms of communication have been studied a great deal in our discipline, as well as in related disciplines; they tend to show up on both women's and men's lists as being critical to relationships, so we review these in the pages that follow.

Opening a New Vein: Self-Disclosure

We will use some important terms in this section. First, *intimacy* is something most people long for in relationships—whether these are family relationships, friendships, or romantic relationships. What exactly is intimacy? Relationship experts Harvey and Weber (2002) provide such descriptions as bonding, closeness, and emotional connection, all based on sharing personal, private information and experiences over time. Our own favorite definition comes from a couples therapist, Jeffrey Fine (2001): "To be intimate is to be totally transparent, emotionally naked in front of another who is equally transparent. You want to see into the other's heart. What people should mean when they say *intimacy* is in-to-me-see" (p. 225). Granted, different kinds of relationships will involve different levels of intimacy, but it appears that some level of intimacy is a goal of most relationships (Canary & Emmers-Sommer, 1997).

You probably know by now that it's hard to make effective decisions or act effectively toward another person without accurate and useful information. The most common means of actively sharing information in order to develop intimacy is known as *self-disclosure*—a concept that was originally researched by psychologist Sidney Jourard (1971). Jourard suggests that self-disclosure occurs when we voluntarily provide information to others that they would not learn if we did not tell them. For example, your height and weight are generally noticeable, but your exact height (and especially) weight will most likely not be known by someone unless you choose to tell him or her. Research suggests that closeness and satisfaction in relationships of all types are closely tied to the level and quality of disclosure by the partners (Afifi & Guerrero, 1995; Prager & Buhrmester, 1998).

Some of our thinking about the sexes and self-disclosure is based on stereotypes, but the stereotypes have been supported by research. Consistent findings indicate that women like to and tend to disclose themselves more than men, especially with regard to their relationships, and they take more risks in disclosure by relating sensitive feelings and personal problems. In contrast, men are more often "strong, silent types" (Derlega, Metts, Petronio, & Margulis, 1993; Dindia & Allen, 1992; Sanders, Wiseman, & Matz, 1990; Shaffer, Pegalis, & Bazzini, 1996). Specifically, in terms of the depth and breadth of information the participants share with each other, female-female relationships have been ranked first in several studies, followed by male-female relationships. Male-male relationships have been rated lowest on degree of intimacy and amount of disclosure (Derlega, Winstead, Wong, & Hunter, 1985; Henley, 1986; Ickes, 1985).

Not only do women tend to disclose more than men, women receive others' disclosures much more often (Aries, 1998; Petronio, Martin, & Littlefield, 1984; Stephens & Harrison, 1985). Gender scholars Perry, Turner, and Sterk (1992) make the point that for most women, disclosure is a positive, welcome aspect of a relationship, and it functions as an invitation to more disclosure. Conversely, men tend to be competitive (even in disclosure) and disclose more about their strengths (such as professional or athletic successes) than about their weaknesses or vulnerability. However, when men do choose to disclose—about sensitive topics or other topics—they most often select women as listeners (Snell, Miller, & Belk, 1988).

Jourard (1971) addressed male-male disclosure (or the lack of it) and the consequences to men's physical health in a book chapter entitled "The Lethal Aspects of the Male Role." He suggested that men who have difficulty expressing their thoughts and feelings also have higher levels of stress-related diseases compared with men who are able to disclose more fully. More recent research supports this finding, indicating that stress related to the male role has not significantly declined since Jourard's work was published (Copenhaver & Eisler, 1996). For many men, expressing their thoughts and feelings suggests weakness and vulnerability, as though one gives up power and control by revealing oneself. In an era when information is power, giving out too much information may give others too much power. In personal relationships, however, a balance between power and disclosure facilitates the development of satisfying friendships, romantic relationships, marriages, and coworker relationships.

Let's stop and think about these sex differences for a moment. Does disclosure need to be expressed in words? Perhaps men disclose themselves through what they *do* in relationships; perhaps they seek and express intimacy nonverbally more than verbally. Research has begun to call into question earlier findings on the sexes and disclosure, and the stereotypes that may accompany them (Borisoff, 2001; Galvin & Bylund, 2001; Reis, 1998). For example, Wood and Inman (1993) make a case for considering joint activities (basketball, watching sports together, etc.) as a path to closeness in male friendships. It is true that women's friendships with other women more often develop and deepen through communication, particularly self-disclosure, rather than shared experiences (Canary & Emmers-Sommer, 1997). But we should not make the judgment that men's relationships with other men are superficial because they involve more doing than talking. We need to avoid using a feminine yardstick to measure intimacy or satisfaction with a relationship.

The Big "E": Empathy

Understanding and responding effectively to another person is critical to long-term relational success. You probably value people who seem to understand you and you probably want to increase contact with them.

Empathy has been called one of the "hallmarks of supportive relationships," yet it remains a difficult concept to define (Beebe, Beebe, & Ivy, 2004, p. 81). Empathizing means trying to understand and feel what another person is feeling; you divorce from self and try to step into the shoes of the other person, to experience as closely as you can what she or he is experiencing. An interesting example is found in pop culture: a recent television show displayed new devices for giving expectant fathers empathy with what expectant mothers experience, particularly in the latter stages of pregnancy. First, a group of willing expectant fathers strapped on a large, heavy device that simulated a belly in the last trimester of pregnancy. Then the handlers attached weights to the men's lower backs to simulate the pressure most pregnant women feel in that area. Finally they strapped amply filled bras onto the men, corresponding to the extra heaviness most women feel when the breasts enlarge during pregnancy and lactation. What a lesson in empathy! The men were astonished by the physical changes their bodies endured during the experiment, as well as their resulting exhaustion.

> *I don't put a gender tag on empathy. I've seen films and read books by men that I would have sworn were written or filmed by women. I think there's elements of the masculine and feminine in all of us.*
>
> —*Natalie Merchant, singer and songwriter*

Research underscores the power of empathy to enhance the quality of close relationships (Ickes, 1993). In one study, the ability to infer a partner's thoughts and feelings correctly and to respond supportively provided the foundation for other relationship-enhancing behaviors, including accommodation, social support, intimacy, and effective communication (Bissonnette, Rusbult, & Kilpatrick, 1997).

One study of empathy identifies three dimensions: *perspective-taking*, a cognitive ability to adopt the viewpoint of the other person; *emotional contagion*, which occurs when one person experiences an emotional response parallel to that of the other person; and *empathic concern*, a sympathetic and altruistic concern for another person (Stiff, Dillard, Somera, Kim, & Sleight, 1988). Empathy is a concept, and a skill, that allows a person to express understanding and concern for another individual at both the cognitive level (content) and the emotional level. Even if you haven't gone through exactly what another person is experiencing, you can relate to that person's emotion. You may not yet have experienced the death of a parent, but if one of your friends loses a parent and seeks your company, you can relate to your friend's sadness and fear, if not to the experience itself.

Beebe, Beebe, and Ivy (2004) offer the following suggestions for developing and demonstrating empathy: First, stop focusing on yourself, your messages, and your thoughts; focus instead on the messages of the other person. Next, pay attention to nonverbal cues as you try to understand the other person's emotions. Then concentrate and listen to what the other person is telling you; imagine how you would feel if you were in his or her situation. Finally, ask appropriate questions and, when suitable, paraphrase the other person's communication to demonstrate your understanding of the situation and how the person feels about the situation. We don't mean to offer an exact formula for empathy; we simply offer some tried-and-true ways to communicate.

Notice that we didn't include "give helpful advice" in our list. Many people believe, incorrectly, that the way to show empathy is to offer advice, to suggest something someone can do to respond to or improve a situation (Harvey

& Weber, 2002; Johnson, 1996). They bypass empathy altogether and try to move the other person into action, typically before that person is ready. When people need empathy, they don't need advice (although advice may come later). Remember that empathy meets people at their emotional level. It doesn't talk them out of what they are feeling, distract them from their emotions or the situation, move them to act, or downplay events by saying, "Well, it'll all blow over soon."

How do women and men show empathy in relationships? The stereotype suggests that women are more empathic than men; however, research has yielded mixed results regarding differences, according to both gender and sex. While some studies have found no significant differences between the sexes' empathic ability (Brehm, Powell, & Coke, 1984; Graham & Ickes, 1997), there seem to be differences in the extent to which men and women are willing to express it. Relationship expert Harry Reis (1998) found that women are more willing to demonstrate empathy and do so more often. Other research has focused on gender rather than sex as related to empathy, finding that androgynous individuals are more empathic, regardless of sex (Fong & Borders, 1985). Perhaps this is one of the variables related to an emphasis on talking over doing. Perhaps men show empathy by just being there—being present at the moment with someone—whereas women express empathy more through conversation.

The ability to both feel and express empathy is a fundamental skill to add to your communication repertoire or to exercise more fully. As you develop and enhance your relationships, empathy will continue to play a significant role.

Are You Listening?

Although many factors come into play during relationship development, one seems to make the most difference: listening. Researchers have estimated that more than 70 percent of adults' waking time is spent in some act of communication. On average, 30 percent of one's communicative energy is spent on speaking and 45 percent is spent on listening (Galvin & Cooper, 1996). As we explained earlier in our section on asking great questions, being deemed a successful conversationalist lies more in your listening skill than your speaking skill. Effective listening and appropriate responding are critical to the development and success of a relationship (Bostrom, 1997; Halone & Pecchioni, 2001; Prager & Buhrmester, 1998).

Have you ever said something to someone whose lack of response made you feel as if you were invisible? Or perhaps the person responded with her or his own ideas, never acknowledging yours (zero empathy). On a more positive note, have you ever found yourself talking more and about more personal things to someone, only to stop and wonder how you got to that depth in the conversation? In both the positive and the negative circumstances, the quality of the listening most likely brought about the result. Not surprisingly, since we are proponents of the receiver orientation to communication, we believe that listening more significantly affects the direction of a relationship than speaking.

Listening is closely related to empathy in that both enhance self-disclosure, increase trust, and decrease the psychological distance between people. Listening and responding to disclosure are obviously important in encouraging or discouraging further disclosure. Listening and responding, however, have been identified as

---

'Net Notes

The Website **www.listencoach.com/LHProfile** offers a way to analyze your listening habits. Your responses to 10 questions provide you with a profile of your effectiveness as a listener.

"women's work." According to gender researchers Borisoff and Merrill (1998), listening is portrayed as a passive (and thus female) behavior, while speaking is portrayed as active (and thus male). Many men and women behave in conversations as if this inaccurate portrayal were true: it's the man's job to talk, the woman's job to listen.

If you ask American women who are in heterosexual romantic relationships about what behavior by their partners makes them angriest, most will respond, "He doesn't listen." That's exactly what noted sex expert Shere Hite (1987) asked in her study of more than 4,000 women. Hite's subjects reported a variety of complaints having to do with listening ability: men's general unwillingness to listen; men's habit of constantly interrupting; men's not asking women questions or not following up on what women say.

There is a limited amount of information about the sexes and listening behavior, but a few key sources agree on a major difference in how men and women listen. It's not that members of one sex don't listen as well as the other but that the sexes tend to listen for different purposes. Just as we discussed in Chapter 4, in the section on content and relational approaches to communication, *why* the sexes listen is more distinctive than *how*. In her book *You Just Don't Understand*, Deborah Tannen (1990) suggests that men tend to listen for facts and the "big picture" (which is why they sometimes say "And your point is . . . ?"), in order to figure out how they can offer advice and solve a problem. Conversely, women tend to listen to enhance their understanding and support the speaker. This parallels Tannen's information on "report talk" and "rapport talk," also discussed in Chapter 4. Tannen also contends that listening behavior is related to power. Men tend to use conversation—speaking and listening—to establish status, whereas women use listening to empower others. Communication researcher Melanie Booth-Butterfield (1984) concluded from her studies that women and men "learn to listen for different purposes

> *Listening to a woman is almost as bad as losing to one. There are only three things that women are better at than men: cleaning, cooking, and having sex.*
>
> *—Charles Barkley, former NBA star*

and have different listening goals. The primary contrast appears in task versus interpersonal understanding; males tend to hear the facts while females are more aware of the mood of the communication" (p. 39).

In expanding their repertoire of communication behaviors, the sexes can learn from each other's tendencies as listeners and unlearn some habits and sex-typed conditioning. While listening to support a speaker is an admirable approach, women can expand their listening ability to more thoroughly track facts and comprehend information, rather than reading into a conversation more than the facts or trying to "take the emotional temperature" of the other person (Beebe, Beebe, & Ivy, 2004, p. 125). Men can demonstrate more active listening by using more nonverbal signals like nodding and eye contact. Research shows that women tend to offer more nonverbal signals of interest in a conversation than men (Aries, 1998). For example, there's a concept in research on nonverbal communication known as the *visual dominance ratio,* which is the amount of eye contact one makes while speaking versus while listening (Knapp & Hall, 2002). Men tend to look more at others when they are speaking and then look elsewhere when others are speaking; in the latter case their behavior can be interpreted as a sign that they have lost interest or are not listening. To take another example, increased use (but not an overuse) of vocalizations such as "uh-huh" and "yeah" can make another person feel that he or she is being listened to. These *back-channel cues* reinforce and draw out more information from a speaker (Guerrero et al., 2001; Knapp & Hall, 2002).

Remember. . .

CONVERSATION STARTERS: The use of opening lines or questions to get a conversation off the ground.

FLIRTING: Means of showing attraction to and interest in another person.

COMMUNICATIVE COMPETENCE: How effectively and appropriately one communicates.

INTIMACY: Sharing personal, private information and experiences over time for the purposes of bonding, developing closeness, and forming an emotional connection.

SELF-DISCLOSURE: Voluntarily providing others with information that they would not learn if you did not tell them.

EMPATHY: Understanding and feeling what another person is feeling.

PERSPECTIVE-TAKING: A dimension of empathy involving the cognitive ability to adopt the viewpoint of another person.

EMOTIONAL CONTAGION: A dimension of empathy which occurs when one person experiences an emotional response parallel to that of another person.

EMPATHIC CONCERN: A dimension of empathy involving a sympathetic and altruistic concern for another person.

VISUAL DOMINANCE RATIO: The amount of eye contact one makes while speaking versus while listening.

BACK-CHANNEL CUES: Vocalizations such as "uh-huh" and "yeah," which indicate listening and can reinforce and draw out more information from a speaker.

Those All-Important Nonverbal Communication Skills

An integral component of the receiver orientation to communication, as well as one of the most useful skills in demonstrating empathy and effective listening, is the development of your ability to nonverbally communicate effectively and appropriately. Effective nonverbal encoding and decoding are directly linked to relationship satisfaction (Miczo, Segrin, & Allspach, 2001). *Nonverbal communication* is message exchange without words, such as the way you use pitch variation and tone of voice to convey sarcasm, your facial expressions, your walk, your stance, and so forth. We explore this important topic in two parts, but the skills are interrelated.

Expressing Yourself Nonverbally

Nonverbal expressiveness pertains to the nonverbal communication you express to others, knowingly or unknowingly. It's not enough just to develop your "gift of gab"; you need to work on expressing yourself appropriately through nonverbal cues, because nonverbal communication facilitates relationship initiation, development, and maintenance.

A set of nonverbal cues critical in relationships has been described by Albert Mehrabian (1970) as nonverbal *immediacy*. These are behaviors which indicate liking or a positive regard for another person. Immediacy generates a positive feeling between people who are meeting for the first time and are beginning to know each other, but conveying positive feelings toward another person is important at all points in a relationship (Hinkle, 1999). Generally, as one person in a relationship uses more immediate and direct nonverbal communication, the other person feels supported and is more likely to value the interaction and the relationship.

Would it surprise you to learn that women tend to use more immediate nonverbal communication than men? We suspect not, since you probably know by now that women's behaviors, both verbal and nonverbal, tend to emphasize their connection to and affiliation with others. Immediacy behaviors displayed frequently by women include leaning forward, direct body orientation (that is, women tend to face people directly when engaged in conversation), closer proximity, nodding, smiling, more animated facial expression, more variation in vocal expression, and increased touching (Deutsch, LeBaron, & Fryer, 1987; Fugita, Harper, & Wiens, 1980; Jones, 1986; Sanders, Wiseman, & Matz, 1990). Again, it's not that women value relationships more than men do, but that women more actively communicate the importance of relationships by utilizing nonverbal channels to adapt to their partner, accommodate his or her nonverbal style, and display greater nonverbal expressiveness (Burgoon, 1994; Knapp & Hall, 2002; Sanders, Wiseman, & Matz, 1990). These findings are supported by social psychologists DePaulo and Friedman (1998) who, in summarizing trends in research, state that "in general, women are more open, expressive, approachable, and actively involved in social interactions than are men. Their faces are more legible than men's, and they smile and gaze at other people and approach them more closely than men" (p. 11).

'Net Notes

The Center for Nonverbal Studies has produced *The Nonverbal Dictionary*, a guide to help you decipher nonverbal cues more accurately. Entries provide examples, descriptions, and possible meanings for a range of nonverbal behaviors.

www.members.aol.com/nonverbal2

Nonverbal research has found that men tend to display indirect nonverbal cues. They tend to talk at angles to each other and look less directly at each other, maintain a turned-out body position, use more nonverbal signals of power, and be generally less nonverbally immediate in conversations, even with people they like (Ellyson, Dovidio, & Fehr, 1981; Hall, 1984; Mulac, Studley, Wiemann, & Bradac, 1987; Tannen, 1990). One explanation for these sex-based trends relates to the differing status of women and men in a patriarchal society, such as ours. Men's nonverbal tendencies may relate to their generally higher status in society, because higher-status persons exhibit many of the same nonimmediate traits ascribed to men (e.g., less direct body orientation, leaning backward rather than forward, making less eye contact, touching less). Women, who still typically have lower status in society than men, are more likely to give a higher-status person more personal space, make more eye contact than is directed at them, and do more nodding and smiling than a higher-status individual (Knapp & Hall, 2002).

These sex-based tendencies appear to be consistent across various ages. Tannen (1994) analyzed conversations of children and young adults of both sexes to compare nonverbal cues during conversation. At each of the four age levels she studied (second-, sixth-, and tenth-grade students, and 25-year-old adults), girls and women sat closer to each other, aligned their bodies more directly facing each other, had greater eye contact, and touched more. At each age level, boys and men sat at angles to each other, looked more at their surroundings than each other, and gave an impression of restlessness and diffused attention or nonengagement in communication. However, Tannen points out that a male's appearance of disengagement does not necessarily mean that he is actually disengaged. In her studies, tenth-grade boys were deeply engaged in conversations that contained a good deal of self-disclosure, but in terms of nonverbal cues the boys looked as though they were anything but engaged. Problems arise when the standard of immediacy is misapplied; that is, feelings of liking may be conveyed rather differently depending on one's sex and the situation or context within which communication occurs.

Becoming more nonverbally expressive doesn't come naturally for many of us; we have to learn what skills work and when to use them, and then practice using them. With enough practice and positive reinforcement from others, your nonverbal expressiveness can become a more natural element of your communication repertoire.

Becoming More Sensitive to Others' Nonverbal Communication

Nonverbal sensitivity refers to our ability to detect and accurately interpret nonverbal cues from others. Some people may be more naturally sensitive and adept at reading nonverbal cues, but—as we said with regard to nonverbal expressiveness—most of us have to work at it. Let us extend a caution here: no one can become a perfect interpreter of others' nonverbal communication. While we encourage you to deepen your understanding of nonverbal communication, sharpen your powers of observation, and develop greater skill in interpreting the meanings behind others' nonverbal actions, you need to realize that nonverbal communication is complex, rooted in culture and context, and very individualized (Beebe, Beebe, & Ivy, 2004). We want to help you catch more clues about others, but don't assume that your read on someone is necessarily correct.

> *When the eyes say one thing, and the tongue another, a practiced man relies on the language of the first.*
>
> —*Ralph Waldo Emerson, poet, essayist, and philosopher*

Surprise, surprise—research conducted over several decades shows that women tend to be better decoders of others' nonverbal cues than men (Friedman & Miller-Herringer, 1991; Rosenthal, Hall, DiMatteo, Rogers, & Archer, 1979; Rotter & Rotter, 1988). In fact, women and men alike believe women to be the superior decoders (Graham, Unruh, & Jennings, 1991). Some scholars contend that this ability may have to do with female socialization, in that females are conditioned, almost at birth, to be attentive and sensitive to others' needs and feelings (Noller, 1986). Another explanation is similar to one posited for sex differences and immediacy cues: women's generally lower status in society and their history of oppression have caused women to develop nonverbal decoding skills for basic survival (Henley, 1986; Leathers, 1997; Miller, 1986; Tavris, 1992).

As we've said, becoming more adept at interpreting nonverbal cues is a skill that takes time and practice to develop. Spending some time watching other people and comparing their nonverbal cues with your own might help you become more self-aware, as well as more astute in reading people's nonverbal cues. For our male readers, it might be helpful to consider whether being more nonverbally expressive and sensitive would improve your relationships. For female readers, it might be a good idea to think about how you would react to a man who uses a higher-than-average degree of immediacy

---

Remember. . .

NONVERBAL COMMUNICATION: Messages exchanged without words.

NONVERBAL EXPRESSIVENESS: The nonverbal communication you express to others, knowingly or unknowingly.

IMMEDIACY: Behaviors that indicate liking or a positive regard for another person.

NONVERBAL SENSITIVITY: The ability to detect and accurately interpret nonverbal cues of others.

---

cues. At what point, if any, might the use of these cues surprise you or make you uncomfortable? Do women really want men to develop nonverbal communication skills, or do they prefer keeping that "edge" or advantage for themselves?

Effective use of the four skills just discussed—self-disclosure, empathy, listening, and nonverbal expressiveness and sensitivity—will probably lead to greater feelings of closeness and less psychological distance between partners in a relationship. When choice points arise that cause you to make decisions about a relationship, these basic communication skills can do much to help you implement effective choices.

When Change Happens (and It Always Does)

Everyone faces countless decisions in relationships, including abstract questions (e.g., Where is this relationship going? Where do I want it to go?) and ideas that arise on the spur of the moment (e.g., You have an opportunity to ask a coworker to have a cup of coffee with you, opening up the possibility of a friendship rather than just a professional relationship). These choice points offer many possibilities for growth, development, and change. Change in a relationship is inevitable; however, some people fear change because they believe it signals the beginning of the end of a relationship. For example, a couple may have a new, intense relationship. If the intensity changes, one or both may view the change with alarm and believe that "something must be wrong." It doesn't have to be. Change and evolution in relationships are natural and expected and can be viewed as signs of potential growth rather than decline.

Relationships also tend to experience periods of relative stability (Shea & Pearson, 1986). People seek comfort in the familiar and in relationships from which consistent benefits can be derived. Change usually comes about when one person or the other feels that the relationship is lacking in some respect, or that it no longer meets his or her needs and some form of change is necessary. If the relationship has a long history, it will be more difficult to change. For example, if you've recently moved away from home to go to college, what was your experience when you returned home and talked to old friends? Did they treat you as they used to treat you, in spite of the fact that you've probably changed since you left?

It's wise for relational partners (friends, coworkers, lovers, etc.) to be cognizant of how their relationship begins, because the patterns developed in the beginning are likely to continue. The longer these patterns have been in place, the more difficult they will be to change. For example, if you feel you no longer get the consideration you deserve from a relational partner, think back: Did you *ever* get that consideration? Did you always hope it would develop, and did you overlook inconsideration in the beginning, simply because the relationship was new? If so, then it will be an uphill challenge to garner more consideration from your partner at this point. If you received more consideration when the relationship began, what changed?

In her book *The Ship That Sailed into the Living Room*, Sonja Johnson (1991) presents an insightful view that casts a relationship itself as a third entity, separate from the two people involved. Johnson describes a "relation Ship" as a large object between two people that develops its own expectations and rules. For example, people in relationships are supposed to do things like "work on the relationship." Johnson says that the "Ship" virtually shouts orders at the two people in it. Her perspective—that it is the relationship which deserves to be examined and possibly changed, not either of the people involved—sheds light on two important and helpful factors: (1) each relationship comes with its own built-in patterns of expectations; and (2) change and movement stem from patterns in the relationship, not the individuals.

Generating Movement in a Relationship

Have you ever felt dissatisfied with a relationship that seemed to have plateaued and wanted to move it to a deeper level? (Likewise, have you ever wanted to "lighten one up"?) Are there strategies you could use to accelerate the rate of change in a relationship? Do sex and gender affect movement in relationships? As you read this material, consider your own relationships and think about whether change or movement is on the horizon.

In the late 1980s, a study was conducted of the communication strategies used to change casual dating relationships into serious dating relationships, and its results have stood the test of time. While this research focused on dating relationships, the strategies identified are applicable to most other contexts. Interpersonal communication scholar James Tolhuizen's (1988) investigation generated a list of 14 strategies people reported using to effect change in a relationship. Note that the strategies (listed below in descending order of use) are intended to propel a relationship to a higher or more intimate stage, not to "notch it back."

1. Increased amount of contact.
2. Relationship negotiation (direct discussion about the relationship, feelings in the relationship, and the future).
3. Social support and assistance (asking for advice, information, and support from others in attempts to intensify a relationship).

4. Increased rewards.
5. Direct definitional bid. (e.g., "Here's what I think we should do with this relationship.")
6. Accepting a direct definitional bid.
7. Tokens of affection.
8. Personalized communication through verbal expressions of affection.
9. Suggestive actions (flirting, teasing).
10. Nonverbal expressions of affection.
11. Social enmeshment. (e.g., "I want you to meet my family.")
12. Changing or improving one's personal appearance.
13. Increased sexual intimacy.
14. Adapting self-presentation (altering how you communicate yourself to others).

In studying men's and women's use of these strategies, Tolhuizen found that men reported using direct definitional bids (e.g., "Let's have this kind of relationship") and verbal expressions of affection more than women. Women reported using relationship negotiation and accepting a definitional bid. Tolhuizen contends that "these results depict males as being more direct and more willing to explicitly express feelings of affection, and females as being less direct, more responsive, and more concerned with the relationship" (p. 5). These findings seem to run counter to stereotypes of men as unwilling to express emotions or to discuss the future of a relationship.

CONCLUSION

The topics explored in this chapter represent a significant challenge for most of us—the challenge of turning a potential relationship into reality. To borrow Sonja Johnson's term, the "relation Ships" that sail into your life can change you in powerful and significant ways. Friendships, workplace relationships, romantic relationships, and committed partnerings all have a significant impact on you. This chapter has explored the other side of that process—your influence on relationship initiation and development through the choices you make. A consistent theme in this text is the acquisition of awareness—awareness of how various factors (e.g., biology, sociology, media, and language) influence you and your choices; awareness of how you can gain control over or manage those influences; and, in this chapter, awareness of how choices may influence your relationships.

Becoming more personally effective in initiating and creating the type of relationships you desire is a worthwhile, important goal. In this chapter, we began with a view of relationship development as "prospecting" and followed through with thoughts on finding prospects, testing a prospect, and developing a "claim." Understanding the skills associated with moving a relationship from one level to another and understanding women's and men's tendencies in such changes can give you greater insight into how positive change might be brought about. It can also keep you from getting the relationship "shaft."

The final section of this text connects these concepts to some specific contexts in your life—friendships, romance, family life, work, and education. Effective gender communication in these contexts involves applying the concepts described in the chapters you have just read.

Discussion Starters

1. Think about the role of information in the initiation of relationships. What information do you use to make decisions about people when initiating a friendship? Do you need different kinds of information when initiating a dating relationship than when initiating a friendship? What information about yourself as a potential relational partner do you think is most important? What's the most important information to learn about someone else as a potential partner?

2. Some people believe that the initiation of a dating or romantic relationship should be men's work. Do you think women should be able to initiate dating relationships in the same ways men can? If you believe they can, and you are a woman, have you ever initiated a relationship with a man? If you are a man who has been "chosen" by a woman, how did you feel when she initiated a relationship with you?

3. Do you know men who disclose more than the typical amount of personal information? What are some reactions to these men? Is the reaction the same as or different from the reaction a woman gets when she discloses more than is expected?

4. Recall a time when you were, or a close friend was, at the point of deciding whether to continue or put a halt to a relationship that was trying to get off the ground—the third stage of relationship initiation discussed in this chapter. Do you recall what factors made the difference or helped you make your decision? Did you (or your friend) make a wise decision at the time? If not, what do you wish had been done differently?

5. In your experience, how do people signal that they want to change the level of a relationship? Do men use different signals from women? Are the signals usually nonverbal? Do people ever say to you, "I'd like to change our relationship?" Have you ever said that to someone? If so, what was the result?

References

Abbey, A. (1982). Sex differences in attributions for friendly behavior: Do males misperceive females' friendliness? *Journal of Personality and Social Psychology, 42*, 830–838.

Abbey, A. (1987). Misperception of friendly behavior as sexual interest: A survey of naturally occurring incidents. *Psychology of Women Quarterly, 11*, 173–194.

Abbey, A. (1991). Misperception as an antecedent of acquaintance rape: A consequence of ambiguity in communication between men and women. In A. Parrot & L. Bechhofer (Eds.), *Acquaintance rape: The hidden crime* (pp. 96–111). New York: Wiley.

Aboud, F. E., & Mendelson, M. J. (1998). Determinants of friendship selection and quality: Developmental perspectives. In N. Burkowski (Ed.), *The company they keep: Friendship in childhood and adolescence*. New York: Cambridge University Press.

Abrahams, M. F. (1994). Perceiving flirtatious communication: An exploration of the perceptual dimensions underlying judgments of flirtatiousness. *Journal of Sex Research, 31*, 283–292.

Adelman, M. B., & Ahuvia, A. C. (1992). Mediated channels for mate seeking: A solution to involuntary singlehood? *Critical Studies in Mass Communication, 8*, 273–289.

Afifi, W. A., & Guerrero, L. K. (1995, June). *Maintenance behaviors in same sex friendships: Sex differences, equity, and associations with relational closeness*. Paper presented at the meeting of the International Network on Personal Relationships, Williamsburg, VA.

Aries, E. (1998). Gender differences in interaction: A re-examination. In D. Canary & K. Dindia (Eds.), *Sex, gender, and communication: Similarities and differences* (pp. 65–81). Mahwah, NJ: Erlbaum.

Arliss, L. P. (2001). When myths endure and realities change: Communication in romantic relationships. In L. P. Arliss and D. J. Borisoff (Eds.), *Women and men communicating: Challenges and changes* (2nd ed.) (pp. 115–131). Prospect Heights, IL: Waveland.

Bar-Tal, D., & Saxe, L. (1976). Perceptions of similarity and dissimilarity of attractive couples and individuals. *Journal of Personality and Social Psychology, 33,* 772–781.

Beebe, S. A., Beebe, S. J., & Ivy, D. K. (2004). *Communication: Principles for a lifetime* (2nd ed.). Boston: Allyn & Bacon.

Bell, R. A., & Roloff, M. E. (1991). Making a love connection: Loneliness and communication competence in the dating marketplace. *Communication Quarterly, 39,* 58–74.

Berger, C. R., & Calabrese, R. J. (1975). Some explorations in initial interaction and beyond. Toward a developmental theory of interpersonal communication. *Human Communication Research, 1,* 99–112.

Berger, C. R., & Douglas, W. (1981). Studies in interpersonal epistemology III: Anticipated interaction, self-monitoring, and observational context selection. *Communication Monographs, 48,* 183–196.

Berscheid, E. (1985). Interpersonal attraction. In G. Lindzey & E. Aronson (Eds.), *Handbook of social psychology* (3rd ed.). New York: Random House.

Berscheid, E., & Reis, H. T. (1998). Attraction and close relationships. In D. T. Gilbert, S. T. Fiske, & G. Lindzey (Eds.), *The handbook of social psychology* (4th ed., vol. 2) (pp. 93–281). New York: McGraw-Hill.

Bissonnette, V. L., Rusbult, C. E., & Kilpatrick, S. D. (1997). Empathic accuracy and marital conflict resolution. In W. Ickes (Ed.), *Empathic accuracy* (pp. 251–281). New York: Guilford.

Blake, S. (1996). *Loving your long-distance relationship.* New York: Anton.

Booth-Butterfield, M. (1984). She hears . . . he hears: What they hear and why. *Personnel Journal, 44,* 36–42.

Borisoff, D. E. (2001). The effect of gender on establishing and maintaining intimate relationships. In L. P. Arliss and D. J. Borisoff (Eds.), *Women and men communicating: Challenges and changes* (2nd ed.) (pp. 15–31). Prospect Heights, IL: Waveland.

Borisoff, D. E., & Merrill, L. (1998). *The power to communicate: Gender differences as barriers* (3rd ed.). Prospect Heights, IL: Waveland.

Bostrom, R. N. (1997). The process of listening. In O. D. W. Hargie (Ed.), *The handbook of communication skills* (2nd ed.) (pp. 236–258). London: Routledge.

Brehm, S. S. (2001). *Intimate relationships* (3rd ed.). New York: McGraw-Hill.

Brehm, S. S., Powell, L., & Coke, J. S. (1984). The effects of empathic instructions upon donating behavior: Sex differences in young children. *Sex Roles, 10,* 415–416.

Breznican, A. (2000, November 26). Internet is not negatively impacting society, study shows. *Corpus Christi Caller Times,* p. A20.

Burch, P. (2001, July 15). Silent judgment: Experts say you have 10 seconds to project your true image. Scripps Howard News Service, as reported in *Corpus Christi Caller Times,* pp. C4, C5.

Burgoon, J. (1994). Nonverbal signals. In M. L. Knapp & G. R. Miller (Eds.), *Handbook of interpersonal communication* (2nd ed.) (pp. 229–285). Thousand Oaks, CA: Sage.

Burleson, B. R., Kunkel, A. W., & Birch, J. D. (1994). Thoughts about talk in romantic relationships: Similarity makes for attraction (and happiness, too). *Communication Quarterly, 42,* 259–273.

Canary , D. J., & Emmers-Sommer, T. M. (1997). *Sex and gender differences in personal relationships.* New York: Guilford.

Coates, J. (1993). *Women, men, and language* (2nd ed.). New York: Longman.

Cooper, A., & Sportolari, L. (1997). Romance in cyberspace: Understanding online attraction. *Journal of Sex Education & Therapy, 22,* 7–14.

Copenhaver, M. N., & Eisler, R. M. (1996). Masculine gender role stress: A perspective on men's health. In P. M. Kato & T. Mann (Eds.), *Handbook of diversity issues in health psychology* (pp. 219–235). New York: Plenum.

Daly, J. A., Hogg, E., Sacks, D., Smith, M., & Zimring, L. (1999). Sex and relationship affect social self-grooming. In L. K. Guerrero, J. DeVito, & M. L. Hecht (Eds.), *The nonverbal communication reader: Classic and contemporary readings* (2nd ed.) (pp. 56–61). Prospect Heights, IL: Waveland.

DePaulo, B. M., & Friedman, H. S. (1998). Nonverbal communication. In D. T. Gilbert, S. T. Fiske, & G. Lindzey (Eds.), *The handbook of social psychology* (4th ed., vol. 2) (pp. 3–40). New York: McGraw-Hill.

Derlega, V. J., Metts, S., Petronio, S., & Margulis, S. T. (1993). *Self-disclosure.* Newbury Park, CA: Sage.

Derlega, V. J., Winstead, B. A., Wong, P., & Hunter, S. (1985). Gender effects in initial encounters: A case where men exceed women in disclosure. *Journal of Social and Personal Relationships, 2,* 25–44.

Deutsch, F. M., LeBaron, D., & Fryer, M. M. (1987). What is in a smile? *Psychology of Women Quarterly, 11,* 341–352.

Dindia, K., & Allen, M. (1992). Sex differences in self-disclosure: A meta-analysis. *Psychological Bulletin, 112* (1), 106–124.

Douglas, W. (1990). Uncertainty, information-seeking, and liking during initial interaction. *Western Journal of Speech Communication, 54,* 66–81.

Egland, K. I., Spitzberg, B. H., & Zormeier, M. M. (1996). Flirtation and conversational competence in cross-sex platonic and romantic relationships. *Communication Reports, 9,* 105–118.

Ellyson, S. L., Dovidio, J. F., & Fehr, B. J. (1981). Visual behavior and dominance in women and men. In C. Mayo & N. M. Henley (Eds.), *Gender and nonverbal behavior* (pp. 63–94). New York: Springer-Verlag.

Feingold, A. (1990). Gender differences in effects of physical attractiveness on romantic attraction: A comparison across five research paradigms. *Journal of Personality and Social Psychology, 59,* 981–993.

Feingold, A. (1992). Gender differences in mate selection preferences: A test of the parental investment model. *Psychological Bulletin, 112,* 125–139.

Fine, G. A. (1996). Friendships in the workplace. In K. M. Galvin & P. Cooper (Eds.), *Making connections: Readings in relational communication* (pp. 270–277). Los Angeles: Roxbury.

Fine, J. (2001, October). Intimacy. *O: The Oprah Winfrey Magazine, 225.*

Flora, J., & Segrin, C. (1999). Social skills are associated with satisfaction in close relationships. *Psychological Reports, 84,* 803–804.

Fong, M. L., & Borders, L. D. (1985). Effects of sex role orientation and gender on counseling skills training. *Journal of Counseling Psychology, 32,* 104–110.

Friedman, H. S., & Miller-Herringer, T. (1991). Nonverbal display of emotion in public and private: Self-monitoring, personality, and expressive cues. *Journal of Personality and Social Psychology, 15,* 766–775.

Fugita, B. N., Harper, R. G., & Wiens, A. N. (1980). Encoding and decoding of nonverbal emotional messages: Sex differences in spontaneous and enacted expressions. *Journal of Nonverbal Behavior, 4,* 131–145.

Galvin, K. M., & Bylund, C. (2001). First marriage families: Gender and communication. In L. P. Arliss and D. J. Borisoff (Eds.), *Women and men communicating: Challenges and changes* (2nd ed.) (pp. 132–148). Prospect Heights, IL: Waveland.

Galvin, K. M., & Cooper, P. (Eds.) (1996). *Making connections: Readings in relational communication* (pp. 91–92). Los Angeles: Roxbury.

Graham, G. H., Unruh, J., & Jennings, P. (1991). The impact of nonverbal communication in organizations: A survey of perceptions. *Journal of Business Communication, 28,* 45–62.

Graham, T., & Ickes, W. (1997). When women's intuition isn't greater than men's. In W. Ickes (Ed.), *Empathic accuracy* (pp. 117–143). New York: Guilford.

Grammer, K. (1990). Strangers meet: Laughter and nonverbal signs of interest in opposite-sex encounters. *Journal of Nonverbal Behavior, 14,* 209–235.

Grammer, K., Knuck, K. B., & Magnusson, M. S. (1998). The courtship dance: Patterns of nonverbal synchronization in opposite sex encounters. *Journal of Nonverbal Behavior, 22,* 3–25.

Guerrero, L. K., Andersen, P. A., & Afifi, W. A. (2001). *Close encounters: Communicating in relationships.* Mountain View, CA: Mayfield.

Hall, J. A. (1984). *Nonverbal sex differences: Communication accuracy and expressive style.* Baltimore: Johns Hopkins University Press.

Halone, K. K., & Pecchioni, L. L. (2001). Relational listening: A grounded theoretical model. *Communication Reports, 14,* 59–71.

Harvey, J. H., & Weber, A. L. (2002). *Odyssey of the heart: Close relationships in the 21st century* (2nd ed.). Mahwah, NJ: Erlbaum.

Henley, N. (1986). *Body politics: Power, sex, and nonverbal communication.* New York: Touchstone.

Hinkle, L. L. (1999). Nonverbal immediacy communication behaviors and liking in marital relationships. *Communication Research Reports, 16,* 81–90.

Hite, S. (1987). *Women and love: A cultural revolution in progress.* New York: Alfred A. Knopf.

Howell, D. (1996, March 24). Women play the dominant role in courtship today: Researcher finds 52 ways males, females flirt to attract attention of potential mate. *Corpus Christi Caller Times,* pp. G1, G3.

Ickes, W. (1985). *Compatible and incompatible relationships.* New York: Springer-Verlag.

Ickes, W. (1993). Empathic accuracy. *Journal of Personality, 61,* 587–609.

Johnson, D. (1996). Helpful listening and responding. In K. M. Galvin & P. Cooper (Eds.), *Making connections: Readings in relational communication* (pp. 91–97). Los Angeles: Roxbury.

Johnson, S. (1991). *The ship that sailed into the living room: Sex and intimacy reconsidered.* Estancia, NM: Wildfire Books.

Jones, S. E. (1986). Sex differences in touch communication. *Western Journal of Speech Communication, 50,* 227–241.

Jourard, S. (1971). *The transparent self.* Princeton, NJ: Van Nostrand.

Kenrick, D. T., Groth, G., Trost, M. R., & Sadalla, E. K. (1993). Integrating evolutionary and social exchange perspectives on relationships: Effects of gender, self-appraisal, and involvement level on mate selection. *Journal of Personality and Social Psychology, 64,* 951–969.

Kenrick, D. T., Neuberg, S. L., & Cialdini, R. B. (2002). *Social psychology: Unraveling the mystery* (2nd ed.). Boston: Allyn & Bacon.

Kenrick, D. T., Sadalla, E. K., Groth, G., & Trost, M. R. (1990). Evolution, traits, and the stages of human courtship: Qualifying the parental investment model. *Journal of Personality, 58,* 97–116.

Kleinke, C. L., Meeker, F. B., & Staneski, R. A. (1986). Preference for opening lines: Comparing ratings by men and women. *Sex Roles, 15,* 585–600.

Knapp, M. L., & Hall, J. A. (2002). *Nonverbal communication in human interaction* (5th ed.). Belmont, CA: Wadsworth.

Koeppel, L. B., Montagne, Y., O'Hair, D., & Cody, M. J. (1999). Friendly? Flirting? Wrong? In L. K. Guerrero, J. DeVito, & M. L. Hecht (Eds.), *The nonverbal communication reader* (2nd ed.) (pp. 290–297). Prospect Heights, IL: Waveland.

Kowalski, R. M. (1993). Inferring sexual interest from behavioral cues: Effects of gender and sexually relevant attitudes. *Sex Roles, 29,* 13–35.

Leathers, D. G. (1997). *Successful nonverbal communication: Principles and applications* (3rd ed.). Boston: Allyn & Bacon.

Limpert, A. (2002). To surf with love. *Entertainment Weekly, 70.*

Lindsey, A. E., & Zakahi, W. R. (1996). Women who tell and men who ask: Perceptions of men and women departing from gender stereotypes during initial interaction. *Sex Roles, 34,* 767–786.

Lindsey, A. E., & Zakahi, W. R. (1998). Perceptions of men and women departing from conversational sex role stereotypes during initial interaction. In D. J. Canary and K. Dindia (Eds.), *Sex differences and similarities in communication* (pp. 393–412). Mahwah, NJ: Erlbaum.

Markham, A. N. (1998). *Life online: Researching real experience in virtual space.* Walnut Creek, GA: AltaMira.

Maurstad, T. (1996, November 17). Strange desires can be fulfilled via the Internet: Cyberspace is making it easier to find people with like interests. *Corpus Christi Caller Times,* pp. A17, A18.

McConnell, D. (1997). Interaction patterns of mixed sex groups in educational computer conferences. *Gender and Education, 9,* 345–363.

Mehrabian, A. (1970). A semantic space for nonverbal behavior. *Journal of Counseling and Clinical Psychology, 35,* 248–257.

Miczo, N., Segrin, C., & Allspach, L. E. (2001). Relationship between nonverbal sensitivity, encoding, and relational satisfaction. *Communication Reports, 14,* 39–48.

Miller, J. B. (1986). *Toward a new psychology of women* (2nd ed.). Boston: Beacon.

Mongeau, P. A. (1992, November). *Relational communication in male- and female-initiated first dates.* Paper presented at the meeting of the Speech Communication Association, Chicago, IL.

Moore, M. M. (1985). Nonverbal courtship patterns in women: Context and consequences. *Ethology and Sociobiology, 6,* 237–247.

Mulac, A., Studley, L. B., Wiemann, J. M., & Bradac, J. J. (1987). Male/female gaze in same-sex and mixed-sex dyads. *Human Communication Research, 13,* 323–343.

Noller, P. (1986). Sex differences in nonverbal communication: Advantage lost or supremacy regained? *Australian Journal of Psychology, 38,* 23–32.

Perry, L. A. M., Turner, L. H., & Sterk, H. M. (Eds.) (1992). *Constructing and reconstructing gender: The links among communication, language, and gender.* Albany: State University of New York Press.

Petronio, S., Martin, J., & Littlefield, R. (1984). Prerequisite conditions for self-disclosing: A gender issue. *Communication Monographs, 51,* 268–272.

Prager, K. J., & Buhrmester, D. (1998). Intimacy and need fulfillment in couple relationships. *Journal of Social and Personal Relationships, 15,* 435–469.

Redmond, M. V., & Vrchota, D. A. (1997). The effects of varying lengths of initial interaction on attraction. *Communication Reports, 10,* 47–53.

Reis, H. T. (1998). Gender differences in intimacy and related behaviors: Context and process. In D. J. Canary and K. Dindia (Eds.), *Sex differences and similarities in communication* (pp. 203–231). Mahwah, NJ: Erlbaum.

Rosenthal, R., Hall, J. A., DiMatteo, R., Rogers, L., & Archer, D. (1979). *Sensitivity to nonverbal communication: The PONS test.* Baltimore: Johns Hopkins University Press.

Rotter, N. G., & Rotter, G. S. (1988). Sex differences in the encoding and decoding of negative facial emotions. *Journal of Nonverbal Behavior, 12,* 139–148.

Sanders, J. A., Wiseman, R. L., & Matz, S. I. (1990). The influence of gender on reported disclosure, interrogation, and nonverbal immediacy in same-sex dyads: An empirical study of uncertainty reduction. *Women's Studies in Communication, 13,* 85–108.

Scheflen, A. E. (1965). Quasi-courtship behavior in psychotherapy. *Psychiatry, 27,* 245–257.

Shaffer, D. R., Pegalis, L. J., & Bazzini, D. G. (1996). When boy meets girl (revisited): Gender, gender-role orientation, and prospect of future interaction as determinants of self-disclosure among same- and opposite-sex acquaintances. *Personality and Social Psychology Bulletin, 22,* 495–506.

Shaikh, T., & Kanakar, S. (1994). Attitudinal similarity and affiliation need as determinants of interpersonal attraction. *Journal of Social Psychology, 134,* 257–259.

Sharma, V., & Kaur, T. (1995). Interpersonal attraction in relation to similarity and help. *Psychological Studies, 39 (2–3),* 84–87.

Shea, C., & Pearson, J. (1986). The effects of relationship type, partner intent, and gender on the selection of relationship maintenance strategies. *Communication Monographs, 53,* 352–363.

Snell, W. E., Miller, R. S., & Belk, S. S. (1988). Development of the emotional self-disclosure scale. *Sex Roles, 18,* 59–73.

Stephens, T. D., & Harrison, T. M. (1985). Gender, sex-role identity, and communication style: A Q-sort analysis of behavioral differences. *Communication Research Reports, 2,* 53–61.

Stiff, J. B., Dillard, J. P., Somera, L., Kim, H., & Sleight, C. (1988). Empathy, communication, and prosocial behavior. *Communication Monographs, 55,* 198–213.

Stone, B. (1999, August 16). Valley of the doll-less: Surfing the Web for dates in America's tech zone. *Newsweek,* 59.

Sutton, L. A. (1996). Cocktails and thumbtacks in the old West: What would Emily Post say? In L. Cherny & E. R. Weise (Eds.), *Wired women: Gender and new realities in cyber space* (pp. 169–187). Seattle: Seal.

Tannen, D. (1990). *You just don't understand: Women and men in conversation.* New York: William Morrow.

Tannen, D. (1994). *Gender and discourse.* New York: Oxford University Press.

Tavris, C. (1992, February). The man/woman thing: Moving from anger to intimacy. *Mademoiselle,* 98–101, 135.

Tolhuizen, J. H. (1988, November). *Intensification strategies in dating relationships: Identification, structure, and an examination of the personality correlates of strategy preferences.* Paper presented at the meeting of the Speech Communication Association, New Orleans, LA.

Trost, M. R., & Alberts, J. K. (1998). An evolutionary view on understanding sex effects in communicating attraction. In D. Canary & K. Dindia (Eds.), *Sex, gender, and communication: Similarities and differences* (pp. 233–255). Mahwah, NJ: Erlbaum.

Turkle, S. (1995). *Life on the screen: Identity in the age of the Internet.* New York: Simon & Schuster.

Turner, R. D. (1990, October). How to attract the opposite sex. *Ebony,* 27–28, 30.

Van Horn, K. R., Arnone, A., Nesbitt, K., Desilets, L., Sears, T., Giffin, M., & Brudi, R. (1997). Physical distance and interpersonal characteristics in college students' romantic relationships. *Personal Relationships, 4*, 15–24.

Varnadore, A. E., Howe, S. C., & Brownlow, S. (1994, March). *Why do I like you? Students' understanding of the impact of the factors that contribute to liking*. Paper presented at the meeting of the Southeastern Psychological Association, New Orleans, LA.

Waldron, V. R., & Applegate, J. L. (1998). Similarity in the use of person-centered tactics: Effects on social attraction and persuasiveness in dyadic verbal disagreements. *Communication Reports, 11*, 155–165.

Walther, J., & Tidwell, L. (1996). When is mediated communication not interpersonal? In K. M. Galvin & P. Cooper (Eds.), *Making connections: Readings in relational communication* (pp. 300–307). Los Angeles: Roxbury.

Warnick, B. (1999). Masculinizing the feminine: Inviting women on line, ca. 1997. *Critical Studies in Mass Communication, 16*, 1–19.

Weber, E. (1970). *How to pick up girls!* New York: Bantam.

Wood, J. T., & Inman, C. C. (1993). In a different mode: Masculine styles of communicating closeness. *Journal of Applied Communication Research, 21*, 279–295.

Yates, S. J. (1997). Gender, identity, and computer mediated communication. *Journal of Computer Assisted Learning, 13*, 281–290.

PART FOUR

THE CONTEXTS FOR OUR RELATIONSHIPS: PERSONAL EFFECTIVENESS IN ACTION

CHAPTER SIX

GENDER COMMUNICATION "JUST AMONG FRIENDS"

CASE STUDY: CAN YOU REALLY BE "JUST FRIENDS"?

RJ and Tamyra were great friends, ever since they discovered they lived two doors down from each other in the neighborhood and began walking to elementary school together. While they didn't play together much during school recess (the boys played with the boys and the girls with the girls), they hung out together after school and on weekends. Occasionally, RJ got teased by the boys for having a "girlfriend" and Tamyra was warned by her female friends to stay away from boys because they had "cooties." Despite the teasing and peer pressure, RJ and Tamyra remained close friends.

As they grew older it seemed harder to maintain this closeness, because their interests diverged and their time became more filled with school activities. In their teen years, as they started to date (others, not each other), they found that social time was taken up by those romantic relationships, leaving little time for their friendship. They talked on the phone and instant-messaged occasionally, but they didn't see each other much. Also, Tamyra began to tire of people's constant comments and questions: Was she secretly in love with RJ but reluctant to risk ruining the friendship? Was there sexual tension between them that now made it hard to be "just friends"? Was she dating other boys just to make RJ jealous? RJ got such questions too, but not as many; his friendship with Tamyra wasn't scrutinized or questioned as much as Tamyra's friendship with him. (It also seems that people are more apt to butt into females' relationships than males'.) After graduating from high school, they headed off to different colleges; even though their friendship wasn't as close as when they were younger, they both felt the pain and uncertainty of a changing relationship, a transition into another chapter of life. They wondered if each would be replaced with a new "best friend."

What's most interesting about Tamyra and RJ's friendship, for the purposes of our discussion, is that, even though they were both heterosexual, there was never an undercurrent of romance between them. Sure, they perceived each other as physically and personally attractive, but there was never any romantic or sexual attraction in this relationship. They had what could be called a truly "platonic" relationship, even though many people exerted subtle (and not so subtle) pressure on them to justify their friendship and even change it into something more recognizable or more expected between men and women—a romance. Even in what you'd consider a modern age, a new millennium, many people's thinking remains characteristic of an earlier time when women and men could not really be friends—there just had to be something else going on. Have you experienced this in the history of your own friendships?

In this chapter we explore friendship, in general, because friendships are among our most important life-sustaining relationships. Specifically, we examine communication that leads to increased personal effectiveness in the contexts of same-sex and cross-sex friendship. As we've said throughout the text, members of both sexes can expand their repertoire of communication behaviors to become more effective in gender communication. A widened range of behaviors, an orientation to the receiver (the friend), and enhanced personal effectiveness can all lead to greater satisfaction, fewer conflicts, and deeper, longer-lasting friendships.

Hot Topics

- Changing patterns of friendship from childhood to adulthood
- Functions and characteristics of same-sex friendship
- Why people form and value same-sex friendships
- Intimacy and self-disclosure in male-male, as compared with female-female, friendships
- Factors that inhibit the development of successful cross-sex friendships
- Factors that enhance cross-sex friendships

A SINGLE SOUL IN TWO BODIES

Aristotle defined a friend as "a single soul who resides in two bodies." More modern definitions are a bit less poetic. Ellen Goodman and Patricia O'Brien (2000), who are friends and coauthors of a book on women's friendships entitled *I Know Just What You Mean*, ask: "What's a friend? If the Eskimos have twenty-six different words for snow, Americans have only one word commonly used to describe everyone from acquaintances to intimates. It is a word we have to qualify with adjectives: school friends, work friends, old friends, casual friends, good friends" (p. 18). In the 1970s, social scientist John Reisman (1979) spoke of the difficulty of defining friendship. He described a friend as "someone who likes and wishes to do well by someone else and who believes those feelings and good intentions are reciprocated" (p. 108). Although this may not sound like a very profound definition, it expresses some central characteristics of friendship.

Friendships are a unique class of relationships. Author Jan Yager (1999) coined the term *friendshifts*, referring to the ways friendships change as persons go from one life stage to another. Yager suggests that "friendship is crucial for school-age children or for singles who are between romantic relationships. However, friends count for even the happiest couples: friendship affirms and validates in a more distinctive way than even the most positive romantic or blood tie. It is now known that friendship is vital *throughout* life" (p. 6). Reisman contrasts friendships with other social relationships, such as business partnerships, marriages, and family ties. Family relationships, in which people are tied to each other by blood or marital lines, or professional situations in which people are committed to a project or business, are embedded within social structures and reinforced by those structures. We're not saying that these relationships are easily maintained, but they do involve a social structure which is conducive for relationship maintenance. This is not the case with friendship. Friends have to set up social structures, such as a weekly bowling night or study session, a pattern of telephoning or e-mailing, and weekend gatherings in order to maintain their relationship. If someone takes friendship for granted, assuming that this form of relationship does not require as much attention and maintenance as other types, that person could find himself or herself with a narrowing circle of friends.

Learning to Be Friends

For many adults, cross-sex friendships are among their most rewarding, but our early patterns as boys and girls do not encourage the formation of these friendships; we have to learn how to develop friendships later in life with persons of the opposite sex. Sex segregation in friendship shows up early among children (Crawford & Unger, 2000). While there are interesting theories about genetics, "hard-wiring," and psychosocial development related to this pattern, it is also clear that society extends its influence in teaching children how to be friends.

Gender scholar Suzanne Romaine (1999) suggests that we need look no further than schools for the roots of sex segregation. Neighborhood kids may play together, but when these kids are at school they are categorized first by age, then by sex. Children have to line up to go from the classroom to the restroom, cafeteria, auditorium, and so forth, and they form separate lines for boys and girls, almost without exception. Granted, separating the sexes for use of the toilet has a basis in fact, in that most schools have separate facilities for females and males. But Romaine notes that this too marks school as a different context for children, because toilets aren't sex-segregated in a typical home. Further sex segregation occurs in playgrounds when students engage in team sports. On some days, schools may offer general recreational activities for everyone, but on most days recess is spent in team games, and girls and boys rarely play together or against each other. School athletic activities are almost always sex-segregated. In addition, children who say that they play in mixed-sex groups in their neighborhoods ignore opposite-sex playmates at school, to avoid being teased (Thorne, 1994). These simple traditions within schools set up a pattern of dichotomies and segregation that affects one's choice of friends, one's understanding of persons of the opposite sex, and one's behavior with same- and cross-sex friends (Romaine, 1999).

Research shows that beginning at about age seven, boys form extended friendship networks with other boys while girls tend to cluster into exclusive same-sex friendship dyads (Rawlins, 2001). In their dyads, girls acquire the social skills of communicating their feelings and being nurturing. In contrast, boys learn to follow rules and get along with groups of people. To varying degrees, these tendencies persist into adulthood.

Reisman (1990) also examined communication in friendship through the formative years, giving particular attention to self-disclosure. In Chapter 5, we defined self-disclosure as voluntarily providing information to others that they would not learn if you did not tell them. As opposed to earlier years, when children disclose almost exclusively with members of their same sex, Reisman found that male adolescents disclose about the same amount of information with friends of either sex, but female adolescents exhibit less self-disclosure with boys than with other girls. This behavior changes again as persons leave their teen years. Young female adults reach similar levels of disclosure with males and females, while males reach higher levels of self-disclosure with females than with other males. The latter finding is consistent with a good deal of research demonstrating that women receive other people's disclosures more often than men do (Aries, 1998; Perry, Turner, & Sterk, 1992; Petronio, Martin, & Littlefield, 1984; Stephens & Harrison, 1985).

During childhood and adolescence, we tend to be drawn to same-sex more than cross-sex friends, but this tendency shifts as we mature. It's interesting to explore the unique properties of each type of friendship, as well as the communication that sustains them. Many people believe that the function of a friendship determines the way the relationship is maintained. For example, many successful married couples say they married their best friends; and some friendships are *functional* in that they serve a certain, perhaps restricted purpose. However, other people contend that communication within a friendship is the distinguishing factor.

COMMUNICATION IN SAME-SEX FRIENDSHIPS: FROM BUTCH AND SUNDANCE TO THELMA AND LOUISE

To many people's thinking, same-sex friendships require less work to maintain than cross-sex friendships. Same-sex friendships are not, for the most part, subject to the same tensions as cross-sex friendships—tensions noted in our opening case study, such as romance versus friendship, sexuality, jealousy, emotional intensity, and how others perceive the relationship. If these tensions appear in same-sex friendships, it is assumed that they will be easier to deal with, or that the relationship might be a special case, such as a homosexual same-sex friendship (Arnold, 1995).

Another assumption about same-sex friendships is that friends are equals; power dynamics that often characterize cross-sex friendships are absent or less of a factor. In one study of power and the quality of friendships, both women and men rated equal-power friendships as more emotionally close, satisfying, enjoyable, disclosing, and rewarding than unequal-power friendships (Veniegas & Peplau, 1997).

Male-Male Friendship: Functions and Characteristics

Friendships between men seem to have evolved from the standard of true friendship to something that writers have begun to critique in recent decades. Part of this critique includes mild teasing about "male bonding" activities and extends to more serious accusations that men's friendships are "impoverished" (Nardi, 1992).

Why Men Form Friendships

For our male readers, why do you form friendships with other men? If you follow the typical pattern, you form such friendships so that you have *something to do* and *someone to do it with*. For many men, male friends are important but replaceable; men tend to have more numerous but less intimate same-sex friendships than women (Basow, 1992). Research has shown that while men and women typically have similar numbers of friends and spend similar amounts of time with friends, men's friendships with other men tend to serve different purposes than women's friendships with other women (Caldwell & Peplau, 1982).

First, men often form friendships through groups because a group satisfies a need to belong to something or to other people. These friendships may form through participation on teams, memberships in clubs and fraternities, involvement with work or study groups, and so forth. Sociologists Orosan and Schelling (1992) describe men's friendships as group-oriented, competitive, and fairly hierarchical. Boys' friendships tend to emerge from larger networks where the boys learn to follow rules and get along with all kinds of people, even people they don't like (Bate & Bowker, 1997). These organized friendships center on group activities and give men a sense of belonging (Strikwerda & May, 1992). For centuries, men have used group belongingness as a source of power and connection. Historically male-dominated religious ceremonies, initiation rituals inherent in such organizations as fraternities and civic groups, and male-only discussions (locker-room conversations, for example) have an air of secrecy and what might be viewed as a code of correct behavior that controls access to these groups and marks women as outsiders (Spain, 1992).

> *Your friends love you anyway.*
>
> —Dave Barry, columnist and author

We all feel a need to belong, but for some people belonging has a price. This sense of belonging is so important to some men that they may value being a team player above self-respect, to the point of humiliation. For example, the male coauthor of this textbook endured a fraternity initiation ritual that was difficult and sometimes humiliating, but it was required to join. The need to belong, to be accepted in a group of other men, can exert a great deal of control over a man's behavior.

Another motivation many men have for forming friendships with other men is to further their own achievement. This may sound manipulative and self-serving, but think about it further. Psychologist Suzanna Rose (1985) suggests that since men still control power and rewards in American society, they value friendships with other men more than friendships with women because they can attain more social and economic rewards from other men. In forming friendships with other men, many men look beyond mere commonality and the opportunity to share activities to consider other, possibly lucrative, benefits of friendship. In the business world, if a man cannot help you get ahead, the possibility of a friendship may decrease—not necessarily disappear, but decrease.

In some instances, male friendships form out of conflict. While we tend to think of conflict as separating people, it can also be cathartic and can clear the air, allowing greater understanding and feelings of closeness. Conflict experienced by persons on the same side—in war, in sports, or in personal disagreements—can also generate significant closeness. Tannen (1994) describes a number of historical and modern male bonding patterns that are based on physical combat against each other or heated verbal sparring. She reports that some men appear to develop powerful friendships with other men against whom they have fought, physically, verbally or both. In one analysis of male friendships in sports, interviews with 30 professional athletes revealed friendships forged through fierce competition both with teammates and competitors (Messner, 1992). In these friendships, men developed "covert intimacy," characterized by doing things together and talking about what they do together, rather than through mutual talk about their lives.

"Doing" versus "Talking"

In the preceding paragraph, we mentioned "doing" rather than "talking" as characteristic of men's friendships. In fact, the activity-orientation of men's friendships is one of its primary characteristics. Men's friendships begin with, are sustained by, and sometimes dissolve over doing things together and sharing (or enduring) experiences (Brehm, 2001; Rawlins, 2001). We've all heard jokes about male bonding, but it is true that through shared experiences and activities, men develop feelings of closeness and express their commonality with male friends. Think of the war stories or fishing tales that your father, uncle, or grandfather tells. Men do talk with their friends, and they may value talk as much as women friends do, but the content of their talk may differ from women's, in that it tends to focus on the activities that men share, not their feelings about those activities or one another (Duck & Wright, 1993; Martin, 1997).

LUANN *BY GREG EVANS*

LUANN © UFS, Reprinted by Permission.

Researchers Bruess and Pearson (1997) extended the analysis of "doing" versus "talking" by conducting a study of friendship rituals. Rituals are repeated events in a relationship that can be described as, "When we get together, we always . . ." Rituals in male-male friendships tend to consist of the "guys' night out," which one group in the study described as a night of barbecuing steaks, smoking cigars, and watching boxing on television. For men, rituals tend to be important because they create a familiar, structured pattern that reduces uncertainty in a friendship and in some situations facilitates the friendship without the need for a great deal of conversation. As it turns out, this may not be a disadvantage. Another study found that people were likely to choose, and be satisfied with, individuals who have similar levels of communication skills. Low-skill pairs were just as satisfied as high-skill pairs; the key was that the levels of communication skills matched (Burleson & Samter, 1996).

As you are no doubt aware, women generally base their friendships less on shared activities than on conversation and an exchange of thoughts and feelings (Brehm, 2001). We will say more about female-female friendships in a subsequent section, but you should be aware of the contrast here. For our male readers, think about your own friendships with other men; for female readers, think about friendships between men you know. Were most of these male friendships initiated through an activity, such as a sport, drinking beer, hunting, working on cars, or the like? Do male friends spend most of their friendship time engaged in these kinds of activities? Do friendships sometimes end because the friends lost interest in the activity that bonded them together?

Intimacy in Male-Male Friendship

Feelings of closeness are important in any friendship, and the expression of closeness between men has changed dramatically over the years (Rawlins, 1992). In his book on men's friendships, Peter Nardi (1992) makes the point that same-sex friendships between men were highly revered in ancient Greece and during the European Renaissance. Nardi quotes Daniel Webster, who, in 1800, called his best male friend "the partner of my joys, grieves, and affections, the only participator in my most secret thoughts."

In Chapter 5, we defined intimacy as bonding, closeness, and emotional connection, based on sharing personal, private information and experiences over time. We offered Fine's (2001) version of intimacy, as "in-to-me-see" (p. 225). Intimacy is something most people long for in their relationships (Canary & Emmers-Sommer, 1997; Harvey & Weber, 2002). But is intimacy actually the goal in male-male friendship?

Gender scholars Strikwerda and May (1992) suggest that "men in America are clearly stymied in pursuing intimacy with other males because of fears involving their sexuality, especially culturally inbred homophobia. The taboo against males touching, except in a firm public handshake, continues these teenage prohibitions" (p. 118). Many of the men in our classes admit that they have difficulty with intimacy, especially when it is operationalized in the form of hugging or otherwise expressing or verbalizing affection for a male friend or family member. In their research regarding affection in nonromantic relationships, Floyd and Morman (1997) found that in situations or relationships where one's motive for affection might be misunderstood, such as male friendships, the parties are more reluctant to express affection because they run the risk of being rejected, teased or made fun of, and seen as odd. Interpersonal communication scholars Knapp and Vangelisti (2000) explain that in cultures in which touch, as a form of affection, is discouraged between men because of implications of homosexuality, most men demonstrate their affection for male friends or family members in subtle, indirect, and even symbolic ways, such as doing favors, helping someone in need, or offering gifts.

The group nature of male friendship may work against intimacy, and it can actually be a way of avoiding intimacy for some men. Strikwerda and May (1992) explored the role of the group, describing male friendship as comradeship. Comrades tend not to reflect on their relationship; they are more bound to each other because of a group than out of individual concern. Strikwerda and May suggest that "what passes for intimate male bonding is really the deep loyalty of comradeship, which is based on so little information about the person to whom one is loyal that it is quite fragile and likely to change" (p. 114).

Regarding male intimacy (or the lack thereof), you might be thinking, "But what about the experience of sitting at a bar, drinking a beer, and just 'BS-ing?' At the end of the evening, you shake hands and head out. Isn't that closeness?" Granted, those can be close, good times; but again, we see the emphasis on doing rather than talking. Do these experiences actually create intimacy in a friendship? One study found that men believed their friendships with other men to be just as intimate as other forms of friendships. These men felt just as close, supported, and satisfied in their male friendships as women did in their female friendships (Botschner, 1996).

Communication researchers Wood and Inman (1993) explored some characteristics traditionally associated with intimacy in relationships, and often included in definitions of intimacy, such as conversations of a deeply personal nature and displays of emotion. What they determined is that these traits may describe female friendship better than male friendship; pronouncements of what "counts" as intimacy in a relationship may be indicative of a feminine bias. In their research, male subjects regarded practical help, mutual assistance, and companionship as marks of caring and closeness. In a subsequent study, Inman (1996) discovered that men characterize their friendships with other men as steeped in "continuity, perceived support and dependability, shared understandings, and perceived compatibility" and as based on "self-revelation and self-discovery, having fun together, intermingled lives, and assumed significance" (p. 100). Men may base their friendships on unspoken assumptions rather than actual conversations about the relationship. Thus we may conclude, regarding male-male intimacy in friendship, that men often gain intimacy by sharing activities and experiences rather than through the more traditional displays of intimacy described in the literature of relationships and self-help (Floyd & Parks, 1995; Reisman, 1990; Yager, 1999).

Self-Disclosure in Male-Male Friendship

In addition to differences in the way same-sex friends achieve intimacy, differences also exist in the amount and type of self-disclosure exchanged between same-sex friends. Researchers generally conclude that men are less self-disclosing than women (Derlega, Metts, Petronio, & Margulis, 1993; Dindia & Allen, 1992; Shaffer, Pegalis, & Bazzini, 1996). Of the three possible types of relationships—male-male, female-female, and female-male—male-male friendships have been found to involve the least disclosure (Derlega, Winstead, Wong, & Hunter, 1985; Henley, 1986; Ickes, 1985).

What might be some reasons for these trends in disclosure within male friendships? One theory relates to topics men tend to discuss. This may sound like a stereotype, but many people recognize it as reality: men tend to talk more about *what* (what they do in their jobs, what happened, etc.) whereas women tend to talk more about *who* (whom they work with, who's doing what, and how the whos are feeling). These trends parallel the content versus relational approaches to communication that we explored in Chapter 4. Relationship scholars Parker and deVries (1993) found that men's same-sex friendships were characterized by less giving and receiving of supportive communication, less empathic understanding, and less talk that deepened the friends' self-awareness. In another study, subjects analyzed transcripts of conversations between pairs of friends; all obvious identifiers of the interactants' sex were removed (Martin, 1997). The results indicated that respondents were able to identify the sex of the interactants from the topics discussed and the openness of the conversation.

The problem arises when we equate disclosure with personal topics, and intimacy with personal disclosure. Let's take an example to make this more clear. If Ted and Emmett are discussing something that happened at work, that's a *what* topic, whereas if Lindsay and Ellen are discussing their spouses, that's a *who* topic. Granted, whats and whos often overlap, but you get the general point. Now if someone overhears those conversations or reads a transcript, and is asked to assess the level of intimacy and decide whether or not an exchange counts as self-disclosure, what would that person say? We hope you'll see that deeming someone's conversation as "disclosing" or not can be arbitrary. Ted and Emmett's friendship may be just as close as Lindsay and Ellen's, but their topics of talk—the substance of their disclosure—may be very different.

Some research suggests that preference, not ability, is responsible for the differing tendencies of disclosure in same-sex friendships. In Reisman's study (1990), male and female college students described disclosure in their same-sex friendships as being equally high. In addition, Reisman found that male subjects believed themselves capable of disclosing as much as women. Perhaps men may *prefer* not to disclose as much with their male friends as they do with their female friends, dating partners, or spouses. The purposes of friendship for men and the social pressures men face explain at least part of this. Gender sociologist James Doyle (1995) speaks about this issue:

> Why should men—granted, some men more than others—hold back their feelings, create false appearances about how they feel, or withhold their real emotions from the very individuals who they openly call their best male friends, their buddies? One possible answer lies in the proscriptive norm that most males in our society subscribe to—under no circumstances let down your emotional guard in the company of other men. To do so would more than likely get one branded as an emotional weakling, a sissy, or the latest in unkind cuts delivered to a man these days, a wimp. (p. 252)

Some men equate disclosure with vulnerability—they believe that if a man discloses his thoughts and feelings to women or to other men, he has made himself powerless. Since powerlessness is undesirable, actions linked to powerlessness are to be avoided, even at the cost of closeness in friendship (Rawlins, 2001).

So, we are left with two conflicting lines of thought regarding intimacy and disclosure. On the one hand, some sources indicate that male-male friendships are deficient owing to a lack of intimacy that can be derived only through personal disclosure. On the other hand, some people argue that the type of closeness men achieve through shared activities and experiences is just as legitimate and beneficial as any other type of closeness. Perhaps we could suggest a combination of perspectives. Intimacy in male-male friendships requires common activities and experiences, but it may be enhanced by disclosure of personal information and displays of emotion.

'Net Notes

The Friendship Page, located at **www.friendship.com.au,** is a Website based in Australia that is "devoted to exploring the topic of friendship in a positive and friendly manner." The site contains information such as quotations from specialists and site visitors, poetry, tributes, interactive advice, and a chat room. If you think you'd like to expand your circle of friends—or at least your circle of cyber-friends—check out this site.

Female-Female Friendship: Functions and Characteristics

Many women can attest to the fact that since the earliest days they can remember as girls, same-sex friendships have been a sustaining, highly significant force in their lives. However, until only recently little research specific to female friendship was available. In fact, sociologist Lionel Tiger (1969) argued that women were not genetically programmed to bond with one another! Psychologists Block and Greenberg (1985) noted the lack of research a few years ago: "It is rare to read of the electricity that suffuses female friendship, of the feelings women develop for one another that intensify their existence. Friendship remains a vast, fertile area of women's lives that is unexplored" (p. 1). In her book *Friendships Between Women,* Pat O'Connor (1992) calls the first chapter "Women's Friendships: The Underexplored Topic?" Gender scholar Fern Johnson (1996) suggests that female-female friendship has been an underresearched area because of stereotypes that women are too competitive, catty, and jealous to have meaningful friendships. More academic and popular attention has been given to female friendships in recent years; researchers have begun to describe, in detail and with insight, friendships between women (Arliss & Borisoff, 1993; Berry & Traeder, 1995; Goodman & O'Brien, 2000; O'Connor, 1992).

The Value of Women's Friendships

Just as men's friendships have changed throughout history, women's friendships have also evolved. Given the social restrictions on male-female interactions in earlier centuries, coupled with the fact that women historically inhabited a world primarily made up of other women and children, close friendships between women became an accepted form of social interaction, albeit one generally discounted by men (O'Connor, 1992). The women's movement ascribed more status to friendships between women and emphasized their value and significance in women's lives (Eichenbaum & Orbach, 1988). Research suggests that women are, in general, more likely than men to form very close same-sex friendships and to value those friendships highly (Wright, 1998).

A friend will tell you she saw your old boyfriend—and he's a priest. A friend will lie about your home permanent and threaten to kill anyone who tries to come into a room where you are trying on bathing suits. But, most of all, a friend will not make every minute of every day count and foul it up for the rest of us.

—Erma Bombeck, columnist and author

Gender scholar Shere Hite (1989) conducted an extensive study of women's relationships and found that approximately 95 percent of single women and 87 percent of married women in her study described their same-sex friendships as "some of the happiest, most fulfilling parts of their lives" (p. 457). Some women feel that their friendships with other women are more intimate, intuitive, rewarding, and accepting than their relationships with men (Basow, 1986; Berry & Traeder, 1995; Fitzpatrick & Bochner, 1981). O'Connor (1992) found that most of the married women in her research would have preferred to have shared their victories, defeats, and even routine activities with their husbands rather than their friends, but they reported that their husbands simply were not interested, and thus that female friendships became more important.

Women also appear to develop friendships that function on multiple levels, as opposed to male friendships that tend to operate around one activity, issue, or function (Barth & Kinder, 1988). Gender development theorist Carol Gilligan (1982) characterizes female friendships as developing an intertwined series of obligations and responsibilities and drawing the participants into a friendship with bonds at multiple levels. Women focus on the individuals involved in the friendship and the pattern of interconnectedness between them. This pattern encourages mutual support, emotional sharing, and increased acceptance (Rawlins, 1992). Earlier, we briefly discussed the role of rituals in men's friendships. Bruess and Pearson (1997) found that women's friendship rituals were markedly different from men's, in that women's rituals involved conversation, emotional expression, and shared support, while men's rituals revolved around shared activities.

Intimacy in Female-Female Friendships

At present, two schools of thought exist on intimacy in women's friendships versus men's. One body of information claims that women's friendships are generally more intimate and close than men's (Caldwell & Peplau, 1982; Eichenbaum & Orbach, 1988; Sherrod, 1989; Wright, 1982). Women tend to value and desire relationships that emphasize intimacy, the sharing of information as well as emotions, and discussion of personal problems (Brehm, 2001). Friendship researcher William Rawlins (1993) suggests that women have greater "intimacy competence" than men, and that this competence stems from women's tendency to embrace the challenge of intimacy and to learn how to communicate closeness with female friends quickly.

Authors of *Girlfriends: Invisible Bonds, Enduring Ties* Carmen Renee Berry and Tamara Traeder (1995) contrast women's friendships with men and women's friendships with women. Women's conversations with male friends tend to focus more on ideas or problem solving than on shared feelings; if women want advice, suggestions, or a "fix it" approach, they are likely to receive that from male friends. However, women most often seek out other women for a listening, sympathetic ear or for empathy regarding what they're going through or feeling. This doesn't mean that women friends don't discuss ideas or help each other solve problems; but female-female friendships may develop stronger bonds of intimacy because a greater range of responses can be obtained; shared feelings, not just information, can lead to greater closeness between women friends. Another element that makes women's friendships with other women different from their friendships with men is men's tendency to withhold personal information. Even though there is evidence that men are more likely to disclose themselves to women than to other men, men tend to disclose less, in general, and to keep things "close to the vest." This tendency can pose a challenge to intimacy between friends (as well as in romantic relationships).

However, another school of thought contends that the difference in intimacy in male-male versus female-female friendships is not so great as previous research suggests, and that in fact there are only minimal differences (Duck & Wright, 1993). Scholar Paul Wright (1998) reexamined earlier findings (including some of his own!) and concluded that men's and women's friendships are more similar than different. Specifically, Wright argues that the "women talk, men do" characterization of friendship is an overgeneralization. On closer inspection of studies that discerned a tendency for women's intimate friendships to develop through communication whereas men's develop through shared activities, Wright found that female subjects also reported shared activities as a mainstay of their friendships with other women. Male subjects reported that they did, in fact, view talk as a central characteristic of their friendships with other men. Wright concludes that "the body of work on the talk-activity issue, as a whole, leaves me convinced that both women and men friends talk a lot and do a lot. Probably they most often talk while doing. However, when reflecting on their friendships, as in responses to interview questions and self-report items, women more often talk about talking and men more often talk about doing" (p. 50).

Again, an assessment of intimacy within a female-female or male-male friendship depends on how you operationalize or define intimacy. If you believe, as many communication scholars do, that genuine intimacy must be achieved and sustained primarily through communication—the sharing of ideas, secrets, fears, and emotions—then you will most likely view women's friendships as epitomizing intimacy and men's friendships as important and satisfying but superficial. However, an expanded definition of intimacy—one that includes experiencing, not just talking—might lead you to conclude that men's and women's friendships can be equally intimate, but that intimacy may emerge or reveal itself in different ways.

Self-Disclosure in Female-Female Friendship

Goodman and O'Brien (2000) explain, regarding their long-time friendship, "We were friends; we had to talk. It was the single most important—and most obvious—connection. Talk is at the very heart of women's friendships, the core of the way women connect. It's the given, the absolute assumption of friendship" (pp. 34–35).

How important is self-disclosure to same-sex friendships? According to Berry and Traeder (1995), "Frequently a woman lets another woman know that she is her most trusted friend by sharing an aspect of herself that she has kept secret from the rest of the world." (p. 71). Reisman (1990) points out that individuals of both sexes who rate their friendships low in disclosure also tend to rate them low in closeness and satisfaction. One study of college students examined the relationship between reported levels of self-disclosure and satisfaction with same-sex friendships; college women participating in the study reported higher levels of self-disclosure in and satisfaction with their same-sex friendships than men did (Jones, 1991).

> *Laugh and the world laughs with you. Cry and you cry with your girlfriends.*
>
> —*Laurie Kuslansky, author*

Research shows, in general, that women are more self-disclosing in their same-sex friendships than men (Clark & Reis, 1988; Dindia & Allen, 1992; Rawlins, 2001; Reis, 1998). However, O'Connor (1992) cautions against using disclosure of personal information and open expression of emotions as defining characteristics of female friendships. The danger, as she describes it, is that if we define women's friendships as operating primarily at a feeling level and "exclude any discussion of ideas or involvement with the world, they [women] abdicate any attempt in changing that world" (p. 31). The concern is that relegating women's friendships to the realm of the emotional reinforces stereotypes of women as purely emotional, with little ability to think rationally or logically.

Same-sex friendships for both men and women offer unique problems and possibilities. In this section, we have introduced you to the major functions of and characteristics in each type of same-sex friendship and explored the role of communication in these relationships. Same-sex friendships are very important to us all, but so are cross-sex friendships. Let's turn our attention to the issues surrounding these sometimes troubling but often fulfilling friendships.

CROSS-SEX FRIENDSHIP: IS IT POSSIBLE TO BE "JUST FRIENDS"?

In the opening case study for this chapter, we described a "just friends" relationship between Tamyra and RJ and mentioned some of the challenges they faced in keeping their friendship intact. For some people, "friends of the opposite sex" is an oxymoron (like "death benefits"). The tendency for contemporary young people to travel in herds, that is, to socialize in groups of both same- and cross-sex friends, is unlike the experience of earlier generations. Just a few decades ago, young men and women socialized together only as dates—rarely if ever as friends. Perhaps young women and men are leading a social change related to cross-sex friendships, because friendships between the sexes have become much more prevalent (Yager, 1999). Research across several decades indicates that we have the greatest number of cross-sex friendships during high school and college years; the number decreases after early adulthood (Kon & Losenkov, 1978; Werking, 1994, 1997b).

'Net Notes

Friendship Force International (FFI) is a nonprofit international cultural exchange organization with headquarters in Atlanta, Georgia. The organization's mission is "to create an environment in which personal friendships are established across the barriers that separate people." FFI has active chapters in more than 60 countries, and they seek to promote goodwill through home-stay exchange programs. For those of you who think you might like to travel abroad and have friendly people to stay with, visit the site for Friendship Force International, located at **www.friendshipforce.org.**

There's an old tune by Michael Bolton with a repeating chorus, "How can we be lovers if we can't be friends?" This lyric suggests that a successful love affair, dating relationship, partnership, or marriage must first be based on friendship. We've all heard folk wisdom that cautions us to like each other as friends before loving each other romantically. Granted, there's merit in such advice, but there's also merit in keeping a male-female relationship at the level of friendship.

As with other aspects of friendship we've discussed, society continues to change its expectations and notions about the appropriateness of cross-sex friendship. While research of the 1970s suggested that both women and men preferred and actually had more same-sex friendships than cross-sex friendships, the experiences of friends today are quite different (Booth & Hess, 1974; Canary & Emmers-Sommer, 1997; Larwood & Wood, 1977; Werking, 1997b). Anecdotal evidence from our students and our own friends suggests that both sexes are seeking friendships with members of the opposite sex. As more and more women continue to enter various walks of life (e.g., business, politics, education), friendships between women and men are increasingly necessary and probable.

What Gets in the Way of Cross-Sex Friendships?

Many of us have experienced the joys that cross-sex friendships can provide, but we also know that these friendships come with their own unique complexities. Let's examine a few issues that typically pose challenges to cross-sex friendships.

The Purpose of Cross-Sex Friendship

One challenge to a successful cross-sex friendship exists in the minds of the friends before they ever meet and decide to become friends. We describe here the differing perceptions of what cross-sex friendship means, or what purpose it serves. Studies over three decades reveal that many men, in contrast to women, consistently report difficulty developing cross-sex friendships that are free of romantic implications and sexual activity, and that men may actually be motivated to form friendships with women because they believe these relationships will lead to "something else" (Bell, 1981; Lipman-Blumen, 1976; Rose, 1985; Rubin, Peplau, & Hill, 1980). Rawlins (2001) explains:

> Typically, males sharply distinguish between same-sex and opposite-sex relationships but view their associations with women rather uniformly. Cross-sex bonds offer more disclosure, intimacy, and emotional involvement, which many males have difficulty interpreting as something other than precursors to romance. Informed by the socially conditioned alternatives of either friendship or romance, they often enact their cross-sex friendships as "not friendship," that is, as possible romances. By contrast, females differentiate less markedly between same-sex and opposite-sex relationships, but make distinctions among their male partners. They are able to form close relationships with females and males. And they clearly distinguish between the males they consider friends and those they regard romantically. Accordingly, their cross-sex friendships are typically enacted as "not romance," that is, as possible friendships. (p. 102)

You can see the potential for conflict and disappointment here, in that the two friends may have very different visions of what the relationship is and where it is heading. Even if the male friend agrees that the relationship is strictly a friendship and nonromantic, he is more likely than the female friend to hold, perhaps in the back of his mind, the hope or expectation that the friendship will lead to romance. While we grant that some men are certainly capable of a truly platonic friendship with a woman and that some women have romantic inclinations toward men who they swear are "just friends," the research consistently shows the first pattern we described.

An Undercurrent of Sexuality

Some research suggests that underlying all heterosexual cross-sex friendships is a pervasive current of sexuality (Egland, Spitzberg, & Zormeier, 1996; Sapadin, 1988). Earlier, we explored the challenge of differing views of the purpose of a cross-sex friendship—the tendency for men more often than women to view friendships with members of the opposite sex as precursors to romantic relationships. In one of the studies that support this finding, female subjects reported that their suspicion of men's sexual motives made them distrustful of men's overtures of friendship and less willing to establish friendships with men (Rose, 1985). In some ways, these findings reflect a remnant from past generations—that relationships with women are for one thing, and that one thing is not friendship.

Cross-sex friends say they are weary of the constant badgering they get from family and other friends as to the true nature of their friendship. Many times people have no sexual attraction or romantic interest at all when they begin hanging out and developing a friendship; it can be a relief to enjoy the company of someone of the opposite sex *without* any sexual tension or romantic expectations. But over time and with repeated "input" from others, the friends may tire of fending off comments, with the result that their friendship erodes or they actually begin to see the other person as a potential romantic partner. This phenomenon can be described as "if everyone else sees potential here, why don't I see it too?"—and it can actually change how one person views the other. For many of us who have developed meaningful cross-sex friendships in our lives, the problem comes when one person develops an attraction and the other doesn't. This is usually followed by the other person's developing an attraction, at just about the time when our attraction for him or her has changed or disappeared. Timing is everything, as they say.

Societal Pressure

Cross-sex friendships face a unique set of societal pressures and judgments, reflected in such comments as "This friendship shouldn't happen at all" and "You must be fooling around." Cross-sex friendships still do not have a strong base of support or approval in American society, as prevalent as this kind of friendship now appears to be. Why can't people let cross-sex friendships alone? Why do people wonder about female-male friendship as though it weren't valid or normal, or as though it were a mere pretense for an underlying romantic or sexual motivation? Why do people think that platonic friends are either lying or fooling themselves when they declare they're "just friends"?

Rawlins (2001) suggests that society actively works to create static for cross-sex friendships, because a "romantic involvement between a man and a woman is much more celebrated than cross-sex friendship in American culture" (p. 95). You've probably heard someone say about a cross-sex friendship, "Oh yeah, their relationship is purely platonic" (wink, wink, nudge, nudge). People frequently use the word *platonic* to describe a friendship that they suspect is something else altogether. Relationships scholar Kathy Werking (1997a) theorizes that since heterosexism is an organizing principle in American society, "romantic relationships between women and men appear to be the 'natural' form of male-female bond" (p. 398). Werking (1997b) maintains that the tension between the cultural model of romantic male-female relationships and the everyday practice of friendship exerts pressure on male and female friends. It is difficult to be friends when the culture does not expect friendship between a man and a woman. In addition, the societal preoccupation with romantic relationships diverts cultural conversations and research away from cross-sex friendships.

Another problem is that we have few ready role models or prototypes of cross-sex friendships; the partners in each friendship seem to make up their own rules as they go. Communication researchers Bell and Healey (1992) suggest that friends look to the images, norms, and rules of society as they attempt to make sense of their connection, but what images of effective cross-sex friendship exist in this society—Hollywood's Harry and Sally? The movement of the whole movie *When Harry Met Sally* was toward romance for the main characters. Hollywood movies rarely let attractive heterosexual people remain friends. It is difficult for two individuals to initiate and develop a relationship in the absence of effective role models. Since no clear prototype exists in this culture for a successful cross-sex friendship, the only conclusion is that the successful ones succeed because the individuals involved have worked to create and communicate to others their own definition of success.

One reason why few role models for successful cross-sex friendships exist is that society places clear limits on what it accepts in this kind of relationship.

Rawlins (2001) describes three somewhat socially approved contexts for cross-sex friendships: (1) male and female coworkers who become friends; (2) non-married female and male friends, because in some circles "friendship" is a euphemism for dating and can be seen as a natural precursor to romance; and (3) a cross-sex friendship that has the approval of the friends' romantic partners. Because of the perception of deviance, Rawlins suggests that "In a frustrating cultural setting, cross-sex friends must orchestrate social perceptions of their relationship as well as develop a shared private definition" (p. 104).

Cross-sex friends have to be cautious and make more conscious choices about messages they give others about their friendship, because misperceptions are likely to have a detrimental effect on the relationship (Aleman, Miller, & Vangelisti, 1993). In earlier sections we discussed friendship rituals, as studied by Bruess and Pearson (1997). These researchers found that cross-sex friends reported fewer rituals, indicating that they may have more difficulty establishing acceptable public and private patterns of behavior. Together with a lack of role models and an undercurrent of sexuality, the issues of public and private definitions may contribute to a shaky base for the development of a relationship. These potential problems led Rawlins (1993) to advocate that cross-sex friends should openly and periodically discuss relational definitions and the challenges their relationship faces.

Interpersonal Communication Patterns

Another source of difficulty in cross-sex friendships arises from interpersonal communication patterns which may relate to gender. For example, how is conflict managed in a cross-sex friendship? Is it handled any differently from the way two female or two male friends might handle disagreement in their friendship? Does one friend consistently exert more influence or power over the other? Is one friend more often the discloser and the other the recipient of disclosure? Could that become a problem?

Research shows that many men seek friendships with women as an emotional outlet and so that they will have someone (other than their romantic partners) who will listen to their disclosure, particularly about personal problems, and respond with empathy (Aukett, Ritchie, & Mill, 1988; Buhrke & Fuqua, 1987; Rose, 1985). As we discussed in an earlier section of this chapter, men typically avoid emotional expression or intimacy with other men; thus, they often seek it with women (Aleman, Miller, & Vangelisti, 1993). In contrast, many women feel that they cannot have their emotional needs met only through their relationships (romantic and other) with men, so they seek relationships with other women to fulfill this purpose. Can you see the potential for difficulty here? If men tend to seek emotional support from women, and women tend to seek emotional support from women, that can create a sort of imbalance of friendship. This may also pose a challenge to the cross-sex friendship: if the male friend views the friendship as an outlet for meeting his emotional needs, but the female friend sees it as unable to serve this function for her, the relationship might be headed for problems. The purposes and parameters of the friendship may need to be discussed directly.

One interpersonal pattern that warrants discussion is not based on research but stems from our own experience, corroborated by numerous experiences our students describe. We have detected a unique form of communication that emerges primarily between men—a form that tends to backfire when men use it with women. In a gender communication class a few semesters ago, this phenomenon received the label "jocular sparring." Here's how it typically works. A guy will see one of his buddies and greet him by saying, "Man, you look *terrible* today; where'd you get that shirt, off somebody who died?! And your hair, geez—put a hat on that." This harmless teasing between male friends can be translated as "I like you; you're my buddy." It's an unthreatening way for men to communicate liking and affection for one another. We realize that the following statement is generalizing a bit, but women don't typically talk this way with their female friends. If a woman greeted a female friend by saying, "Hey, you look like death warmed over today—what happened?! That outfit looks like it's been through the wringer and your hair looks as if the cat's been chewing on it," the female friend would probably feel hurt, get angry, or wonder what in the world had gotten into her friend.

Intrafriendship teasing or jocular sparring just doesn't seem to work the same way with women as it does with men. What happens when a guy teases a female friend, assuming that she'll react the way his male friends do? For example, consider what's likely to happen if a guy greets a female friend by saying, "Not getting enough sleep lately? Your eyes look as though you've been on a four-day drunk. And that outfit—did you get dressed in the dark?!" More often than not, the woman will not take the teasing lightly. She might act as though she is tossing off the comments, but in fact the teasing is probably causing her discomfort because it introduces an element of uncertainty into the relationship. (We hope you're nodding your head while you're reading this—most people find a high level of correspondence between this information and their own experiences.)

This doesn't mean that women have no a sense of humor or that they're fragile creatures who can't take teasing among friends. In fact, after a friendship has been established and the friends understand each other's communication styles better, women can often take jocular sparring (and dish it right back) in the friendly spirit intended. It's not that women can't or don't engage in teasing with both their male and their female friends, but they tend not to prefer it as a form of indicating closeness or affection. When women do engage in teasing, they tend to communicate it differently and with a different effect than when men jocularly spar. If this sounds all too familiar and descriptive of your own experience with friends, then perhaps you will want to reassess this form of communication. Jocular sparring has the potential either to hurt or to engender a sense of playfulness and closeness in a relationship; if you desire the positive outcome, it's wise for friends to negotiate the use of this kind of communication.

What Enhances Cross-Sex Friendships?

A reporter for the *New York Times* suggests that people who have friends they can turn to in troubled times are more likely to lead healthier lives (Brody, 1992). Each of us needs friends, and one of the benefits of the changes over past decades is the increased potential for satisfying friendships between men and women. While many students, both male and female, are aware of some of the problems we just discussed, they also report a desire for more and better friendships with members of the opposite sex. In this final section of the chapter, let's explore some strategies one might follow to increase the chance that a cross-sex friendship will develop successfully.

Defining the Relationship

One of the values we described in Chapter 1, "Talking about it makes it better," is one that we keep coming back to. Within the context of cross-sex heterosexual friendship, it's particularly important that friends discuss their relationship and define it by addressing the question, "Are we just friends or is this leading to something else?" A shared definition—one that can be clearly articulated to others—is critical to long-term success in cross-sex friendship. We hope that platonic friendship will become so commonplace that people won't suspect it of being something else, but research still shows us that society hasn't evolved to a position of complete tolerance on this issue. The sexual dynamics between women and men still form undercurrent, so getting past that issue or negotiating the nature of the relationship is necessary if the friendship is to grow. "State of the relationship" conversations may need to take place more than once if one or both persons change their minds about their intentions or if circumstances change (for example, if one friend gets married).

The question "Where is this relationship headed?" applies to same-sex friends as well, given that one person in a same-sex friendship may want to move the relationship to sexual intimacy. The same suggestions apply here as well: clarity of intentions, open communication, and a willingness to reach a mutually agreed-on definition of the friendship are important to the long-term success of the relationship.

> *It is one of the blessings of old friends that you can afford to be stupid with them.*
>
> —*Ralph Waldo Emerson,*
> *poet*

Cross-Sex Friends as Romance Advisors

One benefit of cross-sex friendship, from a heterosexual perspective, is getting firsthand information and insight into the opposite sex (Canary & Emmers-Sommer, 1997). How many of us have asked an opposite-sex friend to explain that sex and its behavior to us? How many of us have compared a date's behavior with that of our opposite-sex friend and found the date wanting? Our curiosity about the opposite sex is a natural, fun part of life, but when it turns into perplexity because one relational partner cannot understand the other, then we feel we need help. Who better to turn to than an opposite-sex friend?

It's common for men to ask their female friends to help them understand women or just to seek support, empathy, or sympathy. This applies to the guy who is frustrated over his lack of success in the dating market, to the man who wants female insight into his dating relationships, or to the married man who seeks advice about his relationship with his wife, possibly from one of her friends. At times, women remain a mystery to men, so men often feel that a female friend can help them understand women more so than a male friend. As some research we reviewed in the section on male-male friendship indicates, men may not want to disclose their problems, insecurities, or concerns to other men for fear of appearing weak or vulnerable. Thus men often find female friends to be valuable confidantes. Likewise, women who are puzzled or troubled by some situation involving romantic entanglements with men (or the lack thereof) can find their male friends a source of support, strength, and insight.

Of course, like anything else, this function of cross-sex friendships—giving advice, lending an ear—has abuses as well as benefits. For example, if your sole purpose in having an opposite-sex friend is to seek counsel on your romantic relationships, your friend may quickly tire of that. Cross-sex friendships need special kinds of maintenance. Using someone merely as a source of support, a guidance counselor, a spokesperson for all men or all women, or a captive audience for your problems could be considered a selfish, abusive way to conduct a friendship. What if your friend needs your ear sometime? What if your friend is unwilling to be there for you, simply because the friendship has become too one-sided? These important issues warrant sensitive discussion and negotiation between cross-sex friends. If you don't talk about possible abuses of the friendship—or of any relationship, for that matter—you might wind up with one less friend.

Sexual Activity between "Just Friends"

Thus far in this chapter, we have been operating under the assumption that cross-sex friendships are platonic—that is, they do not include sexual activity. Cross-sex friendships often do include sexual tension, as we've also discussed. This tension may be positive or negative, depending on the perception of the individuals involved. Our culture's unspoken dividing line appears to be that as soon as two friends begin to engage in sexual activity, the relationship moves from friendship to some other level. Whatever level that might be, it's not a friendship any longer, so it shouldn't be discussed in this chapter. Perhaps it is time to question that assumption.

Is a physical relationship a logical extension of the intimacy that two people can develop? If a strong friendship includes deep sharing at the psychological level, what about the physical level? If that happens, is the relationship no longer a friendship? (There's a common term for this type of relationship—a friendship-plus-sex relationship—but the words involved may be more suitable to our fairly graphic discussion of language in Chapter 4 than they are here. Suffice it to say, in a PG-13 version, that a person in this type of relationship might be called an "f-buddy.") Definitive answers may not exist for these questions. We raise the point to start you thinking about the qualities of a cross-sex friendship and what it should or shouldn't include.

Hot Button Issue

"LOVERS VERSUS FRIENDS"

Should there be a rule that friends should be only friends, whereas lovers can be friends as well? In the section of this chapter on cross-sex friendship, we briefly discussed the possibility that friends could have a sexual relationship but still remain only friends with no romantic involvement. Do you think that is possible? If so, is it a good idea? Most people think that sex changes a relationship; once a friendship becomes sexual, it morphs into something else—something that will eventually need defining. Perhaps there do exist some special friends who can explore variations on their relationship without risking or damaging the friendship, but we've met very few people who can pull this off. Another concern is the potential for hurt, when one friend believes that sexual activity is a signal that the relationship is moving past friendship into romance, but the other friend doesn't.

Here's a related question our students ask with regularity: Is it possible to go back to being just friends after being lovers? Of course the possibility exists, but it may take some careful conversations about intentions and needs before it becomes a reality. The possibility of "going back to being friends" also depends on the feelings of the parties involved. If you want the relationship to move beyond friendship and if sexual activity becomes part of the equation, then a suggestion from your friend that you cease sexual intimacy and return to being "just friends" may be painful and, frankly, impossible to accomplish. The question of sexual relations in a friendship further complicates the concept. Since this is an area where no clear guidelines exist, we can only suggest to you our earlier advice: talk it over.

The Future for Cross-Sex Friendship

Friendship between men and women has changed. We wonder where these changes will lead, and so we close this chapter with one thought on the direction and future of friendship between the sexes. Buhrke and Fuqua (1987) concluded the following from their research:

> Given that [our research found] women wanted more contact with men, wanted to be closer to men, and wanted more balance in their relationships with men . . . , one could conclude that women more highly value their relationships with men and wish to better those relationships. However, women were already more satisfied with the frequency of contact, closeness, and balance in their relationships with women. Thus it seems women want more from their relationships with men and make efforts to improve the quality of those relationships so that they are more similar to their relationships with women. (p. 349)

This is an interesting thought—that women want better relationships with men but want these relationships to become more like their friendships with other women. Perhaps men would like their cross-sex friendships to become more like their same-sex friendships. We suggest that neither goal is complete. It may not be a good idea to force cross-sex friendships into the mold of the familiar same-sex friendship. Indeed, the terms *cross-sex* and *same-sex* for friendships tend to dichotomize the two types and exaggerate their differences while minimizing their similarities (Arnold, 1994; Werking, 1994). If we classify relationships as same-sex or cross-sex, we may restrict our understanding of communicative practices and experience. Men and women can develop more effective cross-sex friendships by learning to incorporate the patterns of the opposite sex into their communication repertoire and by treating each friendship as a unique entity, not as having come from another planet. The process takes thought, sensitivity, and a willingness to learn and change.

CONCLUSION

This chapter began with the suggestion that the nature of and value placed on same-sex and cross-sex friendships are changing. Research supports that suggestion and provides great insight into friendships and the kind of communication that sustains them. We first explored in this chapter how we learn, as children, what friendship means; we examined gender-related friendship patterns that begin in childhood and change as we progress into adolescence and adulthood. Friendship between the sexes is something we learn to do, because structures in society generally do not teach us how to embrace members of the opposite sex as friends.

We then explored the unique functions and characteristics of male-male friendships, as compared with female-female friendships. While these relationships are more similar than different, researchers have found that some aspects, such as the purpose of the friendship, the approaches to and need for developing intimacy, and the role of self-disclosure in the relationship, do differ.

Finally, we examined cross-sex friendship, in terms of factors that impede the development and satisfaction of this kind of friendship, as well as factors that enhance it. Specifically, such factors as varying purposes or expectations for the friendship, the undercurrent of sexuality, societal pressure, and interpersonal communication patterns—such as who more often discloses versus who more often receives the other's disclosure—may actually impede the success of a cross-sex friendship. We offered some suggestions for enhancing a cross-sex friendship, such as communicating to develop a clear definition of the relationship and being careful not to overuse one's opposite-sex friend as a romantic advisor. We also discussed the murky waters of sexual activity between cross-sex friends, in terms of the effects on a friendship.

Each type of friendship has unique communication issues and unique potential, but one thing is clear: friendships are among our most important relationships in life. We have all probably suffered the consequences of assuming that friends will always be there for us, that we don't have to exert much energy to keep them. Such assumptions will soon leave us friendless, and fast. So, just like other important relationships—with family, coworkers, or romantic partners—friendships need communication, as well as shared experiences, to develop and grow.

Discussion Starters

1. In your experience, how do most male friendships seem to form? What brings the friends together? Are the circumstances different from those that bring female friends together?

2. Some researchers propose that the intimacy men achieve through doing things together is of the same quality as the intimacy women achieve through conversation. Do you believe that men and women are equally capable of forming intimate relationships? Intimate same-sex friendships? Intimate cross-sex friendships? How are women and men different in terms of accomplishing intimacy in their relationships? How are they similar?

3. Think about the issue of sexual activity in heterosexual cross-sex friendships. How is the issue dealt with in most of the cross-sex friendships you know? In your own cross-sex friendships? Is the issue discussed openly, hinted at, or avoided?

4. If you had to write down on a piece of paper the name of the opposite-sex person with whom you've had the best platonic or friendship-type relationship, whose name would come to mind first? What factors about the friendship or the person caused you to think of him or her? What elements characterize your communication with this friend?

5. What do you think are the biggest obstacles to effective cross-sex friendships? What do you think it will take to improve friendships between women and men? Which sex will have to change more, and why? What will the ideal cross-sex friendship look like?

References

Aleman, C. G., Miller, L. L., & Vangelisti, A. L. (1993, February). *Focus of attention as a means of assessing power in relationships: An analysis of cross-sex romantic and friendship conversations.* Paper presented at the meeting of the Western States Communication Association, Albuquerque, NM.

Aries, E. (1998). Gender differences in interaction: A re-examination. In D. Canary & K. Dindia (Eds.), *Sex, gender, and communication: Similarities and differences* (pp. 65–81). Mahwah, NJ: Erlbaum.

Arliss, L. P., & Borisoff, D. J. (1993). *Women and men communicating: Challenges and changes.* Fort Worth, TX: Harcourt, Brace, & Jovanovich.

Arnold, L. B. (1995). Through the narrow pass: Experiencing same-sex friendship in heterosexual(ist) settings. *Communication Studies, 46,* 234–244.

Aukett, R., Ritchie, J., & Mill, K. (1988). Gender differences in friendship patterns. *Sex Roles, 19,* 57–66.

Barth, R. J., & Kinder, B. N. (1988). A theoretical analysis of sex differences in same-sex friendships. *Sex Roles, 19,* 349–363.

Basow, S. A. (1986). *Sex role stereotypes: Traditions and alternatives.* Monterey, CA: Brooks/Cole.

Basow, S. A. (1992). *Gender: Stereotypes and roles* (3rd ed.). Pacific Grove, CA: Wadsworth.

Bate, B., & Bowker, J. (1997). *Communication and the sexes* (2nd ed.). Prospect Heights, IL: Waveland.

Bell, R. R. (1981). *Worlds of friendship.* Beverly Hills, CA: Sage.

Bell, R. A., & Healey, J. G. (1992). Idiomatic communication and interpersonal solidarity in friends' relational cultures. *Human Communication Research, 18,* 307–335.

Berry, C. R., & Traeder, T. (1995). *Girlfriends: Invisible bonds, enduring ties.* Berkeley, CA: Wildcat Canyon.

Block, J. D., & Greenberg, D. (1985). *Women and friendship.* New York: Franklin Watts.

Booth, A., & Hess, E. (1974, February). Cross-sex friendship. *Journal of Marriage and the Family, 36,* 38–47.

Botschner, J. V. (1996). Reconsidering male friendships: A social-developmental perspective. In C. W. Tolman & F. Cherry (Eds.), *Problems in theoretical psychology.* North York, Ontario: Captus.

Brehm, S. S. (2001). *Intimate relationships* (3rd ed.). New York: McGraw-Hill.

Brody, J. E. (1992). Maintaining friendships for the sake of good health. *New York Times, 141,* p. C12.

Bruess, C. J. S., & Pearson, J. C. (1997). Interpersonal rituals in marriage and adult friendship. *Communication Monographs, 64,* 25–46.

Buhrke, R. A., & Fuqua, D. R. (1987). Sex differences in same- and cross-sex supportive relationships. *Sex Roles, 17,* 339–351.

Burleson, B. R., & Samter, W. (1996). Similarity in communication skills of young adults: Foundations of attraction, friendship, and relationship satisfaction. *Communication Reports, 9,* 127–139.

Caldwell, M. A., & Peplau, L. A. (1982). Sex differences in same-sex friendships. *Sex Roles, 8,* 721–732.

Canary, D. J., & Emmers-Sommer, T. M. (1997). *Sex and gender differences in personal relationships.* New York: Guilford.

Clark, M., & Reis, H. T. (1988). Interpersonal processes in close relationships. *Annual Review of Psychology, 39,* 609–672.

Crawford, M., & Unger, R. (2000). *Women and gender: A feminist psychology* (3rd ed.). New York: McGraw-Hill.

Derlega, V. J., Metts, S., Petronio, S., & Margulis, S. T. (1993). *Self-disclosure.* Newbury Park, CA: Sage.

Derlega, V. J., Winstead, B. A., Wong, P., & Hunter, S. (1985). Gender effects in initial encounters: A case where men exceed women in disclosure. *Journal of Social and Personal Relationships, 2,* 25–44.

Dindia, K., & Allen, M. (1992). Sex differences in self-disclosure: A meta-analysis. *Psychological Bulletin, 112* (1), 106–124.

Doyle, J. A. (1995). *The male experience* (3rd ed.). New York: McGraw-Hill.

Duck, S., & Wright, P. (1993). Reexamining gender differences in friendships: A close look at two kinds of data. *Sex Roles, 28,* 709–727.

Eichenbaum, L., & Orbach, S. (1988). *Between women: Love, envy, and competition in women's friendships.* New York: Viking.

Egland, K. L., Spitzberg, B., & Zormeier, M. (1996). Flirtation and conversational competence in cross-sex platonic and romantic relationships. *Communication Reports, 9,* 106–117.

Fine, J. (2001, October). Intimacy. *O: The Oprah Winfrey Magazine, 225.*

Fitzpatrick, M. A., & Bochner, A. (1981). Perspectives on self and other: Male-female differences in perceptions of communication behavior. *Sex Roles, 7,* 523–535.

Floyd, K., & Morman, M. T. (1997). Affectionate communication in nonromantic relationships: Influences of communicator, relational, and contextual factors. *Western Journal of Communication, 61,* 279–298.

Floyd, K., & Parks, M. (1995). Manifesting closeness in the interactions of peers: A look at siblings and friends. *Communication Reports, 8,* 69–76.

Gilligan, C. (1982). *In a different voice.* Cambridge, MA: Harvard University Press.

Goodman, E., & O'Brien, P. (2000). *I know just what you mean: The power of friendship in women's lives.* New York: Simon & Schuster.

Harvey, J. H., & Weber, A. L. (2002). *Odyssey of the heart: Close relationships in the 21st century* (2nd ed.). Mahwah, NJ: Erlbaum.

Henley, N. (1986). *Body politics: Power, sex, and nonverbal communication.* New York: Touchstone.

Hite, S. (1989). *Women and love.* New York: St. Martin's.

Ickes, W. (1985). *Compatible and incompatible relationships.* New York: Springer-Verlag.

Inman, C. (1996). Friendships among men: Closeness in the doing. In J. T. Wood (Ed.), *Gendered relationships* (pp. 95–110). Mountain View, CA: Mayfield.

Johnson, F. L. (1996). Friendships among women: Closeness in dialogue. In J. T. Wood (Ed.), *Gendered relationships* (pp. 79–94). Mountain View, CA: Mayfield.

Jones, D. C. (1991). Friendship satisfaction and gender: An examination of sex differences in contributors to friendship satisfaction. *Journal of Social and Personal Relationships, 8,* 167–185.

Knapp, M. L., & Vangelisti, A. L. (2000). *Interpersonal communication and human relationships* (4th ed.). Boston: Allyn & Bacon.

Kon, L., & Losenkov, V. A. (1978). Friendship in adolescence: Values and behavior. *Journal of Marriage and the Family, 40,* 143–155.

Larwood, L., & Wood, M. M. (1977). *Women in management.* Lexington, KY: Lexington Books.

Lipman-Blumen, J. (1976). Toward a homosocial theory of sex roles: An explanation of the sex segregation of social institutions. In M. M. Blaxall & B. Reagan (Eds.), *Women and the workplace* (pp. 15–22). Chicago: University of Chicago Press.

Martin, R. (1997). "Girls don't talk about garages!" Perceptions of conversations in same- and cross-sex friendships. *Personal Relationships, 4,* 115–130.

Messner, M. A. (1992). Like family: Power, intimacy, and sexuality in male athletes' friendships. In P. M. Nardi (Ed.), *Men's friendships* (pp. 215–238). Newbury Park, CA: Sage.

Nardi, P. M. (1992). *Men's friendships.* Newbury Park, CA: Sage.

O'Connor, P. (1992). *Friendships between women: A critical review.* New York: Guilford.

Orosan, P. G., & Schelling, K. M. (1992). Gender differences in college students' definition and perceptions of intimacy. *Women & Therapy, 12,* 201–212.

Parker, S., & deVries, B. (1993). Patterns of friendships for women and men in same and cross-sex relationships. *Journal of Social & Personal Relationships, 10,* 617–626.

Perry, L. A. M., Turner, L. H., & Sterk, H. M. (Eds.) (1992). *Constructing and reconstructing gender: The links among communication, language, and gender.* Albany: State University of New York Press.

Petronio, S., Martin, J., & Littlefield, R. (1984). Prerequisite conditions for self-disclosing: A gender issue. *Communication Monographs, 51,* 268–272.

Rawlins, W. K. (1992). *Friendship matters: Communication, dialectics, and the life course.* Hawthorne, NY: Aldine de Gruyter.

Rawlins, W. K. (1993). Communication in cross-sex friendships. In L. P. Arliss & D. J. Borisoff (Eds.), *Women and men communicating: Challenges and changes* (pp. 51–70). Fort Worth, TX: Harcourt, Brace, & Jovanovich.

Rawlins, W. K. (2001). Times, places, and social spaces for cross-sex friendship. In L. P. Arliss & D. J. Borisoff (Eds.), *Women and men communicating: Challenges and changes* (2nd ed.) (pp. 93–114). Prospect Heights, IL: Waveland.

Reis, H. T. (1998). Gender differences in intimacy and related behaviors: Context and process. In D. J. Canary and K. Dindia (Eds.), *Sex differences and similarities in communication* (pp. 203–231). Mahwah, NJ: Erlbaum.

Reisman, J. J. (1979). *Anatomy of friendships.* New York: Irvington.

Reisman, J. J. (1990). Intimacy in same-sex friendships. *Sex Roles, 23,* 65–82.

Romaine, S. (1999). *Communicating gender.* Mahwah, NJ: Erlbaum.

Rose, S. M. (1985). Same- and cross-sex friendships and the psychology of homosociality. *Sex Roles, 12,* 63–74.

Rubin, Z., Peplau, L. A., & Hill, C. T. (1980). Loving and leaving: Sex differences in romantic attachments. *Sex Roles, 6,* 821–835.

Sapadin, L. A. (1988). Friendship and gender: Perspectives of professional men and women. *Journal of Social and Personal Relationships, 5,* 387–403.

Shaffer, D. R., Pegalis, L. J., & Bazzini, D. G. (1996). When boy meets girl (revisited): Gender, gender-role orientation, and prospect of future interaction as determinants of self-disclosure among same- and opposite-sex acquaintances. *Personality and Social Psychology Bulletin, 22,* 495–506.

Sherrod, D. (1989). The influences of gender on same-sex friendships. In C. Hendrick (Ed.), *Close relationships* (pp. 164–186). Newbury Park, CA: Sage.

Spain, D. (1992). The spatial foundations of men's friendships and men's power. In P. M. Nardi (Ed.), *Men's friendships* (pp. 59–73). Newbury Park, CA: Sage.

Stephens, T. D., & Harrison, T. M. (1985). Gender, sex-role identity, and communication style: A Q-sort analysis of behavioral differences. *Communication Research Reports, 2,* 53–61.

Strikwerda, R. A., & May, L. (1992). Male friendship and intimacy. *Hypatia, 7,* 110–125.

Tannen, D. (1994). *Gender and discourse.* New York: Oxford University Press.

Thorne, B. (1994). *Gender play: Girls and boys in school.* New Brunswick, NJ: Rutgers University Press.

Tiger, L. (1969). *Men in groups.* New York: Random House.

Veniegas, R. C., & Peplau, L. A. (1997). Power and the quality of same-sex friendships. *Psychology of Women Quarterly, 21,* 279–297.

Werking, K. J. (1994, May). *Barriers to the formation of cross-sex friendship.* Paper presented at the meeting of International Network for Personal Relationships, Iowa City, IA.

Werking, K. J. (1997a). Cross-sex friendship research as ideological practice. In S. Duck (Ed.), *Handbook of personal relationships: Theory, research, and interventions* (2nd ed.) (pp. 391–410). Chichester: John Wiley & Sons.

Werking, K. J. (1997b). *We're just good friends: Women and men in nonromantic relationships.* New York: Guilford.

Wood, J. T., & Inman, C. C. (1993). In a different mode: Masculine styles of communicating closeness. *Journal of Applied Communication Research, 21,* 279–295.

Wright, P. (1982). Men's friendships, women's friendships, and the alleged inferiority of the latter. *Sex Roles, 8,* 1–19.

Wright, P. (1998). Toward an expanded orientation to the study of sex differences in friendships. In D. J. Canary & K. Dindia (Eds.), *Sex differences and similarities in communication* (pp. 41–63). Mahwah, NJ: Erlbaum.

Yager, J. (1999). *Friendshifts: The power of friendship and how it shapes our lives* (2nd ed.). Stamford, CT: Hannacroix Creek Books.

CHAPTER SEVEN

BEYOND FRIENDSHIP:

Gender Communication in Romantic Relationships

CASE STUDY: PERSISTENT TRADITIONS
IN THE REALM OF ROMANCE

"You know one thing that still really bothers me? Guys are still the ones who have to ask girls out. With all this liberation we're supposed to have had, why do we still have to put ourselves on the line all the time?" This was Cliff's complaint in class one day about something he doesn't see changing—the continued responsibility a man feels to put his ego on the line and ask a woman for a date. Bonnie countered with, "Wait a second. You don't know what it's like to wait or hope you'll be asked out. That's really hard, too." This led Nicole to chime in, "Hey, if you don't like waiting for a guy to ask you out, ask *him* out. I know lots of women who ask guys out on dates. I've called a few myself." At this point, an informal class poll showed that the traditional model, in spite of changing times, was still very much in evidence. Few men get asked out by women (even though they'd *like* to); few women actually ask men out (even though they know they *can*). Men feel responsible for doing the asking, and while some women do take the initiative, most are uncomfortable with it.

As the class discussion continued, Bonnie asked, "Why haven't things changed much? The way it used to be still seems to be the way it is." Jawarren responded, "I think you're right. A couple of friends of mine got married this summer, and even though they had a pretty balanced relationship in college, when they graduated, got married, and he got a job, all of a sudden he's the breadwinner and she's taking care of the house. They're behaving just like their parents!" Bonnie answered, "Yeah, I know what you mean. It seems as if there are lots of opportunities to change, but when it comes right down to it, there's a lot of pressure to keep things they way they've been."

In this chapter, we discuss some things that have changed and some things that haven't, in the realm of romantic relationships. It seems that despite changes in many areas of male-female relationships, romantic partnerings often cling to some old patterns. Do you think things have changed, in terms of female and male roles in dating and romantic relationships? Does the traditional model still make its presence felt? Changing our patterns, expectations, and communication within romantic relationships takes conscious effort and an awareness of options.

We could discuss a whole host of issues regarding this topic; instead, we've selected what we consider the most pertinent gender-related information to present to you. As you're reading, do what we've asked you to do before—put yourself and your experiences into your reading. Compare the research and ideas with your own views about romantic relationships and your own experiences. Maybe you'll find that your approach is on the money. Or maybe you'll find some things you want to do differently.

Hot Topics

- The language of romance
- The pressure to establish romantic relationships
- How stereotypical notions of romance impede relational success
- Tensions in romantic relationships, including autonomy versus connection, power versus empowerment, acceptance versus change, developing comparable views of intimacy, expressing love, and making a commitment
- The role of relational talk and metacommunication in the development of couples' communication patterns
- Conflict management in romantic relationships
- The effects of gender and the role of communication in relationship termination
- Attitudes and communication about sexual activity in a romantic relationship

AH, LOVE AND ROMANCE (AND GENDER)

Hollywood movies would have us believe that romantic relationships happen almost by magic, as though we all know what it takes to make them happen and how to keep them going. Movies throughout the years have also shown us various faces of pain when romantic relationships have gone awry. Given the idealized, overdrawn images in our heads, it may sometimes come as a shock, or at least a rude awakening, to find a different reality when we embark on romantic relationships of our own. Romantic relationships bring their own unique communication and challenges to men and women who venture into them. But even when we are in the midst of a breakup, when a relationship seems doomed and we wonder why we ever wandered into such uncharted territory, we'd probably say we'd do it all over again if given the chance. Humans are innately romantic creatures, and for many of us, the opportunity for romance and love is one of life's greatest experiences.

What kinds of gender issues and communication make this relational context so special and unique? That's exactly the focus of this chapter. Few things motivate individuals more strongly than the emotions that surround romance, love, sex, and marriage; and few topics are so strongly evidenced in our cultural artifacts such as movies, television, art, books, and other media. Because romantic relationships tap such strong emotions and because our culture has such a strong interest in them, communication within them is critical and complex.

The Language of Romance

Romantic relationships are complicated (an understatement). To begin, consider the terms used to describe the nature of a romantic relationship and the two people in it. For heterosexual couples, the term *girlfriend* is still the most common usage of traditionally-aged male students, but use of *boyfriend* seems to be on the decline among their female counterparts. Instead, college women often say "the guy I'm dating" or, less often, "a man I'm seeing"

> *A guy knows he's in love when he wants to grow old with a woman. When he wants to stay with her in the morning. When he starts calling sex "making love" and afterward wants a great big hug. When he loses interest in the car for a couple of days. It's that simple, I swear.*
>
> *—Tim Allen, actor*

(which may imply that he's somewhat older than the woman). Homosexual couples face this problem as well, if not to a more difficult degree. Most often they refer to each other as *partners,* a term that some heterosexual couples have begun to co-opt, because it communicates the sense of equality and cooperativeness inherent in a partnership. Sometimes, if the relationship or the sexual orientations of the partners are closeted, homosexual cohabitating couples may refer to each other as *roommates.* Older adults especially cringe when they refer to a romantic involvement, given the choices of descriptors available to them: juvenile terms (such as *boyfriend* and *girlfriend*), ambiguous and nondescript terms (e.g., *my friend*), terms that are too personal (*lovers*), or clinical psychobabble terms (such as *significant other,* a term widely used in the 1970s).

Gender researcher Laurie Arliss (2001) describes the gap in our language regarding terms for relationships that involve more than being "just friends" but are not marital (and perhaps not likely to be). We've seen a number of people stumble in introductions. A newspaper editorial once gave this example: "I'd like you to meet my . . . uh . . . " Sadly, the English language hasn't progressed much past calling these relationships "uh." (The best option in a situation like this is to simply introduce the person by her or his name, leaving out the "my.") For the purposes of this chapter, the term *relational partner* is used to refer to members of romantic relationships and *marital partner* or *spouse* to refer to married partners. We believe that *relational partner* is the best option. It sounds a bit clinical, but not as clinical as *significant other*. We use the term *romantic relationship* to include the range of relationships from dating to longer-term commitments (where the term *dating* doesn't seem to fit) and nonmarital relationships that include sexual activity. (We don't mean to insinuate that marital relationships are somehow not romantic; we're just trying to be clear.) On occasion, we use the term *monogamous relationship*, in reference to a romantic relationship in which the partners date only each other. Some usages of the term imply a sexual relationship, meaning that partners are involved romantically and sexually only with each other, but it can apply to couples whose relationship does not (or not yet) involve sexual activity. The more these terms work their way into common usage, the more easily people will be able to connect them with the kind of relationship described.

The Pressure to Partner

Communication researchers Hendrick and Hendrick (1992), in their extensive review of romantic love, make the point that romantic love in our culture has become the overwhelming reason for entering into long-term relationships, such as marriage or homosexual partnerings. Love, as a reason for partnering, is a relatively recent occurrence in our culture. As recently as the early twentieth century in America, economic and social reasons were more important than love in choosing a mate. In many parts of the world, love and romance are not significant parts of marriage; business opportunities, the furtherance of family, and tradition override love as motivations for marrying.

As "liberated" as we are now as a culture (some people believe we aren't very liberated at all), many people still feel a great deal of pressure to partner or couple, as though they can't be taken seriously or haven't really arrived until they're in a committed monogamous relationship. Traditionally-aged college students probably don't experience much of this pressure while completing their education. In fact, our students tell us that they feel pressure in the opposite direction—they feel pressure, primarily from peers, to stay single and play the field. If they do involve themselves in a monogamous relationship, they may actually take heat or teasing from their friends, and may even feel pressure to cheat or end the relationship and begin dating lots of people again. However, students report that they do feel increasing pressure to find the "right" person and commit to a romantic relationship the closer they get to graduation. They begin to hear well-meaning voices—perhaps the voices of family members—asking when they're going to get a job and settle down. If you stay single through graduation and beyond, you may really feel pressure when you begin your career because you may not be considered as stable or as reliable a bet for the future as a married colleague. Gays and lesbians are stereotyped as "playing the field" and also feel actual pressure to play the field, but the people who tend to receive the most respect and envy in gay and lesbian communities are those in committed monogamous relationships.

In American society, we still see evidence of strong cultural pressure to marry and raise a family, even though a government report in 2002 predicted that one in three marriages would end within 10 years (ABC *World News Tonight*, 2002). Statistics suggest that although there are alternatives to marriage (living together, remaining single, etc.), approximately 95 percent of heterosexual Americans will get married (*Information Please*, 1998). (They may not stay married, but research says that they will at least get married.) This form of societal pressure led author Gerri Hirshey (1989) to explore the "tyranny of the couple," one result of a culture that has "commitment obsession" (p. 49). Hirshey jokes about the situation: "Question: How does a single woman get rid of roaches in her apartment? Answer: She asks them for a commitment" (p. 49).

Author Barbara Yost (1996) quips, "Single Americans are as welcome as pot-smoking hippies at a Bob Dole party" (p. H1). The pressure to couple is embodied in the often-asked question, "So how come you're still single?" This attitude, Yost says, is hard on singles. Couples become so self-involved that they tend to forget or gravitate away from their single friends, perceiving that they'll have less in common. (A few episodes of *Friends* addressed this issue after Monica and Chandler's marriage.) Some married women see single women as potential threats. Some single men may find their sexual orientation questioned, especially if they have male roommates (Yost, 1996). Yost sees a shift in American culture and a return to the idea that "People are expected to grow up, get married, and stay married—or risk the wrath of politicians who brandish spouse and children like banners of morality" (p. H1).

Stereotypical Notions of Romance

Social psychologist Caryl Avery (1989) states, "Given one wish in life, most people would wish to be loved—to be able to reveal themselves entirely to another human being and be embraced, caressed, by that acceptance" (p. 27). The strength, depth, and pervasiveness of this wish cause our culture to be highly romantic (Arliss, 2001).

As with other aspects of gender communication, women and men tend to approach romance from different points of view, dating back to early influences on their notions of what romance is supposed to be. Children form stereotypical notions about romance very early through viewing such movies as *Beauty and the Beast, Aladdin,* and other legends of princes and princesses. Girls, in particular, learn about romance from such stories as *Cinderella* and *Snow White,* as we explore in depth in Chapter 10. Most romantic literature and movies are aimed at women—young and old. Typically, males do not have the same experience; instead, they more often learn about romance (as such) from sources like comic books, locker-room talk, action or adventure stories in which the girl is the reward at the end, and, perhaps later, from magazines like *Playboy.*

For many women, the romance novel contains the stereotypical cultural script. These novels follow a predictable formula of "woman meets a (perfect) stranger, thinks he's a rogue but wants him anyway, runs into conflicts that keep them apart, and ends up happily in his arms forever" (Brown, as in Crawford & Unger, 2000, p. 279). The man is usually cold, rejecting, even brutal at the beginning, but through the woman's love, we learn that his cold demeanor hides his true emotions and character. While the culture is changing slowly, these images still predominate. They tend to lead men to focus on sex and women to focus on being swept away in a romantic rush. Clearly, neither focus is very accurate, yet these romantic images remain a powerful force.

By the time you're an adult, you've seen and read countless stories of passionate, engulfing, magical love between, typically, very attractive people. These images and legends that you grew up with may have formed powerful, albeit unrealistic models for romantic relationships. Such images lead our culture to place a high value on finding, winning, and keeping a desirable partner. The situation is particularly challenging for gays and lesbians who have grown up with—if not exclusively, primarily—images of heterosexual romance. Homosexuals often grow up without role models, in life or in the media, of romantic same-sex couplings, with the result being that the learning curve is greater for establishing and maintaining romantic relationships than what heterosexual persons typically experience. No matter what one's sexual orientation is, the contrast between the myth and the reality of romantic relationships can lead to a high degree of frustration, disillusionment, and even violence (Arliss, 2001).

Tensions within Romantic Relationships

In comparison with friendships, romantic relationships engender a different set of issues, perhaps more aptly described as *tensions* within a relationship. By *tensions*, we don't mean to imply the negative connotation you might normally

'Net Notes

With so many of today's college students working and taking full loads of classes, it's hard to meet people and get romantic relationships off the ground. If you find you have little time for bars or clubs and little faith in dating services or personal ads, you might want to try a couple of websites created just for the purpose of helping people connect with other people. Remember: There are pluses and minuses to connecting with people in cyberspace, so use the same precautions you would if you were meeting someone face to face. Here are three sites to try:

www.ecrush.com

www.match.com

www.matchmaker.com

Remember . . .

RELATIONAL PARTNER: A preferred term for someone involved in a romantic, non-marital relationship.

ROMANTIC RELATIONSHIP: A nonmarital relationship that may range from dating to a longer-term committed relationship including or not including sexual activity.

SIGNIFICANT OTHER: A term that emerged in the 1970s to describe a relational partner in nonsexist terms, defying societal conventions.

MONOGAMOUS RELATIONSHIP: A romantic relationship in which the partners date only each other; may also imply a sexual relationship in which partners are involved sexually only with each other.

---

associate with the word. Romantic relationship tensions arise from the decisions couples face in developing and defining their relationship, not necessarily because of the individuals in the relationship (Baxter & Montgomery, 1996). These tensions are usually expressed in questions related to "Should I (we) do this or that?" and "Should our relationship be this or that?" These tensions are not unique to romantic relationships, but they seem to intensify in a romantic context.

Communication researcher Daena Goldsmith (1990) describes five types of tensions that come into play as a relationship moves into the romantic stage:

1. Whether to get involved and get to know the other person on this level.
2. Whether or not to date others, especially if the relationship is a long-distance one.
3. Trade-offs with other priorities, such as spending time with one's friends.
4. Whether or not one person's will should be imposed on the other (such as "I wish you wouldn't drink").
5. The degree of commitment.

Subjects in Goldsmith's study found these tensions unpleasant. Some of them dealt with the tension by going totally one way (complete submersion into the relationship) or the other (breaking the relationship off altogether). Most people tried to find a middle ground, although it can be difficult for two people to find the same middle ground. Identifying these issues or tensions in your own relationships may give you the opportunity to talk about them with your partner.

Communication researchers Bell and Buerkel-Rothfuss (1990) also describe a number of relational issues or tensions, cast in the form of alternatives:

1. Honesty versus the protection of feelings. (Should I tell you everything I think and feel about you?)
2. Self-disclosure versus privacy. (Should I tell you my secrets?)
3. Personal autonomy versus interdependence. (How often can I pursue my own interests?)
4. Integration versus differentiation. (How alike do we need to become in our attitudes, values, and beliefs?)

5. Reciprocity versus generosity. (Do I do things for you because I care about you or do I expect something in return?)
6. Commitment versus voluntarism. (Do I do things with you because I have to or because I want to?)
7. Novelty versus predictability. (How unpredictable should I be to keep your interest alive?)

These are issues that couples will probably face. Talking about them may make resolving them easier, or it may lead two people to decide that they just aren't suited for each other. The earlier couples talk about these issues, the sooner they can make a wise decision. From these two long lists, as well as our own thoughts, we have identified a few tensions to discuss in more detail.

Autonomy versus Connection

Philosopher Robert Nozick (1993) believes that a defining characteristic of love is the "declaration of *we*"; he states that the primary feature of *we* is the close *connection* of one person's well-being with that of another person. Connection has its trade-off; it comes with limits on *autonomy*. Some decisions can no longer be made alone but must be made as a couple, because they affect both persons. Gender scholar Letitia Peplau (1994) describes autonomy as the extent to which a person values individual pursuits apart from an intimate relationship. The degree of autonomy partners desire within a relationship varies widely; thus autonomy is one of the most difficult issues to confront within a relationship. In the early stages of romance, the tendency is to spend as much time together as possible. This creates a sense that your life together almost operates in a vacuum, sheltered from the outside world. Have you ever experienced this kind of immersion in a relationship, to the point that you may realize you haven't seen a newspaper or heard a news broadcast for days? A major event could have happened and you wouldn't know it, nor would you particularly care. After a period like this, the rest of life usually intrudes and begins to whittle time away from the people in the relationship. It is at this point that a couple may first experience the tension created by autonomy versus connection.

Goldsmith (1990) suggests, "Each of us wants the support and companionship that come from connection with others, yet we simultaneously want independence, privacy, an individual identity" (p. 538). At one point, the issue for a couple might be time spent in independent activities versus time spent together. At another point in the relationship, the couple might deal with autonomy and connection more abstractly in terms of identity and commitment (e.g., "Who am I? What am I doing here?"). Relational partners will be likely to feel needs in both directions at different times.

How do couples manage the transition from the constant togetherness that often typifies the beginning stages of romantic relationships to a more balanced blend of togetherness and separateness? How can partners enjoy their necessary autonomy while avoiding the possible hurt or rejection the other person might feel when the first clues of separateness arise? How do they avoid the possibility that issues surrounding independence won't degenerate into power struggles?

Conventional wisdom regarding romantic relationships says that self-interest should become secondary to "other-interest," that romantic relationships are supposed to be demonstrations of unconditional love. But you know as well as we do that conventional wisdom doesn't always match reality.

To understand this first tension in romantic relationships, let's work through a real-life example. Mary and Don met, fell in love, and spent a significant amount of time together. Then they encountered the first major hurdle in their relationship. Mary had a long-standing interest in the theatre, so she auditioned for a play and was awarded a part. Rehearsals were scheduled for six nights a week for five weeks. When Don learned of this, he hit the roof: "That's too much time! You're putting a *play* ahead of me? You're putting your interests ahead of our relationship?" Don wanted Mary to quit the play, but Mary felt she would be giving up an important interest under pressure from Don. After all, she was talking only about a five-week rehearsal period away from their normal routine together as a couple. Don's reaction led to some serious concerns for Mary. Would Don try to control all her activities? Would he always insist that she put the relationship above everything else, requiring her to check with him before making decisions? On the other hand, Don felt that he needed reassurance from Mary that the relationship was as important to her as it was to him. He reacted strongly to Mary's taking a part in the play because he thought it meant she didn't really care about him; she hadn't talked to him about it before auditioning, so he felt left out of the situation. Also, Don had been dumped before; he was worried that this new turn of events signaled an impending end to the relationship, and he just didn't want to go through that again. The outcome of this story is that Mary and Don were able to work through this tension by having a heart-to-heart conversation (and Mary stayed in the play). Mary admitted that she was wrong not to at least let Don know before she auditioned for the play, and she offered reassurance that the relationship was important to her. Don agreed to ask questions and talk a situation out next time before jumping to angry conclusions and before letting his insecurity and past hurts affect his behavior. They both realized that negotiating time spent apart versus time spent together required honest, loving communication, so that their insecurities or actions wouldn't be a dividing point.

Have you experienced a situation like Don and Mary's? Have you seen your friends go through such a situation? What did you or they do to work it out? Since this balance between personal freedom and shared activities is one of the single toughest issues in a relationship, talking it out isn't easy. It's particularly problematic in the initial stages of romantic relationships, when a pattern of spending great amounts of time together has been set and conflict is the last thing either partner wants. When a time-consuming activity occurs, or even when the "first night out without you" arises, a relational partner is likely to feel a degree of betrayal or have problems dealing with the contrast between this new factor and doing everything together. To keep the relationship alive, partners can benefit from an honest, open, nondefensive conversation about the amount of time they expect to spend together versus time spent apart. Talking about this tension won't necessarily ensure a perfect balance or prevent the problem from arising again, but it will allow partners to know each other better and open the door for discussions if the problem repeats itself.

The notion that women are more likely to have problems with men's assertion of autonomy in heterosexual romantic relationships than the reverse may be more a myth than a reality (Wood, 1998). As more women pursue career goals, as they continue to explore the range of options open to them, and as they enjoy friendships with other women, their dependence on men and the significance they attach to relationships with men have decreased. This doesn't mean that romantic relationships aren't as important to women as they once were; it simply means that there is more competition for women's attention now than in the past, as well as less emphasis on "getting and keeping a man" as a way to achieve happiness. More structures in society exist today than in the past to support women's autonomy in relationships.

Power Versus Empowerment

Another source of tension that becomes a factor in long-term effectiveness is the pattern of control or *power* within a romantic relationship. For many couples, this boils down to making decisions, ranging from the simplest of things to the future of the relationship. At the root of decision making is a measure of power, control, or influence over another person. According to one set of scholars, "power resides in the actual resources an individual can wield to influence others, and one's latitude of influence depends on one's power bases in operation" (Canary & Emmers-Sommer, 1997, p. 75).

Traditional stereotypes suggest that men hold more power than women in heterosexual relationships, because of men's generally higher status in society and greater income. To many people, financial success confers greater power and more potential to exert influence. Thus, in many couplings—particularly in marriages or cohabiting relationships in which finances are shared—the stereotype rings true and the breadwinner, typically the man, may control more of the decision making. However, in committed relationships financial accomplishment is not as much of a basis for power or control as it once was. In many modern heterosexual relationships, the person who manages the household, in terms of caring for children, handling food purchases and preparation, paying the bills, and generally keeping the household running smoothly, is the woman. She may be seen as the powerful person in the couple, because without her efforts the household and the structure of the family might fall apart.

Power complicates the issue of autonomy. In most instances, the person with the most relational power is also the person with the most autonomy. In our culture, men still tend to hold more power than women; thus it follows that in many heterosexual romantic relationships the man has more autonomy than the woman. Peplau (1994) compares heterosexual romantic relationships with lesbian relationships and suggests that lesbians are more likely to develop qualities of independence, self-actualization, and strength than straight women. The emphasis on autonomy in lesbian relationships might lead women to emphasize equality as a means of preserving independence. At least some women believe it is easier to balance equality and autonomy in a same-sex relationship than an opposite-sex romantic relationship.

In keeping with the values we described in Chapter 1, we believe that a pattern of equality of control in a relationship, particularly a committed relationship like a marriage, is the most effective for both people. This type of coupling has been termed *egalitarian,* in that partners have equal power and authority and share responsibilities equally, without regard for gender roles, income levels, job demands, and so forth (Crawford & Unger, 2000; Guerrero, Andersen, & Afifi, 2001). Egalitarian relationships are characterized by *empowerment*—power *to* rather than power *over*—which involves a shared approach that capitalizes on the strengths of each relational partner (Bate & Bowker, 1997; Schwartz, 1994; Thorne, Kramarae, & Henley, 1983). Interpersonal communication scholars Guerrero, Andersen, and Afifi (2001) describe egalitarian marriages as "deep and true friendships, as well as romances" and as more intimate and committed than traditional marriages (p. 309). In virtually all committed relationships, shared decision making is a benefit. Researchers have found a positive correlation between equality in decision making and satisfaction with decision making (Rosenbluth, Steil, & Whitcomb, 1998; Ting-Toomey, 1984). Conversely, inequitable decision making is related to low satisfaction with the decisions and, ultimately, the relationship.

Acceptance versus Change

One unfortunate belief that often exists in romantic relationships is, "I can change this person. I know she or he has faults, but I can fix those faults." This is so much a part of relational folklore that, even though your friends will warn you that you can't change a person, deep down inside you might be saying, "I'll be the exception; I'll be the one to do it." Family communication experts Galvin and Bylund (2001) describe this phenomenon in relation to the early stages of marriage: "Newlywed couples frequently make allowances for behavior that isn't quite acceptable because spouses focus on what they are getting, and differences seem enhancing. Later, differences become annoying and call out for resolution" (p. 141). It's safe to say—though it may be a stereotype—that more heterosexual women declare that they will change their men than the reverse. If you overhear two men talking about a relationship, you'll rarely hear either of them say, "My honey has her faults, but over time, I can change that."

How do you feel when you know another person wants to change you or change the relationship? The tendency is to resist the person's attempt or to view it as a power play designed to exert control over you. Consider an example: Anthony and Arthur were in the middle of the powerful, exhilarating emotions that exist early on in a romantic relationship. But the intense romantic feelings subsided a bit for Arthur before they did for Anthony. He didn't care for Anthony any less, but he wasn't as caught up in the emotional rush as he once was. Anthony was really bothered by this subtle change in Arthur; he tried several ways to restore the initial level of feeling. Arthur neither wanted nor was able to change his feelings. The more Anthony pushed to get things back to the way they were, the more Arthur resisted and began to resent Anthony's pressure. It wasn't until Anthony stopped putting on the pressure and relaxed enough to accept the change in Arthur that Arthur regained some of his positive feelings about the relationship. They didn't return to the early phase, but they attained a new degree of closeness.

The importance of acceptance in a romantic relationship can hardly be overemphasized. It's a great feeling to have complete confidence in another person, and it's quite disconcerting when such confidence is lacking. Humanistic psychologist Carl Rogers (1970) based much of his highly successful client-centered counseling on what he called "unconditional positive regard." In describing how human beings change, Rogers noted a paradox—that real change in people seems to be possible only when they feel completely secure and accepted in a relationship. Nozick (1993) maintains that a fundamental source of happiness in love is to be loved for ourselves. It seems that we all want to be accepted and loved for who we are—not for our money, appearance, or social position. Within that acceptance, we can decide to change to please ourselves and to improve the relationship.

Comparable Views of Intimacy

In Chapter 5, we explored varying definitions of and perspectives on intimacy, but one thing most people can agree on is that intimacy—however you define it—is the goal of almost all committed romantic relationships (Brehm, 2001; Canary & Emmers-Sommer, 1997). As we discussed in Chapter 5, research shows that women and men often have differing views of what intimacy is and how much intimacy is desirable in a relationship (Harvey & Weber, 2002). In fact, one partner may view a relationship as highly intimate while the other partner does not; at the root of this common problem is a difference in the basic perception of what intimacy is.

Psychologists Heller and Wood (1998) conducted research on intimacy among committed heterosexual couples and found that women perceived higher levels of intimacy in their relationships than their male partners; these women were also better at predicting a partner's feelings. The researchers concluded that, at least among the subjects in their study, men were less attuned to intimacy within a relationship. These sex differences—perceived or real—can lead to diminished intimacy and less satisfaction with the relationship. However, it may be that the women and men in this study simply had differing views of what constituted intimacy; that basic difference led to varying perceptions of the level of intimacy and varying degrees of satisfaction with that level among the couples.

To achieve an increased level of relational satisfaction, common definitions of intimacy are critical (Gottman, Katz, & Hooven, 1997). One way to agree on what constitutes intimacy is to use what Galvin and Brommel (1991) call "relational currencies"—agreed-on ways of conveying affection, information, caring, and so on. The key is the shared definition of the "currency," because through this definition couples become able to be more empathic toward each other, and empathy leads to greater clarity and shared expression of emotion in the relationship (Gaines, 1996; Ickes & Simpson, 1997). For instance, if a husband thinks he is expressing affection through an activity like tuning up his wife's car, but she doesn't see that act as affectionate, then these two have not yet achieved a shared definition for the currency of affection.

Expressions of Love

One of the clearest expressions of a desire to move a relationship to a more intimate level is saying the words, "I love you." These words can bring a reaction of intense pleasure or of nervous questioning like, "What do you mean by that?" A consistent theme throughout this text is the need to verbalize intentions, desires, and goals with your relational partner, including the expression of love.

The statement, "I love you" has many different meanings. In the 1950s, one researcher penned this truly memorable description of the range of meanings for the phrase:

> Sometimes it means: I desire you or I want you sexually. It may mean: I hope you love me or I hope that I will be able to love you. Often it means: It may be that a love relationship can develop between us or even I hate you. Often it is a wish for emotional exchange: I want your admiration in exchange for mine or I give my love in exchange for some passion or I want to feel cozy and at home with you or I admire some of your qualities. A declaration of love is mostly a request: I desire you or I want you to gratify me, or I want your protection or I want to be intimate with you or I want to exploit your loveliness. "I love you"—wish, desire, submission, conquest; it is never the word itself that tells the real meaning here. (Meerloo, 1952, pp. 83–84)

In heterosexual relationships, who is more likely to express love and under what circumstances? Contrary to romance novels, movies, and stereotypes which tend to cast women as the first to say "I love you," research has showed otherwise (Brehm, 2001). Communication scholar William Owen (1987) found that men more often initiated a declaration of love, a critical communication event in a romantic relationship. Owen offered the following reasons for this tendency:

Brevity may be the soul of wit, but not when someone's saying "I love you." When someone's saying "I love you," he always ought to give a lot of details. Favorable comparisons with all the other women he ever loved are also welcome. And even though he insists it would take forever to count the ways in which he loves you, let him start counting.

—Judith Viorst,
television writer

1. It is a way to coerce commitment from women.
2. Men are less able than women to withhold expressions of love when they feel love.

3. Women are more capable of discriminating between love and related emotions.
4. Women wait until they hear the phrase from men, because they often play a reactive rather than an active (or proactive) role in a romantic relationship.

The stereotype that men in romantic relationships don't say "I love you" is still evident. Some men believe that actions speak louder than words. ("I'm here. I don't need to tell you that I love you.") Research, however, indicates that actually saying the words is a predictor of a positive future for the relationship. Communication scholars Dainton, Stafford, and Canary (1994) found that saying "I love you" was among a group of behaviors positively associated with predicting long-term love; other behaviors included assuring the partner of one's feelings, keeping a positive outlook, and practicing maintenance strategies such as being patient and forgiving, being cooperative during disagreements, and avoiding criticism.

If you've ever been (or are currently) in a heterosexual romantic relationship that involves love, who said the three words first—the woman or the man? Another difficult issue in all relationships concerns whether or not you'll hear "I love you, too" in response to a declaration of love. Not having the sentiment reciprocated may signal an imbalance of emotion or level of commitment in a relationship, which may in turn signal troubled waters for the relationship.

Making a Commitment

Commitment involves the decision to stay in a relationship, but it also implies a coordinated view of the future of the relationship (Wood, 1998). In many ways, being in a relationship is largely a matter of coordination—a meshing of the language, gestures, and habits of daily life, primarily through attentiveness, courtesy, and a common desire to make the relationship work. Research findings suggest that such variables as the anticipated duration of the relationship (short-term versus long-term), gender roles enacted by the partners, and the level and quality of disclosure within the relationship interact to influence the level of commitment (Cline & Musolf, 1985; Kenrick, Sadalla, Groth, & Trost, 1990).

Commitment also represents a level of seriousness about one's relational partner (Harvey & Weber, 2002). It indicates a deeper level of regard and intimacy in a relationship. What are some factors related to the decision to commit? Sometimes a trial or crisis causes people to make the decision to commit to each other. Here's a real-life example (with altered names) involving friends of the authors. Fred and Jacquie had been going together for about three years and were considering marriage when Fred met another woman and had a brief affair with her. This affair was not just about sex; it involved strong emotions. Because of Fred's feelings for Jacquie, he told her about his affair. As you might well imagine, this event precipitated a crisis in Jacquie and Fred's relationship. After hours of very emotional discussion, Fred and Jacquie decided they wanted to stay together. Fred felt that if he wasn't going to leave Jacquie for this other woman, he wasn't going to leave her for anyone. Jacquie couldn't imagine a more stressful crisis and decided that if they could get through this one, they could get through anything. The crisis resulted in a renewed commitment to each other.

Achieving a matched or equal level of commitment within romantic relationships appears to be related to how well couples handle *turning points*—critical moments in the life of a relationship that alter it in some way (Baxter & Pittman, 2001; Graham, 1997). Communication researchers Bullis, Clark, and Sline (1993) analyzed 17 factors related to various turning points in relationship development; one factor they examined was *relational talk,* or conversation about the relationship itself. They found that more mature relationships with greater levels of commitment involved a higher amount of relational talk, which was used as a means of handling the turning points. Relational talk and commitment seemed to nourish each other; positive relational talk increased commitment, which increased positive relational talk, and so on. In most situations and relationships, talking about the relationship actually does make it better. Particularly in the context of romance, where emotions and issues of self-esteem are heightened, couples need to have periodic conversations about the quality of their relationship, because these conversations clear the air and reinforce commitment (Sillars, Shellen, McIntosh, & Pomegranate, 1997).

*"Of course I care about how you imagined I thought
you perceived I wanted you to feel."*

The long-standing stereotype about commitment in heterosexual relationships suggests that women are more willing to commit than men. Do you think the stereotype holds true in relationships today? Are men just as likely as women to desire a committed relationship and work to maintain one? A social psychologist in the 1980s called the general condition of being unable to commit "commitmentphobia," and defined it as "a social disease characterized by fear of the opposite sex, inability to establish a long-term intimate relationship, and unsatisfying sexual encounters and loneliness" (Schnall, 1981, p. 37). She contended that commitmentphobia was "first noticed among men in the 1970s," but had "spread to the female population" (p. 37).

The tension surrounding commitment is similar to what we described in our discussion of autonomy versus connection: more options mean greater flexibility and more complex decision making (Galvin & Bylund, 2001). Some of you who are reading this text may be nontraditional students who married at a young age and are now returning to college to start or complete a degree at a later point in life. It used to be more common to marry in one's teens or twenties. College-educated men and women frequently married in the last year of college or upon graduation. Indeed, only a few decades ago it was quite common for couples to marry as soon as they graduated from high school. For many people today, getting married at around age 18 would be unthinkable. Granted, teenagers still marry, but nowhere near as commonly as they did in past generations. According to Galvin and Bylund (2001), "A sharp increase in age at first marriage has occurred over the last three decades from 20 for women and 23 for men in 1965 to 24 for women and 26 for men in 1988" (p. 133). And among African Americans marriage rates are actually declining, leading to estimates that about 25 percent of African Americans will never marry (Dickson, 1993; Steil, 1997). Expanded opportunities, especially for women, in a culture that increasingly encourages women to experience life's options beyond home and family, complicate one's choice to commit to a relationship.

Other factors, such as the competitiveness of the marketplace, economic pressures that cause people to emphasize their jobs over their personal lives, disillusionment brought on by rising divorce rates, and an enhanced knowledge of health risks related to sexual activity continue to contribute to postponement of commitment and marriage. While you might think that the fear of health risks associated with sexual promiscuity would lead to a greater incidence of committed, monogamous relationships, it also has a converse effect—causing people to choose abstinence or celibacy, to immerse themselves more deeply in their careers, and to become even more fearful of connecting with others.

Talking about Communication, or Communicating about Talking

Research shows overwhelmingly that highly satisfied couples engage in significantly more communication than less satisfied couples (Burleson & Denton, 1997; Richmond, 1995; Teichner & Farnden-Lyster, 1997). Every relationship develops its own communication patterns. These patterns make a situation more predictable, and predictability fosters security in the relationship (Bruess &

Pearson, 1997). At times, the patterns change, owing to circumstances outside the couple's relationship. The arrival of a child, a change in employment, a move to a new city, and other changes will have a clear (and sometimes negative) impact on the communication patterns in a relationship (Sinclair & McCluskey, 1996). According to Galvin and Bylund (2001), communication patterns are especially critical in first marriages, because the patterns of each spouse's family of origin will be incorporated into the new marriage (sometimes causing conflict), spouses' interaction patterns reflect gender differences, and these patterns will change over developmental stages of a family, as affected by peers and culture. Most of the time, communication patterns evolve on their own, influenced by societal rules and norms and by the individuals' needs and desires. For the most part, people in relationships don't sit down together and say, "Let's work out our patterns of communication." You may have noticed, however, that we have advocated exactly this in more than one place in the text.

It is important to *talk about talking;* in communication research, the term for this activity is *metacommunication.* What do you like or prefer, in terms of communication with a relational partner? Various researchers and marriage therapists have studied the value of this type of conversation in marriage enrichment groups and have found significant increases in marital satisfaction for couples who talked openly about the communication patterns in their relationships (Bodermann, 1997; Hickmon, Protinsky, & Singh, 1997; Worthington, McCullough, Shortz, & Mindes, 1995). It takes courage to sit down and carefully examine the communication patterns of your relationship, especially if the patterns are ineffective. Author Sonja Johnson (1991) suggests that people who say their relationship is good usually will not look at it carefully and will not see all the major and minor frustrations. Johnson writes, "the longer they have been together, the more built-up pressure there is, the more terrified they are of breakup, and therefore the more resistance they have to seeing themselves truthfully" (p. 74). In a relationship, the sooner a metaconversation occurs, the more likely it is that patterns will be formed purposefully rather than by accident.

A discussion about the kinds of communication that work well and are supportive in a relationship is critical, yet many couples avoid this kind of conversation until a disagreement or major conflict arises (Wilmot & Hocker, 2001). Some don't even talk about their communication tendencies and patterns in the event of a conflict. It's easier just to let the event play out and hope that things fix themselves or get back to normal. But many times this can breed resentment, as partners simply bury their feelings and "go along to get along," and resentment builds. The most obvious communication behavior to discuss is how each partner approaches and deals with conflict (we deal with this more specifically in the next section of this chapter), but other aspects of couple communication also need to be discussed. For instance, married or cohabiting couples often experience tension when they are reunited at the end of the workday. Whether both partners work outside the home or just one of them does, the period of time they see each other after hours apart can create tension. Typically, tension arises when one or the other partner arrives home last, has had a tough or long day, and simply wants some time to herself or himself and some peace and quiet before starting the evening's activities. The other person wants to jump right into conversation, because she or he has had some time to decompress from the day. Rather than having a fight and hurting feelings over something like this, the better strategy is to discuss it, preferably before a potential conflict arises or as a result of the first conflict over this situation.

Other preferences, tendencies, and idiosyncrasies can also benefit from metacommunication. For example, one partner isn't a morning person and the other can't wait to greet the day and chat over breakfast. One partner likes to discuss the day's events before turning out the light and falling asleep; the other finds this kind of conversation stimulating instead of relaxing, so the "pillow talk" keeps that person from actually ending his or her day. Before a pattern gets established that works well for one partner, but less well for the other, talking about talking can be helpful.

The stereotype is that in heterosexual romantic partnerings women raise the issue of communication and stage the discussion about communication preferences and patterns. This is related to the view that women, more often than men, take the "temperature" of a relationship—that women are more likely to raise issues about the relationship and are more likely to ask their partners or husbands "How do you think we're doing?" However, research shows that this is more than a stereotype (Acitelli, 1992; Messman & Mikesell, 2000; Ragsdale, 1996; Tannen, 1990; Weigel & Ballard-Reisch, 1999). In Chapter 4 we discussed the relational and content approaches to communication. Given research which shows that women tend to approach communication in order to connect and establish or strengthen the relationship, and that men tend to approach communication for the purpose of exchanging information, one can see this trend in evidence in the typical patterns within romantic relationships (Beebe, Beebe, & Ivy, 2004). Granted there certainly are exceptions, but the tendency to "let things blow over" or avoid talking about talking isn't advisable, and it shouldn't be only up to women in heterosexual romantic relationships to seek opportunities to discuss the relationship and the communication within it.

Conflict: The Inevitable in a Relationship

Why do we say that conflict is inevitable in a relationship? We've simply never witnessed a healthy relationship that was free from conflict; in fact, a relationship may achieve its apparent health because the partners cope with conflict in an effective way. Interpersonal scholar David Johnson (2000) compares conflicts to natural storms:

> Interpersonal storms are a natural and unavoidable aspect of life that vary in intensity from mild to severe. . . . When individuals work together to achieve shared goals, participate in a division of labor, have complementary roles, and depend on each other's resources, storms will arise. Two people in a relationship are interdependent. What each does influences what the other does. But at the same time, each person has different perspectives, goals, and needs. The combination of interdependence and differing perspectives makes it impossible for a relationship to be free from conflict. (pp. 249–250)

Conflict arises when two persons cannot agree on a way to meet their needs (Beebe, Beebe, & Ivy, 2004; Wilmot & Hocker, 2001). These needs may simply be incompatible or too few resources may exist to satisfy them; however, conflict often arises or intensifies because relational partners compete rather than cooperate to resolve the difference. And the more important the relationship, the greater the potential for conflict because more is at stake. To put this another way, we're less likely to disagree with people who don't matter much to us. Conflict with people who matter a great deal to us is to be expected, but it is extremely important that the conflict be handled in an effective way because it has the potential to damage the relationship, as well as the potential for real growth to emerge (Beck, 2001; McGraw, 2002; Tannen, 2001). The ability to discover negative conflict patterns in a relationship and to make them more positive is critical to long-term relationship success (Gottman, Coan, Carrere, & Swanson, 1998).

Communication scholars Duck and Wood (1995) make the point that conflict and happiness in a relationship are not necessarily opposites but are intertwined: "Relationships are complex experiences in which grief and joy, pleasure and pain, enjoyment and irritation, ease and discomfort, satisfaction and frustration are recurrent and paired elements" (p. 6). Psychotherapist David Richo (2002), author of *How to Be an Adult in Relationships*, describes conflict as it emerges in a relationship:

> Once blinded by romance, now we are free to see all sides of the partnership. We confront pettiness, lack of consideration, self-serving choices, and the arrogant ego with its need to be right, to get its way, and to avenge itself. We notice all the things in our partner that we cannot abide or hide. What was cute in romance may become acute in conflict. (p. 126)

Are there gender differences in approaches to conflict? Some research finds evidence of gender differences in conflict in adult heterosexual relationships, and those differences seem to be due to physiology and socialization (Ruble & Schneer, 1994; for a discussion of this perspective, see Sagrestano, Heavey, & Christensen, 1998). Communication scholars Taylor and Miller (1994) believe: "Girls are socialized to value relationships and maintain harmony while boys are socialized to value status and seek victory. This is thought to translate into women taking a cooperative stance in conflict situations, whereas men are more competitive" (p. 155). However, other researchers contend that women and men do not approach and handle conflict differently, especially within marital relationships (Burggraf & Sillars, 1987; Fitzpatrick, 1988). One summary of studies of heterosexual couples found few gender differences in preferred conflict-management styles (Keashly, 1994). Across a variety of studies, male and female subjects preferred to handle conflict through the following strategies, in descending order: accommodation, avoidance, compromise, collaboration, and, least of all, competition.

In addition to gender, race has been studied for its effects on approaches to conflict in ongoing, committed relationships. In one study of conflict management among married couples, gender scholar Judi Beinstein Miller (1994) found that African American married couples held more traditional beliefs about marriage than white couples, but those traditional beliefs were difficult to maintain,

Remember . . .

RELATIONSHIP TENSIONS: Issues that arise within romantic relationships and require negotiation, whether or not they create tension for relational partners.

AUTONOMY: A need for independence and time alone from one's partner.

CONNECTION: A need for affiliation and association with one's romantic partner, which often involves time spent together.

EGALITARIAN RELATIONSHIP: A romantic relationship or marriage in which partners have equal power and authority and share responsibilities equally, without regard for gender roles, income levels, job demands, etc.

POWER: Power *over,* instead of power *to,* in which one partner exerts control or influence over the other.

EMPOWERMENT: Power *to,* versus power *over;* joint control or shared influence within a relationship.

COMMITMENT: A decision to stay in a relationship, which also involves a coordinated view of the future of the relationship; a level of seriousness about one's relational partner.

TURNING POINTS: Critical moments in the life of a relationship that alter it in some way.

RELATIONAL TALK: Conversation between relational partners about the relationship itself.

METACOMMUNICATION: Talking about communication; having a conversation about how one communicates, one's preferences in communicating and being communicated to, how communication functions, etc.

CONFLICT: Communication which arises when people cannot agree on a way to meet their needs.

DEMAND-WITHDRAW PATTERN: A relational conflict pattern in which one partner raises a problem, criticizes and blames the other partner for the problem, and asks for or demands a change; the other partner tries to avoid the discussion, becomes defensive regarding the criticism and blame, and eventually withdraws from the conflict altogether.

given the reality of day-to-day married life. As a result, these couples were generally less happy with marriage than white couples in the study. In addition, an adherence to traditional beliefs about marriage was associated with the tendency of African American couples to avoid conflict more than white couples in the study. Of the participants in the study, African American husbands were the most likely to avoid conflict with their spouses.

Research has identified one very interesting conflict pattern in particular—the *demand-withdraw pattern* (Julien, Arellano, & Turgeon, 1997; Klinetob & Smith, 1996). In this pattern, one partner tries to discuss a problem, criticizes and blames the other partner for the problem, and asks for or demands a change. The other partner tries to avoid the discussion, becomes defensive regarding the criticism and blame, and eventually withdraws from the conflict altogether (Harward & Cavanaugh, 1997; Sagrestano, Heavey, & Christensen, 1998). In most research on this pattern in heterosexual relationships, men are more likely to avoid conflict and women are more likely to approach it. Communication scholars Harward and Cavanaugh (1997) explain that women tend to confront conflict because they perceive confrontation as problem solving and as an opportunity to get closer to their partner, whereas men tend to view the women's behavior as nagging and unproductive. Marriage scholars Klinetob and Smith (1996) point out that "the spouse with the most to gain by maintaining the status quo is likely to withdraw, and the discontented spouse demands change. Insofar as the status quo in marriage generally tends to favor men, men will appear most frequently as withdrawers" (p. 954). Breaking out of such a negative pattern is quite difficult, especially if the status quo works well for the dominant person.

Ending a Relationship

As a culture, are we getting better at resolving problems in relationships? Listen to the responses of high school students who were asked, "How did you solve a problem with the opposite sex?" in an article in *Parade* magazine (Minton, 1997). One 16-year-old girl said, "How I deal with a problem with the opposite sex is that I really don't. I'll most likely just call the whole thing off." A 16-year-old boy said, "One way to deal with your problems is to get a car. I promise you that the minute you're behind the wheel, a hot chick will be next to you." A 15-year-old girl stated, "I work out problems with the opposite sex by yelling, because males don't know how to listen." A 14-year-old boy said, "I have worked out my problems by sucking up. They (girls) get mad over anything, but all you have to do is give them a sad face, say you're sorry, and they will forgive you in a heartbeat." If the teens interviewed for this article are any indication, our culture is still not very effective at resolving problems in relationships.

Not all relationships can be salvaged. We realize that a discussion of ending relationships can be depressing, but you're probably realistic and experienced enough to know that not all relationships make it. Although we may enter a romantic relationship with a vision of forever and ever in mind, relationships often don't work out as we first imagine. Thus it's wise to consider some effective communication strategies for ending romantic relationships.

Who Does the Breaking Up?

Breakups can cause stress and anguish for both persons involved—and that may be the understatement of the year! Who is more likely to end a heterosexual romantic relationship? The

> *I never thought that I'd yearn for a breakup, but damn it, I want one!*
>
> —*Laura Dern, actor (about an affair that ended with a whimper and not a bang)*

'Net Notes

Interested in getting some advice on your love life? Need some help *getting* a love life? Check out **www.love-sessions.com.** This site offers all kinds of advice on love, dos and don'ts of dating, romantic ideas for a partner, marriage, sexual health, how to cope with cheating, solutions for insecurity, and much more. If you might like more exclusive sites, which offer dating services to groups of people who have something in common, try:

www.romancetips.com, a Christian dating service and the official site of an organization called Faith Friends

www.jdate.com, a dating service for Jewish persons

www.planetout.com, a gay and lesbian dating service

www.mediabistro.com, a dating service that links people who work in journalism and other media-related fields.

stereotype suggests that women are more interested in relationships and thus suffer more than men when a relationship ends; however, that stereotype is not supported by research. Research from two decades shows that men more often initiate relationships and women more often terminate them (Peplau, 1994; Rubin, Peplau, & Hill, 1981). (Maybe this is why so many country-and-western tunes involve a jilted male lover.) Findings also indicate that women tend to foresee a breakup sooner than men, but men tend to be more deeply affected by the breakup. Peplau (1994) found that men reported being depressed and distressed after a relationship ends, while women reported feeling relief and even joy. Feminist psychologists Crawford and Unger (2000) suggest that men fall in love more readily than women; feel more depressed, lonely, and unhappy after a breakup; and are less likely to initiate a breakup than their female partners.

Perhaps the stereotype relates more to the difference in the ways men and women express themselves regarding relationships than to an actual value placed on relationships in general. As we discussed in our chapter on friendship, women usually deal with things and make sense of their world through talking. Men typically deal with things by distracting themselves with activities or by withdrawing and isolating themselves until the situation is resolved. When men do choose to talk out a relational issue such as a breakup, the conversation is typically not as long, profound, detailed, or emotional as a woman's conversation on the subject. Think about how female friends talk to each other for hours, either in person or over the phone, about a relationship. They'll explore what happened, what was said, how it was said, how it made the woman feel, what she thinks she'll do next, and so on. The male equivalent of the breakup aftermath might look like this: A guy learns about his buddy's breakup. He consoles his friend by saying, "Hey, forget about her, man. She's not worth it. Let's go shoot some hoops and have a few beers. I guarantee you'll feel better." This is an overgeneralized example to emphasize the contrast, but does it sound familiar?

Communicating to End a Relationship

You may be wondering whether there is one personally effective way to end a romantic relationship. Romantic relationships are so situation- and person-specific that proposing one optimum termination strategy would be unwise. However, as we've said time and again, to communicate is better than not to communicate.

From our own experiences and those shared by our students, the worst way to end a relationship is the "Dear John (or Joan) letter" or, given our modern technology, the "Dear John email." One of our students revealed in class that his girlfriend broke up with him in an email message. (The class decided that this method was "chicken," inappropriate, and needlessly hurtful.) Another method that can lead to hurt and disillusionment is the silent treatment. Even a screaming match, while traumatic, doesn't seem to carry the same sting as noncommunication or one-sided communication. It's quite painful to be ignored, or to realize that increasing distance is signaling that a relationship is over. While distancing from one's partner is typical as a relationship comes apart, expanding distance—physical and psychological—so that a person "gets the hint," without ever communicating about the breakup, is ill-advised (Knapp & Vangelisti, 2000). It's painful also to be told it's over with no explanation, no chance for negotiation, and no opportunity for the one who gets "terminated" to express her or his feelings. Many people would rather talk it out—even argue it out—than be shut out and left to wonder what went wrong, an experience that is likely to plunge a person's self-esteem to a new low. Adopting a receiver orientation to communication, which we described in Chapter 1 and adhere to throughout this book, implies that partners would do well to think through their breakups, consider what strategy is best to use—given the person who will be on the receiving end of the upsetting information—and communicate as sensitively and clearly as possible. Not only is this kind of communication likely to lessen the blow; it will also keep the person who's breaking up from feeling like a louse, schmuck, or downright terrible person for hurting someone and communicating poorly.

Just for the record, let's all agree on something related to ending a romantic relationship: The line "I still want to be friends," extended from the "terminator" (one doing the dumping) to the "terminated" (one getting dumped), should NEVER be used. If you're nodding your head in agreement, then you've probably experienced this terrible utterance—perhaps you've said it yourself as a way to soften the blow of a breakup. But never again, right? The problem is that the terminator is in the dominant position; his or her wish or will is being imposed on the other person. It isn't typical for terminators to say that they want to break up, then for their partners try to talk them out of it, and then for the terminators to agree to resume the relationship. For most of us in the position of being dumped, the last thing we want to try to do, or even conceive of, is act like friends with our former romantic partners. A request that a relationship regress into something less intimate is understandable if you're doing the dumping, because you may genuinely want a friendship with your former romantic partner and offering friendship makes you feel as though you're easing the sting of the breakup. But it is completely self-serving and unreasonable to expect that someone will be able to shift relationship definitions as quickly as you'd like.

The tensions we've discussed in this section are by no means all the issues relational partners may have to face, but they represent some of the more prominent, common, and troublesome ones examined by research. One remaining issue connected to romantic relationships surrounds sexual activity—more specifically, how gender communication plays a significant role in a relationship that becomes sexual.

GENDER ISSUES SURROUNDING SEXUAL ACTIVITY

Passionate love is one of the most intense feelings a person can experience. Anthropologists Hatfield and Rapson (1996) describe it this way: "Passionate love is a 'hot,' intense emotion, sometimes called a crush, obsessive love, lovesickness, head-over-heels in love, infatuation, or being in love" (p. 3). They go on to describe passionate love as associated with fulfillment and ecstasy generally expressed through sexual union. It is difficult to separate considerations of passionate love from considerations of sex. Freud, in fact, believed they were one and the same (as in Hendrick & Hendrick, 1992); at the very least, the two are deeply intertwined.

At some point in a romantic relationship, the issue of sexual activity will probably develop (Guerrero, Andersen, & Afifi, 2001). Then the questions become, "What does sex mean to us?" and "What do we do about it?" Hendrick and Hendrick (1992) point out that for some individuals, sex without love is unthinkable, while for others sex is intrinsically good and can be an end in itself. Most couples are likely to have different meanings for sex within their relationship. Regarding the question "what to do about it," a number of answers are possible, ranging from "absolutely nothing" to "absolute passion." We're not making any assumptions about how the question should be answered, for obvious reasons. What's more important is the communication of a clear and mutually agreed-on decision about what course to take.

Women need a reason to have sex. Men just need a place.

—Billy Crystal, actor and director

In Chapter 8, we explore the downside of sexual activity, specifically when sex is used as a weapon or power play. But to close this chapter, we focus on the positive side of consensual sex, in an attempt to understand varying attitudes toward sexual activity, learn more effective ways of talking about sex with a relational partner, and develop a broader repertoire of communication behavior in dealing with problematic sexual situations.

Attitudes toward Sexual Activity

Many factors affect our views of sex and sexuality: cultural values, upbringing (primarily in terms of lessons our parents or other family members taught us), childhood experimentation, exposure to media, and peer group influences. Research shows that even at early ages, when we are first thinking about ourselves as sexual creatures, the likelihood that we will engage in sexual activity is highly influenced by whether or not we perceive that our peers are having sex (DiBlasio & Benda, 1992; Miller, Norton, Curtis, Hill, Schvaneveldt, & Young, 1997). One study of middle-school children found that those who were sexually active believed their peers to be active too, and that being sexually active would make them popular (Kinsman, Romer, & Schwartz, 1998). (Many of us didn't even know what sex *was* when we were in middle school, and it's sad to think that times have changed so much.)

In considering your options, it may be helpful to know what some research over a couple of decades has said about the sexes' attitudes toward sexual activity. One of the most widely cited series of studies of misperceptions of

Hot Button Issue

"SEXUAL SAFETY OR SEXUAL CORRECTNESS?"

Have you heard the term "sexual correctness"? It emerged several years ago, in association with a controversy that arose when the student government at Antioch College in Ohio proposed a Sexual Offense Policy, a set of guidelines regarding sexual activity for its students. In reaction to several instances of sexual assault and harassment on campus, the university adopted the policy which required that permission be sought at each stage in a sexual situation. For example, in a heterosexual situation, if a man wants to unbutton his partner's blouse, he has to ask her permission. If he wants to remove her bra, he has to ask for permission. These guidelines may seem like an overreaction, but the intent is to make sure that persons are engaging in sexual activity *with their consent*. If someone says no to any request for sexual activity to continue, then the activity must stop—according to the policy.

Many students objected to the policy, stating that it was sexual correctness run amok and that the administration was trying to legislate how they managed their personal lives. One critic of the policy believes that it "criminalizes the delicious unexpectedness of sex" and that advocates of sexual correctness are "trying to take the danger out of sex, but sex is inherently dangerous" (Crichton, 1993, p. 54). Other students see it as a strong stance in favor of sexual safety—the university's serious attempt to deal with a rampant problem on campus. What's your view? Is a policy like this reasonable? How would it be received on your campus? Does it send a message about the seriousness with which the university views the problem—even if the reality may be that few people actually follow the policy?

sexual interest was produced by Antonia Abbey (1982, 1987, 1991). In her first study, opposite-sex dyads conversed for five minutes while hidden male and female subjects observed the interaction. Results indicated that, in comparison with female observers, male observers more often perceived a woman's friendliness as seduction, made more judgments that female interactants were promiscuous, and frequently reported being sexually attracted to female interactants. Male observers also rated male interactants' behavior as sexual in nature, whereas female observers did not perceive as much sexuality in male subjects' behavior. From these results, Abbey concluded that "men are more likely to perceive the world in sexual terms and to make sexual judgments than women are" (1982, p. 830).

Communication scholars Mongeau, Yeazell, and Hale (1994) conducted similar research on heterosexual subjects' interpretations of behavior on first and second dates. Men in the study tended to perceive interaction in more intimate and sexual ways than women. Thus research suggests that men appear to be more likely to perceive sexual interest when, in fact, it may not be there. For our male readers, it may be worth checking your perceptions before you assume them to be true; this could forestall some inappropriate behavior.

In her review of the literature about heterosexual men and women in love, Peplau (1994) examined the cultural stereotype that men initiate increases in sexual intimacy and women set the limits and control the progress toward that intimacy. She wondered if this stereotype had changed since it was first researched in the 1950s. She concluded that it had not: "Despite the sexual permissiveness of many couples, a traditional pattern of male initiation and female limit-setting was apparent. The traditional pattern provides a familiar and well-rehearsed script that enables the partners to interact comfortably" (p. 28). Hendrick and Hendrick (1992) suggest that this tendency may be based in biology. Males of many species develop reproductive strategies to maximize the number of offspring they have, while females develop strategies to maximize the probability that offspring will grow to adulthood. This leads females to be more choosy about their partners, with the result that males compete for sexual access to females while females are the guardians of that access. We are not suggesting that this pattern should change, but couples shouldn't assume that the stereotype will hold for them or be shocked if the roles are reversed. It is possible for women to initiate and men to set limits.

> *You know that look women get when they want sex? Me neither.*
>
> —*Drew Carey, actor and comedian*

Research has produced consistent findings regarding motives for engaging in sexual activity: Women (heterosexual and homosexual) are more likely to connect sex with emotional involvement and intimacy, whereas men (heterosexual and homosexual) more often connect sex with lust and physical gratification (Allegeier & Royster, 1991; Basow, 1992; Carroll, Volk, & Hyde, 1985; Clark, 1990;

'Net Notes

Budding authors should check out **www.genders.org,** a Website that publishes essays about gender and sexuality in relation to social, political, artistic, and economic concerns.

Peplau & Gordon, 1983; Whitley, 1988). This doesn't mean that women don't use sex to fulfill their lustful needs or that men don't view sex as building intimacy and closeness in a relationship, but the trend has persisted in research findings across decades. For example, in a study sponsored by the Medical Research Institute of San Francisco, Barbara Critchlow Leigh (1989) found differences related to gender and sexual orientation between subjects, concerning reasons for engaging in sexual activity. Among the reasons for having sex, male subjects emphasized pleasure, pleasing one's partner, and relieving tension, while female subjects viewed the expression of emotional closeness as primary. Differences between men and women emerging in Critchlow Leigh's study were consistent across sexual orientations. Gay male subjects and straight men reported similar reasons for engaging in sexual activity. Lesbians and straight women connected sexual activity closely to love and emotional involvement. These findings led Critchlow Leigh to conclude that "men's and women's motivations for sex are different, no matter the sex of their partners" (p. 205).

These research findings suggest gender differences in both the perception of sexual interest and the motivations for having and avoiding sexual activity. Do the researchers' findings match your experience or the experiences of your friends? Is it your perception that men tend to read more sexuality into things than women do? Or do you think that the difference is more a stereotype than a reality? One thing seems obvious to us: Stereotypes or not, given findings that reveal potential differences in women's and men's approaches to sexual activity, it seems to be even more critical for relational partners to communicate openly and honestly about sex—preferably *before* they engage in it.

Women, Men, Communication, and Sex

Communicating about sexual activity represents a proactive approach to what can be a turning point in a relationship, although some people may see it as taking the romance out of the act or the situation. Communication scholars Cupach and Metts (1991) encourage interaction on sexuality because research consistently finds that the quality of a couple's communication about sexuality is linked to the quality of their relationship, and an individual's skill in communicating about sexuality is central to successful relationships.

Some research suggests that a romantic approach to sexual activity involves a web of ambiguity, game playing, or a sort of dance—a dangerous concept in and of itself (Baxter, 1987). Among heterosexuals, the woman's role in the sexual game has traditionally been to hint, to convey subtly or nonverbally, whether or not she is sexually interested. Then the man is supposed to catch the clue and either abstain from or initiate sexual involvement (Anderson, Schultz, & Staley, 1987; Harvey & Weber, 2002; Perper & Weis, 1987). If a woman is interested in having sex, she's expected to offer some form of token resistance to a man's advances, as a way of testing her partner, but mainly so as to not appear too willing or "easy" (Muelenhard & Rodgers, 1998). Then the man's response is to work past the token resistance, and sex is the result—a result that supposedly pleases both partners. In Chapter 8 we explore in more depth the many devastating outcomes that can occur from just such a "gaming" scenario. But for now, we wonder: Could it be that this hinting, guessing, and resisting game in the name of preserving romance causes more problems than it's worth?

Talking about Sex

One of the earliest and most revealing studies of college students' dating and sexual behavior was conducted by sociologists Knox and Wilson (1981), who asked their subjects "What do university men and women do to encourage their partners to become more sexually intimate?" (p. 257). One-third of the female respondents and one-fourth of the male respondents said that they preferred to "be open about sexual desires and expectations" (p. 257). Other, less direct methods of expressing sexual expectations included "creating an atmosphere" for sexual intimacy, "expressing love," "moving closer" to a partner, and "hinting" (p. 257). Additional research has shown that couples who can talk about sex have higher levels of sexual satisfaction, and that the inability to talk about sex leads to serious problems (Baus & Allen, 1996; Wheeless & Parsons, 1995). These findings suggest that direct, open discussion of sexual activity isn't a first option for many people, but it's becoming a genuine alternative to the guessing games that often cause misunderstanding. Honest communication appears to be preferable to trying to read each other's minds (and nonverbal cues), expecting sexual activity to be as it's portrayed on television or in the movies, or taking the plunge only to discover that one's haste was a real mistake—and may cost a relationship.

> *It seems that talking about sex requires more intimacy than actually doing it.*
>
> —Jane Fonda, actor and political activist

Just how do you approach the topic of sex with someone you're involved with or dating? When we say "approach the topic of sex," we mean having a conversation about sexual activity in a relationship—no matter what your views are on whether sexual activity outside marriage is wrong in general, inadvisable for you and a partner, or something that might occur in your relationship. This also involves discussing topics related to sexual activity, such as birth control, monogamy versus multiple partners, and views about protection from sexually transmitted diseases (Edgar & Fitzpatrick, 1988).

Sexual activity is an awkward topic to talk about with another person; it may be an especially uncomfortable topic to discuss with your relational partner. One study analyzed the ways in which one partner persuaded the other that condoms should be used in sexual activity; the results indicated that persuasive appeals related to caring, responsibility, and pleasure were the most effective (Sheer, 1995). Even though awareness of the need to use a condom has vastly increased, this topic remains difficult to discuss for many persons. In one study of Australian students' use of condoms in heterosexual activity, 39 percent reported that they never used condoms with a new partner, even though they knew that their behavior was risky (Galligan & Terry, 1993). The students explained that their primary reason for avoiding any discussion of protection was a concern that such a conversation would destroy the romance of the moment and make their partners think they were strange. The findings of the Australian study can be compared with a study of heterosexual American college students, of whom 38 percent reported never using condoms (Boyd & Wandersman, 1991). Other studies show that heterosexuals may use condoms with new partners, but once they're in an ongoing relationship, they choose not to use protection because they believe they no longer have to worry about contracting AIDS and other sexually transmitted diseases, or STDs (Hammer, Fisher, Fitzgerald, & Fisher, 1996; Joffe, 1997; Misovich, Fisher, & Fisher, 1997). Such assumptions are very dangerous—to one's health, one's partner's health, and the relationship. Granted, it's difficult, in what might be the heat of passion, to stop and talk about the advisability of advanced sexual activity and the use of protection. Yet there are many reasons for doing so, not the least of which is the threat of AIDS and other STDs.

Even if you believe that this kind of discussion is important, you will not necessarily find actually talking over sexual issues any easier. Many of us were raised in the belief that honest discussion about sexual acts was somehow improper, particularly in "mixed company." Communication researchers Anderson, Schultz, and Staley (1987) explored some of the issues involved when a heterosexual woman must become assertive in a sexual situation. Women are not usually taught or encouraged to talk about sex or to use sexual words in normal conversation; thus, their societal conditioning may work against them when they confront the need to be assertive. But Anderson et al. conclude that initiating a conversation about sexual activity with one's partner isn't a role one sex rather than the other is expected to take. It is equally appropriate for the female or the male partner to initiate a discussion of this kind. This is becoming easier for many women, who now have more role models—perhaps primarily in the media, but role models nonetheless—who demonstrate that strong self-reliant women assert their sexual rights and preferences rather than hinting, gameplaying, or giving in to the preferences of their partners.

The Language of Sex

Another factor complicating sex and communication is that our language doesn't provide much help; in fact, it often works against honest, serious discussion (Potorti, 1992). What language can you use in a frank discussion with your partner about sex? Your options are: (1) to use clinical, scientific terms, such as "You believe that sexual intercourse and oral sex should be postponed until marriage, but heavy petting of clothed genitalia is okay?"; (2) to speak in euphemisms (terms that substitute for other terms), which may sound immature or condescending, such as "When I get close to you, my 'thing' reacts"; or (3) to use "gutter" terms for sexual acts and body parts, examples of which you're probably well aware. Many of us are uncomfortable using clinical terms, as though we'll come off sounding like we're quoting the latest anatomy textbook. But euphemisms can bring about such embarrassment or laughter that the discussion goes off-track, and they can be extremely ambiguous (e.g., just what "thing" are you referring to?). Gutter terms may be acceptable (even enjoyable) once sexual activity has been initiated and has become an ongoing part of a relationship. But the use of such terms in the initial stages of a relationship doesn't represent an option that many of us are comfortable with; such language can make sexual activity sound crude and unappealing. There's no perfect way to talk to a partner about sex and for now at least, it appears there's no way around the language problems. We encourage you to acknowledge the linguistic limitations with your partner, maybe even to have a good laugh about them, and then to make the best of them as you work your way through an honest discussion about sexual activity. Defects in the language don't have to become an excuse for avoiding a discussion about sex.

CONCLUSION

Gender communication in love, romance, marriage, and sex is complicated by a wide range of sociological, physiological, linguistic, and relational factors. Success in these relationships is never guaranteed, but the chances for success can be increased by broadening the range of communication behaviors that you bring to these contexts.

Autonomy, change, power, commitment, intimacy, conflict—these are just some of the integral issues and sources of tension within a romantic relationship. Although the tensions in romance aren't particularly easy to write or talk about, they're easier to talk about than to negotiate in an actual relationship. Your own experience, the experiences of your friends, and what we've described in this chapter should reemphasize the considerable complexities inherent in romantic relationships.

Patterns of communication within intimate relationships are particularly critical because effective patterns lead to success and feelings of satisfaction, whereas ineffective patterns may lead to any number of destructive outcomes. It may sound simple, for example, to read about negotiating a balance between your sense of independence apart from a relationship versus time spent with your partner. However, when you actually confront that first discussion and witness the hurt resulting from one partner's assertion of independence, you find that it's a much harder and more complex issue to manage. It's easy to give lip service to the sentiment, "I love you for what you are; I'll never want to change you," but what happens when you really, honestly think your way is better? Even understanding the complexity involved in these kinds of relationships, however, isn't enough to scare us away from romance and marriage. When it's going well, when it's right, there's hardly anything comparable.

Here, as in other chapters in this text, we continue to suggest that communicating is preferable to *not* communicating. Most of us function better when we have information than when we feel we've been left out of the loop, and romantic partners definitely need information. It's fairly safe to say that an expanded communication repertoire and a willingness to openly communicate with one's partner in a way that's not stereotyped by gender constitute a more successful approach to romantic relationships than a narrow repertoire and an unwillingness to communicate. This approach doesn't mean you'll be successful every time—you know there are no guarantees, especially in a romantic context. But, given the chances that your success in relationships could improve, it's probably well worth it to attempt to expand the range of your gender communication in this unique context.

Discussion Starters

1. Consider the language used to refer to special people in our lives. How did you refer to the person in your first romantic relationship, like the first boy or girl you really liked in a different way from the rest? How did those references change as you grew up and experienced different types of relationships? Does the term *relational partner* work for you, or can you suggest a better term?

2. Think of an example—in your own life or the life of someone close to you—that epitomizes the tension of autonomy versus connection. If you're married or in a committed romantic relationship, was it difficult when you and your partner experienced that first attempt at independence? How did you both handle it? Do you think this issue is more easily negotiated between married partners than between people who are only steadily dating?

3. Review the information in this chapter on "commitmentphobia." Did this information change your views regarding commitment and the sexes? Is it your current opinion that men are generally more fearful of commitment in a heterosexual romantic relationship than women, or the reverse, or neither? Could it be that commitmentphobia has more to do with personality and family background, for instance, than with gender?

4. What's the best pattern of communication you've seen in a marriage? What made it effective? Did the two people involved develop this consciously, or did the pattern tend to evolve out of trial and error? How should decisions be made in a marriage or a similar relationship? Should each decision be a 50–50 proposition, or should different partners take the lead in different matters?

5. Do you think that navigating the sexual waters with a relational partner is a difficult communication challenge? If so, why is it that heterosexual women and men may have difficulty openly discussing sexual activity in their relationships? Do you think that same-sex partners have an easier time discussing sexual activity, since they have similar physiology? What are the barriers to a successful discussion of this kind?

References

Abbey, A. (1982). Sex differences in attributions for friendly behavior: Do males misperceive females' friendliness? *Journal of Personality and Social Psychology, 42,* 830–838.

Abbey, A. (1987). Misperception of friendly behavior as sexual interest: A survey of naturally occurring incidents. *Psychology of Women Quarterly, 11,* 173–194.

Abbey, A. (1991). Misperception as an antecedent of acquaintance rape: A consequence of ambiguity in communication between men and women. In A. Parrot & L. Bechhofer (Eds.), *Acquaintance rape: The hidden crime* (pp. 96–111). New York: Wiley.

ABC *World News Tonight.* (2002, July 24). Government report on marriage.

Acitelli, L. K. (1992). Gender differences in relationship awareness and marital satisfaction among young married couples. *Personality and Social Psychology, 18,* 102–110.

Allegeier, E. R., & Royster, M. J. T. (1991). New approaches to dating and sexuality. In E. Grauerholz & M. Koralewski (Eds.), *Sexual coercion* (pp. 133–147). Lexington, MA: Lexington Books.

Anderson, J., Schultz, B., & Staley, C. C. (1987). Training in argumentativeness: New hope for nonassertive women. *Women's Studies in Communication, 10,* 58–66.

Arliss, L. P. (2001). When myths endure and realities change: Communication in romantic relationships. In L. P. Arliss & D. J. Borisoff (Eds.), *Women and men communicating: Challenges and changes* (2nd ed.) (pp. 115–131). Fort Worth, TX: Harcourt Brace Jovanovich.

Avery, C. S. (1989, May). How do you build intimacy? *Psychology Today,* 27–31.

Basow, S. A. (1992). *Gender: Stereotypes and roles* (3rd ed.). Pacific Grove, CA: Brooks/Cole.

Bate, B., & Bowker, J. (1997). *Communication and the sexes* (2nd ed.). Prospect Heights, IL: Waveland.

Baus, R. D., & Allen, J. L. (1996). Solidarity and sexual communication as selective filters: A report on intimate relationship development. *Communication Research Reports, 13,* 1–7.

Baxter, L. A. (1987). Cognition and communication in the relationship process. In R. Burnett, P. McGhee, & D. Clarke (Eds.), *Accounting for relationships: Explanation, representation, and knowledge* (pp. 192–212). London: Methuen.

Baxter, L. A., & Montgomery, B. M. (1996). *Relating: Dialogues and dialectics.* New York: Guilford.

Baxter, L. A., & Pittman, G. (2001). Communicatively remembering turning points of relational development in heterosexual romantic relationships. *Communication Reports, 14,* 1–17.

Beck, M. (2001, October). Fighting for intimacy. *O Magazine,* 73–76.

Beebe, S. A., Beebe, S. J., & Ivy, D. K. (2004). *Communication: Principles for a lifetime* (2nd ed.). Boston: Allyn & Bacon.

Beinstein Miller, J. (1994). Conflict management and marital adjustment among African-American and white middle-class couples. In A. Taylor & J. Beinstein Miller (Eds.), *Conflict and gender* (pp. 141–153). Cresskill, NJ: Hampton.

Bell, R. A., & Buerkel-Rothfuss, N. L. (1990). S(he) loves me, s(he) loves me not: Predictors of relational information-seeking in courtship and beyond. *Communication Quarterly, 38,* 64–82.

Bodermann, G. (1997). Can divorce be prevented by enhancing the coping skills of couples? *Journal of Divorce & Remarriage, 27,* 177–194.

Boyd, B., & Wandersman, A. (1991). Predicting undergraduate condom use with the Fishbein, Ajzen, and Triandis attitude-behavior models: Implications for public health interventions. *Journal of Applied Social Psychology, 21,* 1810–1830.

Brehm, S. S. (2001). *Intimate relationships* (3rd ed.). New York: McGraw-Hill.

Bruess, C. J. S., & Pearson, J. C. (1997). Interpersonal rituals in marriage and adult friendship. *Communication Monographs, 64,* 25–46.

Bullis, C., Clark, C., & Sline, R. (1993). From passion to commitment: Turning points in romantic relationships. In P. J. Kalbfleisch (Ed.), *Interpersonal communication: Evolving interpersonal relationships* (pp. 213–236). Hillsdale, NJ: Erlbaum.

Burggraf, C., & Sillars, A. L. (1987). A critical examination of sex differences in marital communication. *Communication Monographs, 54,* 276–294.

Burleson, B. R., & Denton, W. H. (1997). The relationship between communication skill and marital satisfaction: Some moderating effects. *Journal of Marriage & the Family, 59,* 884–902.

Canary, D. J., & Emmers-Sommer, T. M. (1997). *Sex and gender differences in personal relationships.* New York: Guilford.

Carroll, J. L., Volk, K. D., & Hyde, H. S. (1985). Differences between males and females in motives for engaging in sexual intercourse. *Archives of Sexual Behavior, 14,* 131–139.

Clark, R. D. (1990). The impact of AIDS and gender differences on willingness to engage in casual sex. *Journal of Applied Psychology, 20,* 771–782.

Cline, R. J., & Musolf, K. E. (1985). Disclosure as social exchange: Anticipated length of relationship, sex roles, and disclosure intimacy. *Western Journal of Speech Communication, 49,* 43–56.

Crawford, M., & Unger, R. (2000). *Women and gender: A feminist psychology* (3rd ed.). New York: McGraw-Hill.

Crichton, S. (1993, October 25). Sexual correctness: Has it gone too far? *Newsweek,* 52–56.

Critchlow Leigh, B. (1989). Reasons for having and avoiding sex: Gender, sexual orientation, and relationship to sexual behavior. *Journal of Sex Research, 26,* 199–209.

Cupach, W. R., & Metts, S. (1991). Sexuality and communication in close relationships. In K. McKinney & S. Sprecher (Eds.), *Sexuality in close relationships* (pp. 93–110). Hillsdale, NJ: Erlbaum.

Dainton, M., Stafford, L., & Canary, D. (1994). Maintenance strategies and physical affection as predictors of love, liking, and satisfaction in marriage. *Communication Reports, 7,* 88–98.

DiBlasio, F. A., & Benda, B. B. (1992). Gender differences in theories of adolescent sexual activity. *Sex Roles, 27,* 221–239.

Dickson, L. (1993). The future of marriage and family in Black America. *Journal of Black Studies, 23,* 472–491.

Duck, S., & Wood, J. T. (1995). For better, for worse, for richer, for poorer: The rough and the smooth of relationships. In S. Duck & J. T. Wood (Eds.), *Confronting relationship challenges* (pp. 1–21). Thousand Oaks, CA: Sage.

Edgar, T., & Fitzpatrick, M. A. (1988). Compliance-gaining in relational interaction: When your life depends on it. *Southern Speech Communication Journal, 53,* 385–405.

Fitzpatrick, M. A. (1988). *Between husbands and wives: Communication in marriage.* Newbury Park, CA: Sage.

Gaines, S. O. (1996). Impact of interpersonal traits and gender-role compliance on interpersonal resource exchange among dating and engaged/married couples. *Journal of Social & Personal Relationships, 13,* 241–261.

Galligan, R. F., & Terry, D. J. (1993). Romantic ideals, fear of negative implications, and the practice of safe sex. *Journal of Applied Social Psychology, 23,* 1685–1711.

Galvin, K., & Bylund, C. (2001). First marriage families: Gender and communication. In L. P. Arliss & D. J. Borisoff (Eds.), *Women and men communicating: Challenges and changes* (2nd ed.) (pp. 132–148). Prospect Heights, IL: Waveland.

Galvin, K. M., & Brommel, B. J. (1991). *Family communication: Cohesion and change* (3rd ed.). New York: HarperCollins.

Goldsmith, D. (1990). A dialectic perspective on the expression of autonomy and connection in romantic relationships. *Western Journal of Speech Communication, 54,* 537–556.

Gottman, J. M., Coan, J., Carrere, S., & Swanson, C. (1998). Predicting marital happiness and stability from newlywed interactions. *Journal of Marriage and the Family, 60,* 5–22.

Gottman, J. M. K., Katz, L. F., & Hooven, C. (1997). *Meta-emotion: How families communicate emotionally.* Mahwah, NJ: Erlbaum.

Graham, E. E. (1997). Turning points and commitment in post-divorce relationships. *Communication Monographs, 64,* 350–368.

Guerrero, L. K., Andersen, P. A., & Afifi, W. A. (2001). *Close encounters: Communicating in relationships.* Mountain View, CA: Mayfield.

Hammer, J. C., Fisher, J. D., Fitzgerald, P., & Fisher, W. A. (1996). When two heads aren't better than one: AIDS risk behavior in college-age couples. *Journal of Applied Social Psychology, 26,* 375–397.

Harvey, J. H., & Weber, A. L. (2002). *Odyssey of the heart: Close relationships in the 21st century* (2nd ed.). Mahwah, NJ: Erlbaum.

Harward, H. L., & Cavanaugh, D. (1997, November). *Men, women, and interpersonal relationships: A qualitative analysis of the first big fight.* Paper presented at the meeting of the National Communication Association, Chicago, IL.

Hatfield, E., & Rapson, R. L. (1996). *Love and sex: Cross-cultural perspectives.* Boston: Allyn & Bacon.

Heller, P. E., & Wood, B. (1998). The process of intimacy: Similarity, understanding, and gender. *Journal of Marriage & Family Counseling, 24,* 273–288.

Hendrick, S. S., & Hendrick, C. (1992). *Romantic love.* Newbury Park, CA: Sage.

Hickmon, W. A., Jr., Protinsky, H. O., & Singh, K. (1997). Increasing marital intimacy: Lessons from marital enrichment. *Contemporary Family Therapy: An International Journal, 19,* 581–589.

Hirshey, G. (1989, March/April). Coupledom über alles: Tyranny of the couples. *Utne Reader,* 48–55.

Ickes, W. J., & Simpson, J. A. (1997). Managing empathic accuracy in close relationships. In W. J. Ickes (Ed.), *Empathic accuracy* (pp. 218–250). New York: Guilford.

Information please almanac. (1998). Boston: Information Please.

Joffe, H. (1997). Intimacy and love in late modern conditions: Implications for unsafe sexual practices. In J. M. Ussher (Ed.), *Body talk: The material and discursive regulation of sexuality, madness, and reproduction* (pp. 159–175). New York: Routledge.

Johnson, D. W. (2000). *Reaching out: Interpersonal effectiveness and self-actualization.* Boston: Allyn & Bacon.

Johnson, S. (1991). *The ship that sailed into the living room: Sex and intimacy reconsidered.* Estancia, NM: Wildfire Books.

Julien, D., Arellano, C., & Turgeon, L. (1997). Gender issues in heterosexual, gay, and lesbian couples. In W. K. Halford, H. J. Markman, & H. J. K. Halford (Eds.), *Clinical handbook of marriage and couples' interventions* (pp. 107–127). Chichester, England: John Wiley & Sons.

Keashly, L. (1994). Gender and conflict: What does psychological research tell us? In A. Taylor & J. Beinstein Miller (Eds.), *Conflict and gender* (pp. 168–190). Cresskill, NJ: Hampton.

Kenrick, D. T., Sadalla, E. K., Groth, G., & Trost, M. R. (1990). Courtship: Qualifying the parental investment model. *Journal of Personality, 58,* 97–115.

Kinsman, S. B., Romer, D., & Schwartz, D. F. (1998). Early sexual initiation: The role of peer norms. *Pediatrics, 102,* 1185–1192.

Klinetob, N. A., & Smith, D. A. (1996). Demand-withdraw communication in marital interaction: Tests of interpersonal contingency and gender role hypotheses. *Journal of Marriage & the Family, 58,* 945–957.

Knapp, M. L., & Vangelisti, A. L. (2000). *Interpersonal communication and human relationships* (4th ed.). Boston: Allyn & Bacon.

Knox, D., & Wilson, K. (1981). Dating behaviors of university students. *Family Relations, 30,* 255–258.

McGraw, P. C. (2002, August). Couples combat: The great American pastime. *O Magazine,* 42–43.

Meerloo, J. A. (1952). *Conversation and communication.* New York: International Universities Press.

Messman, S. J., & Mikesell, R. L. (2000). Competition and interpersonal conflict in dating relationships. *Communication Reports, 13,* 21–34.

Miller, B. C., Norton, M. C., Curtis, T., Hill, E. J., Schvaneveldt, P., & Young, M. H. (1997). The timing of sexual intercourse among adolescents. *Youth and Society, 29,* 54–83.

Minton, L. (1997, October 12). Fresh voices. *Parade Magazine,* 18.

Misovich, S. J., Fisher, J. D., & Fisher, W. A. (1997). Close relationships and elevated HIV risk behavior: Evidence and possible underlying psychological processes. *Review of General Psychology, 1,* 72–107.

Mongeau, P. A., Yeazell, M., & Hale, J. (1994). Sex differences in relational message interpretations on male- and female-initiated first dates. *Journal of Social Behavior and Personality, 9,* 731–742.

Muelenhard, C. L., & Rodgers, C. S. (1998). Token resistance to sex: New perspectives on an old stereotype. *Psychology of Women Quarterly, 22,* 443–463.

Nozick, R. (1993). Love's bond. In A. Minas (Ed.), *Gender basics: Feminist perspectives on women and men* (pp. 152–159). Belmont, CA: Wadsworth.

Owen, W. F. (1987). The verbal expression of love by women and men as a critical communication event in personal relationships. *Women's Studies in Communication, 10,* 15–24.

Peplau, L. A. (1994). Men and women in love. In D. L. Sollie & L. A. Leslie (Eds.), *Gender, families, and close relationships* (pp. 19–49). Newbury Park, CA: Sage.

Peplau, L. A., & Gordon, S. L. (1983). The intimate relationships of lesbians and gay men. In E. R. Allgeier & N. B. McCormick (Eds.), *Changing boundaries: Gender roles and sexual behavior.* Palo Alto, CA: Mayfield.

Perper, T., & Weis, D. L. (1987). Proceptive and rejective strategies of U.S. and Canadian college women. *Journal of Sex Research, 23,* 455–480.

Potorti, P. (1992). Personal communication, October.

Ragsdale, J. D. (1996). Gender, satisfaction level, and the use of maintenance strategies in marriage. *Communication Monographs, 6,* 354–369.

Richmond, V. P. (1995). Amount of communication in marital dyads as a function of dyad and individual marital satisfaction. *Communication Research Reports, 12,* 152–159.

Richo, D. (2002). *How to be an adult in relationships: The five keys to mindful loving.* Boston: Shambhala.

Rogers, C. (1970). *On becoming a person.* Boston: Houghton Mifflin.

Rosenbluth, S. C., Steil, J. M., & Whitcomb, J. H. (1998). Marital equality: What does it mean? *Journal of Family Issues, 19,* 227–244.

Rubin, A., Peplau, L. A., & Hill, C. T. (1981). Loving and leaving: Sex differences in romantic attachments. *Sex Roles, 7,* 821–835.

Ruble, T. A., & Schneer, J. A. (1994). Gender differences in conflict-handling styles: Less than meets the eye? In A. Taylor & J. Beinstein Miller (Eds.), *Conflict and gender* (pp. 155–166). Cresskill, NJ: Hampton.

Sagrestano, L. M., Heavey, C. L., & Christensen, A. (1998). Theoretical approaches to understanding sex differences and similarities in conflict behavior. In D. J. Canary & K. Dindia (Eds.), *Sex differences and similarities in communication* (pp. 287–302). Mawhah, NJ: Erlbaum.

Schnall, M. (1981, May). Commitmentphobia. *Savvy,* 37–41.

Schwartz, P. (1994). *Peer marriage.* New York: Free Press.

Sheer, V. C. (1995). Sensation seeking predispositions and susceptibility to a sexual partner's appeals for condom use. *Journal of Applied Communication Research, 23,* 212–229.

Sillars, A., Shellen, W., McIntosh, A., & Pomegranate, M. (1997). Relational characteristics of language: Elaboration and differentiation in marital conversations. *Western Journal of Communication, 61,* 403–422.

Sinclair, I., & McCluskey, U. (1996). Invasive partners: An exploration of attachment, communication, and family patterns. *Journal of Family Therapy, 18,* 61–78.

Steil, J. M. (1997). *Marital equality: Its relationship to the well-being of husbands and wives.* Thousand Oaks, CA: Sage.

Tannen, D. (1990). *You just don't understand.* New York: William Morrow.

Tannen, D. (2001). *I only say this because I love you.* New York: Ballantine Books.

Taylor, A., & Beinstein Miller, J. (Eds.) (1994). *Conflict and gender.* Cresskill, NJ: Hampton.

Teichner, G., & Farnden-Lyster, R. (1997). Recently married couples' length of relationship marital communication, relational style, and marital satisfaction. *Psychological Reports, 80,* 490.

Thorne, B., Kramarae, C., & Henley, N. (1983). Language, gender, and society: Opening a second decade of research. In B. Thorne, C. Kramarae, & N. Henley (Eds.), *Language, gender, and society* (pp. 7–24). Rowley, MA: Newbury.

Ting-Toomey, S. (1984). Perceived decision-making power and marital adjustment. *Communication Research Reports, 1,* 15–20.

Weigel, D. J., & Ballard-Reisch, D. S. (1999). How couples maintain marriage: A closer look at self and spouse influences upon the use of maintenance behaviors in marriages. *Family Relations, 48,* 263–270.

Wheeless, L. R., & Parsons, L. A. (1995). What you feel is what you might get: Exploring communication apprehension and sexual communication satisfaction. *Communication Research Reports, 12,* 39–45.

Whitley, B. E., Jr. (1988). The relation of gender-role orientation to sexual experience among college students. *Sex Roles, 19,* 619–638.

Wilmot, W. W., & Hocker, J. L. (2001). *Interpersonal conflict* (6th ed.). New York: McGraw-Hill.

Wood, J. T. (1998). *But I thought you meant . . . : Misunderstandings in human communication.* Mountain View, CA: Mayfield.

Worthington, E. L., McCullough, M. E., Shortz, J. L., & Mindes, E. J. (1995). Can couples' assessment and feedback improve relationships? Assessment as a brief relationship enrichment procedure. *Journal of Counseling Psychology, 42,* 466–475.

Yost, B. (1996, November 17). Alone in a world of couples: Society's aversion to singlehood remains strongly rooted in tradition. *The Arizona Republic,* as reported in *Corpus Christi Caller Times,* pp. H1, H5.

CHAPTER EIGHT

POWER ABUSES IN HUMAN RELATIONSHIPS

A NON-CASE STUDY

The information in this chapter is difficult to write about, and it's going to be difficult to read. Certainly it isn't the first time you've read or heard about sexual harassment, sexual assault and rape, and partner violence. But this chapter may be the most concentrated presentation of these topics you've been assigned in college. The chapter focuses on power abuses in human relationships, the downside of interacting with others, and how communication creates options for those situations.

It doesn't seem appropriate to start this chapter the way we start the others—with a case study to engage your thinking and energize you for the pages to come. Many cases could be included because many people suffer abuses in relationships. But we prefer to tell some of those stories in context, along with the information on each topic. Here's why: it's very hard to focus on how people abuse one another; it takes us out of our comfort zones to think or talk about it. Even when we do decide to think or talk about it, we still tend to distance ourselves from it—to view it as a social problem, a bunch of statistics, or something that happens to someone else. These are understandable ways to protect ourselves from having to confront the tough issues. But you don't really understand a problem until you put a face on it. That's what the cases in the chapter are designed to do—to make these issues real by putting human faces on them. You may be able to put the face of a relative, friend, or coworker into the situations we describe. While that's painful, we encourage you to do just that, because it will enable you to more fully understand these problems and what can be done about them.

We also realize that some of you reading this material *are* those human faces—your case could be substituted for the cases here. The abuses we discuss don't just happen to someone else; they happen to *us*. We hope that none of you has experienced what we examine in this chapter, but it's very likely that some of you have. If you've lived through power abuses in the past, reading this chapter will no doubt bring up unpleasant reminders for you. But perhaps you will gain a deeper understanding of what you went through or a comparison for how you coped with your situation. If you're currently in an abusive situation, our sincere hope is that this information will help you realize that you do not deserve or cause the abuse, and that you have options.

Not-So-Hot Topics

- The role of power and communication in abusive situations
- Statistics and types of sexual harassment at work and school
- A receiver-oriented view of sexual harassment
- Strategies for how to respond to and report sexual harassment, including legal updates
- Forms of rape and the language of survivors
- The prevalence of date rape and date rape drugs in American society
- Myths about rape and sexual aggression
- Rape prevention programs and the status of rape laws
- The language of partner violence
- Statistics and types of partner violence, including gay and lesbian partner abuse
- Myths about battering, including the blame-the-victim stance
- Battered woman's syndrome, one explanation of why victims stay with abusers
- Laws and women's shelters that provide hope

AT THE CENTER OF ABUSIVE SITUATIONS: COMMUNICATING POWER

What do sexual harassment, sexual assault, and partner (domestic) violence have in common? None of them is primarily about sex, but instead they are about power (Berryman-Fink, 1993). While the gender or sexuality of the target of abuse may be an issue or play a role in the offense, an abuser's behavior is more often related to an attempt to control, influence, and dominate the other person (Angier, 2000). Harassers, rapists, and batterers all have varying degrees of anger and needs for power that they inflict on their targets in the worst way, by preying on their sexuality, physicality, or insecurities.

Another common thread throughout these issues is that they all involve communication. In his introduction to a collection of articles on sexual harassment, Gary Kreps (1993) states: "Communication is the primary medium through which sexual harassment is expressed; it is the means by which those who are harassed respond to harassment, and it is also the primary means by which policies for eliminating sexual harassment in the workplace can be implemented" (p. 1). Acquaintance sexual assault or rape and partner violence usually involve a context of communication that precedes the assault, as well as follows it. Most important, full recovery from these abuses must involve communication. Not talking about sexual harassment doesn't make the harassment go away or allow the victim to get past it. One of the worst things a victim can do, but something that happens frequently, is to hide in shame and guilt and not tell anyone what happened. Communication makes an experience real, which is frightening but necessary for recovery. So these abuses are things that communication people—especially people with an interest in gender communication—should study.

> *Once, power was considered a masculine attribute. In fact, power has no sex.*
>
> *—Katherine Graham, author and The Washington Post publisher*

A final element before we address the first topic of this chapter: we are aware, from having written previous editions of this text, from talking to instructors who use the text across the country, and from teaching the gender communication course many times, that students have concerns about male-bashing. Men and women alike have difficulty with material that seems to criticize men and favor women or that addresses men as the oppressors and women as the oppressed. In this book and in our teaching we work to be balanced and fair in our representation of research and discussion of trends. Much of the effort that has been made to bring these problems to the forefront has been done by women, because it is usually the case that members of a historically oppressed group raise issues in order to change their plight and create more options for themselves. The same holds true for women's liberation and feminism, movements that are primarily made up of women concerned with upgrading women's status and increasing their opportunities.

But whether someone's claims of male-bashing are legitimate isn't the issue. Feeling bashed isn't ever a good feeling. For our male readers, you may indeed feel bashed when reading this chapter. For our female readers, you may feel protective or defensive toward men you perceive are being bashed. But, for this chapter, we ask that you attempt to suspend the male-bashing reaction for the greater good of truly understanding these difficult societal problems. Gentlemen, could you try not to take the statistics and research findings about male harassers, rapists, and batterers personally, as though the information was an indictment of you and your entire sex? Could we all just view these problems as *human* problems and look them squarely in the face? As you'll see, the fact is that 95 percent of reported sexual harassment in businesses and academic institutions *is* perpetrated by males against females. The fact is that most rapists of women and of other men *are men.* The fact is that far more partner abuse is committed by men against women than the reverse. In this chapter we want to talk about both "the rule" and, when appropriate, "exceptions to the rule." Instead of feeling bashed, we hope that men *and* women feel deeply concerned about these problems, appalled by what's happening, and challenged to do something about it.

ATTENTION? COMPLIMENTING? FLIRTING? SEXUAL HARASSMENT?

Some of you may have to jog your memories to recall the dramatic events that played out on national television in the fall of 1991. For others of you, the image of Anita Hill claiming she was sexually harassed by now Supreme Court Justice Clarence Thomas is permanently etched into your memory. No matter which party you believed or your reaction to this event, the Hill-Thomas hearing had profound effects. First, it sparked a great deal of discussion and research on sexual harassment. It also empowered persons who had experienced harassment to come forward and seek assistance. The Equal Employment Opportunity Commission (EEOC) experienced a 23 percent increase in sexual harassment complaints and a 150 percent increase in inquiries within weeks after Hill-Thomas (Baker, 1992).

Many people like to think that we've solved the problem of sexual harassment since the nation's collective conscience was jolted by Hill-Thomas. Instead, we may be witnessing fatigue over the issue or a backlash of sorts. A 1998 Time/CNN poll found that 52 percent of American women and 57 percent of men believe "we have gone too far in making common interactions between employees into cases of sexual harassment" (as in Steinem, 1998, p. 62). The poll also found that only 26 percent of those surveyed viewed sexual harassment as "a big problem," compared to 37 percent in 1991 (Cloud, 1998).

But here are some statistics that show we're not past the problem of sexual harassment, much as we'd like to be. Between 1991 and 2001, charges filed with the EEOC increased 127 percent; about 7000 complaints were filed in 1991, compared to 16,000 complaints registered in each of the first two years of the new millennium (Equal Employment Opportunity Commission, 2002). In 2001, complainants were awarded $53 million, not counting any benefits obtained through litigation (EEOC, 2002). Stanford law professor Deborah Rhode (1997) discusses the current status of workplace sexual harassment in her article "Harassment Is Alive and Well and Living at the Water Cooler." Rhode contends that the denial that serious workplace harassment still frequently occurs is a "variation on the traditional view that it didn't happen at all" (p. 28). Take a look at the case study below and think about whether sexual harassment or mere inappropriate behavior occurred.

Olivia's Great New Job

Olivia landed a great job right after college graduation as a manager at a medium-sized company. She was hired by Bernie, her supervisor, and in her first year on the job, she'd come to trust Bernie's advice, to value the mentoring relationship they'd developed, and to appreciate the opportunities he'd given her to excel at her work. Then things took a downturn.

At the end of a meeting on sales strategy, Bernie steered the conversation to more personal topics. He asked Olivia if she was dating or sexually involved with anyone at the time, if she thought her work went more smoothly when her sex life was running smoothly, if she found older men sexy, and so forth. Bernie and Olivia always maintained a friendly, informal working relationship, so at first Olivia laughed off Bernie's questions—until they began to make her feel uncomfortable. When Bernie pushed for sexual information, Olivia masked her discomfort by saying "Well, now that this conversation is going downhill, I think we should end our meeting because customers are waiting, sales are out there to be made, ha, ha, ha. . . ." Olivia made her way back to her office, knowing that something very wrong had just happened. But she couldn't make sense out of it or out of what she was feeling. She felt as if she'd been punched in the stomach.

Over the next few weeks, Olivia tried to operate in a "business as usual" manner, but Bernie continued to show romantic interest. He got close to Olivia when talking to her; occasionally he would touch her arm or try to hug her while praising the good job she was doing. Once, in a meeting with several other managers, Bernie leaned over to Olivia, put his arm around her waist, and whispered to her about a colleague's ideas. By this time, Olivia was really bothered by Bernie's unprofessional behavior. She'd always thought Bernie a somewhat attractive man, but he was at least 20 years her senior and he was married—happily, or so she thought.

Finally, over lunch one day, Olivia told a coworker about her problem with Bernie. She explained that it was the first time a supervisor had said anything personal or sexual to her; it bothered her to think that maybe Bernie had been looking at her all along in a sexual way, rather than as a professional colleague. She wondered if this was sexual harassment. Olivia's coworker didn't exactly offer what you'd call a textbook empathic response. She teased Olivia about her boss having a crush on her, saying she ought to be complimented that someone in the company of such status as Bernie had shown her special attention. But Olivia didn't feel complimented.

What's your reaction to this story? Was Bernie's attention nothing more than complimentary? Was he merely being friendly or flirtatious—nothing serious enough to warrant the stigmatizing label of sexual harassment? Or was this sexual harassment on the job? Is your opinion affected by the fact that Bernie is married?

The Basics of Sexual Harassment

Olivia and Bernie's case illustrates several key elements related to sexual harassment. Before we explore them, let's make sure we're all on the same page in how we talk about and define sexual harassment.

The Power of Naming

Just exactly what *is* sexual harassment? Gloria Steinem (1983) answered that question like this: "A few years ago this was just called life" (p. 149). There actually was no term for this age-old problem until feminists in the 1970s coined the term *sexual harassment* (Wise & Stanley, 1987). There's power in naming—just ask medical people who get to assign their names to discoveries or diseases. Naming something makes it real, gives it significance, and brings it from silence to voice (Spender, 1984).

An inspection of the language surrounding sexual harassment justifies the struggle of many people to bring this problem into the open. Harassing behavior used to be described (and probably still is) in romantic language, such as seduction," "overtures," "advances," or "passes." But as gender scholar Julia Wood (1993) suggests, "Using terminology associated with amorous contexts obscures the ugliness, unwantedness, violation, repugnance, and sheer darkness of sexual harassment" (p. 14).

Other ways to excuse sexual harassment besides a "boys will be boys" attitude include viewing unwanted attention as merely complimenting the target. If the victim didn't view it as such, she or he wasn't being "gracious" and accepting of the compliment. A prime way to blame a target of harassment and direct attention away from a harasser's behavior is the "just kidding" suggestion. If you couch communication as kidding, joking, or teasing, then when it's interpreted as harassment, a harasser can blame the victim for "not getting the joke" or "not having a sense of humor." A prime example of this blame-shifting technique is telling a victim to "lighten up."

The language of sexual harassment has changed since the 1980s, so that we now have "targets," "victims," and "survivors" instead of "objects of attention," "whistle-blowers," "prudes," "complainers," and "whiners." "Pushy" or "forward" people are now named "harassers" and in some cases, "defendants." What once was an "advance" is now a "violation of individual rights" (Wood, 1992; 1993). But we've also seen a resurgence of euphemisms for sexual harassment, such as "inappropriate behavior," "disrespect," "personal misconduct," and "poor decision making," stemming from various scandals involving such politicians as former Senator Bob Packwood and former President Bill Clinton (Ivy, 1999; Woodward, 1995).

First the Name, Then the Legal Definition

The definition of sexual harassment is fairly straightforward; however, the interpretation as to what behaviors constitute sexual harassment is much more complicated. Let's track back in time a bit, before a definition was available. The fight against sexual harassment in the workplace was led by women of color and working-class women. The first victory came in the form of Title VII of the Civil Rights Act of 1964, which protected citizens from discrimination based on a variety of factors, one of which was sex. In essence, this law made sexual harassment illegal. Under Title VII, Congress gave the EEOC formal authority to investigate claims of workplace sexual harassment (Peach, 1998). Later, with the passage of Title IX in 1972, educational institutions were mandated by law to avoid sex discrimination (Wood, 1992). Title IX defined sexual harassment as "the use of authority to emphasize the sexuality or sexual identity of students" (Peach, 1998, p. 291). But, as you can well imagine, sexual harassment continued despite the legislation.

In 1980 the EEOC produced the following set of guidelines on sexual harassment:

Unwelcome sexual advances, requests for sexual favors, and other verbal or physical conduct of a sexual nature constitute sexual harassment when (1) submission to such conduct is made either explicitly or implicitly a term or condition of an individual's employment, (2) submission to or rejection of such conduct by an individual is used as the basis for employment decisions affecting such individual, or (3) such conduct has the intention or effect of unreasonably interfering with an individual's work performance or of creating an intimidating, hostile, or offensive working environment. (EEOC, 1980)

Up to this time, most documented cases of sexual harassment were *quid pro quo,* the "have sex with me or lose your job" type of harassment (Gerdes, 1999). In 1986 the U.S. Supreme Court acted upon the third clause in the EEOC guidelines, the *hostile climate* clause, extending and legitimizing complaints of sexual harassment beyond quid pro quo (*Meritor Savings Bank* v. *Vinson,* as in Paetzold & O'Leary-Kelly, 1993). Hostile climate harassment is difficult for organizations and institutions to address, but it is far more prevalent than quid pro quo. In fact, estimates indicate that less than five percent of harassment cases today involve quid pro quo situations (Hill, 2002). Hostile climate harassment often taps into sexist structures, policies, and practices long ignored, overlooked, or even accepted as a part of the organizational culture (Carroll, 1993). Quite often the intent is to put someone in a one-down position or to emphasize the harasser's status or power over another person. If the offending behavior falls short of actually threatening something tangible (like one's job, promotion, or raise), it may be termed hostile climate harassment. The EEOC recognized this as sexual harassment because it pervades the target's working or learning environment enough to create a hostile situation.

> *Sexual harassment on the job is not a problem for virtuous women.*
>
> *—Phyllis Schlafly,*
> *anti-feminist activist*

Sexual Harassment Is Power Play

Sexual harassment can occur between individuals with differing statuses or power bases, and who function within clearly structured hierarchies. These relationships are termed *status-differentiated* (such as boss-employee, teacher-student, doctor-patient). A status-differentiated relationship may be distant and impersonal, so that harassment introduced into such a relationship is bewildering. But other such relationships may be well-established and trusting, like a mentor relationship in which the lower-status person looks up to, believes, and confides in the higher status person (Taylor & Conrad, 1992). Harassment in these relationships is devastating. Some receivers of harassment, most often called *targets,* *victims,* or *survivors,* describe a "grooming" process in which the harasser (who desires a sexual connection) slowly develops a friendly relationship with the target, winning her or his trust and admiration before attempting to extend the relationship into a sexual arena. This type of power abuse damages a target's self-esteem and professional development.

Peer sexual harassment, harassment occurring between persons of equal status, occurs on the job as well. In academic settings—from elementary schools to universities—it is much more prevalent than teacher-to-student harassment (Ivy & Hamlet, 1996; Loredo, Reid, & Deaux, 1995; Zirkel, 1995). Yet another form has been termed *contrapower harassment,* which involves a person of lower rank or status sexually harassing someone of higher rank or status (Benson, 1984). Sexual harassment has gone "high tech" as well, meaning that *electronic* or *virtual harassment* is becoming a problem (Brail, 1996; Salaimo, 1997). A survey of 700 female computer scientists and programmers found that 19 percent reported experiencing some form of sexual harassment on-line, through the use of e-mail, computer bulletin boards or conferences, and chat rooms (King, 1993). In the mid-1990s, four Cornell University students found themselves in a great deal of legal trouble for sending an e-mail message that included joking about rape and a list of "75 reasons why women (bitches) should not have freedom of speech" (E-mail, 1995). These forms of harassment are based in power as well, since one person attempts to control another, making him or her uncomfortable or vulnerable.

Hot Button Issue

"HARASSMENT AT THE HOSPITAL"

When Stephen was a child, he had a serious illness for which he was hospitalized for a fairly lengthy period. During his stay, he was especially touched by the kindness and care he received from hospital nurses, so he grew up always wanting to be a nurse—not a doctor, lawyer, or fire fighter—but a nurse, so that he could help people the way he was helped. When he finally achieved his dream and began working on a hospital ward with mostly female nurses, he was surprised and dismayed at the treatment he received. One of only a handful of male nurses in the whole hospital, he was treated disrespectfully by the female nurses. Some made a point to use sexual language around him, as they talked casually about their husbands or boyfriends and their sex lives. It was as though they were testing Stephen, to see if he could cut it in a female-dominated environment. They often complimented Stephen and looked at him in sexual ways, told sexual jokes, criticized men they knew for their sexual "shortcomings," and quizzed Stephen about his personal and sexual life. Was this a case of hostile work climate sexual harassment, or merely a "rites of passage" for the new kid on the hospital block?

Documented cases of sexual harassment with a female harasser and a male target do exist, although they are few in number. Do you think it's more difficult in our society for a man to admit that he's been sexually harassed by a woman or several women, as in Stephen's case? Does society assume that a man won't be offended by sexual talk, joking, or innuendo? If Stephen filed a complaint with the hospital personnel office about the behavior of his coworkers, what do you think would be the hospital's reaction? Are we more aware now of sexual harassment, in all its forms, such that Stephen's complaint would be taken seriously? Or is there a different standard for men who are targets of harassment?

UH, SHARON, YOU LOOK NICE TODAY... BUT UM... NOT IN A SEXUAL HARASSMENT KIND OF WAY

Most reported and researched sexual harassment involves heterosexuals, with a male-harasser, female-target profile (Markert, 1999; McKinney & Maroules, 1991; Reilly, Lott, Caldwell, & DeLuca, 1992). Female sexual harassment of men does occur, but it is reported and pursued in the courts with far less frequency than male-to-female harassment and has historically been neglected by research (Clair, 1998; Romaine, 1999; Wayne, Riordan, & Thomas, 2001). In 2001, 14 percent of EEOC sexual harassment complaints were filed by men (EEOC, 2002). Incidences of same-sex or homosexual harassment are being reported with increasing frequency (Bennett-Alexander, 1998; Dubois, 1998; MacKinnon, 2002).

A Target Orientation to Sexual Harassment

We trust that you know the principles of the receiver orientation to communication backwards and forwards by now. In a nutshell, a receiver view of communication places more importance on a listener's interpretation of a message than it does on a sender's intentions or what a sender meant to convey. Sexually harassing communication exemplifies the receiver orientation so well that we used a harassment example to illustrate it in Chapter 1. But did you know that the law takes a receiver view also?

Sexual harassment is different from other kinds of offenses in that the laws and courts tend to take a receiver approach, meaning that when someone believes communication directed to her or him is sexually harassing, that receiver's perception carries more weight than the sender's intentions. The sender may have meant his or her comments as a joke, a mere compliment, or simple teasing among friendly coworkers or classmates. Or the sender may have been trying to "get a rise" out of the target or "put out a feeler," just to see what the response would be. Certainly courts take into account the context of the situation, the history of the relationship between the parties, and any past behavior by the accused that might indicate a pattern of harassment rather than an isolated incident. But the laws are primarily designed to favor a target's perception of harassment.

Two Sides to Every Story

Consider our example of Olivia and Bernie. From a sender's perspective, one could argue that Bernie was not sexually harassing Olivia. His questions about her sexual life were simply ways to get to know her better, meant to create closeness between a boss and an employee. His nonverbal actions of coming close and touching Olivia were merely expressions of a mentor's affection, ways of communicating his positive regard for a valued employee. If you knew Bernie, if you'd seen him around other employees, then you might think "He's like that with lots of people; he didn't single her out for special attention. "She's going too far if she thinks that's harassment."

On the receiver's side, Olivia didn't interpret Bernie's verbal and nonverbal communication in a benign way. On the contrary, she deemed his questions unwelcome, unwarranted intrusions into her personal life. His nonverbal actions of touch and space invasion were designed to make him look powerful and make her feel uncomfortable and powerless. In fact, a recent study determined that two touches in particular—the face touch and arm around waist touch—are interpreted as the most inappropriate and harassing touch-related behaviors (Lee & Guerrero, 2001). These actions put a target in a classic double bind—a damned if you do, damned if you don't situation. How could Olivia have reacted to Bernie? If she answered his questions, she would have fallen into the trap of revealing personal information when she really didn't want to. And that conversation would likely have opened the door for more questions. If she refused to answer, she could have been accused of being rude and disrespectful to her boss who, after all, was simply trying to get to know her better. If she'd recoiled at his touch, the dramatic rejection might have caused her worse problems with her boss.

One could say that Bernie and Olivia's situation was a simple case of "he said, she said." But describing it this way is unproductive; it clouds the issue because *most* harassment is one person's word against another's. Harassment most often occurs in private, without any witnesses. Research also consistently shows that women view harassment much more seriously than men (Alberts, 1992; Berryman-Fink & Vanover Riley, 1997; Dougherty, 2001). So minimizing or dismissing harassment by calling it "he said, she said" perpetuates a power imbalance, especially for women, who are more frequently targets of sexual harassment.

Reexamining Communication at Work

The Olivia-Bernie example illustrates one of the main problems surrounding sexual harassment: What is deemed sexual harassment by one person may not be viewed as harassment by another. One person's flirtation is another person's sexual harassment (Haunani Solomon & Miller Williams, 1997). Even the most off-the-top-of-your-head comment can be taken differently than you intended. For example, if you extended a simple, one-time compliment to a coworker to make her or him feel good, but it was taken by that coworker as too personal and an unwelcome entrance of sexuality into a professional setting, then your coworker may claim sexual harassment. Proving it or obtaining legal recourse will likely be unsuccessful, given that it was a one-time incident; typically a pattern of behavior is the level necessary for a successful claim (Bingham, 1996; Paetzold & O'Leary-Kelly, 1996). But the point is that the person may have grounds. You can conclude that the employee is paranoid and insecure, out to get you, or hates members of your sex. But given the tense climate surrounding this issue and the litigious country we live in, some action toward you, such as a reprimand from a superior ranging up to a civil lawsuit, could result.

Concerns over sexual harassment have led to a sense that we're "walking on eggshells" at work. Instead of viewing this climate as inhibiting freedom, however, we could look at it as an opportunity for everyone on the job to "clean up their act" and learn some sensitive communication. A reporter for *M Magazine* described men's reactions after the Hill-Thomas situation hit the airwaves: "All the men I talked to told me they had reexamined their conduct in the office. Many were appalled at the things they remembered saying and doing. One company executive said that the Clarence Thomas hearings marked 'one of those pivotal moments, and the office will never be the same' " (Baker, 1992, p. 70). If the threat of being deemed "Neanderthal" or being sued for sexual harassment causes us to think about the effects of our words and actions on others, then perhaps that's the impetus we need to learn to communicate in a more professional, respectful, and equitable manner.

Remember . . .

SEXUAL HARASSMENT: Unwelcome sexual advances, requests for sexual favors, and other verbal or physical conduct of a sexual nature which is made a condition of one's employment or advancement, or which creates a hostile or intimidating working environment.

QUID PRO QUO SEXUAL HARASSMENT: "This for that" harassment, meaning that one's job, promotion, raise, grades, or other inducement is the trade off for sexual favors.

HOSTILE CLIMATE SEXUAL HARASSMENT: Sexual conduct which creates an intimidating or offensive working or learning environment.

STATUS-DIFFERENTIATED RELATIONSHIPS: Relationships in which there are clear-cut lines of status between persons or a well-delineated hierarchy.

PEER SEXUAL HARASSMENT: Sexual harassment occurring between persons of equal status.

CONTRAPOWER SEXUAL HARASSMENT: A person of lower rank or status sexually harassing someone of higher rank or status.

ELECTRONIC OR VIRTUAL SEXUAL HARASSMENT: Sexual harassment that occurs in virtual reality, through on-line channels such as e-mail, bulletin boards, and chat rooms.

Initial Reactions to Sexual Harassment

Research documents the serious toll sexual harassment takes on its victims—emotionally, physically, academically, professionally, and economically. The emotional harm leaves victims angry, afraid, alternatively passive and aggressive, anxious, nervous, depressed, and with extremely low self-esteem (Cochran, Frazier, & Olson, 1997; Hippensteele & Pearson, 1999). They are more likely to abuse substances and become dysfunctional in relationships, and may develop serious health problems such as severe weight loss, stomach problems, and sleeplessness (Clair, 1998; Taylor & Conrad, 1992). There are even documented diagnoses of *post traumatic stress disorder*, characterized by nightmares, muscle tremors, cold sweats, hallucinations, and flashbacks (Castaneda, 1992). Professional impairment includes missing work, being less productive on the job, and feeling isolated and ostracized by coworkers (Hickson, Grierson, & Linder, 1991). Economic costs are mostly associated with changes in or the loss of employment. If a grievance or lawsuit is filed, the obvious legal costs are exacerbated in many cases by the fact that the target may be out of work or on leave (many times without pay) until the situation is resolved. In general, frivolous claims of sexual harassment are few because, as you can see, the economic hardships are real.

Calling It What It Is

It's important to know when to call something sexual harassment, which sounds simpler than it really is. Research indicates that one of the more common reactions to sexual harassment is a reluctance to call it harassment (Cochran, Frazier, & Olson, 1997; Cortina, Swan, Fitzgerald, & Waldo, 1998; Ivy & Hamlet, 1996). This is particularly true of women who report becoming numb to harassing behavior because they grew up with it. They adopt a "boys will be boys" attitude because they see so much harassment around them or they discount harassment and other forms of sexual abuse with a "nothing happened" response, often because they believe that they shouldn't rock the boat (Kelly & Radford, 1996).

Targets of sexual harassment may doubt or deny the event occurred as they remember it. Since sexual harassment is power play, a harasser intends to cause the target doubt, discomfort, and "loss of face." When a target becomes befuddled or embarrassed over a comment or touch, for example, then the harasser's power play has had its intended effect. If you're a target of sexual harassment, realize that questioning the reality of the situation and your feelings of embarrassment or shame are common, understandable reactions. Also realize that you have an empowering right to label the behavior "sexual harassment." You're not exaggerating, stirring up trouble, or making something out of nothing.

Blaming Oneself

Another quite common, understandable reaction is for the receiver of sexual harassment to blame herself or himself for the situation (DeJudicibus & McCabe, 2001; Valentine-French & Radtke, 1993). Targets report negative self-messages, such as "If I'd only seen it coming" and "Did I encourage this person, or somehow give off clues that it was okay to talk to me like that?" It's not uncommon for a target to replay the event later, wondering in hindsight if another response would have been better (the old "I should have said . . ." dilemma). The thing to remember is that sexual harassment, by its very definition, involves *unwarranted, unwelcome* behavior. If the target deserved or welcomed the behavior, if the target brought about the behavior, it wouldn't be considered harassment.

However—and this is a *big* however—there are certain behaviors that increase the possibility that someone will become a target of sexual harassment (Jacobs, 1993). For example, the odds go up that a female employee will be seen as a sex object when she wears unprofessionally short skirts, extremely high heels, overdone makeup and hair, and flashy jewelry to work. A man who tolerates sexual teasing from female coworkers or who engages in sexual banter as a way to be accepted or to deflect attention may be tacitly condoning and contributing to that kind of atmosphere. Understand that this is not a *blame the victim* stance; we're not saying that people who dress provocatively or join in sexual joking deserve to be harassed. We're saying that people who present themselves in an unprofessional, sexual manner in the workplace or classroom are "playing with fire." They don't deserve unprofessional treatment, but their behavior increases the likelihood that they'll be taken any way but seriously.

After the Deed's Been Done: Responding to Harassment

Research has explored personal, professional, and legal responses to harassment (Adams-Roy & Barling, 1998). Keep in mind that, particularly for female targets, the prime motivation or goal is to get a harasser to leave her alone (Bingham, 1991; Payne, 1993). When counseled, most targets say, "I just want it to stop."

A Range of Responses

Sociologist James Gruber (1989) adapted conflict resolution strategies to develop a range of responses to sexual harassment. Ranging from least assertive to most assertive, these responses include *avoidance, defusion, negotiation,* and *confrontation.* There is no "best" response to sexual harassment. Being assertive is not necessarily wiser than avoiding a harasser; a judgment of a best response is up to the target because there are pros and cons to each.

Given targets' discomfort and feelings of powerlessness, along with perceptions of potential threats by harassers, it's understandable that the most common response is to *avoid* or ignore harassment. Most targets of harassment try to get out of the situation as quickly and gracefully as they can, putting as much distance between themselves and the harasser as possible. Some people feel forced to go to great lengths to get this distance, including transferring units within a company (or the military), quitting a job, dropping a class in which they've been harassed by a teacher or classmate, transferring schools, and even moving to another residence or city (Becker, 2000). But the problem is that when targets passively try to "let it go," they usually suffer great personal loss of self-esteem, confidence, and comfort at work or in school. Ignoring the situation does not make it go away; on the contrary, it increases the likelihood that it will happen again to the same victim, someone else, or both.

'Net Notes

For the latest information on sexual harassment laws and procedures for filing complaints or lawsuits, one source to turn to is **www.lawguru.com**. This site offers helpful advice on how to prove your case if you're being harassed, what to do if sexual harassment occurs at work, and ways to protect yourself while you're pursuing a case. For sexual harassment occurring in educational settings, **www.ed.gov**, a Website from the U.S. Department of Education and Office of Civil Rights, offers information about sexual harassment that occurs at all educational levels—from elementary to university. The site explains Title IX protections, overviews current laws governing academic harassment, and provides answers to frequently asked questions about harassment.

A second common strategy, one step away from avoidance, is to attempt to *defuse* or "take the sting out" of a situation by joking about it or trivializing it with one's peers (Clair, McGoun, & Spirek, 1993; Cochran, Frazier, & Olson, 1997). Many times targets simply laugh off a comment, act as though they don't understand what was said, or stumble out a "thank you" to a compliment that wasn't really appreciated. However, these actions may simply delay the process of confronting the problem (if not the harasser). Defusion responses often leave targets feeling dissatisfied, anxious about the future, and concerned about themselves (Maypole, 1986). Downplaying an event may reduce emotional stress and create a perception that there's no longer a need for negotiation or confrontation with the harasser. But then the harassment and the harasser aren't labeled as such publicly, so the behavior is likely perpetuated.

Some targets *negotiate* with a harasser, typically in the form of directly requesting that the behavior stop. A negotiating response might be, "I think that kind of talk is inappropriate and it makes me uncomfortable, so I'd appreciate it if you would stop talking to me like that." Organizational communication scholar Shereen Bingham (1991) suggests that "More frequent and effective use of interpersonal communication for dealing with sexual harassment may improve relationships between men and women at work and reduce costs to organizations" (p. 110). However, for many targets, saying anything at all directly to a harasser is a tall order. Remember that harassment is, by design, a show of power. The person in the less powerful position is often unable to summon enough will to comment directly to a harasser. If the harasser is a supervisor or professor—someone who can hold one's professional, economic, or academic future as a type of ransom—the wisest thing in the target's estimation may be to do nothing.

The final level of response is to *confront* the harasser by issuing an ultimatum such as "Keep your distance and stop asking me personal questions or else I'll have to talk to the boss about it." Assertive tactics like negotiation and confrontation are more likely to be used in closer relationships that have a longer history, one in which trust was set up and then violated, than when the harasser is an acquaintance. Confrontation is the least often reported response, but what's confusing is that this is the advice targets often get from people. People say, "Stand up for yourself. Just tell him to back off, that you're not going to put up with that crap." Those of us who have experienced sexual harassment know just how difficult it is to take that advice. Most of the time, harassment is so surprising, disgusting, and upsetting that a target has a hard time saying *anything*. Perhaps after some time passes a target might feel empowered enough to directly confront or negotiate with a harasser, but that's an individual choice. Our hope is that more and better information about sexual harassment will cause targets to feel more empowered, to believe that they can use assertive responses to stop a harasser's behavior without serious jeopardy to themselves. But we should all be careful about being quick or cavalier in our advice to receivers of harassment.

The Downside of Secrecy

Keeping harassment bottled up is an understandable immediate, reaction. In fact, research documents a characteristic time-lag for responding to harassment, due to the target's feelings of helplessness and shame and because it takes many people time to realize that sexual harassment has actually occurred (Clair, 1998; Taylor & Conrad, 1992). People who have researched and experienced sexual harassment understand why, for example, Anita Hill waited 10 years before going public with her claims of sexual harassment (whether they believe her allegations or not) (Foss & Rogers, 1992). In Hill's case, she did not actually file a sexual harassment complaint against Clarence Thomas; she would not have gone public were it not for the fact that the press was about to expose her story.

But we suggest that if you are a target of sexual harassment—if you even just *think* that you may have been harassed—*tell someone.* We're not necessarily talking about reporting the harassment here, but making it real by saying it out loud. It's critical to tell a friend, family member, clergy member, classmate, or coworker what happened, what you interpreted from the incident, how it made you feel, how you currently feel about yourself and your job or schooling, and so forth. Communication allows a target to gain back confidence and get useful perspectives from others (Witteman, 1993). It also creates documentation that can be used for possible professional and legal action in the future (Booth-Butterfield, 1986; Payne, 1993).

One caution regarding confiding in someone about harassment: *Be careful whom you select to talk to.* In both Chapters 5 and 6, we discussed gender differences in listening and responding—how men tend to react to women's communication by problem solving, rather than responding empathically to what women feel. If you're a female target of sexual harassment—at work, school, wherever—think long and hard before deciding that the first person you'll tell is your husband, boyfriend, or father. We're not suggesting that you shouldn't tell one of these persons, but it's wise to apply the principles of the receiver orientation here. Consider what a man's reaction might be to your sexual harassment experience. If you do decide to confide in him, think about *how* you will tell him. You may have heard stories like those we've heard of men who took on women's problems by confronting the harasser (often violently) or by going to the woman's or the harasser's boss—actions that often made the situation worse. It's more empowering for people to fight their own harassment battles, with as many sources of support as possible *behind* them. This strategy will do more to repair their self-esteem and enhance their respectability in others' eyes.

If you're the person a target speaks to about a sexually harassing experience, your knowledge of the issue will be a great comfort. Apply the principles of the receiver orientation and your understanding of gender communication to help you respond in a helpful way, keeping in mind that the problem belongs to the target and it is her or his decision about what to do. The best thing you can do for someone who confides in you is to listen—with your eyes as well as your ears, watching for nonverbal cues about what the target is feeling and needing.

Going a Step Further: Reporting Sexual Harassment

After you've told someone about the incident, think about how you want to deal with it. For example, if the harasser is one of your professors, how will you handle being in his or her class the rest of the semester? Will you drop the class, become passive and withdrawn so as to endure the class, confront the professor and possibly risk your grade, report the harassment to the professor's department chair, or file an official grievance? If the harasser is a coworker, will you report the harassment? Ask for a transfer? Quit your job?

We don't mean to lay guilt trips here by saying that targets must report their harassment. Reporting is an individual decision because there are always costs involved. In fact, research shows that less than five percent of targets report harassment to an authority; fewer still bring state or federal charges against harassers or their organizations (Fitzgerald, 1993). But a target also has to weigh the costs of *not* reporting harassment. Unreported harassment leaves the harasser free from responsibility for her or his behavior, and free to harass again. As communication scholar Kay Payne (1993) contends, "The failure to report suggests that nothing is wrong and extends the power imbalance" (p. 142).

Preparing to Claim Sexual Harassment

Remembering our old friends Olivia and Bernie, let's say that Olivia decides to make a claim of sexual harassment. Many targets initiate an internal grievance, rather than using less familiar, higher profile measures such as filing a complaint with the EEOC or launching a lawsuit. Whether Olivia decides to use an internal route involving her company in the problem or an external process, the first thing she should do is ask herself this question: "What do I want to happen?" Knowing one's expectations or goals before starting the grievance process is critical; it can save some emotional toll down the road.

Once she is clear on her goals, Olivia should inventory the whole experience. Did she make any notes on the harassment, meaning how often it occurred, what Bernie said and did and what Olivia said and did, if she responded? Creating a paper trail is a good idea, even if you don't expect harassment to recur and don't anticipate filing a grievance. But many targets are so taken aback by the behavior and reluctant to view it as sexual harassment that requiring written documentation is unrealistic. It's not necessary to have a paper trail, but it no doubt strengthens a case. If Olivia doesn't have any notes, she should write an account of harassing events, recalling specific dates, what was said and done, and other details with as much accuracy and information as possible.

Were there any witnesses to the conversations and events Olivia considers harassing? Did she ever tell Bernie directly that his behavior was unwelcome, and did anyone else witness or know about her telling him such? Notifying a harasser that the behavior is unwelcome is a key element courts look for; it's not a requirement, but again, it strengthens one's claims. Did Olivia tell anyone about the experiences, at the time they happened or later? If so, could those people be relied upon to verify Olivia's claims?

The Hunt for the Handbook

Olivia's next action might logically be to consult an employee handbook for a policy on sexual harassment and procedures for filing a grievance. Employees and students are often unaware that some company and university policies impose time limits for filing grievances (which are usually unreasonable, given the toll harassment takes on its victims) (Geist & Townsley, 1997). However, Olivia might have the rude awakening that her company doesn't have such a document, hasn't developed a policy, or has guidelines that are so vague or outdated that they make her situation more difficult to pursue (Cloud, 1998). A target's options will either be more limited because of ignorance among the organization's leaders or enhanced because the organization was caught unprepared to handle this situation. In some instances, organizations' ignorance on this issue has cost them dearly.

If there is a sexual harassment policy, the company probably advises employees to report the problem to an immediate supervisor. Since Bernie *is* Olivia's supervisor, she will have to go further up the chain of command to Bernie's supervisor. Another option is to report harassment to human resources personnel or an EEO office, if the company or institution has these departments. Many targets only request that their complaint be taken seriously and that the supervisor take action to stop the behavior from recurring. However, in some instances the target asks that the harasser be fired, transferred, or sanctioned. Our sincere hope is that the target's complaint will be taken seriously and the policy (if there is one) will be followed carefully and fairly, for the sake of all parties involved. If not, Olivia can take her complaint to the courts.

Of Laws and Lawsuits

Legal recourse for victims of sexual harassment is costly and time consuming, and it offers no guarantee of a desired outcome. But as charges continue to be filed, harassment is taken more seriously, laws and policies are strengthened, and more victims are compensated. Remember the statistic we cited earlier, indicating that complaints of sexual harassment filed with the EEOC more than doubled between 1991 and 2001 (EEOC, 2002). Today's organizations are taking more seriously the prospect of sexual harassment litigation by reviewing or creating policies and grievance procedures and by conducting training sessions (Gruber, 2002). One survey indicates that 97 percent of American organizations report having sexual harassment policies on file; 84 percent of employees surveyed say that their organizations have adequately informed them of such policies (Sexual Harassment, 1999).

U.S. Supreme Court rulings and case law continue to change the way sexual harassment is viewed, victims are compensated, and liability is assessed. Some rulings are contradictory, just to make things more confusing. A law passed in 1991 made it possible for sexually harassed individuals to sue for both punitive and compensatory damages (Clair, 1992; Wood, 1992). Prior to 1991, victims could only sue for compensation, such as lost wages and benefits; the law enabled victims to receive remuneration for the personal, psychological, and physical effects of harassment.

Another area of concern is legal liability, meaning who is responsible and who must compensate for harassment. Several rulings indicate that managers and companies can be held legally liable for harassment among their employees. In the late 1990s, three Supreme Court rulings dealt with employer liability and victim compensation. First, the court ruled that recipients of sexual harassment need not demonstrate psychological pain and suffering in order to receive compensation; in other words, it is a given or expected that victims of harassment will suffer psychological consequences (Laabs, 1998). In *Ellerth* v. *Burlington Industries,* the court held that even if an employee did not suffer financial or career-related harm as a result of sexual harassment, the employer was still liable for other forms of injury to the victim, such as psychological damage. Findings in *Faragher* v. *The City of Boca Raton* made the previous ruling more specific, stating that employers are not liable for supervisory harassment if (1) they exercise reasonable care to prevent and correct the behavior, and (2) they can show that the victim of harassment failed to take advantage of an available remedy for the situation, such as a company policy or training program (Casey, Desai, & Ulrich, 1998). In Chapter 10, we discuss laws that pertain to schools and universities; one ruling on peer sexual harassment has far-reaching implications. Other laws deal with some of the same issues as in workplace harassment, such as compensation for victims and who can be held legally liable for sexual harassment in educational settings.

So if Olivia pursues an internal grievance but isn't satisfied with the outcome, she can file a civil suit against the company. She should do so only after weighing the risks and getting legal advice about the current status of the law and her chances of winning a case, however. Some people go as far as they can with their claims; others never report harassment. Let's remember that as outsiders to a situation, we aren't really in a position to judge a target's decision regarding action (or inaction) after the fact. So many factors depend on circumstances that advising a specific response to sexual harassment is inappropriate and unhelpful. The best advice is for targets to get as much information as possible in order to make the best decision possible. Having options, and knowing what they are, is critical.

Parting Considerations about Sexual Harassment

When students ask how to avoid sexual harassment, here's our answer: Communicate professionally—not personally or sexually—with bosses, coworkers, professors, and classmates. Including classmates in that list may seem harsh, but at least start out on this track until you're very sure (and we mean *very, very* sure) that personal communication is appropriate. This is not a suggestion that you "walk on eggshells," but that you exercise personally effective communication. You now know what your options are and how you can respond if you're in the unfortunate circumstance of being sexually harassed. Put your knowledge of gender communication to work to minimize the likelihood of being accused of harassment. If someone reacts nonverbally with embarrassment or discomfort, or says that she or he doesn't appreciate what you've said or done, try not to get defensive. Be responsible for your own behavior and try to rectify the situation, not by explaining what you meant or trying to justify your behavior, but by apologizing and offering to make amends. If the person won't accept your apology, then *leave her or him alone*. Accept the person's interpretation of the event, rather than asserting your will into the situation. Chalk up that experience and learn some lessons from it; perhaps you'll get a chance to start anew if the person is ready at some future point.

One final suggestion is to communicate equally and consistently, meaning in the same professional manner with members of the same and opposite sex. For example, it's unwise for women to communicate professionally with female coworkers but flirtatiously with male coworkers. It's unwise to communicate with deference to a male professor, but talk to a female professor as though she were "just one of the girls." For the men, would you tell a joke with equal comfort in "mixed company"? Do you speak to male colleagues with respect, but treat female coworkers like girls, rather than professionals? Do you compliment

---

Remember . . .

POST TRAUMATIC STRESS DISORDER: A psychological stress-related disorder, characterized by nightmares, muscle tremors, cold sweats, hallucinations, and flashbacks.

AVOIDANCE: A response to sexual harassment in which a target ignores harassment and avoids any form of confrontation with a harasser.

DEFUSION: A response to sexual harassment in which a target tries to distract or "take the sting out" of a situation, through joking or changing the subject, etc.

NEGOTIATION: A response to sexual harassment in which a target works with the harasser, harasser's boss, or other entity internal or external to an organization so as to arrive at a resolution.

CONFRONTATION: A response to sexual harassment in which a target confronts the harasser directly, usually insisting that the harassing behavior stop and possibly issuing an ultimatum.

a male colleague's suit just as often as you compliment a female colleague's dress? These are just a few important things that will help you initiate and maintain more respectful, successful relationships at school and on the job.

PERSONAL RIGHTS AND SEXUALITY

Although significant strides have been made in recent years toward gender equity in sexual matters, the goal is not yet reached. As teachers, we see vestiges of older attitudes in some students who express in overt or subtle ways an expectation that men have a right to assert their sexual needs. Recall our discussion in Chapter 2 about biology becoming a cop-out from focusing on sociocultural factors to explain gender communication. The belief that some men commit sexual assault because their physical urges overtake their reason, that "men just have to have it," is a similar cop-out. This is blaming biology again, but taken to the extreme. In this section of the chapter, we explore the difficult topic of sexual assault and rape and the critical role of communication in sexual encounters.

Power at the Core, Again

We've said that the abuses explored in this chapter have to do primarily with power, not about sex. Of the three offenses we're studying, rape is the most closely associated with sex. As Pulitzer Prize–winning author Natalie Angier (2000) explains, "rape is about sex and power and a thousand other things as well . . . rape is not a monolithic constant but varies in incidence and meaning from culture to culture and epoch to epoch" (p. 81). The role of power is obvious in stranger rape, because a stranger must render a target powerless in order to assault. Here's how power emerges when the assaulter is someone the target knows: When sexual expectations and interests in a romantic or social situation differ, when one person's sexual intentions or desires don't match another's, then the sexual motive becomes a power motive, a case of someone getting his or her way no matter the cost or the wishes of the other person. One person engages in sexual conduct against the will of another person; someone's personal rights are violated.

Changing Language as We Learn More

The law recognizes different types of rape, some of which, unfortunately, are hard to prove. *Forcible rape,* as defined by the Federal Bureau of Investigation, is "the carnal knowledge of a female forcibly and against her will" (FBI, 1989). However, the FBI's outdated and conservative view of rape has been roundly criticized because it narrowly defines rape as vaginal intercourse without consent. Their definition does not mention male victims of rape, nor does it include forced oral sex, anal sex, and penetration with an object, which are a part of many researchers' definitions when studying this problem (Crichton, 1993). A very broad definition of rape is "taking possession of another's sexuality" (Moore, 2000, p. 25). A complicating factor in discussions and research, as well as laws about rape, is disagreement on a definition.

Stranger rape is just what the term says—rape by a person unknown to the victim. You may recall hearing news accounts on a particularly gruesome day in June of 2000, when approximately 60 women were victimized in Central Park on the day of the Puerto Rican Day Parade in New York City (Moore, 2000; Zia, 2000). Some were verbally harassed, stripped of their clothing, and robbed, while others were sexually assaulted by 40 or so men in the park. While people used to associate the general term rape primarily with stranger rape, research has shown us that this form of rape occurs with far less frequency than rape by a person known to the victim.

Date rape (also termed *acquaintance rape*) occurs in the context of persons who know one another, even if they have just met. Researchers Jean Hughes and Bernice Sandler (1987) define date rape as "forced, unwanted intercourse with a person you know. It is a violation of your body and your trust" (p. 1). They also offer another important distinction—the difference between seduction and rape: "Seduction occurs when a woman is manipulated or cajoled into agreeing to have sex; the key word is 'agreeing.' Acquaintance rape often occurs when seduction fails and the man goes ahead and has sex with the woman anyway, despite any protests and without her agreement" (p. 2). After years of being ignored, attention is now being paid to the very serious societal problem of acquaintance rape. We spend a good deal of time in this chapter on this form, because it's the most common sexual offense college students experience. While cases of same-sex date rape continue to be documented, few targets of date rape are male; the vast majority of targets are female. (The exception to this trend might be found among prison populations, where male-to-male rape occurs frequently but is rarely reported.) Some claim, in fact, that "the possibility of being raped is certainly *one* of the defining characteristics of being a woman in our culture" (Peach, 1998, p. 295). Thus, most of the literature refers to the rapist as "he" and the person raped as "she."

The word *rape* is the historical term for this crime, but that term can be a *trigger word* for people who've experienced it. By *trigger word*, we mean that simply hearing the term can remind targets of the trauma they went through, sometimes making them feel victimized again. This is one of the primary reasons you hear the term *sexual assault* instead of *rape.* The impact of trigger words for our readers who have survived rape is a concern, but part of the healing process is calling the act what it is rather than using a euphemism that can dilute or trivialize the experience. Another factor in word choice is that in some information on the topic, sexual assault refers to a category of behavior that includes forced kissing or petting, but stops short of intercourse (Crawford & Unger, 2000). In other usages, *sexual assault* is the term for a range of offenses that includes rape (defined as vaginal intercourse) as well as other forms of sexual invasion, such as forced sodomy (oral sex) and anal penetration. We realize this is confusing and difficult language on an uncomfortable topic, but it's important to be clear on terms so that we can accurately and honestly discuss these life-altering experiences.

Remember . . .

FORCIBLE RAPE: The carnal knowledge of a female forcibly and against her will (FBI definition).

STRANGER RAPE: Rape by a person unknown to the target.

DATE/ACQUAINTANCE RAPE: Rape by a person who is known by the target, even if they have just met.

TRIGGER WORD: The use of a term which can remind a target of past trauma, sometimes making her or him feel victimized again.

SEXUAL ASSAULT: A range of offenses that includes rape as well as other forms of sexual invasion, such as forced sodomy (oral sex) and anal penetration.

The preferred term for persons who've lived through the ordeal of rape and sexual assault is *survivors,* which is a great term because it signals respect and hope. Rape also occurs among marital partners (together or separated) and between persons who used to be married. At long last, all 50 states have laws on the books addressing this form of rape (*Wife Rape Information Page,* 1998). Other terms include *marital rape, spousal rape,* and *wife rape,* defined as "sexual acts committed without a person's consent and/or against a person's will, when the perpetrator (attacker) is the woman's husband or ex-husband" (*Wife Rape Information Page,* 1998, p. 1). We prefer the term *partner rape,* because homosexual partners and people who are cohabiting can be raped just as persons who are legally married, separated, or divorced.

Other forms of rape include *gang rape,* which involves multiple rapists and a single target (although there are accounts of gang rapes of multiple targets). In most gang rapes, the perpetrators are acquaintances of the target (Ehrhart & Sandler, 1985; O'Sullivan, 1991). *Statutory rape* is the rape of a minor, someone who has not yet attained the age of consent (Eaves, 1992). Finally, a form of rape even exists on the Internet, although it involves only psychological, not physical, assault and is not legally recognized or prosecuted. In a provocative yet disturbing article in *Ms.* magazine, Debra Michals (1997) describes entering an on-line chat room in which a gang rape was taking place. As Michals explains, *cyber-rape* or *virtual rape* "is not the same as the rape a woman experiences in the physical world. But something as yet unnamable is going on in chat rooms where an erotic scenario can shift to a gang bang with a few keystrokes" (p. 69). Now that we've defined the terms, how bad is the problem?

Underestimates of an Underreported Problem

Although we start with a few numbers to illustrate the extent of the problem, realize that numbers do not tell even half of the story when it comes to rape and sexual assault. FBI crime statistics for 2002 indicate that rates of violent crimes (murders, robberies, and rapes) remained relatively unchanged nationwide from the previous year (U.S. Department of Justice, 2002). Forcible rape rates showed a minimal increase of .2 percent in this period. But remember: Rape rates reflect *reported* cases. The crime least likely to be reported and least likely to result in a conviction in America is rape (Crawford & Unger, 2000). Journalist Annette Fuentes (1997) contends, "By all accounts, rape remains the most underreported violent crime. The U.S. Department of Justice, using FBI data, says only 36 percent of rapes are reported. Because the FBI's Reporting Program reflects only crimes reported to police, its rape numbers may be off by almost two thirds" (p. 20).

Underreporting is particularly the case for partner rape because many women do not consider sexual assaults by their husbands to be rape (*Wife Rape Information Page*, 1998). Research estimates that one in every seven married women will be sexually assaulted by her husband (Koss & Harvey, 1991). Studies also reveal that 62 percent of all forcible rapes occur to girls younger than 18, with 29 percent occurring before age 11, primarily committed by persons known to these girls (Fuentes, 1997). The FBI's Uniform Crime Reporting Program (2002) estimates that one forcible rape occurs in the U.S. every 5.8 minutes.

Statistics on Date Rape

It's a devastating fact that most women are raped by persons they know; only one in five rapes are committed by strangers (FBI, 1995). The effects of date rape on younger women are enormous, especially in the damage done to their ability to trust or form intimate relationships. Mary Pipher, author of *Reviving Ophelia: Saving the Selves of Adolescent Girls* (1994), provides some statistics on the aftermath of rape: 41 percent of survivors expect to be raped again; 30 percent consider suicide; 31 percent seek therapy; 22 percent enroll in self-defense courses; 82 percent say they are permanently changed by the experience.

Date rape situations are extremely difficult for survivors to understand and grapple with, because many persons who are victimized by someone they know

> *Once in cabinet we had to deal with the fact that there had been an outbreak of assaults on women at night. One minister suggested a curfew: women should stay home after dark. I said, "But it's the men who are attacking the women. If there's to be a curfew, let the men stay home, not the women."*
>
> —Golda Meir, former Israeli prime minister

are especially reluctant to call what happened rape. They often call it a "bad date." They blame themselves for getting into the situation in the first place, not seeing it coming, using substances that altered their judgment or impaired their ability to resist (since alcohol and/or drugs are involved in most date rape situations), and being generally unable to prevent the assault. This is similar to how targets of sexual harassment blame themselves for a harasser's illegal behavior. Author Noelle Howey (2001) told of her date rape experience in an article for *Ms.* magazine; she explains: "I feared claiming that I had been raped because I felt far less traumatized than I thought a rape victim was supposed to feel. All those TV specials showed rape as unambiguous and brutal. The heroine fights back—even if she's barely conscious—and emerges with bruises and ripped clothing. She scrubs herself raw, doesn't tell anyone what happened, and eschews formfitting clothes—not to mention sex—for months" (p. 89). Howey's experience with date rape was alcohol-affected and ambiguous, which made recovering from it very difficult. Nonetheless, she didn't feel she could move on from the experience until she called it what it really was, and then actively dealt with the fact that she was now a survivor of rape.

One name that repeatedly surfaces in research on this topic is Mary Koss, author of multiple studies on rape and a principal investigator for the Arizona Rape and Sexual Assault Surveillance Project. Koss and colleagues surveyed 7,000 students across 32 American college campuses and found the following:

1. One out of every 12 men responding to the survey said they had tried or actually succeeded in forcing a woman to have sexual intercourse.
2. None of the men who admitted such behavior called themselves rapists.
3. One in eight women responding to the survey revealed that she was a survivor of rape.
4. Only a little over half of these rape survivors actually called their experiences rape; the others had a hard time viewing their experience as rape.
5. Five percent of the women who reported surviving rape had been raped by multiple offenders (gang raped).
6. The rate of college student victimization is about three times the rate for the general population (Koss, Gidycz, & Wisniewski, 1987).

More recent research has produced similar results, in terms of college students' sexual experiences related to rape, coercion, and aggression (Calhoun, Bernat, Clum, & Frame, 1997; Elliott & Brantley, 1997).

Slip 'Em a Mickey

Some of you are too young to know what "slipping a Mickey" means, but it's a reference to a Mickey Finn, a substance used to involuntarily sedate someone for the purpose of assaulting or taking advantage of her or him. The old phrase "get her drunk and take advantage of her" has a 21st-century incarnation in the form of date rape drugs.

You may have heard or read about this, but the practice of placing substances in people's drinks without their knowledge is increasing at an alarming rate. According to the Washington DC Rape Crisis Center Website (1998), the mostly commonly used, easily obtained drugs are as follows (street names included): Rohypnol

(Roofies, Roachies, La Rocha, The Forget Pill); Gamma Hydroxybutyrate or GHB (Grievous Bodily Harm, Easy Lay); and Ketamine (Special K). The most well-known of these, Rohypnol, is a medication prescribed internationally for people with severe and debilitating sleep disorders. It's illegal in the U.S., but it's being smuggled in and sold as a street drug. The Swiss-based company that manufactures Rohypnol has reformulated the drug so that it releases a blue dye when dissolved in a liquid. While this is a step in the right direction, the problem is that the blue dye is difficult to detect in dark drinks and dark settings, such as bars and clubs.

When this tasteless, odorless drug is slipped into a person's drink, within 20 to 30 minutes the person will show symptoms of being sedated. Limited motion and voice production are two common effects; drugged rape survivors report feeling like they were in a daze, as though they were too heavy to move or call out. But perhaps the most devastating effect of the drug is its memory impairment. The DC Rape Crisis Center describes it this way: "Because survivors will have been heavily sedated, they may not have complete recall of the assault. It is likely that they will be uncertain about exactly what happened and who was involved. The unknowns may create tremendous anxiety as survivors are left to fill in the gaps with their imagination" (pp. 4–5). Some persons who've been drugged have no memory of the incident; they wake up, sometimes in a hospital, to learn that they've been raped, but can't remember how it happened or who raped them.

If you or a friend suspect you've been drugged because you feel dizzy or confused after drinking something, try to get to a hospital. If you believe you've been raped (and there are reported cases of men being drugged with Rohypnol and raped), crisis centers recommend that you get to a safe place and call a crisis center or 911. If you decide to report the assault to the police, be sure not to shower, bathe, douche, change clothes, or straighten up the area where you suspect the rape took place until medical and legal evidence is collected. Then go to a hospital or other facility where you can receive treatment for injuries, tests for pregnancy and sexually transmitted diseases, a urine test, and counseling. The urine test is important because Rohypnol can be found in urine up to 72 hours after ingestion, depending on someone's metabolism and the dose of the drug. The Drug-Induced Rape Prevention and Punishment Act, passed in October 1996, punishes persons who commit rape by administering a controlled substance without the target's knowledge.

Who Are the Rapists?

The normal, gentle, nice-looking guy sitting next to you in class could be a rapist. Does that sound paranoid or absurd? The point we're trying to make is that persons capable of committing date or partner rape look just like all of us. Their profiles cross racial and ethnic, class, age, and religious lines. Research has isolated a number of characteristics more common among date rapists, such as the use or abuse of alcohol, athletic affiliation, fraternity affiliation, a history of family violence, and early and varied sexual experience (Crawford & Unger, 2000). But a date rapist *could be anybody.*

We don't want to make you overly suspicious, so you see potential rapists everywhere you look, but we do want you to realize that the "crazed man jumping out of the bushes" to rape is much more the exception than the rule. Most rapists are people you know: family members, friends of the family, classmates, boyfriends, teachers, coworkers, bosses, doctors, lawyers, ministers. As a reporter for the *San Antonio Express-News* asserted, in an article educating the community about rape, "In 80% of sexual assaults, the victim is acquainted with the rapist in some way. Most rapists don't break into homes to terrorize their victims. More often than not, they are welcomed at the front door or they already live there" (Aaron, 1997).

Contributing Effects of Gender Socialization

In Chapter 2, we defined *socialization* as the process through which individuals learn their culture, develop their potential, and become functioning members of society. Part of this socialization process is *gender socialization,* or the way individuals learn gender—their own and others' identity in terms of biological sex and psychological gender. Many cultures socialize men to be aggressive and competitive and women to be submissive and not "rock the boat." While we are making progress on some of that socialization, change in the sexual arena hasn't kept pace. For example, we are increasingly more aware of serious health risks associated with sexual activity, but our culture still reinforces men for expressing and exploring their sexuality.

Women hear a variety of mixed messages about sexuality. On the one hand, they are encouraged to take responsibility for sex, for example, by carrying condoms rather than expecting a sexual partner to have them. They may be told that they can be sexual creatures and that they need to learn to express their sexual desires and openly discuss the limits they want to place on sexual activity. On the other hand, they see people become squeamish and prudish when such subjects as female anatomy, masturbation, and orgasm arise. They see rape laws that encourage men's sexuality and question women's. They see constant attempts in rape trials to determine if a woman behaved in a sexual manner that brought about her own rape. There is still much more openness and acceptance of male sexuality in our society than female sexuality, which adds to the power imbalance.

Along with differences in socialization, other structures in society reinforce the woman-as-victim role. For example, only recently have we witnessed an increase in women's participation in self-defense courses and other instruction aimed at teaching women to protect and defend themselves against assault. And while women are being encouraged to develop their bodies and strength, they still get the message that they should limit that development so that they're not stronger than men (which would be "unfeminine"). Women are bombarded with fashion messages, including those that constantly encourage them to wear tight clothing and high-heeled shoes that inhibit their movement and prevent easy escape. Finally, there's the age-old message that women need men for financial support (Crawford & Unger, 2000).

Common Myths about Rape

Research conducted by psychologist Martha Burt (1980) led to the discovery of a set of rape myths, beliefs people hold about rape that aren't based in fact. While these myths emerged 20 years ago, people still adhere to them in surprising numbers today. These myths include the following:

1. Women say "no" when they mean "yes" to avoid being seen as promiscuous.
2. Men must overcome women if they resist.
3. Some women deserve to be raped.
4. Some women actually enjoy rape, because it fulfills one of their sexual fantasies.
5. Some men just can't help themselves when they are aroused; they *have* to have sexual intercourse, even if they have to be aggressive to get it.
6. "Good girls" don't get raped—a myth related to prior sexual activity. A man may believe that if a woman has been sexually active, she will willingly have sex with anyone, including him. The "only virgins can be raped" myth suggests that sexually active women cannot be raped.

A related myth is the belief that if a woman has had sex with a man but refuses to have sex with him again, it's not rape if he forces her (Shotland & Goldstein, 1992). This couldn't be further from the truth. Unwanted, nonconsensual sex is rape, no matter if there have been instances of prior consent.

From this research, Burt developed a Rape Myth Acceptance Scale, an instrument that asks subjects questions about their experiences with sexual violence and determines to what level an individual accepts or believes certain myths about rape. Subsequent studies measuring rape myth acceptance consistently find that men who score high on scales of traditional masculine traits, hold traditional attitudes about gender roles, and view feminism negatively are likely to believe in rape myths and to describe past or future aggression toward women (Abbey & Harnish, 1995; Good, Heppner, Hillenbrand-Gunn, & Wang, 1995; Malamuth, Sockloskie, Koss, & Tanaka, 1991; Meyer & Johnson, 1999; Schwartz & DeKeseredy, 1997; Truman, Tokar, & Fischer, 1996). Other research has determined a connection between a belief in rape myths and exposure to pornography, sexually violent media, and mainstream media depictions (such as in R-rated movies) of women acting aroused during rape or being objectified in degrading ways (Milburn, Mather, & Conrad, 2000; Mullin, 1995; Zillman & Bryant, 1982).

The Washington DC Rape Crisis Center (1998) contributes a few more myths about rape:

1. Rape is not a big deal; it is only sex.
2. Most rapes are interracial; most rapes are committed by black men against white women or white men against black women. (The reality is that about 90 percent of all rapes occur between members of the same race.)
3. Most rapists are psychotic men. (Actually, most rapists are not mentally ill.)

Changing sexual standards may lead some men to expect sex from women, almost as a given or a reward for having dated someone a few times. Some men believe that they are entitled to sex when they have spent money on a date—that somehow sex and money are an even exchange.

Sexually Aggressive Tendencies

Studies have attempted to predict some of the characteristics of men who are likely to be sexual aggressors. Keep in mind that the term *sexual aggression* describes a continuum of behaviors, with consensual sexual activity on one end (meaning that consensual sex can involve aggressive behavior) and violent rape on the other (Crawford & Unger, 2000). Prominent sexual assault researcher Neil Malamuth and colleagues found that sexually aggressive men were incompetent in decoding women's negative emotions and had more suspicious interpretations of women's verbal communication (as in doubting that a woman's "no" really meant "no"). They failed to distinguish between assertiveness and hostility, and between friendliness and seduction in women's communication (Malamuth & Brown, 1994). Sexually aggressive men also tend to be more domineering in casual conversation, using one-up messages, bragging, criticizing others, and attempting to dominate conversation by controlling the topic and interrupting others. The researchers suggest that a sexually aggressive man might be domineering in conversation as a way to assess the vulnerability of a female target (Malamuth & Thornhill, 1994). Other studies find that physically aggressive men who hold traditional views of gender roles are more likely to have sexually aggressive tendencies toward women (Cachie & deMan, 1997; Muehlenhard & Falcon, 1990) and that men who accept rape myths and have poor argumentation skills are likely to resort to verbal aggression, which has the potential to lead to physical aggression, sexual aggression, or both (Andonian & Droge, 1993).

Remember . . .

SURVIVOR: A term for a person who has survived sexual harassment, sexual assault or rape, or partner violence.

MARITAL/SPOUSAL/WIFE RAPE: Sexual acts committed without a person's consent and/or against a person's will, when the rapist is the woman's husband or ex-husband.

PARTNER RAPE: A broader term for rape committed by one person in a relationship against the other; applies to homosexual and cohabiting partners as well as married, separated, or divorced persons.

GANG RAPE: Rape involving multiple rapists and either a single target or multiple targets.

STATUTORY RAPE: Rape of a minor, someone who has not yet attained the age of consent.

CYBER/VIRTUAL RAPE: A sexual conversation or scenario occurring on-line, which may turn from sexual to sexually abusive.

GENDER SOCIALIZATION: The way individuals learn gender—their own and others' identity in terms of biological sex and psychological gender.

RAPE MYTHS: Beliefs about rape that aren't based in fact.

SEXUAL AGGRESSION: A continuum of behaviors, with consensual sexual activity on one end (aggressive sex) and violent rape on the other.

An Evening Out with Annie and Kris

Besides being a professor of communication, the female co-author of this text (whom we'll just refer to as "the professor") served as the director of the Women's Center at her university. In that capacity, she frequently made presentations on gender-related topics on campus and in her community. One campus event will stay in her memory because it so clearly illustrates our discussion of socialization and sexuality. The professor was asked by a dorm resident assistant (RA) to speak to a group of her residents about gender communication. The event drew about 20 or so students on a week night, with more women than men in attendance. The discussion started generally, but as usual in addressing gender communication in an informal setting, it fairly quickly turned to topics of sex. At one point, the RA said that a friend of hers (whom we'll call Annie) was studying and couldn't attend the gathering, but had an important question she was going to call in.

Annie did phone in and her question was about "blue balls" (pardon the bluntness and use of this term). She said that at the end of a date, she'd been making out with her boyfriend (whom we'll call Kris) in his car and the activity went a bit further than usual, at which point she resisted. She told Kris "You know I'm not into that; I'm not ready to do it with you yet." He got flustered, as she said was typical of him, but this time he became angry as well. Kris said Annie was responsible for him having a "permanent case of blue balls" and that she had to have sex with him or it would hurt his health. His claim was that being sexually aroused but ungratified caused an uncomfortable and unhealthy condition for men. He said Annie owed it to him not to tease him, and he knew she really wanted sex as much as he did.

As best she could, not being a physician (or a man), the professor explained Kris's condition. A state of pressure, swelling, and discomfort can develop in men as a result of arousal that doesn't consummate in ejaculation, and, over time, it can actually cause the testicles to take on a pale blueish tint. But the condition isn't permanent, as Kris claimed. It goes away shortly, as the build-up of fluid due to arousal retreats, is absorbed, or is ejaculated via masturbation. But here's the main point the professor tried to get across to Annie: The physical state termed "blue balls" is in no way a justification for sexual coercion or aggression. Kris had no right to make Annie feel guilty for arousing him by kissing and then not giving in to his insistence on sex because of the threat of some debilitating condition. On hearing this, Annie started to cry over the phone.

There was more to the story. Annie said she felt bad about making Kris angry, she cared about him, and she didn't want to do something that would hurt him physically because she really didn't know anything about blue balls. She'd had sex before in a prior relationship, but wasn't ready to have sex with Kris. But it turned out that Annie did have intercourse with Kris that night in the car. In Annie's perception, she didn't really say yes, she didn't say no—she just didn't resist when Kris started in again. But she kept saying no all the time in her head. She didn't enjoy the experience because she wasn't ready to go that far with Kris and she was worried someone would see them in the car. It wasn't until later that she started to question what had happened.

Was this a case of consensual sex or date rape? One could argue that this was a classic case of date rape because Annie felt coerced into sex; although she complied with Kris's desires, she didn't really consent because she kept saying no in her head. He should have stopped when she first said she didn't want to have sex. But what about Kris's point of view? What if he thought he was just being honest with Annie by telling her that he was frustrated and needed to have sex? He first got a "no" to sex, but later Annie didn't resist or say no, so things continued. Kris may have thought that he was just fulfilling his male role—that it's up to the guy to make the first move and the woman to resist. Then when the man keeps pressing, the woman gives in and gets what she really wanted all along. Whose interpretation is the right one? Is there a right one?

Answers to these questions reveal the complexity of the issue. A court dealing with a situation like this might find merit in both Annie's and Kris's interpretations. On Annie's side, the incident could be considered date rape because she initially said no to Kris's advances and later said no in her head as Kris continued. She may have felt powerless to stop Kris, since they had argued and he had gotten angry. However, a court might find merit in Kris's interpretation by believing that Annie was inconsistent—at first saying no, but when physical activity continued she made no attempt to push Kris away or say no again. If she was saying no in her head, Kris couldn't read her mind. At the core of this example, and so many like it, is the issue of consent. Communication—and the lack of it—is also at the core of the problem.

One lesson among many emerges from this story: A sexual situation like this involves power, but that power isn't always easy to detect or counter. In this situation, Kris used the power of persuasion by talking about a male condition he knew Annie probably wouldn't understand and by making it sound like a dire situation if she didn't comply. This is a classic "men have to have it" example in which one person controls events by declaring a "need," then claiming that the other person is at fault if she doesn't meet his needs. The result is that someone felt she had to do something she really didn't want to do. In Kris's mind, the incident was just sex, certainly not rape. Annie knew what had happened was wrong, but she had a hard time calling it rape. She couldn't fathom charging Kris with rape, but she ended their relationship right after this experience. It was clear that the event would stay with Annie a long time.

Communication and the Abuse of Power in Sexual Assault

Of special interest to our study of gender communication is the miscommunication that occurs in situations that end up as sexual assault and date rape. Just to be clear, we aren't labeling date rape a simple situation of miscommunication. That's as bad as calling sexual harassment "misbehavior," as we discussed earlier in this chapter. But some communication elements common to abusive episodes are worth talking about.

When Women Say "Yes" and "No"

Research indicates that men tend to interpret sexual messages from flirtatious behavior, while women tend to distinguish between behavior that is flirtatious or playful versus sexual (Abbey, 1982; Lee & Guerrero, 2001; Metts & Cupach, 1989). Communication scholars Lim and Roloff (1999) explored the critical issue of consent in sexual situations; their research indicated that verbal statements of consent are more clear and less likely to lead to misunderstanding than nonverbal actions. This research suggests that simply acting in a way that suggests consent or nonconsent is risky; it is wiser to use consistent verbal and nonverbal messages that clearly communicate what sexual activity is desired and acceptable and what isn't. Women and men alike are learning how critical it is to be as clear as possible when it comes to sex—even though this kind of communication is tough for many people.

We don't want to insinuate that women who are date raped are at fault for poor communication that somehow confused men. But as writer Stephen Schulhofer (1998) suggests, "Beneath the surface, in the messy, emotionally ambiguous real world of dating, petting, and sexual exploration, 'no' doesn't always mean no" (p. 59). Some women do give mixed messages about sexual activity, like saying no when their actions say yes or feigning resistance to sexual overtures in an effort to tease a man they want to have sex with. Some men think that a woman's no really doesn't mean no, but means "maybe," "try harder," or "try again."

Research at different universities from across two decades found evidence of mixed messages in sexual situations. Surveys of university students in Hawaii, Pennsylvania, Texas, and the Midwest found that upwards of 39 percent of women surveyed revealed "token resistance," meaning that they first said no to a man they had every intention of having sex with. These women reported that they wanted their initial no to be respected and their dates to wait for sex, and that they wanted to be "talked into" sex. If this is the case, then the mantra "no means no" that feminists and rape prevention activist groups have worked to get across is meaningless, or at least greatly undermined (Schulhofer, 1998).

Sometimes women send mixed signals for fear that, if they agree to sex too easily or quickly, they'll be seen as easy or slutty. They may even avoid discussing sex for the same reason, worried that a frank conversation will make them appear either nerdy or too overt about sex, as though they have "been around." But as all the research on this topic advocates, the best approach for women is to say no when they mean no and yes when they mean yes, avoiding game playing and pretense in romantic or sexual situations. Even if women think that sexual teasing and sending mixed signals heightens their own and the man's arousal, they should avoid such teasing because this behavior contributes to a greater problem: When a man who has been teased is with his next woman, will she handle things differently? If her no really means no, will the guy believe her or will he think she's playing a game?

When a Man Hears "No"

On the flip side, in some situations women say no and mean no, but the man chooses to reject that no. In sexual encounters, these men may try to turn a woman's no into a yes, by continuing to physically arouse their partner or by displaying anger or frustration with the intent of making the woman feel nervous, uncomfortable, or guilty enough to give in (as in Kris's behavior). However, some men work to unlearn these responses and to interpret a woman's no as actually meaning no. Researchers' advice is to take a woman's no at face value, assuming that no really does mean no—no questions asked nor disagreement voiced. Any actions beyond the woman's no are sexual violations, and sexual activity without agreement or consent is rape.

Everything you've learned about gender communication and personal effectiveness from this text applies with even more urgency to this situation of negotiating sexual waters with a relational partner. The principles behind the receiver orientation to communication and the value of expanding one's repertoire of communication to provide alternatives for confronting different situations are highly applicable and useful in sexual contexts.

Date Rape Prevention Programs

Many colleges and universities have implemented programs to prevent date rape. Research describes both the content and results of some of these programs designed to raise awareness in women and men about the definition of date rape and ways to avoid it (Baker & Meadows, 1997; Becky & Farren, 1997; Earle, 1996; Holcomb & Seehafer, 1996; Kier, 1996). One consistent tendency that emerged in these programs was that many students, both men and women, were unaware of the fact that some dating incidents were actually rape.

Something that engenders a great deal of resentment, regarding this whole topic of rape and sexual assault, is the focus on women in educational programs and literature, as though women are to blame for rape. Rapists are to blame for rape. The constant suggestion that women should learn how to prevent rape, as though they are responsible for whether or not a date ends in rape, contributes to the belief that rape is just a women's issue. Granted, women *should* become educated in preventing date rape; they *should* be clear and consistent with their communication with men. But date rape is another area, like sexual harassment, in which blame-the-victim attitudes are rampant. Most of the educational programs, films, and literature on date and stranger rape are aimed at teaching women how to walk defiantly, talk clearly, dress appropriately, and not do "stupid" things, like walking alone to their cars at night after class. This places the burden on women to prevent men from raping. As Ron Aaron (1997) wrote (in his article about rape in San Antonio, referenced earlier): "The extraordinary focus on what women should do to prevent rape reinforces one of the most troubling myths about rape, that victims not perpetrators are responsible for sexual assault. That's simply not true. Failing to lock doors and windows or going out alone at night doesn't cause rape. Indeed, it's not her responsibility to prevent rape. It's his obligation to stop doing it." So we ask: Where are the programs that teach men not to rape?

'Net Notes

One of the worst aspects of date rape is the silence—the silence someone experiences when they've survived a sexual assault, the way our society often silences persons on this topic, efforts even well-meaning people may make to downplay the "incident" or "sweep it under the rug." A non-threatening way to break the silence is to contact the National Crime Prevention Council at **www.ncpc.org**. This site offers current, easy-to-access information on the crimes of rape and sexual assault. The extensive section on date rape may be especially helpful to survivors, their family members, and their friends—to help all of us better understand this terrible problem.

Even greater silence is often experienced by male survivors of rape and sexual assault, because of a societal stigma about male victimization. If you or someone you know has survived this terrible crime, you may find assistance, in the privacy of your own computer, at **www.xris.com**. This Website offers links, books, educational films, and bibliographies on the topic, as well as a hotline for men who have been sexually assaulted and a listing of organizations that can assist survivors.

Crawford and Unger (2000) describe some innovative programs on college campuses that target all-male groups, such as fraternities and athletic teams, as well as community-based, male-led campaigns to stop sexual assault. But materials and programs geared for men on the topic of date rape are seriously lacking, and men need good information about this problem. So we start this section with advice to men, drawn from the limited available information from this point of view; we then move to advice for women.

Attention: Men

An excellent Website, simply entitled *Sexual Assault and Rape: Advice for Men* (1998), offers this current, helpful information.

1. Think about whether you really want to have sex with someone who doesn't want to have sex with you; how will you feel afterwards if your partner tells you she or he didn't want to have sex?
2. If you are getting a double message from a woman, speak up and clarify what she wants. If you find yourself in a situation with a woman who is unsure about having sex or is saying "no," back off. Suggest talking about it.
3. Be sensitive to women who are unsure whether they want to have sex. If you put pressure on them, you might be forcing them.
4. Do not assume you both want the same degree of intimacy. She might be interested in some sexual contact other than intercourse. There may be several kinds of sexual activity you might mutually agree to share.
5. Stay in touch with your sexual desires. Ask yourself if you are really hearing what she wants. Do not let your desires control your actions.

6. Communicate your sexual desires honestly and as early as possible.
7. Do not assume her desire for affection is the same as a desire for sex.
8. A woman who turns you down for sex is not necessarily rejecting you as a person; she is expressing her decision not to participate in a single act at that time.
9. No one asks to be raped. No matter how a woman behaves, she does not deserve to have her body used in ways she does not want.
10. The fact that you were intoxicated [or high] is not legal defense for rape. You are responsible for your actions, whether you are drunk or sober.
11. Be aware that a man's size and physical presence can be intimidating to a woman. Many victims report that the fear they felt based on the man's size and presence was the reason they did not fight back or struggle. (p. 1)

Attention: Women

Hughes and Sandler (1987) offer useful guidelines that are still applicable today to help minimize the potential for date rape. While this advice is aimed at women, men need to understand these points and be aware that acting on this advice may not come easily for some women. Hughes and Sandler suggest the following:

1. Examine your feelings about sex.
2. Set sexual limits for yourself and your partner or date.
3. Decide early if you would like to have sex, and communicate your decision clearly and firmly.
4. Do not give mixed messages; be alert to other unconscious messages you may be giving.
5. Be forceful and firm; don't worry about being "polite."
6. Be independent and aware—you can have input on dates about where you'd like to go, what you think is appropriate, and so on.
7. Do not do anything you do not want to just to avoid a scene or unpleasantness.
8. Be aware of specific situations in which you do not feel relaxed or in charge.
9. If things start to get out of hand, protest loudly, leave, or go for help.
10. Realize that drugs and alcohol are often present in date rape situations. (p. 3)

A Word about Rape Laws

In 1994, Congress passed the *Violence Against Women Act* (VAWA), a law created to provide federal protections for women because prosecutions of cases involving violence against women weren't being vigorously pursued in state courts (Tracey, 2000). Since its passage, various court rulings have affected the power of VAWA to protect women from sexual crimes. The laws governing the prosecution of various forms of rape are very complex and beyond the parameters of this chapter. As a whole, they are also archaic; our frustration with the status of rape laws also leads us to abbreviate a discussion of them. Rape laws seem to be at least two decades behind sexual harassment laws in terms of understanding the problem, placing blame where it appropriately belongs, and vindicating the abused. These laws are sender based, as opposed to the receiver-based laws for sexual harassment. Rape laws focus on a rapist's intentions, meaning what was in the mind of the accused during the incident.

Author Stephen Schulhofer (1998) outlines many problems with current laws, mainly their conceptualizations of force and consent. He explains, "Standards remain extraordinarily murky, especially for determining when a man's behavior amounts to prohibited force or when a woman's conduct signals her consent" (p. 56). The problem is an archaic view of force, meaning that jurors often don't view a woman's unwillingness as enough to prove rape. Even if she objects, "intercourse is still not considered rape or any other form of felonious assault unless the assailant used physical force or threatened bodily injury" (p. 56). Such actions as coerced penetration or pinning a victim down aren't considered force, in and of themselves. The force must be "something beyond the acts involved in intercourse—something that physically 'compels' the woman to submit" (p. 56). So if a rapist doesn't exert any force beyond subduing and penetrating a woman, the victim's only recourse, if she's going to successfully prosecute her attacker, is to fight back. And fighting back can sometimes cost someone her life.

Even if a rapist uses the "right" kind of force (in a court's view), many prosecutors won't go near rape cases because they are so difficult to win. The least frequent form of rape—stranger rape—has the best chance of being successfully prosecuted (Buzawa, 1995). Date rape prosecutions are prone to the same kind of "he said-she said" problem we discussed regarding sexual harassment. Except for situations of gang rape, most rapes occur in private. As law professor and rape survivor Susan Estrich (1993) explains, the "he said-she said" aspect that emerges in many rape trials has led to the so-called *nuts and sluts defense* of the accused rapist. According to Estrich, "Today, if you're trying to destroy a woman's credibility, you argue that she's sexually permissive (so she consented) and unstable (so she lied about it)" (p. 64).

Schulhofer (1998) reports that rape law reformers are working to extend the legal definition of force from physical violence to other types of coercion. But rape survivors face uphill battles trying to prove rape, punish rapists, and receive justice. We encourage rape survivors to seek justice in the courts and prosecutors to find the guts and determination to prosecute offenders, rather than instantly deciding a case doesn't have a chance. Rape laws in this country do little to deter rape, so we must work to try to reform them. Outdated rape laws are overturned or rewritten when survivors and prosecutors bring cases forward and persevere through the court system.

Parting Considerations about Sexual Assault and Rape

It's obvious that members of both sexes need to become more aware of the different forms of sexual assault, how prevalent rape is in our culture, what elements embedded in our society actually condone and reinforce the problem, how devastating rape is (particularly date rape), and what all of us can do to help combat this crime. It should be obvious to you that rape laws are in serious need of reform. But let us not be deterred by lousy laws; there are things that all of us can do on our campuses.

See if your campus has literature and educational programs on date rape, such as a "Take Back the Night" march. These marches exist on many campuses, typically as part of a celebration of Women's History Month. They honor survivors of rape and generate awareness of the problem. If there are no such programs on your campus, start one. Educate yourself about the best procedure to follow in the unfortunate chance you or a friend are sexually assaulted. For example, certain hospitals might have agreements with your institution to examine students and provide rape counseling. If you drive a friend or a friend drives you somewhere to get help, you need to know where to go. And what will be your response if you learn that someone is a date rapist? What are the legal responsibilities and implications of such knowledge?

As Hughes and Sandler (1987) explain, "Rape is violence. It strikes at the heart of the personal relationship between a man and a woman, how they treat each other, and how they respect each other's wishes" (p. 2). We can't bury our heads in the sand about this problem, pretending it doesn't happen. Look around your classrooms; there are rape survivors sitting there. Maybe you're one of them, but we hope not. Like sexual harassment, sexual assault isn't a woman's or a man's problem; it's a human problem that we all must work to overcome.

PARTNER VIOLENCE

What do the three areas we discuss in this chapter have in common? Certainly, the primary commonality is that sexual harassment, sexual assault and rape, and partner violence are all extreme abuses of power. They all involve one person's attempt to control, dominate, and render powerless another person. Another commonality is privacy, meaning that most abusive episodes occur behind closed doors, not in front of witnesses. Partner violence is a bit different from harassment and rape, in that it may occur within earshot or eyeshot of children. But there is a closed-doors quality to this too, in that violence in the home may be kept within the family and rarely spoken about outside the home. As we'll see in the next few pages, this closed-doors quality is one of the main problems in situations of domestic violence (as it is with harassment and rape as well).

Another common element across the three abuses is the tendency to blame the victim. We described this tendency in sexual harassment and assault contexts, but it is very typical of partner abuse as well. Most harassment, rape, and battering is done by men upon women. But remember, as we said in the opening pages of this chapter, it's important to try to keep any feelings of male-bashing to a minimum (if you have them at all), realizing that this material does not indict all *man*kind. Remember, because statistics show that the overwhelming majority of harassers, rapists, and batterers are male, we choose to talk about the problem in those terms. But we don't want to send the message that *all* men are abusive or that women *cannot be* abusive; we want men and women alike to become more outraged about these problems so that we can all do something about them. The final commonality across the three areas is that the laws for each are complex and in a constant state of flux as society continues to learn about and unmask these crimes. Let's first work on our language, then look at how pervasive the problem of domestic violence is in our culture.

The Language of Violence

Before we explore the many different terms for this kind of abuse, we want to ask you to join us in ridding the language of the phrase *rule of thumb*. You may not know the historical derivation of that phrase, but it refers to an old English law that made it legal for a husband to beat or whip his wife, as long as he used a stick or switch no larger than the width of his thumb (Hirshman, 1994). A statement like "A good rule of thumb is to . . ." can easily be rephrased to say "A good guideline to follow is to . . . ."

Family violence is probably the widest-ranging term because it encompasses child, spousal, and elderly abuse. Family violence is defined as "an act carried out by one family member against another family member that causes or is intended to cause physical or emotional pain or injury to that person" (Heffernan, Shuttlesworth, & Ambrosino, 1997, p. 364). Our focus is on abuse between adults, so terms such as *domestic violence, marital abuse, spousal abuse, battering,* and the most blatant term, *wife beating,* are more descriptive. But there are problems with these terms, too.

> *I tend to agree that celibacy for a time is worth considering, for sex is dirty if all it means is winning a man, conquering a woman, beating someone out of something, abusing each other's dignity in order to prove that I am a man, I am a woman.*
>
> —Toni Cade Bambara,
> author

It's Not about Political Correctness

Discussions about language don't arise out of a need to find the most politically correct term for this problem; it is important to use language that allows people to accurately, honestly communicate about the problem (Ashcraft, 2000). *Domestic violence* has been defined as "a crime of power and control committed mainly by men against women, a crime in which the perpetrator does not consult the victim's wishes and from which he will not let her escape" (Jones, 1994, p. 126). But one problem is that the term *domestic* tends to sanitize the abuse. As feminist scholar bell hooks (2000) explains, "For too long the term domestic violence has been used as a 'soft' term which suggests it emerges in an intimate context that is private and somehow less threatening, less brutal, than the violence that takes place outside the home" (p. 62). *Battering* is a term you hear often and one that we will use in this discussion, but it typically implies only physical abuse rather than other forms. Ann Jones (1994), author of *Next Time She'll Be Dead: Battering and How to Stop It,* describes problems with these two terms: "It makes the violence sound domesticated, like a special category of violence that is somehow different from other kinds—less serious. The more difficult term is 'battered woman,' because it suggests a woman who is more or less permanently black and blue and helpless. And of course most women who are abused and controlled by men don't think of themselves as battered women" (as in Jacobs, 1994, p. 56).

Wife beating leaves out husbands and other male partners, as well as persons in homosexual relationships who are abused. While the overwhelming majority of victims of abuse are female, a small percentage involves female abusers and male victims (Crary, 2001; Robinson, 1994). *Marital* or *spousal abuse* isn't as inclusive a term as *partner violence* because persons in both heterosexual and homosexual nonmarital relationships (those who cohabitate, date, or are separated or divorced) also suffer abuse. Abusers are referred to as *batterers, wife beaters,* or, as we found at one interesting Website, *intimate enemies* (*Women Killed,* 1998).

Yet another form of abuse is *courtship violence,* also known as *dating violence* or *premarital violence.* This abuse involves "acts of aggression occurring between young unmarried women and men" (Crawford & Unger, 2000, p. 492). Because the predominance of this abuse is carried out by young men on young women, it's also been termed *boyfriend violence.* Estimates are that between 25 and 40 percent of female teens have been assaulted by dates; over 70 percent of pregnant or parenting teens are beaten by their boyfriends. Most of these assaults involve pushing, shoving, slapping, and grabbing (Libby, 2001). A study conducted by the Family Research Laboratory at the University of New Hampshire showed that up to 28 percent of teenagers suffer dating violence, from verbal abuse to slaps in the face to battering and rape (Harris, 1996). In another national survey, over one-third of college women and men reported being physically aggressive

---

'Net Notes

Parents may be the last to know if their son or daughter is experiencing violence at the hands of a boyfriend or girlfriend. Dating or courtship violence is a very real problem, one which groups across the country have been addressing. Since 1991, Liz Claiborne Inc. has turned their attention to this issue; their newest offering to help parents is entitled "A Parent's Guide to Teen Dating Violence: 10 Questions to Start the Conversation." The guide and other educational materials can be found at **www.loveisnotabuse.com**. Another helpful resource can be found at **www.breakthecycle.org,** the site for a domestic violence prevention program entitled Break the Cycle, founded by Meredith Blake, who experienced an abusive relationship as a high school student.

Remember . . .

FAMILY VIOLENCE: An act perpetrated by one family member against another family member that causes or is intended to cause physical or emotional pain or injury.

DOMESTIC VIOLENCE: A crime of power and control in which a perpetrator does not consult a target's wishes and from which he or she will not let the target escape.

BATTERING: A form of domestic violence that implies only physical abuse rather than other forms.

PARTNER VIOLENCE: The broadest term, which can encompass psychological and/or physical violence occurring among married, separated, divorced, unmarried, homosexual, or cohabiting persons.

COURTSHIP/DATING/PREMARITAL VIOLENCE: A form of domestic violence that involves persons who are dating or in committed romantic relationships, but who have not yet legally formalized those relationships.

---

toward a date and receiving physical aggression from a date (White & Koss, 1991). Because the previous section of the chapter focused mostly on date rape, we're going to emphasize partner abuse in this last section. Much of the patterns and problems inherent in partner abuse apply to courtship violence as well.

Two Ways to Hurt Your Lover

Partner abuse is usually discussed in two forms: *physical* and *psychological*. Physical abuse ranges from a push or slap to a beating to the use of a weapon. Psychological abuse is a broad category that subsumes emotional and verbal abuse. Communication researchers have become interested in ways in which women and men exhibit verbal aggression, typically manifested in such things as severe criticism, intimidation, threats, humiliation (private and public), isolation, and degradation (Infante & Rancer, 1995; Infante, Sabourin, Rudd, & Shannon, 1990; Marshall, 1994). Research has also determined a connection between verbal aggression and physical violence (Olson, 2002; Sabourin, 1995; Sabourin & Stamp, 1995; White & Humphrey, 1994). While psychological abuse is more harmful and long-lasting than physical abuse, in most instances, the two go hand in hand. Psychological abuse destroys self-esteem and leaves devastating emotional scars; physical abuse often leaves more than emotional scars (Crawford & Unger, 2000).

The Extent of the Problem

How long has it taken you to read this far in this chapter? Twenty or thirty minutes? Forty-five minutes? Statistics indicate that a woman is battered in the United States every 15 seconds (Women's Action Coalition, WAC, 1993). Let's say you've worked through this material in 30 minutes. We'll do the math for you; in the time it's taken you to read this far in the chapter, 120 women have been beaten in this country.

An "Epidemic"

That's what the American Medical Association called partner violence in 1992 (Peach, 1998). FBI statistics (1995) show that in an average year, about 600,000 violent victimizations of women at the hands of intimates occur, compared to about 49,000 such victimizations against men. This rate of violence is consistent across racial and ethnic groups. But again, domestic violence is an underreported crime, mainly because of attitudes victims hold about this form of violence, as well as embarrassment and social pressures that can be roadblocks for victims who need help (Schneider Shevlin, 1994). Women are more likely to suffer violence from people they know than from strangers, whereas for men, it is the opposite (FBI, 1995). Ninety-five percent of partner abuse is perpetrated by men on women and 60 percent of beaten women are pregnant at the time of the abuse (Davis, 1995; WAC, 1993). Research has estimated that over half of all women, either in a marriage or a long-term relationship, will be hit at least once by their partners. In various studies, 25 to 35 percent of women visiting hospital emergency rooms and clinics had injuries resulting from partner violence (Davis, 1995; Hamberger, Saunders, & Hovey, 1992). Domestic violence is the leading cause of injury to American women aged 15 to 44—more than muggings, rapes, and car accidents combined (Attune, 2000).

From Abuse to Death

Many victims of partner abuse die at the hands of their abusers or as a result of severe injuries. According to FBI crime statistics, over 1000 women were murdered by their boyfriends or husbands in 1997 (FBI, 1998). Over twice as many women are murdered by their boyfriends or husbands as are killed by strangers (Kellerman, 1992). During the 1990s, estimates of women who were killed by their husbands, ex-husbands, or boyfriends constituted 28 percent of the total number of homicides of women in a given year at the low end (over 1,400 women) and 55 percent at the high end (Colburn, 1994; FBI, 1995). This compares to a low estimate of 3 percent (over 600 men) and a high of 20 percent of homicides in which men were killed by their wives, ex-wives, or girlfriends. Other statistics show that over half of the total murders of women are committed by former or current partners (Browne & Williams, 1993). One study found that half of the homicides of female partners were committed by abusive men from whom these women were separated (*General Facts*, 1998).

Abuse during Separation or Divorce

From a survey of middle-class marriages, 22 percent of divorced couples cited violence as the number one reason for their divorce (*General Facts*, 1998). But being separated or divorced doesn't exempt or protect a person from abuse. About 75 percent of calls to police for assistance and intervention with domestic violence occur after separation from a batterer (*General Facts*, 1998). (If you followed the O. J. Simpson criminal trial, you'll remember that Nicole Brown placed a 911 call for assistance after O. J. kicked down her door and threatened her; they were separated at the time.) Women who are separated suffer twice as much violence from their partners as divorced women, six times as much as married women, and 12 times as much as never-married women (*Sex Differences,* 1997).

Common Myths about Battering

Statistics for partner violence, like those for sexual assault and rape, are much lower than the reality because so much goes unreported. A high degree of shame and guilt is associated with partner violence, on both the part of the batterer and the battered. But a primary reason for underreporting this crime relates to *battering myths*—outdated, non-factual beliefs about relationships and the violence that can occur within them.

Myth #1: Everybody Does It

You'll be surprised at how many people still believe that wife beating is a normal part of marriage (Browne, 1993). Men used to joke with one another (and we fear some still do) about needing to "give the old lady a pop" or "a good thrashing," and keeping a woman in line by "smacking her around a bit." Only recently has society begun to treat partner violence as a crime and to decry those who batter their partners. Some of you are old enough to remember the greatly loved television series, *The Honeymooners.* While no physical domestic violence was portrayed on that show, Jackie Gleason's character, Ralph Cramden, used to pump his fist near his wife's face and yell "To the moon, Alice!" Lots of us thought that bit was hilarious, but would it be hilarious now?

Myth #2: The Victim Is to Blame, Again

Another myth about partner abuse is that the person being abused deserves it or is to blame for the abuse. This parallels blame-the-victim attitudes in both sexual harassment and sexual assault, but it is probably most often heard in relation to battering. As sociologists Heffernan, Shuttlesworth, and Ambrosino (1997) explain, "It is much easier for the general public to become concerned about abused children than abused women. Many individuals still subscribe to the myth that women who are beaten somehow deserve it, or that they must enjoy it or they would not put up with it" (p. 365). One study found that a significant number of ministers who counseled women in abusive marriages tended to hold traditional attitudes about marital roles and actually blamed battered victims for causing marital strife (Wood & McHugh, 1994).

A few researchers have interviewed male batterers for their accounts of how domestic violence occurred in their homes. In one study, male abusers blamed the victim, in that they described their wives (or partners) as the abusers and attempted to justify, excuse, minimize, or deny their own abusive behavior (Stamp & Sabourin, 1995). These findings parallel other studies. For example, sociologists Anderson and Umberson (2001) interviewed men in court-mandated domestic violence educational programs. These men believed that they were victims of a biased judicial system and that their female partners were responsible for the violence in their relationships. In another study, only a third of male abusers held themselves accountable for physical violence; 40 percent asserted that the violence was mutually provoked and 27 percent blamed their wives and denied any responsibility for their brutality (Sirles, Lipchik, & Kowalski, 1993). Researchers Dobash, Dobash, Cavanagh, and Lewis (1998) found that male abusers underestimated both their use of particular forms of violence and the frequency of that use.

One factor that leads some people to blame victims or to suggest that they make their plight worse relates to victims' communication. Communication researchers Rudd and Burant (1995) found that battered women used two main strategies during arguments that escalated into violence: (1) submissive strategies in an attempt to smooth over a conflict, and (2) aggressive strategies to escalate the conflict. These aggressive strategies fuel the perception that women are to blame for the battering they receive, but they are actually not inappropriate strategies. As Rudd and Burant explain, "Perhaps battered women's use of aggressive strategies are a means for them to escalate the inevitable violence so that the conflict will end. Abused women have often reported that the fear of not knowing when the violence is going to occur is as frightening as the violent act itself" (p. 141).

Myth #3: Only the Poor Are Abusive

Some people believe that partner abuse only occurs in low-income and minority families. While more abuse does occur among lower-income families in which one or both spouses are unemployed, partner abuse extends across all social classes, races, and ethnicities (FBI, 1995; Gelles & Straus, 1988). Again, the Simpson case reminds us that partner violence can occur within the wealthiest of households and among marriages of persons from different racial groups.

Myth #4: Gay and Lesbian Partners Are Never Abusive

Many of us adhere to the myth that partner abuse occurs only within heterosexual relationships, yet another disturbing aspect of this problem is its existence among gay and lesbian couples (Peach, 1998). Studies show that upwards of 37 percent of lesbians report having been in abusive relationships (Lie & Gentlewarrior, 1991; Lie, Schilit, Bush, Montagne, & Reyes, 1991). According to one study, gay men experience less frequent abuse than lesbians, but the violence inherent in their abuse is more severe (Waterman, Dawson, & Bologna, 1989). In one study, the brutality lesbian subjects reported involved pushing; shoving; hitting with fists or open hands; scratching or hitting the face, breasts, or genitals; and throwing things (Renzetti, 1989). These subjects reported psychological abuse as well as physical, primarily in the form of verbal threats.

Researchers Morrow and Hawxhurst (1989) provide four myths about women, in general, and lesbian relationships, in specific, that lead to secrecy surrounding lesbian abuse. First is the myth that because women are socialized to be less aggressive than men, they are incapable of brutalizing other women. While women tend to exhibit less aggression than men as a rule, they are certainly capable of being physically aggressive as a means of exerting power and control over another person. A second myth is that battering only occurs as a result of substance abuse or in clubs or bars. Substances may lead to or expedite a battering incident, but an urge to batter isn't necessarily prompted by substance abuse. A third is that because feminist lesbians are committed to equality in relationships, they do not batter. Don't equate homosexuality with a belief in equality in relationships (meaning not all lesbians are feminists). It is a stereotype to believe that a "nontraditional" relationship is automatically steeped in nontraditional thinking. Also, someone might believe in equality, but still be a batterer; the two aren't necessarily related because one is an ideological stance, the other is a behavior based on an emotional and psychological state. A final myth is that since lesbians are women, they are incapable of inflicting serious physical harm. Some say that, compared to opposite-sex violence, the brutality that members of the same sex can inflict on each other is worse because they know best how to hurt each other.

The violence within gay male relationships also tends to be shrouded in secrecy. Many gay men report having had more than one relationship in which they experienced physical violence. That violence typically includes punching with fists, beating the head against a wall or floor, and brutal rape. One victim recounted that his partner tried to run him down with his car. One of the reasons gay men batter relates to something we talked about back in Chapter 1, in our discussion of homophobia. The third definition we gave of homophobia was an in-group use of the term to mean gays' own hatred toward homosexuals and toward themselves for being homosexual. One of the causes of battering is rage that is an outgrowth of homophobia and self-hatred. Also, because gays are often ostracized or isolated in a society that's predominantly straight and because many are made to feel they must keep their sexual orientation a secret, they may turn their resulting rage onto one another.

Unlike for lesbian victims of violence, there are few, if any, men's shelters, or societally sanctioned places where gay men can get counseling or safe haven from an abusive partner. But as a society, we are becoming more aware of this unspoken problem, as books on the subject of gay and lesbian partner violence show. Some titles include David Island and Patrick Letellier's (1991) *Men Who Beat the Men Who Love Them: Battered Gay Men and Domestic Violence* and Kerry Lobel's (1986) *Naming the Violence: Speaking Out About Lesbian Battering.*

One thing to keep in mind is that, just like in heterosexual partner violence, one partner tends to be the dominant member of the relationship and does most, if not all, of the battering. You might think that in a same-sex abusive relationship both partners batter, but the reality is otherwise. In Renzetti's (1989) study, 78 percent of the subjects said that they did try at some point in the relationship to defend themselves against their batterers, but that most often these attempts were unsuccessful or only temporarily successful in stopping the abuse. A final, sad note to this topic is this: Because of homophobia and lack of training in same-sex abuse, abused gays and lesbians report that institutional sources of support, such as police officers, attorneys, and physicians, prove to be very unhelpful (Renzetti, 1992). Most of the help they are able to locate comes from women's shelters and community groups that support gay and lesbian causes (Morrow & Hawxhurst, 1989; Renzetti, 1992).

Abused Partners: How Do They Stand It? Why Do They Stay?

Explanations of the dynamic between an abuser and a victim vary. One body of literature suggests that women stay with abusers because their self-esteem is so low, their powerlessness so pervasive, that they blame themselves for their victimization. Another line of thought suggests that abused women don't blame themselves; they blame external factors or their abusers, which causes them to stay in abusive relationships as well. Let's explore both of these explanations.

Blaming Oneself

It's very hard for those who haven't experienced battering to understand the dynamic between abuser and abused. One group of authors explain it this way:

> Battering relationships are extreme versions of the traditional marriage relationship characterized by male dominance and female subordination. The subordinate wife in a battering relationship feels helpless and consequently develops unrealistically low self-esteem plus anxiety and depression. The dominant husband develops unrealistically inflated self-esteem and is dependent on the subordinate to maintain the feelings of power and self-aggrandizement. Each partner comes to require the other to satisfy needs developed as a consequence of the power imbalance. (Graham, Rawlings, & Rimini, 1988, pp. 220–221)

Important contributions in this area have been made by Lenore Walker, whose research coined the terms *learned helplessness* and *battered woman's syndrome.* Walker (1979, 1984, 1993) describes battered woman's syndrome as including a feeling of helplessness when battered women realize they cannot change their partners or their relationships with them. When a violent episode is followed by the batterer's guilt and begging for forgiveness, followed by acts of kindness, followed again by more brutality, battered women feel they have no way of protecting themselves or escaping. Many also fear that their partners will kill them (and possibly their children) if they leave, have their abuser arrested, or attempt to get a restraining order. This is a very real fear, because many abusive husbands threaten to kill their wives if they leave. For many women, economic pressures and commitments to children heighten the perception that they cannot leave the abusive relationship. This cycle creates a learned helplessness, which is so overpowering that some battered women see no solution but to kill their abusers or themselves.

Battered woman's syndrome helps us understand why women remain in abusive relationships. Abused women often believe they are so worthless and unlovable that they deserve the anger and violent displays their partners perpetrate on them. They tear themselves down psychologically, saying things like, "If I was just prettier (thinner, sexier, younger), he wouldn't be so disgusted with me" and "If I just say and do the right things, if I become a better housekeeper and cook and mother, he won't treat me this way." Lest you are thinking, "How pathetic that someone could let themselves get so low," think again. Even persons with the strongest of self-concepts and most optimistic of dispositions are susceptible to power abuses from ones they love.

In abusive episodes, targets tend not to panic or fly into an uncontrolled rage, but to exhibit what's been termed "frozen fright," a hysterical, emotional state of numbness or paralysis (Graham, Rawlings, & Rimini, 1988, p. 220). The most important thing is survival. When targets realize that their abuser holds power over their very lives, and when abusers allow targets to live, the targets' response is often a strange sort of gratitude. The shell-shock type of reaction after an abusive episode affects the psyche, causing the target to realize that she or he may be physically free for the moment, but still not psychologically free. The chronic physical and psychological trauma battered women experience may lead to *post traumatic stress disorder* (as we discussed with sexual harassment), not unlike victims of catastrophe, hostage crises, or other forms of violence report.

Studies conducted with women in shelters have taught us a good deal about how difficult it is to leave an abuser, since most situations involve a series of leaving and returning episodes, before a successful and final departure can be accomplished (Heise, Ellsberg, & Gottemoeller, 2002). Sheltered women have also helped us understand how violent episodes occur, including the forms of communication present before, during, and after a violent encounter. One of the main things we've learned backs up Walker's observations: Battered women can recall almost every detail of every violent incident, including what blows landed where, how he looked when he started the beating, the terrible things he said, and how he acted afterward (Rudd, Dobos, Vogl-Bauer, & Beatty, 1997).

Blaming the Abuser, Not the Abused

Another view about responses to abuse, one that differs from responses to both sexual harassment and assault, is that battered partners tend *not* to blame themselves for the violence they receive. Research from this perspective shows that abused wives are much more likely to blame external factors (such as their husband being unemployed or having a bad day at work) or their abuser's

---

Remember . . .

PHYSICAL ABUSE: Violent behavior that ranges from a push or slap to a beating to the use of a weapon.

PSYCHOLOGICAL ABUSE: A broad category of behavior that includes emotional and verbal abuse.

BATTERING MYTHS: Beliefs about partner violence that aren't based in fact.

LEARNED HELPLESSNESS: A sense that one cannot escape or protect oneself from an abusive partner, which causes self-esteem to plummet and dependency on the batterer to increase.

BATTERED WOMAN'S SYNDROME: A condition that battered women often experience which makes them feel they cannot escape or protect themselves; a result of repeatedly going through a cycle of being battered by a partner, begged for forgiveness, extended acts of kindness, followed by more acts of brutality, etc.

personality or behaviors (his feeling guilty about being a poor provider, his drinking, or his bad temper, which cause him to turn violent) (Cantos, Neidig, & O'Leary, 1993). While these are interesting responses that seem better than blaming the self, don't adopt a rosy interpretation too quickly. Those same external factors or character flaws often give women reasons to stay with their abusers. If the battered partner perceives the cause as external or about the abuser rather than about oneself, the partner thinks that these things can change. Thinking like "once he gets a job, this will stop" or "if he'd stop drinking we'd be happier" causes women to persevere in dangerous, dead-end (often literally) relationships.

Living Happily Ever After

Leah (not her real name) was an attractive woman in her mid-30s who came back to school to get her degree after her divorce. She (wisely) chose communication as her major and (wisely) enrolled in a gender communication course. On the day when the class focused on issues of violence and abuse, the instructor encouraged some of the students who had not yet entered the discussion to speak up if they had something to say or ask. At that point the instructor made eye contact with Leah, and she started to tell her story. This was clearly one of those instances where you could put a face to a problem.

Leah told us of her "picture perfect" courtship with her now ex-husband (whom we'll call Matt), how he seemed like the perfect man, or near perfect anyway. The couple was the envy of all their friends and they certainly made their parents proud when they married. But less than a year into the marriage, when their first child was six weeks old, Leah's husband erupted during an argument. She really didn't see it coming; she had no hints that he was capable of being brutal. In all the time they'd dated and been engaged he'd never raised a hand to her. But it happened with her infant son just down the hall in their home.

Matt's anger was exacerbated by his drinking. The episodes became more frequent, as many days he would leave work early and head to a bar, drink for the rest of the afternoon, and arrive home that night in an abusive rage. A typical evening involved Matt slapping and punching Leah, yelling and calling her obscene names, and threatening to "really teach her a lesson" if she left him. She learned quickly how to cover bruises with makeup. A day or two later, Matt would show the typical batterer's remorse for "losing his temper" and Leah would try to convince herself that it wouldn't happen again. But it did happen again; she never knew what would trigger a violent episode. Her self-esteem plummeted; she constantly questioned herself about what she was doing wrong and what she could do better to stave off Matt's anger. She tiptoed through her life, but it seemed that nothing she tried worked.

Finally, Leah contacted Matt's parents and told them what was going on. At first they denied that their precious son could be capable of such horrible behavior. Then they downplayed it, calling it a "misunderstanding," "a show of temper," and "having a bad day." On several occasions they blamed Leah, saying that she must have done something to make Matt act this way. After Leah made repeated calls to Matt's parents to report yet another beating, they finally offered to help, but this is how: When Matt went out drinking or came home drunk, Leah would call his parents; they would pick him up, take him to their house, and keep him there until the next day when he sobered up. That way they could keep him from "misbehaving" or "throwing a fit."

Knowing that Leah was divorced, the instructor in the class asked how Leah finally managed to pull herself out of the relationship and get a divorce. She said, "Well, after about 10 years of this, I decided...." The instructor had to interrupt because she, and no doubt the other students in the class, were thinking, "TEN years?" Leah said, "Yes, I put up with it for 10 years, all the while thinking it would stop." It took her another year to untangle from the relationship. She still has tremendous emotional scars from the experience, not only from Matt but from his parents as well for their role in protecting the abuser and leaving their daughter-in-law and grandchild in a life-threatening situation.

Leah experienced much of what Walker describes as battered woman's syndrome—feelings of helplessness, terror, dependency, and rage, mixed with strange feelings of love and commitment. Those mixed emotions allowed her to tolerate for 10 years what seems to us—those of us who haven't experienced battering—to be an intolerable situation. She received a divorce and custody of their son and began putting herself and her life back together. She told everyone in class that she'd often heard the phrase "never say never," but she wanted to reject that and say that she would never, NEVER again tolerate a man who tried to control her. If she stayed single the rest of her life, if she never had another romantic relationship with a man, that was fine. She hoped she might meet someone wonderful and was open to the possibility, but she didn't feel less of a woman because she wasn't in a relationship or marriage. She knew that she'd never put up with an abuser again.

A Word about Partner Violence Laws

Statistics show that police are more likely to respond within five minutes if an offender is a stranger than a person known to a female victim (Bureau of Justice Statistics, 1994). One study found that a majority of battered women actively attempt to secure help and protection from an abuser by contacting police, lawyers, shelters, counselors, and ministers (Hutchison & Hirschel, 1998). But approximately 90 percent of all family violence defendants are never prosecuted (*Response from the Criminal Justice System*, 1993).

Feminist attorneys are working to reform partner violence laws, the primary impetus being that many battered women who suffer repeated physical and psychological abuse, and fear their children will be the next victims, resort to killing their abusive partners. According to one source, women serving prison sentences for homicide convictions are twice as likely to have killed an abusive partner than a relative, friend, or stranger (Snell, 1991). Many attorneys consider battered woman's syndrome to be a mitigating circumstance that should cause judges and juries to view these homicides differently. However, as author Martha Mahoney (1998) explains, "litigation and judicial decision-making in cases of severe violence reflect implicit or explicit assumptions that domestic violence is rare or exceptional" (p. 324).

A significant legal development was the passage in 1994 of the *Violence Against Women Act* (VAWA), which we alluded to in the earlier section on sexual assault and rape. This act makes it a criminal offense to cross state lines to inflict violence upon one's spouse; it also enforces protection orders from state to state (Hirshman, 1994). A civil rights component of the VAWA allows women to sue their attackers in federal court for both punitive and compensatory damages. The civil nature of this component increases the chances of victims successfully prosecuting batterers because the standards of proof in civil actions are less stringent than in criminal actions. Law professor Linda Hirshman (1994) asserts, "The VAWA marks the first time in history that the violence women face in their own homes will be taken seriously by the government whose mandate it is to protect them" (p. 47).

Shelters Give Support and Hope

Women's shelters are safe havens for victims of partner violence and their children. Besides providing temporary room and board, as well as counseling for abused women (and in some locations for abused men as well), most offer 24-hour crisis hotlines so that abuse survivors can call and receive support and advice. In 1964, a group of women in San Gabriel Valley, California, opened the first refuge for battered women in the United States, called Haven House. In the early 1970s, the first hotline for battered women was created in St. Paul, Minnesota (Gillespie, 1994a). In the mid 1990s, one successful shelter-sponsored program was the Clothesline Project, in which battered women designed T-shirts to depict their experiences with abuse. Many locations in the country displayed clotheslines of these T-shirts on hangers as a means of creating awareness of the problem (Garza, 1996).

Not all cities have women's shelters. Here's a revealing statistic: There are three times as many animal shelters in the United States as there are battered women's shelters (Majority Staff of the Senate Judiciary Committee, 1992). As one authority explains, "Unfortunately we need a lot more shelters, because the problem is so great that they're turning away many women. They do save a great many lives. But what they've really done is save the lives of *men*. The rate of women killing men has gone down, and its decline began with the advent of battered women's shelters" (Jones, as in Jacobs, 1994, p. 59).

Parting Considerations about Partner Violence

As you now realize, partner violence is an enormous problem that crosses boundaries of sex, sexual orientation, race, class, educational level, age, and nationality. It's becoming less and less a silent destroyer of families and lives as survivors emerge, tell their stories, and give other abused persons hope. From outsiders' perspectives, none of us can truly know the depth of despair this kind of victimization causes. We'll have to take the word of people who have experienced it—and there are far more of them than we'd like to think.

A recent magazine article had some great words of advice about bringing men into the conversation about violence against women (Edgar, 2002). The author points out that, like programs for sexual assault and rape, much of the educational efforts on partner violence are aimed at women. Public service ads tend to focus on raising women's awareness, encouraging them to get out of abusive relationships, and offering information on where to get help. While these efforts have been successful, as polls indicate that women's understanding of the problem has increased, they reinforce the belief that domestic violence is a woman's issue. As we've seen for other forms of power abuses, that belief isn't helpful. So, our challenge to readers is for us all—men and women alike—to give our attention to this issue and decide what we can do about it. If you're in an abusive relationship, perhaps the information in this chapter will give you options and maybe some hope. If you know someone who is being abused, perhaps you now know more about the problem, what to do, and how to help. We'll end this section with the eloquent words of Marcia Ann Gillespie, editor of *Ms.,* as she wrote for a special edition of the magazine about the crime of partner violence:

> For the sake of all the women in this world who've been killed—whose names we will never know—for all the women who are beaten, who have been beaten and brutalized, for my sake, and yours, and for our daughters, and their daughters, and yes, for the sake of men's souls, let us mobilize as never before to ensure that women are protected, abusers are truly held accountable for their actions, our communities are held responsible for putting an end to the violence, and our nations acknowledge that men's violence against women is a human rights violation. Society is responsible for allowing domestic violence to flourish—and for making it stop. (1994b, p. 1)

CONCLUSION

You're probably glad you made it through this chapter; we realize it's a drain to consider all the terrible things people do to one another. It was a drain to research these topics and write about them, but we're sure you'll agree they're extremely important. We provided statistics and research findings in an effort to bring you the most relevant information possible, but we also put a face on each of these problems. Many of you were probably able to substitute a more familiar face for the people in our stories—Olivia and Bernie, Annie and Kris, Leah and Matt. The faces of the people who have suffered abuse are more real, more meaningful than all the statistics and research in the world.

We have to think about ways people use and abuse power in our society and across the world. Burying our heads in the sand, not wanting to believe that our fellow human beings commit such atrocities, not wanting to do anything to stop it, makes us part of the problem, not the solution. One of the co-authors of this text often uses this adapted phrase, "Pick ye rebellions where ye may." Perhaps one of your own personal rebellions against injustice may be to see that sexual harassment, sexual assault and rape, or partner violence never happen to you and the ones you love.

Discussion Starters

1. Imagine that you were an attorney representing either Olivia or Bernie from our sexual harassment case study in this chapter. Knowing what you now know about harassment, how would you prosecute or defend Bernie and the company in a harassment suit? What would be the weaknesses or gray areas you might point out?

2. Whether you are female or male, think about how you would react if you were sexually harassed on the job. (Perhaps some of you have experienced it. If so, how did you react?) Do you imagine you'd respond by avoiding or defusing the situation or would you attempt to negotiate or confront the harasser? What would be some possible risks of confronting the harasser, if he or she is your boss rather than a coworker?

3. Imagine that you (and an organization you belong to on campus) were asked to present a date rape awareness and prevention program on campus. Knowing what you now know about this serious problem, what would you choose to highlight in such a program? Would you spend equal amounts of time teaching men not to rape as you might teaching women how to prevent their own victimization?

4. Why do you think people continue to adhere to myths about rape and battering? Are these forms of abuse just too terrible to face, so we manufacture false ideas about them? Knowing that these myths exist because somebody believes them, how can you expose and debunk them?

5. If it were in your power to change the existing laws or write new ones for sexual harassment, sexual assault and rape, or partner violence (or all of these problems), what laws would you write? What gaps exist in current law that need to be covered?

References

Aaron, R. (1997, February 25). Don't blame victim of sexual violence. *San Antonio Express-News.* [On-line]. Feminista! Available: http://www.feminista.com

Abbey, A. (1982). Sex differences in attributions for friendly behavior: Do males misperceive females' friendliness? *Journal of Personality and Social Psychology, 42,* 830–838.

Abbey, A., & Harnish, R. J. (1995). Perception of sexual intent: The role of gender, alcohol consumption, and rape supportive attitudes. *Sex Roles, 32,* 297–314.

Adams-Roy, J., & Barling, J. (1998). Predicting the decision to confront or report sexual harassment. *Journal of Organizational Behavior, 19,* 329–336.

Alberts, J. K. (1992). Teasing and sexual harassment: Double-bind communication in the workplace. In L. A. M. Perry, L. H. Turner, & H. M. Sterk (Eds.), *Constructing and reconstructing gender: The links among communication, language, and gender* (pp. 185–196). Albany: State University of New York Press.

Anderson, K. L., & Umberson, D. (2001). Gendering violence: Masculinity and power in men's accounts of domestic violence. *Gender & Society, 15,* 358–380.

Andonian, K. K., & Droge, D. (1993, February). *Verbal aggressiveness and sexual violence in dating relationships: An exploratory study of antecedents of date rape.* Paper presented at the meeting of the Western States Communication Association, Albuquerque, NM.

Angier, N. (2000, June/July). Biological bull. *Ms.,* 80–82.

Ashcraft, C. (2000). Naming knowledge: A language for reconstructing domestic violence and systemic gender inequity. *Women & Language, 23,* 3–10.

Attune. (2000, Fall). Newsletter of the Tennessee Technological University Women's Center and the Commission on the Status of Women Attuned to Today's Woman, 7, 1; 4.

Baker, B. J., & Meadows, M. (1997). Two year college students and date rape: An empowerment model. (ERIC Document Reproduction Service No. ED 409 067)

Baker, M. (1992, February). Sexual shock and the emergence of the new man. *M Magazine,* 69–75.

Becker, E. (2000, May 14). Sexual harassment kept under wraps, female officers say. *New York Times* News Service, as reported in *Corpus Christi Caller Times,* p. A20.

Becky, D., & Farren, P. M. (1997). Teaching students how to understand and avoid abusive relationships. *School Counselor, 44,* 303–308.

Bennett-Alexander, D. (1998). Same-gender sexual harassment: The Supreme Court allows coverage under Title VII. *Labor Law Journal, 49,* 927–948.

Benson, K. (1984). Comment on Crocker's "An analysis of university definitions of sexual harassment." *Signs, 9,* 516–519.

Berryman-Fink, C. (1993). Preventing sexual harassment through male-female communication training. In G. L. Kreps (Ed.), *Sexual harassment: Communication implications* (pp. 267–280). Cresskill, NJ: Hampton.

Berryman-Fink, C., & Vanover Riley, K. (1997). The effect of sex and feminist orientation on perceptions in sexually harassing communication. *Women's Studies in Communication, 20,* 25–44.

Bingham, S. G. (1991). Communication strategies for managing sexual harassment in organizations: Understanding message options and their effects. *Journal of Applied Communication, 19,* 88–115.

Bingham, S. G. (1996). Sexual harassment: On the job, on the campus. In J. T. Wood (Ed.), *Gendered relationships* (pp. 233–252). Mountain View, CA: Mayfield.

Booth-Butterfield, M. (1986). Recognizing and communicating in harassment-prone organizational climates. *Women's Studies in Communication, 9,* 42–51.

Brail, S. (1996). The price of admission: Harassment and free speech in the wild, wild west. In L. Cherny & E. R. Weise (Eds.), *Wired women: Gender and new realities in cyberspace* (pp. 141–157). Seattle: Seal.

Browne, A. (1993). Violence against women by male partners: Prevalence, outcomes, and policy implications. *American Psychologist, 48,* 1077–1087.

Browne, A., & Williams, K. R. (1993). Gender, intimacy, and lethal violence: Trends from 1976 to 1987. *Gender & Society, 7,* 78–98.

Bureau of Justice Statistics. (1994). *Violence against women: A national crime victimization survey report.* [On-line]. Available: http://www.ojp.usdoj.gov

Burt, M. R. (1980). Cultural myths and supports for rape. *Journal of Personality and Social Psychology, 38,* 217–230.

Buzawa, E. (1995). Responding to crimes of violence against women: Gender differences versus organization imperatives. *Crime and Delinquency, 41,* 443–466.

Cachie, L., & deMan, A. F. (1997). Correlates of sexual aggression among male university students. *Sex Roles, 37,* 451–457.

Calhoun, K. S., Bernat, J. A., Clum, G. A., & Frame, C. L. (1997). Sexual coercion and attraction to sexual aggression in a community sample of young men. *Journal of Interpersonal Violence, 12,* 392–406.

Cantos, A. L., Neidig, P. H., & O'Leary, K. D. (1993). Men's and women's attributions of blame for domestic violence. *Journal of Family Violence, 8,* 289–302.

Carroll, C. M. (1993, Winter). Sexual harassment on campus: Enhancing awareness and promoting change. *Educational Record,* 21–26.

Casey, T., Desai, S., & Ulrich, J. (1998, Fall). Supreme Court unpredictable on harassment and sex. *National NOW Times,* pp. 6, 15.

Castaneda, C. J. (1992, August 3). Tailhook investigation "no help." *USA Today,* p. 3A.

Clair, R. P. (1992, November). *A critique of institutional discourse employed by the "Big Ten" universities to address sexual harassment.* Paper presented at the meeting of the Speech Communication Association, Chicago, IL.

Clair, R. P. (1998). *Organizing silence.* Albany: State University of New York Press.

Clair, R. P., McGoun, M. J., & Spirek, M. M. (1993). Sexual harassment responses of working women: An assessment of current communication-oriented typologies and perceived effectiveness of the response. In G. L. Kreps (Ed.), *Sexual harassment: Communication implications* (pp. 209–233). Cresskill, NJ: Hampton.

Cloud, J. (1998, March 23). Sex and the law. *Time,* 48–54.

Cochran, C. C., Frazier, P. A., & Olson, A. M. (1997). Predictors of responses to unwanted sexual attention. *Psychology of Women Quarterly, 21,* 207–226.

Colburn, D. (1994, March 15). When violence begins at home: AMA conference addresses "problem of shocking dimension." *The Washington Post.*

Cortina, L. M., Swan, S., Fitzgerald, L. F., & Waldo, C. (1998). Sexual harassment and assault: Chilling the climate for women in academia. *Psychology of Women Quarterly, 22,* 419–441.

Crary, D. (2001, August 12). Male victims of domestic violence are asking for more support. Associated Press, as reported in *Corpus Christi Caller Times,* p. A25.

Crawford, M., & Unger, R. (2000). *Women and gender: A feminist psychology* (3rd ed.). New York: McGraw-Hill.

Crichton, S. (1993, October 25). Sexual correctness: Has it gone too far? *Newsweek,* 52–56.

Davis, L. (1995). Domestic violence. In *Encyclopedia of social work* (Vol. 1, pp. 780–789). Washington, DC: National Association of Social Work (NASW).

DeJudicibus, M., & McCabe, M. P. (2001). Blaming the target of sexual harassment: Impact of gender role, sexist attitudes, and work role. *Sex Roles, 44,* 401–417.

Dobash, R. P., Dobash, R. E., Cavanagh, K., & Lewis, R. (1998). Separate and intersecting realities: A comparison of men's and women's accounts of violence against women. *Violence Against Women, 4,* 382–414.

Dougherty, D. S. (2001). Sexual harassment as [dys]functional process: A feminist standpoint analysis. *Journal of Applied Communication Research, 29,* 372–402.

Dubois, C. (1998). An emotional examination of same- and other-gender sexual harassment in the workplace. *Sex Roles, 39,* 731–747.

Earle, J. P. (1996). Acquaintance rape workshops: Their effectiveness in changing the attitudes of first year college students. *NASPA Journal, 34,* 2–18.

Eaves, M. H. (1992, November). *A male-dominated legal system: A feminist response to statutory rape.* Paper presented at the meeting of the Speech Communication Association, Chicago, IL.

Edgar, J. (2002, Summer). Stopping violence against women: Bring men into the conversation. *Ms.,* 7.

Ehrhart, J. K., & Sandler, B. R. (1985). *Campus gang rape: Party games.* Washington, DC: Project on the Status and Education of Women, Association of American Colleges.

Elliott, L., & Brantley, C. (1997). *Sex on campus: The naked truth about the real sex lives of college students.* New York: Random House.

E-mail has men in trouble. (1995, November 16). Associated Press, Ithaca, NY.

Estrich, S. (1993, October 25). Balancing act. *Newsweek,* 64.

Equal Employment Opportunity Commission. (1980). Guidelines on discrimination because of sex. *Federal Register, 45,* 74676-74677.

Equal Employment Opportunity Commission. (2002). [On-line]. *Sexual harassment charges: EEOC & FEPAs combined, FY 1992-FY 2002.* Available: http://www.eeoc.gov/stats/harass

Federal Bureau of Investigation. (1989). *Crime in the United States: Uniform crime reports.* Washington, DC: U.S. Department of Justice.

Federal Bureau of Investigation. (1995). *Violence against women: Estimates from the redesigned survey, August 1995.* [On-line]. Available: http://www.ojp.usdoj.gov

Federal Bureau of Investigation. (1998). *Uniform Crime Reports.* Washington, DC: U.S. Department of Justice.

Federal Bureau of Investigation. (2002). *Summary of the Uniform Crime Reporting (UCR) Program.* [On-line]. Available: http://www.fbi.gov

Fitzgerald, L. F. (1993). Sexual harassment: A research analysis and agenda for the 1990s. *Journal of Vocational Behavior, 42,* 5–27.

Foss, K. A., & Rogers, R. A. (1992, February). *Observations on the Clarence Thomas-Anita Hill hearings: Through the lens of gender.* Paper presented at the meeting of the Western States Communication Association, Boise, ID.

Fuentes, A. (1997, November-December). Crime rates are down . . . but what about rape? *Ms.,* 19–22.

Garza, T. Z. (1996, April 30). Women's Shelter gives students a dose of reality. *Island Waves,* p. 9.

Geist, P., & Townsley, N. (1997, November). *"Swept under the rug" and other disappearing acts: Legitimate concerns for university's sexual harassment policy and procedures.* Paper presented at the meeting of the National Communication Association, Chicago, IL.

Gelles, R. J., & Straus, M. A. (1988). *Intimate violence.* New York: Simon & Schuster.

General facts about domestic violence. (1998). [On-line]. Available: http://www.newcountrycanada.com

Gerdes, L. I. (1999). Introduction. In L. I. Gerdes (Ed.), *Sexual harassment: Current controversies* (pp. 12–14). San Diego: Greenhaven.

Gillespie, M. A. (1994a, September-October). Domestic violence. *Ms.,* 33.

Gillespie, M. A. (1994b, September-October). Memories to keep. *Ms.,* 1.

Good, G. E., Heppner, M. J., Hillenbrand-Gunn, T. L., & Wang, L. (1995). Sexual and psychological violence: An exploratory study of predictors in college men. *Journal of Men's Studies, 4,* 59–71.

Graham, D. L. R., Rawlings, E., & Rimini, N. (1988). Survivors of terror. In K. Yello & M. Bograd (Eds.), *Feminist perspectives on wife abuse* (pp. 217–233). Newbury Park, CA: Sage.

Gruber, J. E. (1989). How women handle sexual harassment: A literature review. *Sociology and Social Research, 74,* 3–7.

Gruber, J. E. (2002). The impact of male work environments and organizational policies on women's experiences of sexual harassment. In P. J. Dubeck & D. Dunn (Eds.), *Workplace/women's place: An anthology* (2nd ed.) (pp. 90–97). Los Angeles: Roxbury.

Hamberger, L. K., Saunders, D. G., & Hovey, M. (1992). The prevalence of domestic violence in community practice and rate of physician inquiry. *Family Medicine, 24,* 283–287.

Harris, L. (1996, September 22). The hidden world of dating violence. *Parade Magazine,* 4–6.

Haunani Solomon, D., & Miller Williams, M. L. (1997). Perceptions of social-sexual communication at work: The effects of message, situation, and observer characteristics on judgments of sexual harassment. *Journal of Applied Communication Research, 25,* 196–216.

Heffernan, J., Shuttlesworth, G., & Ambrosino, R. (1997). *Social work and social welfare* (3rd ed.). New York: West.

Heise, L., Ellsberg, M., & Gottemoeller, M. (2002). Is domestic violence best treated as a gender crime? In E. L. Paul (Ed.), *Taking sides: Clashing views on controversial issues in sex and gender* (2nd ed.) (pp. 226–234). New York: McGraw-Hill/Dushkin.

Hickson, M. III., Grierson, R. D., & Linder, B. C. (1991). A communication perspective on sexual harassment: Affiliative nonverbal behaviors in asynchronous relationships. *Communication Quarterly, 39*, 111–118.

Hill, A. (2002, Spring). The nature of the beast: What I've learned about sexual harassment. *Ms.*, 84–85.

Hippensteele, S., & Pearson, T. C. (1999). Responding effectively to sexual harassment. *Change, 31*, 48–54.

Hirshman, L. (1994, September-October). Making safety a civil right. *Ms.*, 44–47.

Holcomb, D. R., & Seehafer, R. W. (1996). Enhancing dating attitudes through peer education as a date rape prevention strategy. *Peer Facilitator Quarterly, 12*, 16–20.

hooks, b. (2000). *Feminism is for everybody: Passionate politics.* Cambridge, MA: South End Press.

Howey, N. (2001, February/March). By any other name. *Ms.*, 87–89.

Hughes, J. O., & Sandler, B. R. (1987). *"Friends" raping friends: Could it happen to you?* Washington, DC: Project on the Status and Education of Women, Association of American Colleges.

Hutchison, I. W., & Hirschel, J. D. (1998). Abused women. *Violence Against Women, 4*, 436–456.

Infante, D. A., & Rancer, A. S. (1995). Argumentativeness and verbal aggressiveness: A review of recent theory and research. *Communication Yearbook, 19*, 319–351.

Infante, D. A., Sabourin, T. C., Rudd, J. E., & Shannon, E. A. (1990). Verbal aggression in violent and nonviolent marital disputes. *Communication Quarterly, 38*, 361–371.

Island, D., & Letellier, P. (1991). *Men who beat the men who love them: Battered gay men and domestic violence.* Binghamton, NY: Haworth.

Ivy, D. K. (1999). *"Monica madness": A feminist look at language in the Clinton sex scandal.* Unpublished manuscript.

Ivy, D. K., & Hamlet, S. (1996). College students and sexual dynamics: Two studies of peer sexual harassment. *Communication Education, 45*, 149–166.

Jacobs, C. (1993, February). *Giving students a corporate picture: Sexual harassment in the workplace.* Paper presented at the meeting of the Western States Communication Association, Albuquerque, NM.

Jacobs, G. (1994, September-October). Where do we go from here? An interview with Ann Jones. *Ms.*, 56–63.

Jones, A. (1994). *Next time she'll be dead: Battering and how to stop it.* Boston: Beacon.

Kellerman, A. (1992). Men, women, and murder. *Journal of Trauma*, 1–5.

Kelly, L., & Radford, J. (1996). "Nothing really happened": The invalidation of women's experiences of sexual violence. In M. Hester, L. Kelly, & J. Radford (Eds.), *Women, violence, and male power: Feminist activism, research, and practice.* Buckingham, England: Open University Press.

Kier, F. J. (1996, January). *Acquaintance rape on college campuses: A review of the literature.* Paper presented at the meeting of the Southwest Education Research Association, New Orleans, LA.

King, J. (1993, September-October). Harassment on-line. *New Age Journal*, 20.

Koss, M. P., Gidycz, C. A., & Wisniewski, N. (1987). The scope of rape: Incidence and prevalence of sexual aggression and victimization in a national sample of higher education students. *Journal of Consulting and Clinical Psychology, 55*, 162–170.

Koss, M. P., & Harvey, M. R. (1991). *The rape victim.* New York: Sage.

Kreps, G. L. (1993). Introduction: Sexual harassment and communication. In G. L. Kreps (Ed.), *Sexual harassment: Communication implications* (pp. 1–5). Cresskill, NJ: Hampton.

Laabs, J. (1998). Sexual harassment: New rules, higher stakes. *Workforce, 34–42.*

Lee, J. W., & Guerrero, L. K. (2001). Types of touch in cross-sex relationships between coworkers: Perceptions of relational and emotional messages, inappropriateness, and sexual harassment. *Journal of Applied Communication Research, 29, 197–220.*

Libby, L. (2001, February 11). Many endure abuse to fit in and feel loved. *Corpus Christi Caller Times,* pp. H1, H3.

Lie, G-Y., & Gentlewarrior, S. (1991). Intimate violence in lesbian relationships: Discussion of survey findings and practical implications. *Journal of Social Service Research, 15,* 41–59.

Lie, G-Y., Schilit, R., Bush, J., Montagne, M., & Reyes, L. (1991). Lesbians in currently aggressive relationships: How frequently do they report aggressive past relationships? *Violence and Victims, 6,* 121–135.

Lim, G. Y., & Roloff, M. E. (1999). Attributing sexual consent. *Journal of Applied Communication Research, 27,* 1–23.

Lobel, K. (Ed.). (1986). *Naming the violence: Speaking out about lesbian battering.* Seattle: Seal.

Loredo, C., Reid, A., & Deaux, K. (1995). Judgments and definitions of sexual harassment by high school students. *Sex Roles, 32,* 29–45.

MacKinnon, C. A. (2002). Should Title VII apply to sexual harassment between individuals of the same sex? In E. L. Paul (Ed.), *Taking sides: Clashing views on controversial issues in sex and gender* (2nd ed.) (pp. 152–163). Guilford, CT: McGraw-Hill/Dushkin.

Mahoney, M. R. (1998). Legal images of battered women (excerpt). In L. J. Peach (Ed.), *Women in culture: A women's studies anthology* (pp. 323–338). Malden, MA: Blackwell.

Majority Staff of the Senate Judiciary Committee. (1992). *Violence against women: A week in the life of America.* Washington, DC: Congressional Printing Office.

Malamuth, N. M., & Brown, L. (1994). Sexually aggressive men's perceptions of women's communication: Testing three explanations. *Journal of Personality and Social Psychology, 47,* 699–712.

Malamuth, N. M., Sockloskie, R. M., Koss, M. P., & Tanaka, J. S. (1991). Characteristics of aggressors against women: Testing a model using a national sample of college students. *Journal of Consulting and Clinical Psychology, 59,* 670–681.

Malamuth, N. M., & Thornhill, N. W. (1994). Hostile masculinity, sexual aggression, and gender-biased domineeringness in conversations. *Aggressive Behavior, 20,* 185–194.

Markert, J. (1999). Sexual harassment and the communication conundrum. *Gender Issues, 17,* 34–52.

Marshall, L. L. (1994). Physical and psychological abuse. In W. R. Cupach & B. H. Spitzberg (Eds.), *The dark side of interpersonal communication* (pp. 281–311). Hillsdale, NJ: Erlbaum.

Maypole, D. E. (1986). Sexual harassment of social workers at work: Injustice within? *Social Work, January-February,* 29–34.

McKinney, K., & Maroules, N. (1991). Sexual harassment. In E. Grauerholz & M. A. Koralewski (Eds.), *Sexual coercion* (pp. 29–44). Lexington, MA: Lexington Books.

Metts, S., & Cupach, W. R. (1989). The role of communication in human sexuality. In K. McKinney & S. Sprecher (Eds.), *Human sexuality: The societal and interpersonal context* (pp. 139–161). Norwood, NJ: Ablex.

Meyer, M., & Johnson, R. (1999, October). *The "F- word" as a predictor of date rape myth acceptance.* Paper presented at the meeting of the Organization for the Study of Communication, Language, and Gender, Wichita, KS.

Michals, D. (1997, March-April). Cyber-rape: How virtual is it? *Ms.,* 68–73.

Milburn, M. A., Mather, R., & Conrad, S. D. (2000). The effects of viewing R-rated movie scenes that objectify women on perceptions of date rape. *Sex Roles, 43,* 645–664.

Moore, B. M. (2000, October/November). License to rape. *Ms.,* 25.

Morrow, S. L., & Hawxhurst, D. M. (1989). Lesbian partner abuse: Implications for therapists. *Journal of Counseling and Development, 68,* 58–62.

Muehlenhard, C. L., & Falcon, P. L. (1990). Men's heterosexual skill and attitudes toward women as predictors of verbal sexual coercion and forceful rape. *Sex Roles, 23,* 241–259.

Mullin, C. R. (1995). Desensitization and resensitization to violence against women: Effects of exposure to sexually violent films on judgments of domestic violence victims. *Journal of Personality & Social Psychology, 69,* 449–459.

Olson, L. N. (2002). Exploring "common couple violence" in heterosexual romantic relationships. *Western Journal of Communication, 66,* 104–128.

O'Sullivan, C. S. (1991). Acquaintance gang rape on campus. In A. Parrot & L. Bechhofer (Eds.), *Acquaintance rape: The hidden crime* (pp. 140–156). New York: Wiley.

Paetzold, R. L., & O'Leary-Kelly, A. M. (1993). Organizational communication and the legal dimensions of hostile work environment sexual harassment. In G. L. Kreps (Ed.), *Sexual harassment: Communication implications* (pp. 63–77). Cresskill, NJ: Hampton.

Paetzold, R. L., & O'Leary-Kelly, A. M. (1996). The implications of U.S. Supreme Court and circuit court decisions for hostile environment sexual harassment cases. In M. S. Stockdale (Ed.), *Sexual harassment in the workplace: Perspectives, frontiers, and response strategies* (pp. 85–104). Thousand Oaks, CA: Sage.

Payne, K. E. (1993). The power game: Sexual harassment on the college campus. In G. L. Kreps (Ed.), *Sexual harassment: Communication implications* (pp. 133–148). Cresskill, NJ: Hampton.

Peach, L. J. (1998). Sex, sexism, sexual harassment, and sexual abuse: Introduction. In L. J. Peach (Ed.), *Women in culture: A women's studies anthology* (pp. 283–301). Malden, MA: Blackwell.

Pipher, M. (1994). *Reviving Ophelia: Saving the selves of adolescent girls.* New York: Ballantine.

Reilly, M. E., Lott, B., Caldwell, D., & DeLuca, L. (1992). Tolerance for sexual harassment related to self-reported sexual victimization. *Gender & Society, 6,* 122–138.

Renzetti, C. M. (1989). Building a second closet: Third party responses to victims of lesbian partner abuse. *Family Relations, 38,* 157–163.

Renzetti, C. M. (1992). *Violent betrayal: Partner abuse in lesbian relationships.* Newbury Park, CA: Sage.

Response from the criminal justice system. (1993). [On-line]. Available: http://www.newcountrycanada.com

Rhode, D. L. (1997, November-December). Harassment is alive and well and living at the water cooler. *Ms.,* 28–29.

Robinson, V. (1994). Denial and patriarchy: The relationship between patriarchy and abuse of women. In A. Taylor and J. Beinstein Miller (Eds.), *Conflict and gender* (pp. 25–44). Cresskill, NJ: Hampton.

Romaine, S. (1999). *Communicating gender.* Mahwah, NJ: Erlbaum.

Rudd, J. E., & Burant, P. A. (1995). A study of women's compliance-gaining behaviors in violent and non-violent relationships. *Communication Research Reports, 12,* 134–144.

Rudd, J. E., Dobos, J. A., Vogl-Bauer, S., & Beatty, M. J. (1997). Women's narrative accounts of recent abusive episodes. *Women's Studies in Communication, 20,* 45–58.

Sabourin, T. C. (1995). The role of negative reciprocity in spouse abuse: A relational control analysis. *Journal of Applied Communication Research, 23,* 271–283.

Sabourin, T. C., & Stamp, G. H. (1995). Communication and the experience of dialectical tensions in family life: An examination of abusive and nonabusive families. *Communication Monographs, 62,* 213–242.

Salaimo, D. M. (1997). Electronic sexual harassment. In B. R. Sandler & R. J. Shoop (Eds.), *Sexual harassment on campus: A guide for administrators, faculty, and students* (pp. 85–103). Boston: Allyn & Bacon.

Schneider Shevlin, J. (1994). Wife abuse: Its magnitude and one jurisdiction's response. In A. Taylor and J. Beinstein Miller (Eds.), *Conflict and gender* (pp. 45–71). Cresskill, NJ: Hampton.

Schulhofer, S. (1998, October). Unwanted sex. *The Atlantic Monthly,* 55–66.

Schwartz, M. D., & DeKeseredy, W. S. (1997). *Sexual assault on campus: The role of male peer support.* Thousand Oaks, CA: Sage.

Sex differences in violent victimization, 1994. (1997, September). Washington, DC: U.S. Department of Justice, Office of Justice Programs and Bureau of Justice Statistics.

Sexual assault and rape: Advice for men. (1998). [On-line]. Available: http://www.ncf.carleton.ca/freenet

Sexual harassment charges (and dismissals) escalate. (1999, April). *HR Focus, 76,* 4.

Shotland, R. L., & Goldstein, L. (1992). Sexual precedence reduces the perceived legitimacy of sexual refusal: An examination of attributions concerning date rape and consensual sex. *Personality and Social Psychology Bulletin, 18,* 756–764.

Sirles, E. A., Lipchik, E., & Kowalski, K. (1993). A consumer's perspective on domestic violence intervention. *Journal of Family Violence, 8,* 267–276.

Snell, T. (1991). *Bureau of Justice statistics special report: Women in prison.* Washington, DC: U.S. Department of Justice.

Spender, D. (1984). Defining reality: A powerful tool. In C. Kramarae, M. Schultz, & W. O'Barr (Eds.), *Language and power* (pp. 9–22). Beverly Hills: Sage.

Stamp, G. H., & Sabourin, T. C. (1995). Accounting for violence: An analysis of male spousal abuse narratives. *Journal of Applied Communication Research, 23,* 284–307.

Steinem, G. (1983). *Outrageous acts and everyday rebellions.* New York: Holt, Rinehart, & Winston.

Steinem, G. (1998, May-June). Yes means yes, no means no: Why sex scandals don't mean harassment. *Ms.,* 62–64.

Taylor, B., & Conrad, C. (1992). Narratives of sexual harassment: Organizational dimensions. *Journal of Applied Communication, 20,* 401–418.

Tracey, P. (2000, April/May). Christy's crusade. *Ms.,* 53–61.

Truman, D. M., Tokar, D. M., & Fischer, A. R. (1996). Dimensions of masculinity: Relations to date rape supportive attitudes and sexual aggression in dating situations. *Journal of Counseling & Development, 74,* 555–562.

U.S. Department of Justice, Federal Bureau of Investigation. (2002). *Crime trends, 2001 preliminary figures.* Available: http://www.fbi.gov

Valentine-French, S., & Radtke, H. L. (1993). Attributions of responsibility for an incident of sexual harassment in a university setting. *Sex Roles, 21,* 545–555.

Walker, L. (1979). *The battered woman.* New York: Harper Colophon.

Walker, L. (1984). *The battered woman syndrome.* New York: Springer.

Walker, L. (1993). The battered woman syndrome is a psychological consequence of abuse. In R. J. Gelles & D. R. Loseke (Eds.), *Current controversies on family violence* (pp. 133–153). Newbury Park, CA: Sage.

Washington DC Rape Crisis Center. (1998). *Myths about rape.* [On-line]. Available: http://www.dcrcc.org

Waterman, C., Dawson, L., & Bologna, M. (1989). Sexual coercion in gay and lesbian relationships: Predictors and implications for support services. *Journal of Sex Research,
26,* 118–124.

Wayne, J. H., Riordan, C. M., & Thomas, K. M. (2001). Is all sexual harassment viewed
the same? Mock juror decisions in same- and cross-gender cases. *Journal of Applied
Psychology, 86,* 179–187.

White, J. W., & Humphrey, J. A. (1994). Women's aggression in heterosexual conflicts.
Aggressive Behavior, 20, 195–202.

White, J. W., & Koss, M. P. (1991). Courtship violence: Incidence in a national sample of
higher education students. *Violence and Victims, 6,* 247–256.

The wife rape information page. (1998). [On-line]. Available: http://www.unh.edu

Wise, S., & Stanley, L. (1987). *Georgie porgie: Sexual harassment in everyday life.* New York:
Pandora.

Witteman, H. (1993). The interface between sexual harassment and organizational romance. In G. L. Kreps (Ed.), *Sexual harassment: Communication implications* (pp. 27–62).
Cresskill, NJ: Hampton.

Women killed by partner/spouse. (1998). [On-line]. Available: http://www.
newcountrycanada.com

Women's Action Coalition. (1993). *WAC stats: The facts about women.* New York: The
New Press.

Wood, A. D., & McHugh, M. C. (1994). Woman battering: The response of the clergy. *Pas-
toral Psychology, 42,* 185–196.

Wood, J. T. (1992). Telling our stories: Narratives as a basis for theorizing sexual harassment. *Journal of Applied Communication, 20,* 349–362.

Wood, J. T. (1993). Naming and interpreting sexual harassment: A conceptual framework
for scholarship. In G. L. Kreps (Ed.), *Sexual harassment: Communication implications*
(pp. 9–26). Cresskill, NJ: Hampton.

Woodward, S. (1995, September 10). Packwood his own worst enemy: Case becomes a
watershed event as rules change. *The Sunday Oregonian,* pp. A1, A16, A17.

Zia, H. (2000, October/November). It's a crime. *Ms.,* 18–24.

Zillman, D., & Bryant, J. (1982). Pornography, sexual callousness, and the trivialization of
rape. *Journal of Communication, 32,* 10–21.

Zirkel, P. A. (1995). Student-to-student sexual harassment. *Phi Delta Kappan, 76,* 648–650.

CHAPTER NINE

WOMEN AND MEN IN THE WORKPLACE:

The Challenges of Talking Shop

CASE STUDY: DECISIONS ABOUT CAREERS AND FAMILIES

When Chris took the baby to the park, they got a great deal of attention from mothers and nannies. Was it because the baby was so new and small? Exceptionally beautiful or advanced for its age? Why did the other adults stop their conversations when Chris approached them to sit down? Why did they seem uncomfortable or a bit awkward when Chris walked up? Did Chris just have this effect on people in general?

The effects we describe are due to the fact that Chris is the baby's *father*, not its mother. Granted, you probably know several fathers who take their children to the park, but on weekday mornings or afternoons? How many families do you know in which the father is the primary childcare-giver, while the mother pursues her career? If you know any families like this, that's probably more than you knew even a few short years ago. This new profile of family life has been emerging and gaining prevalence for several years, but it is still far—very far—from the norm.

How does this example apply to communication at work? Think about Chris's life before he had children. What makes men who are successfully pursuing careers or who are in jobs they enjoy decide to step out of that role and stay home to raise children? What happens to working women who become pregnant, take a maternity leave, and then return to work and resume their careers? Do you think these individuals are ridiculed and ostracized or praised and supported for their choices? These choices and how they affect workplace relationships are among the topics in the fascinating area of workplace communication explored in this chapter.

Hot Topics

- The debate over affirmative action and its effect on the workplace
- How gender stereotypes can reduce the likelihood of getting hired
- How relational and content approaches to communication emerge in job interviewing
- Verbal and nonverbal indications of gender bias in job interviews
- Detecting and responding to unethical job interview questions
- Men's and women's advancement on the job
- The status of the glass ceiling for female professionals
- Managerial communication styles of women and men
- An update on the problem of sexual harassment in the workplace

WOMEN AND MEN WORKING TOGETHER: WALKING ON EGGSHELLS?

In this chapter we turn our attention to how gender communication occurs within occupational or workplace settings. Some of you may have quit a full-time job and entered college to finish, or start, earning a degree. For others, work experience may consist of summer jobs or jobs during the year to supplement your income while you're in school. Still others are putting yourselves through college and may be juggling full-time school and a full-time job. If you fit this last description, you know that "personal life" is virtually a thing of the past.

For many of us, our work is our livelihood, our most time-consuming activity. In fact, Americans are working longer hours, spending significantly greater amounts of time on the job than three decades ago (Hochschild, 2002; Toppo, 2000). Work can be a rewarding experience or a real downer for self-esteem. Many things make a job worthwhile and rewarding. However, when asked what makes their jobs enjoyable, most employed persons—men and women alike—say that relationships with people they work with make the most difference between job satisfaction and dissatisfaction. At the same time that people feel coworker relationships are important, they also reveal a sense that coworker communication—especially between female and male coworkers—is complicated. Because some of the rules, roles, and boundaries continue to shift in the world of work, people often feel that they're "walking on eggshells" so as to not say the wrong thing and get themselves or someone else into trouble.

Think about your own work experience—whether in a full-time position of rank within a corporate giant or in occasional baby-sitting for the neighbors' kids. Think about your coworkers and how your communication with them differed from your communication with people outside of work. Think of the most memorable person you worked with at your job and what made her or him memorable. Was that person your boss, a peer, or a subordinate? Was that person the same sex as you or the opposite sex? Now think of the most dramatic or memorable instance of poor communication at this job; think about who was involved and how the situation was resolved (if it was resolved). What variable was most responsible for the miscommunication—a status difference, a simple misunderstanding, a power struggle, something to do with gender?

We're not suggesting that gender is in the center of every instance of ineffective communication at work; however, a considerable number of problems in the workplace that appear to be based on power or status may really be problems between the sexes. What's the likelihood that you will be working with members of both sexes in your next job? Granted, it depends on the job. But generally speaking, if you're a woman, your chance of working with male bosses and coworkers is very good. If you're a man, your chance of having female bosses and coworkers is better than it used to be. Your chance of having female subordinates is as good as it's always been, according to statistics.

U.S. Census data for 2000 revealed that the civilian workforce was 47 percent female, compared with 45 percent in 1990 and 43 percent in 1980. While men still made up a larger percentage of the workforce, the number of women was increasing in virtually all occupations. In addition, the data indicated that women who were employed full-time provided 33 percent of the income of a dual-earner household (Dunn, 2002). However, although things are slowly improving, women—particularly minority women—are still significantly underrepresented in higher-ranking, higher-paying occupations (Guthrie & Roth, 2002).

Department of Labor statistics show that a woman working full time makes, as an average weekly wage, about 76 cents for every dollar a man makes. Women's average yearly salary is about 72 cents to the man's dollar (U.S. Department of Labor, 2002). You may have heard such statistics before, but consider that this earnings gap costs that woman more than $400,000 in lost salary over her lifetime. The wage discrepancy is also affected by race and ethnicity, with a general downward trend in earnings over a 20-year period for members of minority groups (Allen, 2001; U.S. Department of Labor, 2002).

It is beyond the scope of this chapter to interpret trends in workforce statistics, nor do we want to assess the impact of employed women on American society. We do want to explore some possible explanations for the fact that in recent years only a minuscule increase has been achieved among the ranks of female senior managers. We

> *The truth is that women's income, on average, will always be a fraction of men's, so long as America remains free.*
>
> —*Patrick Buchanan, television personality and former presidential candidate*

also want to examine how the increased presence of women in the workplace is affecting professional communication and the dynamics between the sexes, particularly at the management level. However, before tackling these issues, it's a good idea to understand how one's gender may affect getting a job in the first place.

GETTING THAT ALL-IMPORTANT JOB

Gender bias may impede you from getting a chance at a job. Often you don't know that this has happened; you just never get a response from an organization to your resume. If and when you do get job interviews, gender bias may be operating as well.

The Affirmative Action Debate: Equal Opportunity or Discrimination?

The role of such factors as sex, age, and race in creating opportunities for individuals has been hotly debated in recent years. Here we highlight some factors that may be operating in job searches and professional schools.

History and Definitions, in Brief

The Civil Rights Act of 1964, which created the Equal Employment Opportunity Commission (EEOC), was the catalyst for affirmative action. Between 1961 and 1973, presidents Kennedy, Johnson, and Nixon issued executive orders designed to eliminate discrimination. President Johnson was the one who actually attached the term *affirmative action* to his contribution (Daniels, Spiker, & Papa, 1997). These orders were originally applied to federal contractors or firms that conducted business with the government, but they were rapidly expanded to affect recruitment, hiring, training, and promoting practices in business and higher education. Affirmative action has been described as a means of "modifying personnel practices to ensure that minorities and women have job access that is equal to white men's" (Reskin & Padavic, 2002, p. 80), as an effort to force organizations to engage in "vigorous efforts to bring people of color into jobs from which they had previously been excluded" (American Civil Liberties Union, 1995, p. 1), and as a "series of laws intended to overcome such barriers that seemed to exclude minorities and women in a systematic way" (Neher, 1997, p. 67).

> *I believe affirmative action in the area of gender has resulted in jamming many people into roles that are unnatural for them and undesirable for the rest of us.*
>
> —*Laura Schlessinger (AKA Dr. Laura), radio talk show host*

Pros and Cons of Affirmative Action

The American Civil Liberties Union (ACLU) points out four major misconceptions about affirmative action. First, the ACLU contends that affirmative action is not the same as quota systems, which are illegal. Companies or institutions that assume affirmative action forces them into hiring and admitting certain numbers of women and representatives from minority groups are interpreting the goals of affirmative action in a superficial, inaccurate, and harmful way. A second misconception is that affirmative action actually enhances preferential treatment, rather than equalizing opportunity. This perception is echoed in many persons' views that affirmative action creates preferences rather than equality. A third misconception the ACLU discusses regards qualifications, meaning the notion that unqualified women or persons of color are hired or admitted over more qualified white men. Organizational communication experts Daniels, Spiker, and Papa (1997) argue that "Affirmative Action has never been about hiring people *solely* because of their color or sex without concern for their abilities" (p. 240). Finally, the ACLU rejects the notion that affirmative action is reverse discrimination against white males, rather than a "helping hand" to previously disadvantaged or underutilized groups.

In our public speaking classes, students often explore the pros and cons of affirmative action in their speeches. Male students in particular present heated arguments about how unfair and unnecessary they believe affirmative action to be. One student recently argued, "Affirmative action keeps the best people from getting a job. The person who has the toughest time getting a job these days is the white male." Responses across the classroom expressed the sentiment, "Well, it's about time," meaning that white males have had employment privilege for so long, that it's only fair they feel the isolation and discrimination others have felt for a long time. (We don't agree with that sentiment, but it's a deeply-felt stance, just the same.) As an article in *The Chronicle of Higher Education* explained,

> Arguments for and against affirmative action have been summarized like this: Affirmative action fueled the growth of the black middle class, but it has barely touched the problems of the ghetto. It has created workplaces and student bodies that "look like America," but it may have helped slow the country's economic growth. It rectifies past injustices to women and members of minority groups, but it stigmatizes talented people who could get ahead on their own. Equal opportunity. Reverse discrimination. (Analyzing Affirmative Action, 1995, p. A6)

Hot Button Issue

"Affirmative Action—Opportunity Provided or Denied?"

Perhaps you've discussed the pros and cons of affirmative action in the 21st century in one of your classes, or you've written a paper on it. If you have, you understand how far it seems we have gotten away from the original intent of affirmative action, when it was first instituted. We know that this is a difficult issue, one that sparks emotion and debate. One thing to consider, that doesn't often get talked about, is this: If one type of person dominates employment opportunities to the exclusion of other persons, the system insulates and protects itself from change. How can a qualified person who happens to *not* fit a pre-ordained profile ever get a chance?

Some Americans have come to believe that affirmative action is no longer necessary, that we have outgrown the need for guilt-induced, federally mandated standards to protect against discrimination in the workplace and in universities (Franklin, 1997). In fact, presidents Reagan and Bush, Sr., were openly opposed to affirmative action (Reskin & Padavic, 2002). Former House Speaker Newt Gingrich urged the elimination of affirmative action programs, and President Clinton called for a "national conversation on Affirmative Action" and ordered a review of policies (Nacoste, 1995, p. A48). One criticism of particular interest is that affirmative action has helped one group far more than others: white women. Labor statistics show that white women have benefited the most from affirmative action over the 30 years since its creation, at least among entry-level and lower-level management positions (Blum, 1997; St. George, 1995).

The country continues, and probably will continue, its debate about affirmative action. Look for more court rulings and legislation on affirmative action—either upholding it or signaling its doom. Whether or not you've landed that career-type job yet, the debate has already affected you because of its impact on admission standards at colleges and universities. Looking toward the future, you will no doubt want to know how professional schools (like law schools or medical schools) and potential employers view affirmative action and if they have programs in place that enhance the diversification of their student bodies or workforces. Then you will have to weigh that information with your own stance on the issue.

Gender Issues and the Job Interview

There's no doubt about it: Job interviews are extremely important. As communication scholars Kirkwood and Ralston (1999) suggest, "The employment interview is more than just a gateway to the organization. Whatever transpires between parties during interviews is part of their long-term relationship" (p. 56). Once you've landed an interview, your insight into gender communication will be helpful.

Approaches to Talk: Insight into the Interview

How can you apply to the job interview the information in Chapter 4 about *relational* and *content approaches* to communication? First, a caution: don't take the distinction between the relational and content approaches too far by assuming that a person's sex determines his or her preferred approach. Research suggests that there is a *tendency* for men to view conversation as functioning to impart content or information and women to view it as relationship maintenance or a means of connecting with others. You can use this knowledge to better understand yourself and your own approach to communication, and perhaps to help you read clues from an interviewer.

A well-developed communication repertoire, good listening skills, alertness to nonverbal cues, and a flexible communication style will increase the likelihood of success in the interview context (as well as other contexts for communication). It's wise to survey yourself in order to understand your goals in an interview and your own preferences regarding approaches to talk. Then you will be able to detect relational or content approaches and respond, if appropriate, by aligning your behavior with that of the interviewer.

'Net Notes

One thing on the mind of most college students is: "What am I going to do when I graduate?" While there are many Websites to assist you in preparing for your career, we found three particularly helpful.

www.jobhuntersbible.com The job hunter's bible is a companion Website to the popular book *What Color Is Your Parachute?* It offers an extensive library of job-hunting articles, links to helpful employment information, and a guide to conducting job searches on the Internet.

www.jobweb.com The site offers career development assistance; hiring forecasts (extremely useful); regional information; and advice from employers as to necessary job skills and preparation, as well as tips for landing a great job.

www.oxygen.com/buildit From the television network Oxygen, which offers primarily programming for women, this site supports women entrepreneurs and those entering the workforce for the first time. On occasion, Oxygen holds contests in which women wanting to start their own businesses can win $10,000, plus computer equipment and mentoring.

Being Taken Seriously

Unfortunately, a concern about being taken seriously still applies more to female than male candidates for jobs, unless a man applies for a job in a traditionally female-dominated field . Women in the workforce are nothing new, but their presence seems to be noted in a different way than a man's. The expectation still exists that men work out of necessity—they're the breadwinners and *that's just what men do.* Although the corresponding stereotype for women is diminishing, some still believe that women work outside the home for mere distraction, for a secondary supplemental income, or as an interim activity before they settle down and have families. Alternative explanations given for why women work are far more numerous than the simple possibility that they work for the same reasons as men.

Nonverbal Indications of Gender Bias

Nonverbal communication is critical in a job interview; the nonverbal most often carries the true message, rather than the verbal communication (Knapp & Hall, 2002). But just how might gender expectations be revealed nonverbally during a job interview?

A dead give-away (or at least a fairly reliable nonverbal signal that a gender stereotype is in operation) comes in the opening greeting, especially the handshake. We make judgments about someone's personality based on the simple greeting ritual of the handshake. A team of psychologists developed what they called a *handshake index,* a determination based on strength, vigor, completeness of grip, and duration of handshake (Chaplin, Phillips, Brown, Clanton, & Stein, 2000). They studied judgments subjects made about persons with high handshake indexes versus low handshake indexes. Women and men with higher handshake indexes communicated more favorable first impressions, and were deemed extroverted, open to experience, and less shy. Women with high handshake indexes were also perceived to be highly agreeable, in comparison to women with weak or poor handshakes.

Often men and women alike appear awkward when shaking hands with a woman. This situation is improving, but women still get the "cupped fingers, half handshake" (the one that translates into "You sweet, fragile thing; I couldn't possibly grasp your whole hand because it'd fall right off"). A potential employer likely has no intention of conveying negative impressions regarding a female applicant's credibility; the person just has a lousy handshake or has never learned the importance of a firm one. Nonetheless, it should raise the eyebrows of a female applicant when the handshake extended to her is less firm or confidence-inducing than one extended to a male applicant or colleague. This can be a subtle indication of a gender-based value system that is tolerated and perpetuated within the organization. Likewise, job candidates have to exercise care when they extend handshakes to company employees, especially the person doing the hiring. For women, too firm of a handshake may violate expectations, be read as masculine, too forceful, or unconfident, as though the woman is over-compensating by using an overly gripping handshake (Ralston & Kinser, 2001).

Besides the handshake in an interview, gender bias may be subtly communicated through other nonverbal cues. Research has shown that applicant physical attractiveness is an asset for men, but a bit trickier for women (Marlowe, Schneider, & Nelson, 1996). If a woman is highly physically attractive, her looks may be a deterrent to getting a job because of the stereotype that female beauty is accompanied by a lack of intelligence. Another suspicion is that the woman will cause more problems on the job than she is worth by "being a distraction" or inciting male interest. A summary of research on this subject concludes that if a woman's attractiveness is seen as a detriment to the particular job she interviews for, such as a male-oriented management position, then less attractive women are advantaged. If attractiveness is seen as an asset in the job, such as in jobs that stress interpersonal skills, attractive women have the edge in the hiring process (Morrow, 1990). In a perfect world, one's looks shouldn't matter in a decision about who gets the job; one's qualifications should outweigh such things as appearance, but we don't live in a perfect world, do we?

Some negative nonverbal cues that may emerge in job interviews include indications of general lack of interest, such as not making eye contact, which may communicate that you're not being taken seriously for the position. If the interviewer seems unprepared, if she or he rushes through the interview or shows impatience by interrupting or overlapping your answers to questions, or if he or she accepts interruptions from associates or several phone calls, these actions can signal that the candidate is not a serious contender for the job. Granted, you can't always tell whether the behavior has to do with your sex, your qualifications, some idiosyncratic reaction on the part of the interviewer, or some other variable totally unrelated to you and your interview. But it's important to take in as many nonverbal cues as possible and apply caution when interpreting what the cues mean (Beebe, Beebe, & Ivy, 2004).

Verbal Indications of Gender Bias

Another way that gender stereotypes are evidenced in job interviews has to do with the interviewer questioning process. If a potential employer holds some doubt as to whether a person of your sex is serious about a job or is capable of handling the job, the interviewer might reveal these doubts by asking leading questions. *Leading questions* are designed to trap the interviewee into a forced response or a no-win situation. They often take the form of a posed hypothetical situation followed by a question as to what the applicant would do. For example, when men apply for jobs in a currently female-dominated field such as nursing, they may receive leading questions that translate into doubts about their nurturing abilities. Or a woman applying for a position in a male-dominated office might get a leading question such as, "What would you do if a male colleague disagreed with one of your ideas and started to argue with you in front of your coworkers? Would you be able to handle that?"

One of the more overt means of communicating gender bias in a job interview is the use of *unethical questions* to applicants. It is unethical for a potential employer to ask an applicant about his or her marital status, parental status, or sexual orientation, among other things. Most employers know this, so most of them avoid these areas. But if they want to know this information before making a hiring decision, they have to use covert means or be indirect in how they approach these subjects during a job interview. By covert means, we refer to checking out a person's background, learning information in roundabout ways from former employers, and similar tactics.

The female coauthor of this textbook experienced an awkward situation some years ago. During a segment of a job interview with the vice president of an organization, the subject of transition was raised. The interviewer talked about how moving from one job and one state to another was stressful, even more so if one had a spouse and children who were uprooted in the process. After making this statement, he stopped talking, made direct eye contact, and waited for her response. Even though she knew what information he was after, she wanted the job, so her reply revealed her current marital and parental status.

Another woman was put in an awkward position not by her interviewers, but by a man who joined them for lunch. The woman was interviewing for a prestigious position, so you can imagine her surprise and dismay when the lunch guest, a spouse of one of the interviewers, began quizzing her about her private life. He asked whether she was married, whether she had ever been married, whether she had any plans to be married, whether she had or wanted to have children, and so forth. What was unfortunate, and what almost caused the woman to turn down the job, was that the interviewers made no attempt to stop the guest's unethical behavior. It was as though they knew they weren't liable or at fault, since the questions weren't coming from them, so they let a secondary source elicit the information. The woman stammered, hesitated, and somehow managed to avoid answering the guest's intrusive, unethical questions.

The first example is fairly typical of the way an employer might attempt to learn information that cannot be sought directly. In hindsight, the applicant in this example thought, "I wish I hadn't fallen into that trap; I could have simply agreed with him by saying 'Yes, transition can be quite stressful.' " In the second example, the woman defused the situation, choosing not to respond to the unethical questions. There are nonconfrontational ways to communicate effectively to an employer that you know what's going on, but you're not going to play along. One option is to respond to the question with a question, as though you didn't understand what the interviewer was getting at. You may decide to use more confrontational, educative responses, but you have to weigh the risks of such tactics (such as not getting the job). The main thing to think about is whether or not you want to work for a company whose interviewers would use strategies like these, as the woman in the second example had to do. When verbal and nonverbal indications of gender bias surface in a job interview, there is a greater likelihood that gender-biased behavior and attitudes will be in evidence on the job (Ralston & Kinser, 2001).

When Working Women Walk, Talk, and Look Like Working Men

Almost everyone knows the basic message behind the "dress for success" slogan, meaning that you need to dress well and exude confidence in an interview, to appear attractive (physically and in your personality), and to dress in a manner consistent with (or a bit more formal than) the employees who work where you are interviewing. For male job candidates, "dress for success" advice generally works well, but it's not so straightforward for women.

Communication studies have examined what women experience when they must strike some acceptable balance between femininity and masculinity in order to be taken seriously (Nadesan & Trethewey, 2000). Researchers Borisoff and Merrill (1998) explain, "The double bind faced by women applying for professional positions lies in finding how to communicate their 'in-group' status without dressing in a manner regarded as 'too masculine,' which could result in negative hiring decisions. . . . On the other hand, 'too feminine' apparel would be considered too frivolous for the workplace" (pp. 93–94).

Women have reacted in some interesting ways to the realization of this double bind. During the 1970s when American society witnessed a significant increase in women working outside the home, female applicants who wished to be accepted into the male-dominated workforce dressed like little versions of men (as the advice books advocated) (Watkins, 1996). They wore dark, pinstriped suits with skirts instead of pants, and bows or scarves at the neck instead of ties. They wore wing-tipped pumps and carried leather briefcases, because heaven help a woman who showed up in a professional setting carrying a purse! They kept their jewelry, perfume, and makeup to a minimum, generally in

---

'Net Notes

The Women's Alliance is a national organization providing professional attire, career skills training, and related services to low-income women seeking employment.
www.thewomensalliance.org

attempts to play down the fact that they were women vying for the same positions as men. They did everything they could to be taken seriously. What happened?

In some instances women gained some ground, but, in large part, emulating men didn't work. What women have learned since the '70s and '80s, as one scholar terms it "the power pumps era" (Stewart, 2001, p. 178), is this: When women attempt to imitate powerful men—their dress, their verbal displays of aggressiveness and competitiveness, even their joking behaviors or coworker banter—they aren't received in the same manner. This approach can also cause a woman to lose her own identity as a professional (Borisoff & Merrill, 1998). Thus, women have continued to find ways of creating their own paths and making their own voices heard in the world of work. For example, it is now quite common to see working women in attire that combines traditional, conservative lines with softer materials and wider-ranging colors. (Keep in mind that this relates to dress once you are on the job, not during job interviews.)

The best guideline for students regarding job interviewing should sound quite familiar to you by now: develop your communicative repertoire as fully as possible, adopting masculine and feminine behaviors that can be used effectively, given the demands of the interview situation and the particulars of the job and the company. For female readers, realize that society continues to change regarding what is appropriate female professional demeanor. In some settings, communicating confidently and assertively in a job interview will be perceived positively. In other settings and with other interviewers, gender stereotypes may be operating; an interviewer may view some behavior as masculine and therefore inappropriate coming from a female applicant (Borisoff & Merrill, 1998; Ralston & Kinser, 2001). For male readers, think about the possibility that the interviewer may highly value some of the behaviors stereotypically labeled feminine—like verbal and nonverbal affiliative, supportive behaviors—so it will be to your advantage to work these behaviors into how you present yourself in an interview.

Remember...

AFFIRMATIVE ACTION: A governmental effort to help overcome barriers to members of underrepresented groups, in terms of recruiting, hiring, and promoting.

RELATIONAL APPROACH TO COMMUNICATION: The view that communication functions primarily to establish and develop relationships between interactants.

CONTENT APPROACH TO COMMUNICATION: The view that communication functions primarily as an exchange of information between interactants.

HANDSHAKE INDEX: A perception of a handshake, based on strength, vigor, completeness of grip, and duration.

LEADING QUESTION: An interviewer question that traps an interviewee into a forced or no-win response.

UNETHICAL QUESTION: An interviewer question about personal life, such as a question about marital status, parental status, sexual orientation, religious affiliation, etc.

ON THE JOB AND MOVING UP

Congratulations! You got the job. You're on the job. What gender-related variables might emerge at your job? How will you respond?

Advancement within an Organization

Refer back to the statistics cited early in this chapter—you might conclude that the workforce is becoming more equitable since women are increasing their presence in the work arena. But a more careful inspection reveals a problem: While more women are now being hired than in times past, greater numbers of men than women achieve the higher, more responsible and more rewarding ranks (Dunn, 2002; Stewart, 2001; Williams, 2002). Even though *Fortune* magazine continues to produce its "Fifty Most Powerful Women" lists and other indications of gains at higher levels can be cited, significant inequity still exists (Sellers, 1998). For example, statistics show that women now represent over 40 percent of graduating classes at American law schools, a figure that is up from a mere 7 percent in 1972. These women have achieved in all aspects of the practice of law except for one: positions of power, such as partnerships and the management of law firms (Rosenberg, Perlstadt, & Phillips, 2002; Sege, 1996). What factors are connected to the trends regarding advancement?

A Ceiling Still Made of Glass

We expect you've heard the *glass ceiling* term before. It stems from a larger metaphor for working women who operate in "glass houses," whose behavior is not only scrutinized by individuals on every level of the organization, but whose success or failure might affect the status of employed women everywhere. Professional women who look higher, see the possibilities, yet are unable to reach them because of a transparent barrier have encountered the glass ceiling (Kanter, 1977; Reskin & Padavic, 2002).

In the mid-1980s, a group of researchers at the Center for Creative Leadership began a three-year study, the Executive Women Project (Morrison, White, & Van Velsor, 1987). This group coined the term *glass ceiling,* which they described as follows: "Many women have paid their dues, even a premium, for a chance at a top position, only to find a glass ceiling between them and their goal. The glass ceiling is not simply a barrier for an individual, based on the person's inability to handle a higher-level job. Rather the glass ceiling applies to women as a group who are kept from advancing higher *because they are women*" (p. 13).

In 1991 the Federal Glass Ceiling Commission was formed, headed by Secretary of Labor Lynn Martin. This group's Glass Ceiling Initiative studied nine Fortune 500 companies in order to understand the barriers to advancement for women and minorities and to assist corporations in determining strategies for eliminating the barriers. As a result of this study, Martin (1991) issued the following challenge: "The glass ceiling, where it exists, hinders not only individuals but society as a whole. It effectively cuts our pool of potential corporate leaders by eliminating over one-half of our population. If our end game is to compete successfully in today's global market, then we have to unleash the full potential of the American work force. The time has come to tear down, to dismantle the 'Glass Ceiling' " (p. 2). Some factors contributing to the barrier for female and minority advancement include the following:

1. Corporate lack of attention to equal opportunity principles, such as monitoring the progress and development, as well as compensation patterns, for all employees.
2. Discriminatory placement patterns.
3. Inadequate record keeping.
4. Internal recruitment practices that maintain white male-dominated networks.
5. A lack of EEOC (Equal Employment Opportunity Commission) involvement in the hiring processes for middle- and upper-level management positions.

> *If women can sleep their way to the top, how come they aren't there? There must be an epidemic of insomnia out there.*
>
> –Ellen Goodman, columnist

After more than 20 years of awareness of the need to promote women and members of minority groups into higher-level decision-making positions in the workforce, it appears that little progress has been made (Stewart, 2001). The Federal Glass Ceiling Commission (1995) brought together research findings and reported that women were occupying less than 5 percent of senior managerial and executive positions in large American corporations. Surveys of Fortune 1500 companies reveal that in the decade of the '90s, 97 percent of senior managers (vice presidents and above) were men (Federal Glass Ceiling Commission, 1995). At the turn of the new century, the general growth trend for women in the workforce was still not evident at the highest levels of employment. While 47 percent of middle-management positions in American companies were held by women, women held only 17 percent of executive management positions. The disparity was even more extreme at the level of CEOs: only 11 percent of U.S. organizations had female CEOs (Guthrie & Roth, 2002).

The Authority Gap

The discrepancy between the numbers of male and female upper-level managers and executives in the American workforce has been termed an *authority gap* by researchers Reskin and Padavic (1994). They cite three explanations for this gap. The first is the "human-capital inequities" explanation, which suggests that women are still acquiring the education and experience that will enable them to rise to positions of authority. Reskin and Padavic counter with statistics showing that "Women have not advanced into authority-conferring jobs in proportion to their presence in the lower ranks. Women were 15 percent of all managers in 1968, so they should be 15 percent of senior managers today. Instead, in 1990 they were only 3 percent of senior managers. . . . If women's rate of progress proceeds at the present pace, women will not achieve equitable representation and pay at all management levels for another 75 to 100 years" (pp. 95–96).

The second explanation relates to workplace segregation, the finding that the most frequently held managerial positions for women are in personnel and public relations—areas that typically involve little authority or power within an organization. The third explanation for the authority gap stems from cultural bias. Reskin and Padavic contend that many employers still "adhere to an informal segregation code that keeps women from supervising men and that reserves the training slots leading to higher-level jobs for men" (p. 96). Organizational communication researcher Lea Stewart (2001) adds, "Women have not reached the top of the corporate hierarchy in part because of the gender stereotype held by many corporate decision makers that women do not have the personality characteristics necessary for top leadership roles" (p. 180). This reflects the stereotypical judgment that because women are naturally affiliative and nurturing, they choose not to "rock the boat" and cannot make tough decisions that might disappoint others.

To combat the gender differential in upper-level management, organizations must actively ensure that male and female employees' careers are developed with equal attention (Nadler & Nadler, 1987). Teachers, parents, and academic advisers and mentors should work with very young children to eliminate negative gender stereotypes *where they begin.* In addition, women should plan their careers well beforehand and proactively seek advancement, rather than waiting for a superior to notice and reward their accomplishments. Stewart (2001) suggests that networking and developing mentor relationships are excellent strategies to help women overcome barriers in the workplace. Women who use both formal and informal channels for developing contacts, and who actively work to learn from and emulate more experienced professionals, widen their options and heighten their satisfaction and comfort levels in their jobs (Hall, 2001; Sloan & Krone, 2000).

Difficult Choices: Family, Career, or Both?

One of the most obvious factors complicating women's professional advancement is a basic biological function (one we explored in Chapter 2)—women give birth to babies. As a culture, we have moved a bit forward on this front, creating more choices for families. Efforts in the 1970s and 1980s helped to loosen the constricted thinking that women would automatically choose home and family over careers. In the 1990s, women who could afford to sacrifice their paychecks to stay home and raise young children felt more free to do so without feeling that they'd violated some basic tenet of women's liberation. We've witnessed political progress through such laws as Title VII of the Civil Rights Act (1964), the Pregnancy Disability Act (1978), the EEOC's guidelines on sexual harassment (1980), and the Family and Medical Leave Act (1996) (Gerstel & McGonagle, 2002; McDorman, 1998; Paul, 2002).

Changing workplace language indicates changing attitudes toward work and family. In the 1980s, we saw the emergence of "superwomen" who were "doing it all" and "having it all" because they raised children while maintaining their careers (Friedan, 1981). Then the term *second shift* was coined to describe the work of employed women who returned home from their jobs to hours of cleaning, cooking, and childcare (Hochschild, 1989, as in Saltzman Chafetz, 1997). The 1990s brought the term *mommy track* (a variation of "fast track"), which applied to women who sought advancement in the workplace at the same time as they had child-rearing responsibilities. However, for the first time since 1976, we've seen a national decline in the number of employed mothers with infant children (*Texas Labor Market Review,* as in Burns, 2002). The number of mothers working outside the home dropped 4 percentage points between 1998 and 2000. The burden of work and home is even greater for single women; in 1998, 22 percent of families with children under the age of 18 were supported by single women (Dubeck & Dunn, 2002). In 1993, 44 percent of single mothers were employed; by the turn of the century, that figure increased to 65 percent (Pear, 2000). Books such as Arlie Hochschild's (1997) *The Time Bind: When Work Becomes Home and Home Becomes Work,* Betty Holcomb's (2000) *Not Guilty! The Good News for Working Mothers,* Elizabeth Perle McKenna's (1997) *When Work Doesn't Work Anymore,* and Joan K. Peters's (1997) *When Mothers Work: Loving Our Children without Sacrificing Ourselves* offer advice on the realities of juggling family and job.

We also saw in the 1990s greater use of *flextime,* a system some organizations adopt which allows workers to come and go early or late, or to work longer hours fewer days of the week, to better respond to home and family demands (Hochschild & Machung, 2002). We saw an effort to create more *family friendly* workplaces, a descriptor that emerged when *Working Mother* magazine began identifying the best places in the country for women and mothers to work. Organizations attempted to better accommodate workers who had family issues that could affect their job performance (Dubeck & Dunn, 2002). However, evidence shows that family friendly accommodations and flextime opportunities are not readily available for workers across different levels of organizations, particularly low-wage workers, even in those firms deemed at the top of the family friendly lists (Finnigan, 2001; Holcomb, 2002). In some highly competitive workplaces, family friendly initiatives exist as mere public relations devices; the informal internal word is that employees shouldn't actually take advantage of them (Crary, 2002).

> *I think our society is just learning that it's okay for women in their thirties to still be chasing their careers . . . to become mothers and career women. I am just happy letting things happen as they are meant to happen, rather than feeling like I have to be at a certain place at a certain time.*
>
> —Cameron Diaz, actor

Two other relatively recent and positive workplace changes warrant mention. The first is the development of on-site childcare facilities and company-sponsored programs that increase employees' access to childcare, although on-site childcare centers are few and access to these services is problematic (Trei, 2002; Whitehurst, 2002). For example, only about 5000 of the massive number of employers in this country offer on-site childcare, but many of these sites are at headquarters where more upper level management and executives are likely to work than lower level workers—those needing affordable childcare the most (Holcomb, 2002). The second change surrounds the technological innovation of *telecommuting,* gaining steam as we enter the 21st century (Stewart, 2002). The ability to work at home with flexible hours through the wonders of technological devices such as computers and fax machines is liberating to many women, who are among its chief subscribers. However, it sometimes creates a sense that the employee is "on call" or accountable to an employer 24 hours a day (Edley, 2001). It may be more myth than fact that telecommunting saves an employed mother time and grief. Arlie Russell Hochschild, who coined the term "second shift" in the '80s, now describes a *third shift*—the relational repair mothers must do with spouses and children who feel neglected because of a woman's hectic or "on call" work schedule (Hochschild, 1997).

But with all of this awareness and these important innovations, a nagging perception still exists in the minds of many: Women in the workforce just can't be counted on over the long haul. They are likely to want to have children at some point in their careers and that means maternity leaves, a greater potential for absenteeism, and the likelihood that they will vacate their positions in favor of staying home and raising their children (all of which costs organizations money). This is a stereotype—a painful one to write and read about. Our experience and that of many students has been that, no matter how equality based many organizations (including universities) like to believe they are, some persons in authority still retain this stereotype about female employees. They may never say it, but it still crosses many people's minds and causes them to think twice about hiring or promoting women into positions of authority.

At work, you think of the children you have left at home. At home, you think of the work you've left unfinished. Such a struggle is unleashed within yourself. Your heart is rent.

—Golda Meir, former Israeli prime minister

Another complicating factor is the reality of the tension many women feel between their careers and obligations to bear and raise children (Gerson, 2002; Zaslow, 2002). We grant that the stereotype that women contribute significantly to organizational turnover because of pregnancy and childrearing duties has some basis in reality. Women do struggle with multiple demands on their time and energies, particularly if they don't have a spouse or partner, or don't receive much help from one.

A high-profile example bears out the difficult decisions many professional women face. In April of 2002, chief White House aide Karen Hughes announced that she was resigning her position in the Bush administration to return home to Texas for "family reasons," which many suggested included a husband who didn't like Washington DC and a homesick 15-year-old son (Parker, 2002). While Bush spokespersons maintained that Hughes would remain an integral part of the administration, even if at a distance, Hughes' resignation created "another Rorschach test for a culture striving to come to grips with mothers and work" (Toner, 2002, p. A7). ABC's news coverage of the resignation, reported by Jackie Judd, included statistics about women in the workforce, primarily derived from Sylvia Ann Hewlett's (2002) book *Creating a Life: Professional Women and the Quest for Children.* Judd reported that, of American working women over the age of 40 with an income of $100,000 or more, 49 percent do not have children. The comparable figure for men is 10 percent. In addition, of the women, now mothers, who earned Harvard MBA degrees in the 1970s, only 25 percent were still in the workforce by the early 1990s; as regards men in the same category, none had "dropped out" of the workforce. News anchor Peter Jennings commented about these statistics, "That's not good odds for women who want it all."

Let's take a moment to examine some assumptions embedded in the television news coverage we have just described, because the subtle messages reveal a great deal about what's going on in American culture. First, the select statistics in the report paint a picture—accurate or not—of childless women driven to the top of their professions, in contrast to men at the top of their professions, the majority of whom have children, presumably taken care of by their wives. Most of those women who were sufficienty driven in the 1970s to earn Harvard advanced degrees have now not "chosen" to exit the workforce but rather have "dropped out." Would these women want to be called "dropouts"? Women are often chastised for "wanting it all," but that criticism is rarely if ever leveled at men. What's the reality here? Is it true that more and more women are retreating from the workforce to raise families, or are there just some select cases which receive heightened (and skewed) media coverage?

If there's any "truth" here, it's that many mothers feel significant guilt if they choose to continue jobs and careers they enjoy, rather than discard the professional strides they have made in favor of staying home with young children (Jones, 1998). Society magnifies that guilt by repeated insinuations that an employed mother isn't a good mother. There are constant attempts to blame women who work outside the home for the decay of the American family. Career women may also face negative aftereffects of maternity leaves, including learning that their careers have plateaued, their jobs have been rerouted into less attractive trajectories, or their ability to exert influence has been lost or diminished (Miller, Casey, Lamphear-Van Horn, & Ethington, 1993). Another reality is that many two-parent families simply cannot afford the luxury of having only one income while the other parent is the primary childcare giver; for single-parent families, there are few if any choices between work and family.

Hot Button Issue

"PARENTS WHO WORK OUTSIDE THE HOME"

Do you agree that the pull between family and career exerts more pressure on women than men—even in the twenty-first century world of work? While men are assuming greater roles in child rearing than ever before, very few give up or take a break from their careers to raise children. In two-parent families that can afford to function on only one salary, the parent who stays home with the children is usually the mother. There's nothing wrong with this, but there are some cultural assumptions worth taking a look at. Granted, most men's salaries are still higher than women's in our culture, so it makes sense that the higher-salaried person would retain his or her job. But there's also a stereotype, which some people believe has a basis in genetics, that mothers are more nurturing and naturally should be the ones to tend to young children. What is your stance on this issue? Do you know any families in which the father is actually more "naturally" nurturing than the mother, and even though he makes more money, he opts to stay home with the kids while she continues her career? If a woman wants to "have it all," just as most men want to "have it all," how can our culture enable her to do that?

Decisions about home and family must be placed in the context of the persistent fact that few working men experience the same tension as working women when children come into the picture (Kelly, 2002; Reardon, 1997). Feminist activist Gloria Steinem is often quoted as saying, "I have yet to hear a man ask for advice on how to combine marriage and a career." Why don't more men struggle with the career versus family decision? Could it be that society hasn't evolved to the point where men are equal partners in child rearing? Could it be that most people still think in terms of the hunter-gatherer model, the model of male-as-breadwinner and female-as-childcare-giver model we described in Chapter 2?

Women and Men in Leadership Positions

Communication researchers, organizational behavior experts, and gender scholars alike have focused attention for decades on how the sexes approach leadership, management, conflict resolution, and decision making. They have attempted to separate myth from fact in the perception that members of one sex versus the other make better managers.

How Are Male and Female Managers Perceived?

A meaningful discussion on this topic must be placed in the context of the changing workplace. The American workplace, as well as some workplaces abroad, has witnessed a shift away from traditional management approaches, typified by such stereotypical masculine attributes as aggression, competitiveness, control, and individualism. The shift is toward an interactional management approach, reflecting such stereotypical feminine attributes as flexibility, supportiveness, connectedness, and collaborative problem solving (Billing & Alvesson, 2000; Brownell, 2001; Cameron, 1995; Nelton, 1997). Korn/Ferry International, a worldwide executive head-hunting firm, predicted that the omnipotent, controlling boss, termed a "controllasaurus," would be extinct in businesses of the new millennium (as in Nelton, 1997, p. 19). Its report called for a combination of masculine and feminine traits in leaders. Business professor Marie-Therese Claes (2002) explains: "The masculine culture of large corporations cannot easily adapt to a context of uncertainty and constant evolution. The team and supportive behaviors more readily identified with women are perceived as increasingly important for management" (p. 121).

An extensive study of perceptions of female and male managers found that female leaders were rated higher on people-oriented leadership skills and male leaders were rated higher on business-oriented leadership skills (Kabacoff, 1998). In general, bosses rated male and female managers equal in effectiveness; however, peers rated women slightly higher than men. Specifically, the following points emerged from this study: (1) Male managers were perceived as having more of a vision of strategic planning and organization, having a greater sense of tradition (building on knowledge gained from experience), being innovative and willing to take risks, and being more restrained and professional in terms of emotional expression. They were also seen as better delegators, more cooperative, and more persuasive than female managers. (2) Female managers were perceived as being more empathic, being more energetic and enthusiastic, being better communicators (e.g., keeping people informed, providing feedback), and possessing more "people skills" (e.g., sensitivity to others, likability, listening ability, development of relationships with peers and superiors) than their male counterparts. However, they were not perceived as being more outgoing or extroverted, or more cooperative as leaders.

How Do They Communicate as Managers?

Researchers have found readily detectable gender differences in the communication styles of leaders (Helgesen, 1990, 1995; Sloan & Krone, 2000). Generally, a feminine management style involves supportive, facilitative leadership that tends to be effective in participatory, democratic work settings. In contrast, a masculine management style involves control or power over employees and a competitive tone that strives to create winners and losers—a style that may be more effective in a highly autocratic work environment. (Remember that we're talking about gender differences here, not sex differences; a man can demonstrate a feminine style of managing, just as a woman can exhibit masculine leadership behaviors.)

Communication scholar Steven May (1997) describes the "feminization of management," a result of a changing workplace and a changing worker (p. 3). May contends:

> No longer told to "check your brains at the door," workers in high-wage manufacturing and service economies are asked to abandon the idea that their jobs are static and, instead, work more independently, contribute to problem-solving and cost-reduction, be more customer-oriented and vendor-minded, and do what is needed rather than what the job description prescribes. Thus, as workers become self-managing, managers are told to reorient themselves toward a new role of co-ordinating, facilitating, coaching, supporting, and nurturing their employees. (p. 4)

May identifies three themes in current managerial literature, themes that reveal a "thread of feminization" (p. 9). The first theme is advice to managers to replace the notion of control with shared responsibility. Instead of commanding, directing, and deciding, "the new ideal is a manager who relinquishes control and shares responsibility, authority, and the limelight" (p. 10). The second theme is helping and developing employees, as opposed to regulating and supervising them. This theme underlies the team-building approach that is popular in modern American organizations. The third theme is the importance of building meaningful networks of relationships, both within and outside the organization.

While May found these themes consistent with feminine traits identified in our culture, none of the literature he surveyed used the term "feminine style of management." In fact, authors struggled to find another name or metaphor for the style. May contends that a recommended management style based on feminine qualities such as nurturance, along with an unwillingness to call that style feminine, bears witness to continued bias in the workplace. He concludes that "the culture is deeply ambivalent about elevating the status of the female and femininity; doing so would call into question the entire system of gender relations that underpins most organization and management theory" (pp. 22–23).

Can Effective Managers Have It Both Ways?

Research and popular literature on the subject of gender and management describe a blended style, one that draws on both masculine and feminine strengths in communication and leadership (Claes, 2002; Hayes

Andrews, Herschel, & Baird, 1996). This represents a move away from the traditional, male-oriented management style, corresponding to a change to less traditional, less hierarchically based, flatter, and more decentralized organizations that face global competition. As Tom Peters, coauthor of the best-selling management treatise *In Search of Excellence,* explains, "Gone are the days of women succeeding by learning to play men's games. Instead the time has come for men on the move to learn to play women's games" (as in Fierman, 1990, p. 115).

One of the earliest and strongest proponents of the blended management approach was Alice Sargent, author of *The Androgynous Manager* (1981). *Androgynous management* involves blending linear, systematic problem solving with intuitive approaches, balancing competition and collaboration, and dealing with power as well as emotion. Sargent argues that men and women alike have suffered the consequences of a masculine management style, including stress and related health problems.

However, there are some cautions to consider regarding an androgynous or blended management style. This may surprise you, since we are such advocates of androgyny and gender blending throughout this text. In some organizational settings, exhibiting behaviors stereotypically associated with the opposite sex can backfire (Lamude & Daniels, 1990). For example, a male manager who reacts emotionally to bad news at work may be labeled the "corporate wimp," rather than be valued for his honest reaction. A female manager who aggressively communicates her views to colleagues may be labeled the "corporate bitch." When women attempt to emulate the management behaviors of their male counterparts, they perpetuate the male-oriented system and are often devalued for this behavior. In fact, some women explain that they aren't drawn to the upper levels of management in their patriarchal organizations, because of concerns that they will be co-opted or forced into exhibiting the company's masculine value-based behavior (Sloan & Krone, 2000). Sometimes, when a female manager uses stereotypical feminine behaviors, she receives negative reactions as well (Daniels, Spiker, & Papa, 1997). Things are changing and female managers are still finding their way in a male-dominated arena, so the decision to adopt an androgynous management style, or any management style, depends upon the context within which you work.

No matter what jobs men and women hold—from assembly-line workers to schoolteachers to directors of nonprofit agencies to corporate CEOs—they will most likely face some complications related to sex and gender. Right now, members of both sexes are trying to work together productively, trying to decide what kind of woman or man they want to be on the job, and trying to communicate effectively and be received positively. All this "trying" represents the current struggle in the workplace, but this struggle is manifested most dramatically by the problem of sexual harassment—the subject of the final section of this chapter.

Remember. . .

GLASS CEILING: A transparent barrier in the workplace that allows professional women to look higher and see possibilities for advancement, but that prevents them from attaining higher positions.

AUTHORITY GAP: The discrepancy between the numbers of male and female upper-level managers and executives in the American workforce.

SECOND SHIFT: The work of employed women returning home from their jobs to hours of cleaning, cooking, and childcare.

MOMMY TRACK: A term applied to women who seek advancement in the workplace at the same time as they have child-rearing responsibilities.

FLEXTIME: An organizational innovation that allows employees to work flexible hours, to accommodate the demands of home and family.

FAMILY-FRIENDLY WORKPLACE: A designation that a workplace is accommodating for employees with family responsibilities.

TELECOMMUTING: The ability to work at home with flexible hours through the use of technological advances.

THIRD SHIFT: Relational repair mothers must do with spouses and children who feel neglected because of a woman's hectic or "on call" work schedule.

ANDROGYNOUS MANAGEMENT: A leadership style exhibiting a blend of masculine and feminine approaches to management.

THE PROBLEM OF SEXUAL HARASSMENT IN THE WORKPLACE

Just reading this heading may make you want to put the book down. As difficult as sexual harassment is to think about, it's important to examine this topic because many of you are nearing graduation and will be launching careers. We hope you don't encounter sexual harassment at work, but whether or not you experience it firsthand, you need to be current and knowledgeable on the topic if you want to function successfully on the job. Sexual harassment is discussed thoroughly in Chapter 8; we briefly discuss how it occurs and is dealt with in educational settings in Chapter 10. Here we summarize current information particularly pertinent to the workplace.

The Pervasiveness of the Problem

Sexual harassment in the workplace continues to be talked about and researched, because it continues to be a problem. Charges filed with the EEOC increased 127 percent between 1991 and 2001, with almost 16,000 complaints filed each year in 2000 and 2001. In 2001, 14 percent of complaints were filed by men, and $53 million in benefits were awarded to complainants, not counting any benefits obtained through litigation (Equal Employment Opportunity Commission, 2002). Don't get the idea that sexual harassment is a recent phenomenon, one that only gained attention in the 1990s because of Anita Hill's sexual harassment claims during the Clarence Thomas Supreme Court confirmation hearings, the Navy's Tailhook scandal, or Paula Jones' lawsuit against President Bill Clinton (Violanti, 1996). In the late 1970s, feminists coined the label *sexual harassment*, but one can imagine that as long as men and women have worked together in many diverse settings, sexual harassment has occurred.

In her article "Harassment Is Alive and Well and Living at the Water Cooler," Stanford law professor Deborah Rhode (1997) asks why, after highly publicized cases and "after two decades of enforcing prohibitions on harassment, are we still seeing so many egregious examples of it?" (p. 28) The popular media say that the public is tired of hearing about harassment, leading to the perception that we have "fixed the problem" in today's modern and highly informed society. Rhode contends that this denial that workplace harassment still occurs, and frequently occurs, is a "variation on the traditional view that it didn't happen at all" (p. 28). Frivolous claims and particularly lurid, headline-grabbing cases tend to deflect or camouflage the real problem.

Most reported and researched workplace sexual harassment is heterosexual, with a male-harasser, female-target profile (Markert, 1999; Reilly, Lott, Caldwell, & DeLuca, 1992). Female sexual harassment of men does occur, but it is reported and pursued in the courts with far less frequency than male-to-female harassment (Romaine, 1999; Wayne, Riordan, & Thomas, 2001). Incidences of same-sex harassment occur also and have begun to receive research attention (Bennett-Alexander, 1998; Dubois, 1998; MacKinnon, 2002). Many instances of sexual harassment occur between individuals who function within clearly drawn power lines, such as in relationships of boss-employer, teacher-student, doctor-patient, lawyer-client. However, research shows that peer harassment—sexually harassing communication between coworkers of equal or similar rank and power—also occurs within organizations (Ivy, 1993; Ivy & Hamlet, 1996; Paetzold & O'Leary-Kelly, 1993).

In Chapter 8, we defined sexual harassment in some detail. For the purpose of a quick review, here is the Equal Employment Opportunity Commission's definition (1980) of sexual harassment, the standard still used today:

> Unwelcome sexual advances, requests for sexual favors, and other verbal or physical conduct of a sexual nature constitute sexual harassment when (1) submission to such conduct is made either explicitly or implicitly a term or condition of an individual's employment, (2) submission to or rejection of such conduct by an individual is used as the basis for employment decisions affecting such individual, or (3) such conduct has the intention or effect of unreasonably interfering with an individual's work performance or of creating an intimidating, hostile, or offensive working environment.

The first two forms reflect "quid pro quo" harassment, which means "this for that" or "something for something." This is the more traditional or historical view of harassment, involving a threat by superiors that unless subordinates engage in some form of sexual behavior, they will lose their jobs, be overlooked for promotions and raises, be transferred to less desirable units or locations, and so forth. Because it is overt and tangible, quid pro quo harassment is more easily recognizable by the courts as a form of illegal sex discrimination than the third form of harassment, hostile climate (Paetzold & O'Leary-Kelly, 1993).

Working in a Hostile Environment

Hostile climate or work environment sexual harassment began to be viewed as illegal sex discrimination by the U.S. Supreme Court in 1986. To date, this form of harassment has generated the largest number of court cases and has also produced the most confusion regarding what actions could or could not be regarded as sexual harassment (Berryman-Fink & Vanover Riley, 1997; Gerdes, 1999; Jacobs & Bonavoglia, 1998). Research provides some examples from the workplace that can substantiate claims of hostile climate harassment: posters, flyers, calendars, and other "decorative" materials that contain nudity or sexual representations (including screen savers on office computers); lewd or insulting graffiti in workplace areas; pornographic or sexually explicit materials; vandalism of one's personal belongings or work space; and behaviors such as making repeated phone calls; leaving e-mail or voice mail messages; placing intimidating or sexist materials in an employee's mailbox; staring, following, or stalking someone; and performing office pranks (Paetzold & O'Leary-Kelly, 1993).

One element that makes this situation so difficult and causes people to feel that they are walking on eggshells is the fine line between flirting and harassment. The average American spends much more time at work today than in decades past, so more of us are likely to look to the workplace for friendship and romantic liaisons (Fine, 1996). While an office romance can make you look forward to getting out of bed and going to work each day, it can also create huge problems. As we mentioned in Chapter 5, one person's friendly, teasing, or flirtatious behavior is another person's sexual harassment (Alberts, 1992; Haunani Solomon & Miller Williams, 1997). While some organizations believe workplace romances are private and not causes for concern, worries about romantic workplace relationships and potential liability have led some organizations to create policies banning office romance (Buzzanell, 1992; Eisenberg, Goodall, & Goodall, 2001; Witteman, 1993).

Researchers Jacobs and Bonavoglia (1998) addressed the question, "When does harmless workplace behavior morph into a potentially hostile environment?" (p. 51) They provided the following examples, asking readers what is and is not "hostile climate" harassment: a man accidentally e-mailing a list called "The 50 Worst Things about Women" to everyone in his organization (instead of his closest buddies); a man using various communication channels (e.g., e-mail, voice mail, fax) to repeatedly ask a female coworker for a date; a male manager whispering compliments and invading the space of a female coworker; guys in a mail room exchanging the latest raunchy joke within earshot of a female worker; a male professor who uses a copy of *Hustler* magazine to teach female anatomy; and a female administrator, whose office contains male-bashing posters and cartoons, who is assigned a male office mate. Jacobs and Bonavoglia concluded that all these situations could involve sexual harassment, with the exception of the first one—the accidental e-mail. They contended that if this was indeed a one-time, unintentional incident, a claim of sexual harassment would be a stretch. Typically, a pattern of behavior is the threshold for a successful suit (Paetzold & O'Leary-Kelly, 1996).

As if what we've outlined thus far wasn't enough, there's yet another complicating factor about workplace sexual harassment. Consistent research findings indicate that women react more strongly to inappropriate sexual behavior and view more behaviors as potential sexual harassment than men (Berryman-Fink & Vanover Riley, 1997; Ivy & Hamlet, 1996; LaRocca & Kromrey, 1999; Mongeau & Blalock, 1994).

In her investigation of workplace sexual harassment, communication scholar Debbie Dougherty (2001) offers insight into why women and men tend to perceive sexual behavior in the workplace so differently. Previous research typified sexual harassment as being dysfunctional to an organization (Kreps, 1994). However, through discussion groups and recall interviews conducted at a large healthcare organization, Dougherty discovered that sexually harassing behavior is perceived by women as dysfunctional but by men as functional. If you wonder how sexual harassment could be "functional," here's Dougherty's explanation. Male subjects in her study, like most men in sexual harassment studies, viewed certain behaviors as sexual, but not sexual harassment (which implies one has done something wrong). Dougherty's study describes sexual behavior as being "verbally or nonverbally sexually explicit or implicit," and offers such examples as "sexual jokes," "references to sexuality," "references to body parts," "touching beyond socially functional behaviors," and "threats to touch" (p. 380). As male subjects spoke about their workplace environment, three "functions" of sexual behavior began to emerge. The first function is sexual behavior as a coping mechanism. Male subjects reported using sexualized behavior as a means of coping with job stress, so that they could continue to work in the healthcare context. A second function is termed by Dougherty "therapeutic touch" (p. 386). When male subjects discussed touch in workplace, they first emphasized the therapeutic benefits of touching patients. However, they suggested that therapeutic touch also comforted their fellow employees; thus, touching behavior on the job (e.g., backrubs, comforting hugs) served a function and should not be interpreted as sexual harassment. The final function that emerged from the study is termed "camaraderie," in reference to the way that sexualized behavior was seen by men as being conducive to group cohesion and team building.

Dougherty explains how her female subjects saw male sexualized behavior in a very different light in this organization. At best, it was something to be endured and at worst, it was sexual harassment. These women did not discuss job stress, nor did they mention sexualized behavior as being a means of stress reduction. To the contrary, the sexualized behavior male coworkers described *created* a stressful working environment for women; it did not reduce their stress. As for the second function, research has long documented men's and women's differing meanings for and responses to touch, concluding that touches from men, meant to be comforting to women, are often interpreted as signals of power or control (Henley, 1977; Jones & Yarbrough, 1985; Knapp & Hall, 2002). Consistent with earlier research findings, female subjects in Dougherty's study viewed male coworker touch as an attempt to control them and make them un-comfortable. For the final function of camaraderie, Dougherty explains:

> For the male participants, sexualized behavior tended to serve a functional and normative role of creating and demonstrating a sense of cohesion for a group to which they felt a strong commitment. For the women, on the other hand, groups were a means of preventing sexualized behavior. So while the men enacted sex-ualized behavior to demonstrate group cohesion, women used a cohesive group to prevent the enactment of sexualized behavior. (p. 388)

Dougherty's study sheds light on how women and men tend to view the same behaviors on the job so differently; it also underscores the complicated na-ture of men's and women's communication and relationships on the job. Do you hear echoes of these research findings in your workplace environment? What ef-forts are your employers making to protect themselves, their employees, and their organizations from sexual harassment?

A Proactive Approach to the Problem of Workplace Sexual Harassment

How can an organization educate its employees, create a respectful working cli-mate free of hasassment, and protect the rights of its workers if and when ha-rassment occurs? Everything we have experienced and read about sexual harassment calls for a proactive approach: that is, organizations and workers shouldn't bury their heads in the sand as if sexual harassment didn't exist or couldn't happen to them or their businesses (Gruber, 2002). Ignoring the prob-lem is very risky because employers are legally liable for sexual harassment in their workplaces whether or not they knew the harassment was occurring. In fact, two rulings by the U.S. Supreme Court in 1998 further expanded the scope of the employer's liability (Casey, Desai, & Ulrich, 1998). The proactive approach we recommend for organizations involves a four-part strategy, including the de-velopment and updating of a sexual harassment policy, the institution of a train-ing program, use of mediation services, and the establishment and maintenance of a supportive, open communication climate in the workplace.

Getting Something on Paper

National attention to sexual harassment has brought about some impor-tant changes, one being the widespread development of company harassment policies. One national human relations publication indicates that 97 percent of organizations currently have sexual harassment policies; 84 percent of em-ployees say that their organizations have adequately informed them of such policies (Sexual Harassment, 1999). However, Ellen Bravo, codirector of the Na-tional Association of Working Women, contends that many company policies are brief, vague, incomplete, out of date, and weak (as in Cloud, 1998). Lax or outdated policies can greatly imperil an organization, in terms of worker pro-ductivity and satisfaction and in potential costs of employee turnover, litiga-tion, and settlements.

Organizations must develop clear and comprehensive policies on sexual harassment and review those policies frequently. Along with a statement of the organization's philosophical stance on equality in the workplace and on freedom from discrimination, the policy should detail procedures for both reporting and responding to claims of sexual harassment. A thorough explanation of the range of behaviors that could constitute sexual harassment in the workplace, especially "hostile climate" harassment, should be provided; the policy should educate workers about sexual harassment in general and outline the organization's procedures in particular. Policies—and the managers and trainers who explain those policies—need to be as specific and blatant as possible in educating employees about what behaviors reflect professionalism and what behaviors do not. However, Dougherty (2001) contends that merely having a company policy and some sort of enforcement mechanism is inadequate, since, as her study revealed, it is likely that men and women within an organization will not view the same set of behaviors the same way. She points out that managers need to have a clear understanding of sexual harassment's connection to other issues in the organization, such as the connection between sexual behavior and stress reduction for male healthcare workers in her study. Gruber's (2002) research shows that the presence of a sexual harassment policy within an organization does affect men's and women's behavior; however, policies are more effective at curtailing environmental harassment, in such forms as denigrating sexual comments made by men about women or the presence of sexual posters or materials in workplaces. A policy alone is not effective in deterring more serious and more personal forms of harassment.

Management researchers Paetzold and O'Leary-Kelly (1993) suggest two important provisions which typically do not appear in most policies but which every policy should contain: (1) a description of the variety of ways an employee can indicate that a harasser's conduct is unwelcome and offensive, and (2) a clear statement of the consequences for harassers, enumerating steps the organization will take once a claim of harassment is made or a person's behavior is called into question. Finally, since harassment court rulings and laws continue to change, organizations should institute a procedure for a periodic review and update of the policy.

Providing Meaningful, Useful Training

We put these adjectives in the heading because we've been to some training programs that seemed to be conducted for appearances' sake—token attempts at dealing with a problem that they didn't really believe was a problem, but that someone else (in a higher or influential position) *said* was a problem. Have you been to sessions like this? One of the first things that reveals the seriousness of a training session is who is involved, meaning both who puts on the training and who is expected (or required) to attend. For example, internal trainers may be more trusted and familiar, thereby increasing the potential for meaningful discussion of a difficult subject. However, external consultants may be viewed as more credible, with their fees signaling how seriously the organization views the subject. Probably the best option is a team of internal and external trainers, also mixed by sex so as to diminish the potential for gender stereotypes.

A mandated training program sends a different message than a voluntary program; voluntary programs sometimes suffer from low attendance because of employees' fears that they'll be perceived as either victims of harassment or as harassers who were "advised" to attend. Training only human resources personnel and supervisors is commendable but incomplete (Berryman-Fink, 1993). A training program that targets lower-level employees while exempting upper levels certainly sends the wrong message. And it doesn't help an organization much, since research indicates that sexual harassment occurs at all levels within organizations, regardless of the salary, status, or power of an employee (Dougherty, 2001). Training programs that involve everyone in an organization produce the best results. This includes temporary workers, who, as research documents, are especially vulnerable to workplace sexual harassment (Henson, 1996; Rogers & Henson, 2002). Plans need to be instituted for repeating training sessions as an organization experiences turnover, with provisions for including sexual harassment information in new employee orientation sessions and personnel interviews. In an insightful chapter on effective training, communication scholar Cynthia Berryman-Fink (1993) offers this suggestion: "In addition to teaching supervisors how to recognize, detect, and deal with sexual harassment, organizations need to educate employees about professional behavior that is neither sexually intimidating nor sexually inviting" (p. 268). This is a reference to such behaviors as teasing and banter among coworkers, which can sometimes be sexual, may involve flirtation, and is in any case unprofessional.

One approach to training that has received recognition is DuPont Industries' program "A Matter of Respect." Role playing, videos, and groups discussions are used with employees at all levels within the company to help them understand risks to safety in the workplace, such as sexual harassment and sexual assault (Jacobs & Bonavoglia, 1998). This company also established a 24-hour hot line through which counselors provide callers with advice and information (Hayes Andrews, Herschel, & Baird, 1996). One factor that makes training programs like this successful is having employees participate actively instead of delivering information in a lecture format. Because research finds gender-based and individual differences in perceptions of sexual harassment, employees need to have forums where they can comfortably discuss their perspectives (Haunani Solomon & Miller Williams, 1997).

Mediation Services

Organizations might want to consider the wisdom of developing in-house mediation services. Mediation, which some agencies, courts, and organizations require, is a middle step between a complaint and litigation. It calls for complaining parties to have a conversation—a highly structured conversation controlled (mediated) by an impartial third party. Many times situations can be rectified and compromises reached before they escalate into expensive and time-consuming lawsuits. Of course, in-house mediation services are more feasible for larger organizations than small because of the costs involved and the potential

---

'Net Notes

If you're interested in learning more about mediation services, check out **www.mediation.com.** This site offers referral services and information on how to locate a mediator or mediation service that will help you with your particular issue. For example, some mediators who work specifically with divorce disputes, others handle employment disputes, and so forth. The site also provides articles on mediation, information about careers in mediation, and descriptions of and links to mediation centers across the country, many of which are on college and university campuses.

---

frequency of usage. But mediation services are springing up in many communities, small and large, typically offering services at no or low cost.

An Open and Supportive Communication Climate

Finally, but probably most importantly, organizations must develop communication climates in which employees feel safe bringing their concerns to the attention of employers. This is neither easily nor quickly accomplished in an organization. But as Paetzold and O'Leary-Kelly (1993) suggest, "Employers bear the responsibility of communicating a desexualized and degendered culture to their employees" (p. 70). Organizational leaders must work continually with managers and employees at all levels to create and foster open lines of communication so that an organizational climate is established and maintained in which concerns can be communicated. Sexual harassment is a difficult problem to discuss; for harassment survivors it is deeply personal, emotional, and often embarrassing, and so it is even harder to talk about with anyone. An organizational climate of openness—one in which female employees, in particular, know that their problems will be taken seriously—contributes more to successful employee relations than extensive policies, great training programs, and mediation.

Whether we want to believe it or not, sexual harassment is a reality in the workplace—not in all workplaces, but in more than you'd imagine. Sometimes it arises out of ignorance, sometimes out of sincere intentions to get acquainted or to compliment, and many times out of a desire to embarrass and outpower another individual. Most of the time it comes from men and is aimed at women, but it does happen in the reverse as well as between same-sex individuals. The best advice we can give on this point is to communicate professionally, not personally and certainly not sexually, with all coworkers—subordinates, peers, and superiors. Sexual innuendo, the dissemination of sexual material, sexist language and jokes, excessive compliments about appearance rather than professional performance, questions about private life, requests for social contact, invasive and unwelcome nonverbal behaviors—anything of this sort basically

---

Remember. . .

SEXUAL HARASSMENT: Unwelcome sexual advances, requests for sexual favors, and other verbal or physical conduct of a sexual nature.

QUID PRO QUO SEXUAL HARASSMENT: A request for sexual favors, backed up by a threat, implicit or explicit, that one will lose one's job, promotion opportunity, salary increase, etc., if one doesn't comply.

HOSTILE ENVIRONMENT SEXUAL HARASSMENT: Sexual conduct that has the intention or effect of interfering with an individual's work performance or creating an intimidating or offensive working environment.

MEDIATION: A middle step between a complaint and litigation, in which complaining parties have a highly structured conversation controlled (mediated) by an impartial third party.

---

has no place at work. Consultants advise, "If what you're thinking even vaguely involves sex, keep it to yourself" (Cloud, 1998, p. 52). It's best to avoid this kind of communication unless, and *only* unless, you have negotiated these "dangerous waters" with persons at work and you all feel *completely* comfortable with this kind of communication. But, as a caution, there are very few of us who feel completely comfortable with this kind of communication with all of our coworkers, across all situations, at all times. You can never really know what is in someone's mind or how someone will react.

CONCLUSION

This chapter has presented some predominant issues that challenge today's working women and men. We've explored this particular context with students in mind, considering situations and concerns that may arise when students launch, restart, or redirect their careers. We've examined affirmative action, job interviewing, on-the-job communication, advancement opportunities and barriers, and management styles. The complicated topic of sexual harassment has also been explored for its effects on work relationships and the work environment. Are you now magically equipped with a solution for every problem and a strategy for overcoming every obstacle you might encounter at work? Will you be able to confront gender bias and gender-related communication perplexities with skill and ease? The answers are "probably not" to the first question, and "we hope so" to the second one.

Again, when it comes to gender communication, to the unique and complex dynamics of communication between women and men, there are no magical formulas, no surefire remedies, no easy answers. But by ridding your professional communication of stereotypes and personal or sexual elements that are inappropriate in the workplace and by assuming a flexible communicative style with colleagues, bosses, and clients that is not gender-specific, you will have gone a long way toward projecting a professional, successful image at work.

Discussion Starters

1. Have you formed an opinion about whether affirmative action is still necessary today or whether its time has passed? Think about your own profile, considering sex, gender, race, religion, and sexual orientation. Are you a person who has benefited or will benefit from affirmative action? How would the job market be affected if affirmative action no longer existed in your state?
2. Think of a time when you interviewed for a job you really wanted. It could be any kind of job—paper route, baby-sitter, part-time waiter, and so on. Now imagine yourself in the same interview, but as a member of the opposite sex. Would the person who interviewed you treat you any differently? If so, how so? Do you think your sex had anything to do with getting or not getting that job?
3. In this chapter, we discussed a double bind for professional women—how they are "damned if they do" and "damned if they don't" act like men. Do you think this double bind is real for working women? Have you ever experienced it, or do you know of a woman who has faced this kind of challenge in her job? Is there a corresponding double bind for male managers? Are there any options for getting out of a double bind?
4. Think of a person who holds a position of power and authority at work. This person might be one of your parents, your doctor, someone you've worked for, and so on. What is the sex of the person? If the person is male, do you think he'd have as much power and respect in his job if he were female? Would he have to change his communication style or the way he deals with coworkers, subordinates, and clients if he were female? If the person is female, what barriers or challenges has she faced in achieving her position of respectability? Do you see evidence of an authority gap among professional people?
5. Think about the difference between quid pro quo and hostile climate sexual harassment. Have you ever known anyone who experienced quid pro quo harassment? Think about jobs you've had; was there anything in your workplace that someone could have interpreted as contributing to a hostile sexual environment?

References

Alberts, J. K. (1992). Teasing and sexual harassment: Double-bind communication in the workplace. In L. A. M. Perry, L. H. Turner, & H. M. Sterk (Eds.), *Constructing and reconstructing gender: The links among communication, language, and gender* (pp. 185–196). Albany: State University of New York Press.

Allen, B. J. (2001). Gender, race, and communication in professional environments. In L. P. Arliss & D. J. Borisoff (Eds.), *Women and men communicating: Challenges and changes* (2nd ed.) (pp. 212–231). Prospect Heights, IL: Waveland.

American Civil Liberties Union. (1995). *Affirmative Action: Still effective, still needed in the pursuit of equal opportunity in the '90s.* New York: American Civil Liberties Union Press.

Analyzing Affirmative Action. (1995, November 17). *The Chronicle of Higher Education,* p. A6.

Beebe, S. A., Beebe, S. J., & Ivy, D. K. (2004). *Communication: Principles for a lifetime* (2nd ed.). Boston: Allyn & Bacon.

Bennett-Alexander, D. (1998). Same-gender sexual harassment: The Supreme Court allows coverage under Title VII. *Labor Law Journal, 49,* 927–948.

Berryman-Fink, C. (1993). Preventing sexual harassment through male-female communication training. In G. L. Kreps (Ed.), *Sexual harassment: Communication implications* (pp. 267–280). Cresskill, NJ: Hampton.

Berryman-Fink, C., & Vanover Riley, K. (1997). The effect of sex and feminist orientation on perceptions in sexually harassing communication. *Women's Studies in Communication, 20,* 25–44.

Billing, Y. D., & Alvesson, M. (2000). Questioning the notion of feminine leadership: A critical perspective on the gender labeling of leadership. *Gender, Work, and Organization, 7,* 144–157.

Blum, L. M. (1997). Possibilities and limits of the comparable worth movement. In D. Dunn (Ed.), *Workplace/women's place: An anthology* (pp. 88–99). Los Angeles: Roxbury.

Borisoff, D., & Merrill, L. (1998). *The power to communicate: Gender differences as barriers* (3rd ed.). Prospect Heights, IL: Waveland.

Brownell, J. (2001). Gender and communication in the hospitality industry. In L. P. Arliss & D. J. Borisoff (Eds.), *Women and men communicating: Challenges and changes* (2nd ed.) (pp. 289–309). Prospect Heights, IL: Waveland.

Burns, S. (2002, May 26). Workplace moms may have hit a peak. *Corpus Christi Caller Times,* p. D5.

Buzzanell, P. M. (1992). Sex, romance, and organizational taboos. In L. A. M. Perry, L. H. Turner, & H. M. Sterk (Eds.), *Constructing and reconstructing gender: The links among communication, language, and gender* (pp. 175–184). Albany: State University of New York Press.

Cameron, D. (1995). *Verbal hygiene.* London: Routledge and Kegan Paul.

Casey, T., Desai, S., & Ulrich, J. (1998, Fall). Supreme Court unpredictable on harassment and sex. *National NOW Times,* pp. 6, 15.

Chaplin, W. F., Phillips, J. B., Brown, J. D., Clanton, N. R., & Stein, J. L. (2000). Handshaking, gender, personality, and first impressions. *Journal of Personality and Social Psychology, 79,* 110–117.

Claes, M. T. (2002). Women, men, and management styles. In P. J. Dubeck & D. Dunn (Eds.), *Workplace/women's place: An anthology* (2nd ed.) (pp. 121–125). Los Angeles: Roxbury.

Cloud, J. (1998, March 23). Sex and the law. *Time,* 48–54.

Crary, D. (2002, May 12). Corporate ladder might still be more male-friendly. Associated Press Wire Service, as reported in *Corpus Christi Caller Times,* p. A5.

Daniels, T. D., Spiker, B. K., & Papa, M. J. (1997). *Perspectives on organizational communication* (4th ed.). New York: McGraw-Hill.

Dougherty, D. S. (2001). Sexual harassment as (dys)functional process: A feminist standpoint analysis. *Journal of Applied Communication Research, 29,* 372–402.

Dubeck, P. J., & Dunn, D. (2002). Introduction to unit four: Work and family—seeking a balance. In P. J. Dubeck & D. Dunn (Eds.), *Workplace/women's place: An anthology* (2nd ed.) (pp. 141–145). Los Angeles: Roxbury.

Dubois, C. (1998). An emotional examination of same- and other-gender sexual harassment in the workplace. *Sex Roles, 39,* 731–747.

Dunn, D. (2002). Preface to the second edition. In P. J. Dubeck & D. Dunn (Eds.), *Workplace/women's place: An anthology* (2nd ed.) (pp. xiii–xv). Los Angeles: Roxbury.

Edley, P. P. (2001). Technology, employed mothers, and corporate colonization of the lifeworld: A gendered paradox of work and family balance. *Women & Language, 24,* 28–35.

Eisenberg, E. M., Goodall, H. L. Jr., & Goodall, H. L. (2001). *Organizational communication: Balancing creativity and constraint* (3rd ed.). New York: Bedford/St. Martin's.

Equal Employment Opportunity Commission. (2002). [Online]. *Sexual harassment charges: EEOC & FEPAs combined, FY 1992-FY 2002.* Available: http://www.eeoc.gov/stats/harass

Federal Glass Ceiling Commission. (1995). *A solid investment: Making full use of the nation's human capital.* Washington, DC: U.S. Government Printing Office.

Federal Glass Ceiling Commission. (2002). The glass ceiling. In P. J. Dubeck & D. Dunn (Eds.), *Workplace/women's place: An anthology* (2nd ed.) (pp. 98–104). Los Angeles: Roxbury.

Fierman, J. (1990, December 17). Do women manage differently? *Fortune,* 115–117.

Fine, G. A. (1996). Friendships in the workplace. In K. M. Galvin & P. Cooper (Eds.), *Making connections: Readings in relational communication* (pp. 270–277). Los Angeles: Roxbury.

Finnegan, A. (2001, October). The inside story: Are the 100 best as good as they say they are? *Working Mother Magazine.* Available: http://workingmother.com

Franklin, S. (1997, March 30). The angry white male strikes back. *Corpus Christi Caller Times,* p. D4.

Friedan, B. (1981). *The second stage.* New York: Summit Books.

Gerdes, L. I. (1999). Introduction. In L. I. Gerdes (Ed.), *Sexual harassment: Current controversies* (pp. 12–14). San Diego: Greenhaven.

Gerson, K. (2002). Combining work and motherhood. In P. J. Dubeck & D. Dunn (Eds.), *Workplace/women's place: An anthology* (2nd ed.) (pp. 146–162). Los Angeles: Roxbury.

Gertsel, N., & McGonagle, K. (2002). Job leaves and the limits of the Family and Medical Leave Act: The effects of gender, race, and family. In P. J. Dubeck & D. Dunn (Eds.), *Workplace/women's place: An anthology* (2nd ed.) (pp. 205–215). Los Angeles: Roxbury.

Gruber, J. E. (2002). The impact of male work environments and organizational policies on women's experiences of sexual harassment. In P. J. Dubeck & D. Dunn (Eds.), *Workplace/women's place: An anthology* (2nd ed.) (pp. 90–97). Los Angeles: Roxbury.

Guthrie, D., & Roth, L. M. (2002). The state, courts, and equal opportunities for female CEOs in U.S. organizations. In P. J. Dubeck & D. Dunn (Eds.), *Workplace/women's place: An anthology* (2nd ed.) (pp. 105–115). Los Angeles: Roxbury.

Hall, C. (2001, February 11). Mentoring crucial for new employees. *The Dallas Morning News,* as reported in *Corpus Christi Caller Times,* pp. D1, D4.

Haunani Solomon, D., & Miller Williams, M. L. (1997). Perceptions of social-sexual communication at work: The effects of message, situation, and observer characteristics on judgments of sexual harassment. *Journal of Applied Communication Research, 25,* 196–216.

Hayes Andrews, P., Herschel, R. T., & Baird, J. E. Jr. (1996). *Organizational communication: Empowerment in a technological society.* Boston: Houghton-Mifflin.

Helgesen, S. (1990). *The female advantage: Women's ways of leadership.* New York: Doubleday.

Helgesen, S. (1995). *The web of inclusion.* New York: Doubleday.

Henley, N. (1977). *Body politics: Power, sex, and nonverbal communication.* Englewood Cliffs, NJ: Prentice-Hall.

Henson, K. D. (1996). *Just a temp.* Philadelphia: Temple University Press.

Hewlett, S. A. (2002). *Creating a life: Professional women and the quest for children.* New York: Talk Miramax Books.

Hochschild, A. R. (1997). *The time bind: When work becomes home and home becomes work.* New York: Metropolitan Books.

Hochschild, A. R., & Machung, A. (2002). The second shift: Working parents and the revolution at home. In P. J. Dubeck & D. Dunn (Eds.), *Workplace/women's place: An anthology* (2nd ed.) (pp. 163–173). Los Angeles: Roxbury.

Holcomb, B. (2000). *Not guilty! The good news for working mothers*. New York: Touchstone.

Holcomb, B. (2002, Spring). Family-friendly policies: Who benefits? *Ms.*, 102–103.

Ivy, D. K. (1993, February). *When the power lines aren't clearly drawn: A survey of peer sexual harassment*. Paper presented at the meeting of the Western States Communication Association, Albuquerque, NM.

Ivy, D. K., & Hamlet, S. (1996). College students and sexual dynamics: Two studies of peer sexual harassment. *Communication Education, 45,* 149–166.

Jacobs, G., & Bonavoglia, A. (1998, May–June). Confused by the rules. *Ms.*, 48–55.

Jones, D. (1998, July–August). Memo to mothers at work: Stop feeling guilty! *Ms.*, 40–43.

Jones, S. E., & Yarbrough, A. E. (1985). A naturalistic study of the meanings of touch. *Communication Monographs, 52,* 19–56.

Kabacoff, R. I. (1998). *Gender difference in organizational leadership: A large sample study*. Paper presented at the meeting of the American Psychological Association, San Francisco, CA.

Kanter, R. M. (1977). *Men and women of the corporation*. New York: Basic Books.

Kelly, R. M. (2002). Sex-role spillover: Personal, familial, and organizational roles. In P. J. Dubeck & D. Dunn (Eds.), *Workplace/women's place: An anthology* (2nd ed.) (pp. 80–89). Los Angeles: Roxbury.

Kirkwood, W. G., & Ralston, S. M. (1999). Inviting meaningful applicant performances in employment interviews. *Journal of Business Communication, 36,* 55–76.

Knapp, M. L., & Hall, J. A. (2002). *Nonverbal communication in human interaction* (5th ed.). Belmont, CA: Wadsworth.

Kreps, G. L. (1994). Sexual harassment as information equivocality: Communication and requisite variety. In S. G. Bingham (Ed.), *Conceptualizing sexual harassment as discursive practice* (pp. 127–138). Westport, CT: Praeger.

Lamude, K. G., & Daniels, T. D. (1990). Mutual evaluations of communication competence in superior-subordinate relationships. *Women's Studies in Communication, 13,* 39–56.

LaRocca, M. A., & Kromrey, J. D. (1999). The perception of sexual harassment in higher education: Impact of gender and attractiveness. *Sex Roles, 40,* 921–940.

MacKinnon, C. A. (2002). Should Title VII apply to sexual harassment between individuals of the same sex? In E. L. Paul (Ed.), *Taking sides: Clashing views on controversial issues in sex and gender* (2nd ed.) (pp. 152–163). Guilford, CT: McGraw-Hill/Dushkin.

Markert, J. (1999). Sexual harassment and the communication conundrum. *Gender Issues, 17,* 34–52.

Marlowe, C. M., Schneider, S. L., & Nelson, C. E. (1996). Gender and attractiveness bias in hiring decisions: Are more experienced managers less biased? *Journal of Applied Psychology, 81,* 11–21.

Martin, L. (1991). *A report on the Glass Ceiling Initiative*. Washington, DC: U.S. Department of Labor.

May, S. K. (1997, November). *Silencing the feminine in managerial discourse*. Paper presented at the meeting of the National Communication Association, Chicago, IL.

McDorman, T. F. (1998). Uniting legal doctrine and discourse to rethink women's workplace rights. *Women's Studies in Communication, 21,* 27–54.

McKenna, E. P. (1997). *When work doesn't work anymore: Women, work, and identity*. New York: Delacorte.

Miller, V., Casey, M. K., Lamphear-Van Horn, M. J., & Ethington, C. (1993, November). *The maternity leave as a role negotiation process: A conceptual framework*. Paper presented at the meeting of the Speech Communication Association, Miami, FL.

Mongeau, P. A., & Blalock, J. (1994). Student evaluations of instructor immediacy and sexually harassing behaviors: An experimental investigation. *Journal of Applied Communication Research, 22,* 256–272.

Morrison, A. M., White, R. P., & Van Velsor, E. (1987). *Breaking the glass ceiling: Can women reach the top of America's largest corporations?* Reading, MA: Addison-Wesley.

Morrow, P. C. (1990). Physical attractiveness and selection decision making. *Journal of Management, 16,* 45–60.

Nacoste, R. W. (1995, April 7). The truth about Affirmative Action. *The Chronicle of Higher Education,* p. A48.

Nadesan, M. H., & Trethewey, A. (2000). Performing the enterprising subject: Gendered strategies of success. *Text & Performance Quarterly, 20,* 223–250.

Nadler, J. K., & Nadler, L. B. (1987). Communication, gender and intraorganizational negotiation ability. In L. P. Stewart & S. Ting-Toomey (Eds.), *Communication, gender, and sex roles in diverse interaction contexts* (pp. 119–134). Norwood, NJ: Ablex.

Neher, W. W. (1997). *Organizational communication: Challenges of change, diversity, and continuity.* Boston: Allyn & Bacon.

Nelton, S. (1997, May). Leadership for the new age. *Nation's Business,* 18–27.

Paetzold, R. L., & O'Leary-Kelly, A. M. (1993). Organizational communication and the legal dimensions of hostile work environment sexual harassment. In G. L. Kreps (Ed.), *Sexual harassment: Communication implications* (pp. 63–77). Cresskill, NJ: Hampton.

Paetzold, R. L., & O'Leary-Kelly, A. M. (1996). The implications of U.S. Supreme Court and circuit court decisions for hostile environment sexual harassment cases. In M. S. Stockdale (Ed.), *Sexual harassment in the workplace: Perspectives, frontiers, and response strategies* (pp. 85–104). Thousand Oaks, CA: Sage.

Parker, K. (2002, April 28). Karen Hughes and the best of both worlds. *Orlando Sentinel,* as reported in the *Corpus Christi Caller Times,* p. A15.

Paul, E. L. (2002). Introduction to Issue 8. In E. L. Paul (Ed.), *Taking sides: Clashing views on controversial issues in sex and gender* (2nd ed.) (pp. 150–151). Guilford, CT: McGraw-Hill/Dushkin.

Pear, R. (2000, November 5). More single moms taking jobs. *New York Times* News Service, as reported in *Corpus Christi Caller Times,* p. A3.

Peters, J. K. (1997). *When mothers work: Loving our children without sacrificing ourselves.* Reading, MA: Addison-Wesley.

Ralston, S. M., & Kinser, A. E. (2001). Intersections of gender and employment interviewing. In L. P. Arliss & D. J. Borisoff (Eds.), *Women and men communicating: Challenges and changes* (2nd ed.) (pp. 185–211). Prospect Heights, IL: Waveland.

Reardon, K. K. (1997). Dysfunctional communication patterns in the workplace: Closing the gap. In D. Dunn (Ed.), *Workplace/women's place: An anthology* (pp. 165–180). Los Angeles: Roxbury.

Reilly, M. E., Lott, B., Caldwell, D., & DeLuca, L. (1992). Tolerance for sexual harassment related to self-reported sexual victimization. *Gender & Society, 6,* 122–138.

Reskin, B., & Padavic, I. (1994). *Women and men at work.* Thousand Oaks, CA: Pine Forge Press.

Reskin, B., & Padavic, I. (2002). *Women and men at work* (2nd ed.). Thousand Oaks, CA: Pine Forge Press.

Rhode, D. L. (1997, November/December). Harassment is alive and well and living at the water cooler. *Ms.,* 28–29.

Rogers, J. K., & Henson, K. D. (2002). "Hey, why don't you wear a shorter skirt?" Structural vulnerability and the organization of sexual harassment in temporary clerical employment. In P. J. Dubeck & D. Dunn (Eds.), *Workplace/women's place: An anthology* (2nd ed.) (pp. 321–332). Los Angeles: Roxbury.

Romaine, S. (1999). *Communicating gender.* Mahwah, NJ: Erlbaum.

Rosenberg, J., Perlstadt, H., & Phillips, W. R. F. (2002). "Now that we are here": Discrimination, disparagement, and harassment at work and the experience of women lawyers. In P. J. Dubeck & D. Dunn (Eds.), *Workplace/women's place: An anthology* (2nd ed.) (pp. 242–253). Los Angeles: Roxbury.

Saltzman Chafetz, J. (1997). "I need a (traditional) wife!" Employment-family conflicts. In D. Dunn (Ed.), *Workplace/women's place: An anthology* (pp. 116–124). Los Angeles: Roxbury.

Sargent, A. G. (1981). *The androgynous manager.* New York: AMACOM.

Sege, I. (1996, May 30). Sisters in law. *The Boston Globe,* as reported in *Corpus Christi Caller Times,* pp. C1, C2.

Sellers, P. (1998, October 12). The 50 most powerful women in American business. *Fortune,* 76–130.

Sexual harassment charges (and dismissals) escalate. (1999, April). *HR Focus, 76,* 4.

Sloan, D. K., & Krone, K. J. (2000). Women managers and gendered values. *Women's Studies in Communication, 23,* 111–130.

Stewart, L. P. (2001). Gender issues in corporate communication. In L. P. Arliss & D. J. Borisoff (Eds.), *Women and men communicating: Challenges and changes* (2nd ed.) (pp. 171–184). Prospect Heights, IL: Waveland.

St. George, D. (1995, March 19). Analysts: Affirmative Action helps white women. *Corpus Christi Caller Times,* p. A8.

Toner, R. (2002, April 28). Hughes' departure again ignites "having it all" debate. *New York Times* News Service, as reported in *Corpus Christi Caller Times,* p. A7.

Toppo, G. (2000, September 3). Study: Families working harder. Associated Press Wire Service, as reported in *Corpus Christi Caller Times,* p. A6.

Trei, L. (2002, April 10). A feminist economic view of work and family. [Online]. *The Stanford Report.* Available: http://www.stanford.edu/dept/news/report

U. S. Department of Labor, Women's Bureau. (2002). Earnings differences between women and men. In P. J. Dubeck & D. Dunn (Eds.), *Workplace/women's place: An anthology* (2nd ed.) (pp. 57–63). Los Angeles: Roxbury.

Violanti, M. T. (1996). Hooked on expectations: An analysis of influence and relationships in the Tailhook reports. *Journal of Applied Communication Research, 24,* 67–82.

Watkins, P. G. (1996). Women in the work force in non-traditional jobs. In P. Lester (Ed.), *Images that injure* (pp. 69–74). Westport, CT: Praeger.

Wayne, J. H., Riordan, C. M., & Thomas, K. M. (2001). Is all sexual harassment viewed the same? Mock juror decisions in same- and cross-gender cases. *Journal of Applied Psychology, 86,* 179–187.

Whitehurst, T. Jr. (2002). Child care's bottom line: Employers are learning that their participation makes dollars and sense. *Corpus Christi Caller Times,* pp. D1, D4.

Williams, C. L. (2002). Gendered jobs and gendered workers. In P. J. Dubeck & D. Dunn (Eds.), *Workplace/women's place: An anthology* (2nd ed.) (pp. 75–79). Los Angeles: Roxbury.

Witteman, H. (1993). The interface between sexual harassment and organizational romance. In L. A. M. Perry, L. H. Turner, & H. M. Sterk (Eds.), *Constructing and reconstructing gender: The links among communication, language, and gender* (pp. 27–62). Albany: State University of New York Press.

Zaslow, J. (2002, September 2). Moms are rethinking staying at home. *The Wall Street Journal,* as reported in *Corpus Christi Caller Times,* pp. E1, E4.

CHAPTER TEN

A "CLASS ACT":
Gender Communication in Educational Settings

CASE STUDY: TWO COLLEGE EXPERIENCES

Stacy had just transferred to a private university that was much smaller than the state school where she spent her first year in college. She didn't really know what to expect, other than smaller classes. What she really didn't expect was how quickly she relaxed in her classes, how comfortable she felt introducing herself when a professor went around the room. She actually asked one professor a question about the syllabus—on the *first* day. As the semester progressed, Stacy continued to enjoy her classes because they seemed less competitive and pressured than ones she'd had in the past. She felt that she wasn't on display, that her comments or questions didn't seem stupid to her classmates, that what she wore to class didn't matter to anyone, and that nobody cared (or particularly noticed) when she didn't wear makeup or had a "bad hair day." She actually looked forward to going to classes. Stacy was learning and thriving in higher education, and her grades soared.

Javier knew that college wouldn't be anything like high school, and he looked forward to the discipline of life in a military academy. This may sound strange, but Javier knew that the structure and competition would be good for him. He had been bored and a bit of a slacker in high school but had made good enough grades and scored well enough on the SAT to get admitted to a good college. It took a few weeks, but Javier adapted to the strict environment and was accepted into the corps of cadets—quite an achievement for a freshman. He felt less conspicuous in classes, as though he didn't have to show off, be macho, or be the class clown to get attention from girls. There was competition among his classmates, because everyone wanted to be right or to have the best answer for the professor, but Javier expected this. He viewed it as a challenge, one that

Hot Button Issue

"SINGLE-SEX EDUCATION"

Texas Woman's University—the country's largest university primarily for women—is always concerned when another tide rises against single-sex education. TWU is a public university that does admit men, but, historically and currently, its student body and faculty are predominantly female. Their latest concern was prompted by a report from the AAUW (1998a) which concluded that single-sex education was not necessarily better for girls in grades K-12 than coeducation, although they detected trends in single-sex programs that included "a heightened regard by girls for mathematics and science; an increase in girls' risk-taking; and a gain in girls' confidence from academic competence" (*Gender Mindbender*, 1998, p. 1). The controversy will no doubt continue, as opposition to single-sex education emerges from odd places such as the National Organization for Women, which believes that segregated education is discriminatory and a step in the wrong direction toward achieving gender equality (Burk, 1998).

Have you ever thought about what it would be like to attend a predominantly female or male university? Perhaps some of you are taking this course at just such an institution, so this isn't a stretch for you. But most of you attend coeducational institutions, so as you read the material in this chapter, try to imagine how your education would be affected if your classmates and professors were only of your same sex.

would make him smarter and stronger. He found his subjects interesting (well, most of them, anyway), and he earned a decent grade point average during his first semester.

What's going on in these two scenarios? Does this happen only in professors' dreams? No; what you've read are accounts of students attending single-sex institutions of higher learning. This is a topic of considerable controversy, heightened by headline-grabbing cases in the mid-1990s involving two military colleges: the Citadel and the Virginia Military Institute (VMI). Because these institutions accepted public funds, they came under fire for admitting only male students (Jaschik, 1995; Lederman, 1996).

Do you view educational institutions as havens of equality, as places where discriminatory attitudes are left outside the ivy-covered walls? While some of us who have made education our careers like to believe that academic institutions may be more sensitive to diversity issues than other types of organizations, no institution is exempt from discrimination. In this chapter, we examine a few forms of sexism lurking in the halls of education. As you read the information in this chapter, weigh it against your own experience in educational settings—from preschool to college. Consider the contributions of your education and your educators to your gender identity, attitudes, and communication with women and men.

Hot Topics

- Effects of children's fairy tales and nursery rhymes on gender identity and attitudes
- Children's textbooks and literature that contribute to their ideas about gender
- How gender expectations form to affect classroom interaction and student learning
- How textbooks and communication styles affect college classroom interaction
- Factors that contribute to a chilly classroom climate for women in higher education
- Gender-linked teacher and student classroom behaviors
- The problem of peer sexual harassment in educational settings

CHILDREN'S LITERATURE AND
EARLY LESSONS ABOUT GENDER

When you think about your childhood, many experiences come to mind—some good, maybe some not so good. Do your fonder memories include the stories a parent read to you before you went to sleep or stories you read with classmates when you were in grade school? Can you remember imagining yourself as one of the characters in a story, like Gretel, who saves her brother by pushing the witch into the oven, or the prince who kisses Snow White and awakens her from her poison-induced sleep? It may seem silly to think about these things now, but it's possible that who you are as an adult—your view of self, others, relationships, and communication within those relationships—has been affected in some way by the early lessons you received from children's literature at home and at school. Those early lessons contribute to your vision of what it means to be a man or a woman, what roles the sexes should play in society, how relationships ought to work, and the quality of communication it takes to make relationships work.

Fairy Tales, Nursery Rhymes, and Gender

We know what you're thinking: "Hey, don't go getting all analytical with my favorite kids' stories." We ask you to try to suspend any doubts or disbelief for just a moment to consider the potential effects of reading or hearing a number of stories with the same basic plot: The young, beautiful, helpless or abandoned girl encounters a series of obstacles (events or people) that place her in jeopardy. Enter the young, handsome, usually wealthy prince or king who rescues and marries the girl. With minor deviations, this basic theme serves as the plot for such fairy tales as *Cinderella, Snow White and the Seven Dwarfs, Sleeping Beauty, Goldilocks and the Three Bears, Little Red Riding Hood,* and *Rapunzel,* to name only a few of the better-known tales. The attributes of female leading characters in such tales include beauty, innocence, passivity, patience (since they often have to wait a long time for the rescuer to come), dependence, powerlessness, and self-sacrifice (Bottigheimer, 1986). Male characters, as rescuers, have to be handsome, independent, brave, strong, action-oriented, successful, romantic, and kindhearted (for the most part). Do the characters' descriptors reflect stereotypical male and female traits? What's the potential effect of these depictions?

Once upon a Time: Fairy Tale Stereotypes

Researchers continue to examine how stereotypical portrayals in fairy tales affect boys' and girls' developing views of the sexes (Ernst, 1995; Gooden & Gooden, 2001; Trites, 1998; Zipes, 1997). Several studies have focused especially on Disney tales, which are alternatively criticized for their biased depictions of gender roles and praised for their occasional themes of feminine empowerment (Addison, 1995; Sells, 1995; Zipes, 1995). With regard to effects on girls, gender scholar Sharon Downey (1996) suggests: "The fairy tale's popularity in children's literature is unsurpassed. Their joint universalizing and culture-specific themes contribute to the process of 'civilizing' society's young because fairy tales encourage conformity to culturally-sanctioned roles. The 'truths' validated through folktales, however, often reinforce disparaging images of females" (p. 185).

In Chapter 3 on gender and media, we discussed cultivation theory, which suggests that media consumption "cultivates" in us a distorted perception of the world we live in, blurring the lines between reality and fantasy (Fox & Gerbner, 2000; Gerbner, Gross, Morgan, & Signorielli, 1980). Just as someone may grow up expecting relationships to work like they do in Hollywood romance movies or television sitcoms, children may grow up believing that life is somehow supposed to be like the stories they heard and read as a child. Concern arises in the power of these stories to affect a child's sense of self, perceptions about roles women and men should play in our culture, and expectations for relationships. As noted feminist author bell hooks (2000) contends, "Children's literature is one of the most crucial sites for feminist education for critical consciousness precisely because beliefs and identities are still being formed. And more often than not narrow-minded thinking about gender continues to be the norm on the playground" (p. 23).

Consider the story of Cinderella, the beautiful young girl who was terrorized and subjugated by her evil stepmother and two stepsisters after her father's death. She lives virtually as a slave until a benevolent fairy godmother transforms her and sends her to the prince's ball. Everyone in the land knows that the handsome and wealthy prince is searching for a wife, so all the eligible women are decked out and positioned at the ball in order to win the prince's favor. You know how the story turns out: Cinderella steals the show and loses her slipper as she exits the ball, causing the now madly-in-love prince to search for her. He gallantly searches near and far for Cinderella, and is finally reunited with her because of her tiny, feminine shoe size, after which he punishes her stepfamily and triumphantly marries Cinderella.

Researchers have analyzed gendered messages that can be drawn from this fairy tale and others (Lieberman, 1986; Rowe, 1986; Trites, 1998). First, the main characters must be physically attractive, in order to be worthy of romance. In many of these stories, love is instantaneous—an uncontrollable reaction to rapturous, extraordinary beauty. Do children, especially young girls, get the message that one must be beautiful to be deserving of love and romance? A second theme in many tales is competition; the primary female character must often compete with other women for the attention and affection of the hero. This message runs counter to the female tendency to cooperate rather than compete to accomplish goals. It also suggests that winning a man is more important than having good relationships with other females. A third theme is that rewards for stereotypically gendered behavior include romance, marriage, wealth, and living happily ever after. This reinforces in girls the notion that the ultimate goal in life is to marry a wonderful man who will protect them and make them completely happy. There's nothing necessarily wrong with this goal, but is it the only appropriate goal? Since many women (even the most postmodern of modern women) feel pressure to be in a relationship and to find a partner, it's important to examine the possible seeds of those thoughts.

Also, consider the messages such fairy tales communicate about male roles. There is an emphasis on males' physical attractiveness (although this is not stressed as much as females' attractiveness). Moreover, the dashing male hero is expected to rescue the girl and turn her unbearable life into wedded bliss. That's a lot of pressure on men! This plot, found over and over again in children's stories (and movies, such as *Pretty Woman*), sets men up to be the rescuers and sets women up to be the rescued—and many men and women believe in and attempt to enact these roles as adults. What happens when women expect princelike qualities, when they form expectations of men that are too high and all-encompassing for any man to fulfill? What happens if the "prince" turns into a "beast"? In fairy tales, you seldom see what happens after the marriage ceremony; you read only the closing line, about living "happily ever after."

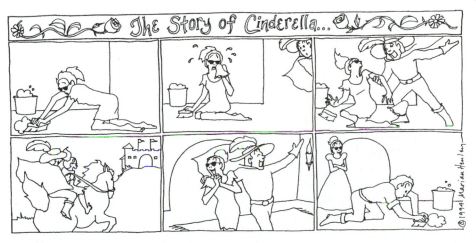

Maxine! Comix by Marian Henley. Reprinted by permission of the artist.

Maybe you're one of the lucky few people whose relational life has turned out like a fairy tale. (We don't know any people or relationships like this, but we acknowledge the possibility.) But have you ever thought that maybe these early, idealized images of what men and women were supposed to be for one another generated some unattainable standards for your adult life? Perhaps the gap between the ideal and the real may have caused you disappointment and disillusionment because life and relationships just didn't turn out the way you thought they were supposed to. Obviously, people learn to cope with the incongruencies of life and fantasy. Most people don't live their lives in complete frustration because relationships don't mirror the movies, romance novels, or childhood fairy tales. We learn—sometimes the hard way—that perfect people and perfect relationships are neither possible, nor particularly interesting for that matter. But should we have to work to dismiss the early images? Could the stories we're exposed to as children better prepare us for the realities we will encounter? Could the female and male characters represent more positive, balanced, realistic images of persons we'll likely deal with as we age and mature?

Contemporary Attempts at Unbiased Children's Tales

Some writers of children's literature are attempting to counter stereotypical images found in traditional fairy tales and nursery rhymes. Consider the following examples:

Jack and Jill Be Nimble

Jack be nimble, Jack be quick,

Jack jump over the candlestick!

Jill be nimble, jump it too,

If Jack can do it, so can you! (*Father Gander,* Larche, 1985)

The Old Couple Who Lived in a Shoe

There was an old couple who lived in a shoe,

They had so many children they didn't know what to do.

So they gave them some broth and some good whole wheat bread,

And kissed them all sweetly and sent them to bed.

There's only one issue I don't understand

If they didn't want so many why didn't they plan? (*Father Gander,* Larche, 1985)

These versions of two well-known nursery rhymes represent one author's attempt to "ungenderize" traditional children's literature. Doug Larche (aka Father Gander) published a book of rewritten, unbiased nursery rhymes in an effort to alter a sexist trend he saw in children's literature. *Father Gander,* as well as Jack Zipes's (1986) *Don't Bet on the Prince,* a collection of feminist fairy tales, are extremely popular among parents who are concerned about perpetuating limited, discriminatory stereotypes of men and women. Sources exist to help parents and teachers locate stories with more realistic, bias-free characterizations and story lines. One such source is *Let's Hear It for the Girls,* a reference guide to 375 books featuring girls in strong, problem-solving, adventurous, and brave roles (Baumeister, 1997).

Depictions of Gender in Textbooks and Children's Literature

As scholars Willis-Rivera and Meeker (2002) suggest, "Books often talk, implicitly or explicitly, about what a culture is, changes cultures might go through, traditions, hardships, and every day life within different groups of people. Books can be referred to again and again, and can be a constant source of information in children's lives" (p. 269). Gender bias in children's textbooks and literature emerges primarily in three ways: (1) the number of depictions of and references to men versus women, (2) representation by female versus male authors; and (3) stereotypical role portrayals of characters.

Depictions Speak Louder Than Words

In *Reviving Ophelia: Saving the Selves of Adolescent Girls,* author Mary Pipher (1994) reports that only one-seventh of illustrations in children's textbooks are of girls. And, according to Pipher, "Girls are exposed to almost three times as many boy-centered stories as girl-centered stories. Boys tend to be portrayed as clever, brave, creative and resourceful, while girls are depicted as kind, dependent and docile. Girls read six times as many biographies of males as of females. Even in animal stories, the animals are twice as likely to be males" (p. 62).

According to instructional communication scholars Simonds and Cooper (2001), male characters, figures, pictures, and references to male authors still greatly outnumber those of females in current public school textbooks. They state that "despite the adoption of nonsexist guidelines during the past decade, textbook publishers have made relatively few changes to increase the visibility of females and decrease the stereotyping of males and females" (p. 235). These authors cite elementary school textbooks in which only one or two books in an entire series contain stories about females; many times these stories are added only to the reading for a single grade level. Other meager attempts include adding gendered examples or female-centric material to the middle or end of a text, with no attempt to integrate the material into the flow of the book. History books—from the elementary to college level—are notorious for focusing on men's history, with a "nod" for women's historical contributions contained in an appendix, occasional in-chapter boxed feature, or tokenized "great women in history" chapter.

High school literature classes rely heavily on anthologies as sources of reading selections. In a study of five widely used high school English literature anthologies, gender scholar Mary Harmon (2000) found serious evidence of gender bias. First, women receive limited representation in the readings, in terms of the numbers of female versus male authors and the amount of pages per each reading. The majority of the female-authored selections contain only one poem apiece or are nonfiction works, few of which are assigned reading. Female authors receive brief introductions to their readings compared to those written for male-authored selections. Harmon's content analysis of these introductions reveals that male authors' accomplishments are highlighted, while female authors' mentors or family relationships are emphasized. This trend parallels research which finds that men are often identified by what they do, while women are identified by who they know, primarily their connections to men (LaRocque, 1997; Maggio, 1988). Finally, Harmon's inspection of language usage in anthologies found little treatment of the topic of sexist language; in fact, all five of the anthologies Harmon examined actually used sexist language, including extensive use of generic masculine terms to stand for all persons and many references to adult women as girls, shrews, and nags. In terms of messages about women that students receive from their textbooks, Harmon concludes:

> Women's works are insignificant, they belong at the back of the book. Women are virtually erased. Although they may write a short poem or two or an essay, the anthologies suggest women do not produce long works or serious works of fiction worth reproducing for a national audience. Women seem to play little or no role in the construction of United States' history. One or two women writers are sufficient to speak for all as well as for all minority persons. Women writers' lives and achievements are of interest primarily in regard to where they lived or which males they knew or were related to. (p. 84)

Dick and Jane: Slow to Change

Research continues to investigate gender stereotypes in children's literature (Cooper, 1987; Ernst, 1995; Heintz, 1987; Peterson & Lach, 1990; Romaine, 1999; White, 1986). A study of gender representation in children's picture books found bias against females, in terms of character prevalence in titles, pictures, central roles, and types of activities engaged in by the characters (Tepper & Cassidy, 1999). In her research on award-winning children's books, communication scholar Pamela Cooper (1991b) found that between the years of 1967 and 1987 (strong decades for women's liberation), a mere 14 of 97 books depicted female characters who worked outside the home. According to consistent research findings, the old "Dick and Jane" breadwinner-homemaker images and gender stereotypical behaviors are alive and well in educational literature for kids.

'Net Notes

Have you heard about Emily the Strange? If you have young female siblings or your own daughters, you may have been introduced to this female character that is all the rage among young teenage girls. Emily is a pop cultural icon invented on the Internet, but she is much more—an alter ego for many girls. She has been described as "part Wednesday Addams, part riot grrl," "cute but not cutesy," "darkly mischievous and clever," the "anti-Hello Kitty," a "postmodern Harriet the Spy," and a "teen Barbie without the perfect body, blond hair, colorful clothes, popularity, and Prozac" (Leibrock, 2000, p. H1). Check out Emily the Strange at **www.emilystrange.com**

Alternative reading materials are being produced to widen the range of experience for schoolchildren (Orenstein, 1997). However, wading through the bureaucracy to gain acceptance in the school systems can be a time-consuming task. One popular alternative to male-dominated textbooks is *My Daddy is a Nurse*, a supplemental reader for elementary grades that depicts nontraditional career paths and roles for men and women. Besides efforts to offer more balanced depictions and information about the sexes in educational texts, authors are making nonsexist contributions to children's literature. Just a sample of titles include *The Serpent Slayer and Other Stories of Strong Women*, a mother-daughter authored book of feminist folktales that feature strong female heroines who vanquish their adversaries; *Dear America*, a series of diary readings portraying women's historical contributions; *Mothers Can Do Anything*, a book by Joe Lasker that describes mothers in traditional and nontraditional jobs; *Winning Kicker*, Thomas Dygard's story of a girl who joins a boys' football team; and Bette Greene's *Philip Hall Likes Me, I Reckon Maybe*, a story about an enduring friendship between a girl and a boy (Jetter, 2001; Steineger, 1993; Vinnedge, 1996).

Some of you may have school-aged children, and you have no doubt confronted issues surrounding sex and gender. How do you or have you used reading material to educate your children about their own gender identities and the roles of the sexes in society? For students yet to raise children, how do you think

Hot Button Issue

"TEACHING KIDS ABOUT SOCIAL REALITIES"

The reading material children are exposed to in school tends to be a hot button issue, especially for parents and school boards. One unfortunate result of restrictions on what children may read and learn about can be a tendency to present only material that offers a very narrow view of reality—stories with stereotyped male and female characters in traditional roles. The controversy arises over who should be responsible for teaching kids about realities in our society, for example, about gays and lesbians. Most people believe that parents should be primarily responsible, but what if the parents aren't doing their job? Should students learn some basic facts in school about "Dick and Jim," not just "Dick and Jane"?

One contribution offers schools the opportunity to help kids understand alternatives in relationships. Michael Willhoite's book, entitled *Daddy's Roommate*, generated controversy across the country, since it is about a young boy whose parents divorce because the father is gay. Its intention is to teach young children how to cope with having a homosexual parent or parents. Children's books, such as this one, that depict or attempt to explain adult situations are often deemed too controversial for adoption by a school district. What's your opinion? Should the decision to expose children to such reading material and enlighten them on forms of diversity in American culture best be made by schools or left to parents' discretion?

you will approach this issue when you have kids? It's important to consider the kinds of subtle messages you may pass on to future generations, either by what you allow your children to read or how you react to what they read in school. We're not insinuating that there's a "correct" message, but it's important to be aware that children get some kind of message from books, stories, fairy tales, and nursery rhymes—just as they do from the programs they watch on television.

EDUCATIONAL EXPECTATIONS AND GENDER BIAS IN THE CLASSROOM

No one begins an education with a clean slate; teachers and students come to the educational setting with their own sets of beliefs, values, and opinions, and with imprints of their experiences, some of which are related to gender. When we allow these imprints to lead us to rigid expectations about the aptitude and appropriate behavior of the sexes, bias may be the result.

Expectations about Academic Achievement: The Early Years

In Chapter 2 we discussed some studies of the brain that suggest differences between the sexes. However, studies do not indicate that girls and boys differ in their capacity for learning. Gender scholars Borisoff and Merrill (1998) contend: "Although girls' and boys' potential for academic learning is equal, several studies suggest that expectations for academic achievement exert a potent influence on the extent to which a child's potential is fulfilled" (p. 83). With effective instruction, equal opportunities for high-quality education, unbiased expectations from teachers and parents, and encouragement free from gender stereotypes, both boys and girls can achieve extraordinary things.

A Gendered Educational Picture

For more than two decades, research has continued to show that the elements necessary for equal achievement by boys and girls in schools are not in place (American Association of University Women, AAUW, 1998b; Brophy, 1983; Cooper & Good, 1983). (The AAUW is a long-standing organization of national repute; its research on trends in education is widely cited.) A study at the turn of the new century found that girls still feel alienated from traditionally male subjects (such as math and science), career aspirations are still highly gendered, boys still dominate the classroom environment, boys' behavior can have a negative effect on girls' learning, and some teachers have lower expectations for girls and find boys more stimulating to teach (Warrington & Younger, 2000).

Sex differences in school children's levels of self-esteem are consistently documented, with girls suffering more self-esteem loss than boys (Chipman & Wilson, 1985; Hyde, Fennema, Ryan, Frost, & Hopp, 1990; Romaine, 1999). Myra and David Sadker, authors of *Failing At Fairness: How America's Schools Cheat Girls* (1994), describe boys' self-esteem as a "self-esteem slide," but girls' self-esteem as a "free-fall" (p. 77). This self-esteem loss often stays with a student through college (and beyond), and profoundly affects achievement, curriculum choices, and career decisions.

Sadker and Sadker (1994) explain the sex difference in self-esteem levels by pointing to such factors as boys believing that they are better able to do things than girls. Girls' belief in their abilities declines steadily over the course of their education (AAUW, 1991). Another factor is the differential reinforcement boys receive from athletics, which helps them cope with changes in their bodies better than girls. This is changing as more and more school systems, colleges and universities, and professional ranks recognize the impact of athletic accomplishment on self-esteem (Sandoz, 2000). Other factors relate to girls' concerns about being popular and liked by boys, compounded by mediated images of "perfect" girls and women, which encourage young girls to focus on appearance rather than academics (Romaine, 1999).

> *I love to see a young girl go out and grab the world by the lapels. Life's a bitch. You've got to go out and kick ass.*
>
> —*Maya Angelou, poet*

Achievement Gaps in the "Hard" Sciences

Studies continue to examine achievement differences among school girls and boys in such areas as math, science, and computer literacy. While one report indicates that the gap has all but disappeared between boys' and girls' abilities in math and science (AAUW, 1998c), most research shows that male students still out-achieve girls in math, science, engineering, and other areas that rely on problem-solving ability (Lakes Matyas, 1997; Romaine, 1999; Warrington & Younger, 2000). Researcher Catherine Paglin (1993) summarizes prevailing explanations for the gap: (1) Boys receive more encouragement from adults to take math and science, plus they have more out-of-school experiences related to these topics than girls; (2) In labs, boys tend to do the experiments while girls fall into the role of recorder; girls have few role models in math and science classes or texts; and (3) Girls lack self-confidence in math and science, often perceiving it as too difficult, unfeminine, and irrelevant.

Here's a pop cultural example that illustrates the problem. The Mattel Corporation produced Teen Talk Barbie in 1992; one of the first lines they put in the doll's mouth was "Math class is tough." The *Washington Post* quickly dubbed the doll "Foot-in-Mouth Barbie" and the AAUW, along with math teachers across the country, registered their disgust (Crawford & Unger, 2000). Since adults create such products, it is clear that some adults (parents and teachers) also carry the attitude that "math is too hard for girls" or "math and science are unfeminine." In turn, they subtly and not-so-subtly communicate these attitudes to students. The detrimental effects on young female students are obvious, in that girls may believe that they cannot and should not achieve in math and science. The effects may also be negative on boys, in that they may feel pressured by the expectation that they are supposed to excel in math and science.

Evidence shows that girls still lag behind boys in interest and competence in computer science (AAUW, 1998c; Quilling, 1999; Sadker, 1999). Janice Weinman, Executive Director of the AAUW, explained: "Girls have narrowed some significant gender gaps, but technology is now the new 'boy's club' in our nation's public schools. While boys program and problem solve with computers, girls use computers for word processing, the 1990s version of typing" (AAUW, 1998d, p. 1). Computers were supposed to be gender-neutral and to level the academic playing field. However, research reveals that three-fourths of children enrolled in computer camps are male; three times as many male students as female students enter school with prior, at-home computer instruction; and the majority of primary figures in educational and recreational computer games are male (Borisoff & Merrill, 1998; Nelson & Watson, 1991; Sadker & Sadker, 1994).

As a result of these trends, efforts have been made to encourage girls' achievement in computer skills, including girls' computer institutes and programs for math and science teachers, like the Computer Equity Expert Project funded by the National Science Foundation (Paglin, 1993). The AAUW has developed *Tech Check for Schools,* a tool that provides a quick but thorough assessment of computer education equity in public schools. One group of educators used *Tech Check* across five school districts in their area and found that boys far outnumber girls in high school computer science and technology courses (AAUW, 2001). Some researchers indicate that it is not a question of aptitude that causes girls to achieve less than boys in computer science; rather, it is a question of interest. Bias in computer software, in such forms as "shoot 'em up themes" and explosions as rewards for correct answers, turns girls off (Paglin, 1993).

Expectations about Academic Achievement: The College Years

The expectations communicated to us as school children have profound effects—so profound that they tend to follow us into our college years. It's hard to "unlearn" early messages that "poetry is for girls" and "math is for boys." But, just like most things in life, those early expectations become more complex and have more serious implications as one ages.

What Does This Professor Expect from Me?

Did you ever sit in a classroom and feel like the teacher had formed an expectation about you before you even had a chance to open your mouth? Did you sense in high school, for example, that a teacher had labeled you a "jock," "bad girl," or "nerd" and then acted toward you based on that label? Did you ever feel that a teacher thought you were a C student in a class and that no matter how hard you tried or what you said or did, you were going to get a C in that class? These things point to the impact of expectations on achievement and enjoyment in a classroom setting, and, once again, gender plays a role.

Scholars of English Jan and Rich Haswell (1995) examined whether sex was a factor in the evaluation of students' writing. Readers critiqued two students' essays—one with an unidentified writer and one that identified the sex of the writer. Reflecting a bias and stereotype that women are better at language skills, readers inflated grades when they knew they were reading a female-authored essay, compared to essays in which the author's sex was unknown. Similarly, readers who knew they were reading a male-authored essay gave lower evaluations than when they did not know the sex of the writer. This is one example of the kind of gender bias that can endanger someone's academic success.

If you're a male reader, have you ever experienced treatment from a college professor that conveyed to you a specific expectation, merely because you were male? Maybe you sensed an attitude that you were more or less valued than female students in a class. For female readers, did you ever feel like a professor held expectations of how women were going to approach his or her course content and achieve in the class, in comparison to male students? Some of our female students give us examples of differential treatment in classes, such as when they are in math classes, where they are not expected to do well, versus communication classes, where they are most often in the majority and tend to excel. These are just a few examples of how teacher expectations can affect your appreciation, involvement, and achievement in a class.

What Does This Student Expect from Me?

Student expectations also play a role in this process. At times, the female co-author of your text attempts to "un-gender" herself, meaning that she encounters some students in gender and interpersonal communication courses who deem the information unimportant, thinking it stems from a "woman's agenda." Female instructors occasionally feel that students hold them up to more scrutiny in the classroom than male colleagues, as if to say "Show me what you know." Some female teachers envy what they perceive to be male teachers' "instant credibility." However, the male co-author of your text also senses that female and male students alike enter his communication classes with a "show me" attitude because he is male and communication is considered more a women's field than a man's. In gender communication classes, in particular, he sometimes senses an attitude from students that translates into, "So what would *you* know about sex discrimination? You're a man in a man's world."

Research has shown that male instructors are viewed by students as significantly more credible than female professors, in general (Anderson & Miller, 1997; Centre & Gaubatz, 2000; Hargett, 1999; Sandler, 1991). Communication researchers Lawrence and Marjorie Nadler (1990) focused on college students' perceptions of their own and their instructors' classroom behavior as a means of examining how expectations translate into behavior. Their results indicated that students brought expectations regarding the behaviors of female and male instructors into class with them. Specifically, "male instructors were depicted as more dominant . . . while female instructors were viewed as more supportive than their male counterparts" (p. 60). Extending those findings to out-of-class communication—conversations you might have with a professor in his or her office, before or after class, or somewhere on campus—research has found more positive results for female than male professors. Communication scholars Jaasma and Koper (2002) examined students' perceptions of teachers' verbal and nonverbal immediacy, based on out-of-class communication. Immediacy refers to behaviors that promote physical and psychological closeness between people. Jaasma and Koper found that female teachers were believed to be more verbally and nonverbally immediate than male teachers.

We know from our discussion in Chapter 1 that a person's sexual orientation is part of her or his gender, as well as biological sex, psychological attributes, and attitudes about sex roles. A recent study examined students' perceptions of straight and gay instructors' credibility (Russ, Simonds, & Hunt, 2002). Since prior research documents many college students' homophobia, the researchers anticipated that heterosexual teachers would be perceived as more credible than homosexual teachers. Indeed, students rated straight teachers as being more credible than gay teachers on two dimensions: competence, or having knowledge or expertise of their given subject area; and character, or the amount of trust the teacher engenders in others. In addition, students believed that they learn significantly more from straight than gay teachers. No studies to date have found a correlation between how much students actually learn from teachers of different sexual orientations; yet, the perception exists in the minds of many students that a teacher's sexual orientation affects their learning.

Many teachers are aware of potential biases students may hold toward members of their sex, and how those expectations may affect the successfulness of their courses. Gay teachers are keenly aware of how students' perceptions of them may affect their teaching and, ultimately, their career success; this awareness asserts a great deal of pressure into the teaching situation.

GENDER COMMUNICATION AND THE COLLEGE CLASSROOM

The history of higher education in America reveals a predominantly male domain. For an interesting account of the struggle women faced when they "invaded" male-dominated higher education, we refer you to Chapter 2 of Sadker and Sadker's book, *Failing At Fairness: How America's Schools Cheat Girls* (1994). Even only a few years ago, it was clear that the ideal of equality for men and women was not achieved in the average college classroom. Through the 1950s, '60s, and into the '70s, men and women had very different educational opportunities. For example, one of your authors overheard a male professor in 1973 say, "Women are not capable of teaching at the college level and should not be admitted to doctoral programs." Certain fields (for example, engineering and accounting) were completely male domains. Women were guided to elementary school teaching, nursing, and home economics. A standard joke of that time period (and you still hear it some today) was that "Women come to college to get their MRS. degree."

How much has changed in the past few decades? While some advances have been made, there is still evidence of significant gender bias in universities. As researchers Wellhousen and Yin (1997) describe, "Gender bias is so prevalent in American society and classrooms that it often goes undetected" (p. 35). For example, how many contributions by women in history are you likely to study in the typical American history course, in comparison to men's contributions? Is this because of sheer numbers, as in the assumption that there were more key men in history than women, so it's appropriate for men to be studied more than women? Were there *really* more key male figures in history than female? Perhaps it's all in how you define the term *key*. Perhaps it relates to the fact that women in American history were not allowed to vote, hold office, or make many political or business decisions, so their accomplishments are overlooked. Many times students aren't aware of women's contributions until they take a women's history course, which to some seems a token gesture that assumes all other history courses are men's history courses.

How close are we to the ideal of equality in education? As a student, do you believe that women and men have equal opportunities to communicate in the average college classroom? That they receive similar treatment from professors? That they have equal access to careers? Research reviewed below suggests that men and women do not have the same experiences in the classroom, which has a profound impact on their education.

Gender Bias in College Textbooks

A significant contributing factor to gender bias in higher education is the reading material used in courses, and textbooks are prime examples. Sadker and Sadker (1994) found that the predominance of teacher education textbooks devoted less than one percent of book space to issues of gender equity. They concluded, "Using these college texts, tomorrow's teachers would actually learn to be more sexist" (p. 174). They also describe token attempts to inject women and their accomplishments into college textbooks, citing English literature texts of "great works" that devote only 15 percent of their content to women writers (and there have been great women writers throughout history). Other texts include devices that give brief mentions of women's issues and experiences, much the same way as we described for children's educational literature.

Many texts across a variety of disciplines rarely mention names of female contributors to these fields; women who are included appear in overtly gender-stereotypical presentations (Hurd & Brabeck, 1997). A content analysis of college economic texts revealed gender stereotypes through exclusive depictions and examples surrounding a traditional family (e.g., husband-breadwinner, wife-homemaker) as an economic unit (Polanyi & Strassmann, 1996). Beyond women's depictions in college textbooks, the use of masculine language as generics reveals sexism as well. Since such key groups as the American Psychological Association and the National Council of Teachers of English established guidelines for nonsexist language usage (in 1977 and 1975, respectively), textbooks have begun to equalize their language, but we have a long way to go in this effort.

Communication textbooks are not immune to gender-stereotyped behavior, although improvements have been made, particularly in the use of nonsexist language. Back in 1975, communication scholar Jo Sprague (1975) reported that most public speaking texts only featured speeches by men. While still far from creating an equal picture, most current public speaking texts and supplements provide examples of female speakers' accomplishments, such as Barbara Jordan's and Ann Richards' keynote speeches at Democratic Party conventions, Elizabeth

Dole's speech at the 1996 Republican Party convention (in which she used a very Oprah-esque style of walking the floor amongst convention-goers while speaking), and various presentations by Hillary Rodham Clinton, Barbara Bush, and Laura Bush.

Communication scholar Trudy Hanson (1999) conducted a study of 20 of the most widely-used university basic public speaking texts. Of special interest to Hanson was the presence of content on gender and diversity issues, as well as the number of pages devoted to these topics. Photos of women and members of minority groups were also analyzed, with particular interest for any power cues depicted in the photos. Hanson's results revealed the following: (1) In five of the 20 texts, no mention of gender was found, although one of the five included sample speeches by female speakers. (2) The fullest coverage of gender in a single text was 32 pages; the average was a little over seven pages. (3) Gender-related topics receiving multiple mentions across various texts included gender considerations in audience adaptation, sexist language, gender differences in delivery styles, and nonverbal communication differences. (4) All of the texts containing photos presented more men than women in those photos, with 94 percent of the photos depicting men in power positions or enacting nonverbal power cues. After surveying the various texts, Hanson concluded: "Women were present, but even the casual undergraduate student reading the text would probably come away with the impression that public speaking is something that men do more often than women" (p. 15).

As you move through your college career, it might be interesting to examine your textbooks for evidence of gender bias. Which sex is represented more in examples and illustrations within a text? Does a text treat both sexes equally in discussing applications of the material or careers? Does it offer other ways of thinking than what might be considered the traditional male pattern? Does it use nonsexist language—for example, do *she* and *he* both appear as personal pronouns? Reading textbooks with these questions in mind may reveal where the ideal we mention is still not being met.

The "Chill" in Higher Education: Students' Classroom Communication

In the ideal college classroom, students of both sexes participate with about the same frequency, ask similar amounts and types of questions, and actively engage in their own learning. However, research over three decades indicates that students' participation continues to be far from this ideal.

"Ice Age" Research

Researchers in the 1970s found that men more often dominated class discussions while women were less verbally aggressive (Karp & Yoels, 1977; Rich, 1979; Sternglanz & Lyberger-Ficek, 1977; Thorne, 1979). Interest in such differences increased throughout the 1980s. Researchers then found that most classrooms tended to favor a traditionally male approach to learning and rejected or did not value a traditionally female approach (Belenky, Clinchy, Goldberger, &

Tarule, 1986; Gilligan, 1982; Treichler & Kramarae, 1983). Studies showed that male students initiated more interactions of greater length with teachers than female students; interrupted professors and other students significantly more often than women, particularly in classes taught by women; and were more likely to control such nonverbal factors as physical space in a classroom (Brooks, 1982; Brophy, 1985; Krupnick, 1985; Sandler & Hall, 1986).

Differences in female and male students' communication in college classrooms and the way professors communicated with these students were so pronounced that they gave rise to the term *chilly climate* as a descriptor for academic settings (Hall & Sandler, 1982, 1984; Sandler & Hall, 1986). Educational researchers Roberta Hall and Bernice Sandler described the difficulties women faced in the average college classroom in the 1980s—difficulties most men did not face. Research they reviewed on classroom interaction determined that men: (1) talked more than women; (2) talked for longer periods and took more turns at speaking; (3) exerted more control over the topic of conversation; (4) interrupted women much more frequently than women interrupted men; and (5) when they interrupted, often introduced trivial or inappropriately personal comments, designed to bring women's discussion to an end or to change its focus. Hall and Sandler concluded that women were silenced in the classroom; they were not given the same opportunity as men to express themselves, verbally or nonverbally. Communication researchers Wood and Lenze (1991) summarize research results on this issue as follows:

> In most classrooms, asserting self is more rewarded than waiting one's turn, individual achievement is valued more highly than collaborative efforts, talking is encouraged more than listening, presenting new ideas is emphasized whereas responding to and synthesizing classmates' ideas is not, competition is stressed more than cooperation, and advancing firm conclusions is more highly regarded than holding tentative ones. (p. 17)

Little Evidence of a Thaw

A 1996 report from the National Association for Women in Education reaffirmed the presence of the chilly climate on college campuses. One of the report's authors, Bernice Sandler, asserts, "The classroom is still quite chilly, but we have more ideas about how to warm it up" (as in Gose, 1996, p. A38). For example, the report describes how male students tend to blurt out answers to teachers' questions, while female students take time to gather their thoughts before raising their hands to be recognized by a teacher. You could interpret these behaviors as male enthusiasm on the one hand or dominance on the other; as female passivity and powerlessness, or thoughtfulness and depth. No matter the interpretation, the report recommends that professors wait a few seconds before taking responses from students or that they pose questions directly to female students in order to balance male contributions.

Higher education is still influenced by a tradition of male dominance in the classroom (Bowker & Regan Dunkin, 1992; Wood & Lenze, 1991). In a 1998 study, a majority of college faculty agreed that male students interrupt more frequently, assume leadership roles more frequently, are less likely to seek outside help, and are less open to constructive criticism than female students (Condravy, Skirboll, & Taylor, 1998). However, fewer male dominance behaviors were detected than in earlier chilly climate studies, according to researchers Kopp and Farr (1999), who found that female students have begun to perceive themselves as emerging leaders in classrooms. Female students perceived that they participated more than men in class, but male students perceived that they participated more than women. Nevertheless, both male and female students perceived males as being more self-confident, especially during class discussion.

Research on *communication apprehension,* defined back in the 1980s as "an individual's level of fear or anxiety associated with either real or anticipated communication," has explored the relationship between student sex and level of apprehension (McCroskey, 1982, p. 127). Scholar Marjorie Jaasma (1997) found that, in general, female students suffered more *classroom communication apprehension* than male students. Younger or traditionally-aged students in this study were more apprehensive than older students, and students from minority groups were more apprehensive than white students. Jaasma concludes: "It appears that females view the forum of the college classroom as one in which they are conspicuous and are judged by peers and instructors" (p. 224).

Based on all this research, most college classroom interaction appears to follow a male pattern. We have noticed, in our teaching, that female students often use stereotypical feminine linguistic patterns (detailed in Chapter 4) in classrooms, such as disclaimers, hesitations, tag questions, and generally deferential patterns of speech that decrease their dominance. Regarding female use of disclaimers, Sadker and Sadker (1994) reveal, "These female preambles of self-deprecation are a predictable part of the college classroom" (p. 171). However, one profile of classes in which we have had extensive experience doesn't fit the male-domination pattern at all—communication courses for majors. In many communication departments in colleges and universities across the country, women outnumber men as communication majors. In courses for majors at our two universities, female students outnumber their male counterparts, and perhaps the old "safety in numbers" adage comes into play. We can vouch for the fact that our female students speak up faster than male students, and generally contribute more in both quantity and quality. Granted, communication majors are a different breed, in that most enjoy communicating and thus are highly interactive in the classroom. Is the interaction pattern in your communication courses different than that of other classes? Do you communicate in classrooms in accord with the research findings for members of your sex? Do you find that members of the opposite sex communicate as the research describes?

The "Chill" in Higher Education: Teachers' Classroom Communication

Besides students' communication patterns in classrooms, researchers have also identified differences in communication from some faculty members to male and female students (AAUW, 1992). Learning in the classroom is mediated through the communication process, and if communication is biased, then the educational opportunities students receive may be biased as well (Cooper, 1991a). Research on classroom interaction, comparing single-sex and coeducational classrooms, has led to a "demand that teachers frame pedagogy specifically in terms of achieving gender equity. Awareness of gender as it plays out in the learning process must inform our teaching" (Allen, Cantor, Grady, & Hill, 1997, p. 46).

Chillin' with Your Professors

In their discussion of classroom communication patterns, Simonds and Cooper (2001) describe how teachers tend to use sexist language, call on male students more often, ask male students more complex questions than female students, and provide male students longer explanations about class assignments and procedures. Other research indicates that male students are perceived as being more fun to teach than female students and that male students are given more opportunities to interact with the teacher, more time to talk, and more attention from teachers, in the form of both praise and discipline (Brophy, 1985; Keegan, 1989; Sadker & Sadker, 1985, 1994).

In their analysis of the chilly climate for women in university settings, Hall and Sandler (1982) began with a realization that most faculty were men and faculty tended to affirm students of their own sex more than students of the other sex. Below we provide some of the teacher behaviors that Hall and Sandler identified as representative of differential treatment of men and women in the classroom:

> *Don't shut yourself up in a bandbox because you are a woman, but understand what is going on, and educate yourself to take part in the world's work for it all affects you and yours.*
>
> *—Louisa May Alcott, author*

1. Calling directly on male students, more often by name, and ignoring female students
2. Addressing the class as if no women were present (e.g., "When you were a boy . . . ")
3. Waiting longer for men to answer a question, and then working toward a fuller answer by probing or coaching the men for additional information
4. Interrupting female students and allowing them to be interrupted by classmates
5. Asking women lower-order, more simplistic questions
6. Responding more extensively to men's comments than to women's
7. Using classroom examples that reflect stereotypical social and professional roles
8. Using sexist, exclusive language

9. Using more encouraging nonverbal behaviors with male students than female, such as making more eye contact, nodding and gesturing more often in response to men's questions and comments, changing vocal tone to indicate a more serious treatment of men's remarks, and assuming a posture of attentiveness when men speak
10. Favoring men as student assistants.

Professor Variables Down Cold

Research spanning multiple decades suggests that a professor's sex may make a difference in how students perceive teachers and in students' classroom interaction patterns (Ryan, 1989). Studies in the 1970s found that male students in male-taught classes were much more likely than female students to be directly questioned by the professor and to respond. In female-taught classes, however, professors were equally likely to directly question male and female students, and participation by students of both sexes was more equal (Karp & Yoels, 1977; Sternglanz & Lyberger-Ficek, 1977). Research in the 1980s determined that classes taught by women incorporated more student input, more teacher and student questions, more feedback, more overall student interaction, and less direct reprimands and confrontation (Macke, Richardson, & Cook, 1980; Richardson, Cook, & Macke, 1981).

In the 1990s, the findings weren't so clear-cut. For example, communication researchers Pearson and West (1991) found that male instructors received more questions from students than female instructors and that male students asked more questions than female students in classes taught by male instructors. However, Nadler and Nadler's (1990) students did not believe they were treated differently by instructors of different sexes, and they reported few differences in their own classroom communication. Male students did not report receiving more supportive behaviors and female students did not report receiving more dominant behaviors from instructors of the opposite sex. Jaasma's (1997) study of classroom communication apprehension revealed that while female students were more apprehensive than male students in general, that trend was unaffected by whether the teacher was male or female.

Students' judgments are also related to perceptions of a teacher as being nonsexist or *egalitarian*, defined as the belief that one's sex does not determine or limit one's abilities or opportunities. Students who perceive that their teachers are sexist generally dislike those teachers and describe their classes as less supportive and innovative than those taught by nonsexist teachers (Cooper, 1993; Rosenfeld & Jarrard, 1986). Students of egalitarian teachers tend to develop more positive attitudes about the class and its subject matter (Petersen, Kearney, Plax, & Waldeck, 1997). Even though research findings reveal different trends, it appears that a professor's sex and her or his attitude toward the sexes may have at least some influence in a classroom. Again, if you are enrolled in courses taught by both sexes, compare the research findings with your own experiences. What patterns can you observe in your classes?

Effects of Educational Sexism on Students

Gender bias also affects students' decisions about courses and careers (AAUW, 1998c; Bem, 1993; Hernandez, 1993; Jamieson, 1995; Simonds & Cooper, 2001). These decisions are related to self-confidence, as well as to how students are advised and reinforced, but not to ability (Borisoff & Merrill, 1998; Crawford & Unger, 2000; Paglin, 1993). Educational researchers Leonard and Sigall (1989) found that women's grades, career goals, and self-esteem decline over the four-year span of college more so than men's. Some effects of gender bias in education, according to Hall and Sandler (1982, 1984), include dropping or avoiding certain classes, minimizing one's relationship with faculty, diminished career aspirations related to certain fields of study, and a general undermining of self-confidence because of suggestions that certain areas within college curricula are too difficult or are inappropriate for members of one's sex.

Changing the Educational Climate for Women and Men

Gender scholars Bate and Bowker (1997) describe college as the most masculine of learning environments. But they also discuss the changing mix of the average college classroom and note that more and more nontraditional students (particularly women) who have high potential in business and in technical areas are returning to college. These changes are evidenced by a greater balance in the numbers of women and men in traditionally male-dominated college majors. As the demographics of the typical university begin to reflect the demographics of society at large, more changes are expected.

How do we change the system? Simonds and Cooper (2001) believe that the " 'male-as-norm' conceptions of educational purposes, of students, of teachers, of curricula, of pedagogy, indeed of the profession of education, must be closely examined" (p. 245). They suggest gathering more information about the diversity of the female experience, reconceptualizing curricula, and infusing alternative approaches into the curriculum. Wood and Lenze (1991) describe the gender sensitive classroom as one that includes "balanced content that highlights the strengths of traditionally masculine and feminine . . . inclinations," texts that "acknowledge and value both women's and men's concerns about interpersonal communication," and an educational climate "that equally values the interaction style women tend to learn . . . , but also advances important social goals such as cooperation, effective listening, and being open minded" (pp. 16–17).

Interestingly enough, gender communication scholar Eric Peterson (1991) found that when a department consciously tried to incorporate gender-balance in the curriculum, student response was mixed. Efforts to affect the climate for women and men included revising courses to include material on gender diversity; incorporating into course content some significant works of female scholars, rather than relying totally or primarily on male contributions; and acknowledging alternative ways of knowing and conducting educational inquiry.

Some students found these changes interesting and valuable, while others found them too oriented toward women or were confused about how they applied to their lives.

The most practical suggestions for change focus on classroom dynamics. The following were adapted from lists written primarily for faculty members to help them bring their classes closer to the ideal we described earlier (Hall & Sandler, 1982). Perhaps you might find yourself in a position to enlighten your teachers and help ensure that these behaviors occur more frequently.

1. Engage in interaction patterns during the first few weeks of classes that draw women into discussions, and then intervene if communication patterns develop that may shut out women.
2. Design and enforce course policy statements to make it clear that biased comments and behavior are inappropriate in the classroom.
3. Make a specific effort to call directly on female as well as male students, give all students an equal amount of time to respond, and then respond to them in similar ways when they make comparable contributions in class.
4. Use terminology that includes both women and men and eliminate sexist materials from course readings and information.
5. Give female and male students the same opportunity to ask for and receive detailed instructions about the requirements for an assignment.
6. When talking about occupations or professions in class discussion, use language that does not reinforce limited views of male and female roles and careers.
7. Use the same nonverbal behaviors when speaking and responding to male and female students.

Integrating different communication styles and continuing to warm up the "chilly climate" in the hallowed halls of the university will not be easy. Different students see different dimensions of the problem; some see no problem at all. If an individual class or an entire university undertakes a discussion of classroom climate and gender bias, it's probably necessary for everyone to realize that "just because it didn't happen to you doesn't mean it didn't happen."

Remember...

CHILLY CLIMATE: An unengaging, sometimes hostile environment in educational institutions, in which communication, expectations, policies, etc., are not conducive to women students' learning.

COMMUNICATION APPREHENSION: An individual's level of fear or anxiety associated with either real or anticipated communication.

CLASSROOM COMMUNICATION APPREHENSION: Fear or anxiety associated with real or anticipated communication in classroom settings.

PEER SEXUAL HARASSMENT:
CLASSMATES WILL BE CLASSMATES?

In Chapter 8, we discussed sexual harassment in some detail. In Chapter 9, we explored the problem of sexual harassment in the workplace, in particular the most complicated aspect of the EEOC's guidelines, the *hostile climate* clause. Many academic institutions have expanded the EEOC definition to reflect their unique concerns, as in the phrase *hostile learning climate.* In this chapter we examine a specific form of harassment that has a pervasive effect on students' lives. As you know from previous reading, the pattern of sexual harassment most often documented in research involves a male harasser and a female target in a *status-differentiated relationship,* such as boss-employee or doctor-patient. But you probably did not know that harassment is far more prevalent among peers than in status-differentiated relationships (Loredo, Reid, & Deaux, 1995; Zirkel, 1995). The treatment you receive from your classmates directly contributes to the creation of a hostile or nonhostile learning climate.

Sexual harassment, just like sexual assault, has much more to do with power than with sex (Berryman-Fink, 1993). However, it appears that we may need to expand our view of power. As educational researcher Katherine McKinney (1990a) contends, "Most researchers in the area of sexual harassment have assumed that harassment occurs only when the offender has more formal or position power than the harasser. Recently, it has been recognized that other types of power can be used by the offender . . ." (p. 435). Sexual harassment between persons of equal status, such as coworkers, classmates, and social acquaintances, has been termed *peer sexual harassment.* Harassment directed from someone of lower status to someone of higher status is called *contrapower sexual harassment* (Benson, 1984).

What people are realizing is that the learning environment is greatly affected by relationships with peers, possibly even more so than relationships with teachers. Yet more attention is paid, in research and discussions about harassment, to situations involving a clearly defined, even institutionalized status or power differential. What about power abuses within relationships in which no clear power lines exist? What about power plays between classmates? Before discussing the current status of this problem, let's think about how the problem got to be a problem.

Back to Basics

Think back to when you were in grade school, when you were on the playground and a boy ran up to some girl and kissed her, to the screams of her friends and the whoops and laughter of his. Maybe this never happened at your school, but it's a common occurrence when kids test the boundaries of acceptable behavior and attempt to engage the opposite sex. If the little boy's kiss was unwelcome, should his behavior be deemed sexual harassment or is this merely an example of "boys being boys"? You may think we've lost our collective marbles here, but just such an incident occurred in a North Carolina elementary school in 1997 and made national headlines. A six-year-old boy was suspended from school for a few days for kissing a girl on the cheek—an action that she (and her parents) viewed as unwarranted and unwelcome. When the boy's mother sued the school district over the suspension, the media picked up the story (of course). News talk shows were full of discussions of "feminism gone overboard" and outrage that a child could be accused of inappropriate "sexual" conduct. We put that term in quotes because it was a central part of the argument—that a child who was not capable of sexual activity could be accused of mischief, but certainly not sexual harassment.

And things have progressed since then (unless you don't believe the following example to be "progress"). A group of sixth grade girls in a Duluth, Minnesota, school complained to the vice principal's office that they had been subjected to "gross" and "disgusting" sexual behavior by male classmates during a lunch break; suffice it to say that the incident involved a milk bag being shaped into the form of male genitalia, with ensuing sexual comments and jokes from the boys. The vice principal's response was to reach into her sexual harassment procedure kit and pull out a harassment complaint form. The girls signed the form and the school system harassment specialist—a position that didn't exist until only recently—was contacted to follow up on the case. The incident resulted in scolding from the principal and detention for the boys, while the girls were made to feel that their concerns were heard and taken seriously by school officials (Gorney, 1999).

One month after this incident, a Supreme Court ruling on peer sexual harassment in the schools changed the thinking on this problem. In *Davis* v. *Monroe County Board of Education,* the Supreme Court ruled that schools receiving federal money can face sex discrimination lawsuits if they show "deliberate indifference" and fail to "intervene energetically enough" in peer sexual harassment situations (Gorney, 1999, pp. A16, A18). Justice Sandra Day O'Connor, writing the majority opinion, stated that "student-on-student sex harassment" was a deeply serious matter, and that school officials who ignored "protracted and serious" harassment could be sued under Title IX, the federal law prohibiting sex discrimination in educational institutions (p. A16). What's your interpretation of these events— a step in the right direction or sexual correctness run amok?

Back to your own school experience: For the female readers, you or a schoolmate may have received unwanted attention from boys because of your developing body (and the boys' developing hormones). How did you respond—with embarrassment, anger, flirtation? Do you remember how such attention made you feel, in a positive or negative way (or both)? Did you tell anyone about it? Would it be a stretch for you to call such attention from boys peer sexual harassment? Hold off answering that question for a moment.

For the male readers, do you remember when a wide variety of surprising things brought about a certain sexual reaction in your body? This is when boys first learned the art of carrying their schoolbooks and papers in front of them, instead of on their hips like girls did. (Now everything's in book bags, so modern boys have no doubt found modern methods of coping with this age-old dilemma.) When you think about this time period in your life, did you ever get teased by a girl because she detected some kind of sexual arousal in you? Did a girl—maybe a girl older than you—come on to you or show you her "new developments"? Would you have called these girls' behavior peer sexual harassment? Here's a tougher question: Could some of your behavior toward girls in your younger years have been deemed sexual harassment?

What we're getting at is this: Sexual harassment doesn't just all of a sudden become a behavior of choice for some people. It doesn't just mysteriously become a problem only adults have to deal with. It starts somewhere. Maybe it should be called something else, something without the sexual implications of the term *sexual* harassment. The term implies that sexual harassment is about sex, when it is really about power. As Peggy Orenstein (1994), author of *Schoolgirls: Young Women, Self-Esteem, and the Confidence Gap*, explains:

> Overwhelmingly boys harass and girls (or other boys) are harassed, indicating that the behavior is less a statement about sexuality than an assertion of dominance. The prevalence of sexual harassment reminds us that boys learn at a very young age to see girls as less capable and less worthy of respect. Middle-class and affluent girls in particular tend to accept sexual harassment as inevitable. And why not? The sexual teasing, stalking, and grabbing merely reinforces other, more subtle lessons: it reminds them that they are defined by their bodies; it underscores their lack of entitlement in the classroom (in fact, the harassment frequently *happens* in the classroom); it confirms their belief that boys' sexuality is uncontrollable while their own must remain in check. (pp. 116–117)

The phrase "boys will be boys" should really be "kids will be kids" because, as the Duluth harassment specialist described, "perps, especially in the vicious mouth department, are just as likely to be girls" (Gorney, 1999, p. A18). A lot of inappropriate behavior gets dismissed as simply part of one's childhood experience, something to be expected and endured. But this is no longer the case in the Duluth school system, and many others around the country. Teasing and disrespecting members of the opposite sex does not have to be a rite of passage. There are things educators and parents can learn from school incidences that make headlines in the papers. Turning our heads and adopting a stance of "they're just being kids" could perpetuate the problem. And the problem does worsen in middle and high school.

The "Hostile Hallways" of Middle and High School

An excerpt from an article in the *Dallas Morning News* reads:

> The four teenagers rattle off examples of lewd acts they've become accustomed to seeing at their Dallas middle school. A boy bit a girl on her breast in a classroom. A girl grabbed a boy's genitals in the hallway. A boy lifted a girl's dress and sent her screaming to the principal's office. In schools around the nation as well as in Texas, children and adolescents are facing sexual harassment and abuse from one another. Girls are usually the victims, but boys sometimes are accosted. Same-sex incidents happen too. (Everbach & Saul, 1998, p. 37A)

According to a school district official interviewed for the story, "It's happening a lot more than people think it is. A lot of young boys don't realize the line is much nearer than they think it is. What some boys think is a friendly touch can be construed as harassment" (p. 37A). Even at these ages, research shows that boys and girls experience and interpret acts of sexual harassment differently (Hand & Sanchez, 2000; Houston & Hwang, 1996).

The AAUW report of 1993, *Hostile Hallways: The AAUW Survey on Sexual Harassment in America's Schools,* was the first national scientific survey of sexual harassment in public schools. From about 1,700 students in grades 8–11 across 79 schools, 85 percent of girls and 76 percent of boys reported experiencing sexual harassment. These figures do not reflect the harassment students indicated they had received from school employees; the AAUW report stated that harassment from employees "was dwarfed by student reports of peer-to-peer harassment" (p. 11). These are alarming figures, the high rate for boys being particularly surprising. While boys and girls are both affected, the research showed a sex difference in terms of frequency of harassment, with girls reporting many more instances of harassment than boys. The sexual harassment also takes a greater toll on girls than boys, according to the study. Harassed girls reported being more afraid in school and feeling less confident about themselves than boys.

An AAUW follow-up study entitled *Hostile Hallways: Bullying, Teasing, and Harassment in School* (2001) found that little had changed since the 1993 study. Four of five students in 8th through 11th grade reported experiencing sexual harassment, with girls experiencing it slightly more frequently than boys. Besides the loss of self-esteem and the fear associated with sexual harassment, the most common outcome of the experience is not wanting to attend school. Harassment leads to absenteeism and truancy, which contribute to the drop-out rate. A second outcome of harassment is a silencing effect, meaning that targets don't want to talk as much in class. This is prime example related to our discussion earlier of a chill in the educational environment. Thirty-two percent of girls, compared to 13 percent of boys, reported this effect, which offers evidence in support of research findings of male dominance in classroom interaction. The AAUW 1993 report states, "Sexual harassment is clearly and measurably taking a toll on a significant percentage of students' educational, emotional, and behavioral lives. And although girls are experiencing more harassment—and suffering graver consequences—in the end, sexual harassment is everyone's problem. For when children's self-esteem and development are hampered, the repercussions echo throughout our society" (p. 21).

So what can be done about this problem? One positive trend was detected in the 2001 study: Sixty nine percent of students said that their schools had a sexual harassment policy, compared to only 26 percent in 1993. How many of those policies specifically address peer sexual harassment is unclear. But despite the school programs and policies on the problem, harassment continues and students rarely tell adults when it happens, especially when it's an incident of same-sex harassment (AAUW, 2001).

The first step for schools is to realize that there is a problem rather than burying their heads in the sand, assuming that their students are not capable of such behavior, which leaves schools vulnerable to litigation. They must approach the problem realistically and involve a *cross-section* of the school and community in the development of a *comprehensive* sexual harassment policy and procedure. We emphasize the cross-section aspect, meaning that administrators, teachers, counselors, and other school personnel should join parents *and* students in the project, because research also shows that administrators do not always offer helpful responses to reports of peer harassment. As Bate and Bowker (1997) suggest, "Explaining the harassing behavior to a person who, from the student's point of view, may or may not understand the vocabulary and nuances of the student's generation adds complicating factors that students may choose to avoid" (p. 253). Students must feel that there is someone they can go to who understands the problem, who will listen and not judge or dismiss the problem, and that their complaints will be taken seriously.

Another proactive approach is to conduct educational programs on the topic. While some schools do hold such sessions, they tend to be provided for school personnel only. Few of these programs involve parents and students, and fewer still educate students about peer sexual harassment—the most prevalent form they are likely to experience. A comprehensive training program—honest, current, conducted in language that engages students, and repeated over time—can help curb the peer sexual harassment trend before it tracks through college and into the workforce.

Peer Sexual Harassment: Another "Chilling" Effect in College

One of the first discussions of the problem of peer sexual harassment on college campuses was co-authored by Hughes and Sandler (1988) of the Association of American Colleges. At that time, only a few colleges and universities had examined the problem. A Cornell University survey indicated that 78 percent of female students had received sexist comments and 68 percent had received unwelcome sexual attention from their male peers. At MIT, 92 percent of women (yikes!) and 57 percent of men (yikes again!) reported having been targets of at least one form of sexual harassment. Hughes and Sandler asserted, "There is a darker side to campus life, often unnoticed. If acknowledged, it is too often brushed off as 'normal' behavior. This darker side is peer harassment, particularly the harassment of female students by male students" (p. 1). The range of behaviors Hughes and Sandler included in their description of peer harassment started with "teasing, sexual innuendoes, and bullying of a sexist nature, both physical and verbal" and ended with "sexual aggression" (p. 1).

Studies continue to reveal a persistent problem with sexual harassment on college campuses (Geist & Townsley, 1997; Kelley & Parsons, 2000; Krolokke, 1998; Sandler, 1997; Seals, 1997). The rates of reported peer sexual harassment are dramatically high, and these are just the reported cases. The actual rate of occurrence is likely to be significantly higher (Gill, 1993). In their survey of harassment at a university with a published policy on harassment, researchers Kelley and Parsons (2000) found that upward of 43 percent of female staff members, faculty members, administrators, and students reported

What we are learning about harassment requires recognizing this beast when we encounter it. We are learning that laws against harassment on the books is not enough. The law, as it was conceived, was to provide a shield of protection for us. Yet that shield is failing us. The law needs to be more responsive to the reality of our experiences.

—Anita Hill, author and law professor

having experienced sexual harassment. Peer sexual harassment was the most prevalent form of harassment reported by staff members and undergraduate students; among graduate students, most complaints were against faculty men. Other studies have reported higher rates of peer sexual harassment, such as in one survey of more than 1,500 undergraduates and 500 graduate students at a large university: researchers found that 76 percent of reported undergraduate sexual harassment came from peers, compared with 14 percent from faculty members (Cochran, Frazier, & Olson, 1997).

To better understand how peer sexual harassment affects college students' lives, the female co-author of your textbook conducted two studies at a large university (Ivy & Hamlet, 1996). A sample of 824 undergraduates, evenly divided by sex, were surveyed about experiences with peer sexual harassment. Almost half of the students reported being targets of peer sexual harassment, with 68 percent of women reporting multiple instances of verbal and nonverbal harassment from male peers. Twenty-five percent of men had experienced peer harassment primarily from women, but with more incidences of same-sex harassment than reported by women. When asked if they perceived peer sexual harassment to be a problem on college campuses, consistent with previous research, more women (81 percent) than men (64 percent) identified a problem.

The main type of verbal harassment aimed at women was sexual innuendo or lewd comments from classmates, like "guys know what it takes for girls to get an A in this class" and remarks about body parts or physical appearance. Other verbal harassment involved sexual jokes, sexual notes or drawings left on desktops, repeated invitations for dates or sex (after having said no), being asked intimate details about personal or sexual life, and descriptions of dreams or fantasies harassers had about targets. Verbal harassment of men also involved repeatedly being asked out and comments about physical appearance and body parts, as well as descriptions of desired sexual activity and offers of sexual favors in exchange for help on assignments or exams. One repeated comment from the men, but not the women, described female classmates talking in sexual ways about their own body parts, which the men said made them uncomfortable.

Nonverbal harassment mainly involved unwanted and repeated touching. Other common forms included invading one's personal space and continual staring from a classmate, especially "staring up and down," the kind that makes someone feel unclothed. Some women reported situations where harassment turned uglier, such as stalking in the parking lot and a tragic account of a beating and date rape in a male student's dorm room. In multiple instances, sexual harassment escalated into date rape.

Many students in our study were unwilling to label their experiences sexual harassment, a tendency described by one female student as "becoming numb to it." This involves becoming so used to bad behavior—being whistled at; hearing rude, often disgusting, comments about appearance and sexuality from male onlookers; being the "butt" of sexual jokes; expecting men's sexual urges to get mildly out of hand—that one is reluctant to call it something as strong as sexual harassment. Research supports this tendency of target's reluctance to label their abuse sexual harassment (Cochran, Frazier, & Olson, 1997; Fitzgerald, Swan, & Magley, 1997; Kelly & Radford, 1996). But what we're finding out is that assigning the label to the behavior is empowering. It vindicates the target in some ways to know that what happened has a name, with all the legitimacy that comes with naming. It's empowering to know that the behavior is illegal, other people have experienced it, and, in almost all instances, it's not the target's fault.

Students participating in the study felt that a complicating factor was a lack of agreement between men and women as to what behaviors constituted harassment. Thus, in a follow-up study, the researchers developed a questionnaire to assess students' perceptions of whether 15 behaviors were peer sexual harassment and the severity of each behavior. Students were asked to assume that the behaviors were directed toward themselves by an opposite-sex casual acquaintance whom they considered a peer. The results showed that only one of the 15 behaviors (humor and jokes) was *not* perceived as sexual harassment by the majority of subjects. Twelve behaviors received high agreement, meaning most students considered these behaviors sexual harassment. For two items on the questionnaire—implied or overt sexual threats and attempted or actual kissing—women assigned much higher levels of severity than men. For nine of the 15 behaviors, women assigned somewhat higher levels of severity. This finding is consistent with other research showing that women take a harsher view of harassment than men (Dougherty, 2001; Gill, 1993; McKinney, 1990b; Mongeau & Blalock, 1994). It's an understatement to say that sexual harassment on college campuses has a chilling effect, especially for women; it contributes significantly to negative perceptions of an academic climate and jeopardizes the sexual safety of all who work and study within its environs (Cortina, Swan, Fitzgerald, & Waldo, 1998).

Profile of a Peer Harasser

Men who connect sexuality and power have a greater predisposition to sexually harass—that's a predisposition, not a foregone conclusion or prediction of future behavior (Crawford & Unger, 2000). Communication researchers have examined the attitudes and communication tendencies that characterize sexual harassers. Bingham and Burleson (1996) proposed, "Because most sexual harassment is perpetrated by men, research that is designed to identify the characteristics that may differentiate men who are and are not likely to engage in particular forms of sexual harassment may suggest important strategies for combating the problem" (p. 309). In their study, 145 male undergraduates completed a questionnaire asking them to imagine themselves as a manager at a large organization who had just hired an "outgoing and friendly" female employee. In the scenario, the manager thought the female employee was attractive, so he asked her out several times but was always turned down. Following the scenario the researchers listed "strategies men said they might use in this situation." Students indicated how likely they would be to use each strategy after being turned down repeatedly for a date. In actuality, the behaviors listed were, by law, highly likely to be considered sexual harassment in a work environment.

Two general categories of strategies emerged: (1) *quid pro quo harassment* (e.g., threatening to fire the employee if she didn't accept a date), and (2) *intrusive harassment* (e.g., commenting on the employee's appearance and asking questions about her personal life). In this study, 7 percent of the male subjects reported that they were likely to use some quid pro quo strategies in order to obtain a date with the female employee. Of this finding, Bingham and Burleson stated, "Although this percentage is small in an absolute sense, any number of respondents who report even a slight likelihood of engaging in such blatant sexual harassment is disturbing. Since the males who participated in this study can be expected to move from the university into full-time employment within the next few years, the finding also suggests the need for strong educational and enforcement efforts by organizations" (pp. 321–322).

The researchers found responses in the intrusive harassment category disturbing as well (as did we), because 70 percent of the men in the study indicated "some likelihood" of engaging in behavior later categorized as intrusive harassment. Another 29 percent said that they would be "more likely than not" to use the strategies listed. Bingham and Burleson relate these findings to the likelihood that men in this study did not view the behaviors they said they would use to actually be sexual harassment. As we have said, the tendency for women to view certain actions as severe and harassing, when men do not, consistently emerges in research (Cochran, Frazier, & Olson, 1997; Dougherty, 2001; Ivy & Hamlet, 1996; LaRocca & Kromrey, 1999; McKinney, 1990b; Mongeau & Blalock, 1994).

The Law and Peer Sexual Harassment

Fewer sexual harassment court cases surround quid pro quo harassment than hostile climate harassment. Blatant "sleep with me or I'll flunk you (or fire you)" situations are the causes of lawsuits less often than in times past, although this type of harassment still does occur. Hostile climate cases are very difficult to try, but in recent years they have become more frequent and successful, from the complainant's point of view. One of the main characteristics of successful hostile climate lawsuits is proving a *pattern* of behavior, not just one instance of harassment. Many people wrongly believe that successful harassment lawsuits stem from hysteria and an overreaction to one ill-chosen comment or one instance of inappropriate humor, but the reality is that a pattern of harassing behavior must be shown (Paetzold & O'Leary-Kelly, 1996).

Managers and companies can be held legally liable for harassment among their employees. Might instructors and institutions be held accountable for peer harassment in their classrooms? In the 1980s, Hughes and Sandler (1988) predicted, "Just as courts have held under Title IX that co-workers and peers can cause an employer to be liable for sexual harassment through the creation of an offensive environment, so, too, it is expected that schools would be held liable under Title IX for sexual harassment of students by students, including the creation of an offensive environment that interferes with a student's learning and well-being" (p. 8). (Since there is no specific law on sexual harassment, most suits are filed under the umbrella of Title IX.)

Court cases in the 1990s examined public schools' liability (with findings that affect colleges and universities as well), but their rulings were inconsistent (Carroll, 1993; Laabs, 1998; Paludi, 1990; Sherer, 1992). When the 1996 *Davis* v. *Monroe County Board of Education* case (alluded to earlier in the section on harassment in public schools) was heard in a federal appeals court, the ruling was that federally-funded school districts could be held liable for peer sexual harassment if they knowingly failed to take action. But then another federal appeals court decided just the opposite, relieving school districts of liability and stating, "Unwanted sexual advances of fellow students do not carry the same coercive effect or abuse of power as those made by a teacher, employer, or co-worker" (*Rowinsky* v. *Bryan Independent School District*, 1997). Subsequent to that decision, a U.S. Supreme Court ruling in 1998—not focused around peer sexual harassment, but with far-reaching implications—held that school officials were not legally liable for a teacher's sexual harassment of a student unless they knew about it and purposefully looked the other way (*Gebser* v. *Lago Vista Independent School District*). And then the pendulum swung back once again, when the *Davis* v. *Monroe County Board of Education* case made it to the Supreme Court and the original ruling was upheld (Gorney, 1999). So, at press time and as far as we can tell, the 1999 Supreme Court ruling holding schools responsible and legally liable for peer sexual harassment is in effect, and has been interpreted to apply to federally funded institutions of higher education.

It's Happening, but What Can We Do?

Classrooms are not exempt locales when it comes to peer sexual harassment. There are no simple solutions, except maybe for one: Treat classmates and coworkers—your peers—as individuals worthy of respect. Keep personal and sexual verbal and nonverbal communication out of your interaction until you're *completely* sure that your actions or words will be received in a positive manner (and even then it's risky). Beyond advice to the individual, the same suggestions as those made earlier for public schools apply to universities. First, naiveté or

Remember...

EGALITARIANISM: The belief that one's sex does not determine or limit one's abilities or opportunities.

HOSTILE CLIMATE SEXUAL HARASSMENT: Sexual conduct that has the intention or effect of interfering with an individual's work or creating an intimidating or offensive working environment.

HOSTILE LEARNING CLIMATE: Sexual conduct that has the intention or effect of interfering with an individual's learning or creating an intimidating or offensive learning environment.

STATUS-DIFFERENTIATED RELATIONSHIP: A relationship in which the lines of status are clearly drawn; one person has higher status than the other.

PEER SEXUAL HARASSMENT: Sexual harassment between persons of equal status, such as coworkers, classmates, and social acquaintances.

CONTRAPOWER SEXUAL HARASSMENT: Harassment of someone of higher status by someone of lower status.

QUID PRO QUO SEXUAL HARASSMENT: A request for sexual favors, backed up by a threat, implicit or explicit, that one will lose one's job, promotion, raise, etc., if one doesn't comply.

denial of the problem, reflected in statements such as "This doesn't happen in my classes," makes students and teachers part of the problem. Even the most well-organized, professionally run, and academically scintillating class contains students who have grown up in a society that socializes them in some negative ways. Many students simply do not know what harassment is and that their behavior might be construed as harassing, but we believe that students are learning.

Colleges and universities, for the most part, have become much more aware of the detrimental effect and legal liability associated with sexual harassment. They've instituted policies and procedures for reporting and responding to claims of sexual harassment, and many conduct educational programs for faculty and other campus personnel. Programs sponsored by such campus organizations as women's centers and offices of student activities, and classes like first-year seminars (the "how to survive college" type of classes) are working to educate students about sexual harassment. But, a word of caution is appropriate: Just like public schools, many, if not most, university policies and programs are more attuned to harassment in status-differentiated relationships than among peers. It's important to develop programs that take a comprehensive approach to the problem (Paetzold & O'Leary-Kelly, 1993).

After reading this material, you may want to do your own "campus inventory." First, note whether your professors include a sexual harassment policy statement in their course syllabi. Do they create and foster a classroom climate of mutual respect, one that allows for safe reporting of harassment should it occur? Next, it might be worthwhile to locate and read your institution's sexual harassment policy. Does it contain any provisions for peer harassment? If a student is harassed by another student, who can she or he talk to for comfort and advice? Are campus counselors available and knowledgeable on this issue so they can help someone suffering the very real pains of sexual harassment? If your campus has student housing and resident advisors, are those RAs trained on this topic? They may have received some training on sexual harassment, but did it cover peer harassment? Where does a target take a complaint? If you find that your campus is lacking in awareness of the peer sexual harassment issue, that may signal it's time for you to get involved and find an avenue for volunteering your considerable knowledge on this topic.

Conclusion

This wraps up this final part of the text on gender communication in specific kinds of relationships and certain contexts. Intuitively, you know that the exact same thing said among family members will be taken differently by a friend, a romantic partner, a classmate, or a coworker. But intuition or what some people like to call common sense isn't common to everyone, as Benjamin Franklin once said. Some people don't realize the power of context to affect a message. We expect that, after reading these chapters, you won't be among these people. We expect that the last several pages of this text have reinforced the importance of context in gender communication.

Learning all you can about communication in educational settings, as well as about how gender communication operates in other contexts and in various types of relationships, will take you a long way toward personal effectiveness as a communicator. Practicing what you've learned, talking with women and men about what you know, making mistakes but being wise enough to stare down those mistakes, learn from them, and avoid repeating them put you even closer to the personal effectiveness goal. Becoming an effective communicator in a world complicated by gender, for starters, is an incredible challenge. We think you're up to it.

Discussion Starters

1. Think about your favorite children's fairy tale, perhaps a Disney story or a favorite story a parent read to you when you were young. Analyze the main characters. Is the main female character the center of the story? How would you describe her character, both physically and in terms of personality? Does her character represent a feminine stereotype? How would you describe the main male character in the story? Is he stereotypically drawn? What interpretations did you make of the story as a child? Do you have different interpretations now, as an adult?

2. If you believe that women and men should have equal opportunities and be treated equally in our society, but you see gender bias around you, how will you communicate an unbiased attitude to your future children? If you already have children, how have you confronted this issue with them? Have you thought about the nursery rhymes, fairy tales, and stories you will expose your children to? Have you thought about how you might discuss gender roles with a child?

3. This chapter discussed some of the effects of teachers' expectations on students' learning and academic achievement. Can you think of a time, either in school or college, when you became acutely aware that one of your teachers had certain expectations of you? Were the expectations positive or negative? (For example, did an instructor expect you to excel or to fail?) Were the expectations in any way related to your sex? How did the realization that those expectations were operating make you feel and affect your learning?

4. Consider some of the specific "chilly" behaviors mentioned in this chapter and see if you detect them in your college classes. For example, when your instructor raises a question, see if men's hands go up first and if more men than women are called on to speak. Do any of your teachers seem to direct more complex questions to male students (rather than female students) and then coach them through the answers?

5. Think about the problem of peer sexual harassment on your campus. Have you experienced any harassment in college classrooms or at social events? Do you know people who believe they've been sexually harassed by a peer? Have friends told you of experiences with sexual harassment but been reluctant to attach the label to the behavior? Knowing what you now know about the problem, will you respond to peer sexual harassment—directed at you or at a friend—any differently?

References

Addison, E. (1995). Saving other women from other men: Disney's *Aladdin. Camera Obscura, 31,* 5–19.

Allen, S., Cantor, A., Grady, H., & Hill, P. (1997). Classroom talk: Coed classes that work for girls. *Women & Language, 20,* 41–46.

American Association of University Women. (1991). *Shortchanging girls, shortchanging America.* Washington, DC: AAUW Educational Foundation.

American Association of University Women. (1992). *The AAUW report: How schools shortchange girls.* Washington, DC: AAUW Educational Foundation and the National Educational Association.

American Association of University Women. (1993). *Hostile hallways: The AAUW survey on sexual harassment in America's schools.* Washington, DC: AAUW Educational Foundation.

American Association of University Women. (1998a). *Separated by sex: A critical look at single-sex education for girls.* Washington, DC: AAUW Educational Foundation.

American Association of University Women. (1998b, October). *Gender gaps: Where schools still fail our children.* Washington, DC: AAUW Educational Foundation.

American Association of University Women. (1998c). *Gender gaps: Where schools still fail our children.* Washington, DC: AAUW Educational Foundation.

American Association of University Women. (1998d). *News release: Technology gender gap develops while gaps in math and science narrow, AAUW Foundation report shows.* [Online]. Available: http://www.aauw.org

American Association of University Women. (2001, Summer). *AAUW in action: American Association of University Women national leadership publication.* Washington, DC: Author.

American Psychological Association. (2001). Guidelines to reduce bias in language. In *Publication manual of the American Psychological Association* (5th ed.) (pp. 61–76). Washington, DC: Author.

Anderson, K., & Miller, E. D. (1997). Gender and student evaluations of teaching. *PS: Political Sciences & Politics, 30,* 216–219.

Bate, B., & Bowker, J. (1997). *Communication and the sexes* (2nd ed.). Prospect Heights, IL: Waveland.

Baumeister, E. (1997). *Let's hear it for the girls: 375 great books for readers 2–14.* New York: Penguin.

Belenky, M., Clinchy, B., Goldberger, N., & Tarule, J. (1986). *Women's ways of knowing.* New York: Basic Books.

Bem, S. L. (1993). *The lenses of gender: Transforming the debate on sexual inequality.* New Haven, CT: Yale University Press.

Benson, K. (1984). Comment on Crocker's "An analysis of university definitions of sexual harassment." *Signs, 9,* 516–519.

Berryman-Fink, C. (1993). Preventing sexual harassment through male-female communication training. In G. L. Kreps (Ed.), *Sexual harassment: Communication implications.* (pp. 267–280). Cresskill, NJ: Hampton.

Bingham, S. G., & Burleson, B. R. (1996). The development of a Sexual Harassment Proclivity Scale: Construct validation and relationship to communication competence. *Communication Quarterly, 44,* 308–325.

Borisoff, D., & Merrill, L. (1998). *The power to communicate: Gender differences as barriers* (3rd ed.). Prospect Heights, IL: Waveland.

Bottigheimer, R. B. (1986). Silenced women in the Grimms' tales: The "fit" between fairy tales and society in their historical context. In R. B. Bottigheimer (Ed.), *Fairy tales and society: Illusion, allusion, and paradigm* (pp. 115–132). Philadelphia: University of Pennsylvania Press.

Bowker, J. K., & Regan Dunkin, P. (1992). Enacting feminism in the teaching of communication. In L. A. M. Perry, L. H. Turner, & H. M. Sterk (Eds.), *Constructing and reconstructing gender: The links among communication, language, and gender* (pp. 261–268). Albany: State University of New York Press.

Brooks, V. (1982). Sex differences in student dominance behavior in female and male professors' classrooms. *Sex Roles, 8,* 683–690.

Brophy, J. E. (1983). Research on the self-fulfilling prophecy and teacher expectations. *Journal of Educational Psychology, 75,* 631–661.

Brophy, J. E. (1985). Interactions of male and female students with male and female teachers. In L. C. Wilkinson & C. B. Marrett (Eds.), *Gender influence in classroom interaction* (pp. 115–142). Orlando, FL: Academic.

Burk, M. (1998, July/August). NOW invokes Title IX to fight an all-girls school. *Ms.,* 24–25.

Carroll, C. M. (1993). Sexual harassment on campus: Enhancing awareness and promoting change. *Educational Record, Winter,* 21–26.

Centre, J. A., & Gaubatz, N. B. (2000). Is there gender bias in student evaluations of teaching? *Journal of Higher Education, 71,* 17.

Chipman, S. F., & Wilson, D. M. (1985). Understanding mathematics course enrollment and mathematics achievement: A synthesis of the research. In S. F. Chipman, L. R. Brush, & D. M. Wilson (Eds.), *Women and mathematics: Balancing the equation* (pp. 275–328). Hillsdale, NJ: Erlbaum.

Cochran, C. C., Frazier, P. A., & Olson, A. M. (1997). Predictors of responses to unwanted sexual attention. *Psychology of Women Quarterly, 21,* 207–226.

Condravy, J., Skirboll, E., & Taylor, R. (1998). Faculty perceptions of classroom gender dynamics. *Women & Language, 21,* 18–27.

Cooper, P. J. (1987). Sex role stereotypes of stepparents in children's literature. In L. P. Stewart & S. Ting-Toomey (Eds.), *Communication, gender, and sex roles in diverse interaction contexts* (pp. 61–82). Norwood, NJ: Ablex.

Cooper, P. J. (1991a). *Speech communication for the classroom teacher* (4th ed.). Scottsdale, AZ: Gorsuch-Scarisbrick.

Cooper, P. J. (1991b). *Women and power in the Caldecott and Newbery winners.* Paper presented at the meeting of the Central States Communication Association, Chicago, IL.

Cooper, P. J. (1993). Communication and gender in the classroom. In L. P. Arliss & D. J. Borisoff (Eds.), *Women and men communicating: Challenges and changes* (pp. 122–141). Fort Worth, TX: Harcourt Brace Jovanovich.

Cooper, H., & Good, T. (1983). *Pygmalion grows up: Studies in the expectation communication process.* New York: Longman.

Cortina, L. M., Swan, S., Fitzgerald, L. F., & Waldo, C. (1998). Sexual harassment and assault: Chilling the climate for women in academia. *Psychology of Women Quarterly, 22,* 419–441.

Crawford, M., & Unger, R. (2000). *Women and gender: A feminist psychology* (3rd ed.). New York: McGraw-Hill.

Dougherty, D. S. (2001). Sexual harassment as (dys)functional process: A feminist standpoint analysis. *Journal of Applied Communication Research, 29,* 372–402.

Downey, S. D. (1996). Feminine empowerment in Disney's *Beauty and the Beast. Women's Studies in Communication, 19,* 185–212.

Ernst, S. B. (1995). Gender issues in books for children and young adults. In S. Lehr (Ed.), *Battling dragons: Issues and controversy in children's literature* (pp. 66–67). Portsmith, NH: Hernemann.

Everbach, T., & Saul, M. (1998, May 23). Confronting peer pressure: Students facing more frequent sexual harassment, abuse from classmates. *Dallas Morning News,* pp. 37A, 41A.

Fitzgerald, L. F., Swan, S., & Magley, V. J. (1997). But was it really sexual harassment? Legal, behavioral, and psychological definitions of the workplace victimization of women. In W. O'Donohue (Ed.), *Sexual harassment: Theory, research, and treatment* (pp. 5–28). Boston: Allyn & Bacon.

Fox, R. F., & Gerbner, G. (2000). *Harvesting minds: How TV commercials control kids.* New York: Praeger.

Geist, P., & Townsley, N. (1997, November). *"Swept under the rug" and other disappearing acts: Legitimate concerns for university's sexual harassment policy and procedures.* Paper presented at the meeting of the National Communication Association, Chicago, IL.

Gender mindbender: Should single sex education remain an option? (1998, Summer). *Texas Woman's University Times,* pp. 1, 8.

Gerbner, G., Gross, L., Morgan, M., & Signorielli, N. (1980). The "mainstreaming" of America: Violence profile no. 11. *Journal of Communication, 30,* 10–29.

Gill, M. M. (1993). Academic sexual harassment: Perceptions of behaviors. In G. L. Kreps (Ed.), *Sexual harassment: Communication implications* (pp. 149–169). Cresskill, NJ: Hampton.

Gilligan, C. (1982). *In a different voice.* Cambridge: Harvard University Press.

Gooden, A. M., & Gooden, M. A. (2001). Gender representation in notable children's picture books: 1955–1999. *Sex Roles, 45,* 89–101.

Gorney, C. (1999, July 4). Sex patrol: Fighting harassment in schools. *The New York Times Magazine,* as reported in *Corpus Christi Caller Times,* pp. A15, A16, A17, A18.

Gose, B. (1996, March 1). Classroom climate found still "chilly" for women. *The Chronicle of Higher Education,* p. A38.

Hall, R., & Sandler, B. (1982). *The classroom climate: A chilly one for women?* Washington, DC: Project on the Status and Education of Women, Association of American Colleges.

Hall, R. M., & Sandler, B. R. (1984). *Out of the classroom: A chilly campus climate for women?* Washington, DC: Project on the Status and Education of Women, Association of American Colleges.

Hand, J. Z., & Sanchez, L. (2000). Badgering or bantering? Gender differences in experience of, and relations to, sexual harassment among U.S. high school students. *Gender & Society, 14,* 718–746.

Hanson, T. L. (1999). Gender sensitivity and diversity issues in selected basic public speaking texts. *Women & Language, 22,* 13–19.

Hargett, J. (1999). Students' perceptions of male and female instructors' level of immediacy and teacher credibility. *Women & Language, 22,* 46.

Harmon, M. R. (2000). Gender/language subtexts as found in literature anthologies: Mixed messages, stereotypes, silence, erasure. In M. J. Hardman & A. Taylor (Eds.), *Hearing many voices* (pp. 75–85). Cresskill, NJ: Hampton.

Haswell, J., & Haswell, R. H. (1995). Gendership and the miswriting of students. *College Composition and Communication, 46,* 223–254.

Heintz, K. E. (1987). An examination of sex and occupational-role presentations of female characters in children's picture books. *Women's Studies in Communication, 11,* 67–78.

Hernandez, B. (1993). Career choices unlimited. *Northwest report: The challenge of sex equity.* Portland, OR: Northwest Regional Educational Laboratory.

hooks, b. (2000). *Feminism is for everybody.* Cambridge, MA: South End Press.

Houston, S., & Hwang, N. (1996). Correlates of the objective and subjective experiences of sexual harassment in high school. *Sex Roles, 34,* 189–204.

Hughes, J. O., & Sandler, B. R. (1988). *Peer harassment: Hassles for women on campus.* Washington, DC: Project on the Status and Education of Women, Association of American Colleges.

Hurd, T. L., & Brabeck, M. (1997). Presentation of women and Gilligan's ethic of care in college textbooks, 1970–1990: An examination of bias. *Teaching of Psychology, 24,* 159–167.

Hyde, J. S., Fenneman, E., Ryan, M., Frost, L., & Hopp, C. (1990). Gender comparisons of mathematics attitudes and affects: A meta-analysis. *Psychology of Women Quarterly, 14,* 299–324.

Ivy, D. K., & Hamlet, S. (1996). College students and sexual dynamics: Two studies of peer sexual harassment. *Communication Education, 45,* 149–166.

Jaasma, M. A. (1997). Classroom communication apprehension: Does being male or female make a difference? *Communication Reports, 10,* 219–228.

Jaasma, M. A., & Koper, R. J. (2002). Out-of-class communication between female and male students and faculty: The relationship to student perceptions of instructor immediacy. *Women's Studies in Communication, 25,* 119–137.

Jamieson, K. H. (1995). *Beyond the double bind: Women and leadership.* New York: Oxford University Press.

Jaschik, S. (1995, April 21). Court orders Citadel to admit woman, but provides escape clause. *The Chronicle of Higher Education,* p. A37.

Jetter, A. (2001, March). The feminists Grimm. *Ms.,* 81–83.

Karp, D. A., & Yoels, W. C. (1977). The college classroom: Some observations on the meanings of student participation. *Sociology and Social Research, 60,* 421–439.

Keegan, P. (1989, August 6). Playing favorites. *New York Times,* p. 26A.

Kelley, M. L., & Parsons, B. (2000). Sexual harassment in the 1990s: A university-wide survey of female faculty, administrators, staff, and students. *Journal of Further and Higher Education, 71,* 548–568.

Kelly, L., & Radford, J. (1996). "Nothing really happened": The invalidation of women's experiences of sexual violence. In M. Hester, L. Kelloy, & J. Radford (Eds.), *Women, violence, and male power: Feminist activism, research, and practice.* Buckingham, England: Open University Press.

Kopp, L. K., & Farr, T. (1999, October 15). *Is the chilly classroom climate still a factor for women as we close the 20th century?* Paper presented at the meeting of the Organization for the Study of Communication, Language, and Gender, Wichita, KS.

Krolokke, C. (1998). Women professors' assertive-empathic and non-assertive communication in sexual harassment situations. *Women's Studies in Communication, 21,* 91–103.

Krupnick, C. (1985). Women and men in the classroom: Inequality and its remedies. *Teaching and Learning: Journal of the Harvard Danforth Center, 1,* 18–25.

Laabs, J. (1998). Sexual harassment: New rules, higher stakes. *Workforce,* 34–42.

Lakes Matyas, M. (1997). Factors affecting female achievement and interest in science and scientific careers. In D. Dunn (Ed.), *Workplace/women's place* (pp. 53–63). Los Angeles: Roxbury.

Larche, D. (1985). *Father Gander.* New York: Methuen.

LaRocca, M. A., & Kromrey, J. D. (1999). The perception of sexual harassment in higher education: Impact of gender and attractiveness. *Sex Roles, 40,* 921–940.

LaRocque, P. (1997, April 7). Sexism slips into language. *Dallas Morning News,* p. 13A.

Lederman, D. (1996, January 26). Supreme Court hears arguments on VMI admissions policy. *The Chronicle of Higher Education,* p. A28.

Leibrock, R. (2000, September 3). Emily the Strange: Little girl with an attitude takes on worlds of Internet, TV. Scripps-McClatchy Western Service, as reported in *Corpus Christi Caller Times,* pp. H1, H3.

Leonard, M. M., & Sigall, B. A. (1989). Empowering women student leaders: A leadership development model. In C. S. Pearson, D. L. Shavlik, & J. B. Touchton (Eds.), *Educating the majority: Women challenge tradition in higher education* (pp. 230–249). New York: ACE/Macmillan.

Lieberman, M. K. (1986). "Some day my prince will come": Female acculturation through the fairy tale. In J. Zipes (Ed.), *Don't bet on the prince: Contemporary feminist fairy tales in North America and England* (pp. 185–200). New York: Methuen.

Loredo, C., Reid, A., & Deaux, K. (1995). Judgments and definitions of sexual harassment by high school students. *Sex Roles, 32,* 29–45.

Macke, A. S., Richardson, L. W., & Cook, J. (1980). *Sex-typed teaching styles of university professors and student reactions.* Columbus: Ohio State University Research Foundation.

Maggio, R. (1988). *The nonsexist word finder: A dictionary of gender-free usage.* Boston: Beacon.

McCroskey, J. C. (1982). Oral communication apprehension: A reconceptualization. In M. Burgoon (Ed.), *Communication yearbook 6* (pp. 136–170). Beverly Hills: Sage.

McKinney, K. (1990a). Sexual harassment of university faculty by colleagues and students. *Sex Roles, 23,* 421–438.

McKinney, K. (1990b). Attitudes toward sexual harassment and perceptions of blame: Views of male and female graduate students. *Free Inquiry in Creative Sociology, 18,* 73–76.

Mongeau, P. A., & Blalock, J. (1994). Student evaluations of instructor immediacy and sexually harassing behaviors: An experimental investigation. *Journal of Applied Communication Research, 22,* 256–272.

Nadler, L. B., & Nadler, M. K. (1990). Perceptions of sex differences in classroom communication. *Women's Studies in Communication, 13,* 46–65.

National Council of Teachers of English. (1975). *Guidelines for nonsexist use of language in NCTE publications.* Urbana, IL: Author.

Nelson, C., & Watson, J. A. (1991). The computer gender gap: Children's attitudes, performance, and socialization. *Journal of Educational Technology Systems, 9,* 345–353.

Orenstein, P. (1994). *Schoolgirls: Young women, self-esteem, and the confidence gap.* New York: Doubleday.

Orenstein, P. (1997). Shortchanging girls: Gender socialization in schools. In D. Dunn (Ed.), *Workplace/women's place* (pp. 43–52). Los Angeles: Roxbury.

Paetzold, R. L., & O'Leary-Kelly, A. M. (1993). Organizational communication and the legal dimension of hostile work environment sexual harassment. In G. L. Kreps (Ed.), *Sexual harassment: Communication implications* (pp. 63–77). Cresskill, NJ: Hampton.

Paetzold, R. L., & O'Leary-Kelly, A. M. (1996). The implications of U.S. Supreme Court and circuit court decisions for hostile environment sexual harassment cases. In M. S. Stockdale (Ed.), *Sexual harassment in the workplace: Perspectives, frontiers, and response strategies* (pp. 85–104). Thousand Oaks, CA: Sage.

Paglin, C. (1993). Girls face barriers in science and mathematics. *Northwest report: The challenge of sex equity.* Portland, OR: Northwest Regional Educational Laboratory.

Paludi, M. A. (Ed.) (1990). *Ivory power: Sexual harassment on campus.* Albany: State University of New York Press.

Pearson, J. C., & West, R. (1991). An initial investigation of the effects of gender on student questions in the classroom: Developing a descriptive base. *Communication Education, 40,* 22–32.

Petersen, T. M., Kearney, P., Plax, T. G., & Waldeck, J. H. (1997). Students' affective evaluations of the professor and course: To what extent is teacher sexism relevant? *Women's Studies in Communication, 20,* 151–165.

Peterson, E. E. (1991). Moving toward a gender balanced curriculum in basic speech communication courses. *Communication Education, 40,* 60–72.

Peterson, S., & Lach, M. (1990). Gender stereotypes in children's books: Their prevalence and influence on cognitive and affective development. *Gender and Education, 2,* 185–197.

Pipher, M. (1994). *Reviving Ophelia: Saving the selves of adolescent girls.* New York: Ballantine.

Polanyi, L., & Strassmann, D. (1996). Story telling and gatekeepers in economics. In V. L. Bergvall, J. M. Bing, & A. F. Freed (Eds.), *Rethinking language and gender research: Theory and practice* (pp. 126–152). New York: Longman.

Quilling, J. I. (1999). Gender, technology, and leadership development. *Journal of Family and Consumer Sciences, 91,* 70–76.

Rich, A. (1979). *On lies, secrets, and silence: Selected prose 1966–1978.* New York: W. W. Norton.

Richardson, L. W., Cook, J., & Macke, A. S. (1981). Classroom management strategies of male and female university professors. In L. Richardson & V. Taylor (Eds.), *Issues in sex, gender, and society.* Lexington, MA: D. C. Heath.

Romaine, S. (1999). *Communicating gender.* Mahwah, NJ: Erlbaum.

Rosenfeld, L. B., & Jarrard, M. W. (1986). Student coping mechanisms in sexist and nonsexist professors' classes. *Communication Education, 35,* 157–162.

Rowe, K. E. (1986). Feminism and fairy tales. In J. Zipes (Ed.), *Don't bet on the prince: Contemporary feminist fairy tales in North America and England* (pp. 209–226). New York: Methuen.

Russ, T. L., Simonds, C. J., & Hunt, S. K. (2002). Coming out in the classroom . . . an occupational hazard? The influence of sexual orientation on teacher credibility and perceived student learning. *Communication Education, 51,* 311–324.

Ryan, M. (1989). Classroom and contexts: The challenge of feminist pedagogy. *Feminist Teacher, 4,* 39–42.

Sadker, D. (1999). Gender equity: Still knocking at the classroom door. *Educational Leadership, 56,* 22–26.

Sadker, M., & Sadker, D. (1985, March). Sexism in the schoolroom of the '80's. *Psychology Today,* 54–57.

Sadker, M., & Sadker, D. (1994). *Failing at fairness: How America's schools cheat girls.* New York: Charles Scribner's Sons.

Sandler, B. R. (1991). Women faculty at work in the classroom, or why it still hurts to be a woman in labor. *Communication Education, 40,* 6–15.

Sandler, B. R. (1997). Student-to-student sexual harassment. In B. R. Sandler & R. J. Shoop (Eds.), *Sexual harassment on campus: A guide for administrators, faculty, and students* (pp. 50–65). Boston: Allyn & Bacon.

Sandler, B. R., & Hall, R. M. (1986). *The campus climate revisited: Chilly for women faculty, administrators, and graduate students.* Washington, DC: Project on the Status and Education of Women, Association of American Colleges.

Sandoz, J. (2000). Victory? New language for sportswomen. *Women & Language, 23,* 33–36.

Seals, B. (1997). Faculty-to-faculty sexual harassment. In B. R. Sandler & R. J. Shoop (Eds.), *Sexual harassment on campus: A guide for administrators, faculty, and students* (pp. 66–84). Boston: Allyn & Bacon.

Sells, L. (1995). Where do the mermaids stand? Voice and body in *The Little Mermaid.* In E. Bell, L. Haas, & L. Sells (Eds.), *From mouse to mermaid: The politics of film, gender, and culture* (pp. 175–192). Bloomington: Indiana University Press.

Sherer, M. L. (1992). School liability under Title IX for peer sexual harassment. *Pennsylvania Law Review, 141,* 2119–2175.

Simonds, C. J., & Cooper, P. J. (2001). Communication and gender in the classroom. In L. P. Arliss & D. J. Borisoff (Eds.), *Women and men communicating: Challenges and changes* (2nd ed.) (pp. 232–253). Prospect Heights, IL: Waveland.

Sprague, J. (1975). The reduction of sexism in speech communication education. *Speech Teacher, 24,* 37–45.

Steineger, M. (1993, September). Gender bias persists in texts and literature. *Northwest report: The challenge of sex equity.* Portland, OR: Northwest Regional Educational Laboratory.

Sternglanz, S. H., & Lyberger-Ficek, S. (1977). Sex differences in student-teacher interactions in the college classroom. *Sex Roles, 3,* 345–352.

Tepper, C. A., & Cassidy, K. W. (1999). Gender differences in emotional language in children's picture books. *Sex Roles, 40,* 265–280.

Thorne, B. (1979). *Claiming verbal space: Women, speech, and language in college classrooms.* Paper presented at the Conference on Educational Environments and the Undergraduate Woman, Wellesley College, Wellesley, MA.

Treichler, P. A., & Kramarae, C. (1983). Women's talk in the ivory tower. *Communication Quarterly, 31,* 118–132.

Trites, R. (1998). *Waking Sleeping Beauty: Feminist voices in children's novels.* Iowa City: University of Iowa Press.

Vinnedge, M. (1996, December 29). Historical novel series aimed at girl readers. *Corpus Christi Caller Times,* p. G13.

Warrington, M., & Younger, M. (2000). The other side of the gender gap. *Gender and Education, 12,* 493–508.

Wellhousen, K., & Yin, Z. (1997). "Peter Pan isn't a girl's part": An investigation of gender bias in a kindergarten classroom. *Women & Language, 20,* 35–39.

White, H. (1986). Damsels in distress: Dependency themes in fiction for children and adolescents. *Adolescence, 21,* 251–256.

Willis-Rivera, J. L., & Meeker, M. (2002). De que colores: A critical examination of multicultural children's books. *Communication Education, 51,* 269–279.

Wood, J. T., & Lenze, L. F. (1991). Strategies to enhance gender sensitivity in communication education. *Communication Education, 40,* 16–21.

Zipes, J. (1986). *Don't bet on the prince: Contemporary feminist fairy tales in North America and England.* New York: Methuen.

Zipes, J. (1995). Breaking the Disney spell. In E. Bell, L. Haas, & L. Sells (Eds.), *From mouse to mermaid: The politics of film, gender, and culture* (pp. 21–42). Bloomington: Indiana University Press.

Zipes, J. (1997). *Happily ever after: Fairy tales, children, and the culture industry.* New York: Routledge.

Zirkel, P. A. (1995). Student-to-student sexual harassment. *Phi Delta Kappan, 76,* 648–650.

Photo Credits

Author Index

I

Subject Index